TOUCHSTONE

ANTHOLOGY OF

CONTEMPORARY

CREATIVE

NONFICTION

WORK FROM 1970 TO THE PRESENT

Edited by Lex Williford and Michael Martone

A Touchstone Book
Published by Simon & Schuster
New York London Toronto Sydney

Touchstone
A Division of Simon & Schuster, Inc.
1230 Avenue of the Americas
New York, NY 10020

First Touchstone trade paperback edition August 2007

TOUCHSTONE and colophon are registered trademarks of Simon & Schuster, Inc.

For information about special discounts for bulk purchases,
please contact Simon & Schuster Special Sales at
1-800-456-6798 or business@simonandschuster.com

Designed by Mary Austin Speaker

Manufactured in the United States of America

10

Library of Congress Cataloging-in-Publication Data

Touchstone anthology of contemporary creative nonfiction : work from 1970 to the present /
[edited by Lex Williford and Michael Martone].
    p.   cm.
  "A Touchstone Book."
  1. American essays—20th century. 2. American essays—21st century. 3. Reportage
literature, American. 4. English essays—20th century. 5. English essays—21st century.
6. Reportage literature, English. I. Williford, Lex, 1954–. II. Martone, Michael.
PS688.T68   2007
814'.5408—dc22   2007039255

ISBN-13: 978-1-4165-3174-6
ISBN-10:   1-4165-3174-2

ACKNOWLEDGMENTS

The editors would like to thank editors Cherise Davis and Meghan Stevenson for their hard work and advocacy for this anthology. Putting the anthology together took much longer than any of us expected—problems with crashed computers, software, long negotiations over authors' permissions, and the like—and we appreciate their patience in the face of delays in fast-approaching production deadlines. We'd also like to thank Jeff Wilson, executive director of contracts at Simon & Schuster, for his calm and generous support with permissions and contracts, as well as Amit Ghosh and his terrific BorderSenses Technology team (http://bstelpaso.com)—Javier Sanchez, Ernesto Flores, and Edevaldo Orozco—who designed the website and the survey's complex databases, administered the surveys, and then compiled all the data for simple-minded literary types who can barely add up a column of numbers.

Thanks also go to Scott Russell Sanders for his marvelous introduction and the many distinguished teaching writers who took time out of their busy summers—the only time many of them could write—to take our survey: Diana Abu-Jaber, Laurie Alberts, Marcia Aldrich, Rilla Askew, Christopher Bakken, Kim Barnes, Helen Barolini, Randolph Bates, David Borofka, Andrea Hollander Budy, Bobby Byrd, David Carkeet, Kelly Grey Carlisle, Christopher Chambers, Kelly Cherry, Rita Ciresi, Elizabeth Cook-Lynn, Burke Davis, Jeffrey DeLotto, Janet Desaulniers, Julie Edelson, David Galef, Albert Garcia, Gaynell Gavin, Denise Gess, Tod Goldberg, Benjamin Grossberg, Marian Haddad, J. C. Hallman, Jane Hammons, Janet Heller, Richard Hoffman, Noy Holland, Sonya Huber, T. R. Hummer, Laura Kasischke, Patricia Kirkpatrick, Wayne Koestenbaum, Martin Lammon, David Leavitt, Sara Levine, Paul Lisicky, Elizabeth Macklin, Lee Martin, Richard McCann, Thomas McConnell, Margaret McMullan, Gregory McNamee, Bart Midwood, Kathleen Volk Miller, Kyle Minor, Roger Mitchell, Dinty W. Moore, Patricia Murphy, James Nolan, Judith Pascoe, Joe Ashby Porter, Lynn Powell, Lia Purpura, Keith Ratzlaff, John Repp, Kathryn Rhett, Natania Rosenfeld, Margaret Rozga,

Andrew Schelling, Marc Sheehan, Sue Silverman, Linda Simone, Floyd Skloot, Ron Smith, Angela Sorby, David St. John, Maureen Stanton, Martin Steingesser, Judith Strasser, Pia Taavila, David Taylor, Richard Terrill, Jessica Treat, Lee Upton, Martha Vertreace-Doody, G. C. Waldrep, Charlotte Walker, Gabriel Welsch, Tom Whalen, Laurance Wieder, Chris Willerton, Paul Winner, and Mark Wunderlich.

Lucky for us, work by many of these same distinguished writers also appears in this anthology, not because they nominated their own work or had friends nominate it for them but because their work is powerful and important.

Without these and other authors, such an anthology as this would never have been possible. Although permissions costs have doubled and even tripled over the last decade, authors, their agents, and their publishers were willing to receive the same low permissions fee to keep the cost of this anthology affordable. We thank them all.

For interested writers who have published at least three essays in nationally distributed literary magazines, please email lex@utep.edu, and we'll add your name to our database so you may participate in surveys for any future editions.

CONTENTS

FOREWORD

TOUCHSTONE ANTHOLOGY OF CONTEMPORARY CREATIVE NONFICTION

Since my coeditor, Michael Martone, and I had already decided to use a sophisticated democratic online survey of teaching writers for the second edition of *The Scribner Anthology of Contemporary Short Fiction*, we thought that another survey like it might also be an excellent opportunity to poll teaching writers about the most compelling contemporary nonfiction they've read and taught in their creative writing workshops and their composition and literature classes. Thus began the long, arduous process of publishing the first edition of the *Touchstone Anthology of Contemporary Creative Nonfiction*.

Not long after September 11, 2001, Simon & Schuster's David Rosenthal described to Edward Wyatt of the *New York Times* what he saw as a recent trend in the reading public away from fiction to nonfiction: "If there's any theme, it's that people only want to read the truth." Following the attacks on the World Trade Center, Rosenthal continued, "readers flocked to nonfiction works."[1] Since the James Frey scandal that began the public debate about the ethical boundaries between fiction and nonfiction, between memory and imagination, this trend, if anything, seems to be accelerating.

Speculation about the causes of this rise in nonfiction's popularity has been wide and varied. In *Many Mountains Moving*, one of the many small literary magazines now regularly publishing creative nonfiction, writer and editor Naomi Horii tells interviewer Andrea Dupree, "Good creative nonfiction has always been important in literature—take Thoreau or Laura Ingalls Wilder." As journalist Deanna Larson of the *Nashville City Paper* speculates in an interview with creative nonfiction guru Lee Gutkind, "Only 50 years ago, Americans didn't talk much about their personal experiences or impressions. . . . But that culture has changed. Readers crave compelling stories about real events that tell them why they should care."

---

1. www.iht.com/articles/2005/12/07/business/booksales.php

While the rise in the reading of nonfiction by the general public is understandable at such a volatile point in history—the end of a millennium during radical global change—it mirrors a similar increase in the number of creative writing programs now teaching the writing of the so-called fourth genre, literary and/or creative nonfiction.

As our survey and anthology bear out, many poets and fiction writers are transforming traditional nonfiction through lyric, scenic, and structural innovations into something altogether new, raising complex questions about "the truth" in its relationship to literary perception and point of view, blurring the lines between "faulty" memory and the vividly rendered details of the imagination that fill in those gaps.

It is an interesting, important time to be reading nonfiction.

Whatever the reasons for its rising popularity, according to the *Associated Writing Programs Official Guide to Writing Programs*, creative nonfiction is now widely taught alongside courses in poetry, fiction, drama, and screenwriting in the more than three hundred writing programs across the United States and Canada, and the number of creative writing programs advertising for new nonfiction teaching positions has risen significantly over the last decade. Furthermore, as the selections in this anthology suggest, many of the country's most gifted poets and fiction writers are also writing remarkable, compelling nonfiction.

Perhaps because of the increased interest by the reading public and the growing number of students reading and writing nonfiction, literary journals such as Gutkind's *Creative Nonfiction* and Michael Steinberg and David Cooper's *Fourth Genre: Explorations in Nonfiction* have proliferated. Despite the rise in books on the writing of nonfiction, however, there are still surprisingly few affordable nonfiction anthologies for professors and students to use in their nonfiction classes and workshops.

For this reason and others, the original premise of *The Scribner Anthology of Contemporary Short Fiction*—to create the highest-quality, most affordable anthology from a democratic selection of teaching writers in universities across the United States and Canada—seemed a perfect starting point for a new anthology of nonfiction, especially when, along with the stunning rise in the costs of a college education over the last decade, the costs of anthologies have almost doubled, some anthologies selling for well over $50 in college bookstores.

Assembling a low-cost, democratically selected anthology like the *Touchstone Anthology of Contemporary Creative Nonfiction* can do much, we hope, to help make the costs of an education more within reach for students and still bring to a wider audience the most compelling contemporary nonfiction written over the last thirty years.

THE ONLINE SURVEYS

For the month of July 2006, we conducted two separate online surveys of free-lance and teaching writers for the second edition of *The Scribner Anthology of Contemporary Short Fiction* and the new *Touchstone Anthology of Contemporary Creative Nonfiction*. After a long, arduous search using many sources including Google, the *Poets & Writers Directory of American Poets and Fiction Writers*, and many university and writers' websites, we obtained the names and email addresses of more than two thousand poets, fiction writers, creative nonfiction writers, and journalists, those with well-established reputations as well as those at the beginning of, we hope, distinguished careers.[2]

From this pool of writers, we received survey responses from just under a hundred, many of them distinguished nonfiction writers, fiction writers, and poets, who nominated a total of more than five hundred essays based on the following two questions:

• What short essays published since 1970 would you most like to see in an anthology of contemporary creative nonfiction? (In other words, what essays do you most often photocopy and bring to discuss in your creative nonfiction classes?)
• Why do you read or teach these essays? What specific technical or thematic concerns do they best illustrate?

At the end of July, we collated the survey's complex results and ranked the essays. Then after several months and no small difficulty in locating the nominated essays, I emailed the same writers who had nominated them to find out where they had found them. Within a matter of days, I'd received stacks of essays via email, snail mail, and fax. It was a remarkably generous response, and we're grateful to all who saved us countless hours looking for essays in small literary magazines and other difficult-to-find publications.

"You've got to read this," everyone told us, and we did.

The nominated essays we've included in this anthology are ranked in this

---

2. We tried as much as possible to respect the privacy of writers, often solitary and protective of their time, and gave all the writers we surveyed the option of having their names removed from our email list, and we did so, if they wished, immediately. We also asked authors to nominate *only* essays by *other* writers, and when a few of them couldn't resist the temptation to nominate their own, we eliminated those nominations. Even so, because some of those we surveyed are also some of our most well-respected nonfiction writers in the United States, we had no trouble publishing their essays based on no other criteria but others' nominations and the high standards of craftsmanship their work represents.

order: Jo Ann Beard's "The Fourth State of Matter" (seven nominations); Thomas Lynch's "The Undertaking" (four); Annie Dillard's "Living Like Weasels," Phillip Lopate's "Portrait of My Body," Tony Earley's "Somehow Form a Family," and Sue William Silverman's "The Pat Boone Fan Club (three each); and Jamaica Kincaid's "A Small Place," Anne Carson's "The Glass Essay," Cheryl Strayed's "The Love of My Life," and Michael W. Cox's "Visitor" (two each).[3]

Choosing among the remaining essays that received a single nomination was incredibly difficult, but the result is, we hope, an anthology that includes a remarkable range of voices unlike any nonfiction anthology we've ever seen.

We live in a time a time of big lies and little lies—one president under fire for lying about sex, another for lying about war—and people are hungry for "the truth." Ask any journalist, essayist, fiction writer, or poet, and he or she might say that striving after truth, the journey itself, is at least as important as the arrival, if not more so, and more often than not it simply raises more questions. Strive as we might for "the truth"—for some certainty *about* it—there are at least as many truths as there are those who believe what they want to believe.

And the rest of us? What can we do? Read everything we can and try to decide the truth in it.

Whether we like it or not, we'll always be stuck with the "factual" truth of observation, faulty memory, and its imaginative interpretation—the fact that, even in physics, just the observation of a quantum event can change it—but the best nonfiction writers take all this as a given. Impatient with lies, especially the lies they tell *themselves*, they give intelligent, critical readers greater freedom by asking questions about the emotional and psychological truths that matter. They try to tell their stories as truthfully as possible, and then they say:

This may not be exactly what happened, but it's exactly how it felt.

—*Lex Williford*

---

3. We also chose several other highly ranked essays, essays we really wanted to include, but we simply couldn't afford their high permissions costs.

INTRODUCTION

Scott Russell Sanders

There is a kind of writing that begins from the impulse to make things up, to invent a situation and see how it unfolds, to create characters and see what they do. Since around 1600, such writing has been called fiction, from a Latin root meaning "to feign" or "to counterfeit." In making fiction, the writer freely goes wherever imagination leads. The only requirement is that the counterfeit be sufficiently compelling to engage the reader's attention from the first line to the last.

Writing may also begin from a contrary impulse, not to make things up, but to record and examine something the writer has actually witnessed, lived through, learned about, or pondered. Such writing can range from history and philosophy to manifestos and memoirs, from the formality of footnoted tomes to the pizzazz of slangy blogs. What all such writing has in common is faithfulness to some reality that the writer did not invent—to a shared history, to real people, to actual events, to places one can visit, to facts one can check. For better or worse, this wildly diverse range of writing has come to be called, by contrast with the freely invented kind, *non*fiction.

Dividing the realm of prose literature into fiction and nonfiction is clumsy at best, rather like dividing the realm of animals into birds and nonbirds. It might be technically correct to describe giraffes and june bugs as nonbirds, but it would not tell us anything about giraffes or june bugs, or birds. Nor is it useful to lump together a four-volume saga of the Crusades and a four-page celebration of croissants under the single label of nonfiction. Judging from the earliest citations of the word in the *Oxford English Dictionary*, the label was imposed by nineteenth-century librarians, who began dividing their books into the twin categories of fiction and nonfiction (originally with a hyphen). I suspect they did so, at least in America, to emphasize the portion of a library's holdings that were solid, sober, useful, uplifting, and, above all, *true*, such as encyclopedias and repair manuals and religious tracts, as opposed to the romances, poetry, mysteries, fantasies, westerns, pirate adventures, thrillers, dime novels, and other frivolous books that wasted readers' time and corrupted youth and made no mill wheels turn.

Whatever the origins of the nonfiction label, the publishers soon picked it up, and then so did bookstores, critics, and teachers, and now, clumsy though it may be, we are stuck with it. One virtue of the term is that the sly little prefix *non-* implies a promise—that such literature is neither feigned nor counterfeit; it is answerable not merely to the writer's imagination but to a world beyond the page, a world that precedes and surrounds and outlasts the act of writing.

Of course, these two contrary impulses—to freely invent a world or to report on the actual world—rarely exist in pure form. Fiction must draw on the familiar world if it is to be comprehensible, and nonfiction must draw on the writer's imagination if it is to come alive. Ask a roomful of writers how far a work may be shaped by imagination before it no longer deserves to be called nonfiction, and you'll receive a roomful of answers. Most likely all will agree on the necessity of choosing, from the myriad of possible details, those that are essential to the story and leaving out the rest; many writers will accept the filling-in of memory's blank spaces with vivid details; some will permit the merging of incidents or characters to streamline the account; and a few will claim the right to add, drop, change, or invent anything that enlivens the work.

While we may debate where the line should be drawn, at some point along that spectrum, nonfiction gives way to fiction. When a writer crosses over the line and still claims to be offering nonfiction, it's usually for the sake of selling more books. Why does it sell more books? Because, in a culture awash with phoniness, we hunger for authenticity. We're so weary of hucksters, talk-show ranters, ideological hacks, inane celebrities, sleazy moralists, and posturing politicians that we long to hear voices speaking from the heart rather than from a script. Amid so much fakery, hypocrisy, and outright fraud, we long for the genuine. Knowing this, television producers manufacture "reality" shows, filmmakers promote movies as "based on a true story," and some authors, with the connivance of their publishers, fabricate a sensational tale and call it a memoir. In a culture besotted by marketing, we shouldn't be surprised by such deceit.

Dressing up a fabrication as a true report is not essentially different from costuming an actor in a white coat to peddle a drug or wrapping a military invasion in the flag to make it appear as a blow for freedom. Lying to sell a book is not as serious an offense as lying to sell a drug or a war, but it's a lie nonetheless.

Beyond insisting on the writer's responsibility to a world outside the page, the nonfiction label doesn't tell us much. To think and speak in a more precise way about this rich array of literature, we need more precise language. Just as we have names for a host of animals, from aardvarks to zebras, that might be grouped under "nonbirds," so we have names for many species of nonfiction: biographies, profiles, travelogues, spiritual writing, sports writing, science writing, literary journalism, documentaries, speeches, letters, memoirs, and essays, to list a few.

Of all these nonfiction species, the most versatile and exemplary is, in my view, the essay. This quirky and inquisitive mode of writing was named, and more or less invented, by a sixteenth-century Frenchman, Michel de Montaigne. He derived the name *essai* from a French verb meaning to make a trial of something, the way one assays an ore to determine its value. The term suggests an experiment, a testing, a weighing out. For Montaigne, an essay was an effort to make sense of life—not the whole of life, but some confusing or intriguing portion of it. Thus he wrote about the pleasures of idleness and the rigors of old age, about cannibals and warfare and thumbs. His motto was, "What do I know?" Read ironically, that question is self-effacing, as if to say, "Who am I to have an opinion on such matters?" Read straight, the question challenges the writer to discover what, at this moment and within the inevitable constraints of ignorance, he takes to be true—about himself, about our baffling existence, about the universe. It's not coincidental that Montaigne invented the essay at roughly the same time as Francis Bacon, Descartes, Galileo, and others were inventing the modern scientific method. Instead of relying on scripture, mythology, astrology, or past authority to explain the workings of nature, scientists conducted experiments. They formulated a hypothesis, carefully tested it, published their results for others to confirm or refute, and then went on to create a more refined hypothesis. Since it is a collective endeavor in a way that art rarely is, science might take as its motto, "What do *we* know, and how do we know it?"

Experiments in language are messier than experiments in laboratories, because words do not parse the universe as neatly as numbers do, but the spirit behind both kinds of experiment is the same: to discover a tentative truth. For the essayist as for the scientist, the truth must be tentative rather than final, because further inquiry may deepen or clarify or overturn our understanding. The essay is not the only kind of literature that seeks to discover and articulate provisional truths about our existence. Poems and plays, stories and novels, along with other kinds of nonfiction do so as well. But the essay seems to me the purest expression of this impulse, which is why I call it exemplary. With a lineage stretching back five centuries and including such noteworthy practitioners as Henry David Thoreau, Virginia Woolf, George Orwell, and James Baldwin, the essay has enjoyed a flowering in our own time. It is a wide-open form, skeptical and reflective, lending itself to humor as well as solemnity, well suited to an age of multiplying possibilities and dwindling certainties. Readers as well as writers are drawn to the form because it allows for an examination of our most powerful and bewildering experiences. The worthiest essays are ventures into the unknown, from which we return bearing fresh insights and delights.

We are a question-asking animal. That is our burden and our glory. It's a burden because, unlike creatures governed entirely by instinct, we puzzle over how to behave, we wonder about where we've come from and where we're going and what, if anything, the journey means. This inveterate questioning is also our glory because it leads to our finest achievements—to physics and philosophy, to poetry and painting, to cosmologies and essays—to all the ways we ponder and praise this life, this universe, into which we've been so mysteriously born.

TOUCHSTONE
ANTHOLOGY OF
CONTEMPORARY
CREATIVE
NONFICTION

Jo Ann Beard

THE FOURTH STATE OF MATTER

JO ANN BEARD is the author of *The Boys of My Youth*, a collection of autobiographical essays, as well as other works of fiction and nonfiction that have appeared in magazines, literary journals, and anthologies. She was a recipient of the Whiting Foundation Award, and was a 2005 fellow in nonfiction literature for the New York Foundation for the Arts and the John Simon Guggenheim Memorial Foundation.

The collie wakes me up about three times a night, summoning me from a great distance as I row my boat through a dim, complicated dream. She's on the shoreline, barking. Wake up. She's staring at me with her head slightly tipped to the side, long nose, gazing eyes, toenails clenched to get a purchase on the wood floor. We used to call her the face of love.

She totters on her broomstick legs into the hallway and over the doorsill into the kitchen, makes a sharp left at the refrigerator—careful, almost went down—then a straightaway to the door. I sleep on my feet, in the cold of the doorway, waiting. Here she comes. Lift her down the two steps. She pees and then stands, Lassie in a ratty coat, gazing out at the yard.

In the porchlight the trees shiver, the squirrels turn over in their sleep. The Milky Way is a long smear on the sky, like something erased on a chalkboard. Over the neighbor's house, Mars flashes white, then red, then white again. Jupiter is hidden among the anonymous blinks and glitterings. It has a moon with sulfur-spewing volcanoes and a beautiful name: Io. I learned it at work, from the group of men who surround me there. Space physicists, guys who spend days on end with their heads poked through the fabric of the sky, listening to the sounds of the universe. Guys whose own lives are ticking like alarm clocks getting ready to go off, although none of us is aware of it yet.

The collie turns and looks, waits to be carried up the two steps. Inside the house, she drops like a shoe onto her blanket, a thud, an adjustment. I've climbed back under my covers already but her leg's stuck underneath her, we can't get comfortable. I fix the leg, she rolls over and sleeps. Two hours later I wake up again and she's gazing at me in the darkness. The face of love. She wants to go out again. I give her a boost, balance her on her legs. Right on time: 3:40 A.M.

There are squirrels living in the spare bedroom upstairs. Three dogs also live in this house, but they were invited. I keep the door of the spare bedroom shut at all times, because of the squirrels and because that's where the vanished husband's belongings are stored. Two of the dogs—the smart little brown mutt and the Labrador—spend hours sitting patiently outside the door, waiting for it to be opened so they can dismantle the squirrels. The collie can no longer make it up the stairs, so she lies at the bottom and snores or stares in an interested manner at the furniture around her.

I can take almost anything at this point. For instance, that my vanished husband is neither here nor there; he's reduced himself to a troubled voice on the telephone three or four times a day.

Or that the dog at the bottom of the stairs keeps having mild strokes which cause her to tilt her head inquisitively and also to fall over. She drinks prodigious amounts of water and pees great volumes onto the folded blankets where she sleeps. Each time this happens I stand her up, dry her off, put fresh blankets underneath her, carry the peed-on blankets down to the basement, stuff them into the washer and then into the dryer. By the time I bring them back upstairs they are needed again. The first few times this happened I found the dog trying to stand up, gazing with frantic concern at her own rear. I praised her and patted her head and gave her treats until she settled down. Now I know whenever it happens because I hear her tail thumping against the floor in anticipation of reward. In restraining her I've somehow retrained myself, bustling cheerfully down to the basement, arms drenched in urine, the task of doing load after load of laundry strangely satisfying. She is Pavlov and I am her dog.

I'm fine about the vanished husband's boxes stored in the spare bedroom. For now the boxes and the phone calls persuade me that things could turn around at any moment. The boxes are filled with thirteen years of his pack-rattedness: statistics textbooks that still harbor an air of desperation, smarmy suit coats from the Goodwill, various old Halloween masks, and one giant black papier-mâché thing that was supposed to be Elvis's hair but didn't turn out. A collection of ancient Rolling Stones T-shirts. You know he's turning over a new leaf when he leaves the Rolling Stones behind.

What I can't take are the squirrels. They come alive at night, throwing terrible parties in the spare bedroom, making thumps and crashes. Occasionally a high-pitched squeal is heard amid bumps and the sound of scrabbling toenails. I've taken to sleeping downstairs, on the blue vinyl dog couch, the sheets slipping off, my skin stuck to the cushions. This is an affront to two of the dogs, who know the couch belongs to them; as soon as I settle in they creep up and find their places between my knees and elbows.

I'm on the couch because the dog on the blanket gets worried at night. During the day she sleeps the catnappy sleep of the elderly, but when it gets dark her eyes open and she is agitated, trying to stand whenever I leave the room, settling down only when I'm next to her. We are in this together, the dying game, and I read for hours in the evening, one foot on her back, getting up only to open a new can of beer or take peed-on blankets to the basement. At some point I stretch out on the vinyl couch and close my eyes, one hand hanging down, touching her side. By morning the dog-arm has become a nerveless club that doesn't come around until noon. My friends think I'm nuts.

One night, for hours, the dog won't lie down, stands braced on her rickety legs in the middle of the living room, looking at me and slowly wagging her tail. Each time I get her situated on her blankets and try to stretch out on the couch she stands up, looks at me, wags her tail. I call my office pal, Mary, and wake her up. "*I'm weary*," I say, in italics.

Mary listens, sympathetic, on the other end. "Oh my God," she finally says, "*what* are you going to do?"

I calm down immediately. "Exactly what I'm doing," I tell her. The dog finally parks herself with a thump on the stack of damp blankets. She sets her nose down and tips her eyes up to watch me. We all sleep then, for a bit, while the squirrels sort through the boxes overhead and the dog on the blanket keeps nervous watch.

I've called in tired to work. It's midmorning and I'm shuffling around in my long underwear, smoking cigarettes and drinking coffee. The whole house is bathed in sunlight and the faint odor of used diapers. The collie is on her blanket, taking one of her vampirish daytime naps. The other two dogs are being mild-mannered and charming. I nudge the collie with my foot.

"Wake up and smell zee bacons," I say. She startles awake, lifts her nose groggily, and falls back asleep. I get ready for the office.

"I'm leaving and I'm never coming back," I say while putting on my coat. I use my mother's aggrieved, underappreciated tone. The little brown dog wags her tail, transferring her gaze from me to the table, which is the last place she remembers seeing toast. The collie continues her ghoulish sleep, eyes partially open, teeth exposed, while the Labrador, who understands English, begins howling miserably. She wins the toast sweepstakes and is chewing loudly when I leave, the little dog barking ferociously at her.

· · ·

Work is its usual comforting green-corridored self. There are three blinks on the answering machine, the first from an author who speaks very slowly, like a kindergarten teacher, asking about reprints. "What am I, the village idiot?" I ask the room, taking down his number in large backward characters. The second and third blinks are from my husband, the across-town apartment dweller.

The first makes my heart lurch in a hopeful way. "I have to talk to you right *now*," he says grimly. "Where *are* you? I can never find you."

"Try calling your own house," I say to the machine. In the second message he has composed himself.

"I'm *fine* now," he says firmly. "Disregard previous message and don't call me back, please; I have meetings." Click, dial tone, rewind.

I feel crestfallen, the leaping heart settles back into its hole in my chest. I say damn it out loud, just as Chris strides into the office.

"What?" he asks defensively. He tries to think if he's done anything wrong recently. He checks the table for work; none there. He's on top of it. We have a genial relationship these days, reading the paper together in the mornings, congratulating ourselves on each issue of the journal. It's a space physics quarterly and he's the editor and I'm the managing editor. I know nothing about the science part; my job is to shepherd the manuscripts through the review process and create a journal out of the acceptable ones.

Christoph Goertz. He's hip in a professorial kind of way, tall and lanky and white-haired, forty-seven years old, with an elegant trace of accent from his native Germany. He has a great dog, a giant black outlaw named Mica who runs through the streets of Iowa City at night, inspecting garbage. She's big and friendly but a bad judge of character and frequently runs right into the arms of the dog catcher. Chris is always bailing her out.

"They don't understand dogs," he says.

I spend more time with Chris than I ever did with my husband. The morning I told him I was being dumped he was genuinely perplexed.

"He's leaving *you*?" he asked.

Chris was drinking coffee, sitting at his table in front of the chalkboard. Behind his head was a chalk drawing of a hip, professorial man holding a coffee cup. It was a collaborative effort; I drew the man and Chris framed him, using brown chalk and a straightedge. The two-dimensional man and the three-dimensional man stared at me intently.

"He's leaving *you*?" And for an instant I saw myself from their vantage point across the room—Jo Ann and a small bubble of self-esteem percolated up from the depths. Chris shrugged. "You'll do fine," he said.

During my current turmoils, I've come to think of work as my own kind of Zen practice, the constant barrage of paper hypnotic and soothing. Chris lets me work an erratic, eccentric schedule, which gives me time to pursue my non-existent writing career. In return I update his publications list for him and listen to stories about outer space.

Besides being an editor and a teacher, he's the head of a theoretical plasma physics team made up of graduate students and research scientists. During the summers he travels all over the world telling people about the magnetospheres of various planets, and when he comes back he brings me presents—a small bronze box from Africa with an alligator embossed on the top, a big piece of amber from Poland with the wings of flies preserved inside it, and, once, a set of delicate, horrifying bracelets made from the hide of an elephant.

Currently he is obsessed with the dust in the plasma of Saturn's rings. Plasma is the fourth state of matter. You've got your solid, your liquid, your gas, and then your plasma. In outer space there's the plasmasphere and the plasmapause. I like to avoid the math when I can and put a layperson's spin on these things.

"Plasma is blood," I told him.

"Exactly," he agreed, removing the comics page and handing it to me.

Mostly we have those kinds of conversations around the office, but today he's caught me at a weak moment, tucking my heart back inside my chest. I decide to be cavalier.

"I wish my *dog* was out tearing up the town and my *husband* was home pee-ing on a blanket," I say.

Chris thinks the dog thing has gone far enough. "Why are you letting this go on?" he asks solemnly.

"I'm not *letting* it, that's why," I tell him. There are stacks of manuscripts everywhere and he has all the pens over on his side of the room. "It just *is*, is all. Throw me a pen." He does, I miss it, stoop to pick it up, and when I straighten up again I might be crying.

You have control over this, he explains in his professor voice. You can decide how long she suffers.

This makes my heart pound. Absolutely not, I cannot do it. And then I weaken and say what I really want. For her to go to sleep and not wake up, just slip out of her skin and into the other world.

"Exactly," he says.

I have an ex–beauty queen coming over to get rid of the squirrels for me. She has long red hair and a smile that can stop trucks. I've seen her wrestle goats, scare off a giant snake, and express a dog's anal glands, all in one afternoon. I told her on the phone that a family of squirrels is living in the upstairs of my house and there's nothing I can do about it.

"They're making a monkey out of me," I said.

So Caroline climbs in her car and drives across half the state, pulls up in front of my house, and gets out carrying zucchinis, cigarettes, and a pair of big leather gloves. I'm sitting outside with my sweet old dog, who lurches to her feet, staggers three steps, sits down, and falls over. Caroline starts crying.

"Don't try to give me zucchini," I tell her.

We sit companionably on the front stoop for a while, staring at the dog and smoking cigarettes. One time I went to Caroline's house and she was nursing a dead cat that was still breathing. At some point that afternoon I saw her spoon baby food into its mouth and as soon as she turned away the whole pureed mess plopped back out. A day later she took it to the vet and had it euthanized. I remind her of this.

"You'll do it when you do it," she says firmly.

I pick the collie up like a fifty-pound bag of sticks and feathers, stagger inside, place her on the damp blankets, and put the other two nutcases in the backyard. From upstairs comes a crash and a shriek. Caroline stares up at the ceiling.

"It's like having the Wallendas stay at your house," I say cheerfully. All of a sudden I feel fond of the squirrels and fond of Caroline and fond of myself for heroically calling her to help me. The phone rings four times. It's the husband, and his voice over the answering machine sounds frantic. He pleads with whoever Jo Ann is to pick up the phone.

"Please? I think I might be freaking out," he says. "Am I ruining my life here, or what? Am I making a *mistake*? Jo?" He breathes raggedly and sniffs into the receiver for a moment, then hangs up with a muffled clatter.

Caroline stares at the machine like it's a copperhead.

"Holy fuckoly," she says, shaking her head. "You're *living* with this crap?"

"He wants me to reassure him that he's strong enough to leave me," I tell her. "Else he won't have fun on his bike ride. And guess what; I'm too tired to." Except that now I can see him in his dank little apartment, wringing his hands and staring out the windows. He's wearing his Sunday hairdo with a baseball cap trying to scrunch it down. In his rickety dresser is the new package of condoms he accidentally showed me last week.

Caroline lights another cigarette. The dog pees and thumps her tail.

I need to call him back because he's suffering.

"You call him back and I'm forced to kill you," Caroline says. She exhales smoke and points to the phone. "That is evil shit," she says.

I tend to agree. It's blanket time. I roll the collie off onto the floor and put the fresh ones down, roll her back. She stares at me with the face of love. I get her a treat, which she chews with gusto and then goes back to sleep. I carry the blankets down to the basement and stuff them into the machine, trudge back up the stairs. Caroline has finished smoking her medicine and is wearing the leather gloves which go all the way to her elbows. She's staring at the ceiling with determination.

The plan is that I'm supposed to separate one from the herd and get it in a corner. Caroline will take it from there. Unfortunately, my nerves are shot, and when I'm in the room with her and the squirrels are running around all I can do is scream. I'm not even afraid of them, but my screaming button is stuck on and the only way to turn it off is to leave the room.

"How are you doing?" I ask from the other side of the door. All I can hear is Caroline crashing around and swearing. Suddenly there is a high-pitched screech that doesn't end. The door opens and Caroline falls out into the hall, with a gray squirrel stuck to her glove. Brief pandemonium and then she clatters down the stairs and out the front door and returns looking triumphant.

The collie appears at the foot of the stairs with her head cocked and her ears up. She looks like a puppy for an instant, and then her feet start to slide. I run down and catch her and carry her upstairs so she can watch the show. They careen around the room, tearing the ancient wallpaper off the walls. The last one is a baby, so we keep it for a few minutes, looking at its little feet and its little tail. We show it to the collie, who stands up immediately and tries to get it.

Caroline patches the hole where they got in, cutting wood with a power saw down in the basement. She comes up wearing a toolbelt and lugging a ladder. I've seen a scrapbook of photos of her wearing evening gowns with a banner across her chest and a crown on her head. Curled hair, lipstick. She climbs down and puts the tools away. We eat nachos.

"I only make food that's boiled or melted these days," I tell her.

"I know," she replies.

We smoke cigarettes and think. The phone rings again but whoever it is hangs up.

"Is it him?" she asks.

"Nope."

The collie sleeps on her blankets while the other two dogs sit next to Caroline on the couch. She's looking through their ears for mites. At some point she gestures to the sleeping dog on the blanket and remarks that it seems like just two days ago she was a puppy.

"She was never a puppy," I say. "She's always been older than me."

When they say good-bye, she holds the collie's long nose in one hand and kisses her on the forehead; the collie stares back at her gravely. Caroline is crying when she leaves, a combination of squirrel adrenaline, and sadness. I cry, too, although I don't feel particularly bad about anything. I hand her the zucchini through the window and she pulls away from the curb.

The house is starting to get dark in that terrible early-evening twilit way. I turn on lights, get a cigarette, and go upstairs to the former squirrel room. The black dog comes with me and circles the room, snorting loudly, nose to floor. There is a spot of turmoil in an open box—they made a nest in some old disco shirts from the seventies. I suspect that's where the baby one slept. The mean landlady has evicted them.

Downstairs, I turn the lights back off and let evening have its way with me. Waves of pre-nighttime nervousness are coming from the collie's blanket. I sit next to her in the dimness, touching her ears, and listen for feet at the top of the stairs.

They're speaking in physics so I'm left out of the conversation. Chris apologetically erases one of the pictures I've drawn on the blackboard and replaces it with a curving blue arrow surrounded by radiating chalk waves of green.

"If it's plasma, make it in red," I suggest helpfully. We're all smoking illegally in the journal office with the door closed and the window open. We're having a plasma party.

"We aren't discussing *plasma*," Bob says condescendingly. He's smoking a horrendously smelly pipe. The longer he stays in here the more it feels like I'm breathing small daggers in through my nose. He and I don't get along; each of us thinks the other needs to be taken down a peg. Once we had a hissing match in the hallway which ended with him suggesting that I could be fired, which drove me to tell him he was *already* fired, and both of us stomped into our offices and slammed our doors.

"I had to fire Bob," I tell Chris later.

"I heard," he says noncommittally. Bob is his best friend. They spend at least half of each day standing in front of chalkboards, writing equations and arguing about outer space. Then they write theoretical papers about what they come up with. They're actually quite a big deal in the space physics community, but around here they're just two guys who keep erasing my pictures.

Someone knocks on the door and we put our cigarettes out. Bob hides his pipe in the palm of his hand and opens the door.

It's Gang Lu, one of their students. Everyone lights up again. Gang Lu stands stiffly talking to Chris while Bob holds a match to his pipe and puffs fiercely; nose daggers waft up and out, right in my direction. I give him a sugary smile and he gives me one back. Unimaginable, really, that less than two months from now one of his colleagues from abroad, a woman with delicate, birdlike features, will appear at the door to my office and identify herself as a friend of Bob's. When she asks, I take her down the hall to the room with the long table and then to his empty office. I do this without saying anything because there's nothing to say, and she takes it all in with small, serious nods until the moment she sees his blackboard covered with scribbles and arrows and equations. At that point her face loosens and she starts to cry in long ragged sobs. An hour later I go back and the office is empty. When I erase the blackboard finally, I can see where she laid her hands carefully, where the numbers are ghostly and blurred.

Bob blows his smoke discreetly in my direction and waits for Chris to finish talking to Gang Lu, who is answering questions in a monotone—yes or no, or I don't know. Another Chinese student named Shan lets himself in after knocking lightly. He nods and smiles at me and then stands at a respectful distance, waiting to ask Chris a question.

It's like a physics conference in here. I wish they'd all leave so I could make my usual midafternoon spate of personal calls. I begin thumbing through papers in a businesslike way.

Bob pokes at his pipe with a bent paper clip. Shan yawns hugely and then looks embarrassed. Chris erases what he put on the blackboard and tries unsuccessfully to redraw my pecking parakeet. "I don't know how it goes," he says to me.

Gang Lu looks around the room idly with expressionless eyes. He's sick of physics and sick of the buffoons who practice it. The tall glacial German, Chris, who tells him what to do; the crass idiot Bob who talks to him like he is a dog; the student Shan whose ideas about plasma physics are treated with reverence and praised at every meeting. The woman who puts her feet on the desk and dismisses him with her eyes. Gang Lu no longer spends his evenings in the computer lab, running simulations and thinking about magnetic forces and invisible particles; he now spends them at the firing range, learning to hit a moving target with the gun he purchased last spring. He pictures himself holding the gun with both hands, arms straight out and steady; Clint Eastwood, only smarter. Clint Eastwood as a rocket scientist.

He stares at each person in turn, trying to gauge how much respect each of them has for him. One by one. Behind black-rimmed glasses, he counts with his eyes. In each case the verdict is clear: not enough.

The collie fell down the basement stairs. I don't know if she was disoriented and looking for me or what. But when I was at work she used her long nose like a lever and got the door to the basement open and tried to go down there except her legs wouldn't do it and she fell. I found her sleeping on the concrete floor in an unnatural position, one leg still awkwardly resting on the last step. I repositioned the leg and sat down next to her and petted her. We used to play a game called Maserati, where I'd grab her nose like a gearshift and put her through all the gears, first second third fourth, until we were going a hundred miles an hour through town. She thought it was funny.

Now I'm at work but this morning there's nothing to do, and every time I turn around I see her sprawled, eyes mute, leg bent upward. We're breaking each other's hearts. I draw a picture of her on the blackboard using brown chalk. I make *X*s where her eyes should be. Chris walks in with the morning paper and a cup of coffee. He looks around the clean office.

"Why are you here when there's no work to do?" he asks.

"I'm hiding from my life, what else," I tell him. This sounds perfectly reasonable to him. He gives me part of the paper.

His mother is visiting from Germany, a robust woman of eighty who is depressed and hoping to be cheered up. In the last year she has lost her one-hundred-year-old mother and her husband of sixty years. She mostly can't be cheered up, but she likes going to art galleries so Chris has been driving her around the Midwest, to our best cities, showing her what kind of art Americans like to look at.

"How's your mom?" I ask him.

He shrugs and makes a flat-handed so-so motion.

We read, smoke, drink coffee, and yawn. I decide to go home.

"Good idea," he says encouragingly.

It's November 1, 1991, the last day of the first part of my life. Before I leave I pick up the eraser and stand in front of the collie's picture on the blackboard, thinking. I can feel him watching me, drinking his coffee. He's wearing a gold shirt and blue jeans and a gray cardigan sweater. He is tall and lanky and white-haired, forty-seven years old. He has a wife named Ulrike, a daughter named Karcin, and a son named Goran. A dog named Mica. A mother named Ursula. A friend named me.

I erase the *X*s.

Down the hall, Linhua Shan feeds numbers into a computer and watches as a graph is formed. The computer screen is brilliant blue, and the lines appear in red and yellow and green. Four keystrokes and the green becomes purple. More keystrokes and the blue background fades to the azure of a summer sky. The wave lines arc over it, crossing against one another. He asks the computer to print, and while it chugs along he pulls up a golf game on the screen and tees off.

One room over, at a desk, Gang Lu works on a letter to his sister in China. *The study of physics is more and more disappointing*, he tells her. *Modern physics is self-delusion and all my life I have been honest and straightforward, and I have most of all detested cunning, fawning sycophants and dishonest bureaucrats who think they are always right in everything.* Delicate Chinese characters all over a page. She was a kind and gentle sister, and he thanks her for that. He's going to kill himself. *You yourself should not be too sad about it, for at least I have found a few traveling companions to accompany me to the grave.* Inside the coat on the back of his chair are a .38-caliber handgun and a .22-caliber revolver. They're heavier than they look and weigh the pockets down. *My beloved elder sister, I take my eternal leave of you.*

The collie's eyes are almond-shaped; I draw them in with brown chalk and put a white bone next to her feet.

"That's better," Chris says kindly.

Before I leave the building I pass Gang Lu in the hallway and say hello. He has a letter in his hand and he's wearing his coat. He doesn't answer and I don't expect him to. At the end of the hallway are the double doors leading to the rest of my life. I push them open and walk through.

Friday afternoon seminar, everyone is glazed over, listening as someone explains something unexplainable at the head of the long table. Gang Lu stands up and leaves the room abruptly; goes down one floor to see if the chairman, Dwight, is sitting in his office. He is. The door is open. Gang Lu turns and walks back up the stairs and enters the meeting room again. Chris Goertz is sitting near the door and takes the first bullet in the back of the head. There is a loud popping sound and then blue smoke. Shan gets the second bullet in the forehead, the lenses of his glasses shatter. More smoke and the room rings with the popping. Bob Smith tries to crawl beneath the table. Gang Lu takes two steps, holds his arms straight out, and levels the gun with both hands. Bob looks up. The third bullet in the right hand, the fourth in the chest. Smoke. Elbows and legs, people trying to get out of the way and then out of the room.

Gang Lu walks quickly down the stairs, dispelling spent cartridges and loading new ones. From the doorway of Dwight's office: the fifth bullet in the head, the sixth strays, the seventh also in the head. A slumping. More smoke and ringing. Through the cloud an image comes forward—Bob Smith, hit in the chest, hit in the hand, still alive. Back up the stairs. Two scientists, young men, crouched over Bob, loosening his clothes, talking to him. From where he lies, Bob can see his best friend still sitting upright in a chair, head thrown back at an unnatural angle. Everything is broken and red. The two young scientists leave the room at gunpoint. Bob closes his eyes. The eighth and ninth bullets in his head. As Bob dies, Chris Goertz's body settles in his chair, a long sigh escapes his throat. Reload. Two more for Chris, one for Shan. Exit the building, cross two streets, run across the green, into building number two and upstairs.

The administrator, Anne Cleary, is summoned from her office by the receptionist. She speaks to him for a few seconds, he produces the gun and shoots her

in the face. The receptionist, a young student working as a temp, is just beginning to stand when he shoots her in the mouth. He dispels the spent cartridges
in the stairwell, loads new ones. Reaches the top of the steps, looks around. Is
disoriented suddenly. The ringing and the smoke and the dissatisfaction of not
checking all the names off the list. A slamming and a running sound, the shout
of police. He walks into an empty classroom, takes off his coat, folds it carefully,
and puts it over the back of the chair. Checks his watch; twelve minutes since it
began. Places the barrel against his right temple. Fires.

The first call comes at four o'clock. I'm reading on the bench in the kitchen, one
foot on a sleeping dog's back. It's Mary, calling from work. There's been some
kind of disturbance in the building, a rumor that Dwight was shot; cops are
running through the halls carrying rifles. They're evacuating the building and
she's coming over.

Dwight, a tall likable oddball who cut off his ponytail when they made him
chair of the department. Greets everyone with a famous booming hello in the
morning, studies plasma, just like Chris and Bob. Chris lives two and half blocks
from the physics building; he'll be home by now if they've evacuated. I dial
his house and his mother answers. She tells me that Chris won't be home until
five o'clock, and then they're going to a play. Ulrike, her daughter-in-law, is
coming back from a trip to Chicago and will join them. She wants to know why
I'm looking for Chris; isn't he where I am?

No, I'm at home and I just had to ask him something. Could he please call
me when he comes in.

She tells me that Chris showed her a drawing I made of him sitting at his
desk behind a stack of manuscripts. She's so pleased to meet Chris's friends, and
the Midwest is lovely, really, except it's very brown, isn't it?

It is very brown. We hang up.

The Midwest is very brown. The phone rings. It's a physicist. His wife, a
friend of mine, is on the extension. Well, he's not sure, but it's possible that I
should brace myself for bad news. I've already heard, I tell him, something happened to Dwight. There's a long pause and then his wife says, Jo Ann. It's possible that Chris was involved.

I think she means Chris shot Dwight. No, she says gently, killed, too.

Mary is here. I tell them not to worry and hang up. I have two cigarettes going. Mary takes one and smokes it. She's not looking at me. I tell her about the
phone call.

"They're out of it," I say. "They thought Chris was involved."

She repeats what they said: I think you should brace yourself for bad news.
Pours whiskey in a coffee cup.

For a few minutes I can't sit down. I can't stand up. I can only smoke. The phone rings. Another physicist tells me there's some bad news. He mentions Chris and Bob and I tell him I don't want to talk right now. He says okay but to be prepared because it's going to be on the news any minute. It's 4:45.

"Now they're trying to stir Bob into the stew," I tell Mary. She nods; she's heard this, too. I have the distinct feeling there is something going on that I can either understand or not understand. There's a choice to be made.

"I don't understand," I tell Mary.

We sit in the darkening living room, smoking and sipping our cups of whiskey. Inside my head I keep thinking *Uh-oh*, over and over. I'm in a rattled condition; I can't calm down and figure this out.

"I think we should brace ourselves in case something bad has happened," I say to Mary. She nods. "Just in case. It won't hurt to be braced." She nods again. I realize that I don't know what *braced* means. You hear it all the time but that doesn't mean it makes sense. Whiskey is supposed to be bracing but what it is is awful. I want either tea or beer, no whiskey. Mary nods and heads into the kitchen.

Within an hour there are seven women in the dim living room, sitting. Switching back and forth between CNN and the special reports by the local news. There is something terrifying about the quality of the light and the way voices are echoing in the room. The phone never stops ringing, ever since the story hit the national news. Physics, University of Iowa, dead people. Names not yet released. Everyone I've ever known is checking in to see if I'm still alive. California calls, New York calls, Florida calls, Ohio calls twice. All the guests at a party my husband is having call, one after the other, to ask how I'm doing. Each time, fifty times, I think it might be Chris and then it isn't.

It occurs to me once that I could call his house and talk to him directly, find out exactly what happened. Fear that his mother would answer prevents me from doing it. By this time I am getting reconciled to the fact that Shan, Gang Lu, and Dwight were killed. Also an administrator and her office assistant. The Channel 9 newslady keeps saying there are six dead and two in critical condition. They're not saying who did the shooting. The names will be released at nine o'clock. Eventually I sacrifice all of them except Chris and Bob; they are the ones in critical condition, which is certainly not hopeless. At some point I go into the study to get away from the terrible dimness in the living room, all those eyes, all that calmness in the face of chaos. The collie tries to stand up but someone stops her with a handful of Fritos.

The study is small and cold after I shut the door, but more brightly lit than the living room. I can't remember what anything means. The phone rings and I pick up the extension and listen. My friend Michael is calling from Illinois for the second time. He asks Shirley if I'm holding up okay. Shirley says it's hard to tell. I go back into the living room.

The newslady breaks in at nine o'clock, and of course they drag it out as long as they can. I've already figured out that if they go in alphabetical order Chris will come first. Goertz, Lu, Nicholson, Shan, Smith. His name will come on first. She drones on, dead University of Iowa professors, lone gunman named Gang Lu.

Gang Lu. Lone gunman. Before I have a chance to absorb that she says, The dead are.

Chris's picture.

Oh no, oh God. I lean against Mary's chair and then leave the room abruptly. I have to stand in the bathroom for a while and look at myself in the mirror. I'm still Jo Ann, white face and dark hair. I have earrings on, tiny wrenches that hang from wires. In the living room she's pronouncing all the other names. The two critically wounded are the administrator and her assistant, Miya Sioson. The administrator is already dead for all practical purposes, although they won't disconnect the machines until the following afternoon. The student receptionist will survive but will never again be able to move more than her head. She was in Gang Lu's path and he shot her in the mouth and the bullet lodged in the top of her spine and not only will she never dance again, she'll never walk or write or spend a day alone. She got to keep her head but lost her body. The final victim is Chris's mother, who will weather it all with a dignified face and an erect spine, then return to Germany and kill herself without further words or fanfare.

I tell the white face in the mirror that Gang Lu did this, wrecked everything and killed all those people. It seems as ludicrous as everything else. I can't get my mind to work right, I'm still operating on yesterday's facts; today hasn't jelled yet. "It's a good thing none of this happened," I say to my face. A knock on the door and I open it.

The collie is swaying on her feet, toenails clenched to keep from sliding on the wood floor. Julene's hesitant face. "She wanted to come visit you," she tells me. I bring her in and close the door. We sit by the tub. She lifts her long nose to my face and I take her muzzle and we move through the gears slowly, first second third fourth, all the way through town, until what happened has happened and we know it has happened. We return to the living room. The second wave of calls is starting to come in, from those who just saw the faces on the news. Shirley screens. A knock comes on the door. Julene settles the dog down again on her blanket. It's the husband at the door, looking frantic. He hugs me hard but I'm made of cement, arms stuck in a down position.

The women immediately clear out, taking their leave, looking at the floor.

Suddenly it's only me and him, sitting in our living room on a Friday night, just like always. I realize it took quite a bit of courage for him to come to the house when he did, facing all those women who think he's the Antichrist. The dogs are crowded against him on the couch and he's wearing a shirt I've never seen before. He's here to help me get through this. Me. He knows how awful this must be. Awful. He knows how I felt about Chris. Past tense. I have to put my hands over my face for a minute.

We sit silently in our living room. He watches the mute television screen and I watch him. The planes and ridges of his face are more familiar to me than my own. I understand that he wishes even more than I do that he still loved me. When he looks over at me, it's with an expression I've seen before. It's the way he looks at the dog on the blanket.

I get his coat and follow him out into the cold November night. There are stars and stars and stars. The sky is full of dead men, drifting in the blackness like helium balloons. My mother floats past in a hospital gown, trailing tubes. I go back inside where the heat is.

The house is empty and dim, full of dogs and cigarette butts. The collie has peed again. The television is flickering *Special Report* across the screen and I turn it off before the pictures appear. I bring blankets up, fresh and warm from the dryer.

After all the commotion the living room feels cavernous and dead. A branch scrapes against the house and for a brief instant I feel a surge of hope. They might have come back. And I stand at the foot of the stairs staring up into the darkness, listening for the sounds of their little squirrel feet. Silence. No matter how much you miss them. They never come back once they're gone.

I wake her up three times between midnight and dawn. She doesn't usually sleep this soundly but all the chaos and company in the house tonight have made her more tired than usual. The Lab wakes and drowsily begins licking her lower region. She stops and stares at me, trying to make out my face in the dark, then gives up and sleeps. The brown dog is flat on her back with her paws limp, wedged between me and the back of the couch.

I've propped myself so I'll be able to see when dawn starts to arrive. For now there are still planets and stars. Above the black branches of a maple is the dog star, Sirius, my personal favorite. The dusty rings of Saturn. Io, Jupiter's moon.

When I think I can't bear it for one more minute I reach down and nudge her gently with my dog-arm. She rises slowly, faltering, and stands over me in the darkness. My peer, my colleague. In a few hours the world will resume itself, but for now we're in a pocket of silence. We're in the plasmapause, a place of equilibrium, where the forces of the Earth meet the forces of the sun. I imagine it as a place of silence, where the particles of dust stop spinning and hang motionless in deep space.

Around my neck is the stone he brought me from Poland. I hold it out. *Like this?* I ask. Shards of fly wings, suspended in amber.

Exactly, he says.

Wendell Berry

GETTING ALONG WITH NATURE

WENDELL BERRY, novelist, poet, essayist, philosopher, and farmer, is the author of fourteen books of poems, eleven novels and short story collections, and sixteen volumes of essays, including *The Unsettling of America*. A recipient of a Wallace Stegner Fellowship, Berry studied creative writing at Stanford University. He has received numerous awards, including a Guggenheim Fellowship. He lives on the family farm at Port Royal, Kentucky.

1982

The defenders of nature and wilderness—like their enemies the defenders of the industrial economy—sometimes sound as if the natural and the human were two separate estates, radically different and radically divided. The defenders of nature and wilderness sometimes seem to feel that they must oppose any human encroachment whatsoever, just as the industrialists often apparently feel that they must make the human encroachment absolute or, as they say, "complete the conquest of nature." But there is danger in this opposition, and it can be best dealt with by realizing that these pure and separate categories are pure ideas and do not otherwise exist.

Pure nature, anyhow, is not good for humans to live in, and humans do not want to live in it—or not for very long. Any exposure to the elements that lasts more than a few hours will remind us of the desirability of the basic human amenities: clothing, shelter, cooked food, the company of kinfolk and friends—perhaps even of hot baths and music and books.

It is equally true that a condition that is *purely* human is not good for people to live in, and people do not want to live for very long in it. Obviously, the more artificial a human environment becomes, the more the word "natural" becomes a term of value. It can be argued, indeed, that the conservation movement, as we know it today, is largely a product of the industrial revolution. The people who want clean air, clear streams, and wild forests, prairies, and deserts are the people who no longer have them.

People cannot live apart from nature; that is the first principle of the conservationists. And yet, people cannot live in nature without changing it. But this is true of *all* creatures; they depend upon nature, and they change it. What we call nature is, in a sense, the sum of the changes made by all the various creatures and natural forces in their intricate actions and influences upon each other and upon their places. Because of the woodpeckers, nature is different from what it would be without them. It is different also because of the borers and ants that live in tree trunks, and because of the bacteria that live in the soil under the trees. The making of these differences is the making of the world.

Some of the changes made by wild creatures we would call beneficent: beavers are famous for making ponds that turn into fertile meadows; trees and prairie grasses build soil. But sometimes, too, we would call natural changes destructive. According to early witnesses, for instance, large areas around Kentucky salt licks were severely trampled and eroded by the great herds of hoofed animals that gathered there. The buffalo "streets" through hilly country were so hollowed out by hoof-wear and erosion that they remain visible almost two centuries after the disappearance of the buffalo. And so it can hardly be expected that humans would not change nature. Humans, like all other creatures, must make a difference; otherwise, they cannot live. But unlike other creatures, humans must make a choice as to the kind and scale of the difference they make. If they choose to make too small a difference, they diminish their humanity. If they choose to make too great a difference, they diminish nature, and narrow their subsequent choices; ultimately, they diminish or destroy themselves. Nature, then, is not only our source but also our limit and measure. Or, as the poet Edmund Spenser put it almost four hundred years ago, Nature, who is the "greatest goddesse," acts as a sort of earthly lieutenant of God, and Spenser represents her as both a mother and judge. Her jurisdiction is over the relations between the creatures; she deals "right to all . . . indifferently," for she is "the equall mother" of all "and knittest each to each, as brother unto brother." Thus, in Spenser, the natural principles of fecundity and order are pointedly linked with the principle of justice, which we may be a little surprised to see that he attributes also to nature. And yet in his insistence on an "indifferent" natural justice, resting on the "brotherhood" of *all* creatures, not just of humans, Spenser would now be said to be on sound ecological footing.

In nature we know that wild creatures sometimes exhaust their vital sources and suffer the natural remedy: drastic population reductions. If lynxes eat too many snowshoe rabbits—which they are said to do repeatedly—then the lynxes starve down to the carrying capacity of their habitat. It is the carrying capacity of the lynx's habitat, not the carrying capacity of the lynx's stomach, that determines the prosperity of lynxes. Similarly, if humans use up too much soil—

which they have often done and are doing—then they will starve down to the carrying capacity of *their* habitat. This is nature's "indifferent" justice. As Spenser saw in the sixteenth century, and as we must learn to see now, there is no appeal from this justice. In the hereafter, the Lord may forgive our wrongs against nature, but on earth, so far as we know, He does not overturn her decisions.

One of the differences between humans and lynxes is that humans can see that the principle of balance operates between lynxes and snowshoe rabbits, as between humans and topsoil; another difference, we hope, is that humans have the sense to act on their understanding. We can see, too, that a stable balance is preferable to a balance that tilts back and forth like a seesaw, dumping a surplus of creatures alternately from either end. To say this is to renew the question of whether or not the human relationship with nature is necessarily an adversary relationship, and it is to suggest that the answer is not simple.

But in dealing with this question and in trying to do justice to the presumed complexity of the answer, we are up against an American convention of simple opposition to nature that is deeply established both in our minds and in our ways. We have opposed the primeval forests of the East and the primeval prairies and deserts of the West, we have opposed man-eating beasts and crop-eating insects, sheep-eating coyotes and chicken-eating hawks. In our lawns and gardens and fields, we oppose what we call weeds. And yet more and more of us are beginning to see that this opposition is ultimately destructive even of ourselves, that it does not explain many things that need explaining—in short, that it is untrue.

If our proper relation to nature is not opposition, then what is it? This question becomes complicated and difficult for us because none of us, as I have said, wants to live in a "pure" primeval forest or in a "pure" primeval prairie; we do not want to be eaten by grizzly bears; if we are gardeners, we have a legitimate quarrel with weeds; if, in Kentucky, we are trying to improve our pastures, we are likely to be enemies of the nodding thistle. But, do what we will, we remain under the spell of the primeval forests and prairies that we have cut down and broken; we turn repeatedly and with love to the thought of them and to their surviving remnants. We find ourselves attracted to the grizzly bears, too, and know that they and other great, dangerous animals remain alive in our imaginations as they have been all through human time. Though we cut down the nodding thistles, we acknowledge their beauty and are glad to think that there must be some place where they belong. (They may, in fact, not always be out of place in pastures; if, as seems evident, overgrazing makes an ideal seedbed for these plants, then we must understand them as a part of nature's strategy to protect the ground against abuse by animals.) Even the ugliest garden weeds earn affection from us when we consider how faithfully they perform an indispensable duty in covering the bare ground and in building humus. The weeds, too, are involved in the business of fertility.

We know, then, that the conflict between the human and the natural estates really exists and that it is to some extent necessary. But we are learning, or re-learning, something else, too, that frightens us: namely, that this conflict often occurs at the expense of *both* estates. It is not only possible but altogether prob-able that by diminishing nature we diminish ourselves, and vice versa.

The conflict comes to light most suggestively, perhaps, when advocates for the two sides throw themselves into absolute conflict where no absolute differ-ence can exist. An example of this is the battle between defenders of coyotes and defenders of sheep, in which the coyote-defenders may find it easy to forget that the sheep ranchers are human beings with some authentic complaints against coyotes, and the sheep-defenders find it easy to sound as if they advo-cate the total eradication of both coyotes and conservationists. Such conflicts—like the old one between hawk-defenders and chicken-defenders—tend to occur between people who use nature indirectly and people who use it directly. It is a dangerous mistake, I think, for either side to pursue such a quarrel on the assumption that victory would be a desirable result.

The fact is that people need both coyotes and sheep, need a world in which both kinds of life are possible. Outside the heat of conflict, conservationists probably know that a sheep is one of the best devices for making coarse foliage humanly edible and that wool is ecologically better than the synthetic fibers, just as most shepherds will be aware that wild nature is of value to them and not lacking in interest and pleasure.

The usefulness of coyotes is, of course, much harder to define than the useful-ness of sheep. Coyote fur is not a likely substitute for wool, and, except as a last resort, most people don't want to eat coyotes. The difficulty lies in the difference between what is ours and what is nature's: What is ours is ours because it is directly useful. Coyotes are useful *indirectly*, as part of the health of nature, from which we and our sheep alike must live and take our health. The fact, moreover, may be that sheep and coyotes need each other, at least in the sense that neither would prosper in a place totally unfit for the other.

This sort of conflict, then, does not suggest the possibility of victory so much as it suggests the possibility of a compromise—some kind of peace, even an al-liance, between the domestic and the wild. We know that such an alliance is necessary. Most conservationists now take for granted that humans thrive best in ecological health and that the test or sign of this health is the survival of a diversity of wild creatures. We know, too, that we cannot imagine ourselves apart from those necessary survivals of our own wildness that we call our in-stincts. And we know that we cannot have a healthy agriculture apart from the teeming wilderness in the topsoil, in which worms, bacteria, and other wild creatures are carrying on the fundamental work of decomposition, humus making, water storage, and drainage. "In wildness is the preservation of the world," as Thoreau said, may be a spiritual truth, but it is also a practical fact.

On the other hand, we must not fail to consider the opposite proposition— that, so long at least as humans are in the world, in human culture is the preservation of wildness—which is equally, and more demandingly, true. If wildness is to survive, then *we* must preserve it. We must preserve it by public act, by law, by institutionalizing wildernesses in some places. But such preservation is probably not enough. I have heard Wes Jackson of the Land Institute say, rightly I think, that if we cannot preserve our farmland, we cannot preserve the wilderness. That said, it becomes obvious that if we cannot preserve our cities, we cannot preserve the wilderness. This can be demonstrated practically by saying that the same attitudes that destroy wildness in the topsoil will finally destroy it everywhere; or by saying that if *everyone* has to go to a designated public wilderness for the necessary contact with wildness, then our parks will be no more natural than our cities.

But I am trying to say something more fundamental than that. What I am aiming at—because a lot of evidence seems to point this way—is the probability that nature and human culture, wildness and domesticity, are not opposed but are interdependent. Authentic experience of either will reveal the need of one for the other. In fact, examples from both past and present prove that a human economy and wildness can exist together not only in compatibility but to their mutual benefit.

One of the best examples I have come upon recently is the story of two Sonora Desert oases in Gary Nabhan's book *The Desert Smells Like Rain*. The first of these oases, A'al Waipia, in Arizona, is dying because the park service, intending to preserve the natural integrity of the place as a bird sanctuary for tourists, removed the Papago Indians who had lived and farmed there. The place was naturally purer after the Indians were gone, but the oasis also began to shrink as the irrigation ditches silted up. As Mr. Nabhan puts it, "an odd thing is happening to their 'natural' bird sanctuary. They are losing the heterogeneity of the habitat, and with it, the birds. The old trees are dying. . . . These riparian trees are essential for the breeding habitat of certain birds. Summer annual seed plants are conspicuously absent. . . . Without the soil disturbance associated with plowing and flood irrigation, these natural foods for birds and rodents no longer germinate."

The other oasis, Ki:towak, in old Mexico, still thrives because a Papago village is still there, still farming. The village's oldest man, Luis Nolia, is the caretaker of the oasis, cleaning the springs and ditches, farming, planting trees:

"Luis . . . blesses the oasis," Mr. Nabhan says, "for his work keeps it healthy." An ornithologist who accompanied Mr. Nabhan found twice as many species of birds at the farmed oasis as he found at the bird sanctuary, a fact that Mr. Nabhan's Papago friend, Remedio, explained in this way: "That's because those birds, they come where the people are. When the people live and work in a place, and plant their seeds and water their trees, the birds go live with them. They like those places, there's plenty to eat and that's when we are friends to them."

Another example, from my own experience, is suggestive in a somewhat different way. At the end of July 1981, while I was using a team of horses to mow a small triangular hillside pasture that is bordered on two sides by trees, I was suddenly aware of wings close below me. It was a young red-tailed hawk, who flew up into a walnut tree. I mowed on to the turn and stopped the team. The hawk then glided to the ground not twenty feet away. I got off the mower, stood and watched, even spoke, and the hawk showed no fear. I could see every feather distinctly, claw and beak and eye, the creamy down of the breast. Only when I took a step toward him, separating myself from the team and mower, did he fly. While I mowed three or four rounds, he stayed near, perched in trees or standing erect and watchful on the ground. Once, when I stopped to watch him, he was clearly watching me, stooping to see under the leaves that screened me from him. Again, when I could not find him, I stooped, saying to myself, "This is what he did to look at me," and as I did so I saw him looking at me.

Why had he come? To catch mice? Had he seen me scare one out of the grass? Or was it curiosity?

A human, of course, cannot speak with authority of the motives of hawks. I am aware of the possibility of explaining the episode merely by the hawk's youth and inexperience. And yet it does not happen often or dependably that one is approached so closely by a hawk of any age. I feel safe in making a couple of assumptions. The first is that the hawk came because of the conjunction of the small pasture and its wooded borders, of open hunting ground and the security of trees. This is the phenomenon of edge or margin that we know to be one of the powerful attractions of a diversified landscape, both to wildlife and to humans. The human eye itself seems drawn to such margins, hungering for the difference made in the countryside by a hedgy fencerow, a stream, or a grove of trees. And we know that these margins are biologically rich, the meeting of two kinds of habitat. But another difference also is important here: the difference between a large pasture and a small one, or, to use Wes Jackson's terms, the difference between a field and a patch. The pasture I was mowing was a patch—small, intimate, nowhere distant from its edges.

My second assumption is that the hawk was emboldened to come so near because, though he obviously recognized me as a man, I was there with the team of horses, with whom he familiarly and confidently shared the world.

I am saying, in other words, that this little visit between the hawk and me happened because the kind and scale of my farm, my way of farming, and my technology *allowed* it to happen. If I had been driving a tractor in a hundred-acre cornfield, it would not have happened.

In some circles I would certainly be asked if one can or should be serious about such an encounter, if it has any value. And though I cannot produce any hard evidence, I would unhesitatingly answer yes. Such encounters involve another margin—the one between domesticity and wildness—that attracts us irresistibly; they are among the best rewards of outdoor work and among the reasons for loving to farm. When the scale of farming grows so great and obtrusive as to forbid them, the *life* of farming is impoverished.

But perhaps we do find hard evidence of a sort when we consider that *all* of us—the hawk, the horses, and I—were there for our benefit and, to some extent, for our *mutual* benefit: The horses live from the pasture and maintain it with their work, grazing, and manure; the team and I together furnish hunting ground to the hawk; the hawk serves us by controlling the field mouse population.

These meetings of the human and the natural estates, the domestic and the wild, occur invisibly, of course, in any well-farmed field. The wilderness of a healthy soil, too complex for human comprehension, can yet be husbanded, can benefit from human care, and can deliver incalculable benefits in return. Mutuality of interest and reward is a possibility that can reach to any city backyard, garden, and park, but in any place under human dominance—which is, now, virtually everyplace—it is a possibility that is *both* natural and cultural. If humans want wildness to be possible, then they have to make it possible. If balance is the ruling principle and a stable balance the goal, then, for humans, attaining this goal requires a consciously chosen and deliberately made partnership with nature.

In other words, we can be true to nature only by being true to human nature—to our animal nature as well as to cultural patterns and restraints that keep us from acting like animals. When humans act like animals, they become the most dangerous of animals to themselves and other humans, and this is because of another critical difference between humans and animals: Whereas animals are usually restrained by the limits of physical appetites, humans have mental appetites that can be far more gross and capacious than physical ones. Only humans squander and hoard, murder and pillage because of notions.

The work by which good human and natural possibilities are preserved is complex and difficult, and it probably cannot be accomplished by raw intelligence and information. It requires knowledge, skills, and restraints, some of which must come from our past. In the hurry of technological progress, we have replaced some tools and methods that worked with some that do not work. But we also need culture-borne instructions about who or what humans are and how and on what assumptions they should act. The Chain of Being, for instance—which gave humans a place between animals and angels in the order of Creation—is an old idea that has not been replaced by any adequate new one. It was simply rejected, and the lack of it leaves us without a definition.

Lacking that ancient definition, or any such definition, we do not know at what point to restrain or deny ourselves. We do not know how ambitious to be, what or how much we may safely desire, when or where to stop. I knew a barber once who refused to give a discount to a bald client, explaining that his artistry consisted, not in the cutting off, but in the knowing when to stop. He spoke, I think, as a true artist and a true human. The lack of such knowledge is extremely dangerous in and to an individual. But ignorance of when to stop is a modern epidemic; it is the basis of "industrial progress" and "economic growth." The most obvious practical result of this ignorance is a critical disproportion of scale between the scale of human enterprises and their sources in nature.

The scale of the energy industry, for example, is too big, as is the scale of the transportation industry. The scale of agriculture, from a technological or economic point of view, is too big, but from a demographic point of view, the scale is too small. When there are enough people on the land to use it but not enough to husband it, then the wildness of the soil that we call fertility begins to diminish, and the soil itself begins to flee from us in water and wind.

If the human economy is to be fitted into the natural economy in such a way that both may thrive, the human economy must be built to proper scale. It is possible to talk at great length about the difference between proper and improper scale. It may be enough to say here that that difference is *suggested* by the difference between amplified and unamplified music in the countryside, or the difference between the sound of a motorboat and the sound of oarlocks. A proper human sound, we may say, is one that allows other sounds to be heard. A properly scaled human economy or technology allows a diversity of other creatures to thrive.

"The proper scale," a friend wrote to me, "confers freedom and simplicity . . . and doubtless leads to long life and health." I think that it also confers joy. The renewal of our partnership with nature, the rejoining of our works to their proper places in the natural order, reshaped to their proper scale, implies the reenjoyment both of nature and of human domesticity. Though our task will be difficult, we will greatly mistake its nature if we see it as grim, or if we suppose that it must always be necessary to suffer at work in order to enjoy ourselves in places specializing in "recreation."

Once we grant the possibility of a proper human scale, we see that we have made a radical change of assumptions and values. We realize that we are less interested in technological "breakthroughs" than in technological elegance. Of a new tool or method we will no longer ask: Is it fast? Is it powerful? Is it a labor saver? How many workers will it replace? We will ask instead: Can we (and our children) afford it? Is it fitting to our real needs? Is it becoming to us? Is it un-healthy or ugly? And though we may keep a certain interest in innovation and in what we may become, we will renew our interest in what we have been, real-izing that conservationists must necessarily conserve *both* inheritances, the natural and the cultural.

To argue the necessity of wildness to, and in, the human economy is by no means to argue against the necessity of wilderness. The survival of wilderness—of places that we do not change, where we allow the existence even of creatures we perceive as dangerous—is necessary. Our sanity probably requires it. Whether we go to those places or not, we need to know that they exist. And I would ar-gue that we do not need just the great public wildernesses, but millions of small private or semiprivate ones. Every farm should have one; wildernesses can oc-cupy corners of factory grounds and city lots—places where nature is given a free hand, where no human work is done, where people go only as guests. These places function, I think, whether we intend them to or not, as sacred groves—places we respect and leave alone, not because we understand well what goes on there, but because we do not.

We go to wilderness places to be restored, to be instructed in the natural economies of fertility and healing, to admire what we cannot make. Sometimes, as we find to our surprise, we go to be chastened or corrected. And we go in order to return with renewed knowledge by which to judge the health of our human economy and our dwelling places. As we return from our visits to the wilderness, it is sometimes possible to imagine a series of fitting and decent transitions from wild nature to the human community and its supports: from forest to woodlot to the "two-story agriculture" of tree crops and pasture to orchard to meadow to grainfield to garden to household to neighborhood to village to city—so that even when we reached the city we would not be entirely beyond the influence of the nature of that place.

What I have been implying is that I think there is a bad reason to go to the wilderness. We must not go there to escape the ugliness and the dangers of the present human economy. We must not let ourselves feel that to go there is to escape. In the first place, such an escape is now illusory. In the second place, if, even as conservationists, we see the human and the natural economies as necessarily opposite or opposed, we subscribe to the very opposition that threatens to destroy them both. The wild and the domestic now often seem isolated values, estranged from one another. And yet these are not exclusive polarities like good and evil. There can be continuity between them, and there must be.

What we find, if we weight the balance too much in favor of the domestic, is that we involve ourselves in dangers both personal and public. Not the least of these dangers is dependence on distant sources of money and materials. Farmers are in deep trouble now because they have become too dependent on corporations and banks. They have been using methods and species that enforce this dependence. But such a dependence is not safe, either for farmers or for agriculture. It is not safe for urban consumers. Ultimately, as we are beginning to see, it is not safe for banks and corporations—which, though they have evidently not thought so, are dependent upon farmers. Our farms are endangered because—like the interstate highways or modern hospitals or modern universities—they cannot be inexpensively used. To be usable at all they require great expense.

When the human estate becomes so precarious, our only recourse is to move it back toward the estate of nature. We undoubtedly need better plant and animal species than nature provided us. But we are beginning to see that they can be too much better—too dependent on us and on "the economy," too expensive. In farm animals, for instance, we want good commercial quality, but we can see that the ability to produce meat or milk can actually be a threat to the farmer and to the animal if not accompanied by qualities we would call natural: thriftiness, hardiness, physical vigor, resistance to disease and parasites, ability to breed and give birth without assistance, strong mothering instincts. These natural qualities decrease care, work, and worry; they also decrease the costs of production. They save feed and time; they make diseases and cures exceptional rather than routine.

We need crop and forage species of high productive ability also, but we do not need species that will not produce at all without expensive fertilizers and chemicals. Contrary to the premise of agribusiness advertisements and of most expert advice, farmers do not thrive by production or by "skimming" a large "cash flow." They cannot solve their problems merely by increasing production or income. They thrive, like all other creatures, according to the difference between their income and their expenses.

One of the strangest characteristics of the industrial economy is the ability to increase production again and again without ever noticing—or without acknowledging—the *costs* of production. That one Holstein cow should produce 50,000 pounds of milk in a year may appear to be marvelous—a miracle of modern science. But what if her productivity is dependent upon the consumption of a huge amount of grain (about a bushel a day), and therefore upon the availability of cheap petroleum? What if she is too valuable (and too delicate) to be allowed outdoors in the rain? What if the proliferation of her kind will again drastically reduce the number of dairy farms and farmers? Or, to use a more obvious example, can we afford a bushel of grain at a cost of five to twenty bushels of topsoil lost to erosion?

"It is good to have Nature working for you," said Henry Besuden, the dean of American Southdown breeders. "She works for a minimum wage." That is true. She works at times for almost nothing, requiring only that we respect her work and give her a chance, as when she maintains—indeed, improves—the fertility and productivity of a pasture by the natural succession of clover and grass or when she improves a clay soil for us by means of the roots of a grass sod. She works for us by preserving health or wholeness, which for all our ingenuity we cannot make. If we fail to respect her health, she deals out her justice by withdrawing her protection against disease—which we *can* make, and do.

To make this continuity between the natural and the human, we have only two sources of instruction: nature herself and our cultural tradition. If we listen only to the apologists for the industrial economy, who respect neither nature nor culture, we get the idea that it is somehow our goodness that makes us so destructive: The air is unfit to breathe, the water is unfit to drink, the soil is washing away, the cities are violent and the countryside neglected, all because we are intelligent, enterprising, industrious, and generous, concerned only to feed the hungry and to "make a better future for our children." Respect for nature causes us to doubt this, and our cultural tradition confirms and illuminates our doubt: No good thing is destroyed by goodness; good things are destroyed by wickedness. We may identify that insight as Biblical, but it is taken for granted by both the Greek and the Biblical lineages of our culture, from Homer and Moses to William Blake. Since the start of the industrial revolution, there have been voices urging that this inheritance may be safely replaced by intelligence, information, energy, and money. No idea, I believe, could be more dangerous.

Eula Biss

THE PAIN SCALE

EULA BISS, author of *The Balloonists*, teaches nonfiction writing at Northwestern University and is coeditor of Essay Press, a new press dedicated to publishing innovative nonfiction. Her essays have recently appeared in *Gulf Coast*, *Hotel Amerika*, *Columbia*, *Ninth Letter*, *American Poet*, the *North American Review*, the *Massachusetts Review*, the *Seneca Review*, and *Harper's*.

No Pain

The concept of Christ is considerably older than the concept of zero. Both are problematic—both have their fallacies and their immaculate conceptions. But the problem of zero troubles me significantly more than the problem of Christ.

I am sitting in the exam room of a hospital entertaining the idea that absolutely no pain is not possible. Despite the commercials, I suspect that pain cannot be eliminated. And this may be the fallacy on which we have based all our calculations and all our excesses. All our sins are for zero.

Zero is not a number. Or at least, it does not behave like a number. It does not add, subtract, or multiply like other numbers. Zero is a number in the way that Christ was a man.

Aristotle, for one, did not believe in Zero.

If no pain is possible, then, another question—is no pain desirable? Does the absence of pain equal the absence of everything?

Some very complicated mathematical problems cannot be solved without the concept of zero. But zero makes some very simple problems impossible to solve. For example, the value of zero divided by zero is unknown.

I'm not a mathematician. I'm sitting in a hospital trying to measure my pain on a scale from zero to ten. For this purpose, I need a zero. A scale of any sort needs fixed points.

The upper fixed point on the Fahrenheit scale, ninety-six, is based on a slightly inaccurate measure of normal body temperature. The lower fixed point, zero, is the coldest temperature at which a mixture of salt and water can still remain liquid. I myself am a mixture of salt and water. I strive to remain liquid.

Zero, on the Celsius scale, is the point at which water freezes. And one hundred is the point at which water boils.

But Anders Celsius, who introduced the scale in 1741, originally fixed zero as the point at which water boiled, and one hundred as the point at which water froze. These fixed points were reversed only after his death.

The deepest circle of Dante's *Inferno* does not burn. It is frozen. In his last glimpse of Hell, Dante looks back and sees Satan upside down through the ice.

There is only one fixed point on the Kelvin scale—absolute zero. Absolute zero is 273 degrees Celsius colder than the temperature at which water freezes. There are zeroes beneath zeroes. Absolute zero is the temperature at which molecules and atoms are moving as slowly as possible. But even at absolute zero, their motion does not stop completely. Even the absolute is not absolute. This is comforting, but it does not give me faith in zero.

At night, I ice my pain. My mind descends into a strange sinking calm. Any number multiplied by zero is zero. And so with ice and me. I am nullified. I wake up to melted ice and the warm throb of my pain returning.

Grab a chicken by its neck or body—it squawks and flaps and pecks and thrashes like mad. But grab a chicken by its feet and turn it upside down, and it just hangs there blinking in a waking trance. Zeroed. My mother and I hung the chickens like this on the barn door for their necks to be slit. I like to imagine that a chicken at zero feels no pain.

←———————— 1 ————————→

Major things are wind, evil, a good fighting horse, prepositions, inexhaustible love, the way people choose their king. Minor things include dirt, the names of schools of philosophy, mood and not having a mood, the correct time. There are more major things than minor things overall, yet there are more minor things than I have written here, but it is disheartening to list them. . . .
—Anne Carson

My father is a physician. He treats patients with cancer, who often suffer extreme pain. My father raised me to believe that most pain is minor. He was never impressed by my bleeding cuts or even my weeping sores. In retrospect, neither am I.

Every time I go to the doctor and every time I visit the physical therapist, I am asked to rate my pain on a scale from zero to ten. This practice of quantifying pain was introduced by the hospice movement in the 1970s, with the goal of providing better care for patients who did not respond to curative treatment.

My father once told me that an itch is just very mild pain. Both sensations simply signal, he told me, irritated or damaged tissue.

But a nasty itch, I observed, can be much more excruciating than a paper cut, which is also mild pain. Digging at an itch until it bleeds and is transformed into pure pain can bring a kind of relief.

Where does pain worth measuring begin? With poison ivy? With a hang nail? With a stubbed toe? A sore throat? A needle prick? A razor cut?

When I complained of pain as a child, my father would ask, "What kind of pain?" Wearily, he would list for me some of the different kinds of pain, "Burning, stabbing, throbbing, prickling, dull, sharp, deep, shallow . . ."

Hospice nurses are trained to identify five types of pain: physical, emotional, spiritual, social, and financial.

The pain of feeling, the pain of caring, the pain of doubting, the pain of parting, the pain of paying.

Overlooking the pain of longing, the pain of desire, the pain of sore muscles, which I find pleasurable . . .

The pain of learning, and the pain of reading.

The pain of trying.

The pain of living.

A minor pain or a major pain?

There is a mathematical proof that zero equals one. Which, of course, it doesn't.

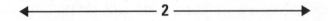

The set of whole numbers is also known as "God's numbers."

The devil is in the fractions.

Although the distance between one and two is finite, it contains infinite fractions. This could also be said of the distance between my mind and my body. My one and my two. My whole and its parts.

The sensations of my own body may be the only subject on which I am qualified to claim expertise. Sad and terrible, then, how little I know. "How do you feel?" the doctor asks, and I cannot answer. Not accurately. "Does this hurt?" he asks. Again, I'm not sure. "Do you have more or less pain than the last time I saw you?" Hard to say. I begin to lie to protect my reputation. I try to act certain.

The physical therapist raises my arm above my head. "Any pain with this?" she asks. Does she mean any pain in addition to the pain I already feel, or does she mean any pain at all? She is annoyed by my question. "Does this cause you pain?" she asks curtly. No. She bends my neck forward. "Any pain with this?" No. "Any pain with this?" No. It feels like a lie every time.

On occasion, an extraordinary pain swells like a wave under the hands of the doctor, or the chiropractor, or the massage therapist, and floods my body. Sometimes I hear my throat make a sound. Sometimes I see spots. I consider this the pain of treatment, and I have come to find it deeply pleasurable. I long for it.

The International Association for the Study of Pain is very clear on this point—pain must be unpleasant. "Experiences which resemble pain but are not unpleasant," reads their definition of pain, "should not be called pain."

In the second circle of Dante's *Inferno*, the adulterous lovers cling to each other, whirling eternally, caught in an endless wind. My next-door neighbor, who loves Chagall, does not think this sounds like Hell. I think it depends on the wind.

Wind, like pain, is difficult to capture. The poor windsock is always striving, and always falling short.

It took sailors more than two hundred years to develop a standardized numerical scale for the measure of wind. The result, the Beaufort scale, provides twelve categories for everything from "Calm" to "Hurricane." The scale offers not just a number, but a term for the wind, a range of speed, and a brief description.

A force 2 wind on the Beaufort scale, for example, is a "Light Breeze" moving between four and seven miles per hour. On land, it is specified as "wind felt on face; leaves rustle; ordinary vanes moved by wind."

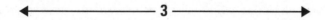

Left alone in the exam room I stare at the pain scale, a simple number line complicated by only two phrases. Under zero: "no pain." Under ten: "the worst pain imaginable."

The worst pain imaginable . . . Stabbed in the eye with a spoon? Whipped with nettles? Buried under an avalanche of sharp rocks? Impaled with hundreds of nails? Dragged over gravel behind a fast truck? Skinned alive?

My father tells me that some things one might expect to be painful are not. I have read that starving to death, at a certain point, is not exactly painful. At times, it may even cause elation. Regardless, it is my sister's worst fear. She would rather die any other way, she tells me.

I do not prefer one death over another. Perhaps this is because I am incapable of imagining the worst pain imaginable. Just as I am incapable of actually understanding calculus, although I could once perform the equations correctly.

Like the advanced math of my distant past, determining the intensity of my own pain is a blind calculation. On my first attempt, I assigned the value of ten to a theoretical experience—burning alive. Then I tried to determine what percentage of the pain of burning alive I was feeling.

I chose 30 percent—three. Which seemed, at the time, quite substantial.

Three. Mail remains unopened. Thoughts are rarely followed to their conclusions. Sitting still becomes unbearable after one hour. Nausea sets in. Grasping at the pain does not bring relief. Quiet desperation descends.

"Three is nothing," my father tells me now. "Three is go home and take two aspirin." It would be helpful, I tell him, if that could be noted on the scale.

The four vital signs used to determine the health of a patient are blood pressure, temperature, breath, and pulse. Recently, it has been suggested that pain be considered a fifth vital sign. But pain presents a unique problem in terms of measurement, and a unique cruelty in terms of suffering—it is entirely subjective.

Assigning a value to my own pain has never ceased to feel like a political act. I am citizen of a country that ranks our comfort above any other concern. People suffer, I know, so that I may eat bananas in February. And then there is history. . . . I struggle to consider my pain in proportion to the pain of a napalmed Vietnamese girl whose skin is slowly melting off as she walks naked in the sun. This exercise itself is painful.

"You are not meant to be rating world suffering," my friend in Honduras advises. "This scale applies only to you and your experience."

At first, this thought is tremendously relieving. It unburdens me of factoring the continent of Africa into my calculations. But the reality that my nerves alone feel my pain is terrifying. I hate the knowledge that I am isolated in this skin—alone with my pain and my own fallibility.

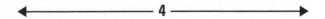

The Wong-Baker Faces scale was developed to help young children rate their pain.

| 0 | 1 | 2 | 3 | 4 | 5 |
| No Hurt | Hurts Little Bit | Hurts Little More | Hurts Even More | Hurts Whole Lot | Hurts Worst |

The face I remember, always, was on the front page of a local newspaper in an Arizona gas station. The man's face was horrifyingly distorted in an open-mouthed cry of raw pain. His house, the caption explained, had just been destroyed in a wildfire. But the man himself, the article revealed, had not been hurt.

Several studies have suggested that children using the Wong-Baker scale tend to conflate emotional pain and physical pain. A child who is not in physical pain but is very frightened of surgery, for example, might choose the crying face. One researcher observed that "hurting" and "feeling" seemed to be synonymous to some children. I myself am puzzled by the distinction. Both words are used to describe emotions as well as physical sensations, and pain is defined as a "sensory and emotional experience." In an attempt to rate only the physical pain of children, a more emotionally "neutral" scale was developed.

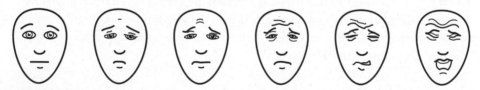

A group of adult patients favored the Wong-Baker scale in a study comparing several different types of pain scales. The patients were asked to identify the easiest scale to use by rating all the scales on a scale from zero, "not easy," to six, "easiest ever seen." The patients were then asked to rate how well the scales represented pain on a scale from zero, "not good," to six, "best ever seen." The patients were not invited to rate the experience of rating.

I stare at a newspaper photo of an Israeli boy with a bloodstained cloth wrapped around his forehead. His face is impassive.

I stare at a newspaper photo of a prisoner standing delicately balanced with electrodes attached to his body, his head covered with a hood.

No face, no pain?

A crying baby, to me, always seems to be in the worst pain imaginable. But when my aunt became a nurse twenty years ago, it was not unusual for surgery to be done on infants without any pain medication. Babies, it was believed, did not have the fully developed nervous systems necessary to feel pain. Medical evidence that infants experience pain in response to anything that would cause an adult pain has only recently emerged.

There is no evidence of pain on my body. No marks. No swelling. No terrible tumor. The X-rays revealed nothing. Two MRIs of my brain and spine revealed nothing. Nothing was infected and festering, as I had suspected and feared. There was no ghastly huge white cloud on the film. There was nothing to illustrate my pain except a number, which I was told to choose from between zero and ten. My proof.

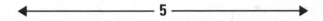

"The problem with scales from zero to ten," my father tells me, "is the tyranny of the mean."

Overwhelmingly, patients tend to rate their pain as a five, unless they are in excruciating pain. At best, this renders the scale far less sensitive to gradations in pain. At worst, it renders the scale useless.

I understand the desire to be average only when I am in pain. To be normal is to be okay in a fundamental way—to be chosen numerically by God.

When I could no longer sleep at night because of my pain, my father reminded me that a great many people suffer from both insomnia and pain. "In fact," he told me, "neck and back pain is so common that it is a cliché—a pain in the neck!"

The fact that 50 million Americans suffer from chronic pain does not comfort me. Rather, it confounds me. "This is not normal," I keep thinking. A thought invariably followed by a doubt, "Is this normal?"

The distinction between test results that are normal or abnormal is often determined by how far the results deviate from the mean. My X-rays did not reveal a cause for my pain, but they did reveal an abnormality. "See this," the doctor pointed to the string of vertebrae hanging down from the base of my skull like a loose line finding plumb. "Your spine," he told me, "is abnormally straight."

I live in Middle America. I am of average height, although I have always thought of myself as short. I am of average weight, although I tend to believe I am oddly shaped. Although I try to hide it, I have long straight blond hair, like most of the women in this town.

Despite my efforts to ignore it and to despise it, I am still susceptible to the mean—a magnet that pulls even flesh and bone. For some time I entertained the idea that my spine might have been straightened by my long-held misconception that normal spines were perfectly straight. Unknowingly, I may have been striving for a straight spine, and perhaps I had managed to disfigure my body by sitting too straight for too many years. "Unlikely," the doctor told me.

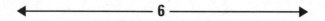

A force 6 wind on the Beaufort scale, a "Strong Breeze," is characterized by "large branches in motion; telegraph wires whistle; umbrellas used with difficulty."

Over a century before preliminary scales were developed to quantify the wind, serious efforts were made to produce an accurate map of Hell. Infernal cartography was considered an important undertaking for the architects and mathematicians of the Renaissance, who based their calculations on the distances and proportions described by Dante. The exact depth and circumference of Hell inspired intense debates, despite the fact that all calculations, no matter how sophisticated, were based on a work of fiction.

Galileo Galilei delivered extensive lectures on the mapping of Hell. He applied recent advances in geometry to determine the exact location of the entrance to the underworld and then figured the dimensions that would be necessary to maintain the structural integrity of Hell's interior.

It was the age of the golden rectangle—the divine proportion. Mathematics revealed God's plan. But the very use of numbers required a religious faith, because one could drop off the edge of the earth at any point. The boundaries of the maps at that time faded into oceans full of monsters.

Imagination is treacherous. It erases distant continents, it builds a Hell so real that the ceiling is vulnerable to collapse. To be safe, I think I should only map my pain in proportion to pain I have already felt.

But my nerves have short memories. My mind remembers crashing my bicycle as a teenager, but my body does not. I cannot seem to conjure the sensation of lost skin without actually losing skin. My nerves cannot, or will not, imagine past pain—this, I think, is for the best. Nerves simply register, they do not invent.

After a year of pain, I realized that I could no longer remember what it felt like not to be in pain. I was left anchorless. I tended to think of the time before the pain as easier and brighter, but I began to suspect myself of fantasy and nostalgia.

Although I cannot ask my body to remember feeling pain it does not feel, and I cannot ask it to remember not feeling pain it does feel, I have found that I can ask my body to imagine the pain it feels as something else. For example, with some effort I can imagine the sensation of pain as heat.

Perhaps, with a stronger mind, I could imagine the heat as warmth, and then the warmth as nothing at all.

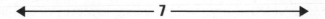

I accidentally left a burner on the stove going for two and a half days—a small blue flame, burning, burning, burning . . .

The duration terrified me. How incredibly dangerous, so many hours of fire.

I would happily cut off a finger at this point if I could trade the pain of that cut for the endless pain I have now.

When I cry from it, I cry over the idea of it lasting forever, not over the pain itself. The psychologist, in her rational way, suggests that I do not let myself imagine it lasting forever. "Choose an amount of time that you know you can endure," she suggests, "and then challenge yourself only to make it through that time." I make it through the night, and then sob through half the morning.

The pain scale measures only the intensity of pain, not the duration. This may be its greatest flaw. A measure of pain, I believe, requires at least two dimensions. The suffering of Hell is terrifying not because of any specific torture, but because it is eternal.

The square root of seven results in a decimal that repeats randomly into infinity. The exact figure cannot be known, only a close approximation. Rounding a number to the nearest significant figure is a tool designed for the purpose of making measurements. The practicality of rounding is something my mind can fully embrace. No measurement is ever exact, of course.

Seven is the largest prime number between zero and ten. Out of all the numbers, the very largest primes are unknown. Still, every year, the largest known prime is larger. Euclid proved the number of primes to be infinite, but the infinity of primes is slightly smaller than the infinity of the rest of the numbers. It is here, exactly at this point, that my ability to comprehend begins to fail.

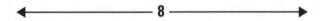

Although all the numbers follow each other in a predictable line, many unknown quantities exist.

I do not know how long I have been clenching my teeth when I notice that I am clenching my teeth. My mind, apparently, has not been with my body. I wonder why, when I most want to, I cannot seem to keep my mind from my body.

I no longer know who I am, or if I am in charge of myself.

Experts do not know why some pain resolves and other pain becomes chronic. One theory is that the body begins to react to its own reaction, trapping itself in a cycle of its own pain response. This can go on indefinitely, twisting like the figure eight of infinity.

My father tells me that when he broke his collarbone it didn't hurt. I would like to believe this, but I am suspicious of my father's assessment of his own pain.

The problem of pain is that I cannot feel my father's, and he cannot feel mine. This, I suppose, is also the essential mercy of pain.

Several recent studies have suggested that women feel pain differently than men. Further studies have suggested that pain medications act differently on women than they do on men. I am suspicious of these studies, so favored by *Newsweek*, and so heaped upon waiting-room tables. I dislike the idea that our flesh is so essentially unique that it does not even register pain as a man's flesh does—a fact that renders our bodies, again, objects of supreme mystery.

But I am comforted, oddly, by the possibility that you cannot compare my pain to yours. And, for that reason, cannot prove it insignificant.

The medical definition of pain specifies the "presence or potential of tissue damage." Pain that does not signal tissue damage is not, technically, pain.

"This is a pathology," the doctor assured me when he informed me that there was no definitive cause of my pain, no effective treatment for it, and very probably no end to it. "This is not in your head."

It would not have occured to me to think that I was imagining the pain. But the longer the pain persisted, and the harder it became for me to imagine what it was like not to be in pain, the more seriously I considered the disturbing possibility that I was not, in fact, in pain.

Another theory of chronic pain is that it is a faulty message sent by malfunctioning nerves. "For example," the Mayo Clinic suggests, "your pain could be similar to the phantom pain some amputees feel in their amputated limbs."

I walked out of a lecture on chronic pain after too many repetitions of the phrase, "We have reason to believe that you are in pain, even if there is no physical evidence of your pain." I had not realized that the fact that I believed myself to be in pain was not reason enough.

We have reason to believe in infinity, but everything we know ends.

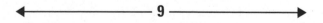

"I have a very high pain threshold," my mother mentions casually. This is undoubtedly true.

I stand by uselessly and cover my ears as my mother, a very small woman, lifts the blunt end of a pick axe over her head and slams it down on a metal pipe she is driving into the frozen ground. Any portrait of my mother should include a blue-black fingernail.

"I breathe, I have a heartbeat, I have pain . . ." I repeat to myself as I lie in bed at night. I am striving to adopt the pain as a vital sensation. My mother, I know, has already mastered this exercise.

Her existence, like my father's, pains me. This is the upper fixed point of love.

Once, for a study of chronic pain, I was asked to rate not just my pain but also my suffering. I rated my pain as a three. Having been sleepless for nearly a week, I rated my suffering as a seven.

"Pain is the hurt, either physical or emotional, that we experience," writes the Reverend James Chase. "Suffering is the story we tell ourselves of our pain."

Yes, suffering is the story we tell ourselves.

"At the moment we are devoid of any standard criteria as to what constitutes suffering," Reverend Chase writes in his paper on genetic therapy, which is more a meditation on suffering. "Since we do not have agreed-upon criteria, it would be negligent to make decisions for others regarding suffering. We might be able to answer this for ourselves, but not for others. . . .

"If we come to the point where we have no place for suffering, to what lengths will we go to eradicate it? Will we go so far as to inflict suffering to end it?"

Christianity is not mine. I do not know it and I cannot claim it. But I've seen the sacred heart ringed with thorns, the gaping wound in Christ's side, the weeping virgin, the blood, the nails, the cross to bear. . . . Pain is holy, I understand. Suffering is divine.

In my worst pain, I can remember thinking, "This is not beautiful." I can remember being disgusted by the very idea.

But in my worst pain, I also found myself secretly cherishing the phrase, "This too shall pass." The longer the pain lasted, the more beautiful and impossible and absolutely holy this phrase became.

 **10**

The Worst Pain Imaginable

Through a failure of my imagination, or of myself, I have discovered that the pain I am in is always the worst pain imaginable.

But I would like to believe that there is an upper limit to pain. That there is a maximum intensity nerves can register.

There is no tenth circle in Dante's Hell.

The digit ten depends on the digit zero, in our current number system. In 1994 Robert Forslund developed an Alternative Number System. "This system," he wrote with triumph, "eliminates the need for the digit zero, and hence all digits behave the same."

In the Alternate Number System, the tenth digit is represented by the character A. Counting begins at one: 1, 2, 3, 4, 5, 6, 7, 8, 9, A, 11, 12 . . . 18, 19, 1A, 21, 22 . . . 28, 29, 2A . . . 98, 99, 9A, A1, A2, A3, A4, A5, A6, A7, A8, A9, AA, 111, 112 . . .

"One of the functions of the pain scale," my father explains, "is to protect doctors—to spare them some emotional pain. Hearing someone describe their pain as a ten is much easier than hearing them describe it as a hot poker driven through their eyeball into their brain."

A better scale, my father thinks, might rate what patients would be willing to do to relieve their pain. "Would you," he suggests, "visit five specialists and take three prescription narcotics?" I laugh because I have done just that. "Would you," I offer, "give up a limb?" I would not. "Would you surrender your sense of sight for the next ten years?" my father asks. I would not. "Would you accept a shorter life span?" I might. We are laughing, having fun with this game. But later, reading statements collected by the American Pain Foundation, I am alarmed by the number of references to suicide.

". . . constant muscle aches, spasms, sleeplessness, pain, can't focus . . . must be depression . . . two suicide attempts later, electroshock therapy and locked-down wards. . . ."

The description of hurricane-force winds on the Beaufort scale is simply "devastation occurs."

Bringing us, of course, back to zero.

Mary Clearman Blew

THE UNWANTED CHILD

MARY CLEARMAN BLEW is the author of *Lambing Out and Other Stories, Runaway: Stories, All But the Waltz, Balsamroot, Circle of Women* (with Kim Barnes), *Bone Deep in Landscape, Sister Coyote: Montana Stories,* and *Written on Water: Essays on Idaho Rivers.* She teaches at the University of Idaho.

December 1958. I lie on my back on an examination table in a Missoula clinic while the middle-aged doctor whose name I found in the Yellow Pages inserts his speculum and takes a look. He turns to the sink and washes his hands.

"Yes, you're pregnant," he says. "Congratulations, Mommy."

His confirmation settles over me like a fog that won't lift. Myself I can manage for, but for myself and *it?*

After I get dressed, he says, "I'll want to see you again in a month, Mommy."

If he calls me Mommy again, I will break his glasses and grind them in his face, grind them until he has no face. I will kick him right in his obscene fat paunch. I will bury my foot in his disgusting flesh.

I will walk through the glass doors and between the shoveled banks of snow to the parking lot where my young husband waits in the car.

"You're not, are you?" he says.

"Yes."

"Yes, you're not?"

"Yes, I am! Jeez!"

His feelings are hurt. But he persists: "I just don't think you are. I just don't see how you could be."

He has a theory on the correct use of condoms, a theory considerably more flexible than the one outlined by the doctor I visited just before our marriage three months ago, and which he has been arguing with increasing anxiety ever since I missed my second period. I stare out the car window at the back of the clinic while he expounds on his theory for the zillionth time. What difference

43

does it make now? Why can't he shut up? If I have to listen to him much longer, I will kill him, too.

At last, even his arguments wear thin against the irrefutable fact. As he turns the key in the ignition his eyes are deep with fear.

"But I'll stand by you," he promises.

Why get married at eighteen?

When you get married, you can move into married student housing. It's a shambles, it's a complex of converted World War II barracks known as the Strips, it's so sorry the wind blows through the cracks around the windows and it lacks hot-water heaters and electric stoves, but at least it's not the dormitory, which is otherwise the required residence of all women at the University of Montana. Although no such regulations apply to male students, single women must be signed in and ready for bed check by ten o'clock on weeknights and one on weekends. No alcohol, no phones in rooms. Women must not be reported on campus in slacks or shorts (unless they can prove they are on their way to a physical education class), and on Sundays they may not appear except in heels, hose, and hat. A curious side effect of marriage, however, is that the responsibility for one's virtue is automatically transferred from the dean of women to one's husband. Miss Maurine Clow never does bed checks or beer checks in the Strips.

When you get married, you can quit making out in the backseat of a parked car and go to bed in a bed. All young women in 1958 like sex. Maybe their mothers had headaches or hang-ups, but *they* are normal, healthy women with normal, healthy desires, and they know the joy they will find in their husbands' arms will—well, be better than making out, which, though none of us will admit it, is getting to be boring. We spend hours shivering with our clothes off in cars parked in Pattee Canyon in subzero weather, groping and being groped and feeling embarrassed when other cars crunch by in the snow, full of onlookers with craning necks, and worrying about the classes we're not attending because making out takes so much time. We are normal, healthy women with normal, healthy desires if we have to die to prove it. Nobody has ever said out loud that she would like to go to bed and *get it over with* and get on with something else.

There's another reason for getting married at eighteen, but it's more complicated.

By getting married I have eluded Dean Maurine Clow only to fall into the hands of in-laws.

"We have to tell the folks," my husband insists. "They'll want to know."

His letter elicits the predictable long-distance phone call from them. I make him answer it. While he talks to them I rattle dishes in the kitchen, knowing exactly how they look, his momma and his daddy in their suffocating Helena living room hung with mounted elk antlers and religious calendars, their heads together over the phone, their faces wreathed in big grins at his news.

"They want to talk to you," he says finally. Then, "Come on!"

I take the phone with fear and hatred. "Hello?"

"Well!!!" My mother-in-law's voice carols over the miles. "I guess this is finally the end of college for you!"

She uses a Maytag washing machine with a wringer and a monotonous, daylong chugging motor which, she often says, is a damn sight better than a washboard. She starts by filling the tub with boiling water and soap flakes. Then she agitates her whites for twenty minutes, fishes them out with her big fork, and feeds them sheet by sheet into the wringer. After she rinses them by hand, she reverses the wringer and feeds them back through, creased and steaming hot, and carries them out to the clothesline to freeze-dry. By this time the water in the tub has cooled off enough for the coloreds. She'll keep running through her loads until she's down to the blue jeans and the water is thick and greasy. My mother has spent twenty-five years of Mondays on the washing.

I know I have to tell her I'm pregnant.

She's talking about college, she's quoting my grandmother, who believes that every woman should be self-sufficient. Even though I'm married now, even though I had finished only one year at the University of Montana before I got married, my grandmother has agreed to go on lending me what I need for tuition and books. Unlike my in-laws, who have not hesitated to tell me I should go to work as a typist or a waitress to support my husband through college (after all, he will be supporting me for the rest of my life), my grandmother believes I should get my own credentials.

My mother and grandmother talk about a teaching certificate as if it were a gold ring which, if I could just grab it, would entitle the two of them to draw a long breath of relief. Normally I hate to listen to their talk. They don't even know you can't get a two-year teaching certificate now, you have to go the full four years.

But beyond the certificate question, college has become something that I never expected and cannot explain: not something to grab and have done with but a door opening, a glimpse of an endless passage and professors who occasionally beckon from far ahead—like lovely, elderly Marguerite Ephron, who lately has been leading four or five of us through the *Aeneid*. Latin class has been my sanctuary for the past few months; Latin has been my solace from conflict that otherwise has left me as steamed and agitated as my mother's whites, now churning away in the Maytag; Latin in part because it is taught by Mrs. Ephron, always serene, endlessly patient, mercilessly thorough, who teaches at the university while Mr. Ephron works at home, in a basement full of typewriters with special keyboards, on the translations of obscure clay tablets.

So I've been accepting my grandmother's money under false pretenses. I'm not going to spend my life teaching around Fergus County the way she did, the way my mother would have if she hadn't married my father. I've married my husband under false pretenses, too; he's a good fly-fishing Helena boy who has no idea in the world of becoming a Mr. Ephron. But, subversive as a foundling in a fairy tale, I have tried to explain none of my new aspirations to my mother or grandmother or, least of all, my husband and his parents, who are mightily distressed as it is by my borrowing money for my own education.

"—and it's all got to be paid back, you'll be starting your lives in *debt!*"

"—the most important thing is to get *him* through, *he's* the one who's got to go out and face the world!"

"—what on earth do you think you'll do with your education?"

And now all the argument is pointless, the question of teaching certificate over quest for identity, the importance of my husband's future over mine, the relentless struggle with the in-laws over what is most mine, my self. I'm done for, knocked out of the running by the application of a faulty condom theory.

"Mom," I blurt, "I'm pregnant."

She gasps. And before she can let out that breath, a frame of memory freezes with her in it, poised over her rinse tub, looking at me through the rising steam and the grinding wringer. Right now I'm much too miserable to wonder what she sees when she looks at me: her oldest daughter, her bookish child, the day-dreamer, the one she usually can't stand, the one who takes everything too seriously, who will never learn to take no for an answer. Thin and strong and blue-jeaned, bespectacled and crop-haired, this girl could pass for fifteen right now and won't be able to buy beer in grocery stores for years without showing her driver's license. This girl who is too miserable to look her mother in the face, who otherwise might see in her mother's eyes the years of blight and disappointment. She does hear what her mother says:

"Oh, Mary, no!"

My mother was an unwanted child. The fourth daughter of a homesteading family racked by drought and debt, she was only a year old when the sister nearest her in age died of a cancerous tumor. She was only two years old when the fifth and last child, the cherished boy, was born. She was never studious like her older sisters nor, of course, was she a boy, and she was never able to find her own ground to stand on until she married.

Growing up, I heard her version often, for my mother was given to a kind of continuous oral interpretation of herself and her situation. Standing over the sink or stove, hoeing the garden, running her sewing machine with the permanent angry line deepening between her eyes, she talked. Unlike the stories our grandmothers told, which, like fairy tales, narrated the events of the past but avoided psychological speculation ("Great-great-aunt Somebody-or-other was home alone making soap when the Indians came, so she waited until they got close enough, and then she threw a ladle of lye on them ..."), my mother's dwelt on the motives behind the darkest family impulses.

"Ma never should have had me. It was her own fault. She never should have had me if she didn't want me."

"But then you wouldn't have been born!" I interrupted, horrified at the thought of not being.

"Wouldn't have mattered to me," she said. "I'd never have known the difference."

What I cannot remember today is whom my mother was telling her story to. Our grandmothers told their stories to my little sisters and me, to entertain us, but my mother's bitter words flowed past us like a river current past small, ignored onlookers who eavesdropped from its shores. I remember her words, compulsive, repetitious, spilling out over her work—for she was always working—and I was awed by her courage. What could be less comprehensible than not wanting to be? More fearsome than annihilation?

Nor can I remember enough about the circumstances of my mother's life during the late 1940s and the early 1950s to know why she was so angry, why she was so compelled to deconstruct her childhood. Her lot was not easy. She had married into a close-knit family that kept to itself. She had her husband's mother on her hands all her life, and on top of the normal isolation and hard work of a ranch wife of those years, she had to provide homeschooling for her children.

And my father's heath was precarious, and the ranch was failing. The reality of that closed life along the river bottom became more and more attenuated by the outward reality of banks and interest rates and the shifting course of agribusiness. She was touchy with money worries. She saw the circumstances of her sisters' lives grow easier as her own grew harder. Perhaps these were reasons enough for rage.

I recall my mother in her middle thirties through the telescoped eye of the child that distorts the intentions of parents and enlarges them to giants. Of course she was larger than life. Unlike my father, with his spectrum of ailments, she was never sick. She was never hospitalized in her life for any reason but childbirth, never came down with anything worse than a cold. She lugged the armloads of wood and buckets of water and slops and ashes that came with cooking and washing and ironing in a kitchen with a wood range and no plumbing; she provided the endless starchy meals of roast meat and potatoes and gravy; she kept salads on her table and fresh or home-canned vegetables at a time when iceberg lettuce was a town affectation.

She was clear-skinned, with large gray eyes that often seemed fixed on some point far beyond our familiar slopes and cutbanks. And even allowing for the child's telescoped eye, she was a tall woman who thought of herself as oversized. She was the tallest of her sisters. "*As big as Doris* is what they used to say about me!"

Bigness to her was a curse. "You big ox!" she would fling at me over some altercation with my little sister. True to the imperative that is handed down through the generations, I in turn bought my clothes two sizes too large for years.

All adult ranch women were fat. I remember hardly a woman out of her teens in those years who was not fat. The few exceptions were the women who had, virtually, become a third sex by taking on men's work in the fields and corrals; they might stay as skinny and tough in their Levi's as hired hands.

But women who remained women baked cakes and cream pies and breads and sweet rolls with the eggs from their own chickens and the milk and butter and cream from the cows they milked, and they ate heavily from appetite and from fatigue and from the monotony of their isolation. They wore starched cotton print dresses and starched aprons and walked ponderously beside their whiplash husbands. My mother, unless she was going to be riding or helping in the hayfields, always wore those shapeless, starched dresses she sewed herself, always cut from the same pattern, always layered over with an apron.

What was she so angry about? Why was her forehead kneaded permanently into a frown? It was a revelation for me one afternoon when she answered a knock at the screen door, and she smiled, and her voice lifted to greet an old friend of hers and my father's from their single days. Color rose in her face, and she looked pretty as she told him where he could find my father. Was that how outsiders always saw her?

Other ranch women seemed cheerful enough on the rare occasions when they came in out of the gumbo. Spying on them as they sat on benches in the shade outside the horticulture house at the county fair or visited in the cabs of trucks at rodeos, I wondered if these women, too, were angry when they were alone with only their children to observe them. What secrets lay behind those vast placid, smiling faces, and what stories could their children tell?

My mother believed that her mother had loved her brother best and her older sisters next best. "He was always The Boy and they were The Girls, and Ma was proud of how well they did in school," she explained again and again to the walls, the stove, the floor she was mopping, "and I was just Doris. I was average."

Knowing how my grandmother had misjudged my mother, I felt guilty about how much I longed for her visits. I loved my grandmother and her fresh supply of stories about the children who went to the schools she taught, the games they played, and the books they read. School for me was an emblem of the world outside our creek-bottom meadows and fenced mountain slopes. At eight, I was still being taught at home; our gumbo road was impassable for most of the school months, and my father preferred that we be kept safe from contact with "them damn town kids," as he called them. Subversively I begged my grandmother to repeat her stories again and again, and I tried to imagine what it must be like to see other children every day and to have a real desk and real lessons. Other than my little sister, my playmates were mostly cats. But my grandmother brought with her the breath of elsewhere.

My mother's resentment whitened in intensity during the weeks before a visit from my grandmother, smoldered during the visit itself, and flared up again as soon as my grandmother was safely down the road to her next school. "I wonder if she ever realizes she wouldn't even have any grandchildren if I hadn't got married and had some kids! *The Girls* never had any kids! Some people should never have kids! Some people should never get married!"

With a child's logic, I thought she was talking about me. I thought I was responsible for her anger. I was preoccupied for a long time with a story I had read about a fisherman who was granted three wishes; he had used his wishes badly, but I was sure I could do better, given the chance. I thought a lot about how I would use three wishes, how I would use their potential for lifting me out of the present.

"What would you wish for, if you had three wishes?" I prodded my mother.

She turned her faraway gray eyes on me, as though she had not been ranting about The Girls the moment before. "I'd wish you'd be good," she said.

That was what she always said, no matter how often I asked her. With everything under the sun to wish for, that unfailing answer was a perplexity and a worry.

I was my grandmother's namesake, and I was a bookworm like my mother's older sisters. Nobody could pry my nose out of a book to do my chores, even

though I was marked to be the outdoor-working child, even though I was supposed to be my father's boy.

Other signs that I was not a boy arose to trouble us both and account, I
thought, for my mother's one wish.

"Mary's getting a butt on her just like a girl," she remarked one night as I
climbed out of the tub. Alarmed, I craned my neck to see what had changed
about my eight-year-old buttocks.

"Next thing, you'll be mooning in the mirror and wanting to pluck your
eyebrows just like the rest of 'em," she said.

"I will not," I said doubtfully.

I could find no way through the contradiction. On the one hand, I was a boy
(except that I also was a bookworm), and my chores were always in the barns
and corrals, never the kitchen. *You don't know how to cook on a woodstove?* my
mother-in-law was to cry in disbelief. *And you grew up on a ranch?*

To act like a boy was approved; to cry or show fear was to invite ridicule.
Sissy! Big bellercalf! On the other hand, I was scolded for hanging around the
men, the way ranch boys did. I was not a boy (my buttocks, my vanity). What
was I?

"Your dad's boy," my mother answered comfortingly when I asked her. She
named a woman I knew. "Just like Hazel. Her dad can't get along without her."

Hazel was a tough, shy woman who rode fences and pulled calves and took
no interest in the country dances or the "running around" her sisters did on
weekends. Hazel never used lipstick or permed her hair; she wore it cut almost
like a man's. Seen at the occasional rodeo or bull sale in her decently pressed
pearl-button shirt and new Levi's, she stuck close to her dad. Like me, Hazel
apparently was not permitted to hang around the men.

What Hazel did not seem interested in was any kind of fun, and a great resolve arose in me that, whatever I was, I was going to have . . . whatever it was.
I would get married, even if I wasn't supposed to.

But my mother had another, darker reason to be angry with me, and I knew it.
The reason had broken over me suddenly the summer I was seven and had been
playing, on warm afternoons, in a rain barrel full of water. Splashing around,
elbows and knees knocking against the side of the barrel, I enjoyed the rare
sensation of being wet all over. My little sister, four, came and stood on tiptoe
to watch. It occurred to me to boost her into the barrel with me.

My mother burst out of the kitchen door and snatched her back.

"What are you trying to do, kill her?" she shouted.

I stared back at her, wet, dumbfounded.

Her eyes blazed over me, her brows knotted at their worst. "And after you'd drowned her, I suppose you'd have slunk off to hide somewhere until it was all over!"

It had never crossed my mind to kill my sister, or that my mother might think I wanted to. (Although I had, once, drowned a setting of baby chicks in a rain barrel.) But that afternoon, dripping in my underpants, goose-bumped and ashamed, I watched her carry my sister into the house and then I did go off to hide until it was, somehow, all over, for she never mentioned it at dinner.

The chicks had been balls of yellow fuzz, and I had been three. I wanted them to swim. I can just remember catching a chick and holding it in the water until it stopped squirming and then laying it down to catch a fresh one. I didn't stop until I had drowned the whole dozen and laid them out in a sodden yellow row.

What the mind refuses to allow to surface is characterized by a suspicious absence. Of detail, of associations. Memories skirt the edge of nothing. There is for me about this incident that suspicious absence. What is being withheld?

Had I, for instance, given my mother cause to believe I might harm my sister? Children have done such harm, and worse. What can be submerged deeper, denied more vehemently, than the murderous impulse? At four, my sister was a tender, trusting little girl with my mother's wide gray eyes and brows. A younger sister of an older sister. A good girl. Mommy's girl.

What do I really know about my mother's feelings toward her own dead sister? Kathryn's dolls had been put away; my mother was never allowed to touch them.

"I'll never, never love one of my kids more than another!" she screamed at my father in one of her afternoons of white rage. The context is missing.

During the good years, when cattle prices were high enough to pay the year's bills and a little extra, my mother bought wallpaper out of a catalog and stuck it to her lumpy walls. She enameled her kitchen white, and she sewed narrow strips of cloth she called "drapes" to hang at the sides of her windows. She bought a stiff, tight cylinder of linoleum at Sears, Roebuck in town and hauled it home in the back of a pickup and unrolled it in a shiny flowered oblong in the middle of her splintery front room floor.

Occasionally I would find her sitting in her front room on her "davenport," which she had saved for and bought used, her lap full of sewing and her forehead relaxed out of its knot. For a moment there was her room around her as she wanted it to look: the clutter subdued, the new linoleum mopped and quivering under the chair legs that held down its corners, the tension of the opposing floral patterns of wallpaper, drapes, and slipcovers held in brief, illusory harmony by the force of her vision.

How hard she tried for her daughters! Over the slow thirty miles of gumbo and gravel we drove to town every summer for dentist appointments at a time when pulling teeth was still a more common remedy than filling them, when our own father and his mother wore false teeth before they were forty.

During the good years, we drove the thirty miles for piano lessons. An upright Kimball was purchased and hauled home in the back of the pickup. Its carved oak leaves and ivories dominated the front room, where she found time to "sit with us" every day as we practiced. With a pencil she pointed out the notes she had learned to read during her five scant quarters in normal school and made us read them aloud. "F-sharp!" she would scream over the throb of the Maytag in the kitchen as one of us pounded away.

She carped about bookworms, but she located the dim old Carnegie library in town and got library cards for us even though, as country kids, we weren't strictly entitled to them. After that, trips home from town with sacks of groceries included armloads of library books. Against certain strictures, she could be counted on. When, in my teens, I came home with my account of the new book the librarian kept in her desk drawer and refused to check out to me, my mother straightened her back as I knew she would. "She thinks she can tell one of my kids what she can read and what she can't read?"

On our next visit to the library, she marched up the stone steps and into the mote-filled sanctum with me.

The white-haired librarian glanced up inquiringly.

"You got *From Here to Eternity*?"

The librarian looked at me, then at my mother. Without a word she reached into her drawer and took out a heavy volume. She stamped it and handed it to my mother, who handed it to me.

How did she determine that books and dentistry and piano lessons were necessities for her daughters, and what battles did she fight for them as slipping cattle prices put even a gallon of white enamel paint or a sheet of new linoleum beyond her reach?

Disaster followed disaster on the ranch. An entire season's hay crop lost to a combination of ancient machinery that would not hold together and heavy rains that would not let up. A whole year's calf crop lost because the cows had been pastured in timber that had been logged, and when they ate the pine needles from the downed tops, they spontaneously aborted. As my father grew less and less able to face the reality of the downward spiral, what could she hope to hold together with her pathetic floral drapes and floral slipcovers?

· · ·

Bundled in coats and overshoes in the premature February dark, our white breaths as one, my mother and I huddle in the shadow of the chicken house. By moonlight we watch the white-tailed deer that have slipped down out of the timber to feed from the haystack a scant fifty yards away. Cautiously I raise my father's rifle to my shoulder. I'm not all that good a marksman, I hate the inevitable explosive crack, but I brace myself on the corner of the chicken house and sight carefully and remember to squeeze. Ka-crack!

Eight taupe shapes shoot up their heads and spring for cover. A single mound remains in the snow near the haystack. By the time my mother and I have climbed through the fence and trudged up to the haystack, all movement from the doe is reflexive. "Nice and fat," says my mother.

Working together with our butcher knives, we lop off her scent glands and slit her and gut her and save the heart and liver in a bucket for breakfast. Then, each taking a leg, we drag her down the field, under the fence, around the chicken house, and into the kitchen, where we will skin her out and butcher her.

We are two mid-twentieth-century women putting meat on the table for the next few weeks. Neither of us has ever had a hunting license, and if we did, hunting season is long closed, but we're serene about what we're doing. "Eating our hay, aren't they?" says my mother. "We're entitled to a little venison. The main thing is not to tell anybody what we're doing."

And the pregnant eighteen-year-old? What about her?

In June of 1959 she sits up in the hospital bed, holding in her arms a small warm scrap whose temples arc deeply dented from the forceps. She cannot remember birthing him, only the long hours alone before the anesthetic took over. She feels little this morning, only a dull worry about the money, money, money for college in the fall.

The in-laws are a steady, insistent, increasingly frantic chorus of disapproval over her plans. *But, Mary! Tiny babies have to be kept warm!* her mother-in-law keeps repeating, pathetically, ever since she was told about Mary's plans for fall quarter.

But, Mary! How can you expect to go to college and take good care of a husband and a baby?

Finally, *We're going to put our foot down!*

She knows that somehow she has got to extricate herself from these sappy folks. About the baby she feels only a mild curiosity. Life where there was none before. The rise and fall of his tiny chest. She has him on her hands now. She must take care of him.

Why not an abortion?

Because the thought never crossed her mind. Another suspicious absence, another void for memory to skirt. What she knew about abortion was passed around the midnight parties in the girls' dormitory: *You drink one part turpentine with two parts sugar.* Or was it the other way around? . . . *two parts turpentine to one part sugar. You drink gin in a hot bath . . .*

She has always hated the smell of gin. It reminds her of the pine needles her father's cattle ate, and how their calves were born shallow-breathed and shriveled, and how they died. She knows a young married woman who begged her husband to hit her in the stomach and abort their fourth child.

Once, in her eighth month, the doctor had shot her a look across his table. "If you don't want this baby," he said, "I know plenty of people who do."

"I want it," she lied.

No, but really. What is to become of this eighteen-year-old and her baby?

Well, she's read all the sentimental literature they shove on the high school girls. She knows how the plot is supposed to turn out.

Basically, she has two choices.

One, she can invest all her hopes for her own future in this sleeping scrap. *Son, it was always my dream to climb to the stars. Now the tears of joy sprung at the sight of you with your college diploma . . .*

Even at eighteen, this lilylicking is enough to make her sick.

Or, two, she can abandon the baby and the husband and become really successful and really evil. This is the more attractive version of the plot, but she doesn't really believe in it. Nobody she knows has tried it. It seems as out of reach from ordinary daylight Montana as Joan Crawford or the Duchess of Windsor or the moon. As she lies propped up in bed with the sleeping scrap in her arms, looking out over the dusty downtown rooftops settling into noon in the waning Eisenhower years, she knows very well that Joan Crawford will never play the story of her life.

What, then? What choice is left to her?

What outcome could possibly be worth all this uproar? Her husband is on the verge of tears these days; he's only twenty himself, and he had no idea what trouble he was marrying into, his parents pleading and arguing and threatening, even his brothers and their wives chiming in with their opinions, even the minister getting into it, even the neighbors; and meanwhile his wife's grandmother firing off red-hot letters from her side, meanwhile his wife's mother refusing to budge an inch—united, those two women are as formidable as a pair of rhinoceroses, though of course he has no idea in the world what it took to unite them.

All this widening emotional vortex over whether or not one Montana girl will finish college. What kind of genius would she have to be to justify it all?

Will it be enough that, thirty years later, she will have read approximately 16,250 freshman English essays out of an estimated lifetime total of 32,000?

Will it be enough, over the years, that she remembers the frozen frame of her mother's face over the rinse tub that day after Christmas in 1958 and wonders whether she can do as much for her son as was done for her? Or that she often wonders whether she really lied when she said, *I want it*?

Will it be enough? What else is there?

Charles Bowden

TORCH SONG

CHARLES BOWDEN, a recipient of the Lannan Foundation award and a contributing editor to *GQ* magazine and contributing writer to *Mother Jones*, is the author of many books, including *A Shadow in the City: Confessions of an Undercover Drug Warrior; Down by the River: Drugs, Money, Murder and Family*, a *New York Times* Notable Book; *Blues for Cannibals: The Notes from Underground; Juárez: The Laboratory of Our Future; Blood Orchid: An Unnatural History of America; Desierto: Memories of the Future; Red Line; Blue Desert;* and *Trust Me: Charles Keating and the Missing Billions* (with Michael Binstein). His next book is *Café Blood: Going over Jordan.*

I can't tell much from her silhouette. She's sitting off to one side, her shoulders hunched, and toward the front is the box with the teddy bears. Or at least I think they're teddy bears. Almost twenty years have passed, and I've avoided thinking about it. There are some things that float pretty free of time, chronology, the book of history, and the lies of the experts. In the early eighties I went to a funeral as part of my entry into a world, a kind of border crossing.

It started as the gold light of afternoon poured through the high, slit windows of the newsroom. I had no background in the business and I'd lied to get the job. I was the fluff writer, the guy brought on to spin something out of nothing for the soft features and the easy pages about how people fucked up their marriages or made a quiche or found the strength to go on with their lives because of God, a diet, or a new self-help book. Sometimes they wrote the book, sometimes they just believed the book. I interviewed Santa Claus, and he told me of the pain and awkwardness of having held a child on his fat lap in Florida as ants crawled up his legs and bit him. One afternoon the newsroom was empty, and the city desk looked out and beckoned me. I was told to go to a motel and see if I could find anything to say.

The rooms faced a courtyard on the old desert highway that came into town and were part of a strip of unhappy inns left to die after the interstate lanced Tucson's flank. When I was twelve this belt still flourished, and my first night in this city was spent in a neighboring motel with a small pool. I remember swimming until late at night, intoxicated with the idea of warm air, cool water, and palm trees. My sister was fourteen, and the son of the owners, a couple from the East with the whiff of Mafia about them, dated her; later, I read a newspaper story that cited him as a local purveyor of pornography. But the row of motels had since lost prosperous travelers to other venues and drifted into new gambits, most renting by the day, week, or month, as old cars full of unemployed people lurched into town and parked next to sad rooms where the adults scanned the classifieds for a hint of employment. The children always had dirty faces and anxious eyes. The motel I was sent to was a hot-sheet joint, with rooms by the hour or day, and featured water beds (WA WA BEDS, in the language of the sign), in-room pornographic movies, and a flock of men and women jousting through nooners.

The man at the desk had a weasel face and the small frame of the angry, smiling rats that inhabit the byways of America; the wife was a woman of some heft, with polyester pants and short-cropped hair. They seemed almost delighted to have a reporter appear, and after a few murmured words in the office, where I took in the posters for the featured films of cock-sucking, butt-fucking, and love, ushered me across the courtyard, with its unkempt grass, to the room. As we entered, she apologized and said she was still cleaning up. The linoleum floor looked cool, and the small chamber offered a tiny kitchenette and a small lavatory with shower, the old plastic curtain stained by years of hard water. The water bed, stripped of its sheets, bulged like a blue whale, and as the woman and I talked—he was quiet, she seemed nice, they didn't cause any fuss, the kid was a charmer—a dirty movie played soundlessly on the screen hanging off the wall and confronting the bed. I seem to remember a mirror of cheap streaked tiles on the ceiling.

I walked around aimlessly and popped open the door of the old refrigerator—shelves empty—and then the little door to the freezer, where two bottles of Budweiser, frozen solid, nestled as if someone with a powerful thirst had placed them to chill in a hurry and then been distracted. I heard the woman's voice in my ear explaining how the mother had gone to work—she danced at a strip joint, one of the new gentlemen's clubs that featured college-looking girls instead of aging women with bad habits—and so was gone when it happened. I nodded, purred soothing words, closed the freezer door, and strolled back by the water bed; the blue of its plastic had the gaiety of a flower in the tired room. I looked at a big splotch on the cinder block wall, and she said, "I haven't had time to clean that off yet."

That's where the head had hit, the skull of the toddler just shy of two years, as the man most likely held him by the legs and swung him like a baseball bat.

He probably killed the kid out of boredom or frustration with the demands of a small child, or because he'd been bopped around himself as a child, or God knows why. The man had taken off, then been caught by the cops, and was sitting in jail as they figured out what level of murder he'd scored. The dancer they'd found wandering in the desert, and they'd flung some kind of charges at her. As I stared at the block wall, the proprietress bubbled up in my ear again and said, with that small, cooing voice American women sometimes favor when indicating feeling, "We kind of made a collection and customers chipped in and we bought him an outfit for the burial." She told me they got the clothes at K-mart. I drove back to the paper, wrote an impressionistic piece pivoting on the frozen bottles and all the hopes and basic desires found in a beer chilling for a thirsty throat, and then phones started ringing at the city desk and I was hurled at the funeral.

So I sit through the service studying the mother's profile. She has fine hair, a kind of faint red. I once knew a woman with hair like that, and as I stare I can smell this other woman and feel my hands tracing a path through the slender strands. I can smell the soap, the scent of the other woman; the small smile and fine bones and clean, even teeth. In my memory the coffin is open, the boy's small face very pale and blank, and he is surrounded by donated teddy bears that came from a town that told itself these things are not supposed to happen, and if such things do happen they're not supposed to happen in our town.

Just before the service ends, I have a hunch that the cops are going to take the mother out the back so that the press cannot snap her image and I cannot scan her face. So I get up and leave the chapel of the cheap mortuary and go to the back, and, sure enough, suddenly the metal door opens and two cops burst through with the lap dancer handcuffed and sagging between their grip. The light is brilliant at 1:15 P.M. and merciless as it glares off the woman. Her face is small, with tiny bones, and her age is no longer possible to peg—somewhere between nineteen and one thousand. She is wearing tight pants on slender, girlish hips and a black leather vest over her blouse. The waist is small, the hair falls to her shoulders, the lips are very thin. A moan comes off her, a deep moan, and I sense that she is unaware of the sound she is making, just as she is unaware of what has happened to her. The only thing she knows is what I know. There is a toddler in a box with teddy bears, and the box sits in a room full of strangers from this town where she has bagged a job dancing for other strangers.

The cops look at me with anger, drag her slumping form away, and toss her into the back of a squad car. I stand still, make no notes. Then I go back to the newsroom and write up the funeral. That is when it begins. The toddler's death probably didn't have anything to do with child molestation, but for me this child became the entry point to rape and other categories of abuse. For the next three years I live in a world where the desire of people, almost always men, to touch and have their way with others makes them criminals. Gradually I began to lose the distinction between the desires of criminals and the desires of the rest of us. I am told I can't get off this kind of beat, because most reporters won't do it. This may be true, I don't really know, because those three years are the only ones I ever spent working for a newspaper and practically the only ones I ever spent working for anyone besides myself. I would quit the paper twice, break down more often than I can remember, and have to go away for a week or two and kill, through violent exercise, the things that roamed my mind. It was during this period that I began taking one-hundred- or two-hundred-mile walks in the desert far from trails. I would write up these flights from myself, and people began to talk about me as a nature writer. The rest of my time was spent with another nature, the one we call, by common consent, deviate or marginal or unnatural.

I can still see the woman coming through the metal door, slumping between the paws of the cops. I am standing northwest of her and about twenty feet away. It is 1:15 P.M., the glare of the sun makes her squint, her hips are bound in impossible pants, her face has never seen anything brighter than the dim lights of a strip joint, and her wrists, in the chrome gleam of cuffs, are tiny. I can remember this with photographic detail, only I can't remember what became of her or her lover. Just the boy, the splotch on the wall, the blue water bed, and the frozen Budweiser.

Until this moment, I've avoided remembering what became of me.

Night, the warm night of early fall, and they form up in the park, the women and their supporters, with candles and flashlights, banners and the will to take back the night. The green pocket of trees and grass hugs the road. They go a few blocks and swing down one of the city's main thoroughfares. Safety in numbers, group solidarity, sisterhood is powerful, protest, demands, anger, laughter, high spirits.

They find her later in a narrow slot between two buildings, more a gap in the strip of commercial façades than a planned path or walkway, the kind of slot that sees hard sun a few minutes a day and then returns to shadow. She is seven and dead. While the march to take back the night was passing through here, she apparently left her neighbor's yard nearby and came over to see the spectacle. The police and press keep back one detail: she has been eviscerated. That is part of what a newsroom feeds off, the secret facts that others do not know or cannot be told, the sense of being where the action is and where the knowing people gather. So we say to one another: opened up from stem to stern that night.

I come in the next morning ignorant of all this and am called into a meeting. The city editor, the managing editor, and the publisher are agitated. They have children; they want to do something, but they don't know what. I'm told to make a difference in the slaughter of our children. I nod and say, You'll have to give me time. The exchange is very short; this paper has no long meetings. I go back to my desk and remember another night long ago: the man crying. And when I remember, I don't want to take this assignment, but I do.

He speaks in a small voice as his hands cradle his face in the hospital waiting room, and he says, "My baby girl, my baby girl." His wife looks on stoically. The call came in the middle of the night, and when I arrive there is the cool of fluorescent lights, the sterile scent of linoleum floors, and the memory of her going down the corridor on a gurney with her face pulverized into raw flesh. She had gone to visit a friend near campus and stepped out of her car onto the quiet street.

That is when he took her. He forced her back into her car, and they drove out of town into the open ground. He raped her, pistol-whipped her, pumped two rounds into her, and then left her for dead. She saw a house light and crawled toward it. The people inside feared her pounding in the night and did not want to open up. Somehow an ambulance came, and now she is in surgery as I sit with her weeping father and stoical mother. At the time, I am related by marriage. But that does not help. I am a man, but that does not help. I am not a rapist, and that does not help at all. Nothing really helps—not words, not anger, not reflection. For days afterward, as the hospital reports come in, as the visits to the room present a bandaged and shaved head, as the unthinkable becomes normal for all of us, nothing really helps. We have stepped over a line into a place we refuse to acknowledge, a place of violence and danger, where the sexual impulses that course through our veins have created carnage.

I was in my late twenties then, and I remember my male friends all coming to me with visions of violence, scripts about what should be done to the rapist, what they would do to him, how these instances should be handled. I would nod and say very little.

I'm over at a house where friends live, the kind of male dormitory that has a dirty skillet festering on the stove, clothes tossed here and there, and empty beer bottles on the coffee table giving off stale breath. It is precisely 10:00 A.M., and one guy is just getting up from the mattress on the floor of his room. He is a Nam vet with a cluster of medals and has two interests after his war: hunting and women. A stack of skin magazines two feet high towers over the mattress, and a fine .270 with a polished walnut stock leans in the corner. He tells me they should take those guys out and cut their dicks off, and then he staggers down the hall with his hangover to take a piss. I feel that I am watching something happening on a screen but that I am not really here.

Eventually, a red-faced detective comes by to placate the victim's family and express his sense of urgency as we sit in the quiet kitchen. He explains all the things being done, but he convinces no one. How do you find a rapist when half the population is suspect? This is when I first hear the police read on rape: "Fifteen minutes for the guy, five years for the woman."

I had a vegetable garden then, and this was the only place where things made sense and fell into some kind of order. So I sit on the dirt amid the rows of bell peppers, tomatoes, eggplant, marigolds, and squash, sip red wine, and let my mind flow. I wonder if there is a monster lurking in all of us. I never cease, I realize, scanning faces when I prowl the city, and what I wonder is, Are you the one? I look over at the other cars when I am at a stoplight. This becomes an unconscious habit. Sometimes I think I have adopted the consciousness of a woman. Now I think like prey.

Later, a year or two later, a guy goes to a party near the campus, drinks and whoops it up, and leaves with a woman he meets there. He takes her out and rapes her and tries to kill her. Turns out he is the one, and they send him off to prison. By then, it hardly matters to me. I know he will be back and he will be older, and that that will be the only change. I bury the memories and go on pretty much as if nothing had ever happened. As does the woman who was raped, pistol-whipped, shot, and left for dead. You can know some things and the knowing seems to help you not at all.

"My baby girl, my baby girl." These memories resurface as I leave the editorial meeting with my instructions to figure out something for the paper to do about the slaughter of a seven-year-old girl during a march to take back the night. I sit at my gray desk and stare at the clock on the east wall. It is early in the morning, 7:00 or 8:00 A.M. I have no delusions that I will magically crack the case. But I decide to look into the world where such acts come from, though I do not consciously know what such a desire means in practical terms. I have no plan, just this sensation of powerlessness and corruption and violation and grief. I can feel my eyes welling with tears, and I know instantly that this feeling will do nothing for me or anyone else.

After that I follow my instincts, which is what the predators do also.

There are five things I know to be true. These rules come to me out of my explorations.

1. No one can handle the children.
2. Get out after two years.
3. Always walk a woman to her car, regardless of the hour of the day or the night.
4. Don't talk about it; no one wants to hear these things.
5. No one can handle the children.

The fourth lesson is the iron law. We lie about sex crimes because we lie about sex. We lie about sex because we fear what we feel within ourselves and recoil when others act out our feelings. American society has always been more candid about murder ("I felt like killing him," we can say out loud) than about the designs we have on each other's bodies. What destroys people who have to deal with sex crimes is very simple: you lose the ability to lie to yourself about your feelings, and if you are not careful you fail to lie appropriately to others. When we are in bed with each other we find it difficult to say what we want, and when we brush up against sex crimes we find it difficult to stomach what we see and even more difficult to acknowledge the tug of our fantasies. In the core of our being live impulses, and these impulses are not all bright and not all as comfortable as an old shoe.

Soon after I embark on this assignment, I am at the home of a friend, a very learned man who is elderly. When we sit and drink he is open to any topic—the machinations of the Federal Reserve, the mutilation of young girls in Africa, male menopause, or the guilt/innocence of Alger Hiss. I have just written a story for the newspaper on child molestation that runs four solid pages without one advertisement because no merchant wants products next to such a story. I vaguely remember the lead. I must do this from memory, because regardless of the passage of years, with their gentle soothing effect, I cannot look at the clips yet: "The polite term is child molestation. The father said he had done nothing but fondle his son. The boy had gonorrhea of the mouth. The polite term is child molestation."

As I sit with my friend and we ponder the intricacies of the world and swap lifetimes of reading, he suddenly turns to me and says, "I want you to know I didn't read your story. I don't read things like that."

I am not surprised. After the story hits the press, women at the newspaper come up to me for soft conversations and want to have lunch or drinks. They murmur that they are part of the sisterhood or secret society of the maimed. The men avoid me, and I can sense their displeasure with what I have written and the endless and relentless nature of the piece. I realize that if I had not written it, I would avoid reading it, too.

Another revelation comes from having drinks with a retired cop. We are kind of friends: cops and reporters are natural adversaries and yet, in some matters, have no one else to talk with (see rule number four). I ask him how the local police handled rape during his time.

He says, "Well, the first thing we'd do is take the suspect out of the house and into the carport, and then we'd beat the shit out of him with our saps. Then we'd take him downtown and book him for assault." He does not read the piece either.

Then there is the woman who is passionately into nonviolence and vegetarianism and speaks softly as if she embodied a state of grace. She comes to my door one night after a couple of my stories have run, and we make love on the cement floor. Afterward, she tells me that when she was a girl her father, who was rich and successful, would sit around with his male friends and they would take turns fucking her in the ass. I walk her to her car.

I am sitting on the north end of a back row facing the west wall. The room is institutional and full of therapists, counselors, and other merchants of grief who have gathered to share their experiences treating victims of sex crimes. I scan the crowd, mainly women without makeup wearing sensible shoes. I listen for hours as they outline play therapy, describe predators (with children, usually someone close and accepted by the family; with rape, often as not the mysterious stranger), call for a heightened public consciousness about the size of this plague. Their statistics vary but basically suggest that everyone is either a victim of a sexual crime or the perpetrator of a sexual crime or a therapist treating sexual crimes. They all agree that children do not lie and that more attention must be paid.

Late in the day a woman walks to the podium. I have been noticing her for hours, because she does not fit in with the group. Her lips are lacquered, her hair perfect, and she wears a tasteful lavender dress—one I sense she has bought just for this occasion—and high heels. She is the only woman wearing high heels. She speaks with a southern accent and tells the group that she is not a professional person. She is a mother, and a neighbor molested her daughter, her very young daughter. And she wants something done about it. In her case, she continues, nothing was done. The neighbor still lives a few doors down, and her daughter still lives in terror—they have had to seal her window with duct tape so "he can't look in."

The woman at the podium is on fire and very angry. Her words slap the audience in the face. She has no theory, she says, and no program. She simply wants her government, her police, and her city to pay attention to the problem. And she will not rest. She reads her words off sheets of yellow legal paper, and her articulation is harsh, as if she were drumming her fingers on a Formica kitchen table.

Afterward, I cut through the crowd and find her. I say I am a reporter and would like to talk more. She is flustered. She is not used to talking to audiences and not used to talking to the press. She gives me her number, and we agree to meet. I notice her eye makeup and the sensual nature of her lips.

When I turn, another woman comes up to me. I vaguely noticed her enter when the woman whose child was molested was speaking. She is about thirty and wears leather pants and a motorcycle jacket. Her eyes are very intelligent, and she tells me she is a therapist. Her smile is generous. We walk out and go to a nearby café, which is empty and half-lit in the late afternoon, and sit at a round table with a dark top. We both sip longnecks.

Her life has not been simple lately. She is distancing herself, she explains, from a bad relationship. She has been living with a man, and he is very successful. He came home a few days ago and they made love. He told her she was the sixth woman he had had that day but that he liked her the best. He never comes, she says; anything else, but he never comes. He withholds, don't you see? she asks.

When I go to her place she is in shorts and a shirt and is roller-skating in her driveway. She tells me she wanted me to see her that way, free and skating with delight. We lie on the floor. She says, "Squeeze my nipples hard, squeeze my titties as hard as you can." Later, we are in the bathroom, because she wants to watch us in the mirror. We go back to the bedroom and she rolls over on her stomach.

She says very softly, "Yes."

Somewhere in those hours my second marriage ends. I know why. I, too, tend to say yes. The marriage ends because I do not want to live with her anymore, because she is a good and proper person and this now feels like a cage. I do not want to leave my work at the office. I do not want to leave my work at all. I have entered a world that is black, sordid, vicious. And actual. And I do not care what price I must pay to be in this world.

The therapist has a lot of patients who are fat women, and they fascinate her. She herself has not an extra ounce of fat; she is all curves and muscle, her calves look like sculpture, her stomach is flat, her features are cute. She is very limber. Once at a party, she casually picked up one of her legs while talking to a couple and touched her ear with her foot. She was not wearing panties when she performed this feat. She runs daily, has been part of a female rock and roll band, takes showers three or four times a day, and is proudly bisexual. She tells me one of her best tactics for keeping boyfriends is to seduce and fuck their girlfriends. She smiles relentlessly.

What fascinates her about the fat women is their behavior. Not the eating.

She cannot even fathom the eating part, since she never gains weight and eats whatever she wishes. Her place is always cluttered with bowls of macadamia nuts for guests. No, it's their sexual lives she is interested in. Their sexual lives are very simple: they will do anything. That, she tells me, is why men like fat women. They will do anything; name your fantasy, try out your imagined humiliation.

She tells me how she became a therapist. She went to visit her own therapist once and he questioned her openness, and she wound up doing golden showers in his office. After that she fled to an analytic center on the West Coast and studied very hard. No, she says, she is not bitter about it. She learned he was right: she was not open enough.

I find her smile addictive. We sit in her kitchen and she makes a Greek salad. She becomes a blur cutting up the feta cheese and dicing olives. And then we go to the bedroom. She tells me I have green blood and smiles with the promise that she will make it red.

Here is how play therapy goes. You look through one-way glass at very small children on the floor. The child holds anatomically correct dolls, ones with actual sexual organs, and acts out what has happened in the past. It is something to see. The dolls look like Raggedy Ann. And do pretty much exactly what adults do with each other. My guide in this place is a gray-haired woman who is very well-spoken and has the quiet calm of a Quaker lady. She used to work in a ward with terminally ill children. She tells me this work is harder. Ah, now the child is moving the two dolls.

We talk for twenty-two hours. Not all at once, no one can do that, but for very long stretches at a time. That is how the lady in the lavender dress with the hard words, the lady who stunned the seminar audience, begins. With talk.

We sit across from each other with the coffee table and a patch of rug between our chairs. She is cautious. This is her story and, like most people, she wishes to tell her story but only to the right person—the person who listens. I have no tape recorder, just a pen and a notebook, and we begin spiraling into the tale. It is night, her daughter is in the tub, she mentions pain and points. The mother hides her alarm, asks gentle questions, and it slowly comes out as the minutes crawl past. He is the older man, the pal of neighborhood kids. Always a smile, perfectly normal, you never would have guessed.

As she talks, her daughter, so very young and small, plays out in the yard, and from time to time I catch a glimpse of her as I look up from my notepad or glance away from the woman, her monologue flowing from her full lips. The child is in sunlight, gamboling about without a worry in the world.

For a second, none of it ever happened. I see this apparition through the sliding glass doors, and then the woman's words pull me back to the night, the aftermath, the weeks and now months of coaxing the child back first from terror and then from a sense of betraying her special friend by telling—and, of course, she was warned not to tell, they always make sure to stress this warning.

When I am with the woman, I enter, as she does, a kind of trance. When I am away the trance still holds to a degree, and I talk with no one about what I am doing. I make a point of filing other stories to disguise the hours I spend listening. I live in worlds within worlds, since the child's identity must not be revealed, and so for me things become generic and universal and yet at the same time, looking into one woman's face and taking down one woman's words, specific, exact, and full of color, scent, and feel.

I write the story in one long fury, and the printout runs about twenty feet. I crawl along my floor, reading it and making changes. Sometimes my therapist roller skater drops by and finds me crawling on the floor with my felt pen, and she does not approve of this act. It is too involved, not suitable for things that should be done at a desk with a good lamp and a sound chair. I sense I am failing her by falling into myself, and our sex grows more heated and yet more empty. This goes on for weeks. I don't know what to do with the story, and then finally I turn it in and they print it.

Fifty subscribers cancel in less than an hour, I am told.

I prowl through the police blotter, savoring the rapes of the night: The woman who leaves the bar at 1:00 A.M. with the stranger. No, can't sell her. The woman who decides at 3:00 A.M. to take a walk in short shorts and a halter to the all-night market for a pack of cigarettes and then gets bagged. She's out, too. The girl who goes into the men's room with her boyfriend to give him head and then his friends follow and gangbang her. No sale. I course through the dull sheets of pain, hunting for the right one—the one I can sell, the one to which readers cannot say, "Well, that could never happen to me," the one they can't run away from so easily.

A woman rides the freights into town and then books up with two guys at a café, and they say if you need a place to crash come with us. She does. She decides she needs a shower, and they say go ahead. When she comes out of what she calls "the rain closet" they're on her. She later goes to the cops, describes herself as a motorcycle mechanic, and tells them of the rape. The paper takes one look at my story and says forget it. And, of course, they're right. Rape, like many things, is kind of a class matter. You have to not deserve it for the world to care even a little bit. This I learn.

Sometimes for a break I drop in on a small bookstore where a heavy woman with a British accent sells used volumes. A gray cat is always nestled inside, and the place has the feel of afternoon tea in someone's living room. Then she is attacked and held hostage in her home one night. The store closes; I don't know what happens to the cat. Eventually, she leaves town and settles in a somewhat distant city. Finally, I hear she kills herself.

I keep hunting, talking with fewer and fewer people. Except for those who live in this world or at least understand its dimensions. I'll be somewhere, maybe kicking back, feet up on the coffee table, glass of wine in hand, and someone will play, say, the Stones' "Midnight Rambler," and my mood will sink and go black. Best not to visit people.

The days of the week cease to have meaning, as do the weeks of the month and the months of the year. My life went by clocks and dates and deadlines, but the order implied in paychecks, withholding taxes, dinner at six, and Sunday-morning brunch vanished with my consent. I did not lose control of my life; I gave up the pretense of normal life, and followed crime and appetite. I learned things on the run and without intention. Knowledge came like stab wounds, and pleasure came with the surprise of a downpour from a blue sky in the desert. I remember sitting with some women who had been raped after I wrote a profile of the rapist. Turns out all the guy's co-workers, mainly women, found him to be a polite, nice person.

One woman looked at me and said flatly, "He wasn't that way when I was with him."

Stab wounds.

I have become furious, but mainly with myself. Certain protocols in writing about such matters anger me. I decide never to write the phrase "child molestation" or "sexual assault" except in a context of deliberate mockery. I am angry at the pain I witness and listen to each day as I make my appointed rounds, and I am angry at the hypocrisy of it all. We want to believe that the intersection between sex and crime happens only in an alien country, one that does not touch our lives or feelings or lusts of the midnight hours.

A woman is at the door and she has three balls on a string she wishes to insert in my ass, and then she will pull the string at the moment of orgasm.

A woman is at the door and she says she has cuffs.

A woman is at the door late at night and we make love, and as she leaves she says she can't see me again because she is getting married in the morning.

Two women are at the door . . .

We like to call things that disturb us a jungle, to wall them off from our sense of order and self. But we all inhabit that forest, a dense thicket of desire and dread, both burning bright. We want to categorize: victims or studs, seduced or seducers. And we can hardly look at people who we agree are criminals and admit we feel some of their passions and fantasies within ourselves. My life in those days erased boundaries and paid no attention to whether I was a predator or a victim or a newspaper savior with a byline. I was attractive to women because what I knew made me somehow safe. Ruined people were telling me things they never told anyone else, and the women dealing with ruined people were sharing secrets as well, and some of those secrets were fantasies they wished to act out. There is a way to go so deep into the secrets and hungers of your culture that you live without concern for the mores and with a keen sense of your own needs. I have seen this state most often in the old, who finally realize that the rules of conduct are optional and read what they wish, say what they think, and live in sin without a qualm. I didn't feel guilt. Then or now. I didn't feel love. I didn't seek a cure. Getting in bed with women was a pleasure but not the center of my life. The center of my life was crime. And sex was also an attempt to redeem or exorcise what I saw. As the crimes piled up and corroded my energy and will, I ceased to find even cold comfort in women, and everything in my life became perfunctory except for the crimes. I have hard memories of my life then but not bad memories. But of the work, I still have nightmares. I still drive by commonplace haunts and see weeping women, bodies, a terrified child, an eviscerated girl. There are accepted ways of dealing with such experiences: the secular renunciation of a clinical visit to all the Betty Ford centers out there, the religious rebirth of being born again. I did neither. I simply continued plowing my way into that night.

She sits up in bed and asks, "Aren't my breasts beautiful? Aren't they the best you've ever seen?"

I nuzzle her hair. Time has passed, the story long gone, the woman in the lavender dress with the hard words and the maimed child is now the woman here.

She tells me her husband has been suspicious of me.

I ask her what she told him.

"Don't worry." She smiles. "I told him you were a queer."

Then she slides over, gets up, and rolls a joint.

Rule Number One: No One Can Handle the Children.

I'll tell you something that although not a trade secret is not generally said to others outside the work. The rapes are bad but not that bad. The mind is protected from what adults do to adults. There is a squeamishness about the rapes, an embarrassment among the men who investigate them, and an anger among the women who treat the casualties. But the rapes can be handled to a degree. Of course, it's not as easy as homicide; people stay in homicide forever and never lose pleasure in their work. Sex crimes generally cycle people out in two years. And it is the kids who do it. No one can handle the kids. But then the highway patrol always dreads the car wreck with kids. It goes against nature as we know it.

Once I was helping a guy move—him, his wife, their two young daughters—and a box I was carrying out broke open and small paperbacks spilled to the ground in the bright sunshine. I gathered them up and then idly flipped through one, and then another and another. They were all cheap things from no-name presses about men—daddies, uncles, whoever—fucking kids. I was stunned and did not know what to do. I felt oddly violated, like it was wrong for me to have to know this. So I put them back in the box and put the box in the truck and said nothing and did nothing.

That is part of what I feel as I enter the gray police station and go to the offices where the sex-crimes unit works. They've got a treasure trove of child pornography seized from perps, and in my memory the stack rises six or seven feet. They leave me at a table with it, and what they want is for me to look at it and come out with an article recommending that people who possess such materials go to prison.

The collection mainly features boys, seven, eight, nine from the looks of them, and they are sucking off men, taking it in the ass, being perfect pals about everything. I am struck not by what I feel but by how little I feel. It is like handling the treasured and sacred icons of a dead religion. I have careful constitutional qualms filed in my mind—basically, that to think something is not a crime. Fucking kids and taking pictures—that is already against the law. So I stand firmly on the Constitution of the United States and look at photographs I do not believe should exist made by and for people I do not believe should exist. I look for hours and still feel nothing. I am in a place beyond the power of empathy.

A few months later I get a thick packet of fifty or sixty typed pages. The writer is facing a long prison sentence for having had sex with Scouts, as I recall. He writes with courtesy, clarity, and an almost obsessive sense of detail. Essentially, nothing ever happened except that he tried to comfort and love his charges. I doubt him on his details but come to sense that he means his general thesis about love. He loves children, totally, and locks on them with the same feeling I have for adult women.

That is what I take away from the photos the police want outlawed and the autobiography of the man they eventually send away to be raped and possibly murdered by fellow convicts for being a child molester. A crime is being committed by people who see themselves as the perfect friend. Other things are being committed by people who see themselves as lovers. And, of course, a lot of things are being done by people who have no romantic delusions about their desires but are full of hate, who drag women off into the bushes or a corner because they hate them and are going to get even by causing pain, humiliation, and, at times, death. Cycles of abuse, the role of pornography, the denigration of women by Hollywood and glossy magazines—there is no single, simple explanation for sex crimes. But in the case of the men who use children for sex there is often this fixation, this sense of love, which always leads them to betray the very idea of love itself by using children for their own selfish ends.

During this period of my life my musical taste changes and slowly, without my awareness, starts sliding backward through the decades. One day I decide to look up a style of music I've been listening to in a big Merriam-Webster dictionary. Torch song: from the phrase "to carry a torch for" (to be in love); first appeared 1930; a popular sentimental song of unrequited love.

The walls are block, humming fluorescent lights replace windows, and we sit in rows forming a semicircle as the woman teaching the class speaks. She is very nicely done up in a sedate professional suit, tasteful hair, low-key makeup: she has a serious and clear voice. The prisoners mark time as I go through rape therapy in the joint. I am not here because of a story. I've come to find something beneath the stories or deep within myself. The boundaries between normal, accepted sexual appetite and crime are blurring for me. People get an erotic charge out of playing with consent—holding each other down, tying each other up—indulging in ritualized dominance. Rape is an eerie parody of accepted life, an experience using the same wardrobe but scratching the word "consent" from the script. I am obeying the law and the rules of consent, but I am losing a sense of distance between my obedient self and those who break the law. When I listen to women tell of the horrors they've experienced, the acts they recount are usually familiar to me, and what they recount as true terror, the sense of powerlessness, strikes chords within me also. I can't abide being in the joint even for this class. I can't take the bars, guards, walls.

The men, struggling to earn good time, feign attention. They answer questions appropriately and wear masks of serious thought. I don't believe them for an instant, and I think that this class is a farce and that nothing will deter my colleagues from their appointed rounds when they leave this place. The woman herself, from a good family and with sound religious values, has been attacked—"I am part of the sisterhood," she once told me shyly—and she has brought me here so that I will see hope and share her hope. So I sit with the current crop of convicted rapists—"There are no first-time offenders," a cop once snarled at me, "just sons of bitches that finally get caught"—and feel no hope. Of course, prison is rape culture—"just need a bunk and a punk," one local heroin dealer offered in explaining his lack of concern about doing time.

The session finally ends, and we bleed out the door of the room into the prison corridor. I am ambling along in a throng of convicts, the woman walking just ahead in her prim suit with her skirt snug on her hips. The guy next to me is singing some kind of blues about what he's gonna do to that bad bitch. I've blotted out the actual song. I can remember the corridor (we are strolling east), see her up ahead, hear him singing next to me, his lips barely moving as he floats his protest against the class and her fucking control and all that shit, but not the lyrics themselves. They're gone, erased by my mind, I suspect in self-defense. Afterward, she and I go to a truck stop and eat apple pie, and I can still see the whiteness of her teeth as she smiles and speaks brightly about her work.

Later, I taste child-molestation therapy, a regimen where men who have fucked their own children sit in a circle and talk while their wives run the show. It's either show up at such sessions or the joint—so attendance is rather good. Afterward, I go off with the boys and we have beers. In recounting his lapse from accepted behavior, each and every one of them describes the act itself as fondling. Apparently, there are hordes of diligently caressed children out there. I nurse my beer and say little, pretending to try to understand. But I understand nothing at all. I have seen the end result of fondling, and it does not look at all like fondling to me. I cannot put myself in their place. I cannot see children as sexual objects, it does not seem to be in me. I fixate, I realize, on women. And my fixation is sanctioned, as long as I toe the line. Such thoughts lead to a place without clear light. We all share a biology and deep drives, and what we have created—civilization, courtesy, decency—is a mesh that comes from these drives and also contains and tames them. Whatever feels good is not necessarily good. But what I learn is that whatever is bad is not necessarily alien to me. Or to you.

She loves pornography. It's around midnight, and she is standing in the motel room clutching a bottle of champagne against her black garter belt and peering intently into the screen of the television as fornicating couples, powered by the handyman of American fantasy, the telephone man, frolic. This is one of the seedy motels that cultivate hourly rates, water beds, and hard-core cinema, a place much like the room where my life in this world began with the splotch on the wall left by the toddler's head. She is a counselor, one of the many I now deal with, and she likes sex and is fascinated by pornography. This is not unusual; another woman, a professional woman I deal with, has several hundred pornographic tapes. But the interests of the woman in the black garter belt are kept off the table at her work and left to the night hours and random bouts with me. Days are for the maimed—in her case, children with cigarette burns and sore orifices. Some nights are like this.

I glance at her naked ass, see the serene concentration of her face as she tracks the movie, and I am empty. She and I share the same country, and there is a big hole in us, so we come here. We live in a place past the moral strictures of sin and lust; we run on empty. For us, sex has been drained of its usual charge, delight is beyond our reach. This is a fact. As the months roll past, I feel this slippage within me. I will have lunch or dinner or a drink or coffee with someone and wind up in a place like this. Romance is not a consideration. There is seldom anyone to talk with, and when there is someone, a person like the woman in the black garter belt watching the porn movie, a person stumbling across the same terrain, there is nothing to say, since we both know. So we come here. A proper distance from our appetites has been denied us, so we seek moments of obliteration. I have never regretted those moments or fully understood them. I just knew then, and know now, that they come with the territory.

But the slippage bothers me. I seem to drift, and the drift is downward. Not into sin and the pit but into that emptiness. I am losing all desire and mechanically go through the motions of life. Food also does not tempt me. I flee into the wild country with my backpack, flee again and again for days and days, but increasingly this tactic does not work. Once I am lying by a water hole in July and it is 104 degrees at 1:00 A.M. (I get up with my flashlight and check my thermometer.) I am crawling with crabs. When I go back I buy twelve bottles of the recommended cure and for a day have coffee or drinks with a succession of women, handing each a bottle. I take this in stride, as do they. One woman is briefly anxious because she fears I have called her only to deliver the medicine, but this feeling passes when I assure her that this is not true, that I really wanted to see her. I think we then go to bed. It turns out that this mini-epidemic has come from the therapist who showers three or four times a day. She also is quite calm about it and prefers to talk about her new favorite movie, something entitled *Little Oral Annie*. She tells me she resents the smirks of the male clerks when she rents it at the video store, and I politely sympathize.

The moments of my impotence increase. I am not alarmed by this fact but clinically engaged. I sense that I am walling off everything, all appetites, and have room for nothing but this torrent of pain and squalor that pours through me from the daily and weekly harvest of rapes and killings and molestations. I remember once reading a statement allegedly made by Sophocles in his old age, when sexual desire had left his loins; he said he was glad to be free of the mad master. So I am becoming classic and care not at all. I repeatedly try to leave the work, but the city desk always wins because a part of me feels bound to the crimes. So I protest, and then return. I tell myself it is a duty, but what I feel is the desire to run out my string, to see how much I can stomach and learn. And yet then, and now, I cannot really say what this knowing entails. I can just feel its burden as I lie with caring women in countless cheap motels, the movies rolling on the screen.

The end begins in the bright light of afternoon on a quiet street lined with safe houses. One moment an eight-year-old girl is riding her bicycle on the sidewalk near her home; the next moment the bicycle is lying on the ground and the girl is gone with no one the wiser.

This one is my torch song. The rudiments are simple. The alleged perpetrator is a man in his twenties from a very good home in another city, a man whose life has been a torment of drugs, molestation of himself by others and of others by himself, a man who has slipped from his station in life into dissipation and wound up roaming the skid rows of our nation. None of this concerns me, and I leave ruin in my wake. I fly to that distant city, talk my way through a stout door, and gut his mother like a fish. When I leave she is a wreck, and later that night her husband goes to the hospital for perturbations of his heart. I get into files—legal, psychiatric—that I should not have had access to, and I print them fulsomely. The child favored a certain doll, and I buy one and prowl the city with it on the truck seat beside me, a touchstone. I am standing in the backyard as the mother of the missing girl makes a plea to whoever took her daughter to bring her home safe and sound. The woman's face is grief made flesh, and I note its every tic and sag. It turns out that the alleged perpetrator stayed for a time with a couple in a trailer court. I visit; the man is facing child-molestation charges himself, the woman is a hooker with a coke habit. "Do I have to tell you that?" she whines. I remember leaving them, driving to a saloon, setting my small computer on the bar, and begging a phone for the modem. I sip my drink and write in one quick take. The story flits through the wires and descends into the next edition. The following night a local PTA meeting takes a recess, walks over to the trailer, and then it goes up in flames.

My temper is short, my blood cold. A young mother who works in the newsroom comes over to my desk and asks me what I think the chances are of the girl being alive. I snap, "Fucked, strangled, and rotting out there." And keep typing. The sheriff leaps into the public wound and starts leading marches of citizens holding candles and decrying violence and the rape of children. It is much like the time so long ago when things began for me with a seven-year-old eviscerated while people marched to take back the night. I pay no notice to these marches: they are for others. The reporters on the story all speculate about the girl—even when the arrest comes and still the girl is missing. I do not. I know. Bones bleach out there. It is months and months before her remains turn up, but this hardly matters to me. I know. This is my country.

It ends several times, but at last it finally ends. The city desk asks my help to find a woman whose son, a famous local rapist, has just escaped. I leave, chat up some neighbors, and within an hour I am in a state office, a bullpen of women toiling over desks and processing forms. She has done everything she can—changed her name, told no one of her son, gone on and tried to fashion a life. I approach her desk and tell her my errand. She pleads with me. Don't do this to me. She leans forward and whispers that no one typing away at the other desks, none of them knows anything about this. Leave me in peace, she says. I look into her careworn eyes and I say yes. I tell her I will now leave and she will never read a word of my visit in the newspaper. Nor will I tell anyone of her identity.

When I enter the newsroom, the editor comes over and asks, "Did you find her?"

I say, "Yes."

"When can I have the story?"

"I'm never writing the story."

He looks at me, says nothing, then turns and walks away.

That is when one part of me is finished. I know I must quit. I cannot take the money and decide what goes into the newspaper. I do not believe in myself as censor and gatekeeper. And yet I know I will never write this story, because I have hit some kind of limit in pain. The phone rings. It is a woman's voice. She says, "Thanks to you she has had to go to the hospital. I hope you are happy."

I tell her I am not writing the story. I tell her I told the mother I would not write the story. She does not believe me. This does not matter to me. My hands are cold, and I know from past experience this means I can take no more. I am righteously empty.

The other ending is more important, because it does not involve the work, the little credos and dos and don'ts of journalism. It involves myself. It happens the night the arrests come down for the missing eight-year-old snatched off her bicycle on that safe side street. Around three in the morning, I wrap the story and reach into my desk drawer, where I stashed a fifth of Jack Daniel's bought earlier in the day. I do not drink hard liquor, and I bought the bottle without questioning myself and without conscious intent. So I finish the story, open the drawer, take the bottle, and go home. I sit in my backyard in the dark of the night, those absolutely lonely hours before dawn. I drink, the bite of the whiskey snapping against my tongue, and drink in the blackness.

After a while I feel a wetness and realize that I am weeping, weeping silently and unconsciously, weeping for reasons I do not understand. I know this is a sign that I am breaking down, this weeping without a moan or a sound. I feel the tears trickle, and step outside myself and watch myself clinically in a whiskey-soaked out-of-body experience. That is the other ending.

I quit the paper, never again set foot in a newsroom, and go into the mountains off and on for months and write a book about them. That helps but not enough. I sit down and in twenty-one days write another book about the land, the people, and the city. That helps, but although I barely touch on the world of sex and crimes in this book, it broods beneath the sentences about Indians and antelope and bats and city streets. Nothing really helps.

That is what I am trying to say. Theories don't help, therapies don't help, knowing doesn't help. The experts say they have therapies that are cutting recidivism, and maybe they do, but I doubt it. I live with what I am and what I saw and what I felt—a residue that will linger to the end of my days in the cells of my body. I have never been in an adult bookstore. Two years ago I was at a bachelor party in a lap-dancing place and lasted fifteen minutes before I hailed a cab and fled. This is not a virtue or a position. I have no desire to outlaw pornography, strip joints, blue movies, or much of anything my fellow citizens find entertaining. Nor have I led an orderly life since my time in sex crimes. I write for men's magazines and pass over without comment their leering tone and arch expressions about the flesh. I am not a reformer. So what am I?

A man who has visited a country where impulses we all feel become horrible things. A man who can bury such knowledge but not disown it, and a man who can no longer so glibly talk of perverts or rapists or cretins or scum. A man who knows there is a line within each of us that we cannot accurately define, that shifts with the hour and the mood but is still real. And if we cross that line we betray ourselves and everyone else and become outcasts from our own souls. A man who can be an animal but can no longer be a voyeur. A man weeping silently in the backyard with a bottle of whiskey who knows he must leave and go to another country and yet never forget what he has seen and felt. Just keep under control. And try not to lie too much.

Just before I quit, I am in a bar in a distant city with a district attorney. He shouts to the barkeep, "Hey, give this guy a drink. One of our perverts whacked a kid in his town."

The bartender pours and says, "Way to go."

And I drink without a word. Nobody wants to hear these things.

Janet Burroway

EMBALMING MOM

JANET BURROWAY is the author of eight novels, including *The Buzzards*, *Raw Silk* (runner-up for the National Book Award), *Opening Nights*, *Cutting Stone*, and the forthcoming *Devil's Play*. Her most recent plays are *Medea with Child*, *Sweepstakes*, and *Parts of Speech*. Her book *Writing Fiction*, now in its seventh edition, is the most widely used creative writing text in the United States, and a further text, *Imaginative Writing*, has recently appeared in its second edition. She is the author of a collection of essays, *Embalming Mom*, and the editor of the lectures of Robert Olen Butler, *From Where You Dream*. She is Robert O. Lawton Distinguished Professor Emerita at Florida State University in Tallahassee.

"I want to put you in a story," I say. "Apparently it's a matter of some importance."

She is ironing and her back is to me. She says nothing and does not turn around, but she licks her finger to test the iron. Her spit sizzles like bacon and I can see her hand. Long strong fingers, violet veins, amber freckles. Under the taut freckled flesh of her forearms her narrow bones roll with the maneuvering of the iron.

"I don't mean professional importance," I say, "but psychological. Spiritual, if you like." She rolls the iron along the board.

Things have not been going too well with me lately—a number of breakages, and not all of them for the first time. The compressor on the air conditioner broke down again. The left earpiece of my reading glasses split at the hinge and I can't see to tape it together without my glasses on. Both of my teenaged sons had their hair cut again, for opposing reasons. I got divorced again, and moved again, or at least, I must not have moved, since I live in the same house in Florida, but it seems to feel as if I have moved again.

She rolls the iron along the board, wide end to narrow end in a serpentine path from her belly toward the window sill. It occurs to me that nobody ever sees her own bones, and that she has therefore never seen these bones that twist and roll under her skin, the forearm bones of a bony woman, their mineral and marrow.

"Well," I say, "important to my soul, if you want to put it that way."

"Hmmph," she says. Does she say, "Hmmph?" It seems unlikely. Perhaps what she says is, "Hah!" I think she sighs. Once my brother Bud pointed out to me that when things fall apart you always run home to Mom. He pointed this out because I was fleeing a threatening lover (again) and he thought I wasn't very well hidden in the breakfast bay. But I told him safety is not the point; the point is feeling safe.

She is ironing the skirt of the pima cotton dress with the white and purple pansies, the pin-tucked yoke, the puffed sleeves edged in eyelet. The pansies part at the point of the iron, swirl left and right under the heel of her hand and wheel down the board behind the butt of the iron. I do not, however, say "butt" in her presence. That much is clear.

I cross my legs, sitting at the breakfast bay, which is covered in some orange substance, a precursor of Naugahyde. I am wearing the trouser suit made out of handwoven amber tweed that I bought off the bolt in Galway at an Incredible Bargain. The trouser suit was stolen out of a parked station wagon in New York in 1972, but it is apparently important that I should be wearing it now, partly because it was such a bargain and partly because I designed and made it myself. I feel good in it: cordial, cool. I think of something I can pass on to her. I laugh.

"Do you know what a friend of mine said the other day?" Cordially rhetorical. "He said: Hell is the place where you have to work out all the relationships you couldn't work out in life."

It's all right to say "hell" in this context, not as a swear word but as an acknowledgment of a possible place. My mother's not narrow-minded about the nature of hell. I laugh again, and so although she laughs I don't know if she laughs with me; I miss the tone of her laugh. "Haw, haw!"? I hope it's that one, the swashbuckling one.

"I'd rather work this one out here," I say, but am conscious that I mumble and am not surprised that there is no response. I am sitting on the orange plastic of the nook in the bay window, which my father designed and made, watching my mother at the ironing board that folds up into the wall behind an aluminum door. This also was designed and made by my father, who is not here because he is living in the mountains with his second wife although he was true to my mother right up to the end. And beyond. Outside the desert sun slants through the oleanders, illuminating minute veins in the fuchsia petals. The pansies on the ironing board I remember wearing in the sandbox under the oleanders before I started school, which means that my mother is about thirty-five. I am forty-five and three months by the calendar on the window sill to the left of my typewriter.

"What friend was that?" she asks, eventually, with a palpable absence of malice and a clear implication that any friend who goes under the designation "he" is suspect. It was all right to say "hell" but not "he."

"Nobody in particular; just a friend."

"Your father gets sweeter every day," I think she says, and I am sure that her head angles to one side, a long neck made longer by the tight poodle cut of her hair, already graying, already thinning, the corrugations of her neck where it arches no wider than those on the spine of a hardbound book.

"Yes," I say. "Well." She takes the edge of one puff and twirls the eyelet, arching the iron into each semicircle on the board, expertly smoothing it so that when she releases it each arch buoys into a perfect wave. It occurs to me that I can do this, too.

"You know, I'm not sure I feel too well," she says, as if surprised, mumbling now, but she is an old hand at the audible mumble, and I will not rise to it.

Instead I say, "All we need to do is embark on a minor conflict. Anything will do, any of the old ones. My posture, for instance, or the state of my room. Smoking will do. Or that my hair needs cutting."

My elder son has joined the army and writes that he has had his hair cropped; it never occurred to me before that a crew cut makes one a member of a crew. My younger son has scissored his blond thatch so short that it also seems to have erupted out of World War II, but for him it has an altogether different ideological significance. He does not, however, want it called punk. I am so anxious he should like me that I pay to have his left ear pierced and offer him a diamond-chip stud of which I have lost the mate. He accepts it cheerfully, but most days he wears a diaper pin through the punctured lobe.

She deals with the eyelet of the other sleeve, and she turns to me. I am so startled by this success that I reach into my Italian handbag for a cigarette, and my glance catches no higher than the hand she splays protectively over her stomach; I concentrate on the lighting of my cigarette, and can only suppose the shape of her mouth, narrow-lipped but open wide in the narrow-lipped friendly "hah" shape, large straight teeth except for the crossing of the two lower incisors that I encounter in my own mirror every day of my life. I hear her say, nasal on the vowels, "I just don't want you to be indiscreet, sissy."

This confusingly hits home. I recognize the authenticity of it—the plaint, the manipulation, but also the authenticity. Because I am indiscreet; it is my central fault. I confess to freshman students, junior colleagues, anyone with a dog smaller than a bread box. I expose myself by telephone and telegraph; I say it with ink. I betray the secrets of my friends, believing I am presenting their cases. I embarrass clerks in the Kmart.

But she has her back to me again, and all I can see is the parting of the pin-tucks left and right as she deftly presses them away from the pearl shank buttons. Because she didn't mean the right thing and has no notion that she has hit home.

"What does that mean, indiscreet?" I ask, a little shrill, so that I deliberately draw the smoke in after I've said it, feeling the depth of my lungs, my verbal bottom. "Do you mean sex? Do you mean: lie better?"

"I'm not going to be sidetracked into a discussion of words," my mother says, a thing she would never say.

"It's not a sidetrack," I nevertheless reply. Her forefinger sizzles.

I need an ashtray. I know there are no ashtrays here, but I'm willing to choose carefully among the things I know are here: the amethyst-glass pot with calico flowers set in paraffin; the Carnival glass cup with her name, "Alma," etched in primitive cursive; the California Fiesta pottery in the lurid colors of the zinnias along the front walk. I cross to the cupboard and take the little Depression glass fishbowl because I know it best, because it currently houses a tiny goldfish on the window sill to the left of my typewriter in my house in Florida.

"It's true that I'm indiscreet," I confess, indiscreetly, "but it's not entirely a fault." I tap my ash, and my hair prickles hot against my turtleneck. Both of my husbands liked my hair long, although the second one did not smoke and the first blamed me for indiscretion. The convolutions of authority are confusing. "It's also simply the way I am; it's a negative side of my strength. The thing I want most of all is an understanding audience, a teaching one. The best thing is to tell and be understood. Do you understand?"

"I've never looked at any man but your father," she replies, to the oleanders, to the waffle iron, to the piqué collar that she designed and made and that she now parts into two perfect eyelet-edged arches of Peter Pan.

"Mama!"

No, that won't do. I must not put myself in the hysterical stance because if anything is clear, the clear thing is that she is the hysterical one and I'm the one who copes, deals, functions, and controls. I am the world traveler, the success.

I continue in a more successful tone. "We could start with Dad if you like, but I don't think it's the best place because it's so hard to be honest."

"I *hope* I brought you up to be honest!" Back to me still, she whips the dress from the board and holds it up for her own inspection.

"I mean that there are so many ways of lying apart from words, especially where marriage is concerned. I think it would be better if we just kept it between you and me."

"There's lying and there's telling the truth, especially where marriage is concerned!"

This strikes a false note. She is not speaking to me as she must speak to me because I am not speaking to her as I must speak to her. I tap my ash into the fishbowl while she takes a copper wire hanger and buttons the now-perfect dress onto it at the nape. With one hand she holds the hook and with the thumb of the other she flicks one neat flick at the button while index and middle finger spread the hand-bound buttonhole and the button pops into place. I can see the gesture with magical clarity; I can do it myself. Once when I was caught playing doctor in the tamaracks with crippled Walter Wesch, she sat me in the basin and spread my pink bald mons veneris with the same two fingers, soaping with the flick of her thumb, scourging me with her tongue in terms of Jesus and germs.

"Mama, look," I say, "the reason I want to do this—try to understand—is that I *want* to tell the truth. I want to capture you . . . as you really are." I squirm on the plastic, hair hot at the nape, and add despairingly, "As a *person*."

Does she say, "Hah!"?

"I've tried before, and you came out distorted. I know you're remarkable . . ."

Now she is doing one of Daddy's Arrow shirts, a plain white one with a narrow stitched collar. The point of the iron faces one point of the collar, then the other. The long strong far hand stretches against the stitching so the hot collar lies perfectly flat without any of the tiny corrugations that even a laundry leaves these days. I can do this. My two sons can do it.

She turns again, one eyebrow raised and a mocking smile. "What, then, am I the most unforgettable character you've met?"

Not like her, neither the eyebrow nor the words, which have the cadence of a British education. I'm the one with the British education. I try again. She turns back like the film run backward, the point of the iron faces one point of the collar, then the other, she stretches with the strong far hand, the bones of which she has never seen, and turns again robotlike, profile gashed with a smile. "Honey, write for the *masses*. People need to *escape*. They need to *laugh*."

This is closer. My fist is too big to go in the goldfish bowl, and I have no way to stub out my cigarette. I have to hold it while it burns down to the filter and out. So it turns out to be me who says brightly, "Okay, why don't I do you up as 'The Most Unforgettable Character I've Met'?"

To which, against my will, try as I might, she replies, "Why me? Hah, hah, there are plenty of fish in the sea."

"No!" I slam the bowl down dangerously, but it doesn't break. How could it, when it houses the goldfish next to the calendar on the window sill? Dangerously shrill, I say, "That's exactly what I don't want you to say!"

She hands me a shirt out of the basket, a blue one with the same narrow Arrow collar; I understand that I'm supposed to sprinkle it. I fetch a pan from under the stove and fill it with warm water, holding the hot cigarette filter in the hand that turns on the tap. I run water over the filter, which sizzles, and reach for the garbage bin under the sink, ashamed because my back is to her now and I am doing this in full view. The bin is of the step-on sort, chrome lid on a white cylinder adorned with a bow-tied posy of photographically exact nasturtiums. *Nasty urchums*, Bud and I used to call them in the sandbox years, though I don't remember if we dared to say this in front of Mama. I toss the cigarette in the bin and, when the lid slams, curb the impulse to take the garbage out.

My last love affair was trashed over the question of taking out the garbage. It's a common story. He said, "What can I do to help?" and I said, "Thanks, I'd appreciate it if you took out the garbage." He said, "It makes no sense to take it out now; it isn't full. Do you want the sausage sliced or mashed?" I did not want the sausage sliced or mashed, and said so in no uncertain terms. He said, "What are you on about?" And I was, I admit, a trifle eloquent; it's my job. I put myself in the hysterical stance and he put himself in the imperturbable stance, but it was he who slammed out and that was that. It's common. My mother used to say: common as an old shoe. She meant it for praise, of people who didn't stand on their dignity.

I carry the pan back to the table. "D'you remember when Bud came up with the phrase, 'Mama's Homey Canned Platitudes'?"

At this she swashbuckles; the whole haw-haw comes out and I can hear it from the bottom of her lungs but cannot look at her again because she misses the point; she can laugh at herself but she doesn't know there was real grief in it for us, Bud and me, to whom honesty comes so hard except for money. All I can look at is the linoleum, which is annoyingly and irrelevantly clear, the black outlines of rectangles on a flecked gray ground, the absurdly marbled feather shapes at the upper left corner of each rectangle: it is not the linoleum I want to see.

"Look, you don't understand," I stumble, splashing points of warm water from the pan to the shirt on the table, each spot an instant deeper blue as if I were splashing paint. "The point is that it's become a kind of platitude for us, Bud and me. It's easy to remember your clichés, but they prevent us from remembering you; they only conceal something we never saw because we were kids and kids have to . . . see . . ."

The telephone rings rescuingly. She crosses from the ironing board to the phone, which she pulls through the little sliding door that my dad designed and made so that it, the phone, can be both reached from and closed into both the kitchen and the den; she answers, "Hello?" and swashbuckles the laugh. How can it be that the laugh is false and the pleasure genuine? Can I do this myself? "Why, Lloyd!"

It's the preacher, then. As she stands at the telephone I notice what she wears, which is a green cotton cap-sleeved house smock edged in black piping, sent her one Christmas by Uncle Jack and Aunt Louellen and which has, machine embroidered over the flat left breast, a black poodle dog with a rhinestone stud for an eye. I can see this though her back is to me, and I can see the sharp shadow of the wing blades underneath the cotton, the bones she has never seen. I cannot see her face.

"Lloyd Gruber, how nice of you to call! Oh, as well as can be expected for an old lady, haw haw. Yes, she's home, fat and sassy; you know she's got another book out and she's on a *tour*, well, I wouldn't want to tell you I'd pass it around in the Women's Society for Christian Service but you know it's *those* words that sell nowadays. What? Oh, no, that broke up ages ago. Why, Lloyd, I'm not in the least bit worried about her; you know I was twenty-three myself before I married, yes I was, she's a spring chicken . . ."

"Mama!"

Discouragement appears on me as wrinkles in the elbows of Galway tweed. My mother can embarrass clerks in Kress's five-and-dime. I leave the rolled shirt on the table and escape to the dining room where I watch, in the eight thousand prisms of the glass brick window, eight thousand miniature distortions of the sterile orange tree outside, a bough bobbing under the weight of its puckered fruit. I can taste the acrid taste of these oranges from the time Bud tricked me into lagging a tongue across the wet pebbles of their useless flesh. I think I have changed my mind. I think I will simply cross the living room and thread my way down between the zinnias that line the walk . . .

But there she is, crossing toward the living room herself, with the dress and the shirt flapping from the hooks over her hand. She is there, of course, because she is the pushmi-pullyu of the psychic Midlands. If I go to touch her she will recoil, but if I walk away she will be at my heels. I can do this, too. Somewhere are two teenaged boys and a half a dozen former husbands and lovers who will attest that I can do it, too.

She has hooked the hangers on the knob of the corner cupboard to inspect a possible inch of misturned eyelet, a possible crease in the French seam of the Arrow armhole. She says, "Now *what* it is you want, honey?"

Home is the place where, when you have to go there, they don't understand why you've come.

"I want to put you in a story," I say evenly.

Back to me, she presses a hand over her stomach, she makes a little clucking sound of pain, her back arches in the instinctive position of a Martha Graham contraction and releases, rolling upward from the flat buttocks that I do not mention in her presence. I will not mention Martha Graham, Martha Quest, Billy Graham, Billy Pilgrim, Janet Pilgrim. I may mention graham crackers.

"Sissy, I don't want to fight with you."

"Not a real fight, Mom. That's just a device to get us started. What I really wanted to do is catch your essential . . ."

The ironing has apparently passed muster because she picks up the hangers again and carries on through the living room. The threadbare grape-cluster pattern of the carpet passes before my eyes, the inset knickknack shelf that my father made, the gilded miniature watering can that I broke on the way home from the fourth-grade hobby fair and lied about; the big blond console TV that can't have appeared before I was in high school; the bookcase with *Hurlbut's Stories of the Bible* and the complete works of Edgar Guest. I follow at her heels, black patent Cuban heels, from which emerge the graceful corrugations of the quadruple-A ankles she is so proud of and of which, having the same ankles in spite of my big bone structure, I am so proud. We pass the bulbous, sagging couch, the oversized chartreuse fronds and magenta flowers on the slipcovers that she produced in an awesome lapse of taste, the impossible flowers into which I flung my hot face on the occasion of my first heartbreak: Ace Johnson, yearbook editor, senior class councillor, and jilt. My face sizzles in the flowers as she pronounces the phrases of impossible misunderstanding: "Why, sissy, cheer up, haw haw, there'll be another one along in a minute; there are plenty of fish in the sea."

My elder son is on a transport ship, seeking discipline and the romance of camaraderie. My younger son is the lead singer in a band called Beloved Children, which plays in bars he is legally too young to enter. I am on occasion invited to hear this group, and I do. I sit wondering at the sweet demonic presence of these children, who wail a noise that I like and envy. As a girl I knew nothing better to do than sit a sizzling wallflower and pray that someone would ask me to dance. The Beloved Children crop their heads and embrace freakdom. One of their lyrics praises masturbation, "the central occupation, generation to generation," but they do not have the courage of their erections because one by one the members of the band come by to warn me that I will be shocked. To which generation do they think I belong? I politely assure them that I can take it.

Now we are into the hall, the cupboard where the Bible and the Ansco camera are kept, the laundry cupboard that my father designed so you could put the clothes in from the bathroom or the hall and which we called a chute though nothing chutes from anywhere to anywhere.

"Let me tell you about something," I say, hurrying after her. The trouser suit is an insane thing to be wearing in this heat, long sleeved and cuffed, lined and turtled at the neck. My hot hair prickles; I was thirty-four and living in England before I had the courage to assert that I would wear my hair straight and long. "Once I went back to a house I'd lived in years before. Not this house, you understand, some other house. I went back, and it hadn't been sold, the real estate market was bad, and it was a white elephant of a house, so it was being rented, and a lot of my old things were still there. I went in, the tenant was very nice, and we fell into conversation, and I lit a cigarette . . ."

I wish I hadn't got into this. I remember the first time she caught me with a cigarette, she and Daddy together, and Daddy said, "Aha! Caughtcha!" but Mama said, "You're trying to kill me!" She hangs the dress and shirt, both, in the long closet with the sliding doors, which makes a kind of sense because when I was five this was my room, but later it was hers and Daddy's, and I see from the set of her shoulders that she has drawn in her chin, but I don't know if it's because I mentioned a cigarette or not.

"He set an ashtray in front of me. It was a cheap, simple, glass ashtray in the shape of a spade, like the ace of spades."

She probes her stomach again. I think she sighs again.

"I'd bought a set of those ashtrays in a little country market some dozen years before and I had used them daily for—what?—four or five years; and in the intervening time I had not thought of them once, they did not form any part of my memory. When he set this one down I flicked my ash in it, and I recognized the way the cigarette sounded on the edge of the glass."

She is at the bureau with her back to me, her face averted even from the round rimless mirror, and she begins to lay out things from the drawer, as if for my inspection: the ebony-handled nail buffer, the little pot of waxy rouge that I once stole and lied about, the porcelain doll that sits now on the sill to the left of my typewriter in my house in Florida.

"I was flooded with a whole sense of the reality of that house, and of my life there. I know I'm not explaining myself very well." And I'm not, but I'm not going to make any reference to Proust. "I was homesick, Mama."

She slides the nail buffer along the bureau top toward the window sill where the oleanders nod. The milk of the oleander leaves is poison, Bud and I were taught, as I later taught my boys that the pods of the laburnum were poison, in the garden of the English house that held the glass spade ashtray.

"There's a story," I blurt, inspired, "by John Cheever. In which one of the characters says that fifty percent of the people in the world are homesick all the time."

"Which marriage was that?" she asks, and smiles at me in the mirror while she is putting on her vermilion lipstick so that her mouth is stretched and distorted over the cartilage and the bones.

"Which marriage was what?"

"In that house." She takes out the powder box decorated in peach-colored feathers and opens it in a minor explosion of peach-colored ash, arranges it in front of the buffer, the pot, the doll on my window sill beside the calendar and the goldfish. It was indiscreet to use a name she doesn't know. I could have quoted Edgar Guest, how it takes a heap o' livin' to be homesick all the time. I should have said that Jesus said life is one long longing to go home.

"Which marriage was it in that house?"

"My first. Look, what I'm trying to say . . . Mama, sometimes—usually when I'm driving, for some reason—I think about something that has happened in my life, good or bad, and I think, *I can't wait to tell Mom*, or else I think, *I can't tell Mom* . . .

"And then," I say, "it's like waking up from a dream, a good dream or a nightmare, the sadness or the relief. Do you understand?"

Facing herself in the mirror she places a finger on her nose and deforms it slightly to the right while with the index finger of her same hand pressing downward and the other index finger pressing upward, she produces from her pores several dozen live curling worms of ivory colored wax. I avert my eyes in the old embarrassment and then in the old fascination focus again on the one specific section of the mirror where she places a finger of the other hand on her nose and deforms it slightly to the left. Everyone who grew up in America in the fifties can do this, too.

"*Will* you understand?"

She takes the puff and dabs the peach-colored ash over her nose and cheeks. Minute clogs of powder catch in the emptied pores. She smiles at herself in the mirror, chin tilted, a smile for the PTA or the Women's Society for Christian Service, and as I avert my eyes in the old embarrassment she says, nasal on the vowels, "All I want is your happiness, sissy."

I put my head in my hands. Through my fingers I can see the knees of my trouser suit, baggy and crushed, with the stains of crushed grass on them. My hair is hot and heavy. I will confess to her. I confess, "Nobody knows better than I do how hard it is to make words say what you mean. But it's taken me all these years to know it was just as hard for you."

"All I *ever* wanted was your happiness," she says for the PTA.

"It's not so!" I adjust my tone and say more successfully, "It isn't so." I go to her and try to take her insubstantial shoulders, try to force her toward the mirror and the crossed lower incisors, but am uncertain whether I see her grimace or mine, the powder in her pores or mine. "You wanted me to be happy your way, by your rules: don't smoke, don't wear pink with red, marriage is sacred, the wages of sin. . . . And the truth is you were holding on to a bunch of phrases just like me. You knew they didn't work. The truth is . . ."

The truth is that my elder son is a romantic militarist and my younger a punk rocker. I laugh to my friends: I don't know where they came from! But I know at least one place they are headed, somewhere years hence, to seek for themselves why they are so much, and so threateningly, me.

"Mommy isn't feeling very well, dear. I think the old ulcer is acting up again."

"Don't go to bed. Please don't go to bed."

But she is out of the smock, which she hangs on the brass hook over the shelf of the shoes. She raises a modest and protective hand to her collarbone above the peach satin slip, over the rosily mottled V of flesh below the collarbone she has never seen.

"Don't go to bed!" I say. "It doesn't fool me, I can do it, too. It's a way of getting what you want without asking for it; you've got ulcers and high blood pressure and adrenaline flux, I've got a fibrolated coccyx and chronic otitis and atopic dermatitis; it doesn't fool me, Mama. I can do it, too."

But I notice that my trouser suit is also gone; it has disappeared from my body as abruptly as it disappeared from the parked station wagon in New York in 1972. I am standing in nothing but my ivory satin teddy. My hand goes to my collarbone and the mottled V of flesh. She reaches into her end of the closet for the polished cotton housecoat in stripes of pink and gray sent her one Christmas by Uncle Jack and Aunt Louellen: she sizzles the zipper up, and I reach into my—later Daddy's—end of the closet for the puffed-sleeved pansy dress, which I disengage from the hanger with a deft flick of my thumb at the button at the nape and of course it does not fit; it binds at the armholes and the breast, its hand-stitched hem is above my knees; and yet, it fits so much better than it ought; the time is out of joint.

"Would you get me some milk, sweetie? Funny thing, I always hated milk, and now it's the one thing I can have for my ulcer."

"Don't go to bed."

But she slips under the rose chenille bedspread and lays her tight poodle cut back on the pillow, producing minute wrinkles in the perfectly ironed pink pillowcase, smiling with eyes closed, arms folded over her flat breast. I pull the puffed footstool to her and sit clumsily, crushing the pima pansies as I try to cover my knees, which are stained with grass and tamarack.

"There'll be a brighter day tomorrow," I am almost sure she says. On the nightstand is the photo of her taken on the morning of her wedding day, which now sits beside the doll in my house in Florida. Distractedly I tap my ash; the goldfish attacks it for food. In the photograph she stands beside a mirror in a simple twenties shift of pin-tucked chiffon, her hair marcelled into a shelf so that the profile is half obscured and the mirror image is full-faced, the strand of pearls breaking over the collarbones, the mouth pensive and provocative, the eyes deeply sad. Daddy used to call them bedroom eyes.

"Mama, look at me."

"Sissy, let me tell you, there are so many people in the world worse off than we are."

"Oh, Jesus, Mama, the starving in China, the man who had no feet."

"Don't take the name of the Lord in vain."

"It's the way I talk, for God's sake."

"No child of mine ever talked that way!"

"Don't be an ass, Mama, it's only words."

"I'll wash your mouth out for you!"

"Will you, will you?"

"It kills me to hear you talk that way."

"Does it? Then let me give you something to wash out of my mouth. Daddy's remarried. He's married again!"

Her eyes have been fluttering and slit, but now they open. I have got her now. She glances away and back, her smile parts on the gash of the crossed incisors.

"There are plenty of fish in the sea, haw haw!" I say.

She says, eyes averted, "Your daddy gets sweeter every day."

"Jesus Christ, don't you understand anything? I saw your bones!"

The pima dress is wrinkled, sweaty, and has sand in the pockets. It will have to be washed again, and ironed again. The compressor on the air conditioner will have to be replaced again. "We carried your ashes up to the top of Marble Mountain, Daddy and I; we flung them over the quarry and the foundations of the house you lived in, over the roof of the general store. And do you know, Mama, they're rubble, the marrow looks like dry dog food. I saw the mineral in your bones, blue melted mineral in the chunks!"

Now her eyes widen, the melted hazel and amber of her eyes speak terror, and I know that mine will do this, too.

"We scattered them, Daddy and I!"

"You're trying to kill me," I know she says.

"No!" I grip both her long strong hands in my own. "No, I'm trying to keep you!" I finger the veins and freckles, feel for the bones of her hands and see my own hands long and strong on the black bones of the typewriter keys. I avert my eyes. Beyond the calendar—the fish, the doll, the photo of her bedroom eyes—tropical sun slants through the azaleas, outlining the veins in their fuchsia petals. I hold her eyes.

"Let me see you, Mama!"

But the hands go limp in mine and the eyes begin to close. The lids are delicately veined. I grip her hands. "I've got you now!"

"Not altogether so," my mother says.

A thing she never would say.

Her hair is blued, purpled, and her pores have disappeared. There is an odor of pansies, oleanders, roses, orange blossoms, peach. The planes of her face have been expertly ironed. All the wrinkles of her cheeks are gone, and her mouth, closed, seems fuller in repose. Deep buttoning makes symmetrical creases in the rose satin on the coffin lid. The people passing speak of her; they say: *dear soul*, and *always cheerful*, and *devoted wife and mother*, and *a lady*. Her hands, crossed, are delicate and smooth. There is about her a waxen beatitude.

I don't know how they do this, but everybody says it is an art. Everybody says they have done a splendid job. They have caught her exactly, everybody says.

Kelly Grey Carlisle

PHYSICAL EVIDENCE

KELLY GREY CARLISLE is the managing editor of *Prairie Schooner*, the national literary quarterly published at the University of Nebraska–Lincoln. Her personal essays appear in *River Teeth* and *Tampa Review*, and were named Notable Essays of 2005 in *The Best American Essays 2006*. In 2004, she won an Association of Writers and Writing Programs Intro Journals Award in creative nonfiction and in 2006 was a fellow at the Virginia Center for the Creative Arts. She is a PhD student at the University of Nebraska–Lincoln.

The room into which the attendant has led me is dim, made more so when he pulls the thick shade across the only window. He threads the spool of microfilm into the viewer, turns the machine on, and shows me how to work the controls: forward, backward, focus, zoom. He doesn't talk much, eager, I think, to return to his computer game. I'm glad he hasn't asked me what I'm looking for in these old newspaper reels, but part of me wants to tell him. I'm afraid of what I might find, and I don't want to search on my own. The attendant leaves, and I am left alone with the sound of the machine, the hum of its fan, the clunk and whir of the film as I advance it. Two weeks' worth of the *Los Angeles Times* blur in front of me, the motion making me slightly queasy, until I reach November 29, 1976, three weeks after I was born. I read through headlines, glance at ads for J. C. Penney's Thanksgiving Sale, Safeway's holiday specials. And I laugh a little because not much has changed in all that time: Donald Rumsfeld is still secretary of defense, and depending on whom you ask, Elvis is still alive. What I'm looking for isn't in the big headlines or the ads, so I go back to the front page and read through the smaller items—articles about Amy Carter's high school, a robbery in Fullerton, a blind drum major—but I can't find it. I read on to the next day, and then the next, but still there is nothing. Pretty soon I reach the end of the film: a blank screen and the jarring clack, clack of the tape flapping on its spool.

On November 28, 1976, my mother, Michele Grey, was beaten and strangled, her body abandoned in an empty lot near downtown Los Angeles, about

89

a half mile away from the *Los Angeles Times* headquarters. Her death didn't make the paper.

When I was a little girl, this is the story they told me:

My parents were killed in a car accident when I was three weeks old. My grandmother Spence was half Hawaiian, and that made me special. I lived with her until I was four, when she died, but now she was in heaven watching over me. Her father was full-blooded Hawaiian and a cliff diver, and that was why I liked to swim so much. My grandfather was English and a descendent of the Earl Grey of tea fame, and also of Lady Jane Grey, and somewhere in England our family had a house named Fallodon. And that made me special, too. I had blue blood and Hawaiian blood, and I was going to grow up to be the most beautiful girl in the world, and who knew, maybe I'd become a princess. Sometimes I still let myself believe these things.

I was raised by my grandfather and his second wife, Marilyn. Before I knew the truth about her death I wanted to know everything about my mother, Michele. What did she look like? What was her favorite color? I wanted to know if my mother had curly hair or straight, whether she was tall or thin. Did she like cats or dogs better? Was she pretty? Did she like ice cream? Could she draw well? My grandfather could never really answer my questions. He hemmed and hawed and changed the subject.

I wanted to see a picture of my mother, but all my grandfather had to show me was a snapshot of the back of a little girl who was petting a cat and another one of her blowing out candles on her birthday cake. I couldn't see her face in those pictures, her back was always turned toward the camera. The little girl had red hair, and in both pictures she had on the same dress. I counted the candles on her cake and there were eight of them. I'd always thought of Michele as a tall, graceful woman, with long hair and soft, cool hands, the way Marilyn's hands were cool on my forehead when I was sick. I'd never thought of my mother as an eight-year-old, that she'd ever been a little girl like me.

What I did not know until much later was that my grandfather barely knew his daughter. My grandfather told me that when Spence was pregnant with Michele she pumped gas to earn extra money that he thought would go toward their life together. But a few weeks after Michele was born Spence left him. He said Spence lied to Michele about her parentage, telling her that her father had run off before she was born. The few times my grandfather got to see his daughter he was introduced as "Richard," a family friend. My grandfather admitted that he said nothing and went along with the lie. When she was fourteen Michele figured out that the old family friend to whom she was shipped off once a year for a visit, the old family friend who looked so much like her, was her father. It was not a happy reunion; Michele was furious. She refused to talk to him for months. Four years later she was living on the streets. When my grandfather told me this story he seemed hurt and indignant that Michele would take her anger out at him, as if he thought he was just as much a victim as she was.

One night when I was eight my grandfather and I sat at the dining room table, our empty plates and glasses still before us. Marilyn was out with friends, and he and I were alone. I don't remember what we were talking about or how we got to it, but suddenly there it was, the truth, sitting between us like a round, hard stone.

". . . the man who killed your mother."

"I thought she died in a car crash," I said. I thought maybe he was talking about a drunk driver who'd killed my mother or some teenager who drove too fast.

"No, she was murdered."

I remember how my mind leapt from question to question.

"What about my father? I thought he was killed in the accident, too." The truth was, until that moment, I'd never thought to ask about my father.

"We don't know who your father is."

I pulled my legs up underneath me and fidgeted with Marilyn's orange vinyl placemats.

"Who killed her?"

"We don't know."

"You mean . . . they'll never go to jail?" I was indignant. My notions about fair and unfair were very strong when I was eight.

"The detective on your mother's case thought that maybe she might have been killed by the Hillside Stranglers, but there wasn't any evidence."

"Who were the Hillside Stranglers?"

"No one you need to worry about. They're in jail now. Besides, it was just a guess."

I don't remember what we said after that or what story my grandfather read to me when he tucked me in or what I thought about as I fell asleep. But even though I was only eight I knew everything was different.

For my eleventh birthday Marilyn gave me a picture of my mother. She had spent days looking for it in my grandfather's closet and had had it framed in red lacquered wood. When I first unwrapped it I didn't understand.

"Who is this?" I asked.

"It's Michele," she said.

It was the first time I'd ever seen my mother as an adult.

She had long brown hair and thick arms and eyebrows like mine. She wore a half smile that said, *I don't really want my picture to be taken.* I knew, because I smiled like that, too.

I put that picture up on my dresser, and it was like she was watching me quietly, always with the same shy smile. I kept her picture with me as I grew up. She kept me company during my adolescence, made me feel less alone when I'd convinced myself that no one loved me. I left that picture behind when I moved away to college. I was worried that something might happen to it in my dorm room; worried, too, I think, that my roommate might think me strange because of it. It's still in Los Angeles, and now I am in Nebraska. I find myself wanting to have it again, but Marilyn has moved twice since my grandfather died, and we're not exactly sure which storage space it's in. I'm worried it might have gotten lost in the move, worried that somehow it got thrown away. I hope it's in a box somewhere waiting for me with that quiet smile.

Marilyn remembers how my mother, five months before she died, called my grandfather from a pay phone on Sunset Boulevard and asked for help. She was four months pregnant with me and alone. She needed a place to stay and some money. She said it would be only temporary, that she'd get a job. She even promised to stay sober, a promise both of them knew she couldn't keep. He heard her crying on the other end of the phone, the catch in her voice as she tried to muffle her sobs. It was the first time she had asked him for anything since she had run away from home four years before. My grandfather said *no*. I like to think he was just hurt, angry, when he said, "You've really fucked up now, haven't you?"

It was their last conversation—not that he didn't change his mind a few weeks later and try to get in touch with her. He called her last known number, but the man who picked up couldn't speak English. My grandfather called his ex-wife, my grandmother Spence, and asked if she knew where their daughter was. She hadn't heard from her for two months. She had said *no*, too.

One night three weeks after I was born my mother left me with some friends in a motel room on Wilcox Avenue in Hollywood. Before she left she laid me in a dresser drawer, nestled me between some socks and jeans and a dirty T-shirt, and tucked my baby blanket around me. I like to think she kissed me before she went out into the night. I like to think she loved me, wanted me. I like to think I made her happy.

Her body was found the next day.

Except for that one night when I was eight my grandfather did not talk about my mother's death again. When I was twelve I decided to find out about it for myself. Over the years I had been infatuated with, sequentially, Sherlock

Holmes, Perry Mason (when Raymond Burr was young and trim), Steve Garrett, and Sam Spade. So I snuck into my grandfather's office late at night, slipping folders out of his filing cabinet, paging through documents hurriedly, terrified he might catch me. I found my birth certificate from the hospital. It was printed on heavy paper with a pink border and two cherubs and my real name spelled in calligraphy: Kelly Michelle Archibald. My mother had given me a father, at least on paper. I found my grandmother's state-issued birth certificate, a purple mimeograph that spelled out her full name, Yvonne Kaia Spencer, and said that her father was born in Honolulu, Hawaii. It listed his "race or color" as white. I found my grandfather's birth certificate, an ancient copy creased and folded, worn soft like suede at the edges. I found my mother's birth certificate. And finally, her death certificate, purple ink on shiny paper that listed her cause of death as MANUAL STRANGULATION in thick, bold caps.

The filing cabinet held no other details of her murder, but that didn't matter because soon I found my grandfather's books about the Hillside Stranglers. I read bits and pieces while my grandfather was at work, read passages late at night when I couldn't sleep. Their dust covers were splashed with words like *sensational, shocking, savage.* One of them was written like a novel, and in it I read how Bianchi listened to Buono rape a thirteen-year-old girl, how he got hard imagining his friend thrusting inside her. When I read these things I thought about my mom. Fifteen years later I wonder how many men have been aroused reading those descriptions, and I can't help but wonder if the author was counting on it to sell his book. I wonder if he ever imagined a twelve-year-old girl reading the book, looking for the truth about her mom. I wonder how much money that book has made.

I read those books, and with a morbid fascination of which I am ashamed, I imagined what had happened to my mother, what her body looked like when it was found. I pictured my mother naked, spread-eagled, her foot touching a crumpled bag of Fritos, an empty can of beer by her side. It was 1976, and so I figured it must have been one of those steel cans of Bud with the pull-away tab—the kind I'd found in the woods buried under layers of leaves. I saw my mother lying in a lot overgrown with weeds, littered with trash, within earshot of the 101. I imagined my mother's hair, brown like mine, long like in her picture. I saw it spread around her head, a halo in the grass. Her death certificate says she was found at 8:10 in the morning, and so I always pictured her a few minutes before she was found, in the quiet hush of morning that can happen even in L.A. I imagined purple bruises around her neck, her lips torn, rope burns around her wrists, her eyes, hazel like mine, filled with hate.

But I imagined wrong.

. . .

Because there is nothing in the newspapers about my mother's murder, I decide to call the Los Angeles Police Department and request a copy of her files. It has taken me days to work up the courage to make this call, and I shake as I dial, but the lady in the Cold Case Department who answers the phone is kind.

"All I can do is give you the case summary," she says when I've explained my situation, "because your mom's case is still open. We can't release any other details. Can you hold for a second? I have to go pull a book from the shelf." I imagine leather-bound folios gathering dust on a shelf, or, more likely, huge three-ring binders stamped with LAPD.

"Okay," she says when she gets back. I hear the thump of the book on her desk. "What I have here is a case summary of your mother's file. It's not . . . it's pretty ugly, okay? I really wish you were here in person so that I could be with you to tell you this, but I'll try to read it over the phone."

She pauses a second as if she is trying to control her emotions. "I really wish you were here in front of me."

I had steeled myself to talk to a burned-out detective or a calloused bureaucrat. I wasn't prepared to talk to someone kind. It is her care, and not what follows, that makes me cry.

"In the upper-left-hand corner it says: 'Beating—blunt instrument—unknown. Strangulation—ligature.' That means she was strangled with a ligature, like a rope or a cord or something. Then it says her name: 'Michele Ann Grey.' Your mom was murdered between November 28th and 29th, between 10:00 p.m. and 8:10 a.m., when she was found. It lists the suspects as 'unknown.' Okay, then it says—

"You're gonna hate me," I hear her mutter under her breath, then she continues.

"Victim is a Hollywood prostitute who was living with three companions at the Hollywood Center Motel. At 10:00 p.m. she told her companions she was going next door to turn a trick to help pay the rent because they did not have enough money. Her friends thought she meant a hotel up the street. They did not see the victim alive again."

She clears her throat.

"The victim was discovered by a gardener in the vacant lot at 610 North Hill Place. An autopsy revealed the victim had been beaten and strangled with an unknown ligature. She was fully clothed except for her right shoe. There were no witnesses to the body being dumped or the homicide occurring.

"Status: Investigation Continued."

She takes a breath.

"That means your mom's case is still open. And it always will be until . . . until it's solved. And I'm actually the investigator for homicides in 1976, so I'm the detective on your mother's case. My name is Amelia Chavez."

I don't trust my voice, so all I can say is "Thank you."

Amelia takes down my contact information and tells me she'll read through my mother's file to see if there's anything else we can do. A week later she calls me to tell me that she has sent the available physical evidence to be tested for usable DNA. She is also locating and interviewing all the principal witnesses in the case, including, she says when I ask, my birth father. She also says that the detectives ruled out the Hillside Stranglers long ago.

"This isn't like CSI, okay?" she warns me before we hang up. "It'll take four to five months for the test to come back. And we're probably not going to find anything."

But at least you're trying, I think, at least you care. And suddenly it is like that night when I was eight years old. Everything is different now. In a few months I might know who killed my mother. In a few months I might meet my father.

I try to imagine the physical evidence in my mother's file: her clothes, I imagine, maybe jeans and a sweatshirt, underwear; perhaps her wallet or a watch or earrings; her left shoe, her socks. I keep thinking about her right shoe, the one that was missing. I wonder what happened to it, where it is now. I imagine they store all the items in a big cardboard box, the kind you see on TV mysteries. I think of how more of her belongings are in that box than I will ever possess. The only thing I've ever owned that was hers was the Bible she had when she was a child. It had color illustrations of Moses in the rushes and Mary Magdalene weeping. On the inside cover my mother had written her name, Michele Ann Grey, in big cursive loops. I used to touch that Bible, rub my finger along its spine when I was lonely or sad. I think of the evidence in that big cardboard box, and I want to touch it too, run my finger along the jeans my mom once wore, the hem of the sweatshirt that once kept her warm. I lost that Bible somewhere along the way to adulthood. I wish I had it back.

Hardly anyone cared about my mother while she was alive, and when she died few people took note. All she left behind was a birth certificate, a death certificate, a few pictures, that Bible, and a box of ashes—the only evidence that she ever existed. It is so little with which to reconstruct a life.

This is what I know about my mother: when she was a little girl she had a cat, when she turned eight she had a birthday party. She spelled her name, Michele, with one *l*. On my birth certificate she spelled my middle name,

Michelle, with two. She had brown hair that, like mine, shone red in the sun. She named me after a steak house by the 405 Freeway called Kelly's. She was a prostitute; she was addicted to drugs. Against all reason she carried me to term. She took care of me as best she could. She died at night, with only her murderer for company. This is what I know about my mother: I am her daughter, and her memory rests with me.

Anne Carson

THE GLASS ESSAY

ANNE CARSON, twice a finalist for the National Book Critics Circle Award and winner of the 1996 Lannan Award, was named a MacArthur Fellow in 2000. In 2001 she received the T. S. Eliot Prize for Poetry, the *Los Angeles Times* Book Prize, and the Griffin Poetry Prize. She teaches at the University of Michigan.

I

I can hear little clicks inside my dream.
Night drips its silver tap
down the back.
At 4 A.M. I wake. Thinking

of the man who
left in September.
His name was Law.

My face in the bathroom mirror
has white streaks down it.
I rinse the face and return to bed.
Tomorrow I am going to visit my mother

SHE

She lives on a moor in the north.
She lives alone.
Spring opens like a blade there.
I travel all day on trains and bring a lot of books—

some for my mother, some for me
including *The Collected Works of Emily Brontë*.
This is my favourite author.

Also my main fear, which I mean to confront.
Whenever I visit my mother
I feel I am turning into Emily Brontë,

my lonely life around me like a moor,
my ungainly body stumping over the mud flats with a look of
    transformation
that dies when I come in the kitchen door.
What meat is it, Emily, we need?

THREE

Three silent women at the kitchen table.
My mother's kitchen is dark and small but out the window
there is the moor, paralyzed with ice.
It extends as far as the eye can see

over flat miles to a solid unlit white sky.
Mother and I are chewing lettuce carefully.
The kitchen wall clock emits a ragged low buzz that jumps

once a minute over the twelve.
I have Emily p. 216 propped open on the sugarbowl
but am covertly watching my mother.

A thousand questions hit my eyes from the inside.
My mother is studying her lettuce.
I turn to p. 217.

"In my flight through the kitchen I knocked over Hareton
who was hanging a litter of puppies
from a chairback in the doorway. . . ."

It is as if we have all been lowered into an atmosphere of glass.
Now and then a remark trails through the glass.
Taxes on the back lot. Not a good melon,

too early for melons.
Hairdresser in town found God, closes shop every Tuesday.
Mice in the teatowel drawer again.
Little pellets. Chew off

the corners of the napkins, if they knew
what paper napkins cost nowadays.
Rain tonight.

Rain tomorrow.
That volcano in the Philippines at it again. What's her name
Anderson died no not Shirley

the opera singer. Negress.
Cancer.
Not eating your garnish, you don't like pimento?

Out the window I can see dead leaves ticking over the flatland
and dregs of snow scarred by pine filth.
At the middle of the moor

where the ground goes down into a depression,
the ice has begun to unclench.
Black open water comes

curdling up like anger. My mother speaks suddenly.
That psychotherapy's not doing you much good is it?
You aren't getting over him.

My mother has a way of summing things up.
She never liked Law much
but she liked the idea of me having a man and getting on with life.

Well he's a taker and you're a giver I hope it works out,
was all she said after she met him.
Give and take were just words to me

at the time. I had not been in love before.
It was like a wheel rolling downhill.
But early this morning while mother slept

and I was downstairs reading the part in *Wuthering Heights*
where Heathcliff clings at the lattice in the storm sobbing
Come in! Come in! to the ghost of his heart's darling,

I fell on my knees on the rug and sobbed too.
She knows how to hang puppies,
that Emily.

It isn't like taking an aspirin you know, I answer feebly.
Dr. Haw says grief is a long process.
She frowns. What does it accomplish

all that raking up the past?
Oh—I spread my hands—
I prevail! I look her in the eye.
She grins. Yes you do.

WHACHER

Whacher,
Emily's habitual spelling of this word,
has caused confusion.
For example

in the first line of the poem printed *Tell me, whether, is it winter?*
in the Shakespeare Head edition.
But whacher is what she wrote.

Whacher is what she was.
She whached God and humans and moor wind and open night.
She whached eyes, stars, inside, outside, actual weather.

She whached the bars of time, which broke.
She whached the poor core of the world,
wide open.

To be a whacher is not a choice.
There is nowhere to get away from it,
no ledge to climb up to—like a swimmer

who walks out of the water at sunset
shaking the drops off, it just flies open.
To be a whacher is not in itself sad or happy,

although she uses these words in her verse
as she uses the emotions of sexual union in her novel,
grazing with euphemism the work of whaching.

But it has no name.
It is transparent.
Sometimes she calls it Thou.

"Emily is in the parlour brushing the carpet,"
records Charlotte in 1828.
Unsociable even at home

and unable to meet the eyes of strangers when she ventured out,
Emily made her awkward way
across days and years whose bareness appalls her biographers.

This sad stunted life, says one.
Uninteresting, unremarkable, wracked by disappointment
and despair, says another.

She could have been a great navigator if she'd been male,
suggests a third. Meanwhile
Emily continued to brush into the carpet the question,

Why cast the world away.
For someone hooked up to Thou,
the world may have seemed a kind of half-finished sentence.

But in between the neighbour who recalls her
coming in from a walk on the moors
with her face "lit up by a divine light"

and the sister who tells us
Emily never made a friend in her life,
is a space where the little raw soul

slips through.
It goes skimming the deep keel like a storm petrel,
out of sight.

The little raw soul was caught by no one.
She didn't have friends, children, sex, religion, marriage, success, a salary
or a fear of death. She worked

in total six months of her life (at a school in Halifax)
and died on the sofa at home at 2 P.M. on a winter afternoon
in her thirty-first year. She spent

most of the hours of her life brushing the carpet,
walking the moor
or whaching. She says

it gave her peace.
"All tight and right in which condition it is to be hoped we shall all be this
    day 4 years,"
she wrote in her Diary Paper of 1837.

Yet her poetry from beginning to end is concerned with prisons,
vaults, cages, bars, curbs, bits, bolts, fetters,
locked windows, narrow frames, aching walls.

"Why all the fuss?" asks one critic.
"She wanted liberty. Well didn't she have it?
A reasonably satisfactory homelife,

a most satisfactory dreamlife—why all this beating of wings?
What was this cage, invisible to us,
which she felt herself to be confined in?"

Well there are many ways of being held prisoner,
I am thinking as I stride over the moor.
As a rule after lunch mother has a nap

and I go out to walk.
The bare blue trees and bleached wooden sky of April
carve into me with knives of light.

Something inside it reminds me of childhood—
it is the light of the stalled time after lunch
when clocks tick

and hearts shut
and fathers leave to go back to work
and mothers stand at the kitchen sink pondering

something they never tell.
You remember too much,
my mother said to me recently.

Why hold onto all that? And I said,
Where can I put it down?
She shifted to a question about airports.

Crops of ice are changing to mud all around me
as I push on across the moor
warmed by drifts from the pale blue sun.

On the edge of the moor our pines
dip and coast in breezes
from somewhere else.

Perhaps the hardest thing about losing a lover is
to watch the year repeat its days.
It is as if I could dip my hand down

into time and scoop up
blue and green lozenges of April heat
a year ago in another country.

I can feel that other day running underneath this one
like an old videotape—here we go fast around the last
    corner
up the hill to his house, shadows

of limes and roses blowing in the car window
and music spraying from the radio and him
singing and touching my left hand to his lips.

Law lived in a high blue room from which he could see the sea.
Time in its transparent loops as it passes beneath me now
still carries the sound of the telephone in that room

and traffic far off and doves under the window
chuckling coolly and his voice saying,
You beauty. I can feel that beauty's

heart beating inside mine as she presses into his arms in the high blue room—
No, I say aloud. I force my arms down
through air which is suddenly cold and heavy as water

and the videotape jerks to a halt
like a glass slide under a drop of blood.
I stop and turn and stand into the wind,

which now plunges towards me over the moor.
When Law left I felt so bad I thought I would die.
This is not uncommon.

I took up the practice of meditation.
Each morning I sat on the floor in front of my sofa
and chanted bits of old Latin prayers.

De profudis clamavi ad te Domine.
Each morning a vision came to me.
Gradually I understood that these were naked glimpses of my soul.

I called them Nudes.
Nude # 1. Woman alone on a hill.
She stands into the wind.

It is a hard wind slanting from the north.
Long flaps and shreds of flesh rip off the woman's body and lift
and blow away on the wind, leaving

an exposed column of nerve and blood and muscle
calling mutely through lipless mouth.
It pains me to record this,

I am not a melodramatic person.
But soul is "hewn in a wild workshop"
as Charlotte Brontë says of *Wuthering Heights*.

Charlotte's preface to *Wuthering Heights* is a publicist's masterpiece.
Like someone carefully not looking at a scorpion
crouched on the arm of the sofa Charlotte

talks firmly and calmly
about the other furniture of Emily's workshop—about
the inexorable spirit ("stronger than a man, simpler than a child"),

the cruel illness ("pain no words can render"),
the autonomous end ("she sank rapidly, she made haste to leave us")
and about Emily's total subjection

to a creative project she could neither understand nor control,
and for which she deserves no more praise nor blame
than if she had opened her mouth

"to breathe lightning." The scorpion is inching down
the arm of the sofa while Charlotte
continues to speak helpfully about lightning

and other weather we may expect to experience
when we enter Emily's electrical atmosphere.
It is "a horror of great darkness" that awaits us there

but Emily is not responsible. Emily was in the grip.
"Having formed these beings she did not know what she had done,"
says Charlotte (of Heathcliff and Earnshaw and Catherine).

Well there are many ways of being held prisoner.
The scorpion takes a light spring and lands on our left knee
as Charlotte concludes, "On herself she had no pity."

Pitiless too are the Heights, which Emily called Wuthering
because of their "bracing ventilation"
and "a north wind over the edge."

Whaching a north wind grind the moor
that surrounded her father's house on every side,
formed a kind of rock called millstone grit,

taught Emily all she knew about love and its necessities—
an angry education that shapes the way her characters
use one another. "My love for Heathcliff," says Catherine,

"resembles the eternal rocks beneath—
a source of little visible delight, but necessary."
Necessary? I notice the sun has dimmed

and the afternoon air sharpening.
I turn and start to recross the moor towards home.
What are the imperatives

that hold people like Catherine and Heathcliff
together and apart, like pores blown into hot rock
and then stranded out of reach

of one another when it hardens? What kind of necessity is that?
The last time I saw Law was a black night in September.
Autumn had begun,

my knees were cold inside my clothes.
A chill fragment of moon rose.
He stood in my living room and spoke

without looking at me. Not enough spin on it,
he said of our five years of love.
Inside my chest I felt my heart snap into two pieces

which floated apart. By now I was so cold
it was like burning. I put out my hand
to touch his. He moved back.

I don't want to be sexual with you, he said. Everything gets crazy.
But now he was looking at me.
Yes, I said as I began to remove my clothes.

Everything gets crazy. When nude
I turned my back because he likes the back.
He moved onto me.

Everything I know about love and its necessities
I learned in that one moment
when I found myself

thrusting my little burning red backside like a baboon
at a man who no longer cherished me.
There was no area of my mind

not appalled by this action, no part of my body
that could have done otherwise.
But to talk of mind and body begs the question.

Soul is the place,
stretched like a surface of millstone grit between body and mind,
where such necessity grinds itself out.

Soul is what I kept watch on all that night.
Law stayed with me.
We lay on top of the covers as if it weren't really a night of sleep and time,

caressing and singing to one another in our made-up language
like the children we used to be.
That was a night that centred Heaven and Hell,

as Emily would say. We tried to fuck
but he remained limp, although happy. I came
again and again, each time accumulating lucidity,

until at last I was floating high up near the ceiling looking down
on the two souls clasped there on the bed
with their mortal boundaries

visible around them like lines on a map.
I saw the lines harden.
He left in the morning.

It is very cold
walking into the long scraped April wind.
At this time of year there is no sunset
just some movements inside the light and then a sinking away.

KITCHEN

Kitchen is quiet as a bone when I come in.
No sound from the rest of the house.
I wait a moment
then open the fridge.

Brilliant as a spaceship it exhales cold confusion.
My mother lives alone and eats little but her fridge is always crammed.
After extracting the yogurt container

from beneath a wily arrangement of leftover blocks of Christmas cake
wrapped in foil and prescription medicine bottles
I close the fridge door. Bluish dusk

fills the room like a sea slid back.
I lean against the sink.
White foods taste best to me

and I prefer to eat alone. I don't know why.
Once I heard girls singing a May Day song that went:

> Violante in the pantry
> Gnawing at a mutton bone
> How she gnawed it
> How she clawed it
> When she felt herself alone.

Girls are cruelest to themselves.
Someone like Emily Brontë,
who remained a girl all her life despite her body as a woman,

had cruelty drifted up in all the cracks of her like spring snow.
We can see her ridding herself of it at various times
with a gesture like she used to brush the carpet.

Reason with him and then whip him!
was her instruction (age six) to her father
regarding brother Branwell.

And when she was 14 and bitten by a rabid dog she strode (they say)
into the kitchen and taking red hot tongs from the back of the stove applied
them directly to her arm.

Cauterization of Heathcliff took longer.
More than thirty years in the time of the novel,
from the April evening when he runs out the back door of the kitchen
and vanishes over the moor

because he overheard half a sentence of Catherine's
("It would degrade me to marry Heathcliff")
until the wild morning

when the servant finds him stark dead and grinning
on his rainsoaked bed upstairs in Wuthering Heights.
Heathcliff is a pain devil.

If he had stayed in the kitchen
long enough to hear the other half of Catherine's sentence
("so he will never know how I love him")

Heathcliff would have been set free.
But Emily knew how to catch a devil.
She put into him in place of a soul

the constant cold departure of Catherine from his nervous system
every time he drew a breath or moved thought.
She broke all his moments in half,

with the kitchen door standing open.
I am not unfamiliar with this half-life.
But there is more to it than that.

Heathcliff's sexual despair
arose out of no such experience in the life of Emily Brontë,
so far as we know. Her question,

which concerns the years of inner cruelty that can twist a person into a pain
    devil,
came to her in a kindly firelit kitchen
("kichin" in Emily's spelling) where she

and Charlotte and Anne peeled potatoes together
and made up stories with the old house dog Keeper at their feet.
There is a fragment

of a poem she wrote in 1839
(about six years before *Wuthering Heights*) that says:

> That iron man was born like me
> And he was once an ardent boy:
> He must have felt in infancy
> The glory of a summer sky.

Who is the iron man?
My mother's voice cuts across me,
from the next room where she is lying on the sofa.

Is that you dear?
Yes Ma.
Why don't you turn on a light in there?

Out the kitchen window I watch the steely April sun
jab its last cold yellow streaks
across a dirty silver sky.
Okay Ma. What's for supper?

LIBERTY

Liberty means different things to different people.
I have never liked lying in bed in the morning.
Law did.
My mother does.

But as soon as the morning light hits my eyes I want to be out in it—
moving along the moor
into the first blue currents and cold navigation of everything awake.

I hear my mother in the next room turn and sigh and sink deeper.
I peel the stale cage of sheets off my legs
and I am free.

Out on the moor all is brilliant and hard after a night of frost.
The light plunges straight up from the ice to a blue hole at the top of
    the sky.
Frozen mud crunches underfoot. The sound

startles me back into the dream I was having
this morning when I awoke,
one of those nightlong sweet dreams of lying in Law's

arms like a needle in water—it is a physical effort
to pull myself out of his white silk hands
as they slide down my dream hips—I

turn and face into the wind
and begin to run.
Goblins, devils and death stream behind me.

In the days and months after Law left
I felt as if the sky was torn off my life.
I had no home in goodness anymore.

To see the love between Law and me
turn into two animals gnawing and craving through one another
towards some other hunger was terrible.

Perhaps this is what people mean by original sin, I thought.
But what love could be prior to it?
What is prior?

What is love?
My questions were not original.
Nor did I answer them.

Mornings when I meditated
I was presented with a nude glimpse of my lone soul,
not the complex mysteries of love and hate.

But the Nudes are still as clear in my mind
as pieces of laundry that froze on the clothesline overnight.
There were in all thirteen of them.

Nude #2. Woman caught in a cage of thorns.
Big glistening brown thorns with black stains on them
where she twists this way and that way

unable to stand upright.
Nude #3. Woman with a single great thorn implanted in her forehead.
She grips it in both hands

endeavouring to wrench it out.
Nude #4. Woman on a blasted landscape
backlit in red like Hieronymus Bosch.

Covering her head and upper body is a hellish contraption
like the top half of a crab.
With arms crossed as if pulling off a sweater

she works hard at dislodging the crab.
It was about this time
I began telling Dr. Haw

about the Nudes. She said,
When you see these horrible images why do you stay with them?
Why keep watching? Why not

go away? I was amazed.
Go away where? I said.
This still seems to me a good question.

But by now the day is wide open and a strange young April light
is filling the moor with gold milk.
I have reached the middle

where the ground goes down into a depression and fills with swampy water.
It is frozen.
A solid black pane of moor life caught in its own night attitudes.

Certain wild gold arrangements of weed are visible deep in the black.
Four naked alder trunks rise straight up from it
and sway in the blue air. Each trunk

where it enters the ice radiates a map of silver pressures—
thousands of hair-thin cracks catching the white of the light
like a jailed face

catching grins through the bars.
Emily Brontë has a poem about a woman in jail who says

> A messenger of Hope, comes every night to me
> And offers, for short life, eternal Liberty.

I wonder what kind of Liberty this is.
Her critics and commentators say she means death
or a visionary experience that prefigures death.

They understand her prison
as the limitations placed on a clergyman's daughter
by nineteenth-century life in a remote parish on a cold moor

in the north of England.
They grow impatient with the extreme terms in which she figures
     prison life.
"In so much of Brontë's work

the self-dramatising and posturing of these poems teeters
on the brink of a potentially bathetic melodrama,"
says one. Another

refers to "the cardboard sublime" of her caught world.
I stopped telling my psychotherapist about the Nudes
when I realized I had no way to answer her question,

Why keep watching?
Some people watch, that's all I can say.
There is nowhere else to go,

no ledge to climb up to.
Perhaps I can explain this to her if I wait for the right moment,
as with a very difficult sister.

"On that mind time and experience alone could work:
to the influence of other intellects it was not amenable,"
wrote Charlotte of Emily.

I wonder what kind of conversation these two had
over breakfast at the parsonage.
"My sister Emily

was not a person of demonstrative character," Charlotte emphasizes,
"nor one on the recesses of whose mind and feelings,
even those nearest and dearest to her could,

with impunity, intrude unlicensed. . . ." Recesses were many.
One autumn day in 1845 Charlotte
"accidentally lighted on a MS. volume of verse in my sister Emily's handwriting."

It was a small (4 x 6) notebook
with a dark red cover marked 6d.
and contained 44 poems in Emily's minute hand.

Charlotte had known Emily wrote verse
but felt "more than surprise" at its quality.
"Not at all like the poetry women generally write."

Further surprise awaited Charlotte when she read Emily's novel,
not least for its foul language.
She gently probes this recess

in her Editor's Preface to *Wuthering Heights*.
"A large class of readers, likewise, will suffer greatly
from the introduction into the pages of this work

of words printed with all their letters,
which it has become the custom to represent by the initial and final letter
    only—a blank
line filling the interval."

Well, there are different definitions of Liberty.
Love is freedom, Law was fond of saying.
I took this to be more a wish than a thought

and changed the subject.
But blank lines do not say nothing.
As Charlotte puts it,

"The practice of hinting by single letters those expletives
with which profane and violent persons are wont to garnish their discourse,
strikes me as a proceeding which,

however well meant, is weak and futile.
I cannot tell what good it does—what feeling it spares—
what horror it conceals."

I turn my steps and begin walking back over the moor
towards home and breakfast.
It is a two-way traffic,

the language of the unsaid. My favourite pages
of *The Collected Works of Emily Brontë*
are the notes at the back

recording small adjustments made by Charlotte
to the text of Emily's verse,
which Charlotte edited for publication after Emily's death.
"*Prison* for *strongest* [in Emily's hand] altered to *lordly* by Charlotte."

HERO

I can tell by the way my mother chews her toast
whether she had a good night
and is about to say a happy thing
or not.

Not.
She puts her toast down on the side of her plate.
You know you can pull the drapes in that room, she begins.

This is a coded reference to one of our oldest arguments,
from what I call The Rules Of Life series.
My mother always closes her bedroom drapes tight before going to bed at
    night.

I open mine as wide as possible.
I like to see everything, I say.
What's there to see?

Moon. Air. Sunrise.
All that light on your face in the morning. Wakes you up.
I like to wake up.

At this point the drapes argument has reached a delta
and may advance along one of three channels.
There is the What You Need Is A Good Night's Sleep channel,

the Stubborn As Your Father channel
and random channel.
More toast? I interpose strongly, pushing back my chair.

Those women! says my mother with an exasperated rasp.
Mother has chosen random channel.
Women?

Complaining about rape all the time—
I see she is tapping one furious finger on yesterday's newspaper
lying beside the grape jam.

The front page has a small feature
about a rally for International Women's Day—
have you had a look at the Sears Summer Catalogue?

Nope.
Why, it's a disgrace! Those bathing suits—
cut way up to here! (she points) No wonder!

You're saying women deserve to get raped
because Sears bathing suit ads
have high-cut legs? Ma, are you serious?

Well someone has to be responsible.
Why should women be responsible for male desire? My voice is high.
Oh I see you're one of Them.

One of Whom? My voice is very high. Mother vaults it.
And whatever did you do with that little tank suit you had last year the
    green one?
It looked so smart on you.

The frail fact drops on me from a great height
that my mother is afraid.
She will be eighty years old this summer.

Her tiny sharp shoulders hunched in the blue bathrobe
make me think of Emily Brontë's little merlin hawk Hero
that she fed bits of bacon at the kitchen table when Charlotte wasn't around.

So Ma, we'll go—I pop up the toaster
and toss a hot slice of pumpernickel lightly across onto her plate—
visit Dad today? She eyes the kitchen clock with hostility.

Leave at eleven, home again by four? I continue.
She is buttering her toast with jagged strokes.
Silence is assent in our code. I go into the next room to phone the taxi.

My father lives in a hospital for patients who need chronic care
about 50 miles from here.
He suffers from a kind of dementia

characterized by two sorts of pathological change
first recorded in 1907 by Alois Alzheimer.
First, the presence in cerebral tissue

of a spherical formation known as neuritic plaque,
consisting mainly of degenerating brain cells.
Second, neurofibrillary snarlings

in the cerebral cortex and in the hippocampus.
There is no known cause or cure.
Mother visits him by taxi once a week

for the last five years.
Marriage is for better or for worse, she says,
this is the worse.

So about an hour later we are in the taxi
shooting along empty country roads towards town.
The April light is clear as an alarm.

As we pass them it gives a sudden sense of every object
existing in space on its own shadow.
I wish I could carry this clarity with me

into the hospital where distinctions tend to flatten and coalesce.
I wish I had been nicer to him before he got crazy.
These are my two wishes.

It is hard to find the beginning of dementia.
I remember a night about ten years ago
when I was talking to him on the telephone.

It was a Sunday night in winter.
I heard his sentences filling up with fear.
He would start a sentence—about weather, lose his way, start another.
It made me furious to hear him floundering—

my tall proud father, former World War II navigator!
It made me merciless.
I stood on the edge of the conversation,

watching him thrash about for cues,
offering none,
and it came to me like a slow avalanche

that he had no idea who he was talking to.
Much colder today I guess. . . .
his voice pressed into the silence and broke off,

snow falling on it.
There was a long pause while snow covered us both.
Well I won't keep you,

he said with sudden desperate cheer as if sighting land.
I'll say goodnight now,
I won't run up your bill. Goodbye.

Goodbye.
Goodbye. Who are you?
I said into the dial tone.

At the hospital we pass down long pink halls
through a door with a big window
and a combination lock (5–25–3)

to the west wing, for chronic care patients.
Each wing has a name.
The chronic wing is Our Golden Mile

although mother prefers to call it The Last Lap.
Father sits strapped in a chair which is tied to the wall
in a room of other tied people tilting at various angles.

My father tilts least, I am proud of him.
Hi Dad how y'doing?
His face cracks open it could be a grin or rage

and looking past me he issues a stream of vehemence at the air.
My mother lays her hand on his.
Hello love, she says. He jerks his hand away. We sit.

Sunlight flocks through the room.
Mother begins to unpack from her handbag the things she has brought
     for him,
grapes, arrowroot biscuits, humbugs.

He is addressing strenuous remarks to someone in the air between us.
He uses a language known only to himself,
made of snarls and syllables and sudden wild appeals.

Once in a while some old formula floats up through the wash—
You don't say! or Happy birthday to you!—
but no real sentence

for more than three years now.
I notice his front teeth are getting black.
I wonder how you clean the teeth of mad people.

He always took good care of his teeth. My mother looks up.
She and I often think two halves of one thought.
Do you remember that gold-plated toothpick

you sent him from Harrod's the summer you were in London? she asks.
Yes I wonder what happened to it.
Must be in the bathroom somewhere.

She is giving him grapes one by one.
They keep rolling out of his huge stiff fingers.
He used to be a big man, over six feet tall and strong,

but since he came to hospital his body has shrunk to the merest bone house—
except the hands. The hands keep growing.
Each one now as big as a boot in Van Gogh,

they go lumbering after the grapes in his lap.
But now he turns to me with a rush of urgent syllables
that break off on a high note—he waits,

staring into my face. That quizzical look.
One eyebrow at an angle.
I have a photograph taped to my fridge at home.

It shows his World War II air crew posing in front of the plane.
Hands firmly behind backs, legs wide apart,
chins forward.

Dressed in the puffed flying suits
with a wide leather strap pulled tight through the crotch.
They squint into the brilliant winter sun of 1942.

It is dawn.
They are leaving Dover for France.
My father on the far left is the tallest airman,

with his collar up,
one eyebrow at an angle.
The shadowless light makes him look immortal,

for all the world like someone who will not weep again.
He is still staring into my face.
Flaps down! I cry.
His black grin flares once and goes out like a match.

HOT

Hot blue moonlight down the steep sky.
I wake too fast from a cellar of hanged puppies
with my eyes pouring into the dark.
Fumbling

and slowly
consciousness replaces the bars.
Dreamtails and angry liquids

swim back down to the middle of me.
It is generally anger dreams that occupy my nights now.
This is not uncommon after loss of love—

blue and black and red blasting the crater open.
I am interested in anger.
I clamber along to find the source.

My dream was of an old woman lying awake in bed.
She controls the house by a system of light bulbs strung above her on wires.
Each wire has a little black switch.

One by one the switches refuse to turn the bulbs on.
She keeps switching and switching
in rising tides of very hot anger.

Then she creeps out of bed to peer through lattices
at the rooms of the rest of the house.
The rooms are silent and brilliantly lit

and full of huge furniture beneath which crouch
small creatures—not quite cats not quite rats
licking their narrow red jaws

under a load of time.
I want to be beautiful again, she whispers
but the great overlit rooms tick emptily

as a deserted oceanliner and now behind her in the dark
a rustling sound, comes—
My pajamas are soaked.

Anger travels through me, pushes aside everything else in my heart,
pouring up the vents.
Every night I wake to this anger,

the soaked bed,
the hot pain box slamming me each way I move.
I want justice. Slam.

I want an explanation. Slam.
I want to curse the false friend who said I love you forever. Slam.
I reach up and switch on the bedside lamp. Night springs

out the window and is gone over the moor.
I lie listening to the light vibrate in my ears
and thinking about curses.

Emily Brontë was good at cursing.
Falsity and bad love and the deadly pain of alteration are constant topics in
    her verse.

> Well, thou hast paid me back my love!
> But if there be a God above
> Whose arm is strong, whose word is true,
> This hell shall wring thy spirit too!

The curses are elaborate:

> There go, Deceiver, go! My hand is streaming wet;
> My heart's blood flows to buy the blessing—To forget!

Oh could that lost heart give back, back again to thine,
One tenth part of the pain that clouds my dark decline!

But they do not bring her peace:

Vain words, vain frenzied thoughts! No ear can hear me call—
Lost in the vacant air my frantic curses fall. . . .

Unconquered in my soul the Tyrant rules me still—
Life bows to my control, but *Love* I cannot kill!

Her anger is a puzzle.
It raises many questions in me,
to see love treated with such cold and knowing contempt

by someone who rarely left home
"except to go to church or take a walk on the hills"
(Charlotte tells us) and who

had no more intercourse with Haworth folk
than "a nun has
of the country people who sometimes pass her convent gates."

How did Emily come to lose faith in humans?
She admired their dialects, studied their genealogies,
"but with them she rarely exchanged a word."

Her introvert nature shrank from shaking hands with someone she met on
    the moor.
What did Emily know of lover's lies or cursive human faith?
Among her biographers

is one who conjectures she bore or aborted a child
during her six-month stay in Halifax,
but there is no evidence at all for such an event

and the more general consensus is that Emily did not touch a man in her
    31 years.
Banal sexism aside,
I find myself tempted

to read *Wuthering Heights* as one thick stacked act of revenge
for all that life withheld from Emily.
But the poetry shows traces of a deeper explanation.

As if anger could be a kind of vocation for some women.
It is a chilly thought.

> The heart is dead since infancy.
> Unwept for let the body go.

Suddenly cold I reach down and pull the blanket back up to my chin.
The vocation of anger is not mine.
I know my source.

It is stunning, it is a moment like no other,
when one's lover comes in and says I do not love you anymore.
I switch off the lamp and lie on my back,

thinking about Emily's cold young soul.
Where does unbelief begin?
When I was young

there were degrees of certainty.
I could say, Yes I know that I have two hands.
Then one day I awakened on a planet of people whose hands occasionally
    disappear—

From the next room I hear my mother shift and sigh and settle back down
    under the doorsill of sleep.
Out the window the moon is just a cold bit of silver gristle low on fading
    banks of sky.

> Our guests are darkly lodged, I whispered, gazing through
> The vault . . .

THOU

The question I am left with is the question of her loneliness.
And I prefer to put it off.
It is morning.

Astonished light is washing over the moor from north to east.
I am walking into the light.
One way to put off loneliness is to interpose God.

Emily had a relationship on this level with someone she calls Thou.
She describes Thou as awake like herself all night
and full of strange power.

Thou woos Emily with a voice that comes out of the night wind.
Thou and Emily influence one another in the darkness,
playing near and far at once.

She talks about a sweetness that "proved us one."
I am uneasy with the compensatory model of female religious experience
        and yet,
there is no question,

it would be sweet to have a friend to tell things to at night,
without the terrible sex price to pay.
This is a childish idea, I know.

My education, I have to admit, has been gappy.
The basic rules of male-female relations
were imparted atmospherically in our family,

no direct speech allowed.
I remember one Sunday I was sitting in the backseat of the car.
Father in front.

We were waiting in the driveway for mother,
who came around the corner of the house
and got into the passenger side of the car

dressed in a yellow Chanel suit and black high heels.
Father glanced sideways at her.
Showing a good bit of leg today Mother, he said

in a voice which I (age eleven) thought odd.
I stared at the back of her head waiting for what she would say.
Her answer would clear this up.

But she just laughed a strange laugh with ropes all over it.
Later that summer I put this laugh together with another laugh
I overheard as I was going upstairs.

She was talking on the telephone in the kitchen.
Well a woman would be just as happy with a kiss on the cheek
most of the time but YOU KNOW MEN,

she was saying. Laugh.
Not ropes, thorns.
I have arrived at the middle of the moor

where the ground goes down into a low swampy place.
The swamp water is frozen solid.
Bits of gold weed

have etched themselves
on the underside of the ice like messages.

> I'll come when thou art saddest,
> Laid alone in the darkened room;
> When the mad day's mirth has vanished,
> And the smile of joy is banished,
>
> I'll come when the heart's real feeling
> Has entire, unbiased sway,
> And my influence o'er thee stealing
> Grief deepening, joy congealing,
> Shall bear thy soul away.
>
> Listen! 'tis just the hour,
> The awful time for thee:
> Dost thou not feel upon thy soul
> A flood of strange sensations roll,
> Forerunners of a sterner power,
> Heralds of me?

Very hard to read, the messages that pass
between Thou and Emily.
In this poem she reverses their roles,

speaking not *as* the victim but *to* the victim.
It is chilling to watch Thou move upon thou,
who lies alone in the dark waiting to be mastered.

It is a shock to realize that this low, slow collusion
of master and victim within one voice
is a rationale

for the most awful loneliness of the poet's hour.
She has reversed the roles of thou and Thou
not as a display of power

but to force out of herself some pity
for this soul trapped in glass,
which is her true creation.

Those nights lying alone
are not discontinuous with this cold hectic dawn.
It is who I am.

Is it a vocation of anger?
Why construe silence
as the Real Presence?

Why stoop to kiss this doorstep?
Why be unstrung and pounded flat and pine away
imagining someone vast to whom I may vent the swell of my soul?

Emily was fond of Psalm 130.
"My soul waiteth on Thou more than they that watch for the
     morning,
I say more than they that watch for the morning."

I like to believe that for her the act of watching provided a shelter,
that her collusion with Thou gave ease to anger and desire:
"In Thou they are quenched as a fire of thorns," says the psalmist.

But for myself I do not believe this, I am not quenched—
with Thou or without Thou I find no shelter.
I am my own Nude.

And Nudes have a difficult sexual destiny.
I have watched this destiny disclose itself
in its jerky passage from girl to woman to who I am now,

from love to anger to this cold marrow,
from fire to shelter to fire.
What is the opposite of believing in Thou—

merely not believing in Thou? No. That is too simple.
That is to prepare a misunderstanding.
I want to speak more clearly.

Perhaps the Nudes are the best way.
Nude #5. Deck of cards.
Each card is made of flesh.

The living cards are days of a woman's life.
I see a great silver needle go flashing right through the deck once from end
    to end.
Nude #6 I cannot remember.

Nude #7. White room whose walls,
having neither planes nor curves nor angles,
are composed of a continuous satiny white membrane

like the flesh of some interior organ of the moon.
It is a living surface, almost wet.
Lucency breathes in and out.

Rainbows shudder across it.
And around the walls of the room a voice goes whispering,
Be very careful. Be very careful.

Nude #8. Black disc on which the fires of all the winds
are attached in a row.
A woman stands on the disc

amid the winds whose long yellow silk flames
flow and vibrate up through her.
Nude #9. Transparent loam.

Under the loam a woman has dug a long deep trench.
Into the trench she is placing small white forms, I don't know what they are.
Nude #10. Green thorn of the world poking up

alive through the heart of a woman
who lies on her back on the ground.
The thorn is exploding

its green blood above her in the air.
Everything it is it has, the voice says.
Nude #11. Ledge in outer space.

Space is bluish black and glossy as solid water
and moving very fast in all directions,
shrieking past the woman who stands pinned

to nothing by its pressure.
She peers and glances for some way to go, trying to lift her hand but
    cannot.
Nude #12. Old pole in the wind.

Cold currents are streaming over it
and pulling out
into ragged long horizontal black lines

some shreds of ribbon
attached to the pole.
I cannot see how they are attached—

notches? staples? nails? All of a sudden the wind changes
and all the black shreds rise straight up in the air
and tie themselves into knots,

then untie and float down.
The wind is gone.
It waits.

By this time, midway through winter,
I had become entirely fascinated with my spiritual melodrama.
Then it stopped.

Days passed, months passed and I saw nothing.
I continued to peer and glance, sitting on the rug in front of my sofa
in the curtainless morning

with my nerves open to the air like something skinned.
I saw nothing.
Outside the window spring storms came and went.

April snow folded its huge white paws over doors and porches.
I watched a chunk of it lean over the roof and break off
and fall and I thought,

How slow! as it glided soundlessly past,
but still—nothing. No nudes.
No Thou.

A great icicle formed on the railing of my balcony
so I drew up close to the window and tried peering through the icicle,
hoping to trick myself into some interior vision,

but all I saw
was the man and woman in the room across the street
making their bed and laughing.

I stopped watching.
I forgot about Nudes.
I lived my life,

which felt like a switched-off TV.
Something had gone through me and out and I could not own it.
"No need now to tremble for the hard frost and the keen wind.

Emily does not feel them,"
wrote Charlotte the day after burying her sister.
Emily had shaken free.

A soul can do that.
Whether it goes to join Thou and sit on the porch for all eternity
enjoying jokes and kisses and beautiful cold spring evenings,

you and I will never know. But I can tell you what I saw.
Nude #13 arrived when I was not watching for it.
It came at night.

Very much like Nude #1.
And yet utterly different.
I saw a high hill and on it a form shaped against hard air.

It could have been just a pole with some old cloth attached,
but as I came closer
I saw it was a human body

trying to stand against winds so terrible that the flesh was blowing off the bones.
And there was no pain.
The wind

was cleansing the bones.
They stood forth silver and necessary.
It was not my body, not a woman's body, it was the body of us all.
It walked out of the light.

Bernard Cooper

BURL'S

BERNARD COOPER is the author of five books including *Maps to Anywhere*, *Truth Serum*, *Guess Again*, and *The Bill from My Father*. Cooper is the recipient of the 1991 PEN/USA Ernest Hemingway Award, a 1995 O. Henry Prize, a 1999 Guggenheim grant, and a 2004 National Endowment for the Arts fellowship in literature. His work has appeared in several anthologies, including *The Penguin Book of Gay Short Stories* and *The Best American Essays 1988, 1995, 1997, and 2002*. His work has also appeared widely in magazines and literary reviews including *Harper's* and *The Paris Review*.

I loved the restaurant's name, a compact curve of a word. Its sign, five big letters rimmed in neon, hovered above the roof. I almost never saw the sign with its neon lit; my parents took me there for early summer dinners, and even by the time we left—Father cleaning his teeth with a toothpick, Mother carrying steak bones in a doggie bag—the sky was still bright. Heat rippled off the cars parked along Hollywood Boulevard, the asphalt gummy from hours of sun.

With its sleek architecture, chrome appliances, and arctic temperature, Burl's offered a refuge from the street. We usually sat at one of the booths in front of the plateglass windows. During our dinner, people came to a halt before the news-vending machine on the corner and burrowed in their pockets and purses for change.

The waitresses at Burl's wore brown uniforms edged in checked gingham. From their breast pockets frothed white lace handkerchiefs. In between reconnaissance missions to the tables, they busied themselves behind the counter and shouted "Tuna to travel" or "Scorch that patty" to a harried short-order cook who manned the grill. Miniature pitchers of cream and individual pats of butter were extracted from an industrial refrigerator. Coca-Cola shot from a glinting spigot. Waitresses dodged and bumped one another, as frantic as atoms.

My parents usually lingered after the meal, nursing cups of coffee while I played with the beads of condensation on my glass of ice water, tasted Tabasco sauce, or twisted pieces of my paper napkin into mangled animals. One evening,

132

annoyed with my restlessness, my father gave me a dime and asked me to buy him a *Herald Examiner* from the vending machine in front of the restaurant.

Shouldering open the heavy glass door, I was seared by a sudden gust of heat. Traffic roared past me and stirred the air. Walking toward the newspaper machine, I held the dime so tightly, it seemed to melt in my palm. Duty made me feel large and important. I inserted the dime and opened the box, yanking a *Herald* from the spring contraption that held it as tight as a mousetrap. When I turned around, paper in hand, I saw two women walking toward me.

Their high heels clicked on the sun-baked pavement. They were tall, broad-shouldered women who moved with a mixture of haste and defiance. They'd teased their hair into nearly identical black beehives. Dangling earrings flashed in the sun, as brilliant as prisms. Each of them wore the kind of clinging, strapless outfit my mother referred to as a cocktail dress. The silky fabric—one dress was purple, the other pink—accentuated their breasts and hips and rippled with insolent highlights. The dresses exposed their bare arms, the slope of their shoulders, and the smooth, powdered plane of flesh where their cleavage began.

I owned at the time a book called *Things for Boys and Girls to Do*. There were pages to color, intricate mazes, and connect-the-dots. But another type of puzzle came to mind as I watched those women walking toward me: What's Wrong with This Picture? Say the drawing of a dining room looked normal at first glance; on closer inspection, a chair was missing its leg and the man who sat atop it wore half a pair of glasses.

The women had Adam's apples.

The closer they came, the shallower my breathing. I blocked the sidewalk, an incredulous child stalled in their path. When they saw me staring, they shifted their purses and linked their arms. There was something sisterly and conspirational about their sudden closeness. Though their mouths didn't open, I thought they might have been communicating without moving their lips, so telepathic did they seem as they joined arms and pressed together, synchronizing their heavy steps. The pages of the *Herald* fluttered in the wind; I felt them against my arm, as light as batted lashes.

The woman in pink shot me a haughty glance, and yet she seemed pleased that I'd taken notice, hungry to be admired by a man, or even an awestruck eight-year-old boy. She tried to stifle a grin, her red lipstick more voluptuous than the lips it painted. Rouge deepened her cheekbones. Eye shadow dusted her lids, a clumsy abundance of blue. Her face was like a page in *Things for Boys and Girls to Do*, colored by a kid who went outside the lines.

At close range, I saw that her wig was slightly askew. I was certain it was a wig because my mother owned several; three Styrofoam heads lined a shelf in my mother's closet; upon them were perched a pageboy, an empress, and a baby doll, all in shades of auburn. The woman in the pink dress wore her wig like a crown of glory.

But it was the woman in the purple dress who passed nearest me, and I saw that her jaw was heavily powdered, a half-successful attempt to disguise the telltale shadow of a beard. Just as I noticed this, her heel caught on a crack in the pavement and she reeled on her stilettos. It was then that I witnessed a rift in her composure, a window through which I could glimpse the shades of maleness that her dress and wig and makeup obscured. She shifted her shoulders and threw out her hands like a surfer riding a curl. The instant she regained her balance, she smoothed her dress, patted her hair, and sauntered onward.

Any woman might be a man; the fact of it clanged through the chambers of my brain. In broad day, in the midst of traffic, with my parents drinking coffee a few feet away, I felt as if everything I understood, everything I had taken for granted up to that moment—the curve of the earth, the heat of the sun, the reliability of my own eyes—had been squeezed out of me. Who were those men? Did they help each other get inside those dresses? How many other people and things were not what they seemed? From the back, the impostors looked like women once again, slinky and curvaceous, purple and pink. I watched them disappear into the distance, their disguises so convincing that other people on the street seemed to take no notice, and for a moment I wondered if I had imagined the whole encounter, a visitation by two unlikely muses.

Frozen in the middle of the sidewalk, I caught my reflection in the window of Burl's, a silhoutte floating between his parents. They faced one another across a table. Once the solid embodiments of woman and man, pedestrians and traffic appeared to pass through them.

There were some mornings, seconds before my eyes opened and my senses gathered into consciousness, that the child I was seemed to hover above the bed, and I couldn't tell what form my waking would take—the body of a boy or the body of a girl. Finally stirring, I'd blink against the early light and greet each incarnation as a male with mild surprise. My sex, in other words, didn't seem to be an absolute fact so much as a pleasant, recurring accident.

By the age of eight, I'd experienced this groggy phenomenon several times. Those ethereal moments above my bed made waking up in the tangled blankets, a boy steeped in body heat, all the more astonishing. That this might be an unusual experience never occurred to me; it was one among a flood of sensations I could neither name nor ignore.

And so, shocked as I was when those transvestites passed me in front of Burl's, they confirmed something about which I already had an inkling: the hazy border between the sexes. My father, after all, raised his pinky when he drank from a teacup, and my mother looked as faded and plain as my father until she fixed her hair and painted her face.

Like most children, I once thought it possible to divide the world into male and female columns. Blue/Pink. Roosters/Hens. Trousers/Skirts. Such divisions were easy, not to mention comforting, for they simplified matter into compatible pairs. But there also existed a vast range of things that didn't fit neatly into either camp: clocks, milk, telephones, grass. There were nights I fell into a fitful sleep while trying to sex the world correctly.

Nothing typified the realms of male and female as clearly as my parents' walk-in closets. Home alone for any length of time, I always found my way inside them. I could stare at my parents' clothes for hours, grateful for the stillness and silence, haunting the very heart of their privacy.

The overhead light in my father's closet was a bare bulb. Whenever I groped for the chain in the dark, it wagged back and forth and resisted my grasp. Once the light clicked on, I saw dozens of ties hanging like stalactites. A monogrammed silk bathrobe sagged from a hook, a gift my father had received on a long-ago birthday and, thinking it fussy, rarely wore. Shirts were cramped together along the length of an aluminum pole, their starched sleeves sticking out as if in a halfhearted gesture of greeting. The medicinal odor of mothballs permeated the boxer shorts that were folded and stacked in a built-in drawer. Immaculate underwear was proof of a tenderness my mother couldn't otherwise express; she may not have touched my father often, but she laundered his boxers with infinite care. Even back then, I suspected that a sense of duty was the final erotic link between them.

Sitting in a neat row on the closet floor were my father's boots and slippers and dress shoes. I'd try on his wing tips and clomp around, slipping out of them with every step. My wary, unnatural stride made me all the more desperate to effect some authority. I'd whisper orders to imagined lackeys and take my invisible wife in my arms. But no matter how much I wanted them to fit, those shoes were as cold and hard as marble.

My mother's shoes were just as uncomfortable, but a lot more fun. From a brightly colored array of pumps and sling-backs, I'd pick a pair with the glee and deliberation of someone choosing a chocolate. Whatever embarrassment I felt was overwhelmed by the exhilaration of being taller in a pair of high heels. Things will look like this someday, I said to myself, gazing out from my new and improved vantage point as if from a crow's nest. Calves elongated, hands on my hips, I gauged each step so I didn't fall over and moved with what might have passed for grace had someone seen me, a possibility I scrupulously avoided by locking the door.

Back and forth I went. The longer I wore a pair of heels, the better my balance. In the periphery of my vision, the shelf of wigs looked like a throng of kindly bystanders. Light streamed down from a high window, causing crystal bottles to glitter, the air ripe with perfume. A makeup mirror above the dressing table invited my self-absorption. Sound was muffled. Time slowed. It seemed as if nothing bad could happen as long as I stayed within those walls.

Though I'd never been discovered in my mother's closet, my parents knew that I was drawn toward girlish things—dolls and jump rope and jewelry—as well as to the games and preoccupations that were expected of a boy. I'm not sure now if it was my effeminacy itself that bothered them so much as my ability to slide back and forth, without the slightest warning, between male and female mannerisms. After I'd finished building the model of an F-17 bomber, say, I'd sit back to examine my handiwork, pursing my lips in concentration and crossing my legs at the knee.

One day my mother caught me standing in the middle of my bedroom doing an imitation of Mary Injijikian, a dark, overeager Armenian girl with whom I believed myself to be in love, not only because she was pretty, but because I wanted to be like her. Collector of effortless A's, Mary seemed to know all the answers in class. Before the teacher had even finished asking a question, Mary would let out a little grunt and practically levitate out of her seat, as if her hand were filled with helium. "Could we please hear from someone else today besides Miss Injijikian," the teacher would say. *Miss Injijikian.* Those were the words I was repeating over and over to myself when my mother caught me. To utter them was rhythmic, delicious, and under their spell I raised my hand and wiggled like Mary. I heard a cough and spun around. My mother froze in the doorway. She clutched the folded sheets to her stomach and turned without saying a word. My sudden flush of shame confused me. Weren't boys supposed to swoon over girls? Hadn't I seen babbling, heartsick men in a dozen movies?

Shortly after the Injijikian incident, my parents decided to send me to gymnastics class at the Downtown Athletic Club, a brick relic of a building on Grand Avenue. One of the oldest establishments of its kind in Los Angeles, the club prohibited women from the premises. My parents didn't have to say it aloud: they hoped a fraternal atmosphere would toughen me up and tilt me toward the male side of my nature.

My father drove me downtown so I could sign up for the class, meet the instructor, and get a tour of the place. On the way there, he reminisced about sports. Since he'd grown up in a rough Philadelphia neighborhood, sports consisted of kick-the-can, or rolling a hoop down the street with a stick. The more he talked about his physical prowess, the more convinced I became that my daydreams and shyness were a disappointment to him.

The hushed lobby of the Athletic Club was paneled in dark wood. A few solitary figures were hidden in wing chairs. My father and I introduced ourselves to a man at the front desk who seemed unimpressed by our presence. His aloofness unnerved me, which wasn't hard considering that no matter how my parents put it, I knew that sending me here was a form of disapproval, a way of banishing the part of me they didn't care to know.

A call went out over the intercom for someone to show us around. While we waited, I noticed that the sand in the standing ashtrays had been raked into perfect furrows. The glossy leaves of the potted plants looked as if they'd been polished by hand. The place seemed more like a well-tended hotel than an athletic club. Finally, a stoop-shouldered old man hobbled toward us, his head shrouded in a cloud of white hair. He wore a T-shirt that said INSTRUCTOR, but his arms were so wrinkled and anemic, I thought I might have misread it. While we followed him to the elevator—it would be easier, he said, than taking the stairs—I readjusted my expectations, which had involved fantasies of a hulking drill sergeant barking orders at a flock of scrawny boys.

We got off the elevator on the second floor. The instructor, mumbling to himself and never turning around to see if we were behind him, showed us where the gymnastics class took place. I'm certain the building was big, but the size of the room must be exaggerated by a trick of memory, because when I envision it, I picture a vast and windowless warehouse. Mats covered the wooden floor. Here and there, in remote and lonely pools of light, stood a pommel horse, a balance beam, and parallel bars. Tiers of bleachers rose into darkness. Unlike the cloistered air of a closet, the room seemed incomplete without a crowd.

Next we visited the dressing room, empty except for a naked, middle-aged man. He sat on a narrow bench and clipped his formidable toenails. Moles dotted his back. He glistened like a fish.

We continued to follow the instructor down an aisle lined with numbered lockers. At the far end, steam billowed from the doorway that led to the showers. Fresh towels stacked on a nearby table made me think of my mother; I knew she liked to have me at home with her—I was often her only companion—and I resented her complicity in the plan to send me here.

The tour ended when the instructor gave me a sign-up sheet. Only a few names preceded mine. They were signatures, or so I imagined, of other soft and wayward sons.

When the day of the first gymnastics class arrived, my mother gave me money and a gym bag (along with a clean towel, she'd packed a banana and a napkin) and sent me to the corner of Hollywood and Western to wait for a bus. The sun was bright, the traffic heavy. While I sat there, an argument raged inside my head, the familiar, battering debate between the wish to be like other boys and the wish to be like myself. Why shouldn't I simply get up and go back home, where I'd be left alone to read and think? On the other hand, wouldn't life be easier if I liked athletics, or learned to like them? No sooner did I steel my resolve to get on the bus, than I thought of something better: I could spend the morning wandering through Woolworth's, then tell my parents I'd gone to the class. But would my lie stand up to scrutiny? As I practiced describing phantom gymnastics—*And then we did cartwheels and, boy, was I dizzy*—I became aware of a car circling the block. It was a large car in whose shaded interior I could barely make out the driver, but I thought it might be the man who owned the local pet store. I'd often gone there on the pretext of looking at the cocker spaniel puppies huddled together in their pen, but I really went to gawk at the owner, whose tan chest, in the V of his shirt, was the place I most wanted to rest my head. Every time the man moved, counting stock or writing a receipt, his shirt parted, my mouth went dry, and I smelled the musk of sawdust and dogs.

I found myself hoping that the driver was the man who ran the pet store. I was thrilled by the unlikely possibility that the sight of me, slumped on a bus bench in my T-shirt and shorts, had caused such a man to circle the block. Up to that point in my life, lovemaking hovered somewhere in the future, an impulse a boy might aspire to but didn't indulge. And there I was, sitting on a bus bench in the middle of the city, dreaming I could seduce an adult; I showered the owner of the pet store with kisses and, as aquariums bubbled, birds sang, and mice raced in a wire wheel, slipped my hand beneath his shirt. The roar of traffic brought me to my senses. I breathed deeply and blinked against the sun. I crossed my legs at the knee in order to hide an erection. My fantasy left me both drained and changed. The continent of sex had drifted closer.

The car made another round. This time the driver leaned across the passenger seat and peered at me through the window. He was a complete stranger whose gaze filled me with fear. It wasn't the surprise of not recognizing him that frightened me; it was what I did recognize—the unmistakable shame in his expression, and the weary temptation that drove him in circles. Before the car behind him honked, he mouthed "hello" and cocked his head. What now? he seemed to be asking. A bold, unbearable question.

I bolted to my feet, slung the gym bag over my shoulder, and hurried toward home. Now and then I turned around to make sure he wasn't trailing me, both relieved and disappointed when I didn't see his car. Even after I became convinced that he wasn't at my back (my sudden flight had scared him off), I kept turning around to see what was making me so nervous, as if I might spot the source of my discomfort somewhere on the street. I walked faster and faster, trying to outrace myself. Eventually, the bus I was supposed to have taken roared past. Turning the corner, I watched it bob eastward.

Closing the kitchen door behind me, I vowed to never leave home again. I was resolute in this decision without fully understanding why, or what it was I hoped to avoid; I was only aware of the need to hide and a vague notion, fading fast, that my trouble had something to do with sex. Already the mechanism of self-deception was at work. By the time my mother rushed into the kitchen to see why I'd returned so early, the thrill I'd felt while waiting for the bus had given way to indignation.

I poured out the story of the man circling the block and protested, with perhaps too great a passion, my own innocence. "I was just sitting there," I said again and again. I was so determined to deflect suspicion from myself, and to justify my missing the class, that I portrayed the man as a grizzled pervert who drunkenly veered from lane to lane as he followed me halfway home.

My mother listened quietly. She seemed moved and shocked by what I told her, if a bit incredulous, which prompted me to be more dramatic. "It wouldn't be safe," I insisted, "for me to wait at the bus stop again."

No matter how overwrought my story, I knew my mother wouldn't question it, wouldn't bring the subject up again; sex of any kind, especially sex between a man and a boy, was simply not discussed in our house. The gymnastics class, my parents agreed, was something I could do another time.

And so I spent the remainder of that summer at home with my mother, stirring cake batter, holding the dustpan, helping her fold the sheets. For a while I was proud of myself for engineering a reprieve from the Athletic Club. But as the days wore on, I began to see that my mother had wanted me with her all along, and forcing that to happen wasn't such a feat. Soon a sense of compromise set in; by expressing disgust for the man in the car, I'd expressed disgust for an aspect of myself. Now I had all the time in the world to sit around and contemplate my desire for men. The days grew long and stifling and hot, an endless sentence of self-examination.

Only trips to the pet store offered any respite. Every time I went there, I was too electrified with longing to think about longing in the abstract. The bell tinkled above the door, animals stirred within their cages, and the handsome owner glanced up from his work.

I handed my father the *Herald*. He opened the paper and disappeared behind it. My mother stirred her coffee and sighed. She gazed at the sweltering passersby and probably thought herself lucky. I slid into the vinyl booth and took my place beside my parents.

For a moment, I considered asking them about what had happened on the street, but they would have reacted with censure and alarm, and I sensed there was more to the story than they'd ever be willing to tell me. Men in dresses were only the tip of the iceberg. Who knew what other wonders existed—a boy, for example, who wants to kiss a man—exceptions the world did its best to keep hidden.

It would be years before I heard the word *transvestite*, so I struggled to find a word for what I'd seen. *He-she* came to mind, as lilting as *Injijikian. Burl's* would have been perfect, like *boys* and *girls* spliced together, but I can't claim to have thought of this back then.

I must have looked stricken as I tried to figure it all out, because my mother put down her coffee cup and asked if I was okay. She stopped just short of feeling my forehead. I assured her I was fine, but something within me had shifted, had given way to a heady doubt. When the waitress came and slapped down our check—"Thank you," it read, "dine out more often"—I wondered if her lofty hairdo or the breasts on which her name tag quaked were real. Wax carnations bloomed at every table. Phony wood paneled the walls. Plastic food sat in a display case: fried eggs, a hamburger sandwich, a sundae topped with a garish cherry.

Michael W. Cox

VISITOR

MICHAEL W. COX's essays have appeared in *New Letters, River Teeth, The New York Times Magazine, St. Petersburg Times,* and *The Best American Essays 1999.* His short stories have appeared in *ACM, Columbia, Cimarron Review, Other Voices,* and *Salt Hill,* among other publications, and he has also written a number of academic papers, medical articles, and book reviews. He has won the *New Letters* Literary Award for the Essay and the *Passages North* Waasmode Northern Lights Fiction Prize. He teaches writing at the University of Pittsburgh at Johnstown, where he is coordinator of professional writing.

My father kept a boy in the basement. He'd tell me not to go down there, but I'd go anyway, sometimes, and talk to the boy. He'd smoke a cigarette, usually, while he talked to me. He'd tell me things.

We had two basements, really, one indoor, one out. The boy stayed in the outdoor one, for part of one whole summer. Really, it was a fine basement, the outdoor one. It had been a kind of playhouse for me and my brothers, but by the time the boy had arrived we had forgotten about it, to play instead in a gigantic field of horseweed down below our house, beyond the railroad tracks and before the river. Outside the basement door, in a small alcove, my father kept our trash cans; and at night, you'd hear him out there, beneath the window, taking out the bags of garbage. He would take the bag of trash from our kitchen, through the indoor basement and out its side door, and walk the few steps to the trash can. From there you could look into the dark outdoor basement, the door having long since been removed from its hinges—the house came that way when we moved in, the outdoor basement being doorless, I mean. Inside, the front half of the floor was dirt and, often, especially with the rain that seeped in through the bricks, mud. We boys had laid down planks across the dirt, so we could walk to the back half without getting our shoes wet, where one of the previous owners of the house had built a wooden floor elevated about six inches off the ground. There was a kind of half wall in there, too, and a ceiling above the wall, the whole structure being like an indoor tree house—my brother had taken the stepladder from our bunk bed and put it down there in the basement, so we could climb up to the ceiling and sit between it and the bottom side of the front porch above our heads. Inside the half-room in that basement, I would guess the clearance was about six or seven feet—we were all of us small, but to imagine my father in there, with that boy, he might've had to duck his head down inside that room. There was an old couch in there, I remember, and a blanket for the couch. The boy must've slept on that at night, when he'd come from being out somewhere in the daytime; he'd walk up the railroad tracks— I could hear him, would crawl to my window to watch, unseen, through the screen—up the short hillside path into our yard, in the dark so as not to be seen by neighbors, and on up to the basement, then my father, a while later, taking out the trash and then going on inside for a few minutes, my mother on the other side of the wall from my bedroom, listening to the television set in the summer night, losing track of the time in some mindless plot. And all the while I was supposed to be sleeping, but I'd tick off the minutes my father was inside there—one one-thousand, two one-thousand—keeping time. He never took too long, though more than once I think I heard him, from my bed, go downstairs in the night to get a glass of milk—I'd hear him whisper to mom first, who'd be dead asleep anyway, and then the walking of my father's feet down the stairs in the creaking night and, fifteen seconds later, the basement door clicking open beneath the window of my room, then clicking shut a few minutes later, etc. One morning as I was eating my cereal across from him, he asked me what I was looking at.

"Nothing," I said. "I'm not looking at anything."

He went back to his paper.

"Don't go in the basement," he said from behind it.

"How come?"

"Saw a 'possum there, when I was taking out the trash."

"'Possum?" I said.

"Might be living in that basement," he said. "Might be rabid."

"Might be," I said. And that was that.

But I stepped inside there one day, in broad daylight but dim inside, because I wanted to see how the boy might be living in there. Summer nights were warm, always, never dipping below sixty, so a blanket and dry clothes would be enough. As I walked in along the planks I could smell his cigarette and knew I was not alone—I hadn't expected him in there in the daytime, and most days, I expect, he wasn't there at all—he might be working somewhere, I thought, or maybe be down at the river swimming, I thought, or maybe he'd stop inside the stores down on Main Street and shoplift him a little something—I didn't know, I could only imagine and he said hello to me. I stopped, let my eyes adjust and then I could see him—him, who I'd seen for the most part only the top of as he'd walk beneath my window, a baseball cap on always, which was off now and lying on the couch beside him. His legs were crossed, I could see as my eyes got better at it, and he was wearing dark pants and a jacket and I could see his cigarette brighten when he put it up to his face, his mouth, lips. Hey youngun, he called, but quietly. Come on over, he said, have a seat—he patted the couch beside himself, mashing his cap then realizing that and grabbing it by the bill and popping it out.

Who are you? I asked but without fear in my voice, I'm pretty sure, and he told me his name was Jody, and then he told me, if I wanted to be his buddy, I could go back inside the house and make him a sandwich and bring it on back out here, to his couch. I did exactly what he asked, made him a potted meat sandwich on white bread and even, when he asked, went back inside the house for mustard, so he could spice up the sandwich, he said. I knew right away I would get him real food and not do anything so rank as substitute dog food for potted meat (though some would argue, I knew even then, as to the relative difference between the two), or pee in a glass and tell him that it was lemon-ade—yes, I had done these things to marginal acquaintances, it's true and I am not exactly proud of it, and when I think of these things these days I kind of laugh to myself while grimacing at the same time, hoping no such thing was ever done to me, hoping that they are wrong, whoever they may be, when they say what goes around, etc. But you just can't know sometimes: you cannot file a taste away in your mind and retrieve it, precisely, twenty years later and say my god, that boy fed me dog food, or piss water, or some such thing.

And Jody was grateful and liked my sandwich very much, and then he sent me back inside, promptly, to fix him another and another, telling me that my daddy liked to keep him hungry. You eat good inside there? he asked, and I nodded as he devoured his fourth and, that day, final sandwich, three trips hav-ing been made inside by then (odd trip being the mustard). Well that's good, he said, to eat good, though I must say you are a skinny boy and he was right, I was, it's true, and have remained then to this day, more or less, a couple of periods of drunkenness having led to weight gain, but get sober and it comes right off, pizza boxes and empty bags of chips aside, in the trash, wherever your trash can might be located. And he and I, Jody, I mean, became fast friends, I bringing him sandwiches each day at the same "bat time," as he called it, same bat place (I knew the show he referred to but did not know that the reference was humorous—it all seemed sincerely serious to me, just like my sandwich bringing—he was careful to make sure I brought my mother's plates back in-side, not wanting, as he put it, to tip off the old lady).

I was reading a novel that summer about an alien boy who dropped into our dimension from another—he fell through a portal right into a family's life and, though he did not come to our dimension knowing English, learned it right away, the vocabulary, the grammar, all by listening, processing, and then, one day, by practicing. He was a good boy but frightened, and he wanted, very badly, to find the portal and get back home. I wished my father's boy might be just such an alien, but he wasn't. When he'd strike a match I'd look at him nonetheless, searching for signs: pointed ears, high forehead, hairlessness. He had none of that, and in fact he told me he'd only come from down the road apiece, just a few counties away.

He was a funny boy even so, and by that I mean strange. He laughed at odd times, and not a nice laugh either. He was older than me significantly—had I been a little younger, I'd've thought him a man. But he wasn't a man, just a teenager. He asked me one day what my mother was like, and I asked him what did he mean. Is she pretty, he asked, and I said that yes, I thought she was. Does your father think she's pretty, he asked, and I thought and then I said that yes, I thought that he too thought her pretty. Well that's a pretty picture then, don't you think, he asked, and stuck his tickling fingers against my stomach right then, to get me to laugh.

He wore a jacket, that much I remember. There was a blanket in there, as I have said, and a couch. It is painful sometimes for me, when I think back, to picture him in there in the night, alone, nothing but his cigarettes for company. It is possible he did not have many thoughts, and so was not bothered by the lack of things in there in the night, or possibly he had many thoughts and so he could entertain himself for hours on end. Maybe he'd read books and would remember them, or see, in his mind, TV shows he'd already seen, maybe, or maybe he'd remember his home life and the way his parents and he got along. I cannot know, cannot remember not being, as it were, omniscient. Certainly I could create a life for him, if I wished. At the heart of an enigma is nothing but what you put there yourself. He would tell me tales about the road, for he was, he claimed, a kind of hobo. Did he ride the rails, I'd ask, motioning to the railroad tracks just down the hill, and he told me no, of course not, that hopping trains was dangerous. He would tell me of hitchhiking, and of how you could tell who might be friendly, as a driver, and who might not be. It was always men driving alone, he said, who were the friendly ones, and he made his voice kind of crackle then, he'd start laughing, I mean, like it was a private joke with him and he'd not tell me, precisely, what he meant. I'm a mystery to you, he'd say, and he liked that, I could tell, because he nodded and would take a big pull off his cigarette, blow that smoke into the air, nod again and take another big pull. He taught me how to smoke, that's the one thing he taught me, not being any kind of abuser so much as the object of one or two along the way, or, probably, many.

Your father's a funny man, he'd say, and I could not bring myself to ask Jody to tell me what he meant.

At night sometimes I'd see Jody leave. He would walk beneath my window, where I learned to watch for him or for my father or for them both. He would walk beneath my window, quietly, along the side of the house, his baseball cap turning toward the kitchen window and, as he passed the back porch, the back door. He'd traipse along the short hillside down to the tracks, then head off for downtown. Maybe my father had given him money. Maybe he'd go out to hit the town, paint it red. He came back one night singing something loud and Irish, an eyes-smiling sort of song, sang all the way up the tracks and on up into the yard. Across the lawns I saw a neighbor's light come on, old Mrs. Welch's drapes opening just as he disappeared inside the outdoor basement, her kerchiefed head with rabbit ears twisting in her window—but she wouldn't be able to see him, not with her light turned on—you had to look outside with your lights off, I knew this, having looked outside so many nights and having seen so much. And there was a fight then between my parents, in their bedroom, my father leaving that room with a flashlight, muttering and going down the stairs, my mother hissing to him from the top of the staircase, and then, beneath my window, finally, the basement door opening, and outside my room, my mother's feet sweeping into my bedroom, quietly, so as not to wake me, or so she thought (I was lying in my bed by then, barely breathing). She stood in the window where I had so often stood looking down, and she may or may not have seen him step inside that basement. Then the sound, in the night, of two men murmuring, voices, a slap—my mother putting an ear close to the window.

At night sometimes I'd see him leave. I told you that. And that night, very late, pretty near dawn—I could see the morning star already out my window, on the violet horizon—he slunk away from the basement for what would be the last time, not bothering to check the kitchen window as he passed, and headed away from town, once he got to the tracks, instead of downtown for the beer gardens. My father insisted to my mother that she had been hearing things—there had been no singing, he insisted—and that all there was involved in all this was a rabid 'possum. But I saw her the next day talking to Mrs. Welch by her back door, Mrs. Welch pointing over to our basement. Later, I asked my father over breakfast what happened to Jody. Behind his paper he told me he'd never heard that name before, that he had no idea who I meant. The paper did not move; he studied sports figures the rest of the morning; I know because I waited, and when I left the room, I heard the paper fall to the table.

Except for asking my father about him that one time, I kept my knowledge of Jody to myself. My brothers may have come upon him, for all I knew. Sometimes I played with my brothers down in the field of horseweed, as I have said, but often I preferred to be alone and to go exploring. There was what we called back then an old drunk hole down by the railroad tracks below the house, maybe a hundred feet away—a place where drunks could go and sleep off their cheap wine. At the height of summer once, when the honeysuckle vines rioted across the drunkards' hiding place, covering up nearly everything—the trees there, the broken fence—I journeyed inside the place to study the plant life. I was digging moss up to take back home and plant in the yard, when beside me, from beneath the vines, a sleeping drunk arose and reached for me. I got a good look at the man—old, gray, red-faced—and ran home and told my father (my mother was away just then). He asked me what the man looked like, and I asked him what did he mean. How old was he, my father asked, and I could tell he was thinking of going down there himself, to investigate.

When I was very small, once—once is all I remember of this—my father had me go for a drive with him. He stopped at a store along the road, finally, where a little boy played outside. Two men watched the boy play, one perhaps being the boy's father. He told me, my father, to stay inside the car but that I should act friendly very soon, to look happy when he talked to the men on the porch and pointed my way, where I would be smiling inside the car. And here is what I could hear him telling them: that I was a lonely little boy who had no boys his age living nearby, and that we drove the countryside looking for playmates for me—a lame story now perhaps, but back then, out in the country, it would fly.

We drove the boy up a dirt road far out in the woods, me and my father. He had packed a lunch for us, sandwiches, soda, candy, wrapped in a paper bag that he grabbed quickly, when the road finally stopped, and he told me to wait for them. From the backseat of the car I watched them, hand in hand, disappear into the dark woods. I waited for what seemed like a long, long time. When they returned, my father was practically dragging the boy, who was crying. My father kept telling him, as he loaded him into the front seat, that it was I who had hurt him—me—that I had come along in the dark woods like an Indian and surprised the boy. He stood up in the seat in front of me and began throwing feeble punches my way, and my father shoved him down into the seat and yelled at him to stop crying. He tossed the bag into the backseat beside me; it was empty, crumpled. We drove the boy back to the country store and then sped away.

He took me to carnivals, too, and would buy me a fistful of tickets and make me ride the rides while he wandered the grounds. He'd meet me at the gates when the tickets were gone. He'd rehearse me on the ride back home, in the car, telling me that he had watched me on every ride, standing alongside the other parents, that he had even ridden the Ferris wheel with me. You can see everything from up there, he'd say. What did we see, I asked. The people, he'd say. Popcorn concessions. Candy apples, cotton candy. I see, I said. It's important, he said, that you be able to see it. I can, I said. So how was the tilt-a-whirl, he'd say as we whirled into our driveway. It was fun, I said. And where was I, he asked. Right down in front watching, I said, by the man who worked the gears. That's right, he said. Now tell your mom—and I ran inside the house, eager to tell his stories.

That summer the boy was staying in the basement, I used to wonder what might have happened if my father had gone in there one night and found him gone. Maybe this is why Jody eventually left that plush abode, because he was not available for one of my father's late-night swims. My father would take out the trash, say—he would bag it up in the kitchen, walk across the tiles and into the doorway of the inner basement, his hands clutching the bag, tightening on it. He'd be driven now, moving faster, out the door of the basement to that little alcove where he'd take the lid off that trash can. Upstairs his kids'd be asleep, he'd think, his wife watching TV—a commercial'd be on, the music drifting out the window to where he'd be standing before the gaping hole of the trash can. He'd let the bag drop, loudly, into the can, announcing to the neighbors that all he was doing was taking out the garbage. And then he'd look around, out there in the night, and walk quietly across the planks into the basement. Hey, he'd call out to the small room there in back. But there'd be nothing there but darkness.

Annie Dillard

LIVING LIKE WEASELS

ANNIE DILLARD has written eleven books, including *The Maytrees*, *An American Childhood*, and the Pulitzer Prize–winning *Pilgrim at Tinker Creek*.

A weasel is wild. Who knows what he thinks? He sleeps in his underground den, his tail draped over his nose. Sometimes he lives in his den for two days without leaving. Outside, he stalks rabbits, mice, muskrats, and birds, killing more bodies than he can eat warm, and often dragging the carcasses home. Obedient to instinct, he bites his prey at the neck, either splitting the jugular vein at the throat or crunching the brain at the base of the skull, and he does not let go. One naturalist refused to kill a weasel who was socketed into his hand deeply as a rattlesnake. The man could in no way pry the tiny weasel off, and he had to walk half a mile in water, the weasel dangling from his palm, and soak him off like a stubborn label.

And once, says Ernest Thompson Seton—once, a man shot an eagle out of the sky. He examined the eagle and found the dry skull of a weasel fixed by the jaws to his throat. The supposition is that the eagle had pounced on the weasel and the weasel swiveled and bit as instinct taught him, tooth to neck, and nearly won. I would like to have seen that eagle from the air a few weeks or months before he was shot: was the whole weasel still attached to his feathered throat, a fur pendant? Or did the eagle eat what he could reach, gutting the living weasel with his talons before his breast, bending his beak, cleaning the beautiful airborne bones?

I have been reading about weasels because I saw one last week. I startled a weasel who startled me, and we exchanged a long glance.

Twenty minutes from my house, through the woods by the quarry and across the highway, is Hollins Pond, a remarkable piece of shallowness, where I like to go at sunset and sit on a tree trunk. Hollins Pond is also called Murray's Pond; it covers two acres of bottomland near Tinker Creek with six inches of water and six thousand lily pads. In winter, brown-and-white steers stand in the middle of it, merely dampening their hooves; from the distant shore they look like miracle itself, complete with miracle's nonchalance. Now, in summer, the steers are gone. The water lilies have blossomed and spread to a green horizontal plane that is terra firma to plodding blackbirds, and tremulous ceiling to black leeches, crayfish, and carp.

This is, mind you, suburbia. It is a five-minute walk in three directions to rows of houses, though none is visible here. There's a 55 mph highway at one end of the pond, and a nesting pair of wood ducks at the other. Under every bush is a muskrat hole or a beer can. The far end is an alternating series of fields and woods, fields and woods, threaded everywhere with motorcycle tracks—in whose bare clay wild turtles lay eggs.

So. I had crossed the highway, stepped over two low barbed-wire fences, and traced the motorcycle path in all gratitude through the wild rose and poison ivy of the pond's shoreline up into high grassy fields. Then I cut down through the woods to the mossy fallen tree where I sit. This tree is excellent. It makes a dry, upholstered bench at the upper, marshy end of the pond, a plush jetty raised from the thorny shore between a shallow blue body of water and a deep blue body of sky. The sun had just set. I was relaxed on the tree trunk, ensconced in the lap of lichen, watching the lily pads at my feet tremble and part dreamily over the thrusting path of a carp. A yellow bird appeared to my right and flew behind me. It caught my eye; I swiveled around—and the next instant, inexplicably, I was looking down at a weasel, who was looking up at me.

Weasel! I'd never seen one wild before. He was ten inches long, thin as a curve, a muscled ribbon, brown as fruitwood, soft-furred, alert. His face was fierce, small and pointed as a lizard's; he would have made a good arrowhead. There was just a dot of chin, maybe two brown hairs' worth, and then the pure white fur began that spread down his underside. He had two black eyes I didn't see, any more than you see a window.

The weasel was stunned into stillness as he was emerging from beneath an enormous shaggy wild rose bush four feet away. I was stunned into stillness twisted backward on the tree trunk. Our eyes locked, and someone threw away the key.

Our look was as if two lovers, or deadly enemies, met unexpectedly on an overgrown path when each had been thinking of something else: a clearing blow to the gut. It was also a bright blow to the brain, or a sudden beating of brains, with all the charge and intimate grate of rubbed balloons. It emptied our lungs. It felled the forest, moved the fields, and drained the pond; the world dismantled and tumbled into that black hole of eyes. If you and I looked at each other that way, our skulls would split and drop to our shoulders. But we don't. We keep our skulls. So.

He disappeared. This was only last week, and already I don't remember what shattered the enchantment. I think I blinked, I think I retrieved my brain from the weasel's brain, and tried to memorize what I was seeing, and the weasel felt the yank of separation, the careening splashdown into real life and the urgent current of instinct. He vanished under the wild rose. I waited motionless, my mind suddenly full of data and my spirit with pleadings, but he didn't return.

Please do not tell me about "approach-avoidance conflicts." I tell you I've been in that weasel's brain for sixty seconds, and he was in mine. Brains are private places, muttering through unique and secret tapes—but the weasel and I both plugged into another tape simultaneously, for a sweet and shocking time. Can I help it if it was a blank?

What goes on in his brain the rest of the time? What does a weasel think about? He won't say. His journal is tracks in clay, a spray of feathers, mouse blood and bone: uncollected, unconnected, loose-leaf, and blown.

I would like to learn, or remember, how to live. I come to Hollins Pond not so much to learn how to live as, frankly, to forget about it. That is, I don't think I can learn from a wild animal how to live in particular—shall I suck warm blood, hold my tail high, walk with my footprints precisely over the prints of my hands?—but I might learn something of mindlessness, something of the purity of living in the physical senses and the dignity of living without bias or motive. The weasel lives in necessity and we live in choice, hating necessity and dying at the last ignobly in its talons. I would like to live as I should, as the weasel lives as he should. And I suspect that for me the way is like the weasel's: open to time and death painlessly, noticing everything, remembering nothing, choosing the given with a fierce and pointed will.

I missed my chance. I should have gone for the throat. I should have lunged for that streak of white under the weasel's chin and held on, held on through mud and into the wild rose, held on for a dearer life. We could live under the wild rose wild as weasels, mute and uncomprehending. I could very calmly go wild. I could live two days in the den, curled, leaning on mouse fur, sniffing bird bones, blinking, licking, breathing musk, my hair tangled in the roots of grasses. Down is a good place to go, where the mind is single. Down is out, out of your ever-loving mind and back to your careless senses. I remember muteness as a prolonged and giddy fast, where every moment is a feast of utterance received. Time and events are merely poured, unremarked, and ingested directly, like blood pulsed into my gut through a jugular vein. Could two live that way?

Could two live under the wild rose, and explore by the pond, so that the smooth mind of each is as everywhere present to the other, and as received and as un-challenged, as falling snow?

We could, you know. We can live any way we want. People take vows of pov-erty, chastity, and obedience—even of silence—by choice. The thing is to stalk your calling in a certain skilled and supple way, to locate the most tender and live spot and plug into that pulse. This is yielding, not fighting. A weasel doesn't "attack" anything; a weasel lives as he's meant to, yielding at every moment to the perfect freedom of single necessity.

I think it would be well, and proper, and obedient, and pure, to grasp your one necessity and not let it go, to dangle from it limp wherever it takes you. Then even death, where you're going no matter how you live, cannot you part. Seize it and let it seize you up aloft even, till your eyes burn out and drop; let your musky flesh fall off in shreds, and let your very bones unhinge and scatter, loosened over fields, over fields and woods, lightly, thoughtless, from any height at all, from as high as eagles.

Mark Doty

RETURN TO SENDER
Memory, Betrayal, and Memoir

MARK DOTY is the author of seven books of poems and four volumes of non-fiction prose, most recently *Dog Years: A Memoir*. His work has been honored by the National Book Critics Circle Award, the PEN/Martha Albrand Prize for Nonfiction, and the T. S. Eliot Prize. *Fire to Fire: New and Selected Poems* is his most recent book of poetry.

It wasn't my idea to go to Memphis. It was okay with me, if Paul wanted to drive through, and see if we could find the house on Ramses Street where I lived in 1959, the year I started first grade. We were heading from Houston to Cape Cod, a northward migration we used to make together every year, after my annual teaching stint in Texas. Memphis wasn't exactly on the way, but it wasn't wildly off course either, and if Paul thought that would be an interesting outing, then I was game to give it a try.

Or at least that's the way I put it to myself, that morning in the car, driving north from the Mississippi motel where we'd spent the night. This travel had become ritualized; we'd become skilled at loading the station wagon with our computers, a couple of suitcases, the necessary books. The largest amount of space in the car was, in fact, given over to pets—the rear area for our two retrievers, who pass the time curled up asleep or sitting up staring out windows, awaiting the gift of a livestock sighting, a welcome occasion to perk up and bark. The two cats rode in carriers on the backseat, secure in their contained spaces, sleeping or sitting staring into space from their beds of our old T-shirts. It took at least three days, this long haul, and by the end of it both human and animal travelers were weary and spiritually diminished. Not much side-tripping or sightseeing; we needed to get there, get this pilgrimage over with.

But Memphis, well—that was a temptation. Or it had been, back when I'd been studying the atlas, thinking about the long span of freeway in front of us, and the red letters of the city had caught my eye. I hadn't been to Memphis for exactly forty years. Though I felt I had. I'd been imaginatively revisiting the place not so long ago, in an early chapter of a memoir. The scenes of my life there—the peculiar paste and varnish and wet-jacket smell of Peabody Elementary School, my next-door neighbor Carol gleefully chopping a huge earthworm in half with a trowel, the sickly flap of skin on my father's wounded foot, cut by a shard from a glass I'd broken when I tried to balance it on my head as if I were a model—well, all those scenes had arisen in my memory with a hallucinatory vivacity. My recollections had a kind of intensity that betrayed the way that imagination and memory had fused, which is what happens with our earliest memories—particularly when they concern places and people we can't revisit, times and realms left behind. My family left Tennessee, one of the many places we would leave, when I had just turned seven years old, and so everything about that life remained for me sealed away, as if in a sphere of its own, a set of memories and impressions unrevised by experience, uncorrected by time.

Unrevised? Well, in a way. Ask someone who's lived in the same house all his life what that house is like, and you'll get the adult's perspective, the point of view of now. But when you've left a house years ago, it only changes in your memory, and those changes are different—subtler, dreamier, the past gently rewritten in the direction of feeling. Memory erases the rooms that didn't matter; locations of feeling become intensified, larger. The dream of the past becomes a deeper dream.

Nabokov addresses this in *Speak, Memory*, when he reconstructs a world that cannot be revisited because it no longer exists; the world of prerevolutionary Russia has been atomized, demolished. What exists of the history he knew lies in some photographs, some artifacts—like the traveling valise that becomes an emblem of all the Russian exiles—and in his gorgeous, hammered sentences. In a way, everyone's past shares with Nabokov's its irretrievability, but if there are such things as degrees of vanishing, then his past is gone to a greater extent—memory's players dead, its country houses destroyed, its social fabric swept away.

Odd, then, to think that I'd written a memoir in which I chose not to revisit the places of the past, when, unlike Nabokov, I could. I could have found the sites of childhood scenes and interviewed relatives, seeking corrections or corroboration, but that wasn't my book's project. What interested me was memory itself, the architectures memory constructs, the interpretive act of remembering. There is a passage in a poem by Alfred Corn that says it beautifully:

The idea hard to get in focus
   is not how things
Looked but how the look felt,
   then—and then, now.

"How the look felt" was precisely what I wanted. I didn't realize how much this was the project of my book until I was done. In one passage, I'd wondered about why my sister, who married as a young woman, wore a beige wedding dress. I imagined a number of reasons she might have made this choice, or it might have been made for her—and then, in the margins of the manuscript, a copy editor wrote, Why don't you just *ask* her? (This was not a particularly sympathetic copy editor.) Then I wondered why it had never occurred to me to ask her, and immediately I understood that it simply wasn't that sort of book; my inquiry was into memory, not history: how it was to be that child, as that child rearises in the mind, imaginatively reconstructed, reinhabited. Which is how the past goes on and on in us, changing, developing, its look and meanings built and rebuilt over time.

The past is not static, or ever truly complete; as we age we see from new positions, shifting angles. A therapist friend of mine likes to use the metaphor of the kind of spiral stair that winds up inside a lighthouse. As one moves up that stair, the core at the center doesn't change, but one continually sees it from another vantage point; if the past is a core of who we are, then our movement in time always brings us into a new relation to that core.

It was that sort of movement into "new relation" that seemed to make my book possible. As a young poet, I'd written about my family, but I can't say in retrospect that any of those poems are any good. First I disguised them through surrealist means; I remember, at my first poetry reading at the University of Arizona, reading a poem in which I presented my parents as circus performers, my mother perched on an elaborate trapeze, my father juggling broken dishes. My parents, who were in the audience, didn't know what to make of it, but I remember being so nervous that I stubbed out a cigarette and jammed it into the pocket of my jacket, and had to be told by a concerned audience member, after the reading, that I was smoldering.

Later, I wrote poems about my family that were, if not a by-product of therapy, directly influenced by it; I wanted to arrive at a kind of clarity about who we'd been and what had happened to us, and I wanted to take possession of my story; that's therapy's work, after all, the narration of a tale for the benefit of the teller. These were plainspoken, investigative poems; they were after the truth, and that was an important project for me then, but now the poems seem a bit unidimensional, their point of view finally not complex enough to satisfy.

But I was in my twenties or early thirties when I wrote them, and by the time I came to write a prose book about my family—one that wanted both to enter that child's experience in a lyric way and spin a context around him and his upbringing—I was forty-five or so, around the age my father was when my book begins. I was standing, to return to my spiraling metaphor, on another tread on the stairs; I had a somewhat more detached (or at least differently attached) and inquisitive attitude toward the past. Or at least that was true some of the time; one of the first things writing a memoir teaches you is the startling elasticity of the self: how the perceptions of the seven-year-old and the anxieties of the fifteen-year-old are perfectly available, states of mind into which one can simply slide. Childhood, it seems, is in the next room from this one; adult detachment is gained and lost and gained again, and in the realm of memory, time and location spin like an old-fashioned toy, the kind where still pictures can be suddenly spun into motion.

Somewhere outside of Memphis, we turned to the radio for distraction, and a program began about African music of a particular sort: songs generated by ancestor possession. The singer, in trance, does not write the song but receives it. These are the words of the ancestors, and they must be repeated exactly; to change the song, to improvise, is to betray them. The songs are beautiful and alive, and the program resonates in my imagination on into Memphis. We stop for a street map of the city, and while I drive, Paul, who is fond of maps, searches and studies, turning the unfolded sheet every which way, but he can't find my old street. We stop again, in a shopping center parking lot, and when I step out into the humid sun-struck atmosphere rippling over the asphalt, I suddenly know I want to be in Memphis, I want Memphis intensely, the heat and smell of it, the pressure of its humid air on my scalp, the scent of its leaves and mulch in my nose, its speech in my ears and on my tongue. And at the same time I am suddenly unsteady on my feet and ready to burst into tears: I have betrayed the ancestors, haven't I, writing about them, I have done it the wrong way, I have mis-sung their music; I have, with my words, wounded the powerless dead.

Firebird is a book very much concerned with performance and how experiences of performing lift one out of a self defined by others toward some more joyous, self-generated, more open identity. A series of performances provide structure to the story, and the first of these took place at Peabody Elementary School, in Memphis, when Little Miss Sunbeam, an emblem and spokesperson for the eponymous bread company, appeared at my school to what in memory is a rapt audience of children astonished by her beauty and accomplishment.

We are scouring the map, focusing on older areas of town. There's an amusement park I think I might remember, and there's the Pink Palace, a children's museum I used to visit with my father, and—there! Peabody School. Evidence of the past, it seems, can actually be found. We leave the suburban shopping center behind and find the neighborhood—which doesn't in truth seem all that familiar, though it's interesting and lively: there are old storefronts getting remade into galleries and cafés, a familiar urban dynamic. We try once more to find Ramses Street, but it's no luck, nothing seems right, until we turn a corner and there is the school—limestone or some other yellowy stone, a handsome if somewhat self-important-looking building from the first half of the twentieth century, not a school anymore but a community center. We park, walk across the street, up the steps—and it is only there, when I turn around and stand facing the street, that the body remembers: suddenly it is very clear to me; what I need to do to walk home; I know the way, the turns to take, which had been so important forty years ago, my first long independent walk. It's the strangest sensation, knowing the way on a level that seems to reside beneath thinking—and it leads us down one street (there were big trees there that dripped in the rain), a right turn, another onto—McIlhenny! That was it; the name of our street was never Ramses. I made that up, out of the memory of mummies in the museum, and the word "Memphis," and the fact that our house had fat, tapering columns like diminutive versions of the pillars at Luxor. I loved archaeology as a child, and I'd have to be an excavator to find any remnant of our old house now—gone, torn down to make way for apartments, but all around it are the bungalows of a neighborhood I recognize. It's become a black, working-class neighborhood now, which has preserved it, to some degree, since nobody's had the money to make these houses unrecognizable: same columns and porch swings, same grassy lawns and delicate mimosas and live oaks with their big roots buckling the sidewalks. All vaguely familiar, none of them quite mine, and of course we aren't quite welcome here, we don't really make sense, two white guys in a Volvo full of pets—a car my memoir paid for, incidentally—driving around slowly, looking and looking.

Why did I experience my book as a betrayal?

The lives of other people are unknowable. Period. I wouldn't go as far as a poet colleague of mine who says that "representation is murder," but I would acknowledge that to represent is to maim. When I go to describe the forces that shaped my mother as a girl, I am working from a combination of memory, intuition, evidence, family story; I can make reasonable interpretations and educated guesses, but the fact remains that I must create her as a character in my book, and I am making decisions about how that person—in this case complex, dramatic, haunted—will be presented. I simply can't write a book in which she remains inscrutable, merely the kind of giant shadow on the wall our parents are to us in childhood—the whole *point* of memoir, in a way, is to make these people known. Yet, like any biographer, I sift through what I know and I choose emblematic moments, emphasize one strand over another, and must finally acknowledge that there are threads I can never recover. My picturing will distort its subject; it is, of course, a record and embodiment of a process of knowing; it is "about" the making of knowledge, which is a much larger and more unstable thing than the marshaling of mere facts. This would be true if I'd interviewed every surviving relative and wandered around my mother's little Tennessee hometown like a detective stalking clues—and therefore how much more true if I make a book allegiant to memory, interested in the ways that a child made sense of those people, in how they look and seem "in the then now."

This particular form of distortion—the inevitable rewriting of those we love we do in the mere act of describing them—is the betrayal built into memoir, into the telling of memories. But the alternative, of course, is worse: are we willing to lose the past, to allow it to be erased, because it can be only partially known? For many memoirists, the story we tell is all there'll be of our characters, or at least all there will be of them *as we have known them*. My sister remembers my mother, too, of course, and so does my father, but the person they remember is not *my* mother, not exactly; there are a set of internal relations, a phenomenology, if you will, that only I can name, because only I have known them. This is what my sister meant when she said, charmingly, after reading my book, "The things you got wrong just make it that much more you!" Perfect, and a gift to the memoirist, that response.

My father's response was not such a happy one.

In truth I must here, as Shakespeare says, "admit impediment." I have, so far, been telling you a story—though you have doubtless recognized that the evocation of my visit to Memphis is relayed here in order to allow me to say some things about memory and about memoir. Narration is comforting; as readers, we feel reassured by the presence of a narrator, whose shaping voice assures that things are more or less in control, that there is some reasonable expectation of coherence.

But when it comes to talking about my father and my memoir, I have to choose between honesty and coherence; if I take the former course, then it seems almost inevitable that any sense of stability I've cooked up here will tumble into a morass of contradictory feeling.

He and I have an unsettled history when it comes to my written words. One difficult evening, after I gave him my first book, a slender chapbook of neosurrealist lyrics published in the midseventies, he threw it at me, saying it made no sense. It didn't, save in the refined, oblique way of such poems, but I wasn't prepared for the intensity of his reaction. What did it mean? That he'd spent money on my education only to have it lead to this useless and incomprehensible product? That he felt angry at being excluded from my inner life, whose text was unreadable to him? Or that he was annoyed that he *wasn't* represented there, in the way that Oscar Wilde says that society's rage at art is the rage of Caliban not seeing his face in the mirror?

As my poems grew in clarity, so did my reluctance to show them to my father—not surprisingly, I guess, after that unhappy evening! We maintained a distance around the subject of my work, aided by the fact that we lived on different sides of the country, and this distance only eroded when my work became more visible. When my father could buy a book of mine in Barnes and Noble at the nearby mall, his sense of the value of his son's work shifted.

And that's when he read my first memoir, a book about grief, a love letter to a dead man and a meditation on what the church fathers call "last things." He wrote me a wonderful letter about his sense of emotional connection to the book, about times in his life when he'd felt something like what I'd described. By the time he read the book, he was a widower too, though his letter didn't touch on that; I have no idea if the particular experiences of bereavement I wrote about resonated with his experience, but something did, and he had the forthrightness to say so.

This was partly the gift of prose—which, of course, far more people read, and read because of what it is about, than will ever see a poem. This may seem self-evident, in contemporary America, but I can testify that to a poet it still comes as a shock. Who expects to be read by strangers, much less taken to heart by them? If I'd seriously thought that one of those strangers was my own father, I doubt I could ever have written the book. I wasn't accustomed to being seen by him, and like many gay or lesbian children, I'd protected my inner life from my parents' scrutiny for fear of judgment—quite a reasonable fear, given the level of homophobia in our country and in my family. But that homophobia had simply been washed away, mediated by time and the ways age (and in my father's case, remarriage to a socially liberal woman) rearranges one's priorities and values. I think my father honestly felt that he gained a new kind of access to my life, and for a time we were closer.

Not, I hasten to add, close. There has been a sense of awkwardness between us since—I don't know, the dawn of recorded time?—so it would have been absurd to expect that to shift entirely. But it was fascinating and odd to me to discover that the distance between us was not about sexuality, not really—unless you could say that a lifetime's distance originated there and then we were powerless to revise it. There were some truly odd moments (I mean odd in the sense that they were nothing I could ever have predicted in my life) when my father and stepmother and Paul and I were two couples, going to lunch or for a walk on the beach together. If you'd told me, as a young man, that this could be possible, I'd have probably had some sort of cognitive meltdown; the structure of reality would have to shift first.

Perhaps it was also some element of this sea change that spurred me on to write *Firebird*. If I could be seen this far, if this much honesty were possible . . . ? But early on, when the book was just beginning, I asked my father something about that childhood year in Memphis and heard the tone of his voice shift in his reply, "Why do you want to know?" Now I think he must have already been anticipating the day when I'd write about my growing up, when I'd put my version of the family romance in print. And he must already have dreaded it; every once in a while he'd ask me, "How's that writing about Memphis going?" I never asked him any more questions, in part because I understood I wasn't writing that sort of book, and in part because I knew that if I did so, I would simply inflame his fears.

Fears of? Well, my family never wanted to deal directly with anything, really, and I grew up with the sense that to name a problem was to invite mighty trouble. *The* problem, if there was such a thing, was my mother's alcoholism, the reputed source of which shifted variously: my homosexuality, my sister's misbehavior, my mother's own back pain or loneliness or thwarted creativity or mismatched marriage. None of these "causes" were directly addressed, not quite; they simply floated in the air of our household, or were blurted out in drunken and agonized moments, or were overheard, or were offered as whispered, confidential explanations. I guess that my father was scared that his adult son would do the naming, for all the world to see, and that this revelation of our story would not be told in his favor.

Or afraid that I would say the unspoken thing between us, that I felt he'd failed to protect me? The truth of my high school years is that I was pretty much on my own while my parents were entirely absorbed in the drama of my mother's spectacular collapse. There was about a three-year period when no one remembered, for instance, to buy me shoes. I tried to kill myself, at fifteen, and sometime in there, I can't remember exactly when (who would want to?), my mother tried to shoot me with my father's revolver. In other words, he did fail to protect me. Having left home at seventeen to marry an alcoholic myself, I paid the tough dues necessary to learn childhood's impossible lesson—that you cannot save anyone, not mother or spouse, and the most powerful child in the world, which is surely what I must have imagined myself to be, cannot fix anything, no matter how good or smart he is, or how he disguises himself to try to be who he thinks he's supposed to. No matter how loyal he is to his drunken mother, or how loyally he later behaves toward his father by acting just like him.

No *wonder* my father didn't want me to write another memoir!

But write it I did, holding at bay the awareness that he and my sister would be reading the book. In order to work freely, I needed to behave as if, in the composing process, I was in an arena of pure freedom, of irresponsibility; here I could say anything without consequences. That's the sort of permission the imaginative life requires, and I could allow myself that—increasing, actually, my sense of freedom in successive drafts of the book, which each time seemed to grow riskier and to probe farther. Sometimes I'd catch myself saying, Oh, you don't have to write that, who wants to read it? And then realizing that in projecting these doubts outward onto readers, I was actually protecting not the potential reader but myself; I was the one who didn't want to read about whatever it was that troubled me. And then, once I understood that, I did want to read it, and to write it.

The time came, of course, when I had to show the book to the two living people most implicated therein. I gave it to my sister with some eagerness; I wanted to know what she thought. And I didn't know what she'd told her children and grandchildren about her wild old days, and I certainly didn't want them to learn these stories from my book! Her response—much laughter—was gracious and tender and lovely.

To tell the truth, I simply avoided giving the manuscript to my father, though I told myself I would. I didn't do it and didn't do it, and then my publisher's lawyers told me I had to. Not a wise plan on my part: now my private trepidations about his response were twinned with an external, legal concern. The lawyers asked me to present him with a release to sign, saying he wouldn't sue them, but I declined. I just couldn't imagine handing him the manuscript with a note that would suggest he might want to file a lawsuit!

So I sent the thick pile of pages that comprised my book, an autobiography from the ages of six to sixteen, along with a letter explaining that I understood it might not be the easiest thing to read, and that if there were things in it that he couldn't live with, I wanted to talk about them. I don't know what I would have done had he identified things he wanted me to change; it's difficult for me to imagine, now, what that exchange might have been like, because it never happened. My father simply never answered me at all.

When I wrote to him, a week or two later, my letter came back with a stamp from the post office on the front of the envelope: *Refused, return to sender*. My response to the words was visceral; I felt they were stamped on my face, burning a little there, like a slap or the sensation of rushing air when a door slams in your face.

I tried again, with the same result, and then I didn't try anymore. I didn't want to keep knocking at that door. And I began to feel, justified or not, melodramatic or not, that *Refused, return to sender* was in fact a motto I could have worn on my skin my whole life; it was, in some unspoken way, inscribed upon my childhood, and the ink had never really faded.

My father, who is now in his nineties, hasn't spoken to me for five years. There has been no contact of any sort between us. I ask my sister how he's doing; I don't know if he asks about me. She told me that he once said he thought the book "had an agenda against him," and that she'd said to him that it shouldn't be taken so literally, that things might be shaped "to make a better story." But then I think they had to stop talking about it.

Because my father never talked to me about the book, I have devoted a considerable amount of energy to imagining the specifics of his response. What didn't he like? (Maybe what he *did* appreciate about it would be a more challenging question!) Was it simply that I had told the family secrets, exposing our shame to the neighbors? Was it that he was embarrassed that I talked about how many times we'd moved because he'd shifted jobs again and again, something I'd always understood had to do with government transfers he couldn't control—until he told me that actually he couldn't ever get along with his supervisors or his coworkers, and that was why we'd never stay anywhere long? It is quite possible that my father has told people—my stepmother, for instance— very different versions of the stories I've told.

Was it because I told the darkest moment in the family story—how, when my mother was dying of cirrhosis, my father made a concerted attempt to allow her to die at home, without medical intervention. He said he didn't want her to suffer at the hands of doctors. The physician in the hospital where she died told me he'd never seen a patient brought into the hospital in worse condition. If my father thought he was being heroic, it was a heroism of a profoundly perverse sort—the ultimate codependent's gesture.

For which I do not wish to blame him. Experience teaches us that we could have been these people, that there's no gesture or choice they made that I couldn't have made myself, under the right circumstances, without the luck or grace of some correcting perspective. In fact, I worked very hard, writing *Firebird*, to arrive at empathy. This is the great psychological magic act of memoir; the people you've known become your characters, and you cannot hate your characters—if you treat them as evil, one-dimensional, or even merely inscrutable, the form simply collapses into a narcissistic muddle. Thus, the work of trying to write a good book becomes, unexpectedly, an empathic adventure, a quest to try to see into the lives of others. Even if such a "seeing into" is by nature partial, an interpretive fiction, it's what we have.

Thus, not only because I have also been married to an alcoholic in the face of whose illness I had to admit I was entirely powerless, but also because I have written a book that attempts to understand a bitterness, a human disaster—well, for those reasons I want my father to see my memoir as a gesture of compassion. Or at least as an opportunity to *know* his son, inside and out. In my experience, which is admittedly distorted by the sort of family in which I came of age, it is not usual for children to allow their parents to know them. It doesn't feel safe to do so. If I were a father, I think I would want nothing more than to *know* my children, to see how they understood and experienced their lives, even if it discomfited me.

But that is what I would want, not necessarily what my father wants. And I must also face the possibility, I guess, that he knows me better now and doesn't like what he knows.

The experience I report here is, I suppose, every memoirist's nightmare: that we will lose people in our lives by writing about them. I have replaced an inauthentic relationship—the conversation we had before, with its many elisions—with an authentic silence. Is that better? I can't honestly say that I am sure. My father plans to die, it seems, without talking to me; that is his form of taking power. Because I am an American writer, I don't feel powerful, but I forget that to other people, especially those who don't write, the ability to tell a story, to make language and publish it in a book, is, after all, to be an author; it confers author-ity. I have told the family story now, the author-ized version, and perhaps my father feels powerless to correct it.

It is also perfectly possible that my father dislikes my book for reasons entirely unknown to me. My late editor told me a wonderful story about a memoirist who was a scion of a famous family rife with mental illness and turmoil. She showed her manuscript to family members with the greatest trepidation, and indeed some of them *were* upset, but not because she'd chronicled breakdowns or divorces. The content of their complaints was more like, How dare you tell everyone that I put that underwear on the dog when I was five? Or, I do *not* have a dark mole on my chin.

When my partner Paul published a memoir about growing up in New Jersey, the most surprising letter he received was from a high school math teacher—not even *his* teacher, it turned out—who feared he'd given Paul math anxiety for life and was disturbed and saddened by this report of his own failing. But the passage in question, in Paul's mind, is actually about the way that his fascination with composing liturgical music made him entirely lose interest in school, math included.

Moral: It is a strange and dire thing to be represented, and what the represented make of it is not in the representer's power to control.

Given all this, I have asked myself why I had to write the book. It began with an odd memory—a wonderfully liberating experience of improvisational dance, in 1962, when my fourth-grade teacher in Tucson, Arizona, put Stravinsky's *Firebird* Suite on our classroom phonograph and said to the class, "Now, children, *move*." I danced with abandon, without self-consciousness, and my teacher loved it. Looking back at that bit of memory, I wondered about my education in the creative life, about the relationship between art and survival. And I began to think about other instances of performance in my childhood, and of the sense of joining my little limited and confused self to the larger world of what people make, the traditions of artistic creation in which, for me, there was a sense of safety, permission, and enlargement. That is surely the story of many gay boys of my generation (and of many other kids too, and of a number of generations): the freedom held out by the creative life becomes a refuge, and the sense of accomplishment one might gain there becomes a source of strength and solace. But of course I couldn't tell that story without talking about why I *needed* strength and solace, and thus the waters of my book almost immediately darkened. What is it that art saves us *from*?

Like any life story, mine could be told from many perspectives; a different organizing principle (economic, spiritual, intellectual) would produce a very different story. I wanted to tell the tale through the lens of art (and, concomitantly, of sexual orientation and performance) because that is what I wished to understand better at that moment.

And I wanted to tell the story of my life in order, once again, to take control of it, to shape some comprehensible element of cause and effect, because the instability and complexity of experience mean that this sense of pattern is always slipping away from us. Memoir is a way of reclaiming, at least temporarily, the sense of shapeliness in a life. And it would be disingenuous to deny that there is not some element too, of if not revenge then at least a personal version of setting the record straight. I can't change what happened, but I can tell my side of it, can't I? Tell it with every resource at my disposal, to make it feel real. Did anyone looking at the child me ever think, Oh, that boy's going to write this story? Like that wonderful moment in Sharon Olds's poem "I Go Back to 1933," when the speaker imagines intervening in her parents' relationship before her own birth, warning them off—and then says no, do what you are going to do, and I will write about it.

And one hopes, always, that telling a story out of one's own life becomes useful, that others might see themselves reflected there, in an enlarging and clarifying glass, or at least one that helps them to examine the particular character of their own experience. (Talking to a group of queer kids in Minneapolis on the *Firebird* book tour, young people either homeless or at risk of being on the streets, I felt this so acutely. These kids had been so damaged, so nearly thrown away by the schools and by their parents that most of them couldn't actually read the book, but we could talk about it. And in that conversation I felt such power, for them and for me: I had been a kid who'd come close to being discarded for my sexual difference, and now I was an adult, a working, reasonably happy, thriving adult, who had lived to say so.)

If the reader hears guilt in this attempt at self-justification, she's right. After all, I have wounded an old man, who plans to die without forgiving me; I have made a rupture; I've shone light into dark places and thus brought shame upon my family; I have told the truth, which may indeed set you free, but not without the price of betrayal. You cannot sing your ancestors' songs as they intended them to be sung, as they would have phrased them themselves. If you choose to sing them at all, you will betray your forebears, because you will never understand them as they'd wish to be understood.

This "betrayal" is life giving; it is a condition of truth telling; it is a condition of actual aliveness, which requires emotional honesty with oneself—without that, what on earth is this life? The alternative is silence, a frozen politeness, a fake life. I suppose that being emotionally honest with oneself doesn't necessitate writing a book about it—but for me it has always been the written word that enters where speech cannot, that shapes what would otherwise remain oppressively inchoate. Did I need to publish that book while my father was still alive? I seem to have needed to do so, perhaps simply because of the hungry child in me who wanted to be *seen*.

And, like any artist, when I've made something I believe to be beautiful, what is one to do with it but give it to someone?

If there is a meaning to be taken from this, it is that art cannot be counted on to mend the rifts within or without. Its work is to take us to the brink of clarity. Joy Williams writes, "The writer writes to serve—hopelessly he writes in the hope that he might serve—not himself and not others, but that great cold elemental grace that knows us." Clarity, whether we'd ever have wished for it or not, is a genuine thing. And any instance of the genuine, no matter how discomfiting, and though it may not seem like it at all, is something to be grateful for.

I am used to it, my father's silence, and his silence is a burning in which I reside. In my worst moments I think, Well, now I have no parents. Then I think, I never did. Then I think, Yes, I did, there were moments of affirmation, there were lessons in beauty and making, there were instances of instruction in which I was shown those things that have sustained my life. Both are true. There's the rub, the caught in between–ness of it. I don't care anymore what my father thinks, and I am to some degree crippled by his response. I don't want his presence or his absence. I am proud of my book, and I wouldn't change a word of it. I wish I'd never written it. No, I don't. Yes, I do. No, I don't.

This was about the twin towers...

Brian Doyle

LEAP

BRIAN DOYLE is the editor of *Portland Magazine* at the University of Portland, in Oregon—the best university magazine in America, according to *Newsweek*, and "the best spiritual magazine in the country" according to Annie Dillard. Boyle is the author of five collections of essays, two nonfiction books (including *The Grail*, about a year in an Oregon vineyard), and a new collection of "proems" called *Epiphanies & Elegies*. His books have three times been finalists for the Oregon Book Award, and his essays have appeared in *The Atlantic*, *Harper's*, and *Orion*, and in newspapers around the world. His essays have also been reprinted in four *Best American Essays* anthologies. He is contributing essayist to *The Age* newspaper and *Eureka Street* magazine in Australia.

A couple leaped from the south tower, hand in hand. They reached for each other and their hands met and they jumped. Jennifer Brickhouse saw them falling, hand in hand.

Many people jumped. Perhaps hundreds. No one knows. They struck the pavement with such force that there was a pink mist in the air.

The mayor reported the mist.

A kindergarten boy who saw people falling in flames told his teacher that the birds were on fire. She ran with him on her shoulders out of the ashes.

Tiffany Keeling saw fireballs falling that she later realized were people. Jennifer Griffin saw people falling and wept as she told the story. Niko Winstral saw people free-falling backwards with their hands out, as if they were parachuting. Joe Duncan on his roof on Duane Street looked up and saw people jumping. Henry Weintraub saw people "leaping as they flew out." John Carson saw six people fall, "falling over themselves, falling, they were somersaulting." Steve Miller saw people jumping from a thousand feet in the air. Kirk Kjeldsen saw people flailing on the way down, people lining up and jumping, "too many people falling." Jane Tedder saw people leaping and the sight haunts her at night. Steve Tamas counted fourteen people jumping and then he stopped counting. Stuart DeHann saw one woman's dress billowing as she fell, and he

165

Uses children to make the story innocently chilling

saw a shirtless man falling end over end, and he too saw the couple leaping hand in hand.

Several pedestrians were killed by people falling from the sky. A fireman was killed by a body falling from the sky.

But he reached for her hand and she reached for his hand and they leaped out the window holding hands.

The day of the Lord will come as a thief in the night, in which the heavens shall pass away with a great noise, wrote John the Apostle, *and the elements shall melt with a fervent heat, the earth also and the works that are therein shall be burned up.*

Not driving the piece...

I try to whisper prayers for the sudden dead and the harrowed families of the dead and the screaming souls of the murderers but I keep coming back to his hand and her hand nestled in each other with such extraordinary ordinary succinct ancient naked stunning perfect simple ferocious love.

There is no fear in love, wrote John, *but perfect love casteth out fear, because fear hath torment.*

Their hands reaching and joining are the most powerful prayer I can imagine, the most eloquent, the most graceful. It is everything that we are capable of against horror and loss and death. It is what makes me believe that we are not craven fools and charlatans to believe in God, to believe that human beings have greatness and holiness within them like seeds that open only under great fires, to believe that some unimaginable essence of who we are persists past the dissolution of what we were, to believe against such evil hourly evidence that love is why we are here.

Their passing away was thought an affliction, and their going forth from us utter destruction, says the Book of Wisdom, *but they are in peace. They shall shine, and shall dart about as sparks through stubble.*

No one knows who they were: husband and wife, lovers, dear friends, colleagues, strangers thrown together at the window there at the lip of hell. Maybe they didn't even reach for each other consciously, maybe it was instinctive, a reflex, as they both decided at the same time to take two running steps and jump out the shattered window, but they did reach for each other, and they held on tight, and leaped, and fell endlessly into the smoking canyon, at two hundred miles an hour, falling so far and so fast that they would have blacked out before they hit the pavement near Liberty Street so hard that there was a pink mist in the air.

I trust I shall shortly see thee, John wrote, *and we shall speak face to face.*

Jennifer Brickhouse saw them holding hands, and Stuart DeHann saw them holding hands, and I hold on to that.

I voice is not the main drive. Focused on this third voice.

Tony Earley

SOMEHOW FORM A FAMILY

TONY EARLEY, an MFA in creative writing from the University of Alabama, has been named one of the "twenty best young fiction writers in America" by *The New Yorker* and one of the "Best of Young American Novelists" by *Granta*. His books include a collection of short stories, *Here We Are in Paradise: Stories*; a novel, *Jim the Boy*; and a collection of essays, *Somehow Form a Family: Stories That Are Mostly True*. His stories have also appeared in *The New Yorker, Harper's, Esquire*, and *The Best American Short Stories*. His work has been widely anthologized and translated into many languages. The Samuel Milton Fleming Chair in English, Earley has taught at Vanderbilt University since 1997.

In July 1969, I looked a lot like Opie in the second or third season of *The Andy Griffith Show*. I was a small boy with a big head. I wore blue jeans with the cuffs turned up and horizontally striped pullover shirts. I was the brother in a father-mother-brother-sister family. We lived in a four-room house at the edge of the country, at the foot of the mountains, outside a small town in North Carolina, but it could have been anywhere.

On one side of us lived Mr. and Mrs. White. They were old and rich. Their driveway was paved. Mrs. White was the president of the town garden club. When she came to visit Mama she brought her own ashtray. Mr. White was almost deaf. When he watched the news on television, it sounded like thunder in the distance. The Whites had an aluminum travel trailer in which you could see your reflection. One summer they hitched it to their Chrysler and pulled it all the way to Alaska.

On the other side of us lived Mack and Joan. They had just graduated from college. I thought Joan was beautiful, and still do. Mack had a bass boat and a three-tray tackle box in which lurked a bristling school of lures. On the other side of Mack and Joan lived Mrs. Taylor, who was old, and on the other side of Mrs. Taylor lived Mr. and Mrs. Frady, who had a fierce dog. My sister, Shelly, and I called it the Frady dog. The Frady dog lived a long and bitter life. It did not die until well after I had a driver's license.

On the far side of the Whites lived Mr. and Mrs. John Harris; Mr. and Mrs. Burlon Harris lived beyond them. John and Burlon were first cousins. John was a teacher who in the summers fixed lawn mowers, including ours, in a building behind his house. Burlon reminded me of Mr. Greenjeans on *Captain Kangaroo*. He kept horses and let us play in his barn. Shelly once commandeered one of his cats and brought it home to live with us. Burlon did not mind; he asked her if she wanted another one. We rode our bicycles toward Mr. Harris's house as if pulled there by gravity. We did not ride in the other direction; the Frady dog sat in its yard and watched for us.

In July 1969, we did not have much money, but in the hierarchy of southern poor, we were the good kind, the kind you would not mind living on your road. We were clean. Our clothes were clean. My parents worked. We went to church. Easter mornings, Mama stood us in front of the yellowbell bush and took our picture. We had meat at every meal—chicken and cube steak and pork chops and ham—and plenty of milk to drink. We were not trashy. Mrs. White would not sit with her ashtray in the kitchen of trashy people. Trashy people lived in the two houses around the curve past Mr. Harris's. When Daddy drove by those houses we could see that the kids in the yard had dirty faces. They were usually jabbing at something with a stick. Shelly and I were not allowed to ride our bicycles around the curve.

I knew we were poor only because our television was black and white. It was an old Admiral, built in the 1950s, with the brass knobs the size of baseballs. Its cabinet was perfectly square, a cube of steel with a painted-on mahogany grain. Hoss on *Bonanza* could not have picked it up by himself. It was a formidable object, but its vertical hold was shot. We gathered around it the night Neil Armstrong walked on the moon, but we could not tell what was happening. The picture flipped up and down. We turned off the lights in the living room so we could see better. We listened to Walter Cronkite. In the distance we could hear Mr. White's color TV rumbling. We changed the channel and listened to Huntley and Brinkley. We could hear the scratchy radio transmissions coming down out of space, but we could not see anything. Daddy got behind the TV with a flashlight. He said, "Is that better? Is that better?" but it never was. Mama said, "Just be thankful you've got a television."

After the Eagle had landed but before the astronauts opened the door and came out, Mack knocked on the door and asked us if we wanted to look at the moon. He was an engineer for a power company and had set up his surveyor's transit in the backyard. Daddy and Shelly and I went with him. We left Mama sitting in the living room in the blue light of the TV. She said she did not want to miss anything. The moon, as I remember it, was full, although I have since learned that it wasn't. I remember that a galaxy of lightning bugs blinked against the black pine trees that grew between our yard and that of the Whites. Mack pointed the transit at the sky. Daddy held me up so I could see. The moon inside the instrument was startlingly bright; the man in the moon was clearly visible, although the men on the moon weren't. "You can't see them or anything," Mack said, which I already knew. I said, "I know that." I wasn't stupid and did not like to be talked to as if I were. Daddy put me down. He and Mack stood for a while and talked. Daddy smoked a cigarette. In the bright yard Shelly chased lightning bugs. She did not run, but instead jumped slowly, her feet together. I realized that she was pretending to walk on the moon, pretending that she was weightless. The moon was so bright, it cast a shadow at her feet. I remember these things for sure. I am tempted to say that she was beautiful in the moonlight, and I'm sure she was, but that isn't something I remember noticing that night, only a thing I need to say now.

Eight, maybe nine months later, Shelly and I rode the bus home from school. It was a Thursday, Mama's day off, Easter time. The cherry tree in the garden separating our driveway from that of the Whites was in brilliant, full bloom. We could hear it buzzing from the road. One of us checked the mailbox. We looked up the driveway at our house. Something was wrong with it, but we couldn't tell what. Daddy was adding four rooms on to the house, and we were used to it appearing large and unfinished. We stood in the driveway and stared. Black tar paper was tacked to the outside walls of the new part, but the old part was still covered with white asbestos shingles. In the coming summer, Daddy and a crew of brick masons would finish transforming the house into a split-level ranch-style, remarkably similar to the one in which the Bradys would live. I loved the words *split-level ranch-style*. To me they meant "rich."

Shelly and I spotted what was wrong at the same time. A giant television antenna had attached itself to the roof of our house. It was shiny and tall as a young tree. It looked dangerous, as if it would bite, like a praying mantis. The antenna slowly began to turn, as if it had noticed us. Shelly and I looked quickly at each other, our mouths wide open, and then back at the antenna. We sprinted up the driveway.

In the living room, on the spot occupied by the Admiral that morning, sat a magnificent new color TV, a Zenith, with a twenty-one-inch screen. Its cabinet was made of real wood. *Gomer Pyle, U.S.M.C.* was on. I will never forget that. Gomer Pyle and Sergeant Carter were the first two people I ever saw on a color television. The olive green and khaki of their uniforms was dazzling. Above them was the blue sky of California. The sky in California seemed bluer than the sky in North Carolina.

We said, "Is that ours?"

Mama said, "I'm going to kill your daddy." He had charged the TV without telling her. Two men from Sterchi's Furniture had showed up at the house that morning with the TV on a truck. They climbed onto the roof and planted the antenna.

We said, "Can we keep it?"

Mama said, "I don't know," but I noticed she had written the numbers of the stations we could get on the dial of the Channel Master, the small box which controlled the direction the antenna pointed. Mama would never have written on anything she planned on taking back to the store.

The dial of the Channel Master was marked like a compass. Channel 3 in Charlotte lay to the east; Channel 13 in Asheville lay to the west. Channel 7 in Spartanburg and Channel 4 in Greenville rested side by side below them in the south. For years these cities would mark the outside edges of the world as I knew it. Shelly reached out and turned the dial. Mama smacked her on the hand. Gomer grew fuzzy and disappeared. I said, "Mama, she broke it." When the dial stopped turning, Mama carefully turned it back to the south. Gomer reappeared, resurrected. Jim Nabors probably never looked better to anyone, in his whole life, than he did to us right then.

Mama sat us down on the couch and laid down the law. Mama always laid down the law when she was upset. We were not to touch the TV. We could not turn it on, nor could we change the channel. Under no circumstances were we to touch the Channel Master. The Channel Master was very expensive. And if we so much as looked at the knobs that controlled the color, she would whip us. It had taken her all afternoon to get the color just right.

We lived in a split-level ranch-style house, with two maple trees and a rose bush in the front yard, outside a town that could have been named Springfield. We had a color TV. We had a Channel Master antenna that turned slowly on top of our house until it found and pulled from the sky electro-magnetic waves for our nuclear family.

We watched *Hee-Haw*, starring Buck Owens and Roy Clark; we watched *All in the Family, The Mary Tyler Moore Show, The Bob Newhart Show, The Carol Burnett Show*, and *Mannix*, starring Mike Connors with Gail Fisher as Peggy; we watched *Gunsmoke* and *Bonanza*, even after Adam left and Hoss died and Little Joe's hair turned gray; we watched *Adam-12* and *Kojak, McCloud, Colombo*, and *Hawaii Five-O*; we watched *Cannon*, a Quinn Martin production, and *Barnaby Jones*, a Quinn Martin production, which co-starred Miss America and Uncle Jed from *The Beverly Hillbillies*. Daddy finished the new part of the house and moved out soon thereafter. He rented a trailer in town and took the old Admiral out of the basement with him. We watched *Mutual of Omaha's*

Wild Kingdom and *The Wonderful World of Disney*. After school we watched *Gomer Pyle, U.S.M.C., The Beverly Hillbillies, Gilligan's Island,* and *The Andy Griffith Show*. Upstairs, we had rooms of our own. Mama stopped taking us to church.

On Friday nights we watched *The Partridge Family, The Brady Bunch, Room 222, The Odd Couple,* and *Love American Style*. Daddy came to visit on Saturdays. We watched *The Little Rascals* on Channel 3 with Fred Kirby, the singing cowboy, and his sidekick, Uncle Jim. We watched *The Little Rascals* on Channel 4 with Monty Dupuy, the weatherman, and his sidekick, Doohickey. Mornings, before school, we watched *The Three Stooges* with Mr. Bill on Channel 13. Mr. Bill worked alone. The school year Daddy moved out, Mr. Bill showed Bible story cartoons instead of *The Three Stooges*. That year, we went to school angry.

After each of Daddy's visits, Mama said he was getting better. Shelly and I tried to imagine living with the Bradys but realized we would not fit in. They were richer and more popular at school. They did not have Southern accents. One Saturday Daddy brought me a set of golf clubs, which I had asked for but did not expect to get. It was raining that day. I took the clubs out in the yard and very quickly realized that golf was harder than it looked on television. I went back inside and wiped the mud and water off the clubs with Bounty paper towels, the quicker picker upper. Upstairs I heard Mama say, "Do you think he's stupid?" I spread the golf clubs on the floor around me. I tuned in *Shock Theater* on Channel 13 and turned it up loud.

Shelly had a crush on Bobby Brady; I had a crush on Jan. Jan had braces, I had braces. Jan had glasses, I had glasses. Their daddy was an architect. Our daddy lived in a trailer in town with a poster of Wile E. Coyote and the Road Runner on the living room wall. The Coyote held the Road Runner firmly by the neck. The caption on the poster said, "Beep, Beep your ass." I lay in bed at night and imagined being married to Jan Brady but having an affair with Marsha. I wondered how we would tell Jan, what Marsha and I would do then, where we would go. Greg Brady beat me up. I shook his hand and told him I deserved it. Alice refused to speak to me. During this time Mrs. White died. I heard the ambulance in the middle of the night. It sounded like the one on *Emergency*. I opened the door to Mama's room to see if she was OK. She was embarrassed because our dog barked and barked.

Rhoda left *The Mary Tyler Moore Show*. Maude and George Jefferson left *All in the Family*; Florida, Maude's maid, left *Maude*. Daddy moved back in. He watched the news during supper, the TV as loud as Mr. White's. We were not allowed to talk during the news. This was the law. After the news we watched *Rhoda* or *Maude* or *Good Times*. Daddy decided that cutting the grass should be my job. We had a big yard. I decided that I didn't want to do anything he said. Mr. White remarried. The new Mrs. White's daughter died of cancer. The new

Mrs. White dug up every flower the old Mrs. White had planted; she cut down every tree and shrub, including the cherry tree in the garden between our driveways. Mama said the new Mrs. White broke her heart. Mr. White mowed and mowed and mowed their grass until it was smooth as a golf course. Mack and Joan paved their driveway.

What I'm trying to say is this: we lived in a split-level ranch-style house; we had a Zenith in the living room and a Channel Master attached to the roof. But Shelly and I fought like Thelma and J.J. on *Good Times*. I wanted to live in Hawaii and work for Steve McGarrett. No bad guy ever got away from McGarrett, except the Chinese master spy Wo Fat. Shelly said McGarrett would never give me a job. In all things Shelly was on Daddy's side; I lined up on Mama's. Friday evenings, when Daddy got home from work, I sneaked outside to snoop around in the glove compartment of his car. I pretended I had a search warrant, that I was Danno on a big case. Shelly reported my snooping to Daddy. I was trying to be a good son.

Every Saturday, before he went to work, Daddy left word that I was to cut the grass before he got home. I stayed in bed until lunch. Shelly came into my room and said, "You better get up." I flipped her the bird. She said, "I'm telling." I got up in time to watch professional wrestling on Channel 3. I hated the bad guys. They did not fight fair. They hid brass knuckles in their trunks and beat the good guys until they bled. They won too often. Mama brought me tomato and onion sandwiches. I could hear Mack on one side and Mr. White on the other mowing their grass. I could hear John Harris and Mr. Frady and Mrs. Taylor's daughter, Lucille, mowing grass. Lucille lived in Charlotte, but came home on weekends just to mow Mrs. Taylor's grass. We had the shaggiest lawn on the road. After wrestling, I watched the *Game of the Week* on Channel 4. Carl Yaztremski of the Boston Red Sox was my favorite baseball player. He had forearms like fenceposts. Nobody messed with him. I listened over the lawn mowers for the sound of Daddy's Volkswagen. Mama came in the living room and said, "Son, maybe you should mow some of the grass before your daddy gets home. You know what's going to happen." I knew what was going to happen. I knew that eventually he would make me mow the grass. I knew that when I was through, Mack would come through the pine trees laughing. He would say, "Charles, I swear that is the laziest boy I have ever seen." Mack had a Snapper Comet riding mower, on which he sat like a king. I never saw him on it that I did not want to bean him with a rock. Daddy would shake his head and say, "Mack, dead lice wouldn't fall off that boy." Every Saturday night we ate out at Scoggin's Seafood and Steak House. *Hee-Haw* came on at seven; *All in the Family* came on at eight.

. . .

And then Shelly and I were in high school. We watched *M*A*S*H** and *Lou Grant, Love Boat* and *Fantasy Island*. We watched *Dynasty* and *Dallas*. Opie was Richie Cunningham on *Happy Days*. Ben Cartwright showed up in a black bathrobe on *Battlestar Gallactica*. The Channel Master stopped working, but no one bothered to have it fixed. The antenna was left immobile on the roof in a compromised position: we could almost get most of the channels. One summer Mack built a pool in his backyard. Joan lay in a bikini beside the pool in the sun. The next summer Mack built a fence. This was during the late seventies. Shelly lay in her room with the lights turned off and listened to *Dark Side of the Moon*. On Friday nights she asked me to go out with her and her friends. I always said no. I did not want to miss *The Rockford Files*.

In those days Shelly and I watched *Guiding Light* when we got home from school. It was our soap. I remember that Ed Bauer's beautiful wife Rita left him because he was boring. Shelly said I reminded her of Ed Bauer. She wore her hair like Farrah Fawcett Majors on *Charlie's Angels*. After *Guiding Light* I changed the channel and watched *Star Trek*. I could not stay awake in school. I went to sleep during homeroom. During the day I woke up only long enough to change classes and eat lunch. I watched *Star Trek* when I got home as if it were beamed to our house by God. I did not want to be Captain Kirk, or any of the main characters. I just wanted to go with them. I wanted to wear a red jersey and walk the long, anonymous halls of the Starship Enterprise as it disappeared into space. One day *Star Trek* was preempted by an *ABC After School Special*. I tried to kick the screen out of the TV. I was wearing sneakers, so the glass would not break. Shelly hid in Mama and Daddy's room. I said, "Five-O. Open up." Then I kicked the door off the hinges.

Our family doctor thought I had narcolepsy. He sent me to a neurologist in Charlotte. Mama and Daddy went with me. In Charlotte, an EEG technician attached wires to my head. A small, round amber light glowed high up in the corner of the examination room. I watched the light until I went to sleep. The neurologist said that the EEG looked normal, but that he would talk to us more about the results in a few minutes. He led us to a private waiting room. It was small and bare and paneled with wood. In it were four chairs. Most of one wall was taken up by a darkened glass. I could not see what was on the other side of it. I studied our reflection. Mama and Daddy were trying to pretend that the glass wasn't there. I said, "Pa, when we get back to the Ponderosa, do you want me to round up those steers on the lower forty?"

Daddy said, "What?"

I said, "Damnit, Jim. I'm a doctor."

Daddy said, "What are you talking about?"

Mama said, "Be quiet. They're watching us."

. . .

Shelly died on Christmas Eve morning when I was a freshman in college. She had wrecked Mama's car. That night I stayed up late and watched the Pope deliver the Christmas mass from the Vatican. There was nothing else on. Daddy moved out again. My college almost shut down during the week *The Thorn Birds* was broadcast. Professors rescheduled papers and exams. In the basement of my dorm twenty-five nineteen-year-old guys shouted at the TV when the Richard Chamberlain character told the Rachel Ward character he loved God more than he loved her. At age nineteen, it was impossible to love God more than Rachel Ward. My best friend, a guy from Kenya, talked me into switching from *Guiding Light* to *General Hospital*. This was during the glory days of *General Hospital* when Luke and Scorpio roomed together on the Haunted Star. Laura was supposedly dead, but Luke knew in his heart she was still alive; every time he was by himself he heard a Christopher Cross song.

Going home was strange, as if the Mayberry I expected had become Mayberry, R.F.D. Shelly was gone. Daddy was gone. The second Mrs. White died, then Mr. White went away to a nursing home. The Fradys had moved away. John Harris had a heart attack and stopped fixing lawn mowers. Mama mowed our grass by herself with a rider. I stopped going to see Burlon Harris because he teared up every time he tried to talk about Shelly. Mack and Joan had a son named Timmy. Mack and Joan got a divorce. Mack moved to a farm out in the country; Joan moved to town.

Daddy fell in love with Mama my senior year and moved back in. The Zenith began slowly dying. Its picture narrowed into a greenly tinted slit. It stared like a diseased eye into the living room where Mama and Daddy sat. They turned off the lights so they could see better. I became a newspaper reporter. With my first Christmas bonus, I bought myself a television, a nineteen-inch GE. With my second Christmas bonus I bought Mama and Daddy one. They hooked it up to cable. When I visited them on Thursdays we watched *The Cosby Show, Family Ties, Cheers, Night Court*, and *Hill Street Blues*. Daddy gave up on broadcast TV when NBC cancelled *Hill Street Blues* and replaced it with *L.A. Law*. Now he mostly watches the Discovery Channel. Mama calls it the "airplanes and animals channel." They are in the eighteenth year of their new life together. I bear them no grudges. They were very young when I knew them best.

In grad school I switched back to *Guiding Light*. I had known Ed Bauer longer than I had known all but a few of my friends. It pleased me to see him in Springfield every afternoon, trying to do good. I watched *The Andy Griffith Show* twice a day. I could glance at Opie and tell you what year the episode was filmed. I watched the Gulf War from a stool in a bar.

Eventually I married a woman who grew up in a family that watched television only on special occasions—when Billie Jean King played Bobby Riggs, when Diana married Prince Charles. My wife was a student in a seminary. She did not want to meet Ed Bauer, nor could I explain, without sounding pathetic, why Ed Bauer was important to me. The first winter we were married I watched the winter Olympics huddled beneath a blanket in the frigid basement of the house we had rented. This was in a closed-down steel town near Pittsburgh, during the time I contemplated jumping from a bridge into the Ohio River. My wife asked the seminary community to pray for me. Ann B. Davis, who played Alice on *The Brady Bunch* was a member of that community. One day I saw her in the cafeteria at school. She looked much the same as when she played Alice, except that her hair was white, and she wore small, gold glasses. I didn't talk to her. I had heard that she didn't like talking about *The Brady Bunch*, and I could not think of anything to say to her about the world in which we actually lived. I sat in the cafeteria and stared at her as much as I could without anyone notic- ing. I don't know if she prayed for me or not, but I like to think that she did. I wanted to tell her that I grew up in a split-level ranch-style house outside a small town that could have been named Springfield, but that something had gone wrong inside it. I wanted to tell her that years ago Alice had been impor- tant to me, that my sister and I had looked to Alice for something we could not name, and had at least seen a picture of what love looked like. I wanted to tell her that no one in my family ever raised their voice while the television was on, that late at night even a bad television show could keep me from hearing the silence inside my own heart. I wanted to tell her that Ed Bauer and I were still alive, that both of us had always wanted to do what was right. Ann B. Davis stood, walked over to the trash can, and emptied her tray. She walked out of the cafeteria and into a small, gray town near Pittsburgh. I wanted her to *be* Alice. I wanted her to smile as if she loved me. I wanted her to say, "Buck up, kiddo, everything's going to be all right." And what I'm trying to tell you now is this: I grew up in a split-level ranch-style house outside a town that could have been anywhere. I grew up in front of a television. I would have believed her.

[handwritten annotations: apparent subject: Kissing / Deeper subject: Relationship w/ other women/people]

[handwritten: Read for reading / ↳ Structure & Comprehension.]

Anthony Farrington

KISSING

ANTHONY FARRINGTON teaches creative writing at the Indiana University of Pennsylvania. He is a graduate of the Iowa Writers' Workshop. His most recent work has been nominated for the Pushcart Prize and Best New American Voices, and appears or is forthcoming in *Peculiar Pilgrims: Stories From the Left Hand of God, Georgia Review, Glimmer Train Stories, Salt Hill,* and others. He was the Margaret Bridgman Scholar in Fiction at Bread Loaf in 2006, and he received a 2007 fellowship from the Pennsylvania Council on the Arts.

[handwritten: Goes back & forth.]

> So, go, breake off this last lamenting kisse
> —John Donne, *The Expiration*
> (from the 1669 edition of *Poems*)

This is a story about the mouth and the tongue, about conversations of one kind and another. This is a story about the first girl who ever kissed me. Her name was Lulu, and we were in the second grade. She was—exotically—a twin, and she had long red hair and bell-bottom pants. I still have two pictures of her. One from the first grade and one from the second. In one, I forget which, she is leaning up against me; she is smiling. Even then, especially then, I was terrified of her. Her electric body. Her hair and her fingers and her slender legs everywhere. She was the first.

The secret of good kissing is a relaxed mouth. Never, never pucker your lips, or kiss with the lips and teeth sealed firmly shut. . . . Let your lips go almost limp. Ease the tension from your chin. Automatically your teeth will part slightly and you will be able to slip that teasing tongue of yours into his mouth as the pressure of the kiss (and your passion) mounts.

Naturally . . . the trick is to slip in an embellishment here and there.[1]

---

1. "J." *The Sensuous Woman.* New York: Lyle Stuart, Inc., 1969. pp. 111–2.

Read like newspaper.

Jenny—who eventually married me—said that when she was younger she used to practice by kissing the mirror; she practiced by kissing the bedroom walls. She put on lipstick and kissed the entire room. When we dated, years later, the lipstick was still there—light purple stains, pink; perfect kisses, half kisses, kisses of surprise. There were kisses over her bed and along every wall. Embarrassed, Jenny scrubbed with toothbrushes and hand brushes but could never remove the stains of kisses. Some things stick, no matter what.

Jenny—who eventually divorced me—now lives with another man somewhere in the middle of Arkansas. I raise our children alone. I hear she wears lipstick that doesn't smudge or smear. She told this to our children. She seldom talks to me anymore. They call this lipstick *kissproof.*

Give me a kiss, and to that kiss a score;
Then to that twenty, add a hundred more:
A thousand to that hundred: so kiss on,
To make that thousand up a million.
Treble that million, and when that is done.
Let's kiss afresh, as when we first begun.[2]

INVENTED ADVISE COLUMN:

Question: Help! I'm a virgin. I've never even been kissed! I panic at the thought of touching or being touched. I'm desperate! Any advice?

Answer: Stick to butterfly kisses and Eskimo kisses; avoid the mouth. The first is for foreplay, the second is for post-play. The third—the mouth, my dear—is for yourself and for yourself only.

Question: My partner won't kiss me. All he wants is sex. It's the same routine.

Answer: Only kiss the irresistible. Small children, for example, or aging grandmothers. Or men who love you.

Question: Is it wrong to kiss a boy on the first date?

'Scuse me while I kiss the sky . . .

Answer: Whomsoever I shall kiss, that same is he; hold him fast.[3]

Sometimes, all that's left of love is tied up in song. With Deanne, who kissed me second, it was bubble gum pop and Air Supply—"lost in love" and "every woman in the world"—the music filling the small space of my car while we drove in the early evenings—her body against mine—fifteen years old (me seventeen) and lovely—her head on my shoulder and the windows open, the

---

2. Robert Herrick, from *To Anthea: Ah, My Anthea!*
3. Matt 26:48.

Speaking to past self?

wind and her long yellow hair blowing up and against my face. She was the second. _Reflective._

Now is your chance! The moment you feel the tip of your nose touch her scalp, purse your lips and kiss her, the while you inhale a deep breath of air that is redolent with the exquisite odor of her hair. It is then but a few inches to her ear. Touch the rim of her ear with your lips in a sort of brushing motion. Breathe gently into the delicate shell . . . From the ear to her neck is but another few inches. Let your lips traverse this distance quickly and then dart into the nape of the neck and, with your lips well pursed, nip the skin there, using the same gentleness as would a cat lifting her precious kittens.

Then, with a series of little nips, bring your lips around from the nape of her neck to the curving swerve of her jaw, close to the ear. Gently kiss the lobe of her ear. But be sure to return to the tender softness of her jaw. From then on, the way should be clear to you. . . .

All right. You have subtly kissed the corner of her mouth. Don't hesitate. Push on further to more pleasurable spots. Ahead of you lies that which had been promised in your dreams, the tender, luscious lips of the girl you love. But don't sit idly by and watch them quivering.

Act!

Lift your lips away slightly, center them so that when you make contact there will be a perfect union. Notice, only momentarily, the picture of her teeth in her lips, and, then, like a seagull swooping gracefully down through the air, bring your lips down firmly onto the lips of the girl who is quivering in your arms.

Kiss her!

Kiss her as though, at that moment, nothing else exists in the world. Kiss her as though your entire life is wrapped up into the period of the kiss. Kiss her.[4]

In the car, Deanne sang but she didn't want me to hear. So sometimes she sat facing her own window—the music taking her places—singing just loud enough that I could tell she was singing but just soft enough I couldn't distinguish her voice from the song.

With Jenny, it was Foreigner coming from a tinny cassette player—the ceiling and the walls closing in on us, her bed smelling of skin. Jenny was the third. And I eventually married her. Twelve years later, she kissed me goodbye and left me with two children. She says I must never use the word "abandon."

With April, it was Guns N' Roses. But let's not go there.

Kissing involves more than the mouth. It involves ancient nights, the deep smells of summer turning fall, cars cruising the four lanes on Saturday evenings, and music vibrating the air. In a gas station parking lot with neon lights shimmering on newly washed cars, my older brother tried to act casual. His arm was around his girlfriend, and he flicked the ashes of his cigarette dramatically. By looking at him,

---

4. Hugh Morris. _How to Make Love: The Secret of Wooing & Winning the One You Love._ N.p. 1936 [reprinted 1987]. pp. 16–7.

Uses these to interrupt story. Why?

Tells his story and giving a big picture too.

Teacher & learns in the story.

you would think he was perpetually bored. Or maybe very thoughtful. He was seldom either. Bones, his best friend, was there too, with Teresa—always Teresa. Bones and my brother sneaked me into the drive-in theater once, in the trunk of a purple LeMans. I don't remember a single kiss in the whole movie; but I remember sitting on the hood of the car and gaping at fifty-foot women and yards and yards of skin. When the movie was nearly over, my brother's girlfriend came back from the concession stand with a bag of popcorn to share with me. In the glow of the drive-in lights, her lips were berry; and as she came toward the car, she was pulling her fingers through her hair and walking so the whole wide world took a deep breath. I don't even remember her name.

Sometimes, the longing for those nights is tangible, so intimate, so lonely, that merely the thought of kissing breaks my heart with hope. Back then, let's be honest, my best friends and I rarely told each other about who we were kissing. There was something sacred there, or maybe we sensed our own vulnerabilities. Like most boys, we thought we knew what impressed girls: our cars (jacked-up and unbelievably fast), the nights of stealing beer, our car wrecks, stays at the police station. The smell of peppermint to this day makes me think of Danny Joe and Martha; one night—at Danny Joe's party—they were both drunk off their asses with homemade peppermint schnapps—kissing on the couch, crawling inside each other. What they had looked good, what they had seemed good, I literally stared until I collapsed with laughter; but even then they didn't stop.

Years later—I don't know how many anymore—Danny Joe danced with another woman; I think he kissed her too. And maybe there was more to it. Martha nearly left him for that. And the thought of Martha leaving him fills me with an overwhelming emptiness—a sudden retrospective disappearance of their present two-story house in west Wayland, Iowa, the dematerializing of their two strawberry-blonde girls playing on the swing-set Danny Joe made for them. The sudden loss of Danny Joe and Martha—together, at once—saying (to me) they're so sorry my wife left. They didn't think that could ever happen. Not to us.

Favorite definition: The dictionary says that a kiss is a "salute made by touching with the lips pressed closely together and suddenly parting them." From this it is quite obvious that, although a dictionary may know something about words, it knows nothing about kissing.[5]

• • •

5. Hugh Morris. *The Art of Kissing (1936)*. Qtd. in *The Book of Kisses*. Ed. William Cane. New York: St. Martin's Press, 1993. p. 13.

Lulu's kiss was electric and quick. Just at the corner of my mouth. She was the first.

Deanne was second. With her whole body shivering from the cold, she kissed me by the John Deere tractor in the machine shed at her father's farm.

Jenny wanted to kiss me so bad, she had me backed up against a green refrigerator; her boyfriend was in the next room. I told her to never do that again, and she went home crying. Well, you can imagine, I married her. Jenny was the third girl I kissed.

Robin was number four; she always gave me a friendly peck. She loved the Beatles like I did. Once, while reading the lyrics to "A Day in the Life," she cried at my mother's kitchen table. I was hers for the taking, but we never moved beyond the goodnight kiss. Years later, we got drunk together because we were still great friends. And I wanted to kiss her so badly. But I kept drinking instead and dreamed that many sad years later—

What he wanted.

From the personals:
Single divorced female seeks honest man and soft kisses.
SWM seeks big-breasted blonde. Looks not important.
SM seeks. Call 367-1078. ?

maybe fifteen—she would tell me that she had wanted to kiss me too. And sometimes I still think about that.

April kissed me and I kissed her. In that order. And I nearly broke down. Wondering where my wife was.

Carolyn was number six. She was so beautiful with the softest lips—like petals. I regret kissing her. She left me for her ex-husband. Kissing, like most everything, gets progressively more complicated. She was so beautiful.

Uses pop culture & literary references

Sometimes, the princess kisses the frog. Other times, the frog-prince kisses the sleeping princess. But let's face it, transformative kisses aren't practical. I went out with the prom queen once. But I didn't kiss her. We each loved someone else.

✗ *"And from this slumber you shall wake," said a fairy to Sleeping Beauty, "when true love's kiss the spell shall break."* [6]

From my mouth to yours: Number of women I've kissed: 6. Number of total kisses: 54,978. Excluding Lulu from the second grade: 54,977. Number of hickeys received: 37. Given: 62. Number of times my lips have bled: 33. Hers:

---

6. *Sleeping Beauty.* Walt Disney, 1959.

Each of them focuses on one thing in particular. Hair, lips not eyes... Why?

33. Number of goodbye/hello/goodnight kisses excluding mothers, daughters, sons, yada yada: 10,617. You are wondering how many women I've slept with. The answer is 3. Really, I should say two and a half. But I'll just say 3. Three.

But I don't want to talk about that.

Danny Joe told me that kissing was more intimate than fucking. That's why, he told me, you weren't supposed to kiss a whore. They don't like it. He said this as though he really knew. I think we were twelve or thirteen years old. To be fair, he also told me to never date a woman who played the trumpet. Their lips turn funny, he said. I just nodded. Frankly, he was always talking big. Kissing has a lot to do with bravado.

Favorite aphorism: Kissing a girl is like opening a jar of olives—hard to get the first one, but the rest come easy.[7]

In my hometown in southeast Iowa, most of my friends' first kisses took place during the fourth quarter of the local high school football games—under the bleachers or behind the rows of evenly parked, moonlit cars. The talk was bigger than the kisses. I think it was only kisses. But you know how boys talk.

Carolyn's mouth was soft, April's hard. The one was inviting, the other eager. One talked trash, the other whispered sweet nothings.

The third time my wife left me for good, April and I talked late into the night. She knew Jenny was gone. And I think, maybe, April was bored. We both should have known better. Because we both fell in love hard.

We were so drunk. April was the fifth. *Like this*, she said. And—god bless her—she showed me.

There is nothing wrong about a brief, affectionate goodnight kiss which will not arouse passion. Do not feel, however, that he won't ask you out again unless you kiss him the first night or that you must repay him for the coke and hamburger he bought you. This is too high a price to pay, even if you had a large coke.[8]

He considers a kiss meaning ful.

Mouth-to-mouth resuscitation is called *the kiss of life*. A drop of sealing-wax accidentally fallen beside the seal on a letter is also a *kiss*. There are chocolate kisses. Blown kisses. Air kisses. Continental kisses—which are kisses on both cheeks. A parting kiss is always singular, as in the kiss of death. *Judas came to*

7. Anonymous. Qtd. in *The Book of Kisses*. Ed. William Cane. New York: St. Martin's Press, 1993. p. 49.

8. Anne Culkin. *Charm for Young Women*. New York: Deus Books, 1963. p. 107.

Jesus. And kissed him.[9] My father, whistling appreciatively across the green felt of a pool table—a cue-stick in hand—would say the obvious: "Nice kiss," when one ball gently pushed another into a pocket.

A kiss is just a kiss. But a kiss can also be a smack, a peck, or a buss. Kissing can be smooching, Frenching, or making-out. Kiss me, you fool. Swap slobber. Suck face. Tickle her tonsils. I'm actually quite fond of the *dancing* tongue: the tongue polka and the tongue tango. Here's some advice: Avoid the tongue stranglers but encourage the tongue twisters. Kiss the Blarney Stone. Kiss the ground. Kiss the rod. I've played kiss and tell. And I've certainly kissed ass. If you don't like it, kiss off. Wait. Let's kiss and make up. Both of my children have asked me to, please, kiss it and make it better. But they're too big for that now.

Q: *How do I get my boyfriend to kiss* me?
A: *Take off something you're wearing. I mean like an earring. And toss your hair back and rub your earlobe. Describe the lovely feeling of not having pinched ears any more. Or take off your wristwatch or bracelet and rub your wrist and mention how good that feels.*

Tell him his shoulders look tense. . . . And that it's important to have relaxed shoulders. And to relax his shoulders he should move them in a circle—forward, then up, then back, then down. You demonstrate this, of course, because when your shoulders are back, your chest looks good.

He, of course, isn't doing it quite right, so you can put your hands on his shoulders to show him how. Then you can tell him his shoulders are not only tense, they're muscular.

How else physical contact?

Touch fingers when he hands you a drink. You shouldn't be smoking, because research says you can die from it, but if you are, hold his hand when he lights your cigarette.

When you laugh at something he says, laugh from the torso as you bend over and touch his arm. Or if he's said something serious, you can, wide-eyed, touch his arm as you say, 'You don't mean it!' . . .

Stand very close. Sit very close. (Not right against him; that's being too obvious.) Look very intensely at him.

This is known, in popular parlance, as giving a guy the come-on.

And he nearly always does.[10]

Best kiss: It began with "Truth or Dare" and really began with "Are you going to do it or what?"

Other best kiss: My first real kiss was with Deanne. We were alone and watching *The Muppet Show.* She must have been frustrated with me. We had been

---

9. Matt 26:49.
10. Ellen Peck. *How to Get a Teen-Age Boy and What To Do With Him When You Get Him.* 1969. pp. 230–1.

dating for months, and I hadn't nerve enough to kiss her yet. I was seventeen, and what did I know? So she finally took matters into her own hands. She started kissing my neck. And it was good. I hardly knew what Kermit was saying. And Deanne's lips were getting closer to my mouth. . . . *Whoa*, I was thinking. This is *it*. And that's when her father and mother pulled into the driveway.

Like she was shocked, Deanne shot to the other end of the couch and didn't look at me. I remember that the credits for the end of the show were rolling up and beyond the known universe. Deanne was sulking and mad at me for some reason. I really didn't understand why. Honest. Eventually, she stood up and left the room. I think she was crying.

I looked for her everywhere outside—under the big oak, in the hayloft, in her yellow car. I called her name. Finally, I found her in the machine shed. It was cold outside and she didn't have a coat on like I did. I went to her, and she was crying. I touched her face, her tears, and she began kissing me. Her arms went inside my jacket. She was crawling inside of me for warmth. She was shaking and kissing me. Her cheeks were cold, but her mouth was so warm and her face so wet. She would stop and smile at me—our noses almost touching—and then we would kiss again. I don't really recall how long we stayed in the cold. I remember that there was a dirt floor and that there were sparrows fluttering in the rafters.

When her lose gowne from her shoulders did fall and she me caught in her armes long and small therewithall swetely did me kysse and softely said dere hert howe like you this.[11]

Worst kiss: When Jenny left me for the last time—the real last time—we both knew it. After twelve years, this was it. Jenny left and stopped and left and stopped and came back again and again into the room. I knew what she wanted. But she had to ask first. She asked if she could kiss me goodbye.

For our honeymoon, Jenny and I went to Door County, Wisconsin. I booked a cabin on Lake Michigan for a full week. And, right off, Jenny acted as though she had made a mistake. She had made a mistake marrying me. The first night, she wouldn't kiss me. And she wouldn't let me kiss her either. I couldn't hold still. So I went down to the shore where it was all new to

What is a kiss? Why this, as some approve: The sure, sweet cement, glue, and lime of love.[12]

11. Sir Thomas Wyatt, [*They fle from me that sometyme did me seke*] (#53).
12. Robert Herrick, from *A Kiss*.

me: the waves, the *sound* of the waves, the two black islands in the distance, several lights winking so far away. The sun was setting, nearly gone. And I didn't know if the lights were from ships or from the other shore. I was raised amid cornfields. I had never seen so much water before. And it was cold; the wind was even and strong, going through my jacket.

Jenny must have followed me because she was suddenly there, behind me, still upset. She kept saying *I know*, softly—rubbing my shoulders with her hands. *I know. I know.* And I was lost. I had never seen anything so beautiful.

In the failing light—on the pebbled beach—my new wife wrapped her arms around my waist from behind. She put her head against the center of my back. I think she loved me then. I really do. But I don't know why she stayed there— just holding me so I couldn't hold her—until there was only the dark and the sounds of the waves, and there was nothing to do eventually but go on up the hill home.

It surprises me each time: a woman's hands on my back, on my face, in my hair—encouraging me—as though this is a good thing, this kiss.

And the parting of the lips. The tilt of the head. A type of forerunning gasp as though, "Buddy, I ain't coming up for air this time." And those hard kisses that go from the mouth to the neck back to the mouth. Those kisses that go lightly from the mouth to the cheek to the eyes to the mouth.

Do you want me to stop? April said.
No, I was thinking. God no.
Do you want me to stop?

This is fuzzy, because I was so drunk, but I think of it again and again—the fiercest desire I've ever seen. Out of the mouth. On the floor. Against the wall. God, this could have gone on forever.

But I stopped.

[Advice to the girl:] *Just when to stop [making out] differs among couples and individuals. In general, it's just before the boy begins to be insistent and urgent in his caresses. Up to that point a couple are enjoying their closeness; then suddenly the boy begins to perspire, his heart quickens its beat, his breathing becomes more rapid, and his fondling gets rougher and more intimate. At that time, the responsible girl must push him away . . .*

Or the boy, recognizing that what started as an expression of fondness now has become heightened sexual stimulation, can break the spell of the moment by rising to his feet, getting them both a drink of water, and suggesting a less intimate activity.[13]

---

13. Evelyn Millis Duvall. *The Art of Dating.* New York: Association Press, 1967. *pp. 210–11.*

When I first started kissing April, I thought no way was this going to work. She kissed too hard. Together, we watched entire movies, the ends of which I can't recall.

After our prom, Robin, who kissed me fourth, stayed in my car all night. I can still hear her laugh. I can still smell her perfume. She's the only one whose perfume I remember. She filled my whole mind.

That summer, Robin and I watched movies together, ate pizza; I gave her roses, other gifts. And every night I took her home, we kissed. Lightly. Like friends.

We have kiss'd away Kingdoms and provinces.[14]

Everyone said she was beautiful. But, to be honest, I never thought of her as beautiful until it hit me one day in the face. We grew up together, and that makes you blind sometimes. She was my mom's favorite.

When she worked at Hardees—a few months later—Danny Joe would tell me she came to work with hickeys on her neck—"Big old honking things," he said. And I wondered how I fit into the world. But I know it was my own fault. I knew it even then. If there was ever a chance with Robin, I let it get away.

Rule of life #1: Always kiss your mother goodbye.

Rule of life #2: Kiss often. And remember that KISS is an acronym for "Keep It Simple Stupid."

Rule of life #3: While kissing, keep your eyes closed. Hold your breath. Lose yourself.

The mouth is the most beautiful, the most sensitive, the most active organ you can reach while she's still dressed. The kiss is probably the single most important move toward the bedroom. It's the key! It turns her on—or off—and, since life is a lot better when you turn her on, you can hardly do too much homework in this lesson of love.

1. Don't crush her lips against her teeth to show your passion.

2. Don't squeeze the breath out of her as you're kissing her.

3. Don't try to ram your tongue down her throat in order to stimulate her.

4. Don't bite her lips.

5. Don't use a dry, birdlike, pecking kiss with no pressure at all.

6. Don't kiss with your mouth wide open and slobber all over her.

7. Don't drool as you kiss her.

8. Don't hold a kiss so long that she can't breathe.

9. Don't don't, don't have bad breath.[15]

• • •

---

14. William Shakespeare, *Antony and Cleopatra*, III, viii, 17–18.

15. "M." *The Sensuous Man*. New York: Dell Publishing Co., 1971. pp. 75–6.

The mouth is where the body and language meet. The mouth is also the site of proper language and improper body. The proper body is regulated through language. Our mouths caution us to keep civilized, despite our bodies.

Where does the body begin and end? Kissing is a type of penetration of the body. Kissing is being penetrated. What divides my body from your body? Bodies penetrate; bodies can be penetrated. Bodies can penetrate themselves: tongue in cheek, lick your wounds, practice onanism religiously. But bodies can come inside other bodies in only a few ways. Kissing is one of them.

My mother used to say that the devil could enter any one of our holes: 7 for girls, 6 for boys. The mouth is just one of the gateways. We paint our lips, we decorate our language, we monitor what we say. **Rules of life:** *Keep a civil tongue. Chew with your mouth closed. Never kiss on the first date. Speak only when spoken to. Shut up, shut up.*

Despite what the Victorians might have supposed, the opposite of the mouth is not the asshole. These are both wet places, warm. These are places of fever. To enter the gateway of either is to be consumed. These are matters of the tongue; these are matters of taste.

I am not using my mouth when I write this. I am using my hands. Like kissing, writing is a form of body-language. Later, I'll type this (I'm doing it now). Later, I'll listen to the sentences over and over in my head. I might delete this section. Later, I might read this out loud—to hear how it sounds on my tongue. Later, I will use my mouth. But right now, I am using my hands. Writing and kissing have this—at least—in common. They are both languages of the body.

Here's a grocery list from Carolyn. The list was folded and placed on the kitchen table for me to find. There were caricature lips straddling the tri-fold. "Envelopes. Stamps. Maraschino cherries. Kiwi fruit. Condoms?" We hadn't slept together yet, so she sput a question mark there. After the question mark she wrote, "It's up to you." Then she wrote, "Jumbo pack."

My father kissed my mother three times a day, whether he wanted to or not—once when he left for work, once when he got home from work, and once before he went to bed. My mother (who has been dead for countless years) used to think it was cute when I turned away from couples kissing on the television. "Don't look, Tony," she would yell. "Kissing. Ssik!" (—with an emphasis on snake.

My mother was a devout Christian.) And she would laugh her own particular laugh. I adored her. I thought kissing was gross just to please her. Later, when I got much older, she apparently worried about me (I was a sensitive child and maybe that translated into homophobic hysteria). Mother would tell me how nice kissing was. She would egg me on. "Look at her," my mother would say, pointing to some girl all alone on the football bleachers. "Wouldn't you like to kiss her?"

. . .

Lulu was technically the first. She was a twin. Both Lulu and Sue wore bell-bottoms. Both had deep auburn hair. Both had freckles like my mother; both were gorgeous. Lulu had apparently convinced her twin sister and Jo Jo Leichty to help chase me. Jo Jo Leichty had translucent skin; you could see bluish blood veins on the undersides of her arms and along her neck and jaw line. There was something always very delicate about her. I never kissed Jo Jo, but I thought about it once or twice—many years later.

Each noon, at my elementary school, I ran for my life. It was early May and it was breezy. I was young, and I could find joy in just running, until the day I was trapped behind the merry-go-round. Sue came from one side. Jo Jo came from the other. And they crucified me in the corner. Lulu stepped up and walked over the merry-go-round. She wasn't messing around. Her lips were puckered (dramatically so) and

The opposite of a lover is a dentist. The opposite of kissing is the objectification of the mouth—a focus on bone, enamel, and metal. (We want our lovers in our mouths; we want to be swallowed whole.)

she wasn't aiming for my forehead. She wasn't going for my cheek. She was zeroing in right for the money. Right for the kisser. And this was more than I bargained for.

For a moment I thought yes, no, yes, no; but I didn't have all the time I needed to think this through. So I decided no. And I turned my face.

But Lulu was fast. She lunged forward.

She didn't get me on the cheek as *I* had planned. She didn't get me on the lips as she had planned. Instead, we compromised. She kissed me at the corner of my mouth.

When Jill complains to Jack for want of meat,
Jack kisses Jill, and bids her freely eat.
Jill says, Of what? Says Jack, On that sweet kiss,
Which full of nectar and ambrosia is,
The food of poets.[16]

And I know she was only eight, but it was soft. And it was warm. And little cartoon bluebirds were circling my head, twittering drunkenly. This was my first kiss.

Rule of life #1 (revised): After your mother dies in a traffic accident, on August 4th, 1990, one day before your father's birthday, always kiss those who love you. Remember—upon kissing you, five hours before her death—your mother was weeping because she already missed you.

---

16. Robert Herrick, from *Upon Jack and Jill. Epigram.*

✗ **Rule of life #(n-1):** *Revise.* Mathematically, this is the only equation that has a chance. Also, occasionally let the dishes pile up.

Deanne used to surprise me with secrets in her mouth. Usually it was just a piece of ice tucked under her tongue or a piece of candy. But once, with her tongue, she pushed an unwrapped condom into my mouth with her tongue. It tasted horrible, and she looked at me strangely. I looked back trying to save the moment. But it was all shot to hell. She started laughing, and we couldn't speak to each other for nearly a week without hysterics. We never used that condom, or any other. We were always too scared and never grew out of it.

Regarding Social Graces:
Q: *What's are the rules about public displays of affection?*
A: *Don't.*
Q: *Could you be more specific?*
A: *Kissing is a privilege.*
Q: *Why do social rules about kissing apply primarily to girls? What about boys?*
Q: *Why don't you answer? When is kissing with abandon okay?*
Q: *When you look at your current partner, with what great sadness do you remember a particular kiss?*

What was your longest kiss?
　I don't remember.
What was your sexiest kiss?
　Like I could tell that one. I hate talking about this, if you want the truth. I'm very private.
Most memorable kiss?
　The girl I most wanted to kiss when I was fourteen was a girl who worked with me in the bean fields. She was seventeen and deaf and drop-dead gorgeous. I carried a whistle around my neck which I would blow if I needed to get her attention. She could feel the vibrations. When I spoke to her, she watched my lips move. While *listening* to me, she always smiled. When she spoke to the hearing, she used her hands to sign. I watched her mouth. She had crazy, curly hair that blew across her face; and she would sweep the hair from her eyes, glance back at me, and smile radiant. I thought I was in love with her. And I think she knew that. We never kissed.

　No. This is an essay about kissing. What was your most intimate kiss?

　Didn't I answer that? Maybe when my little girl hung on to me one day after our first Halloween apart (it was Jenny's year for tricking and treating) saying that she missed—

　No. Tell me. What was your most embarrassing most life-changing most wet kiss?

　Listen. This is a story. One time, when I was eighteen—

　No. Who have you kissed since this was written?

·　·　·

Not long after Jenny moved away, I started to get sick. We had been together for twelve years. But I finally got up out of our bed, walked by my son's room, and I saw him surprised—ghost-like in his white T-shirt—running to his bed. He was five years old. And it was two in the morning. He was running to his bed—so quiet, so much like an apparition—that I wasn't even sure I had seen him. I had been preoccupied.

Step one: *Touch her face.*
Step two: *Part your lips.*
Step three: *Kiss her.*
Step four: *Let go.*

My son was awake, pretending to be asleep. I wondered, for a brief drop of a second, how many nights he had been doing this. I wondered how many nights he was pretending when Jenny and I talked about her leaving.

He was nearly crying because he thought he was in trouble. I don't know why. I thought maybe—like me—he couldn't sleep; I wasn't mad. But he didn't know that. He said his sister had made a noise that scared him. He had a bad dream.

He wanted to know why I couldn't sleep. I knew of course, but I told him I didn't know—which, of course, was also true. He had scared me. Anything strange with the kids and I'm frightened.

Before I could shut his door, though, and latch it completely—with sudden passion—he yelled into the darkness, completely terrified. "Wait Daddy wait!" he said. His voice was so sudden and large. "Kiss me," he said. "You forgot to kiss me."

Uses descriptive language well.

Son => By ending here reenforces idea of importance of kiss. Relationship use these as language & contact.

(Kept jumping back & forth...)

Used consistently => Rules in piece piece.

Harrison Candelaria Fletcher

THE BEAUTIFUL CITY OF TIRZAH

HARRISON CANDELARIA FLETCHER is an essayist and journalist whose work has appeared in *New Letters, Fourth Genre, Puerto del Sol*, and *Cimarron Review*. An essay finalist for the 2007 National Magazine Award, Fletcher has also been awarded the 2005 *New Letters* Dorothy Churchill Cappon Prize for best essay and a *New Letters* Readers' Award. He has been a finalist for the PEN Center USA, Eugene S. Pulliam, *Iowa Review*, and *Gulf Coast* awards. He received a BA from the University of New Mexico and an MFA from Vermont College. A native New Mexican, he lives with his wife and two children in Denver, Colorado, and has recently completed a memoir, *Man in a Box*.

Animals arrive after my father dies. Dogs. Cats. Ducks. Geese. A goat. A peacock. They wander into our yard several years into his absence, appearing on our doorstep, or catching our eye from feed store cages. Always, we take them in. We line our laundry room with bath towels, bed sheets and blankets. We fill cereal bowls with tap water, corn scratch and table scraps. We dab cut skin, comb matted fur and smooth broken feathers. Then we flick off the light and watch them sleep. Strays make the best pets, my mother tells the five of us kids. They won't leave.

Beggar's night, 1970. My big brother is late. Again. Our mother has given him permission to play on the ditch behind our house and to see if the neighbors will give him Halloween candy a day early, but when I peek out the back window to check on him, the sun has already set and the shadows drip like ink from the cottonwoods. I don't say anything to our mother, who sits stiffly in her antique rocker chair, tapping a Russian olive switch on the floor. I scoot across the living room on my knees and take my place in front of the TV, where my three sisters are watching *Dr. No*. It's a school night. We've changed into our flannel pajamas. Our hair is damp from the bath.

"Mom!"

The back door thuds open. My brother clomps through the kitchen, breathing hard, as if he's been running. My mother stands, grips the switch and intercepts him in the dining room. The overhead light flicks on, bright as an interrogation lamp.

"Wait!" my brother pleads. "I found something. Look."

I scramble to my feet and jockey for position with my sisters. Our brother reaches into his corduroy jacket, extracts a small bundle, and opens his hands. A baby bird squints at us.

My mother leans the switch against the wall.

"An owl," she says, kneeling. "It's adorable. Where did you find it?"

My brother had been hurrying home along the ditch when he heard a rustling from the bushes. When he slid down the embankment to investigate, he startled a hatchling that skittered through the dust but couldn't fly. He thought it might have broken its wing, so he scooped it up.

"I looked for the nest but couldn't find it," he says. "Then I saw the mother by a tree. Someone shot her or something."

Our mother holds the owl to the warmth of her body. It looks up at her, and blinks.

An ornithologist who lives down the street tells my mother we've adopted a screech owl, probably a female, given the description over the phone. Although it's not allowed under city codes, it should be okay for us to nurse the chick until she gets stronger. She's not a danger to us, although we might want to wear gloves when handling her. Feed her bits of stew meat, the ornithologist suggests, and later mice. Within six months, the owl should grow to her full height of five inches. We should keep her in a large cage or an enclosed room. And watch out for our cats.

My mother follows his advice, but vetoes the cage. She wants the owl to fly freely in her home. She retrieves a cardboard box from Safeway, lines it with towels and places a piñon branch inside before setting the carton atop the dining room pottery case where the cats can't easily reach.

The owl is the size and shape of an upside-down pear. Her feathers are gray with black and white speckles. She has two tufts on her head that look like ears, or horns. Her beak is sharp and shiny black and so are her talons. What I like best are her eyes, a piercing yellow, the size of dimes. When she looks at me, it's as if she's reading my mind, or seeing something I can't. One of my aunts can't even meet her gaze. The owl's eyes, she says, are too human.

My mother considers the bird's name carefully. Usually, she names the pets after artists she admires, like Toshiro, the Japanese actor, for the silky black cat. Sometimes, she chooses characters from her favorite films, like Tonya, from *Dr.*

Zhivago, for the German shepherd cross. Occasionally, she selects Spanish words that just sound nice, like Sol Pavo, sun bird, for the peacock. When I adopt a mallard duckling from the feed store, I pick Hercules, my favorite matinee hero, and the nickname my father gave me because I was stronger than other newborns in the nursery. For the owl, my mother decides upon Tirzah, after a Hopi basket maker.

"Tirzah," my mother says, savoring the syllables, which break like sunlight through her window crystals, turquoise and yellow.

"What does it mean?" I ask.

"It's an old name," she says. "A religious name. From the Bible."

Later, I look it up in a library dictionary: "Tirzah—A city in Palestine, a beautiful place alluded to in the Song of Solomon ('You are as beautiful, my darling, as Tirzah')."

During the first few weeks, Tirzah stays put on the pottery case. But as she gains strength, she flutters from her box, hovers a few seconds, and drops to the floor. Worried the owl will break its wings, my mother drapes the box each night with a sheet. But as soon as morning comes, she throws off the cover and sets the container on the dining room table while she makes breakfast, draws in her sketch pad, or pays bills. Tirzah hops out immediately, waddles over, and nibbles her pen. If my mother leaves the room, the owl tries to follow. The only way my mother can finish her household chores is to wrap the owl in a wash cloth and tuck her in the breast pocket of her denim work shirt. Tirzah remains there for hours, lulled by my mother's heartbeat.

My grandmother grew up on a farm village on the western bank of the Rio Grande, the oldest of nine children. She hated every minute of it, the hard work and the animals, but she learned the old ways despite herself. She knows which herbs make which teas, how to brand cattle and castrate goats, and how to make red wine and corn whiskey. She also knows about spirits, which visit her dreams. Unlike my mother, who also has visions in her sleep, my grandmother sends the specters away for fear they'll claim her. Sometimes I play with my toy knights on the kitchen table while she and my mother make tortillas and gossip. Every so often I hear them whispering in Spanish about dead relatives. When my grandmother catches me eavesdropping, and she always catches me, she laughs under her breath and beckons me with a long arthritic finger. "Come here, *mi hijito*," she says, leaning forward on the edge of her chair, clutching a shiny black handbag. In a low voice, through the Crisco smoke and flour dust, she tells me about the fireballs dancing along the Rio Grande bosque, the footsteps dragging down her hallway at midnight, and the hooded crone who transformed into a banshee and chased two of her brothers home on the irrigation ditch between Alameda and Corrales. "It's true," she says, nodding at my wide eyes, then breaking into a smile of bright red lipstick and crooked teeth. "Did you go to church like I told you?"

On Sunday evenings, my grandmother stops by our house for pot roast. When the owl flutters over her head during one such visit, my grandmother makes the sign of the cross. Owls are bad omens, she grumbles. Navajos consider them evil spirits. *Brujas* use them to deliver messages.

"*Que fea*," she scolds my mother. "What have you brought into your home?"

"I think she's beautiful," my mother replies, shrugging.

When Tirzah settles on a chair back directly across from her, my grandmother holds the owl's gaze. Then she slips a glow-in-the-dark rosary from her purse, turns her head, and spits.

I don't go camping, like the other kids on my block. I don't go fishing, boating, or even to Uncle Cliff's Family Land. My mother doesn't like tourists. She doesn't like to do what everyone else does. On the weekends, we go exploring. We pile into her metallic green '67 Comet and hit the back roads. We visit churches, graveyards, ranch towns and adobe ruins, chasing a culture she says is vanishing before our eyes. She talks to old people and collects antique tables and chairs while I run with my siblings through the juniper and ponderosa pine playing *Last of the Mohicans*.

On a Saturday morning washed clean by spring rain, we take my grandfather's pickup north to Truchas, a farm village so high in the Sangre de Cristos we almost touch the clouds. In a grassy meadow beside the main road, my grandfather discovers a slice of aspen bark, eight feet long, crescent shaped, with a knot hole at one end. My uncle, who lives with us, says it looks like a cobra, but I think it looks like a dragon. My mother says it has character, so we pitch it into the truck bed.

Before heading back to Albuquerque, we stop at the *tiendita* for gas, chile chips and root beer. The old man behind the counter tells us the bark was cut by lightning a few nights earlier. He saw the flash and heard the boom. This makes my mother smile. Great symbolism, she says.

Back home, she and my uncle nail the plank across the living room wall as the centerpiece of her artifact collection. Tirzah notices immediately. She flies from the dining room pottery case and claims the perch as her own, sliding to the knothole, and watching us through the dragon's eye.

My brother finds most of our strays. Or they find him. He'll see a German shepherd digging in a garbage can, walk right up, and it'll lick his hand, a friend for life. He has a way with animals, which soothe him in a way our mother can't.

He was six when our father died. He has the most memories. I was two. I remember almost nothing. We're polar opposites, as our mother likes to say. She's right. My brother loses his temper like the strike of a match, plays hardball without a glove, and keeps a Mexican switchblade in his drawer. He's always moving, always fidgeting, always running, as if he's afraid to look over his shoulder. I'm steady, docile and brooding, like my duck, Hercules, with his blunt beak and orange feet, quite happy never to leave his yard.

On weekday afternoons, Tirzah waits by the front window for my brother to return from school. She hoots when he shuffles through the driveway, flies to his room while he changes into blue jeans, and perches patiently on his shoulder while our mother tethers them together with a strand of yarn; boy's wrist to owl's leg. Task complete, they step outside to straddle his Stingray bike. I watch from the porch as Tirzah's eyes swallow light and motion; the flashing chrome handlebars, the fluttering cottonwood leaf. "Be careful," our mother says, but my brother ignores her. He stands on his pedals and steers a wide circle under the street lamp, gathering speed for the lap around the block. Tirzah grips his jacket, and leans into the wind.

The owl isn't my pet, although I'd like her to be. She won't come when I call, perch on my finger, or accept stew meat from my hand, as she does with my mother, uncle and brother. It's not that I'm afraid. It's more that she's too beautiful to touch. When I get nervous, she flies away.

One afternoon, while I'm doing homework, Tirzah flutters down to the dining room table.

"Hi, pretty girl," says my mother, who sits beside me sewing a blouse. "Are you thirsty?"

Tirzah waddles up to me, ignoring the water bowl my mother slides forward.

I tap the pencil eraser on my teeth.

"Go ahead," my mother says. "Pet her. She won't bite."

"I know. She just doesn't like me."

"That's not true. Scratch her head. She loves that. Rub in little circles."

I extend the pencil. Tirzah flinches, eyes wide, preparing to fly.

"See!"

"Just wait. Try again. Slower this time."

I inch the eraser forward until it touches the owl's head. Tirzah squints, but stays put.

"Good," my mother says. "Use your finger. See how funny it feels? Like a ping pong ball?"

Tirzah closes her eyes and leans into the pressure. The more she relaxes, the more I relax.

After a few minutes, the owl curls her toes and rolls onto her side, asleep.

My grandfather visits us sometimes on the way home from his evening shift as a university security guard. At 65, after raising eight children, picking fruit and paving highways, he insists on holding a job. He nods hello, settles into a corner rocker, hangs his gray fedora on his bony knee, and nurses a cold Coors longneck. My grandfather doesn't talk much. He prefers to watch, listen and absorb the warmth of a family life he never had as a boy. His father died when he was eight. When his mother remarried, she sent him to a boarding school in Santa Fe. He ran away soon afterward, walking a hundred miles through the Rio Puerco badlands to the mining village of Marquez, where he eventually found work. He slept in barns on those nights, bedding down with horses, alfalfa and streaks of moonlight. Owls watched him from the rafters.

On one of his visits to our house, Tirzah flutters over to his armrest. My grandfather extends a finger and she hops on. He raises her to his nose, and smiles.

Each winter, our house fills with the sweet scent of piñon. We have no fireplace or wood-burning stove, so my mother sprinkles trading post incense over the steel grate of our living room floor furnace. It reminds her of childhood, she says of the smell, crumbling sawdust sticks between her fingers, then standing back while orange sparks swirl before her eyes. As a girl, she stoked the potbelly stove in her grandmother's kitchen. Piñon reminds her of black coffee in tin cups, thick cotton quilts and crackling orno flames. Piñon takes her back, she tells me, all the way back.

I take my mother's place when she leaves to prepare supper, standing in the hot current until my blue jeans burn my legs. As Tirzah glides through the room, white smoke curling from her wings, I imagine I'm soaring through the clouds beside her, or drifting like an apparition above the polished tables, brass lamps and Navajo rugs, haunting this room forever.

On nights before art show openings at the state fair, I sleep to the hiss of my uncle's propane torch and the click of his sculptor's tools. He's my mother's youngest brother, fourteen years her junior. He moved in with us four years after my father died because my mother didn't feel safe alone with five children on the ragged edge of northwest Albuquerque. She also wanted a male role model for my brother and me, although my uncle was barely out of his teens at the time. He likes The Doors, Jimi Hendrix and Country Joe and the Fish. He favors a beard and long hair, too, and walks barefoot everywhere, even in the mountains. I think he looks like George Harrison stepping onto the crosswalk of my mother's favorite album, *Abbey Road*. My grandmother thinks he looks like Jesus. She wants him to be a priest, to help atone for her sins, but instead he becomes an artist. With needle-nose pliers and rods of Pyrex glass, he creates intricate figurines of Hopi eagle dancers, Mexican *vaqueros* and Navajo shepherds, then mounts them on driftwood, sandstone and volcanic rock. I watch him from my pillow with his wild hair and welder's glasses spinning solid into liquid into solid again, crafting icy figures from fire. Tirzah perches above his worktable, drawn as I am to his clear blue flame.

My mother wants to bless our pets. Although she left the Catholic Church after my father died, she wants divine protection for our strays. So, on a warm Sunday in February, we load the ducks, geese, peacock, goat and owl into our Comet, and attend the outdoor ceremony.

We stand in line behind a dozen puppies, kitties, gerbils and bunnies. The priest chuckles from the gazebo as he sprinkles holy water. When our turn arrives, he stops mid-motion and appraises us from behind silver-rimmed eyeglasses. My brother slouches before the dais, arms folded, Tirzah on his shoulder. I kneel beside the black Nubian goat, which suckles nosily from its baby bottle. My oldest sister cradles the peacock; the two other girls hold ducks and geese. Our mother lingers on the steps with her eyes hidden behind Jackie O. sunglasses. We're long-haired, tie-dyed and proud of it, in full bloom eight years after my father died, surrounded by the animals who brought new life into our home. Parishioners scowl. A poodle yaps. A news photographer snaps our portrait. After a long pause, the priest mumbles a prayer. The next day, we make the front page.

Tirzah surprises us. When one of the dogs slinks through the house, she contracts her feathers, squints, and becomes as thin as a dry branch, camouflaged completely against the gray aspen plank. She changes direction in mid-flight, too, hovering like a helicopter, swiveling her head, and returning silently the way she came. She's also a hunter. When we place a chunk of stew meat before her, she puffs to twice her normal size, dilates her pupils, and pounces. She thumps the meat hard against the perch then flings it to the floor. Talons scratching hardwood, yellow eyes blazing, she stalks her meal. Finding it, she stretches her beak wide and swallows it whole.

. . .

During the day, the sun is too bright for the owl's eyes, so she seeks dark corners to sleep. One morning, when the temperature hits 85, one of my sisters reaches into the hall closet to flick on the swamp cooler, but leaves the door ajar. The chain is broken on the overhead bulb, and the closet is always pitch black. Tirzah, gazing toward the opening from her living room perch, flutters atop the closet door. I hold my breath. My sister calls our mother. Normally, the closet is off limits to us kids. We're not supposed to disturb the relics inside, the old photos, packaged artwork, and mothballed uniforms, dusty pharmaceutical journals and broken ham radio gear once belonging to our father. We try to shoo Tirzah away, but she won't budge. She will only stare into the cool abyss. After a moment, she lowers her head and hops inside. From then on, the hall closet becomes her sanctuary. To fetch her, I must reach into the darkness, brushing my father's things.

My brother finds another stray, a baby meadowlark that had fallen from a cottonwood into an alfalfa field near his school. He can't find the nest, so he tucks the orphan under his arm and carries it home. Our mother swaddles the chick in a washcloth, fetches some old newspapers and phones the ornithologist. I watch her fill an eyedropper with water and hold it to the bird's beak. She adores meadowlarks, she says after hanging up. As a girl, while staying with her grandparents in Corrales, she often woke to the song of meadowlarks in the apple orchards across the road.

"It was so beautiful," she tells me, puckering her lips to whistle. "But sad, too."

She retrieves an extra birdcage from the back porch, places the chick inside and covers the wire dome with a bed sheet, as the ornithologist instructed. Standing on her tiptoes, she sets the bundle atop the pottery case, away from the cats. Tirzah watches from her living room.

The next morning, I hear my mother scream. In the dining room, I find her holding the birdcage. In the center lies the meadowlark, wet with blood.

"Poor little thing," she cries, swatting a tabby off the table. "See what you did!"

My uncle steps inside from the back yard, examines the bird, and concludes that its skull has been crushed. He checks the cage for damage. Finding none, he snatches up the cat and holds its paw to the wire bars, but its arm is too thick to fit through. Stumped, he searches the house for clues. On the aspen plank, he discovers bits of wet gray fuzz. After retrieving Tirzah from the closet, he holds her tightly with one hand, then uses the other to extend one of her long bony legs, which slips neatly into the cage, within easy reach of where the meadowlark had slept.

"You dirty rat!" my uncle says, holding the owl to his face. "Did you kill that poor bird?"

Tirzah bites his thumb, wriggles away, and flutters to the living room.

She scowls at us the rest of the day. She won't even come to my mother.

I have no bed and no room. I sleep on an aluminum cot beside the antique church pew in our living room. My mother buys me Peanuts sheets to make me feel better but I hate that cot, sliding it down the hallway each night. The foam rubber mattress smells like dirty socks. The joints pinch my pajamas. Be patient, my mother tells me. For my tenth birthday, she'll restore one of the iron headboards on the back porch. Soon, I'll be able to join my uncle and brother in the boys' room.

When she switches off the floor lamp and the ten o'clock news, I'm alone. I lie back under the silver glow of the curb side street light with the clicks from the vintage clock and the creaks of old walls. From the haze of half sleep, I sense Tirzah awaken. I hear scratching. Feel the weight of eyes. Breathe in the aroma of mothballs and dust. I snap awake and sit up, but there's only a whisper, an echo, a slight disturbance of air.

The longer she stays with us, the more stir-crazy Tirzah becomes. Every few weeks or so, she flies into the broad living room window, unable to see the glass, confused when she can't pass through. My mother draws the curtains, then replaces the drapes with bamboo shades, but whenever a sparrow darts by outside, Tirzah chases after it, straight into the glass. My uncle, fearing the owl will crack her skull or break the window, nails a row of Russian olive branches to the outside of the frame. Tirzah settles on a chair back, gazing through the bars.

One afternoon, the owl goes missing. She's not on her perch, in the closet, or in the back rooms. I search under the beds, behind the bookshelves, inside cabinets. I search with my siblings for nearly an hour, but we can't find her. My mother sits in her rocker, jaw muscle flexing.

"She's gone," she mutters. "I know she is. One of you brats must have left the front door open again. How many times have I told you to close that damn door?"

My uncle thumps across the hardwood floor checking behind chairs and tables. When one of the dogs slinks by, he kicks it. "Where's the flashlight? Who took the flashlight?"

I stand with my sisters in the dining room. I didn't leave the door open. I didn't do anything. But I feel like I did, like I always do when one of the pets is in trouble, like something that happened a long time ago is about to happen again.

"Don't just stand there," my mother says. "Look under the table again."

My little sister starts to cry.

Above the scrape and knock of old wooden chairs, we hear a muffled sound.

"Hoo."

"Hush!" my mother says. "Listen. . . ."

"Hoo."

We turn toward the pottery case, to a Zuni water bowl on a back shelf. Inside it, glaring at us over the rim, is Tirzah. She'd settled inside to sleep, but woke during our commotion.

"There you are!" My mother rushes forward. "My Tirzah. . . ."

My sisters gather around her. My uncle snaps a photo.

I hesitate before joining them. I don't like what I see in the owl's eyes. She appears wary, guarded, disapproving, as if she's seeing my family for the first time.

We're late returning home from an outing up north. The horizon burns magenta as we race blue shadows home. We arrive in darkness. My uncle flicks on the house lights while my mother fires the floor furnace. Tirzah, who hasn't eaten since morning, hoots from her perch. My mother squeaks open the refrigerator, scans the shelves, but finds no stew meat, only breakfast steak. She checks the clock. Safeway has just closed. The breakfast steak is fresh, so she chops it for the owl.

The next day, Tirzah won't eat or drink. She barely flies. The ornithologist asks my mother to read the steak label to him over the phone. She does, her voice barely a whisper. The breakfast steak has a chemical protein that stew meat does not, he informs her. Tirzah was poisoned.

My mother paces the living room. Me and my sisters pray to St. Francis of Assisi.

The following morning, I find my mother sobbing at the dining room table. She'd woken up early to check on Tirzah and found her motionless in the water bowl. The thirsty owl had leaned over the rim and fallen inside. Too weak to climb out, Tirzah drowned.

My uncle digs deep in the backyard cactus garden, grunting white puffs of steam. My mother stands beside him holding a shoebox. Inside it lies the owl, wrapped in a washcloth. The air is still. The sky is pink and orange, the colors of dusk, of dawn. My uncle tosses the shovel aside and it clangs against the cold ground. He and my mother shuffle away, heads down, seeking driftwood or a rock to mark the grave. I stare into the hole, another space I will never fill.

After a few minutes, my uncle returns with a piñon branch. Without a word, my mother lowers the shoebox into the fine red sand. We bury Tirzah among the prickly pear, yucca and chamisa, beside the goat, the peacock and the mallard duck named Hercules.

Diane Glancy

SUN DANCE

DIANE GLANCY has published many books of poetry, fiction, and nonfiction. Her newest collection of poems, *Asylum in the Grasslands*, was published in 2007. She is also the author of *Rooms: New and Selected Poems, In-Between Places* (essays), and *The Dance Partner: Stories of the Ghost Dance*. She was awarded a 2003 National Endowment for the Arts Fellowship and the 2003 Juniper Poetry Prize from the University of Massachusetts Press for *Primer of the Obsolete*. Her novels include *Stone Heart: The Journey of Sacajawea on the 1804–06 Lewis and Clark Expedition* and *Pushing the Bear: The 1838–39 Cherokee Trail of Tears*. She is currently working on *Pushing the Bear: Resettlement*. Glancy also received an American Book Award, a Minnesota Book Award, the Pablo Neruda Prize for Poetry, and the Cherokee Medal of Honor. She is a professor at Macalester College in St. Paul, Minnesota, where she has taught Native American literature and creative writing. She is now on a four-year sabbatical/early retirement program. She holds the visiting Richard Thomas Chair at Kenyon College for 2008–2009. She received her MFA from the University of Iowa.

> She practiced both religions at the same time and at random. Her soul was healthy and at peace, she said, because what she did not find in one faith was there in another.
> —*Gabriel García Márquez*,
> Of Love and Other Demons

It was raining when I left St. Paul on Interstate 35 south for the Sun Dance on the Rosebud Reservation just west of Mission, South Dakota. It's 523 miles to the particular dance I was going to. There are others. But this one I knew through Mazakute Native American Mission in St. Paul. I went to the Sun Dance last summer, and wanted to go again to find some words to put it in perspective. To understand more than my own way. To understand why I wanted to return to a ceremony that was not in my culture.

Two hours later, at Interstate 90 in southern Minnesota, I turned west. Another four hours, and I stopped at the lookout above the Missouri River nearly halfway across South Dakota. There isn't much between the low sky and the prairie, except the Missouri River which cuts into the land. The river is green in its valley. Like one of those nineteenth-century landscapes. If you don't look at the bridge. And the traffic.

I read a plaque.

Lewis & Clark / 1804 / ate plums & acorns from the burr oaks / killed a buffalo & magpie / dried equipment / repacked boats / camped again 1806 on the return trip.

I felt the raised letters on the plaque with my hand as if they were the low hills. I ran my finger between them as if my finger were the river. I thought of the site of the Mandan village farther north on the Missouri, where another plaque says the whole tribe was wiped out by smallpox.

A few hours later, I exited Interstate 90 at Murdo. I took Highway 83 south for the last sixty-three miles of the trip. At the junction of Highway 18, I turned west a short distance, then south again at a sign that says *Mission*. Later I turned onto Highway 1, with the *1* on an arrowhead. Somewhere, after one turn or another, the road to Mission goes east and the open land of the Rosebud Reservation is west. The highway descended into a sharp valley, curved around a gas station and convenience store, and a few buildings of Sinte Gleska College, then climbed the hill. No name of the town. No names on streets. Nothing to let you know where you are. At the top of the hill, I turned south again at a sign marked *St. Francis*. Somehow the roads shift and boundaries are not remembered once you passed.

My ears popped and the land seemed high under the sky. I saw a butte to the west and the gray trail of the highway up and down across the land to the south. And it rained. I watched the cattle grazing through the nodding wipers. I passed the Rosebud Timber Reserve, a few clumps of pastel reservation houses, some with satellite dishes, and a trail of smoke from the garbage burn.

In St. Francis, I found the water tower road and turned west on BIA 105. It was about seven miles to the ridge where the Sun Dance is held. Soon I saw the large camp of tents and teepees. I left the road and drove through the rutted field toward the north section where I found people I knew from St. Paul.

The field is on a ridge high above a valley filled with pines. It's pasture except for the third week in July when it's used for the Sun Dance. I passed the vans and trucks and cars, the teepees and tents, the Coleman stoves and campfires. Children ran everywhere and groups of people sat by their tents. It stopped raining and the smell of cedar and sage and cooking fires filled the air.

In the center of the camp is the Sun Dance arena, which looked like an old brush-arbor church-camp meeting in Oklahoma. But this was the Sun Dance and I was going to see it on its own terms.

In the middle of the Sun Dance arena is the cottonwood tree that had been cut and carried into the circle and placed upright again. The cottonwood because it holds water. Its branches were tied up with ropes, and prayer ties or tobacco ties hung from the tree. Black for West. Red for North. Yellow for East. White for South. Green for Earth. Blue for Sky.

It was evening and everyone was resting. After the nine-hour trip from St. Paul by myself, I pulled a borrowed tent from my car and unfolded it. Others helped me set it up.

In the dark, I moved my sleeping bag several places on the hard, uneven ground inside the tent.

I slept, and at 4:30 I heard the wake-up song on the loud speaker. There was no reason to get up. I was an observer. I knew the sun dancers were on their way to the sweat lodges for purification. When I heard the drums, I knew they began in the first light, in their long skirts and bare chests, moving inside the circle of the arena around the cottonwood, singing the Sun Dance songs and blowing their eagle-bone whistles. The women danced in a larger circle around the men.

Soon I got up and walked to the brush arbor, which surrounded both circles of dancers and the tree.

Others watched as the piercing began. A man who had danced and prayed and was in the right frame of mind lay on the buffalo robe by the tree in the center of the circle. Two elk bone skewers were pushed under the skin on his chest. He stood connected to the tree with two small ropes and joined his group of supporters in the circle that surrounded the tree for however many rounds he chose. Then he pulled back on the ropes until the skewers broke free and he was released.

Men are not suspended from a pole, nor do they stare at the sun until they're blind. The Sun Dance is a commitment, more a way of life than a religion. It's keeping a promise. Doing what you say you're going to do. It's a prayer service to the Great Spirit. An intercession for relatives in need. It's humility and respect and supplication. It's a strengthening ceremony. A thanksgiving.

There were testimonies between rounds. And the humor of the announcer mixed with the endurance, the suffering, the seriousness. Over and over, the announcer said to pray for the dancers who were having a difficult time in their fight against heat, thirst, hunger, and tiredness.

There was an assortment of people from several states at the Sun Dance. The Indians are mainly Lakota and Dakota. They open their ceremony to others. There were many white people. Some come from Europe. One family was from Australia. I don't know numbers. Maybe there were four hundred. Probably more. Cars came and went each day.

It was an old ceremony of death and resurrection. A connection to the tree. A release.

The Sun Dance continued all day until about 6:00. Then the dancers sat once more in the sweat lodge and returned to their tents or teepees. They cannot eat or drink water.

There are those who are pierced. There are those who just dance. There are those who watch. I stood in the brush arbor that circled the dance arena. For the second year, I forgot a lawn chair. I watched. Prayed. Thought of my own needs and others. Danced in place. Raised my hands to the tree like the dancers and the other watchers. Sometimes I walked back to the tent. I made tobacco prayer ties that someone would hang on the tree. I was not part of the Sun Dance and could not enter the arena.

There are many rules.

For lunch I ate peanut butter on crackers, remembering somehow the burr oak acorns and magpies from the Missouri River plaque. I drank warm water out of a plastic bottle. You carry your water and food in with you. Whatever you need. I was reminded of church camp in Oklahoma when I had to put on my socks over dirty feet and felt the dust between my toes. There's an outhouse but no bath or shower. You camp in an open field under the sun on a ridge above the valleys of dark pines maybe 150 or 200 miles southeast of the Black Hills. By midafternoon the heat was unbearable inside the tent. The only shade was in the arbor where sometimes a warm breeze moved the prayer ties on the tree.

That night I drove into Mission to hear an Indian leader. He began with a story about a minister who led his congregation in a hymn from the church, only he was walking backward as he led them, and at the edge of the churchyard he fell into a newly dug grave and couldn't get out, his head appearing and disappearing as he jumped. Finally they pulled him out, and he had that white soil even in his eyebrows. The Indian leader used the laughter to enter the hardship of living, the meanness of reservation border towns. When you pray for us, he said, pray for alcoholism, AIDS, drugs, diabetes, joblessness, poverty.

I started back to the Sun Dance ground around 9:30. The sun had gone down and the sky was like a piece of blue tissue paper. Some thought or memory was wrapped in it. The land was dark and wavy beneath the sky. There was one star up there, and the telephone poles were crosses on the hills.

I thought it was about thirty miles back from Mission. I knew it was a long way and I felt unsure. It was hard to see the road in the dark. There was just the prairie and the sky and the centerline on the road and watching the shoulders for deer.

Sometimes, far off in the distance, I saw a few lights on the horizon. I thought it must be St. Francis, but the lights didn't seem in the right direction. The road wasn't headed toward them. I passed a lone building with a yard light. A schoolbus parked in a yard. And where were the stars? The sky in the west still had not turned out its light. Maybe it was too early for them.

Yes, the few lights I saw were St. Francis. The highway finally curved toward them. On the water tower road, right after the post office, I turned west. I wondered if I could see the camp off BIA 501 in the dark. I wondered if I would know when seven miles went by. There was a car behind me and I didn't want to go too slow. But soon I saw car lights coming through a field. I knew the turnoff was just ahead. I signaled, and the car behind me also turned, its headlights on bright.

As I looked from my tent that night, I saw the stars. A sky full of them. I went to sleep on the lumpy ground.

At 4:30 this morning, I got up. I wasn't comfortable. I wanted to leave. I was into something I didn't belong in. A Sun Dance in the Lakota-Dakota tradition. I was in a magnetic field and I felt repelled. But I have felt outside of every tradition I've been in. The Methodist church as a child because I couldn't figure out all the trouble of going to church. What did they preach other than the brotherhood of man and a sense of community? I needed more than that.

I needed salvation to help me out of the hurt and isolation and darkness I felt. The hardship of my own life. The years I'd worked. The invisibility I felt. The reservation border town that writing seemed to be. The weight of years pulling my children through the pitfalls. My daughter in college and law school calling saying she didn't know if she could do it, just think of the student loans she'll be buried under for years.

I had also attended the Presbyterian church through the years, which seemed to me like the Methodist. And later, the fundamentalist church I went to was opposed to the arts and a life of the imagination. Sometimes I attended the Episcopal church.

There was no belonging here either. I was from not the north but a shadow of a place where I used to live, but I wasn't from there either. I was born long ago, to parents of different heritages. I'd lived several places and none of them is where I'm from.

I felt marginalization from both my white and Indian heritages. I was neither of both. Both of neither. My great-grandfather was a full-blood Cherokee born near Sallisaw in Indian Territory in 1843. His parents got there somehow. The only way was the Trail of Tears from the southeast. My mother's people of European descent farmed in Kansas.

Because I didn't have a road, because I was in the process of the journey, I still didn't know why I was between two different cultures. I still had to jump-start an image of my broken self.

The Bible is full of journeys. It's why I think it is home.

That second morning at the Sun Dance, I watched the men lie on the buffalo robe. I watched as the holy men pushed the skewers under their skin. That's where it suddenly connected for me.

My son, when he was 17, had open lung surgery. He had holes in his lungs and they had to be stapled. When his lung first collapsed, the doctor pushed a tube into his chest. I was sitting outside the curtain. The opening for the tube was the size of a yellow jacket stinging with a stinging he couldn't push away.

I was not an outsider to this. I am the mother who listened to him suffer. I smoked and drank when he was conceived, and those habits interfered with his chances for development. I think so anyway. I've had a dream of snow in the yard. He was looking from the window. I tossed the snow at the window calling him until he disappeared.

He was born blue and mottled. Wrapped in the tissue paper of the evening sky. There was also a second surgery. His kidney, that time. He was pierced in the side like Christ, and not all the pages of the Bible can change it.

I wished I could go back and conceive him again. I wished I could put on his overalls and pull a shirt over his chest again. He survived. He went through officer training at Quantico and spent four years in the Marines. He went back to school and now teaches.

That morning in the open field on the Rosebud Reservation in South Dakota, during one of the rest periods between the rounds of dancing, an elder spoke over the loudspeaker. He said the Sun Dance is a form of Christ going to the cross. For me, it was finished on the cross. But the ceremony of linkage to suffering and release is still here, in this manger of sorts, this place where cattle usually graze. This place where boats unload and repack to start back on the river.

In the afternoon, I drove with two friends to the White River, nearly to Murdo. I heard the birds and insects in the grasses from the window of the car as I passed, like Oklahoma and the open places I've traveled. We picked some sage in a field along the road, leaving an offering of tobacco.

We had lunch at the Cook Shack in Mission and returned to the Sun Dance grounds for another hot afternoon. That evening as the dance finished, the announcer said there was a severe storm warning. We could see the clouds to the west because you can see far across the prairie from the ridge where we camped. Less than an hour later, we were in our tents trying to hold them down in the wind.

That evening I rode out the storm in the borrowed tent, the sides puffing as if it were a large bird trying to take flight. I heard the snap and hum of the lightning. I could even smell it.

Afterwards, while it was still light, I heard someone say, *look at the rainbows*. When I looked from the tent, I saw the two rainbows over the camp grounds. I stood in the slight rain that was still falling and the wind still whipping the tents and felt the oneness with the sky and earth. I felt survival. I felt promise. I felt what I hadn't known I'd been looking for. Significance.

Later in the night, I heard the eerie noise of coyotes, the hecklers, laughing at what I had found. But I stuck with it.

I wanted a journey of meaning in ordinary life. I'd always liked the plain land under the sky. The routine of housework and grading papers and writing and teaching and traveling, transformed by the act of its own ordinariness. Just as Jesus walking through the wheat field, these moments became more than themselves.

My mother used to talk about the Maypole dance she experienced as a girl. The ceremony of the tree goes back in history. The cross of Christ. The cottonwood tree of the Sun Dance. It is a connection to the past.

> ... I hung
> on the windy tree ...
> gashed with a blade
> bloodied for Odinn
>   myself an offering to myself
> knotted to that tree
> no man knows
>   wither the roots of it run.
> —Dr. Brian Branston, *The Last Gods of England*

The Sun Dance is also a connection to the Plains Indian culture I had read about in school, which is different from the woodland Cherokee heritage my father had left. It always left me with a sense of confusion as to what an *Indian* was.

I know now I was looking for meaning in the heat and community and sometimes the boredom as a Sun Dance observer.

I knew I already had it. When my son's chest was opened during surgery, when I had come apart, when I needed the construct of strength and meaning and hope, it was Christ. I've always gone to church through the years. I was saved and filled with the Holy Spirit. I spoke in tongues.

I believe in ceremony. There were many ceremonies at the Sun Dance, which is itself a ceremony.

The next morning, the clouds were low when I dismantled my tent and left. It felt as if the day would be cool, but I knew how soon the heat comes.

I watched the road ahead of me as I drove back toward Interstate 90 to the north. I watched the road's reflection on the hood of my car. I had made an expedition to a place I was not from. The low, rolling hills of South Dakota under the sky that lidded them. I felt the air in the window. My hand on the wheel.

I turned east onto Interstate 90 toward Minnesota. The cars and trucks moving along the highway were unaware of the Sun Dance just a few miles over the hills. And the Sun Dancers, when they came in their vans with their teepee lodgepoles tied on top and turned onto the Interstate, would pass along the road with the other traffic. They would carry with them their *significance*, which is a blanket over the pitfalls of the earth. Well, we do fall into them sometimes, but get lifted out.

It's why I wanted to write—to touch words—because the touch of words was alive.

Lucy Grealy

MIRRORINGS

LUCY GREALY, an award-winning poet, was born in Ireland in 1963. She lived in the United Kingdom and in Germany but spent most of her life in New York, where she grew up. She died in 2002. She is the author of a collection of essays, *As Seen on TV: Provocations*.

There was a long period of time, almost a year, during which I never looked in a mirror. It wasn't easy, for I'd never suspected just how omnipresent are our own images. I began by merely avoiding mirrors, but by the end of the year I found myself with an acute knowledge of the reflected image, its numerous tricks and wiles, how it can spring up at any moment: a glass tabletop, a well-polished door handle, a darkened window, a pair of sunglasses, a restaurant's otherwise magnificent brass-plated coffee machine sitting innocently by the cash register.

At the time, I had just moved, alone, to Scotland and was surviving on the dole, as Britain's social security benefits are called. I didn't know anyone and had no idea how I was going to live, yet I went anyway because by happenstance I'd met a plastic surgeon there who said he could help me. I had been living in London, working temp jobs. While in London, I'd received more nasty comments about my face than I had in the previous three years, living in Iowa, New York, and Germany. These comments, all from men and all odiously sexual, hurt and disoriented me. I also had journeyed to Scotland because after more than a dozen operations in the States, my insurance had run out, along with my hope that further operations could make any *real* difference. Here, however, was a surgeon who had some new techniques, and here, amazingly enough, was a government willing to foot the bill: I didn't feel I could pass up yet another chance to "fix" my face, which I confusedly thought concurrent with "fixing" my self, my soul, my life.

Twenty years ago, when I was nine and living in America, I came home from school one day with a toothache. Several weeks and misdiagnoses later, surgeons removed most of the right side of my jaw in an attempt to prevent the cancer they found there from spreading. No one properly explained the operation to me, and I awoke in a cocoon of pain that prevented me from moving or speaking. Tubes ran in and out of my body, and because I was temporarily unable to speak after the surgery and could not ask questions, I made up my own explanations for the tubes' existence. I remember the mysterious manner the adults displayed toward me. They asked me to do things: lie still for X rays, not cry for needles, and so on, tasks that, although not easy, never seemed equal to the praise I received in return. Reinforced to me again and again was how I was "a brave girl" for not crying, "a good girl" for not complaining, and soon I began defining myself this way, equating strength with silence.

Then the chemotherapy began. In the seventies chemo was even cruder than it is now, the basic premise being to poison patients right up to the very brink of their own death. Until this point I almost never cried and almost always received praise in return. Thus I got what I considered the better part of the deal. But now it was like a practical joke that had gotten out of hand. Chemotherapy was a nightmare and I wanted it to stop; I didn't want to be brave anymore. Yet I had grown so used to defining myself as "brave"—i.e., *silent*—that the thought of losing this sense of myself was even more terrifying. I was certain that if I broke down I would be despicable in the eyes of both my parents and the doctors.

The task of taking me into the city for the chemo injections fell mostly on my mother, though sometimes my father made the trip. Overwhelmed by the sight of the vomiting and weeping, my father developed the routine of "going to get the car," meaning that he left the doctor's office before the injection was administered, on the premise that then he could have the car ready and waiting when it was all over. Ashamed of my suffering, I felt relief when he was finally out of the room. When my mother took me, she stayed in the room, yet this only made the distance between us even more tangible. She explained that it was wrong to cry *before* the needle went in; afterward was one thing, but before, that was mere fear, and hadn't I demonstrated my bravery earlier? Every Friday for two and a half years I climbed up onto that big doctor's table and told myself not to cry, and every week I failed. The two large syringes were filled with chemicals so caustic to the vein that each had to be administered very slowly. The whole process took about four minutes; I had to remain utterly still. Dry retching began in the first fifteen seconds, then the throb behind my eyes gave everything a yellow-green aura, and the bone-deep pain of alternating extreme hot and cold flashes made me tremble, yet still I had to sit motionless and not move my arm. No one spoke to me—not the doctor, who was a paradigm of the cold-fish physician; not the nurse, who told my mother I reacted much more violently than many of "the other children"; and not my mother, who, surely overwhelmed by the sight of her child's suffering, thought the best thing to do was remind me to be brave, to try not to cry. All the while I hated myself for having wept before the needle went in, convinced that the nurse and my mother were right, that I was "overdoing it," that the throwing up was psychosomatic, that my mother was angry with me for not being good or brave enough.

Yet each week, two or three days after the injection, there came the first flicker of feeling better, the always forgotten and gratefully rediscovered understanding that to simply be well in my body was the greatest thing I could ask for. I thought other people felt this appreciation and physical joy all the time, and I felt cheated because I was able to feel it only once a week.

Because I'd lost my hair, I wore a hat constantly, but this fooled no one, least of all myself. During this time, my mother worked in a nursing home in a Hasidic community. Hasidic law dictates that married women cover their hair, and most commonly this is done with a wig. My mother's friends were now all too willing to donate their discarded wigs, and soon the house seemed filled with them. I never wore one, for they frightened me even when my mother insisted I looked better in one of the few that actually fit. Yet we didn't know how to say no to the women who kept graciously offering their wigs. The cats enjoyed sleeping on them and the dogs playing with them, and we grew used to having to pick a wig up off a chair we wanted to sit in. It never struck us as odd until one day a visitor commented wryly as he cleared a chair for himself, and suddenly a great wave of shame overcame me. I had nightmares about wigs and flushed if I even heard the word, and one night I put myself out of my misery by getting up after everyone was asleep and gathering all the wigs except for one the dogs were fond of and that they had chewed up anyway. I hid all the rest in an old chest.

When you are only ten, which is when the chemotherapy began, two and a half years seem like your whole life, yet it did finally end, for the cancer was gone. I remember the last day of treatment clearly because it was the only day on which I succeeded in not crying, and because later, in private, I cried harder than I had in years; I thought now I would no longer be "special," that without the arena of chemotherapy in which to prove myself, no one would ever love me, that I would fade unnoticed into the background. But this idea about *not being different* didn't last very long. Before, I foolishly believed that people stared at me because I was bald. After my hair eventually grew in, it didn't take long before I understood that I looked different for another reason. My face. People stared at me in stores, and other children made fun of me to the point that I came to expect such reactions constantly, wherever I went. School became a battleground.

Halloween, that night of frights, became my favorite holiday because I could put on a mask and walk among the blessed for a few brief, sweet hours. Such freedom I felt, walking down the street, my face hidden! Through the imperfect oval holes I could peer out at other faces, masked or painted or not, and see on those faces nothing but the normal faces of childhood looking back at me, faces I mistakenly thought were the faces everyone else but me saw all the time, faces that were simply curious and ready for fun, not the faces I usually braced myself for, the cruel, lonely, vicious ones I spent every day other than Halloween waiting to see around each corner. As I breathed in the condensed, plastic-scented air under the mask, I somehow thought that I was breathing in normality, that this joy and weightlessness were what the world was composed of, and that it was only my face that kept me from it, my face that was my own mask that kept me from knowing the joy I was sure everyone but me lived with intimately. How could the other children not know it? Not know that to be free of the fear of taunts and the burden of knowing no one would ever love you was all that anyone could ever ask for? I was a pauper walking for a short while in the clothes of the prince, and when the day ended, I gave up my disguise with dismay.

I was living in an extreme situation, and because I did not particularly care for the world I was in, I lived in others, and because the world I did live in was dangerous now, I incorporated this danger into my secret life. I imagined myself to be an Indian. Walking down the streets, I stepped through the forest, my body ready for any opportunity to fight or flee one of the big cats that I knew stalked me. Vietnam and Cambodia, in the news then as scenes of catastrophic horror, were other places I walked through daily. I made my way down the school hall, knowing a land mine or a sniper might give themselves away at any moment with the subtle metal click I'd read about. Compared with a land mine, a mere insult about my face seemed a frivolous thing.

In those years, not yet a teenager, I secretly read—knowing it was somehow inappropriate—works by Primo Levi and Elie Wiesel, and every book by a survivor I could find by myself without asking the librarian. Auschwitz, Birkenau: I felt the blows of the capos and somehow knew that because at any moment we might be called upon to live for a week on one loaf of bread and some water called soup, the peanut butter sandwich I found on my plate was nothing less than a miracle, an utter and sheer miracle capable of making me literally weep with joy.

I decided to become a "deep" person. I wasn't exactly sure what this would entail, but I believed that if I could just find the right philosophy, think the right thoughts, my suffering would end. To try to understand the world I was in, I undertook to find out what was "real," and I quickly began seeing reality as existing in the lowest common denominator, that suffering was the one and only dependable thing. But rather than spend all of my time despairing, though certainly I did plenty of that, I developed a form of defensive egomania: I felt I was the only one walking about in the world who understood what was really important. I looked upon people complaining about the most mundane things—nothing on TV, traffic jams, the price of new clothes—and felt joy because I knew how unimportant those things really were and felt unenlightened superiority because other people didn't. Because in my fantasy life I had learned to be thankful for each cold, blanketless night that I survived on the cramped wooden bunks, my pain and despair were a stroll through the country in comparison, I was often miserable, but I knew that to feel warm instead of cold was its own kind of joy, that to eat was a reenactment of the grace of some god whom I could only dimly define, and that to simply be alive was a rare, ephemeral gift.

As I became a teenager, my isolation began. My nonidentical twin sister started going out with boys, and I started—my most tragic mistake of all—to listen to and believe the taunts thrown at me daily by the very boys she and the other girls were interested in. I was a dog, a monster, the ugliest girl they had ever seen. Of all the remarks, the most damaging wasn't even directed at me but was really an insult to "Jerry," a boy I never saw because every day between fourth and fifth periods, when I was cornered by a particular group of kids, I was too ashamed to lift my eyes off the floor. "Hey look, it's Jerry's girlfriend!" they shrieked when they saw me, and I felt such shame, knowing that this was the deepest insult to Jerry that they could imagine.

When pressed to it, one makes compensations. I came to love winter, when I could wrap up the disfigured lower half of my face in a scarf: I could speak to people and they would have no idea to whom and to what they were really speaking. I developed the bad habits of letting my long hair hang in my face and of always covering my chin and mouth with my hand, hoping it might be mistaken as a thoughtful, accidental gesture. I also became interested in horses and got a job at a run-down local stable. Having those horses to go to each day after school saved my life; I spent all my time either with them or thinking about them. Completely and utterly repressed by the time I was sixteen, I was convinced that I would never want a boyfriend, not ever, and wasn't it convenient for me, even a blessing, that none would ever want me. I told myself I was free to concentrate on the "true reality" of life, whatever that was. My sister and her friends put on blue eye shadow, blow-dried their hair, and spent interminable hours in the local mall, and I looked down on them for this, knew they were misleading themselves and being overly occupied with the "mere surface" of living. I'd had thoughts like this when I was younger, ten or twelve, but now my philosophy was haunted by desires so frightening, I was unable even to admit they existed.

Throughout all of this, I was undergoing reconstructive surgery in an attempt to rebuild my jaw. It started when I was fifteen, two years after the chemo ended. I had known for years I would have operations to fix my face, and at night I fantasized about how good my life would finally be then. One day I got a clue that maybe it wouldn't be so easy. An older plastic surgeon explained the process of "pedestals" to me, and told me *it* would take *ten years* to fix my face. Ten years? Why even bother, I thought; I'll be ancient by then. I went to a medical library and looked up the "pedestals" he talked about. There were gruesome pictures of people with grotesque tubes of their own skin growing out of their bodies, tubes of skin that were harvested like some kind of crop and then rearranged, with results that did not look at all normal or acceptable to my eye. But then I met a younger surgeon, who was working on a new way of grafting that did not involve pedestals, and I became more hopeful and once again began to await the fixing of my face, the day when I would be whole, content, loved.

Long-term plastic surgery is not like in the movies. There is no one single operation that will change everything, and there is certainly no slow unwrapping of the gauze in order to view the final, remarkable result. There is always swelling, sometimes to a grotesque degree, there are often bruises, and always there are scars. After each operation, too frightened to simply go look in the mirror, I developed an oblique method, with several stages. First, I tried to catch my reflection in an overhead lamp: the roundness of the metal distorted my image just enough to obscure details and give no true sense of size or proportion. Then I slowly worked my way up to looking at the reflection in someone's eyeglasses, and from there I went to walking as briskly as possible by a mirror, glancing only quickly. I repeated this as many times as it would take me, passing the mirror slightly more slowly each time until finally I was able to stand still and confront myself.

The theory behind most reconstructive surgery is to take large chunks of muscle, skin, and bone and slap them into the roughly appropriate place, then slowly begin to carve this mess into some sort of shape. It involves long major operations, countless lesser ones, a lot of pain, and many, many years. And also, it does not always work. With my young surgeon in New York, who with each passing year was becoming not so young, I had two or three soft-tissue grafts, two skin grafts, a bone graft, and some dozen other operations to "revise" my face, yet when I left graduate school at the age of twenty-five I was still more or less in the same position I had started in: a deep hole in the right side of my face and a rapidly shrinking left side and chin, a result of the radiation I'd had as a child and the stress placed upon the bone by the other operations. I was caught in a cycle of having a big operation, one that would force me to look monstrous from the swelling for many months, then having the subsequent revision operations that improved my looks tremendously, and then slowly, over the period of a few months or a year, watching the graft reabsorb back into my body, slowly shrinking down and leaving me with nothing but the scarred donor site the graft had originally come from.

It wasn't until I was in college that I finally allowed that maybe, just maybe, it might be nice to have a boyfriend. I went to a small, liberal, predominantly female school and suddenly, after years of alienation in high school, discovered that there were other people I could enjoy talking to who thought me intelligent and talented. I was, however, still operating on the assumption that no one, not ever, would be physically attracted to me, and in a curious way this shaped my personality. I became forthright and honest in the way that only the truly self-confident are, who do not expect to be rejected, and in the way of those like me, who do not even dare to ask acceptance from others and therefore expect no rejection. I had come to know myself as a person, but I would be in graduate school before I was literally, physically able to use my name and the word "woman" in the same sentence.

Now my friends repeated for me endlessly that most of it was in my mind, that, granted, I did not look like everyone else, but that didn't mean I looked bad. I am sure now that they were right some of the time. But with the constant surgery I was in a perpetual state of transfiguration. I rarely looked the same for more than six months at a time. So ashamed of my face, I was unable even to admit that this constant change affected me; I let everyone who wanted to know that it was only what was inside that martered, that I had "grown used to" the surgery, that none of it bothered me at all. Just as I had done in childhood, I pretended nothing was wrong, and this was constantly mistaken by others for bravery. I spent a great deal of time looking in the mirror in private, positioning my head to show off my eyes and nose, which were not only normal but quite pretty, as my friends told me often. But I could not bring myself to see them for more than a moment: I looked in the mirror and saw not the normal upper half of my face but only the disfigured lower half.

People still teased me. Not daily, as when I was younger, but in ways that caused me more pain than ever before. Children stared at me, and I learned to cross the street to avoid them; this bothered me, but not as much as the insults I got from men. Their taunts came at me not because I was disfigured but because I was a disfigured *woman*. They came from boys, sometimes men, and almost always from a group of them. I had long blond hair, and I also had a thin figure. Sometimes, from a distance, men would see a thin blonde and whistle, something I dreaded more than anything else because I knew that as they got closer, their tune, so to speak, would inevitably change; they would stare openly or, worse, turn away quickly in shame or repulsion. I decided to cut my hair to avoid any misconception that anyone, however briefly, might have about my being attractive. Only two or three times have I ever been teased by a single person, and I can think of only one time when I was ever teased by a woman. Had I been a man, would I have had to walk down the street while a group of young women followed and denigrated my sexual worth?

Not surprisingly, then, I viewed sex as my salvation. I was sure that if only I could get someone to sleep with me it would mean I wasn't ugly, that I was attractive, even lovable. This line of reasoning led me into the beds of several manipulative men who liked themselves even less than they liked me, and I in turn left each short-term affair hating myself, obscenely sure that if only I had been prettier, it would have worked—he would have loved me and it would have been like those other love affairs that I was certain "normal" women had all the time. Gradually, I became unable to say "I'm depressed" but could say only "I'm ugly," because the two had become inextricably linked in my mind. Into that universal lie, that sad equation of "if only . . ." that we are all prey to, I was sure that if only I had a normal face, then I would be happy.

The new surgeon in Scotland, Oliver Fenton, recommended that I undergo a procedure involving something called a tissue expander, followed by a bone graft. A tissue expander is a small balloon placed under the skin and then slowly blown up over the course of several months, the object being to stretch out the skin and create room and cover for the new bone. It's a bizarre, nightmarish thing to do to your face, yet I was hopeful about the end results and I was also able to spend the three months that the expansion took in the hospital. I've always felt safe in hospitals: they're the one place I feel free from the need to explain the way I look. For this reason the first tissue expander was bearable—just—and the bone graft that followed it was a success; it did not melt away like the previous ones.

The surgical stress this put upon what remained of my original jaw instigated the deterioration of that bone, however, and it became unhappily apparent that I was going to need the same operation I'd just had on the right side done to the left. I remember my surgeon telling me this at an outpatient clinic. I planned to be traveling down to London that same night on an overnight train, and I barely made it to the station on time, such a fumbling state of despair was I in.

I could not imagine going through it *again*, and just as I had done all my life,

I searched and searched through my intellect for a way to make it okay, make it bearable, for a way to *do* it. I lay awake all night on that train, feeling the tracks slip beneath me with an odd eroticism, when I remembered an afternoon from my three months in the hospital. Boredom was a big problem those long afternoons, the days marked by meals and television programs. Waiting for the afternoon tea to come, wondering desperately how I could make time pass, it had suddenly occurred to me that I didn't have to make time pass, that it would do it of its own accord, that I simply had to relax and take no action. Lying on the train, remembering that, I realized I had no obligation to improve my situation, that I didn't have to explain or understand it, that I could just simply let it happen. By the time the train pulled into King's Cross station, I felt able to bear it yet again, not entirely sure what other choice I had.

But there was an element I didn't yet know about. When I returned to Scotland to set up a date to have the tissue expander inserted, I was told quite casually that I'd be in the hospital only three or four days. Wasn't I going to spend the whole expansion time in the hospital? I asked in a whisper. What's the point of that? came the answer. You can just come in every day to the outpatient ward to have it expanded. Horrified by this, I was speechless. I would have to live and move about in the outside world with a giant balloon inside the tissue of my face? I can't remember what I did for the next few days before I went into the hospital, but I vaguely recall that these days involved a great deal of drinking alone in bars and at home.

I had the operation and went home at the end of the week. The only things that gave me any comfort during the months I lived with my tissue expander were my writing and Franz Kafka. I started a novel and completely absorbed myself in it, writing for hours each day. The only way I could walk down the street, could stand the stares I received, was to think to myself, "I'll bet none of them are writing a novel." It was that strange, old, familiar form of egomania, directly related to my dismissive, conceited thoughts of adolescence. As for Kafka, who had always been one of my favorite writers, he helped me in that I felt permission to feel alienated, and to have that alienation be okay, bearable, noble even. In the same way that imagining I lived in Cambodia helped me as a child, I walked the streets of my dark little Scottish city by the sea and knew without doubt that I was living in a story Kafka would have been proud to write.

The one good thing about a tissue expander is that you look so bad with it in that no matter what you look like once it's finally removed, your face has to look better. I had my bone graft and my fifth soft-tissue graft and, yes, even I had to admit I looked better. But I didn't look like me. Something was wrong: was *this* the face I had waited through eighteen years and almost thirty operations for? I somehow just couldn't make what I saw in the mirror correspond to the person I thought I was. It wasn't only that I continued to feel ugly; I simply could not conceive of the image as belonging to me. My own image was the image of a stranger, and rather than try to understand this, I simply stopped looking in the mirror. I perfected the technique of brushing my teeth without a mirror, grew my hair in such a way that it would require only a quick, simple brush, and wore clothes that were simply and easily put on, no complex layers or lines that might require even the most minor of visual adjustments.

On one level I understood that the image of my face was merely that, an image, a surface that was not directly related to any true, deep definition of the self. But I also knew that it is only through appearances that we experience and make decisions about the everyday world, and I was not always able to gather the strength to prefer the deeper world to the shallower one. I looked for ways to find a bridge that would allow me access to both, rather than ride out the constant swings between peace and anguish. The only direction I had to go in to achieve this was to strive for a state of awareness and self-honesty that sometimes, to this day, occasionally rewards me. I have found, I believe, that our whole lives are dominated, though it is not always so clearly translatable, by the question "How do I look?" Take all the many nouns in our lives—car, house, job, family, love, friends—and substitute the personal pronoun I. It is not that we are all so self-obsessed; it is that all things eventually relate back to ourselves, and it is our own sense of how we appear to the world by which we chart our lives, how we navigate our personalities, which would otherwise be adrift in the ocean of *other* people's obsessions.

One evening toward the end of my year-long separation from the mirror, I was sitting in a café, talking to someone—an attractive man, as it happened—and we were having a lovely, engaging conversation. For some reason I suddenly wondered what I looked like to him. What was he *actually* seeing when he saw me? So many times I've asked this of myself, and always the answer is this: a warm, smart woman, yes, but an unattractive one. I sat there in the café and asked myself this old question, and startlingly, for the first time in my life. I had no answer readily prepared. I had not looked in a mirror for so long that I quite simply had no clue as to what I looked like. I studied the man as he spoke; my entire life I had seen my ugliness reflected back to me. But now, as reluctant as I was to admit it, the only indication in my companion's behavior was positive.

And then, that evening in that café, I experienced a moment of the freedom I'd been practicing for behind my Halloween mask all those years ago. But whereas as a child I expected my liberation to come as a result of gaining something, a new face, it came to me now as the result of shedding something, of shedding my image. I once thought that truth was eternal, that when you understood something, it was with you forever. I know now that this isn't so, that most truths are inherently unretainable, that we have to work hard all our lives to remember the most basic things. Society is no help; it tells us again and again that we can most be ourselves by looking like someone else, leaving our own faces behind to turn into ghosts that will inevitably resent and haunt us. It is no mistake that in movies and literature the dead sometimes know they are dead only after they can no longer see themselves in the mirror; and as I sat there feeling the warmth of the cup against my palm, this small observation seemed like a great revelation to me. I wanted to tell the man I was with about it, but he was involved in his own topic and I did not want to interrupt him, so instead I looked with curiosity toward the window behind him, its night-darkened glass reflecting the whole café, to see if I could, now, recognize myself.

William Harrison

PRESENT TENSE AFRICA

WILLIAM HARRISON is the author of eight novels—the last five set in Africa—as well as three volumes of short stories. He taught at the University of Arkansas for a number of years and lives in Fayetteville.

At night in the Bristol Hotel everyone seems to have a key to my room, this little cinderblock cubicle at the rear, two floors above the alleyways of Lagos. I fold a pillow beneath my head and try to sleep facing the door.

A jangle of keys, then a vendor shuffles in, speaking softly as he shows me his magazines. Get out, I tell him, and he nods, but advances to the foot of the bed, smiling and nodding and selling until I raise my voice.

A man with a flit gun arrives to kill insects.

A squat little woman with a kerchief on her head comes to clean the basin.

It's now two o'clock in the morning. The desk clerks all retired at midnight and, besides, this is Africa where complaining only adds stress to your problems.

An Arab boy with a neck brace enters, pointing out that I'll need a tour guide the next day.

Twenty minutes later a young prostitute arrives, asking in broken English if I didn't ask the bartender to send her up. Please, I manage, go away, please.

Exhausted, I stand at the window looking down on hundreds of wayfarers, dark figures in the rainy alleyway out back. Some of them sleep beneath old cartons while others slump in doorways, smoking cigarettes and waiting out the night. Not far off is a rubbish pile as large as a city block. A church bell clanks out a toneless count.

A man in a uniform unlocks my door and peers in, wanting to know if everything is all right. He's the watchman, he tells me, and he suggests money, just a little tip, please, but he smells drunk and unofficial.

An old woman with assorted flowers.

A nearly naked man with a bicycle wheel.

A waiter from the lounge bar.

It's four in the morning when the magazine vendor loudly jangles his keys and tries again. Yes, all right, I tell him, one of those, and I prop myself up after he's gone, turn on the single naked lightbulb, and begin to look at the pictures and read.

At a roadblock near Singida our van is stopped by a trio of ragtag Tanzanian soldiers, one of them carrying a rusty M-1 rifle with an oily rag dangling like a flag from its breech.

The day is scorching, dustdevils everywhere, all the waterholes dry, and the tall soldier in the vest who glances into our van sees that we have six full cases of Tusker, the best Kenyan lager.

The drinking begins.

The third soldier, dressed in short khaki pants and a crushed straw hat, carries the lone bullet for his companion's rifle. Wrapped in dirty string and draped around his neck, its brass casing glints in the sun.

As they drink bottle after bottle of warm lager they ask where we're going. Dodoma, we tell them, then up to Mwanza. But why? No reason, we tell them, and that's clearly reason enough.

The landscape here, north of the lush Iringa Forest, is bleak as the moon: high savannah, rocky, red dust covering the leaves of a few thorny bushes. As our van waits in the raw heat—and we can see ten miles in every direction and there are no other vehicles in sight—we offer the beer as a gift or bribe, no one knows which, and we stand around in the road, everybody waiting to see what will happen. How much will they drink? Do we offer them a full case? When they're drunk, will they become hostile? Or will they soon raise that flimsy crossbar?

What to do? We're rich travelers by their standards, just passing by, a fortune of beer in our possession, plastic cards in our pockets that will buy us the world, and they're small men in tatters who share a common rifle with a single bullet.

We've talked about what to do if the van breaks down out here, how we'll stay close to the vehicle because, as we know, we're the slowest beasts on the landscape. We've talked about emergencies, all the wild animals, how to stay calm. This is a land of cobras and lion, of strange diseases and pestilence, but the great dangers are fleeting authority, vague boundaries, old gods and loyalties, and the oblivion of some unintentional insult in a language no one really understood. Unlike the world we usually inhabit in America, politics here can kill you.

At Cape Point there's an asphalt parking lot, then a steep climb uphill to the promontory where one is supposed to be able to see the Indian Ocean meet the Atlantic.

The day is cool with a bright sun and a steady breeze, so we tuck our windbreakers under our arms and start up. At the top of our climb our perspiration quickly dries and chills us, but we can look miles out to sea and we joke about seeing all the way to Antarctica from here. On such a day and with such a vista, the troubles of South Africa seem far away.

There is an excruciating beauty all around us here. Cape Town, where we started driving from this morning, is a silver city on the edge of civilization, clean as a space station. For Americans, only San Francisco compares to it. The surrounding province is a world of vaulting coastal mountains, white beaches, old Huguenot villages, pastels of wildflowers, and lush vineyards. In recent years the political climate has prevented a lot of people from saying much about the beauty here. There're no packaged travel tours or advertisements in tourist magazines. While tribes fight with one another, while the whites make concessions yet hold onto power, South Africa's celebrated beauty has almost receded into secrecy. One sees a few Japanese with their cameras or a few Germans with theirs, but the land has lost much of its tourist trade.

There are often ugly emotions that go with a country of extraordinary natural vistas such as this. One can argue that the loveliest places on the earth often inspire men to become fanatics—that, say, the splendor of Bavaria had something to do with making the Nazis happen. We know that a beautiful woman often creates male hysteria of a particular lunatic sort, but the same may be true of certain spectacular homelands. Is beauty a curse? One can imagine that it is here.

We can look back to the left at False Bay—a place well named considering all the illusions of South Africa—and see the white beaches of Simon's Town and Muizenburg.

After a while we look back south toward the meeting place of the oceans. The cold breeze continues and we know we won't stay very long.

We try to imagine a dotted line out there: Indian Ocean on the left, Atlantic on the right. We're talking about this when a man in an old ski jacket overhears us and says, "No, it's not out there at all. That's not where the oceans meet. It's far to the east of here."

He's a professional type, maybe a little seedier, with a frayed collar above his jacket, his shoes worn down at the heels, but with an old meershaum between his teeth and an assertive manner. We want to dispute him, but he's got the Afrikaans accent—he's indisputably a native—and he just seems to know.

"Doesn't it say on a brass marker somewhere around here that this is where the oceans meet?" we ask him.

"Nothing's what it seems here," he assures us, smiling with a bit of indulgence. "A willow branch will turn out to be a boomslang. Black isn't black and white isn't white. And what you're looking for is miles to the east." He says this over his shoulder as he strolls away, smiling at us, but finished with his explanation.

After he's gone we look for the marker, but can't find it. The boulders above the lookout platform smell of urine. The wire waste containers are overflowing. In the breeze of the gathering twilight, we begin to shiver.

So what, we ask ourselves, are we looking at? The Atlantic? We do know that it's beautiful: grey and rolling, ancient and mysterious, aglow with the last sheen of the day, it invites the eye to gaze on it.

On the launch going across the Nile to Kitchener Island the *khamsin* begins to blow, that hot desert wind. At first it's just a warm breath, then it picks up and as we begin our little tour of the island it rattles the leaves of the cottonwoods, shakes the palm branches, and becomes a force.

I've fallen in with a group of tourists from the hotel boat *Osiris*. The guide is talking history and myth, but soon the rattling branches obliterate his voice, then sand stings us and we begin to turn away, all of us becoming separated from one another, being driven like stray cattle in a sand blizzard among the curved walkways of this famous garden spot. Eventually I'm alone, out of reach of anyone's voice, and good sense dictates that I should make my way back to the launch, but I take cover behind a broken wall.

There is a way Egypt isn't Africa, yet is.

It's a middle kingdom, embracing the European sea, and for thousands of years it has heard the voices of science and reason. The Coptic religion is here, a blend of Greek thought and Christian mysticism, and the pharaohs always admired order and the rational architectures of the mind. Far south beyond the desert, madness prevailed. On some ancient summer night, one can imagine, an old pharaoh, weary with all he knew and didn't know, might have come to his balcony and thought he heard the drums and soft moans of the continent below him. These would have been fearful notes to his civilized ear, terrifying. Pondering the dark mud of his holy river, he might have considered his origins and destiny. It is a mud, after all, that starts in the lunatic highlands of Ethiopia, that comes out of the heights of the Mountains of the Moon even further south, flowing into the great Nyanza, moving through bloody tribal kingdoms, spreading out into poisonous swamps, then gathering itself once more with feverish vitality in a rush toward Egypt.

If Egypt is the head of Africa, there is a thing in the blood that feeds its brain. The land of the Nile with its carefully tilled fields, its written language, its orderly temples, its yearnings for the philosophic meanings of existence, must have always felt an ancient whisper in the *khamsin* swirling up from the sub-

Sahara. If the ancient Egyptians were introspective, if they inhabited a world of moral and spiritual certainties in their simple desert landscape, they surely must have sensed that on their continent was a wild thoughtlessness, a demonic undertow. If they were the intellectuals of Africa, they must have felt the animal pulse in the body of the continent.

With these thoughts I leave the shelter of the broken wall and run back to the launch just before it starts back. The windstorm has kicked up whitecaps on the river and the boat struggles to stay on course.

This extraordinary burst of nature is the real Africa, I'm thinking, and for a moment history seems clear: this is what blew away the temples at Dendera, Oko Kombo, Esna, Karnak and all the rest. Egypt, the great civilization, was subverted by a chaos in the bloodstream of the continent, a primal fire burning out of control. It's a simple metaphor, I know, but as I cling to the gunwale of the launch and shield my eyes, it seems to hold: we are undone in our progress by something berserk, by the dark jungles, by madness, and it is a madness that is perhaps more truly what we really are.

Lost near Maralal.

Our road became a track, then followed a dry *nullah* for awhile, then became another road, then a small path, then just disappeared. My wife is laughing at us.

Our driver, Patrick, my big cousin Gene and I are all standing on a boulder, passing a pair of binoculars between ourselves, and trying to see where we are. Here in the highlands we can see for thirty miles, but there's nothing out there. We know the time of day and where the sun is, so we know the general direction, we tell each other, and my wife thinks we look funny up there on that boulder together.

A single wisp of smoke rises in the distance: somebody's cooking fire. It's maybe nine miles away.

We get back in the Land Rover and try again. The Land Rover is from Hertz and hardly new. For an additional $10 a day Patrick is included in the deal. He speaks several dialects, but we can't find anybody for him to talk to.

An hour later we're on another road and soon it begins to follow a new barbed wire fence.

Then the young Italian baron arrives. He's barechested—with good-looking pectoral muscles, my wife notes—and riding a Harley Davidson. Strapped on his back is a shiny Winchester rifle and above his tailored safari shorts is an ammunition belt of carved leather. He has a mop of uncombed blond hair and a ready smile. This is all part of his family's ranch, he tells us in pretty good English, and he's hunting lion.

Because my wife is still laughing at us, we're pleased to see him point in the general direction where we assumed Maralal to be. As we chat, my cousin Gene opens a tin of meat and Patrick the driver unwraps a crust of bread he has saved. The baron accepts a beer from our cooler. Suddenly, no one wants to be anyplace else. We enjoy this beautiful young man astride the shiny chrome of his Harley and the day is clear with the special light of the highlands. Maralal is out there, yes, and we'll find it. The lions are somewhere. We talk about motorcycles. I rented a bike, once, I say, and took it on the ferry over to Capri. This gets us talking about Italy and his family who lives just outside Rome.

Africa is in the present tense. Like most Americans, I live in the future or past, planning ahead most of the time, thinking what job I ought to do next, considering the calendar, or thinking and sometimes writing about where I've gone, what I've seen, and who I am because of all that. But here one is in the moment. A peculiar African zen: time becomes itself, not a thing pulling us forward or a psychological thing pushing us back. Journeys, often because they're so difficult, tend to make destinations of little consequence, even foolish.

It is difficult to describe, but Africa is surprise and fate, and all Africans seem to share this sensation and knowledge. In the twilight hush every creature yields to the mystic silence. In a bright noon, a bird of startling primary colors wheels in the sky overhead. Great columns of rain hold up the sky above the Rift Valley. The murmurs of the Jurassic and the Pleistocene surround us. A young Italian arrives on a Harley. The way to Maralal is lost, but no matter.

On the island of Zanzibar we stay in a hotel that used to be the British officers' club during the Victorian period when all the explorers were searching for the source of the Nile.

Nowadays the place is mostly a brothel, but there are rooms available and the verandah and bar are perched out over the water, so that the dhows seem to sail indoors and carry us away. In that open space between the Indian Ocean and the old hotel one gets a heavy case of African *déjà vu* because there's no hint of the twentieth century, just the sound of the surf and distant native voices, the bright sails of the dhows, and the odors of beer and the ancient stench of the sea. Downstairs at reception there are black and white tiles on the floors, dying potted palms, and a general seediness. Like the rest of the island, Afrika House hasn't seen any maintenance since Richard Francis Burton carried on here.

At the top of the landing near the door to our room sits a table with a large spider on it. For the last two mornings our maid has obviously avoided dusting the table, and we give the spider a wide berth when coming or going.

Across town is the other hotel, the somewhat newer one with the ice machine. The building resembles an outworn Holiday Inn and only has a view of the mud flats.

In the late afternoon we stroll through the narrow streets of the town, admiring the studded doors, passing the square near the church, making our way toward the ice machine. By way of saving power, the island authorities don't turn on the electricity until five o'clock, and all the Europeans and many locals know the routine, so line up at the bar, glasses poised and ready, as the machine begins to hum. The cocktail hours produce two dozen cubes every fifteen or twenty minutes. Everyone graciously waits his turn for a cube. Today there are three Scandinavian engineers, a Russian, and a couple of Canadians. There's little business on the island, just cloves and coconuts. The rest is the ghostly history of the slave trade.

They want to know why we're staying at Afrika House. The flies are bad, we admit, and the nights tend to be noisy as the girls ply their trade. The surf has a stench to it, yes, and there's no restaurant or food service. But there are the dhows, we argue, and we have a resident spider. You're staying at the whorehouse, they say, and even when the laughter ends we really can't explain it. It has to do with things long ago.

After supper, a little drunk, we make our way back through the dark and eerie town, entering its maze of streets and passages, but then at last we emerge near Afrika House to see the moonrise on the ocean. It's an immense yellow object tonight, so large that if I extend my hand, stretching out my arm to its full length, my fingers don't even cover the golden surface.

Last night coming back from a swim in the lake our host suddenly put out his arm, stopping my wife. She had narrowly missed stepping barefooted on a sand viper. After that we had trouble sleeping in the heat, breathing becoming a kind of suffocation. We were hungry, too, and worried about drinking up the last of our water and beer.

But this morning, exhilarated, I get into the twenty-foot fishing boat with Ali and Kobo. I've given them petrol for the outboard motor and paid them in advance, so although the wind is too high we're going to brave the whitecaps. They badly need to catch fish and I want to go along to photograph all the crocodiles over on South Island.

The wind gusts to fifty miles an hour all day here, blowing hot out of the east. It remains at our backs this morning, though, and pushes us over the rough waters of the lake.

The visitor to Lake Turkana descends out of the cool highlands of Kenya into desert. The gigantic lake is an elongated mirror held up to the sky. And this morning everything is a torture chamber: a hard sun beating down, a brassy reflection off the water, the swells and whitecaps that pound the boat. Ali, dressed in a pair of jockey shorts and his knitted Moslem skullcap, smiles as he steers us forward. Kobo, the wiry Molo fisherman, rigs our two fiberglass rods.

The tribes here—the Molo, the Turkana, and a few remnants of other tribes including a couple of Dinka—call the lake simply *Ngiza,* the darkness, and their pronunciation is always rich in evil connotations, for this is a relentless environment with powdery volcanic ash in the air, bramble and gorse over the ground, and thousands of crocs infesting the lake and its shores. In the neolithic period the lake was part of the Nile system, but all its links and tributaries dried up in centuries of drouth. As the desert encroached and established itself, a severed body of water more than 150 miles in length remained, and the Nile crocodiles, trapped, multiplied and thrived.

There is an overwhelming solitude here.

Both Ali and Kobo seem to feel it, going about their tasks with very little said. We all seem frail in this immensity of sky and lashing waves.

As we approach the island the crocs slide off the shoreline rocks, avoiding my camera. There are some big specimens: fifteen feet in length and very agile. The tribesmen eat croc, of course, but hunting it is tricky business: they have to flank one of the brutes, cutting off its path back to the lake, and fight to keep it hemmed in while attacking and killing it. They prefer casting their nets when the lake is calm, but this is the season for the east winds. They depend on visitors to the fishing camp, then, but this torrid, windy season few of them show up.

Kobo prepares the lines, attaching big spinners, hooks, cut bait, and lots of weights. When the trolling begins, the boat slows with the drag.

We hope for a catch because the camp food last night—and in the adjacent village—depended largely on provisions out of our Land Rover. A handsome young Kenyan, Jim Robertson, who runs the camp, was in the process of striking the last tents when we arrived, but agreed to stay on as our host. He's the one who suggested the swim and who kept my wife from stepping on the viper. But his supplies are gone and he remarked that even some of the Molo swore they were leaving. They live in small huts that look like sad bird nests thrown upside down to the ground, and their existence up here is precarious at best. Our arrival was virtually a cause for celebration. We brought most of last night's dinner and petrol for the big fishing boat.

If nature is treacherous and uncaring in the bush, it's also occasionally generous. Cassava, the staple root eaten in one form or another by almost everyone in the sub-Sahara, grows whether or not the rains come, whether it's planted properly, and whether it's tended or left to grow wild. In some places antelope are still available. The rivers and lakes provide fish. Apart from the cassava harvests, all over Africa there's a makeshift subsistence farming. Nature remains a paradox in all this, unrelenting and cruel, generous and forgiving: a land of vipers and edible fish, of famine and occasional feasts.

Trolling along, pushed hard against the shore by the wind, we get a strike. Then another, bigger. Kobo has it hooked. As the thick rod bends and nods toward our catch, Kobo hurries to me, getting the rod into my hands, wanting me to feel the thrill of it. Down and reel, pull back hard, bend down and reel, pull back hard again: my rhythm comes and goes, and we're all laughing. At last we see it. Ali jumps around after a net. Kobo leans out and strikes with his homemade gaff. We land a Nile perch of about sixty pounds. Ali begins to whoop and so do I.

That night the fish feeds both camp and village. It is received with great awe and surprise, as if this hasn't happened hundreds of times before. After we finish off the beer, we try sleeping again, and the wind remains fierce and hot all night.

The next morning we pack up to leave, even Jim Robertson, because there's simply nothing left to eat or drink. I ask him what the Molo fishermen will do. Oh, they'll stay on, he assures me, they always stay on, they'll do something.

And it occurs to me that the Molo regard our kind as a benevolent part of nature nowadays: when we arrive we're like a lucky catch, bringing bottled drinks, tins, and perhaps a little money. One wonders if our intrusions are costing the Molo their skills as masters of the lake, as croc killers; if they no longer bother to row themselves across the lake to South Island where the great Nile perch are feeding, and if the arrival of sportsmen and travelers hasn't made them less efficient out here. As we depart this morning the sun is already blistering hot and the Molo are already taking the shade of their huts; none of them are at the shore with their nets or out on the lake.

Our Land Rover climbs the steep track leading away from the lake. Teleki's volcano comes into view. We can see the serpentine sheen of the water below us.

They always stay on, they'll do something, yes, I'm thinking, they'll wait for others like us. It's primitive up here, sure, but to every man, Molo or American, tribesman or tourist, the end of it is in sight.

I'm waiting around in the little airport at Port Harcourt wondering why in hell I have a tennis racquet with me.

The evening plane has been cancelled and there's not a single hotel room back in town, so I've decided to sleep here beside my gear until morning. Tomorrow's planes are all booked, so I've also decided to do what one does in

African airports: take the first available flight going anywhere. Escaping one's present circumstances is an ongoing adventure on the continent.

A young man approaches, grinning. He's an Ibo, speaking with the breathless English by which his tribe is often recognized in the West, and he asks if I happen to know Jennifer Capriati. I smile back and say, well, no, but I've seen her playing tennis on television. He has a letter for her, he says, and can I wait while he goes home to fetch it? I can only answer yes, sure, my pleasure.

After he hurries off, I stroll around the airport, trying to get a little exercise while keeping an eye on my gear. I pause in an open doorway where the odors of the Niger delta are strong: rotted wood, brackish swampwater, and a kind of putrid gardenia. Crickets swarm everywhere, hurling themselves against the lighted windows, and out at the baggage carts a group of locals are cooking up a supply of the insects in an empty tin can held over a small fire of straw and twigs. Pages of the *London Observer, Der Stern, Newsweek* and *Punch* lie around for my entertainment. I take short naps, buy coffee from a vendor who pushes a brass urn fitted with homemade wheels, nod and smile at a weary mother surrounded by her four sleeping children, and take more strolls among the hundred or so passengers stranded for the night.

A greying British gentleman invites me to play gin rummy. He works for a big wildlife fund and he's eager to discuss diminishing herds, endangered species, game reserves and the millions of pounds his outfit has raised to save the animals. He wears a tie—in spite of the humid night—and says he lives in Hampstead. He shows me some brochures. Not much money exchanges hands at cards.

But after a while I'm exhausted with his prattle, even when he talks intelligently about the leopard, my favorite of the animals. I've heard most of it, of course, and I have a prejudice for these wildlife sorts—for one thing, because they're often successful and pious about raising money for the creatures of the continent. Famine in Ethiopia, starvation in Mozambique, disasters everywhere, but save the little lion cubs, pray for the noble elephant, help the snake, monkey, and rodent. It's not that I dislike animals, I want to explain, but please.

As it gets toward morning, I make my excuses. The urinals are broken and the toilets are now overflowing. In another half hour I sit beside the sleeping mother and entertain two of her children with coin tricks, allowing them to keep the money when they correctly guess where I've hidden it.

At sunrise a plane lands. Everyone stirs. Packages and luggage are moved across the terminal, then set down again. We soon learn there are no available seats.

Then the Ibo correspondent returns. His letter is actually a thick packet covered with Nigerian postage, but he's an even more arresting sight: his clothes soaked with perspiration, his eyes wide, his breath coming in uneven bursts.

He lives twelve miles from the airport, he explains. He tries to smile, but he's still breathless. After seeing me he dashed home to fetch the letter. And am I, perhaps, he wonders, a tennis coach? In any case, can I find a proper address for this?

The letter, it turns out, is a long proposal of marriage. Tell me honestly, he asks, do you think Jennifer Capriati would consent to marry a poor man who can only offer his complete love?

I tell him that I just don't know.

He talks about how women athletes practice long hours, how they always want to please their fathers, how their managers exploit them, and how lonely they often are. They are superstars, yes, he argues, but they sacrifice what is most tender in themselves. And can't find good men. Look at Chris Evert, he says, who has been through so many heartbreaks and a divorce. As he goes on, I keep thinking about all the miles he walked, jogged, and ran during these last hours. When the coffee vendor returns, I buy us both a coffee—bitter as dark metal.

By nine o'clock I have a ticket to Lagos and a transfer to London. By the time I move my gear into the crowded departure lounge and before we say goodbye, my Ibo acquaintance has talked about studying in America, working in a brewery, the Biafran war, his family, and his poster of Jennifer. He covets my tennis racquet, but although it has been mostly a nuisance during most of my African visit I don't offer it to him.

In the departure lounge I'm denied a boarding pass and instructed that I'll have to wait for an afternoon flight.

The Brit who works for the wildlife foundation is gone, but the mother and her weary children are still there.

The people, I say to myself, the desperate people, the people, the people.

Robin Hemley

READING HISTORY TO MY MOTHER

ROBIN HEMLEY is the author of seven books of fiction and nonfiction. His stories and essays have appeared in *The New York Times*, *New York Magazine*, *Chicago Tribune*, *Southern Review*, *Conjunctions*, *Boulevard*, *Prairie Schooner*, *Creative Nonfiction*, *Fourth Genre*, *Ploughshares*, *Shenandoah*, and many other literary magazines; and in anthologies including *Sudden Fiction, Continued*, and *New Sudden Fiction*. His work has won first place in the Nelson Algren Award for Fiction from the *Chicago Tribune*, the George Garrett Award for Fiction, *Story* magazine's Humor Award, the Governor's Award for Nonfiction from the State of Washington, the Independent Press Book Award for Nonfiction, *ForeWord* magazine's Award for Nonfiction, the Walter Rumsey Marvin Award from the Ohioana Library Association, and two Pushcart Prizes. He is director of the Nonfiction Writing Program at the University of Iowa and writes a column for *The Believer* magazine on defunct literary journals. He recently finished a new short story collection and is working on a new novel and a work of nonfiction titled *Do Over*.

> Your silence will not protect you.
> —Audre Lourde

"Everything's mixed up in those boxes, the past and the present," my mother tells me. "Those movers made a mess of everything." I'm visiting her at the Leopold late on a Monday night after reading to my kids and being read to by my eldest, Olivia, who at six is rightfully proud of her newfound reading ability. My mother and I have been readers for many years, but in some ways, she finds reading more difficult than does Olivia. At eighty-two, my mother's eyesight has deteriorated. Glaucoma. Severe optic nerve damage to her left eye. Macular degeneration. Tomorrow, I'm taking her to the doctor for a second laser operation to "relieve the pressure." We have been told by the doctor that the surgery won't actually improve her eyesight, but, with luck, will stop it from deteriorating any more. After that there's another operation she'll probably undergo, eighty miles south in Seattle. Another operation that won't actually make her see any better.

"I always had such good eyesight," she tells me. And then, "I wish there was something that could improve my eyesight." And then, "When are we going to go shopping for that new computer?"

"Well, let's make sure you can see the screen first," I say, which sounds cruel, but she has complained to me tonight that she wasn't able to see any of the words on her screen, though I think this has less to do with her eyesight than the glasses she's wearing. Unnaturally thick and foggy. My mother looks foggy, too, almost drunk, disheveled in her dirty sweater, though she doesn't drink. It's probably the medicine she's been taking for her many conditions. My mother owns at least half a dozen glasses, and I know I should have sorted through them all by now (we tried once) but so many things have gone wrong in the last five months since my mother moved to Bellingham that sorting through her glasses is a side issue. I get up from the couch in the cramped living room of her apartment, step over the coffee table—careful not to tip over the cup of peppermint tea I'm drinking out of a beer stein, careful not to bump into my mother—and cross to the bedroom crammed with wardrobe boxes and too much furniture, though much less than what she's used to. On her dresser there are parts of various eyeglasses: maimed glasses, the corpses of eyeglasses, a dark orphaned lens here, a frame there, an empty case, and one case with a pair that's whole. This is the one I grab and take out to my mother who is waiting patiently, always patient these days, or perhaps so unnerved and exhausted that it passes for patience. She takes the case from me and takes off the old glasses, places them beside her beer mug of licorice tea, and puts on the new pair.

She rubs an eye, says, "This seems to be helping. Maybe these are my reading glasses." I should know, of course. I should have had them color-coded by now, but I haven't yet.

She bends down to the photo from the newsletter on the coffee table, and says, "Yes, that's William Carlos Williams."

A little earlier she told me about the photo. "It's in one of those boxes," she told me. "I saw it the other day. I thought I'd told you about it before," but she hadn't, this photo of her with William Carlos Williams, Theodore Roethke, and other famous writers. So I spent fifteen minutes rifling through her boxes of bills and old papers mixed up on the kitchen counter (a Cascade Gas Company bill, final payment requested for service at the apartment she moved into in December, when we still thought she could live on her own; a letter from the superintendent of public schools of New York City, dated 1959, addressed to my grandmother, a teacher at the time, telling her how many sick days she was allowed), looking for the photo, until she explained that it was actually part of a newsletter from the artists' colony, Yaddo, in Saratoga Springs, New York. Armed with that crucial bit of information, I found it.

The photo is captioned "Class picture, 1950."

Can you pick me out? she says.

From left, top: William Osborne, Theodore Roethke, Robel Paris, Harvey Shapiro, Elaine Gottlieb, Beryl Levy, Cid Corman, Simmons Persons, Gladys Farnel, Hans Sahl, Clifford Wright, Richard Eberhart. From left, bottom: Ben Weber, Nicholas Callas, Jessamyn West, Eugenie Gershoy, William Carlos Williams, Flossie Williams, Mitsu Yashima, Charles Schucker, Elizabeth Ames, John Dillon Husband.

Not many of these people are smiling. Eugenie Gershoy, seated next to Jessamyn West, has a little smirk, and Mitsu Yashima, seated next to Flossie Williams, smiles broadly, and also Cid Corman in the back row, whom I met in 1975, when I was a high school exchange student in Japan. My mother visited me in Osaka and we traveled by train to Kyoto, to Cid Corman's ice cream parlor where I ate a hamburger, had an ice cream cone and listened to a poetry reading while my mother and Cid reminisced.

"Don't I look prim?" my mother says, and she does. Or maybe it's something else. Scared? Intimidated? Shocked? My mother was 34 then—This was a year or so before she met my father. My sister, Nola, was three, and my mother was an up-and-coming young writer, one novel published in 1947. John Crowe Ransom liked her work, publishing several of her stories in the *Kenyon Review*. I wasn't born until 1958.

She stands up straight, hands behind her back, a scarf tied loosely around her neck, draping down over a breast, a flower pinned to the scarf. Theodore Roethke stands, huge, imposing, dour. In an accompanying article Harvey Shapiro tells of how publicly Roethke liked to display his wounds, how he told Shapiro of his hurt that John Crowe Ransom had rejected "My Papa's Waltz," though Roethke was famous by then and the poem had been widely anthologized. What remained, still, was Roethke's pain, perhaps the pain of rejection meshed with the pain of the poem's subject matter—abuse at the hands of his drunken father. Shapiro also tells of Roethke's claim that he'd bummed his way to Yaddo after escaping in drag from a mental institution on the west coast earlier that summer. "He liked to romanticize his mental illness," Shapiro writes. Perhaps, but something honest still comes across in that picture, the despair clear for anyone to view head-on.

In the front row, William Carlos Williams sits cross-legged, dignified.

"He dreamed of my legs," my mother tells me.

"William Carlos Williams dreamed of your legs?" I ask.

"At breakfast one day he said he'd had a dream about my legs. 'That girl has nice legs,' he said."

We have to keep going back over histories, our own and the histories of others, constantly revising. There's no single truth . . . except that, perhaps. History is not always recorded and not always written by the victor. History is not always written. We carry our secret histories behind our words, in another room, in the eyeglass case on the dresser in the bedroom. Maybe someone comes along and finds the right pair. Maybe we have too many, unsorted.

My mother's former landlord, Loyce, wants to know the history of the "L." I was gone for the past week in Hawaii, and that's the only reason I haven't called before now. Loyce has left messages on my answering machine twice, ostensibly to see about getting back my mother's deposit to us; minus a charge for mowing, the ad for renting the apartment again, a reasonable charge for her time, and of course, for painting over the "L." She'd also like the keys back from us. But the "L" is the real reason she's called. My mother wrote an "L" on the wall of the apartment in indelible magic marker before she left. "I'm dying to know the story," Loyce says. "I know there's a good story behind it."

Loyce appreciates a good story, and this is one of the things I appreciate about Loyce, that and her compassion. She moved to Bellingham several years ago to take care of her ailing mother, and now lives in her mother's old house on top of a hill with a view of the bay and the San Juan Islands. So she understands our situation. She knows that my mother can't live alone anymore, that all of us were taken by surprise by her condition when she moved here five months ago. Until then, my mother had been living on her own in South Bend, Indiana, where she taught writing until ten years ago. She'd been living on her own since I moved out at the age of sixteen to go to boarding school, and had been taking care of herself since 1966 when my father died. But in the last several months things have fallen apart. Our first inkling was the mover, a man in his sixties who worked with his son. He took me aside on the first day and told me that in his thirty years of moving he'd never seen an apartment as messy as my mother's. When he and his son went to my mom's apartment in South Bend, they almost turned around. "You don't have to do this if you don't want," the mover told his son.

No, the first inkling was my brother's call from L.A., where my mother was visiting a few days prior to her big move. The van had loaded in South Bend and she'd flown off to L.A. to visit him and his family. The night before her flight from L.A. to Seattle he called me near midnight and said, "Mom's hallucinating."

I asked him what he meant, what she was seeing, and he told me that she was seeing all these people who didn't exist and making strange remarks. "When I picked her up at the airport, she said there was a group of Asians having a baby. She said they were a troupe of actors and they were doing a skit."

Still, the next day, he put her on the plane to me, and I picked her up and brought her to her new home. Since then, we have gone to three different doctors and my mother has had brain scans and blood tests and sonograms of her carotid arteries and been placed on a small dose of an anti-psychotic drug. One doctor says her cerebral cortex has shrunk and she's had a series of tiny strokes to individual arteries in her brain.

At three a.m. one morning, the police call me up and tell me that my mother thinks someone is trying to break into her apartment.

"Is there anyone living with her?" the policeman asks.

"No."

"She says a handicapped woman lives with her. You might want to see a doctor about this."

I take her to doctors and try to convince my mother that she needs to live where she can be safe, but she refuses even to consider it. "I should have stayed in New York," she tells me. "I never should have left." And then, "I should never have come here. Why can't you be on my side?" And then, "I'll move down to L.A.. Your brother is much nicer than you are."

I spend a few nights at her apartment, and she tells me about the Middle Eastern couple who have taken over her bedroom and the children who are there, and the landlord comes over and puts a lock on the door from the kitchen to the garage, though we know no one was trying to break in. And homeless people are living on her back porch. And she keeps startling people in the garage who are removing her belongings.

But finally.

After my cousin David flies up from L.A., after visiting a dozen managed care facilities, after my brother says he thinks it's the medicine that's doing this and I talk to the doctors and the doctors talk to each other and they talk to my mother and she says, "The doctor says I'm fine," and I say "No, he doesn't," and she hangs up, turns off her hearing aid.

And coincidentally, a friend of my mother's in South Bend wins second place in a poetry competition run by the literary journal I edit. The poems were all anonymous, and I had nothing to do with the judging, but my mother's friend has won second prize for a poem about her delusional mother, called

"My Mother and Dan Rather." I call her up to tell her the good news of her award, but she assumes, of course, I'm calling to talk about my mother. So that's what we do for half an hour. She tells me she's distanced herself over the last year from my mother because she seemed too much like her own mother, and she tells me that several of my mother's friends wondered if they should call me and let me know what was going on.

I almost forget to tell her about her prize.

No, the first inkling was two years ago. My wife, Beverly, wondered aloud about my mother's memory, her hold on reality. I told Beverly my mother had always been kind of scattered, messy, unfocused.

And finally. After I come into her apartment one day and feel the heat, I go to the stove and turn off the glowing burners. My mother has a blister on her hand the size of a walnut. Beverly tells me that it's insane for my mother to live alone, that somehow we have to force her to move. "What if she sets the apartment on fire? She might not only kill herself, but the people next door."

"I know," I tell her. "I'm trying," but I also know that short of a court order, short of being declared her legal guardian, I can't force her.

And finally. I convince my mother to come with me to the Leopold, an historic hotel in downtown Bellingham that has been converted into apartments for seniors, one wing assisted living, the other independent. We have lunch there one day. My mother likes the food.

And finally, she agrees to spend a couple of weeks there in a guest room.

Famous people stayed at the Leopold, I tell my mother. Rutherford B. Hayes. Jenny Lind, the Swedish Nightingale. This doesn't impress her, of course. She has known more famous people than can fit on a plaque. But she has a nice view of the bay, somewhat blocked by the Georgia Pacific Paper Mill. And she likes the food but the apartment is only two cramped rooms, and across the street at the Greek restaurant, people party until two each night and climb trees and conduct military rituals. And the Iraqi Army rolled through the streets one night. And a truck dumped two bodies, a man and a woman dressed in formal evening attire.

"They sometimes flood the parking lot," she tells me, "and use it as a waterway."

Or, "Look at that," pointing, reaching for nothing.

She keeps returning to the apartment, driven by the woman I've hired to clean it. My mother wants to drive again, and I tell her no, she can't possibly, and I read articles and watch programs that tell me not to reverse roles, not to become the parent, and I wonder how that's possible to avoid. One day, I walk into her apartment and find signs she's posted all around on the bed, in the guest room, on the kitchen counter. "Keep off." "Stay out." "Go Away." I ask her about these signs and she tells me they're just a joke. She's become wary of me. I tell her she's safe, ask her why she feels so threatened. She tells me, "I've never felt safe in my life." During this period, my mother writes her "L" on the wall of the kitchen.

And the weeks at the Leopold have turned to months, and now most of her belongings are stuffed into a heated mini-storage unit. More of her belongings are stuffed into the basement of The Leopold.

Finally.

I almost don't want to tell Loyce the story of the "L" when she calls. I'd like to keep her in suspense, because sometimes that's stronger than the truth. She probably thinks it's about her, that the "L" stands for Loyce, but it doesn't. It stands for Leopold. One day my mother was at the apartment, after we finally convinced her she had to move, and I gave her a magic marker and asked her to mark the boxes she'd like taken to the Leopold. Apparently, she thought she was marking a box, but she was really marking the wall. This is what she really wanted. That was not lost on me. She loved that apartment. She wanted her independence, but this was just too much for me to move.

Loyce and I say goodbye after I assure her I'll return the keys and she assures me she'll return most of the deposit. It's already eight-thirty and I told my mother I'd be over around eight, but I had to read to my kids first. I haven't see them in a week. I've just returned from Hawaii.

In Hawaii, where I've been researching a new book, I probably had more fun than I should have. Not the kind of fun with life-bending consequences, but fun nonetheless, hanging out with a former student, eating out every night, smoking cigars, drinking. For ten dollars a day more, I was told at the airport, I could rent a convertible—a Ford Mustang, or a Caddie, and I'm not ready for that, so I take the Mustang. Stupid. The wife of the friend I'm staying with laughed when she saw it in her driveway. "Oh," she tells me. "I thought maybe Robbie was having a mid-life crisis." No, it's me probably, even though I hate to admit it. I refuse to believe such a thing could happen to me at this pre-ordained age, a month from forty, that I could be saddled with such a cliché crisis, such mediocre regrets.

Olivia wants to read to *me* tonight, all seven stories from an Arnold Lobel book. "They're short," she assures me. We compromise on three, her three favorites. One of these she read last week to her class while I was in Hawaii. Beverly, who sometimes works in Olivia's class as a volunteer, has already told me that the class was enthralled by Olivia. "She acted so confident. She took her time and showed them the pictures."

The one she read to her class, "The Journey," is about a mouse who wants to visit his mother, and in a sequence of transactions, acquires a car, roller skates, boots, sneakers and finally a new set of feet. When he reaches his mother she hugs him, kisses him and says, "Hello, my son, you are looking fine—and what nice new feet you have!" Olivia's whole class broke out in hysterical laughter, she assured me.

I've brought my mother a box of chocolate-covered macadamia nuts. She looks at it, bewildered. "Oh, I thought it was a book," she says.

I make tea for us, but she only has a few tea mugs and they're dirty, so we have to use beer steins. "I've ended up with such an odd assortment of things," she tells me, and she blames this on the movers.

A week before my trip to Hawaii, I visited her and she showed me a notebook in which she'd kept a journal during the mid-seventies. My mother has kept journals from the time she was sixteen, a series of secret histories written in any notebook she can find. But now, she cannot read these histories, and she asks me to read this one to her.

"I might use it in a story," she tells me. "It's about Moe and Helen." Moe is Moe Howard, of the Three Stooges. He was a cousin of ours by marriage, and whenever she visited California, she'd stop by to see them. Moe, who had such a violent on-screen persona: Think of him saying, "Wise guy, eh?" Poking the eyes Larry, Curly, Shemp, or one of the later pseudo-Stooges, Curly Joe and Joe Besser. I met him once, a frail old man with white hair, too quiet to seem like Moe. Off-screen, he was a gentle family man, kind and grateful to his fans, never refusing to sign an autograph. What my mother wants me to read to her is an account of the last time she saw Moe and his wife Helen, when they were both dying.

Seeing Moe and Helen was touching—a beautiful hill of purple flowers outside that Moe said was all theirs—a beautifully furnished, expensively comfortable house through which they glide, ghost-like. They don't kiss me because of the possibility of germs. Helen is in a loose purple nylon dressing gown. She has been recuperating from a breast operation and says in a slightly quaking voice that she will be going to the doctor soon and will probably have cobalt.

Moe is red-faced and very thin. His thinness, wispiness, makes him look elfin— because he used to be heavier, he seemed bigger. His hair is white. He smiles proudly, talking about his appearances at colleges and his memoirs which comprise

many books. Talk about the film I am supposed to have made with him. He re-
minds me that I acted in it (at the age of about 19) 8mm, I think, with his chil-
dren. But it is packed somewhere with thousands of feet of other film.

As I'm reading this to my mother I feel odd, wondering if she notices the simi-
larities between this passage and her own present life—the things packed away,
the memories, the frailty—but I say nothing about this, though it moves me.
Instead, I ask her about this film she was in, and she tells me it was an impromptu home movie in which Moe was cast as the villain, of course, and she
was the protector of his children. She has never seen it but it exists somewhere.
Moe's daughter, Joan, once showed me the huge roll of home movies in her attic. Towards the end of his life, Moe took every home movie he made and
spliced them all together onto one monstrous cumbersome roll that no one
could ever possibly watch in its entirety. Somewhere on this roll exists a movie
with my mother, age nineteen, circa 1935. Silently, I flip through other pages in
my mother's journal, as she sits near me, lost in her memories, needing no journal really. *I am not in fantasy land. I am painfully living out my loneliness and*
nostalgia. I dream of my son every night and wish he were here. Those who have died
are intolerably absent and I feel that all the love I need and want will not come be-
cause I had my chance and lost it, and what man will be responsible for or will react
to my aging, my passion, my intolerable loneliness. . . ?
    I am with her now, but not. We see each other through veils. We have battled
for this moment, and neither sees the other as we would like.

William Carlos Williams dreamed of my mother's legs, as did other men that
summer of 1950 at Yaddo.
    As we bend over the class photo, circa 1950, she tells me the official history
of that summer, how special it was for her, how it was so exciting to be around
such vital intellects, such talented writers. "It was really something, going down
to breakfast and having conversations with all these people. The talent was never
quite the same after that."
    I tell her I'd love to have a copy of this picture. "You could write to Yaddo,"
she says. "They use it for publicity." She tells me I could write to one of the writers pictured with her. "It's the least he could do," she says, with what seems like
bitterness, and I let this remark wash over me because I think I know what's
behind it.
    Once, a number of years ago, Beverly and my mother and I were on a drive,
and I was telling her about a friend of mine who'd done his dissertation on the
poetry of one of the poets pictured in the photo. From the backseat my mother
blurted, "You know, he raped me."

Beverly and I looked at one another. We didn't say anything. We didn't know what to say. The remark was so sudden, so unexpected, we hardly knew how to react. We were silent, all three of us. Neither Beverly nor I mentioned this to each other later.

My mother starts talking about him now, though I haven't asked. She says, "One time, he invited me to a private party, and innocent that I was, I went there." In memory, she's lucid. Only the present is slippery, tricky, untrustworthy.

"There were all these men there. They were all leches. Ted Roethke kept lunging for me, just making grabs. He really had problems," and she laughs. She mentions the name of the poet who was her friend, whom she trusted. He was younger than her, than all these other famous men. "I thought he'd protect me." She laughs again. This time, there's no mistaking the bitterness.

I think about asking her. What term to use? "He assaulted you?"

"Yes," she says.

"Did it happen at Yaddo?" I ask.

She nods.

"Did you ever confront him?"

"No," she says. "I don't want to talk about it."

But then she says, "There wasn't much I could do. In those days, there wasn't much to do. I just pretended it didn't happen. For a little while, he became my boyfriend."

I don't know what to say. I probably shouldn't say anything. I sigh. "He should have been locked up. How could he be your boyfriend after that?"

"He was drunk when it happened," and I want to say that's no excuse, but I keep my mouth shut and let her talk. "I left the party early and he followed me back to my room. I tried to lock the door, but the lock was broken.

"I turned things around. I had to. I was confused. In my mind, he became my protector from the other men there."

I study the picture again. My mother's expression and the expressions of the men. I wonder when this photo was taken, before or after the assault my mother describes. The photo has taken on the quality of a group mug shot to me. I think they look like jerks, most of them—except for Cid Corman, whom my mother says is a wonderful person, and maybe some others, too, maybe William Carlos Williams, who dreamed of my mother's legs and "had an eye for the ladies" as my mother says. Maybe even dour Theodore Roethke, though he lunged at her as though she was something being wheeled by on a dessert tray.

"They weren't famous for their personalities," she tells me.

I think about these people in the photo, how unfair it seems to me that someone can go on to have a career, hide behind his smirk, have dissertations written about him, how the actions of some people seem to have no visible consequences. I think of my mother's secret histories, her journals, her blurted comments, her assertion that she has never felt safe.

I flip the newsletter over to the section titled "Recent works Produced by Yaddo Fellows," and see that the latest works reported are from 1987. For an absurd moment, I believe that none of the Fellows at Yaddo have been productive for over ten years, and this makes me happy, but then I realize the newsletter itself is ten years old.

My mother has taken to carrying a picture of me, Ideal Robin, I call it, skinny, sitting langorously, smiling beside a life-size cardboard cut-out of Rudolph Valentino. The son she longed for in her journal perhaps hardly exists anymore—I was away at boarding school that year, my choice, not hers, and I never returned.

I have come to visit her now. I've knocked lightly. I've used my key. She can barely see me when I walk into her apartment. I've told her I've returned from Hawaii, that she can expect me around eight, but I'm late and as I push open the door she's looking at me almost suspiciously, because really her eyesight is that bad, and until I speak she has no idea who's entering. The Iraqi army? A stranger who wants her belongings? A poet she thinks is her "protector" but means her harm? I half expect to see signs, "Keep Off," "Stay Out," "Go Away." I have brought a box of chocolate-covered macadamia nuts. I am wearing new feet, but she doesn't notice. Tomorrow she will have surgery on her eyes that will not improve anything, but keep things from getting worse. How much worse could things get for this woman who loves words, but can neither see nor write them anymore? Does her history go on inside her, on some gigantic roll of spliced-together home movies? Tell me the story of the "L." Tell me the story of the wall of your apartment. Tell me the story of those talented writers who publicly display their wounds and the writers who secretly wound others. Tell me which is worse. She kisses me lightly and I give her her gift. And she says, once, only once, though I keep hearing it, the disappointment, and strangely, even fear, "Oh, I thought it was a book."

Adam Hochschild

WORLD ON A HILLTOP

ADAM HOCHSCHILD, born in New York City, is the author of *Half the Way Home: A Memoir of Father and Son*; *The Mirror at Midnight: A South African Journey*; *The Unquiet Ghost: Russians Remember Stalin*; *Finding the Trapdoor: Essays, Portraits, Travels*, winner of the 1998 PEN/Spielvogel-Diamonstein Award for the art of the essay; and *King Leopold's Ghost*, a *New York Times Book Review* and *Library Journal* notable book of the year, also awarded the 1998 California Book Awards gold medal for nonfiction. Hochschild's books, translated into five languages, have won prizes from the Overseas Press Club of America, the World Affairs Council, the Eugene V. Debs Foundation, and the Society of American Travel Writers. He has also written for *The New Yorker*, *Harper's*, *The Nation*, *The New York Times Magazine*, *The New York Review of Books*, and *Mother Jones*, which he cofounded. A former commentator on National Public Radio's *All Things Considered*, Hochschild teaches writing at the Graduate School of Journalism at the University of California at Berkeley. In 1997–98 he was a Fulbright Lecturer in India. He lives in San Francisco.

On the night Mel Bancroft was expelled, most of Pomfret School was up past midnight. In a school of only some two hundred boys, you got to know each other well, and we all knew Mel—or thought we did. He was a superb athlete, and at Pomfret this was important: he earned his letters early in soccer and hockey and he danced agilely across the tennis court in a white Pomfret shirt and Bermuda shorts. Mel was popular, but there was an uneasiness in his eyes, and he talked a little too fast. He wore the madras jacket, white socks, chinos, and brown loafers that were the unofficial uniform of New England prep schools in the late 1950s. He let the word get around about how he continued his athletic exploits during vacations: skiing in Europe, rock-climbing expeditions, scuba diving—all trips he was ferried to in his family's limousine and private planes. "No, not plane, *planes*," insisted one boy who had it straight from Mel, the horse's mouth.

One spring day, when the leaves were out on the elms and the crack of baseballs echoed across the school's green lawns and ivy-covered buildings, this whole picture of Mel's life cracked down the middle. Mel Bancroft was found to be embezzling money from the Tuck Shop, the small student-run candy-and-stationery store in the school basement. The same day it was discovered that the sizable array of skis, climbing boots, tennis rackets, and the like in Mel's closet, and some of the cash in his wallet, had been stolen from other boys. Mel Bancroft, it turned out to the astonishment of the entire student body, was not from a wealthy family after all. He was on scholarship. A solemn-faced Mel was interrogated by the headmaster and several teachers. Late that night—in a modest sedan, not a limousine—his parents arrived to pick him up, and his Pomfret career was over.

Mel Bancroft is not his real name, but all other details about him here are unchanged; he went on, incidentally, to became the CEO of a highly successful corporation. Pomfret School is still in business, on a beautiful rural hilltop in northeastern Connecticut. Now, as then, it is basically a school for the rich. Until the day Mel's world collapsed, I never realized how difficult life there must have been for a student whose family did not have money. Since then, I've often wondered what Mel Bancroft must have felt, for it takes vast emotional energy to keep up a façade with all your friends year upon year. Mel felt driven to steal not just ski boots, but an entire biography for himself. Behind his anxious darting eyes lay a desperation. He must have felt like a light-skinned black person who successfully "passes" for white in a Southern town, and who is at last found out.

Pomfret is one of the many boarding schools that were built, mostly between 1850 and 1900, as New England copies of the British model. Both Pomfret's official language and slang were redolent of British class distinctions: teachers were "masters"; freshmen were "weenies." Until the early 1950s, new boys still underwent hazing from the older ones, that ritualistic preparation for distinctions of class and rank in the world outside. At Pomfret, entering freshmen were herded on some pretext into a squash court, then pelted with wet tennis balls by seniors in the spectators' gallery above.

Depending on how far in the air your nose is when you name them, there are one to two dozen American schools like Pomfret. I do not mean private schools in general, or even private boarding schools, whose number is at least in the hundreds. Rather, I mean that select group of well-established schools, mostly in Connecticut and Massachusetts, all a century old or more, with names as familiar as those of the powerful families whose children they educate, so that, in ruling-class circles when somebody asks a mother what her son is doing now, she need only say, "Oh, Danny? He's at Pomfret." And no further explanation is needed. As Danny's life goes on, he will find that the world is laced by a network of other prep school alumni, and that by little signs—a stray reference, a phrase, a touch of accent—they can recognize each other. I have often found this happening to me, particularly when I least expect it, and in those moments of mutual recognition I suddenly see myself as part of a tribe and subtribe to which, however unwillingly, I belong.

Even before I could articulate the feeling, I always thought that my four years at Pomfret were pivotal in my life and in my awareness of the world, or at least of the narrow slice of it into which I was born. I found myself thinking about the school even more once my children grew old enough to be curious. You mean you *lived* there? And there were no blacks? And no *girls?* Today it more and more strikes me how bizarre and unjust is the entire world of prep schools. And yet a significant percentage of the people who run this country are among their graduates. These schools cannot, like monasteries, be dismissed as irrelevant.

I arrived at Pomfret at the age of thirteen, on a crisp fall day at the height of the cold war. Eisenhower was in the White House, God was an Episcopalian, and I was miserably homesick at being away from my parents for the first time. The school was a cluster of red-brick buildings with white trim and a commanding view of the surrounding countryside. The window of my room looked across a football field, down into a wooded valley, and up to the top of a hill on the other side, where an old farmhouse and barn stood out against the horizon. The dormitories had a distinct musty smell, a smell of sweat and steam heat and decades of sunlight seeping into wooden walls. I occasionally catch a whiff of that smell in an old, sun-warmed paneled room that hasn't been dusted, and it brings everything back.

Although I was too nervous to notice it, any other American arriving at Pomfret that day would have been struck by how, side-by-side with only a modest library and science labs, this school for a mere two hundred boys had amazingly lavish sports facilities Squash courts; tennis courts; football, baseball, and soccer fields; a track; a gym with an indoor track and rowing machines; rifles for target shooting; a ski jump on one hill and a slope with a rope tow on another. Today the school also has an indoor hockey rink and four indoor, year-round tennis courts.

The teachers were almost all men. Classes were small, seldom more than fifteen students and often fewer. Three times a day, we donned coats and ties and gathered in the Common Room next to the dining hall. Each night while we were waiting there for the dining hall doors to open for dinner, the same student always played the piano, well enough to draw a little coterie of hovering admirers. He knew only one tune—"Has Anybody Seen My Girl?"—but no one seemed to mind.

We did a great deal of talking at school: announcements to the daily assembly, reports in class, speeches and panel discussions at weekend conferences on current events, meetings of various student-faculty committees, readings at the daily chapel service. Each student ate his three meals a day with half a dozen other boys at a dining table headed by a teacher and his wife—and then was rotated weekly, by roster, to another teacher's table. Years later, a friend asked me if we had had any special training in how to do well in corporate job interviews. No, I replied. But after I had described the daily routine, she said, "Adam, don't you see? The *whole thing* was a practice interview!"

If there is any single thing that stands out in my memory of Pomfret from my first timid weeks at the school, it is the impression that by being there I was somehow beginning a certain path in life, a path whose destination I did not know, but whose existence was as clear as if there had been signposts along my way to class each day.

In fact there were signs everywhere, usually engraved in wood or marble or stone. Plaques in the chapel honoring Pomfret boys who had fallen in the two World Wars. Wooden tablets in the gym listing baseball and football captains back to the 1890s. Signs above the doors to all buildings, naming them after the alumni who had donated money for them. Even the many years' worth of initials carved in the wood-topped desks, spreading across each classroom like a sea of alphabet soup. Often these names were familiar, when there was a son or grandson of the same family just up the dormitory corridor or next to you at soccer practice. It gave you the feeling of entering a web that stretched backward and forward in time, connected both to the past and to the secure future awaiting you as a Pomfret graduate.

No ticket to the future is completely secure, especially today, but a prep school diploma helps. One study of people listed in *Who's Who* found that a graduate of one of the top ten prep schools was thirty-nine times more likely to end up listed in the book than a graduate of the average high school. The twentieth century has seen three prep school alumni as president—George Bush (Andover), John F. Kennedy (Choate), and Franklin Roosevelt (Groton)—and many more among those who tried: Adlai Stevenson (Choate), Robert F. Kennedy (Milton), and Averell Harriman (Groton), to name but a few. Ruling-class families in this country often send their children to the same prep school over the generations: Cabots have usually gone to St. Mark's, Fords to Hotchkiss, Mellons to Choate, Vanderbilts to St. Paul's, DuPonts to Pomfret. When we found names like these among our classmates, or found somebody's father in the newspaper headlines, it did not seem odd. We expected it. That was part of being at Pomfret.

From the Pomfret newsletter over the years, giving news of alumni in each graduating class:

> 1909—*John A. Morris* . . . is a special partner in the New York Stock Exchange member firm of Prescott, Ball and Turben. His interest, aside from that, is thoroughbred racing.

> 1935—*Thibaut de Saint Phalle* is a director of the Export-Import Bank in Washington.

> 1938—*Maxwell Marston, Jr.* is now living in Hilton Head Island, S.C. He reports that the second green of the Dolphin Head Golf Course is about 200 feet from his living room. He is still active in real-estate investment and construction.

> 1964—*Peter Kelsey* writes that after more than eight years practicing environmental law and energy law for the U.S. Department of the Interior, he has decided to get an industry perspective on these issues. He is now assistant general counsel at the Edison Electric Institute [the lobbying arm of the nation's private power companies] "looking for mutual respect and understanding of conflicting priorities."

The segregation that reserves schools like Pomfret mainly for the rich is enforced not by rules but by cost. The percentage is higher at some better-endowed prep schools, but at the time I was there, little more than 10 percent of Pomfret students got any scholarship aid. To send your child to any of the top prep schools as a boarder approaches the cost of tuition at a good private college, something most American families simply can't afford. The total tuition and other charges my parents paid to send me to Pomfret each year was higher than some Pomfret faculty salaries.

From this class gap between students and teachers came some tension. My teachers had generally gone to public high schools themselves; most had worked their way through college or had gone on the G.I. Bill. To make ends meet, they often took summer jobs—two of mine worked in a local lumber yard, for instance. But the students they taught were summering on Martha's Vineyard or visiting Europe. When the teachers saw how boys at the school lived—the style of life Mel Bancroft tried so pitifully hard to mimic—they were appalled. I vividly remember a teacher telling me that one day he had found a boy throwing away a brand new pair of pants, right out of the package, into a dormitory trash barrel. Why? the horrified teacher asked. "Oh," the boy said, "I ordered this suit because I wanted the coat. I don't need the pants." Little incidents like this, confided by teachers, made a deep impression on me, because it was the first time I saw my own social class through the eyes of another.

Some scholars of U.S. ruling circles say that it is precisely to learn those upper-class habits that elite families send their sons to schools like Pomfret. Not so, I think. Pomfret boys learned their values by being born to well-off parents, ranging from doctors and corporate lawyers to people who owned banks or newspapers or the inherited fortunes derived from them. The boys were sent to Pomfret to learn, instead, the middle-class virtues: ambition, hard work, good study habits—those things that the ruling class finds useful to help it keep ruling.

Many boys sorely needed such training. To make big money, especially during an entrepreneurial era like that of the robber barons, requires shrewdness and initiative. But being born into wealth three or four generations later does not engender these qualities. Often, the opposite. One boy during my time at Pomfret, a grandson of a famed turn-of-the-century sugar baron, had to repeat a year. Another, one of the DuPont clan, simply failed to do his homework and—the headmaster gravely announced in the school assembly one day—was put on the train to go home for several weeks until he got it done.

Looking back on it now, I think the school offered something you could call the Pomfret Bargain. From the point of view of parents, the bargain was: I'll pay that astronomical tuition if you'll get my kid into a decent college. From the point of view of Pomfret's teachers, the bargain was: I'll put up with those outrageously low wages so I can teach classes one-third the size of those in a public school. The role of the school administration was to make sure all parts of the bargain were kept and to provide the gloss of uplift and high purpose that covered the bargain's everyday workings. There were prayers in chapel asking God's blessing on "those who teach and those who learn." And there were speeches about the pursuit of excellence and about something called the Pomfret System, which was a lofty way of saying we had a student government.

Everything at Pomfret was covered with that gloss. Instead of saying "Hedley Skeffles gave $100,000 so we'd name the new squash courts after him," the speech at the ribbon-cutting ceremony would thank "Hed Skeffles, who has had the foresight, the courage, and the vision to understand Pomfret's needs in the decades ahead. Especially the needs of our athletic program." It still goes on: at an alumni gathering the last time I was back at school, I heard the headmaster refer to "the many privileges of teaching here at Pomfret and the advantages to us all of being without the *bureaucracy* of public schools." It soon became clear he was talking about the absence of teachers' unions.

The terms of a hidden bargain show more clearly when the bargain breaks down. This began to happen while I was at Pomfret, and it revealed something about changes in America's elite at that time. For the first half of the twentieth century, the Pomfret Bargain had worked: the school did the job it was contracted to do. Unless you were somewhat thickheaded, a Pomfret diploma could get you into an Ivy League college. Then, in the 1950s, several things started to happen. The U.S. population was growing rapidly, while the number of Ivy League and elite colleges, of course, stayed the same. The balance of American economic power began shifting toward the Southwest—people in previously unfashionable places like Phoenix and Houston had the nerve to want to send their kids to Harvard. And high-quality public schools, their curricula as good as any New England prep school's, appeared in well-to-do suburbs, particularly in the mid-West and Far West.

The result was that fairly suddenly the top Eastern colleges had so many qualified applicants that they could pick and choose. Grades and test scores rapidly came to mean a great deal. When I graduated in 1960, 30 percent of my Pomfret class went on to Harvard or Yale; during the following decade, that percentage plummeted, in some years, to zero.

During the years I was at Pomfret, this historic sea change was just beginning. Particularly for fathers, confident that their sons would go on to an Ivy League college just as they had done, it was an unexpected shock. Parents panicked and visited the school for long, anguished conferences with the headmaster: You mean I paid all this money and the best place you can get Johnny into is *Cincinnati?* During the decade or so after I graduated, with the bargain threatened, Pomfret fell into the academic equivalent of an economic depression. Desperate fund-raising appeals went out to alumni in the late sixties and early seventies. Pomfret had never quite been in the topmost rank of New England boarding schools, and so it was hit worse than most. One year it failed to fill all the places in its entering class. Faculty members had to take a temporary 10 percent pay cut, thereby seeing the terms of their part of the Pomfret Bargain eroded. There was even talk of closing down. For college admission purposes, was a Pomfret education still worth anything? Above a sheaf of toilet paper in one of the school men's rooms appeared some graffiti: "Pomfret diplomas. Take one." A *Newsweek* headline in 1972 asked CAN PREP SCHOOLS SURVIVE?

Today, however, prep schools are riding high again. The major reason is that public schools are hard hit. First came state tax-slashing measures like California's Proposition 13, then the Reagan era's cuts in federal aid to public schools. Those families who can afford it are looking for education elsewhere. Private schools all over the country are experiencing a big surge in the number of people trying to get in, the elite New England prep schools most of all. Don't worry, *Newsweek:* privilege endures.

Candidates for Board of Trustees, one to be elected:

Lewis Turner, Jr., '66. In 1973 he ... began working for Bankers Trust Company in New York.... Today [he] is a vice president in Bankers Trust Petroleum Division. He and his wife Beth have one child and live in New York City.

Charles Baker Wheeler II, '40. Charlie Wheeler attended Williams College and served in the U.S. Army.... He subsequently worked for the Central Intelligence Agency, from which he retired in 1976.... His son Gordon graduated from Pomfret in 1969.

The Pomfret chapel is the same: the worn stone steps and dark wooden pews, the grandeur of Bach and stained glass and the Episcopal *Book of Common Prayer.* But something is different this weekend. Many of the students filing into chapel are wearing black arm bands. It is May 1970, the tenth reunion of my Pomfret class and the first time I've been back to the school in almost as many years. Several days ago the United States invaded Cambodia.

The country is swept by student strikes. A hundred thousand angry protesters march in Washington, D.C. At Pomfret, things are more decorous: all that is visible are the black arm bands and solemn knots of students, gathered here and there around the campus, listening to radios reporting body counts from armored columns plunging across the Vietnam-Cambodia border. On the other side of college, everyone knows, lies the draft. For the first time, I'm seeing Pomfret students aware that events in the outside world could affect their own lives.

All this is totally ignored by the returning alumni. On Saturday morning some of them attend panel discussions with guest speakers on subjects like "Does the Independent School Have a Role to Play?" (Surprise conclusion: Yes! The independent school *does* have a role to play.) In the evening the alumni gather for an array of class cocktail parties at a hotel some miles away from school, the nearest that can accomodate everyone. They float from one function to another on a wave of alcohol and reminiscence. Eyes flit furtively to name tags, to refresh rusty memories, hands clap on shoulders; one classmate opens the back of his station wagon to reveal a portable bar, with refrigerator. "Tim, you still at the bank?" "When we were here, sex was dirty and the air was clean. But now it's the other way 'round!" "Adam, I'd like you to meet Candy . . . Penny . . . Muffie . . ." New threads are revealed in the old networks: one alumnus has married another's sister, another has a nephew at school now, a third has come back to teach at Pomfret—an embarrassing come-down, in social-class terms: did he fail in business?

Much of the weekend is spent at this hotel. Despite the navy blue Pomfret School blazers many of them have brought out of the closet for this occasion, the alumni are far more comfortable mingling with each other than with students at the school. The president of Yale addresses us at a banquet. Later in the evening, when most people are watching old Pomfret football movies, several of us slip off to find a TV. Nixon assures the nation the invasion of Cambodia is only to find the secret, elusive communist military headquarters for all of South Vietnam. Four students have been shot dead by the National Guard at Kent State.

The alumni newsletter now reflects the escalation of the war. One schoolmate has flown some fifty missions in Phantom jets. Another, a former Pomfret ski-jump champion, has been killed under enigmatic circumstances in the navy, "in a scuba-diving accident at Guantanamo Bay." Two members of a class just older than mine write that they have run into each other in Saigon: one is working for the State Department and one for Brown and Root, the huge Texas construction firm that does work for the Pentagon. They write of how, over cool drinks on a Saigon villa's patio, they talked about all that had happened "since the class of '58 was loosed upon the world."

Loosed upon the world. The image of that Saigon patio conversation has echoed in my mind ever since. It sums up something important about the school, its ambitions, its arrogance.

The roots of those attitudes go far back. The English schools on which Pomfret and its American counterparts were modeled trained the British Empire's officials. In their mythology, even the school rebels serve king and country in the end. The classic boarding school novel is Rudyard Kipling's *Stalky & Co.*, a high-spirited tale of pranksters always in trouble with the straitlaced school authorities. But in the final chapter Stalky is an army officer in India, heroically fighting another kind of rebel—Himalayan tribesmen resisting the Crown. In the midst of battle, Stalky rallies his troops and officers (who include a few of the old school gang) by playing a song from school days on a bugle.

Most Pomfret graduates went into the more mundane areas of imperial administration: business, banking, or corporate law. Our board of trustees even held most of its meetings at a New York bank. Yet for some students, Pomfret's faculty and administrators had more glamorous aspirations. The school had graduated one secretary of state (Edward Stettinius) and an ambassador or two; teachers always implied that this was a highly desirable type of career. During my time at Pomfret, international relations became something of a theme: there were weekend conferences on the subject and frequent speakers—government officials, foreign students at nearby colleges. A prize catch, the son of the prime minister of Togo, a dapper man speaking Parisian French, once stayed in my room.

I was particularly encouraged to take part in these programs and to give little talks in the daily assembly on the crisis in Kashmir or whatever. One day in my senior year the headmaster was talking to me. "For every boy here," he said, "I like to imagine that we're helping him go in a particular direction, a direction *he* is best suited for. For you, I've always thought it would be something in the realm of foreign affairs, the State Department, something like that."

Suddenly, in a blinding flash of revelation that was one of the turning points of my life, I knew with absolute certainty that whatever I did, it would *not* be in that "realm." So: beneath all the rhetoric about the freedom to make one's choices in life, *they* still had a plan for me after all. Their plans were no doubt hazier and less sinister than I thought then, but it was an important lesson.

Another major lesson I learned at school, and this was a more complicated one, was that *they* had serious divisions in their ranks. The typical Pomfret trustee was a Hartford insurance executive or a Philadelphia banker, large of paunch and gold of watch chain, whose definition of a good school was the one that most closely resembled the dear old Pomfret he had attended forty years before. But during my time the headmaster, like many of the teachers, was in some ways an admirable and progressive man. He wanted to make the school coed, to admit blacks, and to put less emphasis on athletics. To the pinstriped trustees these hopes seemed positively Bolshevik. The crowning insult came when he hired a school chaplain who was not an ordained Episcopalian. The long-simmering conflict finally exploded, and the headmaster resigned. These battles seem antiquated now; almost all these changes have long since been made. But at the time the issues seemed very large indeed. It was my introduction to politics: for the first time I saw that the adult world did not have a united front. Through the cracks in that façade I began for the first time to see the way to some new choices of my own.

A spring day of brilliant sunshine, with bright yellow buttercups bubbling up across the lawns and the scent of fresh-cut grass on the breeze. On the hillcrest opposite the school is still the weathered old farmhouse and barn, home of unknown neighbors from a different world. Returning to Pomfret after another ten years' absence, I would like to feel unsentimental, superior, but despite everything, part of me still loves this place. I notice many familiar buildings are now replaced or rebuilt, and briefly I catch myself feeling, to my amazement, angry: how could they change things so?

I walk along the path with my alumni name tag, nodded at vaguely by young and unfamiliar teachers, perpetrating the great fraud that I have become a grown-up. In the center of the school grounds is a tall flagpole where we used to run up a string of brooms when the football team had an undefeated season: a clean sweep. But today this pole's American flag is at half-mast. It is May 1980, my twenty-year reunion. Several days ago a helicopter crash killed eight commandos in a failed attempt to rescue U.S. hostages in Iran.

Despite this perfunctory acknowledgment of troubles in the outside world, the campus mood is one of celebration. Many students are wearing a pin of crossed hockey sticks; the team won some sort of championship and next winter will play in Finland and Sweden. The sports action today is at the crew regatta. Along the lakeshore are ranged Mercedes, Audis, BMWs with New York, Connecticut, Massachusetts plates. One alumnus, wearing his old letter sweater, stands with a stopwatch and calls out how many strokes a minute a boat is making.

In chapel today prayers ask God's blessing on the work of the school. The chaplain, resplendent in white robes, leads the singing in a strong baritone, then reads the roll of Pomfret alumni who have died in the past year and prays for the welfare of their souls, "these Thy humble servants, whom Thou has called to Thee." But with names like William Ross Proctor, Standish Bourne Taber, and Charles Leo Abry IV, it is hard to imagine them being humble servants of anyone.

Later I'm back in a familiar classroom. A year of chemistry I studied here: into what hidden recess of my mind did that vanish? And a year of trigonometry: what *was* trigonometry, anyway? Something about angles. Today I'm here talking with a group of students interested in careers in journalism. But I also get the chance to question them. One thing I ask about is that tension between middle-class faculty and upper-class students. Is this still as strong as when I was at school?

A young woman in the back row sits up and says with great feeling, "Yes, I know *just* what you mean." I had taken her to be a senior, perhaps, but she turns out to be a new teacher. "It's still the same way," she goes on. "I'll tell you something I don't think the students here know. There has always been a yearly ritual here at Pomfret. When the students go home in June, they're always told to take all their stuff with them; the school isn't responsible for anything left in their rooms. On that last day, we—the faculty—go through all the dorms collecting for ourselves things that the kids have left behind. It's just incredible: brand-new tennis rackets, bicycles, skates, stereo equipment—I'd say about 90 percent of the kids here have better stereos than I could afford. Last year I got a wonderful long wool cape for myself—somebody just didn't want to bother to pack it away during the summer."

That night it is moonless and warm; the stars are out. A teacher's house stands on the other side of a football field. A car drives up; a figure gets out to open the garage door, and for a moment, a woman's body is silhouetted in the light. Back in these familiar surroundings, I feel automatically, for the first time in two decades, the emotion I felt here constantly: the wracking ache of desire and of outrage at this sexless environment. And of envy of those privileged teachers: *they're doing it every night.*

Did those Pomfret faculty wives ever know how much they were lusted after, how often their every attribute was discussed, by two hundred boys? Distant and unattainable, they were the only women we saw. It was only after I graduated that it fully dawned on me how perverse it is to keep someone for four years almost totally isolated from the other sex. You could invite a girl to the school for only one Dance Weekend each term—two days tightly packed with chaperoned activities, during which, legend had it, the school authorities put saltpeter in the milk. Sometimes we had to vacate a dormitory to make room for the girls to stay; afterward, we would go through our rooms carefully to see if we could find anything feminine accidentally left behind—a hairpin, a lipstick, a whiff of perfume. If we did, there was a lot of raucous joshing, but underlying it an unspoken loneliness.

The only other occasion we got to mingle with girls also came only once or twice a term: joint glee-club concerts and dances held with Pomfret's counterparts among girls' boarding schools. You were assigned a blind date for dinner and the evening. The busload of girls from Miss Porter's School, or wherever, would arrive in the afternoon, pulling into a parking lot below the huge bay windows of the dining hall. Thirty or forty boys would stand in the windows, leaning on each other's shoulders, leering and ogling down at the girls as they filed off the bus. But all I felt was total terror. What would I *say* to my date, whom I had never seen before and whom, after five tongue-tied hours, I would likely never see again?

Perhaps only the women who live with male prep school graduates can be the ultimate judges, but my guess is that no man comes out of such an adolescence without some emotional crippling. It was not that we looked on women only as sex objects; it was that they were no kind of object at all. They weren't there. They didn't exist. Except on these rare weekends. Talking to a girl your own age was an *event*, like shaking hands with the president; it was analyzed and discussed and agonized over for months afterward. Should I have said this? Asked her that? To go from such an atmosphere to one in which you live, study, or work with women as equals each day requires a major adjustment, and I think some prep school graduates never made it.

I went to Pomfret about a decade too early. Today it and almost all the other major prep schools are coed. Why did they hold out so long? Even longer, in fact, than it took most of them to become racially integrated? Ultimately these schools were set up with the same hope that is behind all institutions that are by design for men only, from infantry battalions to the Catholic priesthood: the hope that sexuality will be sublimated into zeal for achievement. The appalling thing about this is that it works. I studied harder at Pomfret—sometimes six, seven hours a day, after classes—than I ever have elsewhere, before or since. But the price was too high, and I wish I had never had to pay it. I don't just mean the price in the dammed-up sexuality of those years, but in all the unexperienced gentleness, laughter, and, for want of a better word, roundedness of life, which cannot exist to the full where one half of the human race is kept separate from the other.

I wish I could say that I saw all these problems with prep school while I was there, but I have to admit that my four years at Pomfret were one of the sunniest stretches of my life. Yes, it was the place where I first came to understand something about social class in America. But my experience there had many other layers as well. In traditional classroom terms, I got a superb education. I learned for the first time that words could mean more than their surfaces. I learned that music could say things words could not. I entered as a boy who did his homework; I left as one who read books and, in some rudimentary way, thought about them. I had private tutorials in subjects I was especially interested in. As part of its international affairs focus, Pomfret organized summer seminars involving trips to Asia, Africa, and Latin America; I went on one of these and saw the Third World through nontourist eyes for the first time. Our seminar had three Pomfret boys and seven students from other schools; we studied race relations in the American South and in Africa. For a group of sixteen- and seventeen-year-olds this was an overwhelming, life-changing experience. More than half of us eventually returned to the South as civil-rights workers, or to Africa to work or study.

There you have it: the paradox. Only by being in an elite, able to go to a place like Pomfret, did I gain access to so broadening an opportunity. The real injustice about prep school was not in the content of what we learned in the classroom or in occasional outside ventures like that trip, but in the fact that all that wealth of experience was available, with rare exceptions, only to the few who could pay. For those rich enough to afford them, schools like Pomfret are the greatest affirmative action program in the land.

However, despite occasional windows onto the outside world like that trip to Africa, the school was a little minisociety quite far from the democratic ideal. Of course, American society as a whole falls far short of that ideal also. But certain key parts of it have usually been *socially* democratic: the draft-era military, for example, and many public high schools. There, for at least one portion of their lives, Americans of all classes and colors must rub shoulders with each other, learn to speak with each other, learn that we all share the same country. On our hilltop at Pomfret there was none of this. We knew that poor and black and working-class people existed out there somewhere, but, as if we were vacationers on a yacht, they were invisible.

To spend twenty-four hours a day exclusively with members of your own class from the age of fourteen through eighteen is a recipe for complacency, for conservatism, and, above all, for identifying the welfare of yourself and your friends with that of society in general. In fact, many New England prep schools began precisely because upper-class families did not want their sons and daughters going to school with the children of society in general. The rise and fall in the number of elite boarding schools founded in each decade in the late nineteenth and early twentieth centuries correlates very closely with the rise and fall in the number of immigrants entering the United States.

Certain historical photographs have the power to move us in a particular way: Queen Victoria is proclaimed Empress of India; Tsar Nicholas II reviews his troops. The picture affects us because it captures the arrogance of those who thought they and their descendants would rule forever. I think of New England prep schools in the 1950s as being caught in such a picture. Of my class posing for its group portrait on the chapel steps, where other classes had posed for sixty years before us and where, of course, future classes would pose for decades to come. Everybody line up now. Smile for the camera. Now freeze ...

But the analogy is not complete. For most prep school graduates of my generation and older, the world still *is* that way, and they are still part of its upper reaches. The upheavals of the 1960s washed over Pomfret and its alumni but caused only a few defections and casualties. The school trained its graduates to master a certain world—a world with definite, unspoken borders. And it is that island world they still inhabit, however much it may have changed for their children and grandchildren. On one of those reunion visits, I ran into an old schoolmate. He introduced his wife (Candy or Penny or Muffie) and asked me what I'd been up to. Then I asked him.

"Well," he said cheerfully, "after college and the army, I went into investment banking. First Boston. But now . . ."—he threw his hands wide in a gesture of benign, tolerant acceptance of his own rashness—"I've gone *clear* to the other end of the spectrum. I'm a stockbroker."

1982

Tourism: from perspective of native [handwritten annotation]

Jamaica Kincaid

A SMALL PLACE

JAMAICA KINCAID was born and educated in St. John's, Antigua, in the West Indies. Her first book, *At the Bottom of the River*, a collection of stories, received the Morton Dauwen Zabel Award of the American Academy and Institute of Arts and Letters and was nominated for the PEN/Faulkner Award. Kincaid's other books are *Annie John*; *A Small Place*; *Lucy*; *My Brother*, a finalist for the National Book Award; and *The Autobiography of My Mother*, a nominee for the National Book Critics Circle Award in fiction, a finalist for the PEN/Faulkner Award, and the winner of the Cleveland Foundation's Anisfield-Wolf Book Award as well as the *Boston Book Review*'s Fisk Fiction prize. Her stories have appeared in *The New Yorker, Rolling Stone*, and *The Paris Review*. She lives in Bennington, Vermont.

what? [handwritten annotation]

If you go to Antigua as a tourist, this is what you will see. If you come by aeroplane, you will land at the V. C. Bird International Airport. Vere Cornwall (V. C.) Bird is the Prime Minister of Antigua. You may be the sort of tourist who would wonder why a Prime Minister would want an airport named after him—why not a school, why not a hospital, why not some great public monument? You are a tourist and you have not yet seen a school in Antigua, you have not yet seen the hospital in Antigua, you have not yet seen a public monument in Antigua. As your plane descends to land, you might say, What a beautiful island Antigua is—more beautiful than any of the other islands you have seen, and they were very beautiful, in their way, but they were much too green, much too lush with vegetation, which indicated to you, the tourist, that they got quite a bit of rainfall, and rain is the very thing that you, just now, do not want, for you are thinking of the hard and cold and dark and long days you spent working in North America (or, worse, Europe), earning some money so that you could stay in this place (Antigua) where the sun always shines and where the climate is deliciously hot and dry for the four to ten days you are going to be staying there; and since you are on your holiday, since you are a tourist, the thought of what it might be like for someone who had to live day in, day out in a place that

aren't all ugly? [handwritten annotation]

Repetition of tourist? [handwritten annotation]

257

suffers constantly from drought, and so has to watch carefully every drop of fresh water used (while at the same time surrounded by a sea and an ocean—the Caribbean Sea on one side, the Atlantic Ocean on the other), must never cross your mind.

You disembark your plane. You go through customs. Since you are a tourist, a North American or European—to be frank, white—and not an Antiguan black returning to Antigua from Europe or North America with cardboard boxes of much needed cheap clothes and food for relatives, you move through customs swiftly, you move through customs with ease. Your bags are not searched. You emerge from customs into the hot, clean air: immediately you feel cleansed, immediately you feel blessed (which is to say special); you feel free. You see a man, a taxi driver; you ask him to take you to your destination; he quotes you a price. You immediately think that the price is in the local currency, for you are a tourist and you are familiar with these things (rates of exchange) and you feel even more free, for things seem so cheap, but then your driver ends by saying, "In US currency." You may say, "Hmmmm, do you have a formal sheet that lists official prices and destinations?" Your driver obeys the law and shows you the sheet, and he apologises for the incredible mistake he has made in quoting you a price off the top of his head which is so vastly different (favouring him) from the one listed. You are driven to your hotel by this taxi driver in his taxi, a brand-new Japanese-made vehicle. The road on which you are travelling is a very bad road, very much in need of repair. You are feeling wonderful, so you say, "Oh, what a marvellous change these bad roads are from the splendid highways I am used to in North America." (Or, worse, Europe.) Your driver is reckless; he is a dangerous man who drives in the middle of the road when he thinks no other cars are coming in the opposite direction, passes other cars on blind curves that run uphill, drives at sixty miles an hour on narrow, curving roads when the road sign, a rusting, beat-up thing left over from colonial days, says 40 mph. This might frighten you (you are on your holiday; you are a tourist); this might excite you (you are on your holiday; you are a tourist), though if you are from New York and take taxis you are used to this style of driving: most of the taxi drivers in New York are from places in the world like this. You are looking out the window (because you want to get your money's worth); you notice that all the cars you see are brand-new, or almost brand-new, and that they are all Japanese-made. There are no American cars in Antigua—no new ones, at any rate; none that were manufactured in the last ten years. You continue to look at the cars and you say to yourself, Why, they look brand-new, but they have an awful sound, like an old car—a very old, dilapidated car. How to account for that? Well, possibly it's because they use leaded gasoline in these brand-new cars whose engines were built to use non-leaded gasoline, but you musn't ask the person driving the car if this is so, because he or she has never heard of unleaded gasoline. You look closely at the car; you see that it's a model of a Japanese car that you might hesitate to buy; it's a model that's very expensive; it's a model that's quite impractical for a person who has to work as hard as you do and who watches every penny you earn so that you can afford this holiday you are on. How do they afford such a car? And do they live in a luxurious house to match such a car? Well, no. You will be surprised, then, to see that most likely the person driving this brand-new car filled with the wrong gas lives in a house that, in comparison, is far beneath the status of the car; and if you were to ask why you would be told that the banks are encouraged by the government to make loans available for cars, but loans for houses not so easily available; and if you ask again why, you will be told that the two main car dealerships in Antigua are owned in part or outright by ministers in government. [corruption & monopoly] Oh, but you are on holiday and the sight of these brand-new cars driven by people who may or may not have really passed their driving test (there was once a scandal about driving licenses for sale) would not really stir up these thoughts in you. You pass a building sitting in a sea of dust and you think, It's some latrines for people just passing by, but when you look again you see the building has written on it PIGOTT'S SCHOOL. You pass the hospital, the Holberton Hospital, and how wrong you are not to think about this, for though you are a tourist on your holiday, what if your heart should miss a few beats? What if a blood vessel in your neck should break? What if one of those people driving those brand-new cars filled with the wrong gas fails to pass safely while going uphill on a curve and you are in the car going in the opposite direction? Will you be comforted to know that the hospital is staffed with doctors that no actual Antiguan trusts; that Antiguans always say about the doctors, "I don't want them near me"; that Antiguans refer to them not as doctors but as "the three men" (there are three of them); that when the Minister of Health himself doesn't feel well he takes the first plane to New York to see a real doctor; that if any one of the ministers in government needs medical care he flies to New York to get it?

It's a good thing that you brought your own books with you, for you couldn't just go to the library and borrow some. Antigua used to have a splendid library, but in The Earthquake (everyone talks about it that way—The Earthquake; we Antiguans, for I am one, have a great sense of things, and the more meaningful the thing, the more meaningless we make it) the library building was damaged. This was in 1974, and soon after that a sign was placed on the front of the building saying, THIS BUILDING WAS DAMAGED IN THE EARTHQUAKE OF 1974. REPAIRS ARE PENDING. The sign hangs there, and hangs there more than a decade later, with its unfulfilled promise of repair, and you might see this as a sort of quaintness on the part of these islanders, these people descended from slaves—what a strange, unusual perception of time they have. REPAIRS ARE PENDING, and here it is many years later, but perhaps in a world that is twelve miles long and nine miles wide (the size of Antigua) twelve years and twelve minutes and twelve days are all the same. The library is one of those splendid old buildings from colonial times, and the sign telling of the repairs is a splendid old sign from colonial times. Not very long after The Earthquake Antigua got its independence from Britain, making Antigua a state in its own right, and Antiguans are so proud of this that each year, to mark the day, they go to church and thank God, a British God, for this. But you should not think of the confusion that must lie in all that and you must not think of the damaged library. You have brought your own books with you, and among them is one of those new books about economic history, one of those books explaining how the West (meaning Europe and North America after its conquest and settlement by Europeans) got rich: the West got rich not from the free (free—in this case meaning got-for-nothing) and then undervalued labour, for generations, of the people like me you see walking around you in Antigua but from the ingenuity of small shopkeepers in Sheffield and Yorkshire and Lancashire, or wherever; and what a great part the invention of the wristwatch played in it, for there was nothing noble-minded men could not do when they discovered they could slap time on their wrists just like that (isn't that the last straw; for not only did we have to suffer the unspeakableness of slavery, but the satisfaction to be had from "We made you bastards rich" is taken away, too), and so you needn't let that slightly funny feeling you have from time to time about exploitation, oppression, domination develop into full-fledged unease, discomfort; you could ruin your holiday. They are not responsible for what you have; you owe them nothing; in fact, you did them a big favour, and you can provide one hundred examples. For here you are now, passing by Government House. And here you are now, passing by the Prime Minister's Office and the Parliament Building, and overlooking these, with a splendid view of St. John's Harbour, the American Embassy. If it were not for you, they would not have Government House, and Prime Minister's Office, and Parliament Building and embassy of powerful country. Now you are passing a mansion, an extraordinary house painted the colour of old cow dung, with more aerials and antennas attached to it than you will see even at the American Embassy. The people who live in this house are a merchant family who came to Antigua from the Middle East less than twenty years ago. When this family first came to Antigua, they sold dry goods door to door from suitcases they carried on their backs. Now they own a lot of Antigua; they regularly lend money to the government, they build enormous (for Antigua), ugly (for Antigua), concrete buildings in Antigua's capital, St. John's, which the government then rents for huge sums of money; a member of their family is the Antiguan Ambassador to Syria; Antiguans hate them. Not far from this mansion is another mansion, the home of a drug smuggler. Everybody knows he's a drug smuggler, and if just as you were driving by he stepped out of his door your driver might point him out to you as the notorious person that he is, for this drug smuggler is so rich people say he buys cars in tens—ten of this one, ten of that one—and that he bought a house (another mansion) near Five Islands, contents included, with cash he carried in a suitcase: three hundred and fifty thousand American dollars, and, to the surprise of the seller of the house, lots of American dollars were left over. Overlooking the drug smuggler's mansion is yet another mansion, and leading up to it is the best paved road in all of Antigua—even better than the road that was paved for the Queen's visit in 1985 (when the Queen came, all the roads that she would travel on were paved anew, so that the Queen might have been left with the impression that riding in a car in Antigua was a pleasant experience). In this mansion lives a woman sophisticated people in Antigua call Evita. She is a notorious woman. She's young and beautiful and the girlfriend of somebody very high up in the government. Evita is notorious because her relationship with this high government official has made her the owner of boutiques and property and given her a say in cabinet meetings, and all sorts of other privileges such a relationship would bring a beautiful young woman.

Oh, but by now you are tired of all this looking, and you want to reach your destination—your hotel, your room. You long to refresh yourself; you long to eat some nice lobster, some nice local food. You take a bath, you brush your teeth. You get dressed again; as you get dressed, you look out the window. That water—have you ever seen anything like it? Far out, to the horizon, the colour of the water is navy-blue; nearer, the water is the colour of the North American sky. From there to the shore, the water is pale, silvery, clear, so clear that you can see its pinkish-white sand bottom. Oh, what beauty! Oh, what beauty! You have never seen anything like this. You are so excited. You breathe shallow. You breathe deep. You see a beautiful boy skimming the water, godlike, on a Windsurfer. You see an incredibly unattractive, fat, pastrylike-fleshed woman enjoying a walk on the beautiful sand, with a man, an incredibly unattractive, fat, pastrylike-fleshed man; you see the pleasure they're taking in their surroundings. Still standing, looking out the window, you see yourself lying on the beach, enjoying the amazing sun (a sun so powerful and yet so beautiful, the way it is always overhead as if on permanent guard, ready to stamp out any cloud that dares to darken and so empty rain on you and ruin your holiday; a sun that is your personal friend). You see yourself taking a walk on that beach, you see yourself meeting new people (only they are new in a very limited way, for they

[handwritten margin note top: Using POV of tourist. only to say something else.]

[handwritten margin note left: Takes pretty image cuts in 1/2 w/ the truth.]

are people just like you). You see yourself eating some delicious, locally grown food. You see yourself, you see yourself . . . You must not wonder what exactly happened to the contents of your lavatory when you flushed it. You must not wonder where your bathwater went when you pulled out the stopper. You must not wonder what happened when you brushed your teeth. Oh, it might all end up in the water you are thinking of taking a swim in; the contents of your lavatory might, just might, graze gently against your ankle as you wade carefree in the water, for you see, in Antigua, there is no proper sewage-disposal system. But the Caribbean Sea is very big and the Atlantic Ocean is even bigger; it would amaze even you to know the number of black slaves this ocean has swallowed up. When you sit down to eat your delicious meal, it's better that you don't know that most of what you are eating came off a plane from Miami. And before it got on a plane in Miami, who knows where it came from? A good guess is that it came from a place like Antigua first, where it was grown dirt-cheap, went to Miami, and came back. There is a world of something in this, but I can't go into it right now. *[handwritten: => First time using "I".]*

The thing you have always suspected about yourself the minute you become a tourist is true: A tourist is an ugly human being. You are not an ugly person all the time; you are not an ugly person ordinarily; you are not an ugly person day to day. From day to day, you are a nice person. From day to day, all the people who are supposed to love you on the whole do. From day to day, as you walk down a busy street in the large and modern and prosperous city in which you work and live, dismayed, puzzled (a cliché, but only a cliché can explain you) at how alone you feel in this crowd, how awful it is to go unnoticed, how awful it is to go unloved, even as you are surrounded by more people than you could possibly get to know in a lifetime that lasted for millennia, and then out of the corner of your eye you see someone looking at you and absolute pleasure is written all over that person's face, and then you realise that you are not as revolting a presence as you think you are (for that look just told you so). And so, ordinarily, you are a nice person, an attractive person, a person capable of drawing to yourself the affection of other people (people just like you), a person at home in your own skin (sort of; I mean, in a way; I mean, your dismay and puzzlement are natural to you, because people like you just seem to be like that, and so many of the things people like you find admirable about yourselves—the things you think about, the things you think really define you—seem rooted in these feelings): a person at home in your own house (and all its nice house things), with its nice back yard (and its nice backyard things), at home on your street, your church, in community activities, your job, at home with your family, your relatives, your friends—you are a whole person. But one day, when you are sitting somewhere, alone in that crowd, and that awful feeling of displacedness comes over you, and really, as an ordinary person you are not well equipped to look too far inward and set yourself aright, because being ordinary is already so taxing, and being ordinary takes all you have out of you, and though the words "I must get away" do not actually pass across your lips, you make a leap from being that nice blob just sitting like a boob in your amniotic sac of the modern experience to being a person visiting heaps of death and ruin and feeling alive and inspired at the sight of it; to being a person lying on some faraway beach, your stilled body stinking and glistening in the sand, looking like something first forgotten, then remembered, then not important enough to go back for; to being a person marvelling at the harmony (ordinarily, what you would say is the backwardness) and the union these other people (and they are other people) have with nature. And you look at the things they can do with a piece of ordinary cloth, the things they fashion out of cheap, vulgarly colored (to you) twine, the way they squat down over a hole they have made in the ground, the hole itself is something to marvel at, and since you are being an ugly person this ugly but joyful thought will swell inside you: their ancestors were not clever in the way yours were and not ruthless in the way yours were, for then would it not be you who would be in harmony with nature and backwards in that charming way? An ugly thing, that is what you are when you become a tourist, an ugly, empty thing, a stupid thing, a piece of rubbish pausing here and there to gaze at this and taste that, and it will never occur to you that the people who inhabit the place in which you have just paused cannot stand you, that behind their closed doors they laugh at your strangeness (you do not look the way they look); the physical sight of you does not please them; you have bad manners (it is their custom to eat their food with their hands; you try eating their way, you look silly; you try eating the way you always eat, you look silly); they do not like the way you speak (you have an accent); they collapse helpless from laughter, mimicking the way they imagine you must look as you carry out some everyday bodily function. They do not like you. They do not like me! That thought never actually occurs to you. Still, you feel a little uneasy. Still, you feel a little foolish. Still, you feel a little out of place. But the banality of your own life is very real to you; it drove you to this extreme, spending your days and your nights in the company of people who despise you, people you do not like really, people you would not want to have as your actual neighbour. And so you must devote yourself to puzzling out how much of what you are told is really, really true (Is ground-up bottle glass in peanut sauce really a delicacy around here, or will it do just what you think ground-up bottle glass will do? Is this rare, multicoloured, snout-mouthed fish really an aphrodisiac, or will it cause you to fall asleep permanently?). Oh, the hard work all of this is, and is it any wonder, then, that on your return home you feel the need of a long rest, so that you can recover from your life as a tourist?

That the native does not like the tourist is not hard to explain. For every native of every place is a potential tourist, and every tourist is a native of somewhere. Every native everywhere lives a life of overwhelming and crushing banality and boredom and desperation and depression, and every deed, good and bad, is an attempt to forget this. Every native would like to find a way out, every native would like a rest, every native would like a tour. But some natives—most natives in the world—cannot go anywhere. They are too poor. They are too poor to go anywhere. They are too poor to escape the reality of their lives; and they are too poor to live properly in the place where they live, which is the very place you, the tourist, want to go—so when the natives see you, the tourist, they envy you, they envy your ability to leave your own banality and boredom, they envy your ability to turn their own banality and boredom into a source of pleasure for yourself.

o Very bitter

o Very truthful

Craft elements o Be descriptive (best)

o Painted picture of tourists
↳ Style (painted tourists as uncaring)

Apparent subject: Tourism

Deeper subject: Infrastructure problems w/ tourism.

o Commentary on tourist.

- Layers of CNF
separation between writer, narrator, speaker.

Barbara Kingsolver

HIGH TIDE IN TUCSON

BARBARA KINGSOLVER is the author of twelve books of fiction, poetry, and creative nonfiction, including *High Tide in Tucson: Essays from Now or Never*, and the novels *The Bean Trees* and *The Poisonwood Bible*. Translated into nineteen languages, her work has won many awards, including the National Humanities Medal.

A hermit crab lives in my house. Here in the desert he's hiding out from local animal ordinances, at minimum, and maybe even the international laws of native-species transport. For sure, he's an outlaw against nature. So be it.

He arrived as a stowaway two Octobers ago. I had spent a week in the Bahamas, and while I was there, wishing my daughter could see those sparkling blue bays and sandy coves, I did exactly what she would have done: I collected shells. Spiky murexes, smooth purple moon shells, ancient-looking whelks sandblasted by the tide—I tucked them in the pockets of my shirt and shorts until my lumpy, suspect hemlines gave me away, like a refugee smuggling the family fortune. When it was time to go home, I rinsed my loot in the sink and packed it carefully into a plastic carton, then nested it deep in my suitcase for the journey to Arizona.

I got home in the middle of the night, but couldn't wait till morning to show my hand. I set the carton on the coffee table for my daughter to open. In the dark living room her face glowed, in the way of antique stories about children and treasure. With perfect delicacy she laid the shells out on the table, counting, sorting, designating scientific categories like yellow-striped pinky, Barnacle Bill's pocketbook . . . Yeek! She let loose a sudden yelp, dropped her booty, and ran to the far end of the room. The largest, knottiest whelk had begun to move around. First it extended one long red talon of a leg, tap-tap-tapping like a blind man's cane. Then came half a dozen more red legs, plus a pair of eyes on stalks, and a purple claw that snapped open and shut in a way that could not mean We Come in Friendship.

Who could blame this creature? It had fallen asleep to the sound of the Ca-

265

ribbean tide and awakened on a coffee table in Tucson, Arizona, where the nearest standing water source of any real account was the municipal sewage-treatment plant.

With red stiletto legs splayed in all directions, it lunged and jerked its huge shell this way and that, reminding me of the scene I make whenever I'm moved to rearrange the living-room sofa by myself. Then, while we watched in stunned reverence, the strange beast found its bearings and began to reveal a determined, crabby grace. It felt its way to the edge of the table and eased itself over, not falling bang to the floor but hanging suspended underneath within the long grasp of its ice-tong legs, lifting any two or three at a time while many others still held in place. In this remarkable fashion it scrambled around the underside of the table's rim, swift and sure and fearless like a rock climber's dream.

If you ask me, when something extraordinary shows up in your life in the middle of the night, you give it a name and make it the best home you can.

The business of naming involved a grasp of hermit-crab gender that was way out of our league. But our household had a deficit of males, so my daughter and I chose Buster, for balance. We gave him a terrarium with clean gravel and a small cactus plant dug out of the yard and a big cockleshell full of tap water. All this seemed to suit him fine. To my astonishment our local pet store carried a product called Vitaminized Hermit Crab Cakes. Tempting enough (till you read the ingredients) but we passed, since our household leans more toward the recycling ethic. We give him leftovers. Buster's rapture is the day I drag the unidentifiable things in cottage cheese containers out of the back of the fridge.

We've also learned to give him a continually changing assortment of sea-shells, which he tries on and casts off like Cinderella's stepsisters preening for the ball. He'll sometimes try to squeeze into ludicrous outfits too small to contain him (who can't relate?). In other moods, he will disappear into a conch the size of my two fists and sit for a day, immobilized by the weight of upward mobility. He is in every way the perfect housemate: quiet, entertaining, and willing to eat up the trash. He went to school for first-grade show-and-tell, and was such a hit the principal called up to congratulate me (I think) for being a broad-minded mother.

It was a long time, though, before we began to understand the content of Buster's character. He required more patient observation than we were in the habit of giving to a small, cold-blooded life. As months went by, we would periodically notice with great disappointment that Buster seemed to be dead. Or not entirely dead, but ill, or maybe suffering the crab equivalent of the blues. He would burrow into a gravelly corner, shrink deep into his shell, and not move, for days and days. We'd take him out to play, dunk him in water, offer him a new frock—nothing. He wanted to be still.

Life being what it is, we'd eventually quit prodding our sick friend to cheer up, and would move on to the next stage of a difficult friendship: neglect. We'd ignore him wholesale, only to realize at some point later on that he'd lapsed into hyperactivity. We'd find him ceaselessly patrolling the four corners of his world, turning over rocks, rooting out and dragging around truly disgusting pork-chop bones, digging up his cactus and replanting it on its head. At night when the household fell silent I would lie in bed listening to his methodical pebbly racket from the opposite end of the house. Buster was manic-depressive.

I wondered if he might be responding to the moon. I'm partial to lunar cycles, ever since I learned as a teenager that human females in their natural state—which is to say, sleeping outdoors—arrive at menses in synchrony and ovulate with the full moon. My imagination remains captive to that primordial village: the comradely grumpiness of new-moon days, when the entire world at once would go on PMS alert. And the compensation that would turn up two weeks later on a wild wind, under that great round headlamp, driving both men and women to distraction with the overt prospect of conception. The surface of the land literally rises and falls—as much as fifty centimeters!—as the moon passes over, and we clay-footed mortals fall like dominoes before the swell. It's no surprise at all if a full moon inspires lyricists to corny love songs, or inmates to slamming themselves against barred windows. A hermit crab hardly seems this impetuous, but animals are notoriously responsive to the full moon: wolves howl; roosters announce daybreak all night. Luna moths, Arctic loons, and lunatics have a sole inspiration in common. Buster's insomniac restlessness seemed likely to be a part of the worldwide full-moon fellowship.

But it wasn't, exactly. The full moon didn't shine on either end of his cycle, the high or the low. We tried to keep track, but it soon became clear: Buster marched to his own drum. The cyclic force that moved him remained as mysterious to us as his true gender and the workings of his crustacean soul.

Buster's aquarium occupies a spot on our kitchen counter right next to the coffeepot, and so it became my habit to begin mornings with chin in hands, pondering the oceanic mysteries while awaiting percolation. Finally, I remembered something. Years ago when I was a graduate student of animal behavior, I passed my days reading about the likes of animals' internal clocks. Temperature, photoperiod, the rise and fall of hormones—all these influences have been teased apart like so many threads from the rope that pulls every creature to its regulated destiny. But one story takes the cake. F. A. Brown, a researcher who is more or less the grandfather of the biological clock, set about in 1954 to track the cycles of intertidal oysters. He scooped his subjects from the clammy coast of Connecticut and moved them into the basement of a laboratory in land-locked Illinois. For the first fifteen days in their new aquariums, the oysters kept right up with their normal intertidal behavior: they spent time shut away in their shells, and time with their mouths wide open, siphoning their briny bath for the plankton that sustained them, as the tides ebbed and flowed on the distant Connecticut shore. In the next two weeks, they made a mystifying shift. They still carried out their cycles in unison, and were regular as the tides, but their high-tide behavior didn't coincide with high tide in Connecticut, or for that matter California, or any other tidal charts known to science. It dawned on the researchers after some calculations that the oysters were responding to high tide in Chicago. Never mind that the gentle mollusks lived in glass boxes in the basement of a steel-and-cement building. Nor that Chicago has no ocean. In the circumstances, the oysters were doing their best.

When Buster is running around for all he's worth, I can only presume it's high tide in Tucson. With or without evidence, I'm romantic enough to believe it. This is the lesson of Buster, the poetry that camps outside the halls of science: Jump for joy, hallelujah. Even a desert has tides.

When I was twenty-two, I donned the shell of a tiny yellow Renault and drove with all I owned from Kentucky to Tucson. I was a typical young American, striking out. I had no earthly notion that I was bringing on myself a calamity of the magnitude of the one that befell poor Buster. I am the commonest kind of North American refugee: I believe I like it here, far-flung from my original home. I've come to love the desert that bristles and breathes and sleeps outside my windows. In the course of seventeen years I've embedded myself in a family here—neighbors, colleagues, friends I can't foresee living without, and a child who is native to this ground, with loves of her own. I'm here for good, it seems.

And yet I never cease to long in my bones for what I left behind. I open my eyes on every new day expecting that a creek will run through my backyard under broad-leafed maples, and that my mother will be whistling in the kitchen. Behind the howl of coyotes, I'm listening for meadowlarks. I sometimes ache to be rocked in the bosom of the blood relations and busybodies of my childhood. Particularly in my years as a mother without a mate, I have deeply missed the safety net of extended family.

In a city of half a million I still really look at every face, anticipating recognition, because I grew up in a town where every face meant something to me. I have trouble remembering to lock the doors. Wariness of strangers I learned the hard way. When I was new to the city, I let a man into my house one hot afternoon because he seemed in dire need of a drink of water; when I turned from the kitchen sink I found sharpened steel shoved against my belly. And so I know, I know. But I cultivate suspicion with as much difficulty as I force tomatoes to grow in the drought-stricken hardpan of my strange backyard. No creek runs here, but I'm still listening to secret tides, living as if I belonged to an earlier place: not Kentucky, necessarily, but a welcoming earth and a human family. A forest. A species.

In my life I've had frightening losses and unfathomable gifts: A knife in my stomach. The death of an unborn child. Sunrise in a rain forest. A stupendous column of blue butterflies rising from a Greek monastery. A car that spontaneously caught fire while I was driving it. The end of a marriage, followed by a year in which I could barely understand how to keep living. The discovery, just weeks ago when I rose from my desk and walked into the kitchen, of three strangers industriously relieving my house of its contents.

I persuaded the strangers to put down the things they were holding (what a bizarre tableau of anti-Magi they made, these three unwise men, bearing a camera, an electric guitar, and a Singer sewing machine), and to leave my home, pronto. My daughter asked excitedly when she got home from school, "Mom, did you say bad words?" (I told her this was the very occasion that bad words exist for.) The police said, variously, that I was lucky, foolhardy, and "a brave lady." But it's not good luck to be invaded, and neither foolish nor brave to stand your ground. It's only the way life goes, and I did it, just as years ago I fought off the knife; mourned the lost child; bore witness to the rain forest; claimed the blue butterflies as Holy Spirit in my private pantheon; got out of the burning car; survived the divorce by putting one foot in front of the other and taking good care of my child. On most important occasions, I cannot think how to respond, I simply do. What does it mean, anyway, to be an animal in human clothing? We carry around these big brains of ours like the crown jewels, but mostly I find that millions of years of evolution have prepared me for one thing only: to follow internal rhythms. To walk upright, to protect my loved ones, to cooperate with my family group—however broadly I care to define it—to do whatever will help us thrive. Obviously, some habits that saw us through the millennia are proving hazardous in a modern context: for example, the yen to consume carbohydrates and fat whenever they cross our path, or the proclivity for unchecked reproduction. But it's surely worth forgiving ourselves these tendencies a little, in light of the fact that they are what got us here. Like Buster, we are creatures of inexplicable cravings. Thinking isn't everything. The way I stock my refrigerator would amuse a level-headed interplanetary observer, who would see I'm responding not to real necessity but to the dread of famine honed in the African savannah. I can laugh at my Rhodesian Ridgeback as she furtively sniffs the houseplants for a place to bury bones, and circles to beat down the grass before lying on my kitchen floor. But she and I are exactly the same kind of hairpin.

We humans have to grant the presence of some past adaptations, even in their unforgivable extremes, if only to admit they are permanent rocks in the stream we're obliged to navigate. It's easy to speculate and hard to prove, ever, that genes control our behaviors. Yet we are persistently, excruciatingly adept at many things that seem no more useful to modern life than the tracking of tides in a desert. At recognizing insider/outsider status, for example, starting with white vs. black and grading straight into distinctions so fine as to baffle the bystander—Serb and Bosnian, Hutu and Tutsi, Crip and Blood. We hold that children learn discrimination from their parents, but they learn it fiercely and well, world without end. Recite it by rote like a multiplication table. Take it to heart, though it's neither helpful nor appropriate, anymore than it is to hire the taller of two men applying for a position as bank clerk, though statistically we're likely to do that too. Deference to the physical superlative, a preference for the scent of our own clan: a thousand anachronisms dance down the strands of our DNA from a hidebound tribal past, guiding us toward the glories of survival, and some vainglories as well. If we resent being bound by these ropes, the best hope is to seize them out like snakes, by the throat, look them in the eye and own up to their venom.

But we rarely do, silly egghead of a species that we are. We invent the most outlandish intellectual grounds to justify discrimination. We tap our toes to chaste love songs about the silvery moon without recognizing them as hymns to copulation. We can dress up our drives, put them in three-piece suits or ballet slippers, but still they drive us. The wonder of it is that our culture attaches almost unequivocal shame to our animal nature, believing brute urges must be hurtful, violent things. But it's no less an animal instinct that leads us to marry (species that benefit from monogamy tend to practice it); to organize a neighborhood cleanup campaign (rare and doomed is the creature that fouls its nest); to improvise and enforce morality (many primates socialize their young to be cooperative and ostracize adults who won't share food).

It's starting to look as if the most shameful tradition of Western civilization is our need to deny we are animals. In just a few centuries of setting ourselves apart as landlords of the Garden of Eden, exempt from the natural order and entitled to hold dominion, we have managed to behave like so-called animals anyway, and on top of it to wreck most of what took three billion years to assemble. Air, water, earth, and fire—so much of our own element so vastly contaminated, we endanger our own future. Apparently we never owned the place after all. Like every other animal, we're locked into our niche: the mercury in the ocean, the pesticides on the soybean fields, all come home to our breastfed babies. In the silent spring we are learning it's easier to escape from a chain gang than a food chain. Possibly we will have the sense to begin a new century by renewing our membership in the Animal Kingdom.

Not long ago I went backpacking in the Eagle Tail Mountains. This range is a trackless wilderness in western Arizona that most people would call Godforsaken, taking for granted God's preference for loamy topsoil and regular precipitation. Whoever created the Eagle Tails had dry heat on the agenda, and a thing for volcanic rock. Also cactus, twisted mesquites, and five-alarm sunsets. The hiker's program in a desert like this is dire and blunt: carry in enough water to keep you alive till you can find a water source; then fill your bottles and head for the next one, or straight back out. Experts warn adventurers in this region, without irony, to drink their water while they're still alive, as it won't help later.

Several canyons looked promising for springs on our topographical map, but turned up dry. Finally, at the top of a narrow, overgrown gorge we found a blessed tinaja, a deep, shaded hollow in the rock about the size of four or five claw-foot tubs, holding water. After we drank our fill, my friends struck out again, but I opted to stay and spend the day in the hospitable place that had slaked our thirst. On either side of the natural water tank, two shallow caves in the canyon wall faced each other, only a few dozen steps apart. By crossing from one to the other at noon, a person could spend the whole day here in shady comfort—or in colder weather, follow the winter sun. Anticipating a morning of reading, I pulled *Angle of Repose* out of my pack and looked for a place to settle on the flat, dusty floor of the west-facing shelter. Instead, my eyes were startled by a smooth corn-grinding stone. It sat in the exact center of its rock bowl, as if the Hohokam woman or man who used this mortar and pestle had walked off and left them there an hour ago. The Hohokam disappeared from the earth in A.D. 1450. It was inconceivable to me that no one had been here since then, but that may have been the case—that is the point of trackless wilderness. I picked up the grinding stone. The size and weight and smooth, balanced perfection of it in my hand filled me at once with a longing to possess it. In its time, this excellent stone was the most treasured thing in a life, a family, maybe the whole neighborhood. To whom it still belonged. I replaced it in the rock depression, which also felt smooth to my touch. Because my eyes now understood how to look at it, the ground under my feet came alive with worked flint chips and pottery shards. I walked across to the other cave and found its floor just as lively with historic debris. Hidden under brittlebush and catclaw I found another grinding stone, this one some distance from the depression in the cave floor that once answered its pressure daily, for the grinding of corn or mesquite beans.

For a whole day I marveled at this place, running my fingers over the knife edges of dark flint chips, trying to fit together thick red pieces of shattered clay jars, biting my lower lip like a child concentrating on a puzzle. I tried to guess the size of whole pots from the curve of the broken pieces: some seemed as small as my two cupped hands, and some maybe as big as a bucket. The sun scorched my neck, reminding me to follow the shade across to the other shelter. Bees hummed at the edge of the water hole, nosing up to the water, their abdomens pulsing like tiny hydraulic pumps; by late afternoon they rimmed the pool completely, a collar of busy lace. Off and on, the lazy hand of a hot breeze shuffled the white leaves of the brittlebush. Once I looked up to see a screaming pair of red-tailed hawks mating in midair, and once a clatter of hooves warned me to hold still. A bighorn ram emerged through the brush, his head bent low under his hefty cornice, and ambled by me with nothing on his mind so much as a cool drink.

How long can a pestle stone lie still in the center of its mortar? That long ago—that recently—people lived here. *Here*, exactly, and not one valley over, or two, or twelve, because this place had all a person needs: shelter, food, and permanent water. They organized their lives around a catchment basin in a granite boulder, conforming their desires to the earth's charities; they never expected the opposite. The stories I grew up with lauded Moses for striking the rock and bringing forth the bubbling stream. But the stories of the Hohokam—oh, how they must have praised that good rock.

At dusk my friends returned with wonderful tales of the ground they had covered. We camped for the night, refilled our canteens, and hiked back to the land of plumbing and a fair guarantee of longevity. But I treasure my memory of the day I lingered near water and covered no ground. I can't think of a day in my life in which I've had such a clear fix on what it means to be human.

Want is a thing that unfurls unbidden like fungus, opening large upon itself, stopless, filling the sky. But *needs*, from one day to the next, are few enough to fit in a bucket, with room enough left to rattle like brittlebush in a dry wind.

For each of us—furred, feathered, or skinned alive—the whole earth balances on the single precarious point of our own survival. In the best of times, I hold in mind the need to care for things beyond the self: poetry, humanity, grace. In other times, when it seems difficult merely to survive and be happy about it, the condition of my thought tastes as simple as this: let me be a good animal today. I've spent months at a stretch, even years, with that taste in my mouth, and have found that it serves.

But it seems a wide gulf to cross, from the raw, green passion for survival to the dispassionate, considered state of human grace. How does the animal mind construct a poetry for the modern artifice in which we now reside? Often I feel as disoriented as poor Buster, unprepared for the life that zooms headlong past my line of sight. This clutter of human paraphernalia and counterfeit necessities—what does it have to do with the genuine business of life on earth? It feels strange to me to be living in a box, hiding from the steadying influence of the moon; wearing the hide of a cow, which is supposed to be dyed to match God-knows-what, on my feet; making promises over the telephone about things I will do at a precise hour next *year*. (I always feel the urge to add, as my grandmother does, "Lord willing and the creeks don't rise!") I find it impossible to think, with a straight face, about what colors ought not to be worn after Labor Day. I can become hysterical over the fact that someone, somewhere, invented a thing called the mushroom scrubber, and that many other people undoubtedly feel they *need* to possess one. It's completely usual for me to get up in the morning, take a look around, and laugh out loud.

Strangest of all, I am carrying on with all of this in a desert, two thousand miles from my verdant childhood home. I am disembodied. No one here remembers how I was before I grew to my present height. I'm called upon to reinvent my own childhood time and again; in the process, I wonder how I can ever know the truth about who I am. If someone had told me what I was headed for in that little Renault—that I was stowing away in a shell, bound to wake up to an alien life on a persistently foreign shore—I surely would not have done it. But no one warned me. My culture, as I understand it, values independence above all things—in part to ensure a mobile labor force, grease for the machine of a capitalist economy. Our fairy tale commands: Little Pig, go out and seek your fortune! So I did.

Many years ago I read that the Tohono O'odham, who dwell in the deserts near here, traditionally bury the umbilicus of a newborn son or daughter somewhere close to home and plant a tree over it, to hold the child in place. In a sentimental frame of mind, I did the same when my own baby's cord fell off. I'm starting at the tree right now, as I write—a lovely thing grown huge outside my window, home to woodpeckers, its boughs overarching the house, as dissimilar from the sapling I planted seven years ago as my present life is from the tidy future I'd mapped out for us all when my baby was born. She will roam light-years from the base of that tree. I have no doubt of it. I can only hope she's growing as the tree is, absorbing strength and rhythms and a trust in the seasons, so she will always be able to listen for home.

I feel remorse about Buster's monumental relocation; it's a weighty responsibility to have thrown someone else's life into permanent chaos. But as for my own, I can't be sorry I made the trip. Most of what I learned in the old place seems to suffice for the new: if the seasons like Chicago tides come at ridiculous times and I have to plant in September instead of May, and if I have to make up family from scratch, what matters is that I do have sisters and tomato plants, the essential things. Like Buster, I'm inclined to see the material backdrop of my life as mostly immaterial, compared with what moves inside of me. I hold on to my adopted shore, chanting private vows: wherever I am, let me never forget to distinguish *want* from *need*. Let me be a good animal today. Let me dance in the waves of my private tide, the habits of survival and love.

Every one of us is called upon, probably many times, to start a new life. A frightening diagnosis, a marriage, a move, loss of a job or a limb or a loved one, a graduation, bringing a new baby home: it's impossible to think at first how this all will be possible. Eventually, what moves it all forward is the subterranean ebb and flow of being alive among the living.

In my own worst seasons I've come back from the colorless world of despair by forcing myself to look hard, for a long time, at a single glorious thing: a flame of red geranium outside my bedroom window. And then another: my daughter in a yellow dress. And another: the perfect outline of a full, dark sphere behind the crescent moon. Until I learned to be in love with my life again. Like a stroke victim retraining new parts of the brain to grasp lost skills, I have taught myself joy, over and over again.

It's not such a wide gulf to cross, then, from survival to poetry. We hold fast to the old passions of endurance that buckle and creak beneath us, dovetailed, tight as a good wooden boat to carry us onward. And onward full tilt we go, pitched and wrecked and absurdly resolute, driven in spite of everything to make good on a new shore. To be hopeful, to embrace one possibility after another—that is surely the basic instinct. Baser even than hate, the thing with teeth, which can be stilled with a tone of voice or stunned by beauty. If the whole world of the living has to turn on the single point of remaining alive, that pointed endurance is the poetry of hope. The thing with feathers.

What a stroke of luck. What a singular brute feat of outrageous fortune: to be born to citizenship in the Animal Kingdom. We love and we lose, go back to the start and do it right over again. For every heavy forebrain solemnly cataloging the facts of a harsh landscape, there's a rush of intuition behind it crying out: High tide! Time to move out into the glorious debris. Time to take this life for what it is.

Ted Kooser

SMALL ROOMS IN TIME

TED KOOSER, the thirteenth Poet Laureate Consultant in Poetry to the Library of Congress, is a professor in the English Department of the University of Nebraska–Lincoln and a retired insurance executive. He is the winner of the 2005 Pulitzer Prize in poetry and the author of ten collections of poetry.

Several years ago, a fifteen-year-old boy answered the side door of a house where I once lived, and was murdered, shot twice by one of five people—two women and three men—who had gone there to steal a pound of cocaine. The boy died just inside the door, at the top of a staircase that led to the cellar where I once had set up my easel and painted. The robbers—all but one still in their teens—stepped over the body, rushed down the steps, and shot three people there, a woman and two men.

Somebody called the police, perhaps the people who rented the apartment on the second floor. The next day's front-page story reported that the three in the basement were expected to survive. The boy's father, who was somewhere on the first floor and out of the line of fire, had not been injured.

It's taken me a long time to try to set down my feelings about this incident. At the time, it felt as if somebody had punched me in the stomach, and in ways it has taken me until now to get my breath back. I'm ashamed to say that it wasn't the boy's death that so disturbed me, but the fact that it happened in a place where my family and I had once been safe.

I recently spent most of a month building a Christmas surprise for my wife, a one-inch to one-foot scale replica of her ancestral home in the Nebraska sandhills. The original, no longer owned by her family, was a sprawling fourteen-room, two-story frame house built in 1884. Her great grandparents and grandparents lived there. Her great aunt, still living and 108 years old at the time I am writing this, was born there. Her father and his brothers and sister chased through those rooms as small children, and as a girl my wife and her younger sister spent summers there, taking care of their invalid grandmother.

Day after day as I worked on this dollhouse, pasting up wallpaper, gluing in baseboards and flooring, I would feel my imagination fitting itself into the little rooms. At times I lost all sense of scale and began to feel grit from the sandhills under my feet on the kitchen linoleum, to smell the summer sun on the porch roof shingles. I had never lived in that house but I lived there during those moments, and as I worked, the shadows of wind-tossed trees played over the dusty glass of the windows. Now and then I would hear footsteps on the porch, approaching the door.

Immediately upon seeing the dollhouse on Christmas Eve, my wife began to recall the way it had been furnished when she was a girl, to talk about this piece of furniture being here and that one there. I watched her feed the goldfish in the dirty aquarium and sit down on the stiff, cold leather of the Mission sofa. I saw her stroke-damaged grandmother propped in her painted iron bed under the eaves. Listening to my wife, watching her open the tiny doors and peer into the tiny closets, I began to think about the way in which the rooms we inhabit, if only for a time, become unchanging places within us, complete in detail.

I clipped the article about the shooting and must have read it a hundred times those first few days. In a front-on photograph, like a mug shot, there stood the house, sealed off by yellow police tape, looking baffled, cold, and vacant. Next to the picture was a row of slack-faced mug shots of the five arrested. They looked as empty as the house.

I mailed a copy of the article to my first wife. I wanted her to share the shock that I was suffering, like a distant explosion whose concussion had taken years to reach across a galaxy of intervening happenstance. At the site where only the most common, most ordinary unhappiness had come to us—misunderstandings, miscommunications, a broken marriage like thousands and thousands of others—there had been a murder, three people had been wounded, and five were on their way through the courts and into prison, all for the want of a pound of cocaine that the article reported had never been there.

For several years in the early 1960s we'd rented the first floor, which included the use of the cellar that I used as a study. We'd been married for three years and were then in our early twenties. Diana was a schoolteacher in a nearby town, and I worked as a clerk at an insurance company. While we lived there, Diana became pregnant, our son was born, and when we brought him home from the hospital we carried him in through that same side door where the murder took place.

I remember matted orange shag carpet inside the door and continuing down the steps to the cellar, and more of the same carpet on the damp concrete floor and glued to the walls. (I can't think of it now without seeing bloodstains.) At the foot of the stairs, in a mildewed, overstuffed chair I'd bought at a thrift shop, I studied for night classes at the university. In that room I painted a few amateur pictures by bad basement light, one of a towering grain elevator that I thought was pretty good but which I mislaid long ago. A life-sized nude of Diana disappeared while we were packing to leave that house for another across town. I wonder if someone doesn't have it nailed up over their basement bar. Perhaps over cocktails on football Saturdays their guests try to guess who that pretty young woman might have been.

Two quiet, Latvian women rented the upstairs apartment. They had emigrated from Europe during the Second World War and spent spring, summer, and autumn on their knees beside beds of annual flowers they'd put in along the driveway. Olga was the older, then I suppose in her sixties. She had a badly curved spine, a shy smile, and from a forest near Dresden had seen wave after wave of Allied bombers. She told me that a thousand feet over the city the atmosphere stood in red columns of flame. Alida was handsome, dark-eyed, dark-haired, younger than Olga. Of the two, she was the less approving of the young couple who lived downstairs, who drank too much, who had a very barky dog.

When I think of the exterior of that house, their flowers are always in bloom—petunias, asters, pansies, bachelor buttons, phlox—but when I remember Diana and me living there, it is always winter and we are closed in by heavy snow. The side door where the boy was killed opened onto the driveway, and the first thing I did on those blizzardy winter mornings was to open it to let out our black Schipperke, Hagen, and watch him wade through the snow to pee and then turn back, a miserable look on his sharp little face. It was a cheap, aluminum storm door with loose glass panes, icy to the touch. As I waited there I could hear the kitchen radio behind me, turned up loud so that Diana, who dreaded the twenty-mile drive when the roads were bad, could catch the list of schools that were to be closed for the day.

In a few weeks time I could build a miniature version of that house, using the approximate measurements of memory, and as I worked with plywood and paper and glue I would be able to gradually remember almost everything about it. But I won't need to do that; since the murder I have often peered into those little rooms where things went good for us at times and bad at times. I have looked into the miniature house and seen us there as a young couple, coming and going, carrying groceries in and out, hats on, hats off, happy and sad.

As I stared at the article, every piece of our furniture took its place in the rooms. I could have reached in through the door of that photograph and with the tip of a finger roll our antique dental chair over the floor. A friend's big painting of the Rolling Stones hung on the opposite wall. On the living room floor was the plush, white carpet I bought with money from a literary prize. It was always dirty. Down the hall and through a door to the left, our bed, rumpled and un-made, stood right where it stood when we were young parents, with Jeffrey's crib nearby, and by leaning a little forward I could hear the soft, reassuring sound of his breath.

It has been more than thirty years since we lived at 2820 "R" Street, Lincoln, Nebraska. I write out the full address as if to fasten it down with stakes and ropes against the violence of time. I hadn't thought about it often, maybe a few times a year. But it was our house again the minute I opened the paper that morning and saw its picture and the faces of the people who had struck it with terrible violence. They didn't look sorry, they looked like they'd do it again if they could.

Now and then since the murder I find myself turning into that decaying neigh-borhood and down that street, slowing to look at our house. The window shades are drawn on what were once such bright, welcoming rooms. Nobody lives there now, as far as I can tell. On snowy days there are no tracks up the drive to that flimsy side door.

I lean down, I try to fit myself inside. Even after thirty years there still might be the smell of Olga and Alida's salt herring being cooked upstairs, and on the first floor the fragrance of phlox, a few stalks in a water glass. For thirty years I had put it all firmly behind me, but like a perfect miniature it had waited in a corner of my heart, its rooms packed with memories. The murder brought it forward and made me hold it under the light again. Of course I hadn't really forgotten, nor could I ever forget how it feels to be a young father, frightened by an enor-mous and threatening world, wondering what might become of him, what might become of his wife and son.

Only a year after Diana, Jeff, and I moved away and into another house across town, our marriage came apart, and I began to learn to be a single father. From time to time Jeff came to visit me at the home of friends who had taken me in. The dead boy, too, had gone to visit his father.

If my luck in this life had been worse I might have been that other father, occupied by some mundane task, perhaps fixing a leaky faucet when my son went to answer the door. But I was lucky, and my son was lucky, and today, long after the murder, finding myself imagining that damp cellar room, peering down into it as if looking into a miniature cellar, I don't hear shots or see blood on the steps. I hear only soft sounds: my breath as I sit with my book, Diana's stocking feet as she pads along the hall above me, and water running into the bathtub as she gets ready to give our baby a bath.

. . .

The landlord, who owned a little doughnut shop, died many years ago. They had once lived in that house. His wife had Alzheimer's disease and sometimes arrived bewildered at our door, wanting us to let her in. She too is gone. If I were building a miniature of that house I would stand her at the door, clenching her purse in both hands, her hat on crooked.

The flowers that grew along the driveway are thirty years past their season and their beds are only dust today. My friend who painted the Rolling Stones has died. Olga and Alida, having survived the horrors of war to come to the new world and take a little pleasure in simple flowers, they too are gone. I've noticed lately when I've driven past that the porch has begun to slope toward the street as if to pour our ghosts out the front door and onto the buckled sidewalk. And I am not that young father any more, but a man in his sixties who is slowly becoming a baffled old woman who hammers and hammers at a door, wanting to be let in again, knowing by instinct that something good must still be waiting just inside.

Sara Levine

THE ESSAYIST IS SORRY
FOR YOUR LOSS

SARA LEVINE is associate professor in the Writing Program at the School of the Art Institute of Chicago. Her writing has appeared in *Nerve*, *Sonora Review*, the *Iowa Magazine*, *Alice Blue*, *Fence*, *webConjunctions*, *5-Trope*, and *Denver Quarterly*. She has been awarded a Mellon Fellowship in the Humanities, *Best American Essays* Notable Essays of 2000, 2002, and 2006, and a Pushcart Prize Special Mention for Nonfiction.

I didn't train to be an essayist, but perhaps it can be said that nobody trains—nor is trained, like seal or dog or clematis. I began . . . well, like so many others, by training to do something else, and fell into the essay by accident. It's tempting, of course, to exaggerate the unlikeliness that a person as promising as oneself would wind up practicing this littlest of genres. Once at a party, in the company of her husband, a woman told me that she'd never had any intention of dating—let alone marrying—her husband ("I was dating a *violin performance* major in college, Harry was just some engineering guy who lived down the hallway; I didn't even *notice* him for two years; then one day, what was it, at the laundromat, when I needed *quarters* . . ."). My god, I thought, doesn't she realize what she's saying about Harry?

She probably does, and yet she's baffled. Me and Harry? The essay and me?

The essay is a modest genre. It doesn't mean to change the world. Instead it says: let me tell you what happened to me. The world shrinks and the self bloats. Here in academia, people get bent out of shape about the genre. Not all people. Not the cafeteria workers, not the cleaning staff, not the administrative staff, but COME ON! Who's the university for? Forget those people. We're in the English Department now, we are cruising its halls of hallowedness, we are bumping into people at the mailboxes and saying hello. ("Hello!" "Hello! How's your book going?") And we—a pronoun now rapidly shrinking into me—we are trying to explain to the feminist materialist, and the queer theorist who is also marxist, and the post-colonial scholar who is also friendly, that we study *lol* the essay, a transhistorical *objet d'art*—that this, *this* is what all that fellowship money is going for.

I don't want to exaggerate here. I do want to exaggerate, I love to exaggerate, but I'll do this English department disservice if I pretend they're all against me. They're not. The head of the department waves his handkerchief at me encouragingly, the one and only linguist helps me tell a palatal liquid from a palatal glide, and my advisor is the advisor of all advisors, a guy whose heart is bigger than his nose, which for him is saying a lot, and who gives me no advice but lots of go-get-'ems, and kept me from quitting graduate school when I really, really wanted to quit, by offering me a chance to write essays—a guy who is so magical, so miraculous, and yet so (how does he do it?) masculine, I have no choice but to call him my hairy godmother. So look, this is what I'm saying: Not everyone hates me. But once we put my personality aside, and the quirks of my work, and the little ripples of excitement a well-mannered kid from Ohio managed to cause in a seminar, once we forget the shelter they built for me (because they did build it for me, it wasn't here before), we find that most people here find the essay a bad form, politically suspect, ideologically naive, too excited about language, hopelessly bourgeois, and, like a dirty Kleenex falling out of a handbag, vaguely embarrassing.

Why? I don't know. Believe me, I've pondered it.

Some of the distaste for the essay has nothing to do with the genre, but for the way the personal has insinuated itself into the academic playground. I mean lately. Used to be, all those jungle gyms were covered with theorists. Generalists swung from those bars. People from all kinds of perspectives who had one thing in common. Abstraction. Impersonality. A refusal to say publicly what happened to them in the grocery store. *lol*

Then Jane Tompkins and the Duke group started moving in, talking about their pee and their tenure meetings, and now we find, if we read such things, twenty-six letters in a recent *PMLA* devoted to "the place, nature, or limits (if any) of the personal in scholarship." And in the reaction to this mostly awful personal writing some of its readers cast aspersions on the essay. But the personal, it has to be said, is not particular to the essay. "The personal" is a vague term which says nothing about genre or form.

A friend once told me that it is impossible to be embarrassed about something if no one else is in the room with you, but I find I can embarrass myself all by myself, and do it best that way, and in fact would prefer to do it that way always. *lol* There are lots of memories from college which produce a keen, almost dizzying chagrin which, translated into the physical world, might be compared to being locked for twenty-four hours in a brightly lit Finnish steam bath walled with unsteamable mirrors. I am embarrassed by the pleasure I took in my hair, the violence with which I trembled at an audition for *Midsummer*, the ease with which I decided to "skip over" the readings for a course in political philosophy (something very important in my life must have been going on). I am embarrassed by the savagery I felt toward a woman who wanted to make love to me and climbed into my bed in the middle of the night; and also by the degree to which I suppressed that retrogression. (I expressed no emotion at all. I wriggled out of her embrace after announcing the need to get a drink of water, then paced the dormitory's hallways for an hour. When I came back to bed, she was gone, and even though I saw her every day for a year, we never discussed the incident.)

I'm also embarrassed by the economic fraudulence of those years, the fact that I lived in an apartment with a dishwasher—at that age! a dishwasher! when I only had six dishes to my name—and ate two dinners if I felt like it, if two dinner parties were going on, and loaned Becky Kellum ten dollars and then sat around and stewed about the number of days, hours, seconds, milliseconds it took her to pay it back. I don't think I needed that ten dollars. I think I needed the moral high ground and needed Becky to owe me, *loved* that she owed me, loved that something to me was due. Could somebody dim these lights, please?

At college I was considered a kind of sharpie. Pointed at. Big man on campus. Big man off campus. Not a man at all but nobody seemed to notice. Was winning prizes and making speeches and somebody hung up a flyer that denounced me and my feminist politics. Groovy! They thought I was a man-hater, which I wasn't, but I made the *Chicago Tribune*.

Money was monopoly money then, life was school and I was trying to claw my way through it, not out of it, still trying to cope with the fact that there were boys who were prettier than I was and girls who were smarter than I was, and I think it was no accident that Adrienne Rich was everything to me then. Her essays reduced the world into a gender problem I could squeeze in my fist. Also she writes earnestly, and at that age I was learning how to take myself seriously for the first time.

Then I came to graduate school. Something stopped—probably the attention. Also a sense that things could be done easily, that things could be done. Melancholy, as Burton says, battens when it's just you and a stack of books. (No more girls slipping into my bed, no more rallies on campus, no more Becky Kellums from whom to extract a pound of flesh.)

. . .

[handwritten margin note: has short, an edge, hard to pull off]

In the midwest girls walk around in bright colored parkas and plastic boots to match. In the East the girls don't seem to walk at all; they wisp by you like their own cigarette smoke. They weigh less.

mood

That first year of grad school, I walked around campus in cheap shoes and missed my dog, a very fine mutt who, the following year, would die an unexpected death three days before my mother was diagnosed with cancer. Because his corpse was small and furry and because our anticipated losses were large, that mutt didn't get the mourning he deserved. But I am talking now about the time before his demise, when I wasn't mourning him, just missing him. Walking along the soggy grass in my cheap shoes, I would think wistfully of what I had left behind in the midwest, to come to a fashionable school in the East, and I would also think of the heavy dumb even love that dogs will give you, despite the fact that you don't understand—say, oh come on, just say, this is strictly hypothetical—the construction of power in Foucault.

shifts over, awkward, like she did in grad school

I went home for Thanksgiving and my father said, "Your shoes are cheap. Why don't you buy another pair of shoes?"

Academics, in my experience, are not inclined to be generous to essayists. They are suspicious of humanism, nervous about too much style, and wary of public celebrations of the personal. They assume defensive postures and query: do essayists believe in uniqueness? Once, at a meeting to plan a graduate conference in literary studies, the kind of meeting where inclusivity is the aim, and the group spends three hours and forty minutes worrying about getting enough wheelchairs, ramps, crutches, hearing aids, tofu, baby-sitters, etc., to make "everyone feel welcome" but especially those people who never really are; once I suggested we open the calls to papers to include creative writing on the conference's theme, and people looked at me as if I had requested a naked boy be hired to roller skate in and serve me cotton candy. Essayists are thought to be indulgent.

Which means lenient, messy, loose.

This essayist? Undisciplined? Able to set a perfect table but unable to arrange three consecutive thoughts? One might tackle these accusations in a methodical way, or only pretend to.

The essay seems disorganized, I think, because it has a stake in pretending not to know where it is going. Putting on its hat, heading for the door, it seems to follow the random movement of the mind itself. This looks like laziness, but it smells like epistemology. Because essays offer a way of thinking—a dramatization of process as opposed to a curtain unfurled on the final product, all scrubbed and clean as the newborn on TV. Unlike articles, they give form to the streakiest mental processes. I like to call the essayist a sketch artist for thought, since artistry is an important part of the package. Yes, yeah, right, my thoughts don't really bump along this way, but they do bump somehow, and it's more honest—more pedagogically useful, more truthful—to arrange them in a loose, disconnected, provisional way than to deliver only the conclusions.

Another thing that makes the essay seem like a mess is its refusal to decide the things it feels it cannot decide. The essay is willing to harbor contradictions. Like a hotel for disagreements, like a pillow on which discrepancy can rest her rumpled head. The article likes contradictions too but it starts with them and tries to resolve them; or it starts with something that doesn't look like a contradiction at all, and methodically shows it to be one. Either way contradictions are cunningly displayed in such a way that the contradiction appears to be located outside—outside in a text, outside in the culture, most importantly, outside of the author.

Often an essay ends without any contradiction solved. Often an essay doesn't even push towards resolution. It thinks it is interesting without a big bang.

Like essayists themselves, academics learn to quote E. B. White's self-deprecating remarks about the essayist's self-centeredness, only they quote them without irony. Sometimes they quote them before breakfast. Sometimes in an argument my brother quotes them at me. Personally I can't stand how considerate academics are willing to be. They are clock-watchers and word-counters, all of them! They buckle at the sight of a hasty generalization. They make transitions frank as any handicap. And I know one professor who never considers an article complete until he has checked to make sure all the paragraphs are the same length. ("But why would you want them to be the same length?" I wanted to ask.)

In exchange for the reader's valuable time academics compress their unwieldy thoughts into some sturdy pill the reader can swallow or take away with him, fingering it in his hand, deciding whether or not he should swallow. The essay is not a pill; it is an unwieldy mass; it is fat slime (the phrase is John Donne's) some part of which may stick to the reader's hands, some part of which may evaporate. And this is O.K., I tell myself, since the essay sees all knowledge as provisional.

Imagine a war outside your window and a careless companion who sits with a stack of albums in his lap: "And here's another snapshot of me!" That is a caricature of the essayist, although not a fair one. Some essays move very close to the short story in which the narrator himself is the protagonist. Other essays are personal simply because they move in unconventional ways. They are mum when it comes to life stories. But they digress, they land like a prize frog on the least likely lily pad of a word, they skateboard off into the horizon when you expect them to hop on the horses and ride. The essayist's persona quickens in direct proportion to the reader's inability to predict the next word, argument, mood, or scene.

Essayists get drunk on language. What makes a good essay may have less to do with truth and more to do with what kind of work-out the nouns and verbs get. Art is valued, ease is valued. Because the essay is pessimistic about everything but language. *Life is hard, life is hard,* it says, over and over, like a depressive who fails to fill her prescription. The only thing we can feel good about is the fact that we can talk well and amusingly about how hard everything is, how useless, fleeting, depressing. We rearrange the sounds of our distress. Maybe you've noticed, there are no good *cheery* essayists. When too much optimism comes in, the essay falters. Nancy Mairs writes a convincingly ambivalent description of herself as a cripple, but ruins an essay when she claims at its end, like some sunny Tiny Tim waving his crutch, that she wouldn't exchange anything for "sound limbs and a thrilling rush of energy." She's "getting the hang of being a cripple," she says; that's the essay's last line, in case you didn't hear the music swell or see the credits rolling. Easy resolutions stain the essay, spoil the print of its pessimistic fabric. — *no easy ending*

Outside the academy, people read essays without apology. They pay money for them. In hardback, softback, in newspapers, quarterlies, magazines. Stephen Jay Gould recently read a few essays at a bookstore in Providence, and the store was mobbed. I, a well-dressed graduate student who studies the essay, couldn't get in.

I could get as far as the bookshelves. Gould was beyond the books, in the basement, a room that is usually the temporary housing for the Brown University Computer Store, if anything temporary can be said to be usual, and upstairs seventy-eight science nerds were milling around (I know because I was the seventy-ninth nerd who counted them). We were blinking at each other, through rain-smeared glasses, trying to determine if there was any way we could combine our collective brain power to get down the basement stairs. There was no cordon, but every once in a while an employee would rise up the stairs, like a flame licking the path, a dragon guarding the Gould, and we the nerds stepped fearfully back. I went and hid in the lit section.

And found there one of those huge comprehensive anthologies of literature, the sort of thing which, on a bad day, can induce an inferiority complex, quick as ipecac. But today was a good day. Every author in the book was a familiar, if not an acquaintance, and I felt the professionally heady sense that academia encourages, the sense that I was learning my field. Not just learning it but coming down on it, as elegantly as a linen on a table. This, by the way, is the strategy of the academic article: to cover the field. Or to cover your ass in the field. To point out, with a tick of the tongue and a beam in your eye that the field, in fact, has not been properly covered. In *The Observing Self,* Graham Good explains that the spatial image of covering the field "corresponds to the temporal idea of progress"—as if gradually all the gaps in a discipline could be filled in, as if theoretically (if people didn't have careers to make; if truth didn't keep pursuing them like a doppelgänger) the discipline could be declared "finished."

So there I was, kneeling in the bookstore aisle. (Kneeling is just the first move, an early sign of commitment. Body drops to the floor and then if the pages look good, body is rolling, spreading soft as butter, oozing like oil onto the carpet, never mind the traffic, never mind that oldster with the walker. I'm an uncomfortably comfortable customer, a religious reader—you don't interrupt a girl who is praying, do you; you don't step on a person whose fingers are wrung in prayer?) Perusing this book, this doorstop of a book, which, excluding its index, runs two thousand eight hundred and twenty eight pages long, and professes to be an anthology of American Literature, I find that it includes no essayists besides Emerson and Thoreau. Published in 1996, this book includes no twentieth century or contemporary essays at all.

Because of the Harper American Literature and books like it, because most creative writing departments teach playwriting, fiction, and poetry; because it is raining in Puerto Rico and the cheese has been badly wrapped and the line at the bank is long, and all sorts of other more insidious reasons which I leave you to supply, a cry is sometimes raised to defend the essay. Prick up your ears, as O. B. Hardison says, and you may hear a rumor "that the essay is an endangered species. There have even been calls to 'save the essay,' as there are calls to save whales and condors." Who is O. B. Hardison? Good question. He's a critic at some university. No doubt he is more than that, but we have no time to inquire. Who are the people making the call to save the essay? Another good question, extremely bad timing. I don't like to unfold a long bibliography. I like to play this game like a house game of Scrabble—with a minimum of proper nouns.

Consider Foucault's repressive hypothesis. What Foucault did for sex, I'm doing for the essay. Foucault said we talk on and on about sexual repression and fail to see how much we actually talk about sex. In the academy, people are yakking about whether or not the essay belongs. Our thing is the article, they say. To write essays is to smell of the country; to carry the impression, if not the reality, of being connected to a large sum of money. And yet Derrida writes essays, Cixous writes essays, bell hooks and Leslie Fiedler and Harold Bloom and Jane Gallop and Henry Louis Gates write essays. Basically (correct me if I'm wrong, I don't read everybody), top-ranking tenured academics write essays, and less secure or successful academics write articles.

I am on a date, a blind date. Lodged in some terrible mistake of a sports car, careening on I-95 headed for Newport, with a graduate student in astrophysics who is quizzing me to see what I know about the moon, the stars. I am studying for a Ph.D. in English Language and Literature. That must be Orion, I shrug and give him a smile that means fuck off. Later when the car is parked and the moon is shining its educational glow he will blurt into my ear and out of nowhere, *"I don't spell very well,"* and I will understand why the date had to be an astronomical quiz. (Casting his mind to the orthographical oopsies of his *billet-doux,* he was already worrying about writing "sieze" for "seize," "beasts" for "breasts," fearing I would red-ink his dyslexic letters and return them.) Hoping the reply will be taken as a field-related willingness to articulate a position and not as a sign that I am encouraging him to lean, wet-lipped, across the car, I tell him: "Most people don't spell well. Look at F. Scott Fitzgerald's letters. He couldn't spell worth a damn." People approach writers, assuming we pull a perfect text out of our nose each time (well spelled). Spelling is the least of it.

Academics worry that essayists are naive when it comes to the self—which they call "the subject," to show that they are not naive.

Although it's true you can learn about yourself while writing, the discovery racket, the voyager motif, the Go-Inward-Young-Man conceptualization of the self as a land that you've got to explore, ought to be shelved. Or as the academics say: reexamined. Because it's hard to separate what you are learning from what you are making up along the way. I know—and who am I? One makes discoveries about oneself but more often one makes up discoveries. One does not pull thoughts from the head as easily as laundry from a dryer.

And don't essayists know this? Forget real live personalities, forget interviews, confessions, and intentionalities. I'm extracting the Essence of the Essayist, I'm reading what the essayist knows through the form itself. The essayist knows there is no such thing as a coherent self because the essayist writes short pieces. He does not, as Phillip Lopate points out, write one long autobiography, a book form, with a master narrative. We might say the essayist breaks his life into pieces, but then we would miss the essayist's role in making—as opposed to simply reflecting and shaping—that life. Rather than break his life into pieces the essayist assumes there is no real life, but makes one. Again and again and again. And doesn't worry too much about the contradictions. Never mind Janus-faced, the essayist is a decahedron. I should have ten faces in this essay alone, and at some point each dissolving, like a monster in a movie.

Still, the essayist is often recognized by her voice. "Voice-print," I've heard it said. I am willing to wager that I could tell never-before-read snatches of Edward Hoagland from never-before-read snatches of Joyce Carol Oates, but voice is a linguistic matter. Grammatical habit, tics of diction, penchant for pronouns, a way of winding up the sentence or letting it loosely unravel. If the essayist defines herself by style, then style—a broad term that means the way you do the things you do—for her means deviance. The way you refuse to do the things that everybody *else* does. Even if an essayist is writing as impersonally as Susan Sontag (who unlike Annie Dillard never has a cat on the windowsill or a leg of lamb in the oven), she finds a way to violate the norms of everyday language. Of course you can't deviate the whole nine yards or you would be perfectly incomprehensible. But essayists tend to shudder at anything that sounds conventional, even when they are aiming for an accessible—say, "familiar" persona. So much so that they often exasperate our patience. Edward Hoagland writes, "For the time being the preludes of sex bore me—the whole repetitive preoccupation with the next pair of bobbledeboobs." I only know vaguely what those bobbledeboobs are, and if there weren't a pair of them, I wouldn't have a clue.

Academics have their own style, which accounts for the ease (but not the rancor) with which they are parodied. I know a professor who considers herself a stylist even though every argument she writes begins, "If the blah blah blah, then the blah blah blah." "Trust me," she says (not explicitly; only schmucks and theatre teachers and boyfriends who are about to rob you of your virginity explicitly say "Trust me"), but implicitly: trust that the voice on the page knows whereof it speaks. This professor flashes her style like a policeman flashing a badge. Conformity is a key term here. An academic wants to sound like every other academic—with just a hint of personality (an amusing epigraph, a wry aside, something unexpected, perhaps, put in the expectedly unexpected footnote), but nothing to rock the boat, nothing that suggests there is an ego here who must be heard, whose self-importance is more important than the quest for knowledge, or the subject itself. It takes style to be this self-effacing.

It takes a similar kind of linguistic restraint to write a good sympathy note. *There's* a genre where sincerity counts, where ego really must be broken. Much better to write a formulaic "I am very sorry to hear . . ." than to show how interesting you can be with your prose style. But maybe I'm saying that because in the face of disaster, I often find the inkwell dry. In the last year I have written two letters of condolence. The first was to a woman whose father died after a long slow illness I hardly knew anything about. She is a private type, not one to indulge in window-gazing or acute glances, and never let me know her father was ailing. After he died she spoke of him freely and cheerfully: she showed

she's poking at what an essay should be

me toys he had made for her as a kid, displayed his picture proudly on her desk. It was as if *now* he were alive. But I understand that, the relief she must have felt when he died. Because when my own mother was in chemotherapy I used to fantasize about her dying, not because I wanted her to die but because every hour of the day I felt like I was on the edge of a great grief, and it was the edge that was unbearable, the pitch and sway between despair and relief. I longed to be completely a wreck or completely grateful to the medical profession that saved her. I was too tired and selfish to feel something complicated in between.

So this occurs to me: style-as-deviance is all right in the essay because the essay means to be upfront about the self and *complicated*. When you write a sympathy note you've got to deliver the sympathy in a solid way, without ambivalence, whole hog, or you're a jerk who shouldn't have written a note at all. O.K. Well, the essayist is a jerk. The essayist is tactless. "I am so sorry to hear about the death of your father" becomes, in an essayist's hands, "I am so sorry to hear about the death of your father, even though all those years he wallowed in depression, refused to take his medicine, and drained your mother of what little spirit she had . . .")

lol

The essay doesn't give its reader the relief of life or death, innocent or guilty, he was a good father, he was a bad. A stubborn skeptic, it refuses to let the chips finally fall. That the essay aims for art is what its critics often miss. The best art, said Nabokov, is fantastically deceitful and complex.

telly, reflective

Actually, Nabokov never said anything he said; he wrote what he said, erasing many times.

irony

Although critics have been unable to determine the essay's constituents in the precise and practical way that they can tell a poet to make a sonnet out of fourteen lines, they can say, after years of deliberation, and on pretty good authority, that the essay is like a coat of fur, or Proteus in chains, or a syllable-filled spirit, and has more in common with the German cockroach than the Tennessee snail darter. The essay is like a journey, they say, or a walkabout, or a loose sally of the mind. Because my grandmother wears her blouses unbuttoned, and her name is Sally, this last has always been my favorite definition. My grandmother is a lovely woman, half-cocked, and generous. She seduces indiscriminately. She loves her body, she loves *the* body, and I think it's fair to say (although the deathbed thing tends to distort one's view) that she relates to people through food and touch, as opposed to, say, conversation. Most family pictures feature her in a bathing suit, straps knocked off her shoulders, as if they had just fallen down. Once on the beach she stroked my shoulders and told me how lovely I was. To a kid who wasn't used to being touched, her touch felt strange. "Do I bristle? Do I purr?" I think, because I was young and dull, I acted casual.

grandmother is what essay should be

Break some rules.

lol wandering ——> no clear ending

E. J. Levy

MASTERING THE ART OF
FRENCH COOKING

E. J. LEVY's essays have appeared in *The Best American Essays 2005*, the *2007 Pushcart Prize: Best of the Small Presses, Salmagundi, Orion*, and *Missouri Review*. Her short stories have been published in the *Paris Review, Gettysburg Review*, and *North American Review*, among other places, and two have been recognized as among the year's Distinguished Stories in *The Best American Short Stories 2003* and *2004*. The editor of the Lambda award-winning anthology *Tasting Life Twice: Literary Lesbian Fiction by New American Writers*, Levy holds a BA in history from Yale and earned an MFA in creative writing from Ohio State University. She is currently an assistant professor in the MFA Program in Creative Writing at American University in Washington, DC, where she recently completed a memoir set in the Brazilian rain forest, *Amazons: A Love Story*.

I have no photograph of my mother cooking, but when I recall my childhood this is how I picture her: standing in the kitchen of our suburban ranch house, a blue-and-white-checked terry-cloth apron tied at her waist, her lovely head bent over a recipe, a hiss of frying butter, a smell of onions and broth, and open like a hymnal on the counter beside her, a copy of Julia Child's *Mastering the Art of French Cooking*.

The book's cover is delicately patterned like wallpaper—white with miniature red fleurs-de-lis and tiny teal stars—the title and authors' names modestly scripted in a rectangular frame no larger than a recipe card: a model of feminine self-effacement.

This unassuming book was my mother's most reliable companion throughout my childhood, and from the table laid with a blue cotton cloth, not yet set with flatware and plates and glasses of ice water, not yet laid with bowls of broccoli spears, *boeuf bourguignon*, potatoes sautéed in butter, I observed her as she sought in its pages an elusive balance between the bitter and sweet.

It is a scene less remembered than invoked, an amalgam of the many evenings when I sat and watched my mother cook at the copper gas stove whose handles glowed a soft, burnished, too human pink. Tall and remote as statuary, dressed stylishly in cashmere and pumps, a chestnut bouffant framing her face and its high cheekbones, her pale blue eyes cast down, my mother consulted her recipes night after night. It is a scene suffused in memory with a diffuse golden light and a sense of enormous safety and an awareness that beyond that radiant kitchen lay the shadow-draped lawn, the cold, starry night of another midwestern autumn.

My mother had few pleasures when I was growing up. She liked to read. She liked to play the piano. She liked to cook. Of these, she did a good deal of the first, very little of the second, and a great deal of the third. She was of that generation of women caught in the sexual crossfire of women's liberation, who knew enough to probe for their desires, but not enough to practice them.

Born into the permissive sixties, raised in the disillusioned seventies, the third of three children, I came of age in a world where few rules were trusted, few applied. Of those that did, the rules contained in my mother's cookbooks were paramount.

The foods of my childhood were romantic. *Boeuf bourguignon. Vichyssoise. Salade niçoise. Bouillabaisse. Béarnaise. Mousseline au chocolat.* Years before I could spell these foods, I learned their names from my mother's lips, their smells by heart.

At the time I took no notice of the gustatory schizophrenia that governed our meals. The extravagant French cuisine prepared on the nights my father dined with us; the Swanson TV dinners on the nights we ate alone, we three kids and my mother, nights that came more frequently as the sixties ebbed into the seventies. On those nights we ate our dinners in silence and watched the Vietnam War on television, and I took a childish proprietary delight in having a dinner of my own, served in its aluminum tray, with each portion precisely fitted to its geometrical place. These dinners were heated under thin tinfoil and served on plates, and we ate directly from the metal trays our meals of soft whipped potatoes, brown gravy, sliced turkey, cubed carrots, and military-green peas.

Had I noticed these culinary cycles, I doubt that I would have recognized them for the strategic maneuvers they seem to me in retrospect. Precisely what my parents were warring over I'm not sure, but it seems clear to me now that in the intricate territorial maneuvers that for years defined their marriage, cooking was my mother's principal weapon. Proof of her superiority. My father might not feel tenderness, but he would have to admire her. My mother cooked with a vengeance in those years, or perhaps I should say she cooked for revenge. In her hands, cuisine became a martial art.

. . .

My mother spent herself in cooking. Whipping egg whites by hand with her muscular forearm, rubbing down a turkey with garlic and butter and rosemary and thyme, she sublimated her enormous unfeminine ambition in extravagant hubristic cuisine. Disdainful of the Sisyphean chores of housecleaning, she threw herself into the task of feeding us in style. If we were what we ate, she was hell-bent on making her brood singular, Continental, and I knew throughout my childhood that I would disappoint her.

In the kitchen, my mother could invent for herself a coterie of scent and flavor, a retinue of exquisite associates, even though she would later have to eat them. What she craved in those years was a companion, not children; but my father was often gone, and I was ill suited to the role.

I lacked utterly the romance my mother craved. Indifferent to books, unsociable, I could not master French. Though I would study the language for five years in high school, I would never get beyond the rudiments of ordering in restaurants and asking directions to the municipal pool (*Je voudrais un bifteck, s'il vous plaît. Où est la piscine?*). In the face of my mother's yearning, I became a spectator of desire, passive, watchful, wary. Well into my twenties I remained innocent of my tastes, caught up in observing my mother's passions and fearful too that I might betray her, call into question her unswerving desires with desires of my own.

Julia Child was the only reliable companion my mother had in those years, other than the woman who came once a week to clean the house. Across the street the Segals had a "live-in girl," a local college student who came in to watch the children in the afternoons while Mrs. Segal nursed a nervous breakdown. Each year these live-in girls changed: now blond, now brunette, with names like Stacy and Joanne. They taught us how to shoot hoops, how to ride bikes, how to appreciate soap operas. In our house there was no "live-in girl," there was only Mrs. Williams, the "cleaning lady."

I was quiet on the days when Mrs. Williams came to clean, embarrassed that we needed someone to help us keep our lives in order, embarrassed too by the fact that she was black and we were white. On the afternoons she came to clean I could not help but see my family as White People, part of a pattern of white folks who hired black folks to pick up after them. I felt ashamed when I saw my mother and Mrs. Williams chatting over coffee at our kitchen table. I saw their silhouettes against history, and they made an ugly broken line. I read in it patronage, condescension, exploitation, thwarted rage.

I thought at the time that it was misapplied gentility that prompted my mother to sit with Mrs. Williams while she ate lunch. Their conversations seemed to me a matter of polite routine. They spoke generally. Of the latest space launch. Watergate, the price of oil. The conversation was not intimate. But they shared it. Later, when Mrs. Williams was dying of breast cancer, she told my mother that my mother had been her best friend. Her *best* friend. My mother told me this with wonder, as if she were amazed that anyone had ever considered her a friend. Now I wonder if the declaration moved her too because she understood its corollary, that Mrs. Williams had been her best, perhaps her only, friend.

Cooking was not the only medium in which my mother excelled. She organized birthday parties on an epic scale—fashioning piñatas out of crepe paper and papier-mâché, organizing haunted houses and games of smell and memory—and she made us prizewinning costumes well beyond the point at which we should rightly have given up masquerading.

I was fifteen when I won the final prize in a series of prizes won for her costumes, for a banana suit she'd made me, a full-length, four-paneled yellow cotton shift, worn over a conical cardboard cap to shape the crown, and yellow tights. My mother had ingeniously designed the suit with a triangular front panel that could be secured with Velcro to the crown or "peeled" down to reveal—through a round hole in the cloth—my face.

The prize for this costume, my father reminds me, was a radio designed to look like a box of frozen niblet corn—a square, yellow plastic radio with an authentic Green Giant label. This was the late seventies, and in America you could buy a lot of things that looked like food but weren't. You could buy a scented candle in the shape of a chocolate sundae, sculpted in a tulip glass with piles of frothy false whipped cream and a perfect wax cherry. You could buy a soda glass tipped on its side, out of which a carbonated cola-colored liquid spilled into a puddle of clear plastic. There was shampoo that smelled of herbs or lemons; tiny soaps in the shape of peaches and green apples; paperweights shaped like giant aspirin, four inches in diameter, cast in plaster; the plastic simulacrum of a slice of pineapple or a fried egg dangling at the end of a key chain.

It was an era of food impersonation. A cultural critic might dismiss this as conspicuous consumption: possessed of abundance, we could mock necessity. Food, for us, could be a plaything—revenge for all those childhood admonitions not to play with your food. But I think that there was in this as well a sign of political disaffection—an ironic commentary on the unreliability of appearances in the wake of Watergate and Vietnam (in South Africa such objects were also popular at the time, a Fulbright scholar from Zimbabwe would tell me years later)—and a measure of spiritual dislocation. As if, glutted with comfort and suspicious of appearances, we had lost touch with what sustains us and had relinquished faith in even the most elementary source of life. Food.

Mixed marriage. The phrase itself recalls cuisine: mixed greens, mixed vegetables, "mix carefully two cups sifted flour with . . ." As if marriage were a form of sentimental cookery, a blending of disparate ingredients—man and woman—to produce a new and delectable whole. "She's my honey bun, my sweet pea, my cookie, sugar"; "You can't make an omelet without breaking a few eggs."

English is spiced with phrases that attest to our enduring attachment to food as metaphor, and point to our abiding faith in affection's ability to sustain us as vitally as food does. But the phrase "mixed marriage" also suggests the limits of love, its inability to transform difference, and is a warning. In the mythic goulash of American culture, the melting pot is supposed to inspire amity, not love. One should melt, it seems, not mix. Marriage of the kind my parents ventured to embrace—between gentile and Jew—went, according to the conventions of the time, too far.

It was in part because of their differences that my mother married my father. He must have seemed to her exotic, with his dark skin, jet eyes, his full sensuous mouth. At seventy he will look like Rossano Brazzi, but at age thirty-one, when my parents meet at the University of Minnesota, on the stairs of Eddy Hall, as my beautiful mother descends from a library in the tower where she has finished her day's research and my father ascends to his office where he is a young professor of psychology, he is more handsome even than a movie star—I can see this in photos from the time—because his face is radiant with expectation for his future.

For my father, the son of Russian and Lithuanian immigrants, marrying my mother must have seemed like marrying America itself. Her ancestors had come over in 1620 on that first and famous ship, and though my mother's family was of modest means, her speech and gestures bespeak gentility. Her English is precise, peppered with Latinate words and French phrases; her pronunciations are distinctive and slightly Anglicized (not *cer-EE-bral*, she corrects me, *CER-eh-bral*). She possesses all the Victorian virtues: widely read, she is an accomplished pianist and a gifted painter; she speaks French and Czech, is knowledgeable in art and history, physics, physiology, and philosophy. Although she is a passionate conversationalist, she has a habit of concluding her sentences on a slight descending note, as if she has discovered partway through speech that it is too wearying to converse after all, and so gives up. My mother's verbal inflections are the telltale signs of class in classless America, and marrying her, my father crossed the tracks. He could not know how he would resent the crossing; she could not know how she would resent the role of wife.

My mother's enormous ambitions were channeled by her marriage into a narrow course—like a great roaring river forced against its nature to straighten and be dammed, resulting in floods, lost canyons—and her desires became more powerful for having been restrained. It seemed to me only a matter of time before she'd reassert her claim to wilder, broader terrain. Throughout my childhood, I waited for my mother to leave.

Given the centrality of culinary concerns in my childhood, it is unsurprising perhaps that my first act on leaving home was to codify my eating. My first term at college, I eschewed the freshman ritual of room decoration—the requisite Manet prints, the tacky O'Keeffes—in favor of regulations: I tacked a single notice to the bulletin board beside my desk, specifying what I could and could not eat. My schema was simple: one thousand calories each day, plus, if absolutely necessary, a pack of sugarless gum and as much as a pound of carrots (my skin, in certain photos from the period, is tinted orange from excess carotene). I swam my meals off each morning with a two-mile swim at dawn, followed by a cold shower.

My saporous palette was unimaginative and highly unaesthetic and varied little from an essentially white and brown motif: poached white fish, bran cereal, skim milk, egg whites, with the occasional splash out into carrots. I practiced a sort of secular asceticism, in which repression of desire was for its own sake deemed a virtue.

In time I grew thin, then I grew fat. My senior year, by an inverse of my earlier illogic, I ate almost without cessation: lacking authentic desire to guide me, I consumed indiscriminately. Unpracticed in the exercise of tastes, I lumbered insensibly from one meal to the next. I often ate dinner twice, followed up by a pound bag of M&M's or a slice of pizza. The pop psychology of the day informed me that my eating habits were an effort to "stuff rage," but it seemed to me that I was after ballast. Something to weight me to the world, as love was said to do. Despite my heft, I felt insubstantial as steam, airy and faint as an echo.

Therapy was merely insulting. One waiflike counselor, who had herself been anorexic and spoke in a breathy, childlike voice, insisted earnestly and frequently, whenever I confessed to a thought, "That is your bulimia speaking." She said this irrespective of my statements, like a spiritualist warning of demons in the ether. I raged, I wept, I reasoned. But it was not me, she averred, but my bulimia—*speaking*. She made it sound as if I had a troll living inside me. And I knew it was a lie. I told her I thought this whole thing, my eating and all, was about desire, about being attracted to women. But she set me straight.

In the space of two years I would pass through half a dozen women's hands (none of them a lover's)—therapists, social workers, Ph.D. candidates, even a stern Irish psychiatrist, who looked unnervingly like the actress Colleen Dewhurst—and all of them in short order would assure me that I was not desirous of women. As if it were unthinkable, a thing scripted on the body at birth, a thing you could read in the face, the hands; as if sexual desire were not after all an acquired taste.

I was twenty-five before I went to bed with a woman, and when I did, I found that all along I had been right. Though it strains credulity, the following morning I woke and found that I had lost ten pounds in the night and had recovered my sense of taste. I never again had trouble with food, though my tastes surprised me. Things I never knew I liked suddenly glowed on the gustatory horizon like beacons. Plump oily avocados. The dainty lavender-sheathed teeth of garlic. Ginger. Tonic and Tanqueray gin. Green olives. Blood oranges. Pungent Italian cheese.

If education is ultimately the fashioning of a self through the cultivation of discernment and taste, this was my education, and with it came an acute craving for books and music and film. I discovered in that summer the writings of Virginia Woolf and the films of Ingmar Bergman, the paintings of Jasper Johns and Gertrude Stein's prose and John Cage's symphonies, Italian wines and sex. And I began, tentatively, fearfully, to write (though even the effort to keep a journal was an ordeal; I was tortured by doubt: How could I know what was worthy of recording, what I liked enough, what mattered enough to note and keep?).

"Do you love him?" I once asked my mother, when I was thirteen and still young enough to think that was a simple question, a thing one had or didn't have, the thing that mattered; when I did not yet understand all the other painful, difficult things that bind people more surely than love ever will.

"I like your father," she said. "That is more important."

I do not misremember this. It remains with me like a recipe I follow scrupulously, an old family recipe. And when in my first year of graduate school my lover asks me if I love her, I try to form an answer as precise as my mother's before me; I say, "I am very fond of you, I like and respect you," and watch as pain rises in her face like a leavening loaf. I have learned from my mother and Julia Child how to master French cooking, but I have no mastery when it comes to love. It will take me a long time to get the hang of this; it will take practice.

. . .

In my second year of graduate school, I enroll in an introductory French class. The instructor is a handsome man from Haiti, and the whole class is a little in love with him. In Minneapolis, the home of the sartorially challenged, where a prominent uptown billboard exhorts passersby to "dress like you're not from around here," he is a fashion oasis. An anomaly in these rooms of unmodulated beige, he is dressed this drear January morning in a black turtleneck, chinos, belt, heavy gold chain, ring, watch. He looks like he might go straight from this 11:15 A.M. class to a nightclub—or as if he has just come from one.

Born thirty miles east of Cap Haitien, the second-largest city in Haiti, he is an unlikely figure in these rooms filled with privileged white kids from the suburbs. His own education, he recalls, was "sketchy," snatched from stints in a *lycée* (the equivalent of an American secondary school) in Cap Haitien. His parents did not live together, and life under Duvalier was difficult; he did, he says, what was necessary to survive.

All my adult life I have sought out people like this, people who I sense can instruct me in how to live in the world. Who know how to survive, to hustle. How to make it from one day to the next. The things my mother and father couldn't teach me or never knew. I will spend my twenties and early thirties seeking out people like this, like a junkie; I can't get enough of certitude or attitude.

The questions you ask in an introductory language class are always the important ones, the original ones that the raw fact of language inspires, the ones we ask as children, then forget when we grow up. On the first day of class I dutifully copy into my notebook the questions the instructor has written on the board: *Qui suis-je? Qui êtes-vous?* It is only later, while scanning the pages of this notebook, that I am startled to see the questions I have scribbled there, demanding an answer: Who am I? Who are you?

I had been in junior high or high school when I first began to imagine that my parents would separate as soon as their children left home. I had come to expect this, so when my siblings and I did leave I was genuinely shocked, even disappointed, that my parents stayed together. I didn't understand that they were, after all those years, if not fond of each other, at least established; that they were afraid of loneliness; that, approaching sixty, approaching seventy, they were too tired to fight and so perhaps could make room, as they hadn't previously, for tenderness. I didn't understand that it is not that time heals all, but that in time the simple fact of having survived together can come to outweigh other concerns, that if you're not careful, you can forget that you ever hoped for something more than sustenance.

"Your parents seem so comfortable," a friend of mine commented after we had dined with my parents in New York City a few years back, when my folks were visiting me. "Yes," I said, with something like regret, recognizing in that moment for the first time their surrender in a long-waged battle. "I think they are." These days my mother orders in Thanksgiving dinner from a restaurant in St. Paul. She orders unlikely foods: in place of the traditional turkey with trimmings, there is a large, squat, hatbox-shaped vegetable torte with marinara sauce, green salad, cranberries from the can. At dinner, she presides from the head of the table, opposite my father, smiling. Sedate as a pudding.

In college, I met a young woman who had corresponded throughout her childhood with Julia Child. It was from her that I first heard that Child had been an alcoholic and often was drunk on the set. My mother, if she recognized drunkenness for what it was, nevertheless cast the story differently: she laughed about how Child, having dropped a chicken on the floor during a taping, had had the aplomb to pick it up and cook it anyhow. This delighted my mother, this imperturbability, the ability in the face of disappointment to carry on.

I have asked my mother if she regrets her marriage, her choices, and she has told me it is pointless to regret. That she did what she could do. What more can we ask of ourselves? I want to tell her, but do not, that we must ask for so much more, for everything, for love and tenderness and decency and courage. That we must be much more than comfortable, that we must be better than we think we can be, so if in some foreign tongue we are confronted with those childhood questions—*"Qui êtes-vous?" "Qui suis-je?"*—we will not be afraid to answer.

A few weeks ago, I came across a copy of *Mastering the Art of French Cooking* in a secondhand shop, unused, for $7.49. I bought it and took it home. Fingering its rough pulpy pages, consulting its index for names that conjured my long-ago abandoned childhood, I scanned the book as if it could provide an explanation, as if it were a secret record of my mother's thwarted passion. I held it in my lap, hesitant to read it, as if it were after all a private matter, a diary of those bygone days when it still seemed possible in this country, in our lives, to bring together disparate elements and mix them—artfully, beautifully—and make of them some new and marvelous whole.

Phillip Lopate

PORTRAIT OF MY BODY

PHILLIP LOPATE is the author of three personal essay collections (*Bachelor-hood, Against Joie de Vivre, Portrait of My Body*), *Waterfront: A Walk Around Manhattan* (urban meditation), *Totally Tenderly Tragically* (film criticism), and he is the editor of *The Art of the Personal Essay* and *American Movie Criticism*. The John Cranford Adams Professor of Hofstra University, Lopate lives in Brooklyn, New York.

I am a man who tilts. When I am sitting, my head slants to the right; when walking, the upper part of my body reaches forward to catch a sneak preview of the street. One way or another, I seem to be off-center—or "uncentered," to use the jargon of holism. My lousy posture, a tendency to slump or put myself into lazy, contorted misalignments, undoubtedly contributes to lower back pain. For a while I correct my bad habits, do morning exercises, sit straight, breathe deeply, but always an inner demon that insists on approaching the world askew resists perpendicularity.

I think if I had broader shoulders I would be more squarely anchored. But my shoulders are narrow, barely wider than my hips. This has always made shopping for suits an embarrassing business. (Françoise Gilot's *Life with Picasso* tells how Picasso was so touchy about his disproportionate body—in his case all shoulders, no legs—that he insisted the tailor fit him at home.)

When I was growing up in Brooklyn, my hero was Sandy Koufax, the Dodgers' Jewish pitcher. In the doldrums of Hebrew choir practice at Feigenbaum's Mansion & Catering Hall, I would fantasize striking out the side, even whiffing twenty-seven batters in a row. Lack of shoulder development put an end to this identification; I became a writer instead of a Koufax.

It occurs to me that the restless angling of my head is an attempt to distract viewers' attention from its paltry base. I want people to look at my head, partly because I live in my head most of the time. My sister, a trained masseuse, often warns me of the penalties, like neck tension, that may arise from failing to integrate body and mind. Once, about ten years ago, she and I were at the beach and she was scrutinizing my body with a sister's critical eye. "You're getting flabby," she said. "You should exercise every day. I do—look at me, not an ounce of fat." She pulled at her midriff, celebrating (as is her wont) her physical attributes with the third-person enthusiasm of a carnival barker.

"But"—she threw me a bone—"you do have a powerful head. There's an intensity. . . ." A graduate student of mine (who was slightly loony) told someone that she regularly saw an aura around my head in class. One reason I like to teach is that it focuses fifteen or so dependent gazes on me with such paranoiac intensity as cannot help but generate an aura in my behalf.

I also have a commanding stare, large sad brown eyes that can be read as either gentle or severe. Once I watched several hours of myself on videotape. I discovered to my horror that my face moved at different rates: sometimes my mouth would be laughing, eyebrows circumflexed in mirth, while my eyes coolly gauged the interviewer to see what effect I was making. I am something of an actor. And, as with many performers, the mood I sense most in myself is that of energy-conserving watchfulness; but this expression is often mistaken (perhaps because of the way brown eyes are read in our culture) for sympathy. I see myself as determined to the point of stubbornness, selfish, even a bit cruel—in any case, I am all too aware of the limits of my compassion, so that it puzzles me when people report a first impression of me as gentle, kind, solicitous. In my youth I felt obliged to come across as dynamic, arrogant, intimidating, the life of the party; now, surer of myself, I hold back some energy, thereby winning time to gather information and make better judgments. This results sometimes in a misimpression of my being mildly depressed. Of course, the simple truth is that I have less energy than I once did, and that accumulated experiences have made me, almost against my will, kinder and sadder.

Sometimes I can feel my mouth arching downward in an ironic smile, which, at its best, reassures others that we need not take everything so seriously—because we are all in the same comedy together—and, at its worst, expresses a superior skepticism. This smile, which can be charming when not supercilious, has elements of the bashful that mesh with the worldly—the shyness, let us say, of a cultivated man who is often embarrassed for others by their willful shallowness or self-deception. Many times, however, my ironic smile is nothing more than a neutral stall among people who do not seem to appreciate my "contribution." I hate that pain-in-the-ass half-smile of mine; I want to jump in, participate, be loud, thoughtless, vulgar.

Often I give off a sort of psychic stench to myself, I do not like myself at all, but out of stubborn pride I act like a man who does. I appear for all the world poised, contented, sanguine when inside I may be feeling self-revulsion bordering on the suicidal. What a wonder to be so misread! Of course, if in the beginning I had thought I was coming across accurately, I never would have bothered to become a writer. And the truth is I am not misread, because another part of me is never less than fully contented with myself.

I am vain about these parts of my body: my eyes, my fingers, my legs. It is true that my legs are long and not unshapely, but my vanity about them has less to do with their comeliness than with their contribution to my height. Montaigne, a man who was himself on the short side, wrote that "the beauty of stature is the only beauty of men." But even if Montaigne had never said it, I would continue to attribute a good deal of my self-worth and benevolent liberalism to being tall. When I go out into the street, I feel well-disposed toward the (mostly shorter) swarms of humanity; crowds not only do not dismay, they enliven me; and I am tempted to think that my passion for urbanism is linked to my height. By no means am I suggesting that only tall people love cities; merely that, in my case, part of the pleasure I derive from walking in crowded streets issues from a confidence that I can see above the heads of others, and cut a fairly impressive, elevated figure as I saunter along the sidewalk.

Some of my best friends have been—short. Brilliant men, brimming with poetic and worldly ideas, they deserved all of my and the world's respect. Yet at times I have had to master an impulse to rumple their heads; and I suspect they have developed manners of a more formal, *noli me tangere* nature, largely in response to this petting impulse of taller others.

The accident of my tallness has inclined me to both a seemingly egalitarian informality and a desire to lead. Had I not been a writer, I would surely have become a politician; I was even headed in that direction in my teens. Ever since I shot up to a little over six feet, I have had at my command what feels like a natural, Gregory Peck authority when addressing an audience. Far from experiencing stage fright, I have actually sought out situations in which I could make speeches, give readings, sit on panel discussions, and generally tower over everyone else onstage. To be tall is to look down on the world and meet its eyes on your terms. But this topic, the noblesse oblige of tall men, is a dangerously provoking one, and so let us say no more about it.

The mental image of one's body changes slower than one's body. Mine was for a long while arrested in my early twenties, when I was tall and thin (165 pounds) and gobbled down whatever I felt like. I ate food that was cheap and filling, cheeseburgers, pizza, without any thought to putting on weight. But a young person's metabolism is more dietetically forgiving. To compound the problem, the older you get, the more cultivated your palate grows—and the more life's setbacks make you inclined to fill the hollowness of disappointment with the pleasures of the table.

Between the age of thirty and forty I put on ten pounds, mostly around the midsection. Since then my gut has suffered another expansion, and I tip the scales at over 180. That I took a while to notice the change may be shown by my continuing to purchase clothes at my primordial adult size (33 waist, 15½ collar), until a girlfriend started pointing out that all my clothes were too tight. I rationalized this circumstance as the result of changing fashions (thinking myself still subconsciously loyal to the sixties' penchant for skintight fits) and laundry shrinkage rather than anything to do with my own body. She began buying me larger replacements for birthdays or holidays, and I found I enjoyed this "baggier" style, which allowed me to button my trousers comfortably, or to wear a tie and, for the first time in years, close my top shirt button. But it took even longer before I was able to enter a clothing store myself and give the salesman realistically enlarged size numbers.

Clothes can disguise the defects of one's body, up to a point. I get dressed with great optimism, adding one color to another, mixing my favorite Japanese and Italian designers, matching the patterns and textures, selecting ties, then proceed to the bathroom mirror to judge the result. There is an ideal in my mind of the effect I am essaying by wearing a particular choice of garments, based, no doubt, on male models in fashion ads—and I fall so far short of this insouciant gigolo handsomeness that I cannot help but be a little disappointed when I turn up so depressingly myself, narrow-shouldered, Talmudic, that grim, set mouth, that long, narrow face, those appraising eyes, the Semitic hooked nose, all of which express both the strain of intellectual overachieving and the tabula rasa of immaturity . . . for it is still, underneath, a boy in the mirror. A boy with a rapidly receding hairline.

How is it that I've remained a boy all this time, into my late forties? I remember, at seventeen, drawing a self-portrait of myself as I looked in the mirror. I was so appalled at the weak chin and pleading eyes that I ended up focusing on the neckline of the cotton T-shirt. Ever since then I have tried to toughen myself up, but I still encounter in the glass that haunted uncertainty—shielded by a bluffing shell of cynicism, perhaps, but untouched by wisdom. So I approach the mirror warily, without lighting up as much as I would for the least of my acquaintances; I go one-on-one with that frowning schmuck.

And yet, it would be insulting to those who labor under the burden of true ugliness to palm myself off as an unattractive man. I'm at times almost handsome, if you squinted your eyes and rounded me off to the nearest *beau idéal*. I lack even a shred of cowboy virility, true, but I believe I fall into a category of adorable nerd or absentminded professor that awakens the amorous curiosity of some women. "Cute" is a word often applied to me by those I've been fortunate enough to attract. Then again, I attract only women of a certain lopsided prettiness: the head-turning, professional beauties never fall for me. They seem to look right through me, in fact. Their utter lack of interest in my appeal has always fascinated me. Can it be so simple an explanation as that beauty calls to beauty, as wealth to wealth?

I think of poor (though not in his writing gifts) Cesare Pavese, who kept chasing after starlets, models, and ballerinas—exquisite lovelies who couldn't appreciate his morose coffeehouse charm. Before he killed himself, he wrote a poem addressed to one of them, "Death Will Come Bearing Your Eyes"— thereby unfairly promoting her from rejecting lover to unwitting executioner. Perhaps he believed that only beautiful women (not literary critics, who kept awarding him prestigious prizes) saw him clearly, with twenty-twenty vision, and had the right to judge him. Had I been more headstrong, if masochistic, I might have followed his path and chased some beauty until she was forced to tell me, like an oracle, what it was about me, physically, that so failed to excite her. Then I might know something crucial about my body, before I passed into my next reincarnation.

Jung says somewhere that we pay dearly over many years to learn about ourselves what a stranger can see at a glance. This is the way I feel about my back. Fitting rooms aside, we none of us know what we look like from the back. It is the area of ourselves whose presentation we can least control, and which therefore may be the most honest part of us.

I divide backs into two kinds: my own and everyone else's. The others' backs are often mysterious, exquisite, and uncannily sympathetic. I have always loved backs. To walk behind a pretty woman in a backless dress and savor how a good pair of shoulder blades, heightened by shadow, has the same power to pierce the heart as chiseled cheekbones! . . . I wonder what it says about me that I worship a part of the body that signals a turning away. Does it mean I'm a glutton for being abandoned, or a timid voyeur who prefers a surreptitious gaze that will not be met and challenged? I only know I have often felt the deepest love at just that moment when the beloved turns her back to me to get some sleep.

I have no autoerotic feelings about my own back. I cannot even picture it; visually it is a stranger to me. I know it only as an annoyance, which came into my consciousness twenty years ago, when I started getting lower back pain. Yes, we all know that homo sapiens is constructed incorrectly; our erect posture puts too much pressure on the base of the spine; more workdays are lost because of lower back pain than any other cause. Being a writer, I sit all day, compounding the problem. My back is the enemy of my writing life: if I don't do exercises daily, I immediately ache; and if I do, I am still not spared. I could say more, but there is nothing duller than lower back pain. So common, mundane an ailment brings no credit to the sufferer. One has to dramatize it somehow, as in the phrase "I threw my back out."

Here is a gossip column about my body: My eyebrows grow quite bushy across my forehead, and whenever I get my hair cut, the barber asks me diplomatically if I want them trimmed or not. (I generally say no, associating bushy eyebrows with Balzackian virility, *élan vital*; but sometimes I acquiesce, to soothe his fastidiousness.) . . . My belly button is a modest, embedded slit, not a jaunty swirl like my father's. Still, I like to sniff the odor that comes from jabbing my finger in it: a very ripe, underground smell, impossible to describe, but let us say a combination of old gym socks and stuffed derma (the Yiddish word for this oniony dish of ground intestines is, fittingly, *kish-kas*). . . . I have a scar on my tongue from childhood, which I can only surmise I received by landing it on a sharp object, somehow. Or perhaps I bit it hard. I have the habit of sticking my tongue out like a dog when exerting myself physically, as though to urge my muscles on; and maybe I accidentally chomped into it at such a moment. . . . I gnash my teeth, sleeping or waking. Awake, the sensation makes me feel alert and in contact with the world when I start to drift off in a daydream. Another way of grounding myself is to pinch my cheek—drawing a pocket of flesh downward and squeezing it—as I once saw JFK do in a filmed motorcade. I do this cheek-pinching especially when I am trying to keep mentally focused during teaching or other public situations. I also scratch the nape of my neck under public stress, so much so that I raise welts or sores which then eventually grow scabs; and I take great delight in secretly picking the scabs off. . . . My nose itches whenever I think about it, and I scratch it often, especially lying in bed trying to fall asleep (maybe because I am conscious of my breathing then). I also pick my nose with formidable thoroughness when no one, I hope, is looking. . . . There is a white scar about the size of a quarter on the juicy part of my knee; I got it as a boy running into a car fender, and I can still remember staring with detached calm at the blood that gushed from it like a pretty, half-eaten peach. Otherwise, the sight of my own blood makes me awfully nervous. I used to faint dead away when a blood sample was taken, and now I can control the impulse to do so only by biting the insides of my cheeks while steadfastly looking away from the needle's action. . . . I like to clean out my ear wax as often as possible (the smell is curiously sulfurous; I associate it with the bodies of dead insects). I refuse to listen to warnings that it is dangerous to stick cleaning objects into your ears. I love Q-Tips immoderately; I buy them in huge quantities and store them the way a former refugee will stock canned foodstuffs. . . . My toes are long and apelike; I have very little fellow feeling for them; they are so far away, they may as well belong to someone else. . . . My flattish buttocks are not offensively large, but neither do they have the "dream" configuration one sees in jeans ads. Perhaps for this reason, it disturbed me puritanically when asses started to be treated by Madison Avenue, around the seventies, as crucial sexual equipment, and I began to receive compositions from teenage girl students declaring that they liked some boy because he had "a cute butt." It confused me; I had thought the action was elsewhere.

About my penis there is nothing, I think, unusual. It has a brown stem, and a pink mushroom head where the foreskin is pulled back. Like most heterosexual males, I have little comparative knowledge to go by, so that I always feel like an outsider when I am around women or gay men who talk zestfully about differences in penises. I am afraid that they might judge me harshly, ridicule me like the boys who stripped me of my bathing suit in summer camp when I was ten. But perhaps they would simply declare it an ordinary penis, which changes size with the stimulus or weather or time of day. Actually, my penis does have a peculiarity: it has two peeing holes. They are very close to each other, so that usually only one stream of urine issues, but sometimes a hair gets caught across them, or some such contretemps, and they squirt out in two directions at once.

This part of me, which is so synecdochically identified with the male body (as the term "male member" indicates), has given me both too little, and too much, information about what it means to be a man. It has a personality like a cat's. I have prayed to it to behave better, to be less frisky, or more; I have followed its nose in matters of love, ignoring good sense, and paid the price; but I have also come to appreciate that it has its own specialized form of intelligence which must be listened to, or another price will be extracted.

Even to say the word "impotence" aloud makes me nervous. I used to tremble when I saw it in print, and its close relation, "importance," if hastily scanned, had the same effect, as if they were publishing a secret about me. But why should it be *my* secret, when my penis has regularly given me erections lo these many years—except for about a dozen times, mostly when I was younger? Because, even if it has not been that big a problem for me, it has dominated my thinking as an adult male. I've no sooner to go to bed with a woman than I'm in suspense. The power of the flaccid penis's statement, "I don't want you," is so stark, so cruelly direct, that it continues to exert a fascination out of all proportion to its actual incidence. Those few times when I was unable to function were like a wall forcing me to take another path—just as, after I tried to kill myself at seventeen, I was obliged to give up pessimism for a time. Each had instructed me by its too painful manner that I could not handle the world as I had previously construed it, that my confusion and rage were being found out. I would have to get more wily or else grow up.

Yet for the very reason that I was compelled to leave them behind, these two options of my youth, impotence and suicide, continue to command an underground loyalty, as though they were more "honest" than the devious strategies of potency and survival which I adopted. Put it this way: sometimes we encounter a person who has had a nervous breakdown years before and who seems cemented over sloppily, his vulnerability ruthlessly guarded against as dangerous; we sense he left a crucial part of himself back in the chaos of breakdown, and has since grown rigidly jovial. So suicide and impotence became for me "the roads not taken," the paths I had repressed.

Whenever I hear an anecdote about impotence—a woman who successfully coaxed an ex-priest who had been celibate and unable to make love, first by lying next to him for six months without any touching, then by cuddling for six more months, then by easing him slowly into a sexual embrace—I think they are talking about me. I identify completely: this, in spite of the fact, which I promise not to repeat again, that I have generally been able to do it whenever called upon. Believe it or not, I am not boasting when I say that: a part of me is contemptuous of this virility, as though it were merely a mechanical trick that violated my true nature, that of an impotent man absolutely frightened of women, absolutely secluded, cut off.

I now see the way I have idealized impotence: I've connected it with pushing the world away, as a kind of integrity, as in Molière's *The Misanthrope*—connected it with that part of me which, gregarious socializer that I am, continues to insist that I am a recluse, too good for this life. Of course, it is not true that I am terrified of women. I exaggerate my terror of them for dramatic effect, or for the purposes of a good scare.

My final word about impotence: Once, in a period when I was going out with many women, as though purposely trying to ignore my hypersensitive side and force it to grow callous by thrusting myself into foreign situations (not only sexual) and seeing if I was able to "rise to the occasion," I dated a woman who was attractive, tall and blond, named Susan. She had something to do with the pop music business, was a follower of the visionary religious futurist Teilhard de Chardin, and considered herself a religious pacifist. In fact, she told me her telephone number in the form of the anagram, N-O-T-O-W-A-R. I thought she was joking and laughed aloud, but she gave me a solemn look. In passing, I should say that all the women with whom I was impotent or close to it had solemn natures. The sex act has always seemed to me in many ways ridiculous, and I am most comfortable when a woman who enters the sheets with me shares that sense of the comic pomposity behind such a grandiloquently rhetorical use of the flesh. It is as though the prose of the body were being drastically squeezed into metrical verse. I would not have known how to stop guffawing had I been D. H. Lawrence's lover, and I am sure he would have been pretty annoyed at me. But a smile saying "All this will pass" has an erotic effect on me like nothing else.

They claim that men who have long, long fingers also have lengthy penises. I can tell you with a surety that my fingers are long and sensitive, the most perfect, elegant, handsome part of my anatomy. They are not entirely perfect—the last knuckle of my right middle finger is twisted permanently, broken in a softball game when I was trying to block the plate—but even this slight disfigurement, harbinger of mortality, adds to the pleasure I take in my hands' rugged beauty. My penis does not excite in me nearly the same contemplative delight when I look at it as do my fingers. Pianists' hands, I have been told often; and though I do not play the piano, I derive an aesthetic satisfaction from them that is as pure and Apollonian as any I am capable of. I can stare at my fingers for hours. No wonder I have them so often in my mouth, biting my fingernails to bring them closer. When I write, I almost feel that they, and not my intellect, are the clever progenitors of the text. Whatever narcissism, fetishism, and proud sense of masculinity I possess about my body must begin and end with my fingers.

Barry Lopez

FLIGHT

BARRY LOPEZ is the author of *Light Action in the Caribbean* (stories), *About This Life* (essays and memoir), the novella-length fable *Crow and Weasel*, and *Arctic Dreams* (nonfiction), for which he received the National Book Award. He has traveled extensively in remote regions of the world, and his work has been widely translated and anthologized. He is a recipient of fellowships from the Guggenheim, Lannan, and National Science foundations; the Award in Literature from the American Academy of Arts and Letters; the John Burroughs and John Hay medals; and other honors. He lives in rural western Oregon.

PENGUINS AND LIPSTICK, STRAWBERRIES AND GOLD—ALOFT

One foggy January morning in 1977, a few hours before dawn, a DC-8 freighter crashed on takeoff at Anchorage International Airport, killing the five people aboard and fifty-six head of cattle bound for Tokyo. Reservers found the white-faced Herefords flung in heaps through the thick, snowy woods, their bone-punctured bodies, dimly lit by kerosene fires, steaming in the chill air.

A few days after the accident I happened to land in Anchorage on a flight from Seattle, en route to Fairbanks. The grisly sight of the wreck and the long scar ripped through birch trees off the end of the runway made me philosophical about flying. Beyond the violent loss of human life, it was some element of innocence in the cattle I kept coming back to. Were they just standing there calmly in large metal pens when the plane crashed? And why were they needed in Tokyo? At 35,000 feet over the winter Pacific, cruising that frigid altitude at 400 knots, did their lowing and jostle seem as bucolic?

Like many people who fly often, I have watched dozens of windowless air-freighters lumbering by on taxiways and have wondered at their cargos. In the years after that accident I puzzled over them everywhere—in Quito, in Beijing, in Nairobi, in Frankfurt, in Edmonton. What could warrant such an endless fleet of machines so sophisticated and expensive? It must be more than plasma and vaccines they haul, materials desperately needed; more than cut flowers,

308

gold, and fruit, things highly valued or perishable. Could it be simply the ob-jects people most desire? A fresh strawberry on a winter morning in Toronto?

Watching pallets go aboard on monotonously similar tarmacs around the world, I became more and more curious. I wanted to know what the world craved. I wanted a clarifying annotation of the rag-doll scatter of cattle.

At 2:00 A.M. one night last December, I climbed aboard a 747 freighter in Chicago to begin a series of flights around the world with freight.[1] I would fly in and out of cities like Taipei, Rotterdam, and Los Angeles with drill pipe, pistol targets, frozen ostrich meat, lace teddies, dog food, digital tape machines, pythons, and ball caps; with tangerines from Johannesburg, gold bullion from the Argentine, and orchid clusters from Bangkok. During the hourless penetra-tion of space between continents, I would sidle among the eighty or more tons of airborne freight on the main deck, examining disparate labels like an inquir-ing bird. Out cockpit windows, I would become absorbed in the sprawling still-ness of the earth.

Before I boarded the first flight, however, I wanted to examine the plane.

The assembly building at Boeing's aircraft plant at Everett, Washington, is so large—ninety-eight acres under a single roof more than a hundred feet above the ground—that it is said to have its own weather. Sometimes low clouds form in steelwork near the ceiling, where gantry cranes carrying subassembled sec-tions of 747s, 767s, and 777s glide toward final assembly sites. Over a single November night I watched swing-shift and third-shift crews at the plant com-plete the assembly of a 747–400 freighter, nearly the largest plane ever to fly. I studied it, and listened and touched, as its 68,000-pound wings were joined to a fuselage section, the six fuselage sections slid together, and landing gear at-tached beneath, leaving it to tower above its workers, empty as a cathedral, aloof as the moon.

When I was a boy I raised tumbler pigeons, a breed that at some height above the ground destroys its aerodynamic lift and comes plummeting down like a leathered stone, only to pullout at the very last moment in a terrify-ing demonstration of power and grace. Model airplanes hung by black thread from the ceiling of my bedroom; I was mesmerized by the wind, seething in eucalyptus trees around our house; once I jumped from the roof with an open umbrella.

---

1. The forty flights, covering about 110,000 nautical miles, were made aboard 747 freighters or 747 passenger planes with substantial amounts of cargo in their lower-deck compartments or on the aft portion of their main decks, separated from the passengers by a bulkhead. The flights were arranged by Northwest Airlines in the United States and the Far East, and by KLM Royal Dutch Airlines in India, Africa, the Middle East, Europe, and South America. Both airlines provided cockpit clearance, which permitted me to ride with the pilots.

At seventeen I entered college as an aeronautical engineer, only to discover that it was the metaphors of flight, not its mechanics, that moved me. I was less interested in engineering than in the imagination of Antoine de Saint-Exupery, who wrote of the "tender muslin of the meadows, the rich tweed of the woods," who climbed into the open cockpit of a Sahara-bound mail plane with his tool bag and heavy clothes like a deep-sea diver. I switched to Arts and Letters, but the marvel of flight never diminished for me, and the exotic allure of the earth continued to tug. I pictured the skies as a landscape of winds—West Africa's harmattan, Greece's damp Apeliotes, California's Santa Ana, Japan's Daiboufu ("the wind that knocks horses down").

That night in the Boeing assembly building I admired what I saw come tangibly together: a staggering achievement in engineering, metallurgy, and economy of design. The physical assembly of a 747–400 freighter—232 feet long, 165 tons poised over eighteen tires like a barefoot gymnast on a balance beam, a six-story drop from the apex of its tail—suggests the assembly of a chronometer by tweezer, a sculptor's meaning with a jeweler's fastidiousness. Standing on scaffolding inside a wheel well, I marveled at a set of brass-colored steel screws securing hydraulic lines in a pattern as neat as a musical staff. Not a tool mark, not a misstep was to be seen. (Elsewhere, workers were buffing the plane's aluminum skin to remove scratches I couldn't find with the pad of my finger.) Fuselage sections came together smooth as a cap sliding onto a French fountain pen.

For twelve or thirteen hours that night I watched, wandering off occasionally to sift through a box of buttonhead rivets (three million of the plane's six million parts are fasteners), or to observe agile men disappearing into the recesses of another 747's unfinished wing, or to heft "nuclear hardened" cable—flexible, shielded conduit that carries thick bundles of color-coded wire from the controls on the flight deck to each engine. Then I circled back to the freighter—this particular 747–400 being built for Singapore Airlines—with another bit of understanding, a new appreciation of its elegance. People who saw the 747's first flight, in 1969, were impressed that something so huge could fly. What surprised the pilots were its nimbleness, its fluid response to their foot and hand controls, and the easy way the aircraft absorbed turbulence.

The Boeing 747 is the one airplane every national airline strives to include in its fleet as confirmation of its place in modem commerce, and it's tempting to see it as the ultimate embodiment of what our age stands for. Superficially, it represents an apotheosis in structural engineering, the applied use of exotic metals and plastics. Its avionics and electronics systems incorporate all the speed and efficiency of modem communications, and in terms of manufacturing and large-scale corporate organization, the swift assembly of its millions of parts is a model of streamlining and integration. In action, the object itself is a virtuoso solution to flight, to Icarus's dream of escape and freedom. It operates with as little regard for geography, weather, political boundaries, intimidating physical distance, and time as anything humans have ever devised. If the sophistication of the plane's mechanics was beyond my understanding, the spare grace of its lines was not, nor its ability to navigate and to communicate over any quarter of the planet's surface in almost any sort of weather. (The plane's only enemy, I was told, is rogue winds—the inevitable riptides and flash floods of the troposphere.)

When I measured out the freighter's nearly completed main deck that night—sixty-eight paces down the bare interior—I was thinking of the quintessential symbol of another era: the Gothic cathedral of twelfth-century Europe, and of its emptiness, which we once filled with religious belief. Standing on the main deck, over the stub that joins the wing roots, where "nave" meets "transept," and looking up toward the pilots' "chancel," I recalled the intention behind Lucio Costa's Brasilia, a fresh city, aligned east and west like a cathedral but laid out in the shape of an airplane. But there in the hangar, the issue of spirituality, as serious a consideration as blood in the veins of a people, was too vague. The machine was magnificent, beautiful as staggered light on water, complex as an insoluble murmur of quadratic equations. But what, placed within it, could compare to religious faith?

In the assembly building that night, the 747 came together so quickly that to be away even for half an hour meant missing lines in a sketch that soon became a painting. I would stand in one place, then another amid the cocoon of jigs, cradles, floor jacks, elevated walkways, and web slings surrounding the plane, watching while teams of men, some with ponytails and tattoos, polished off a task neat as a snap of dry fingers in slow motion. They were glad for the work. They knew it could disappear in a trice, depending on the banks, the market, or a lone securities trader in Singapore.[2]

An aircraft will give away some of its character to a slow walkabout. If you stare nose-on at a 747, you can tell whether the plane is fueled by the angle at which the wings sag. This vertical flexibility partly explains the sensation of unperturbed agility one feels as a passenger. If you let your eye run to the tip of either wing, you can see another key: a slight horizontal twist apparent in the

2. As a singular icon the 747 also symbolizes huge economic risk, brutal financial efficiency, and despotic corporate ego. Boeing president William Allen and Pan American's Juan Trippe dared each other to take the then mind-boggling steps of contracting for and building the 747. Who would go first? In 1969, when Boeing's total debt after developing the plane was thought to be larger than its net worth, it eliminated 60,000 jobs to save the company, pushing Seattle's unemployment to 17 percent.

last thirty feet or so—an engineer's quick, intuitive solution to damping a troublesome oscillation. A similar intuition once compelled Wilbur Wright to warp the leading edge of the wing on an experimental glider, lending it critical lateral stability. The glider metamorphosed into Flyer, in which, on December 17, 1903, at Kill Devil Hills on the North Carolina coast, Orville Wright achieved powered, sustained, controllable flight for the first time.

That flight carried him about half the length of a 747–400 freighter's main deck. He was airborne for twelve seconds in a craft stripped of all excess weight. The plane I was standing under can carry 122 tons 50,000 nautical miles in ten hours. The Wrights had little inkling of commercial advantage; the 747 freighter, without the support of government subsidies for initial research and development, without the promise of private profit, without corporations competing fiercely for a share in the marketplace, without a continuous turnover in all that is considered fashionable in consumer goods, might very easily have gotten no further than a draftsman's table.

Yet my last impression of the plane, the rainy morning I drove away from the assembly building, was of accomplishment. Whatever people might do with it, however they might fill this empty vessel, it gleamed, to my way of thinking, as an ideal. It was an exquisite reification of the desire for beauty.

Sometime later, I returned to Everett to inspect the finished cockpit. I wanted to crawl into every space that would admit me: low, tight bays on either side of the nosewheel doghouse that hold tiers of maintenance computers; the transverse avionics bay aft of them, where the plane's triple-redundant inertial navigation system and flight-deck computers are located (and from where, through separate hatches, one can either drop to the tarmac below or emerge on the main deck above). I wanted to orient myself among banks of Halon bottles (the firefighting system) and emergency oxygen tanks on the lower cargo deck. I wanted to enter the compartment aft of the rear pressure bulkhead and see the massive jackscrew that tilts the horizontal stabilizer (the fins that protrude from a plane's tail).

Once the plane was fitted with its four Pratt & Whitney engines—each developing up to 56,000 pounds of thrust (about 21,000 horsepower)—Singapore Airlines would take it away. At something like $155 million, it was an enormous capital investment. But with an international airfreight market currently expanding at about three times the rate of the passenger market, Boeing's plane number RR835 would soon pay for itself. After which, grossing upward of $750,000 per load against an operating cost of roughly $15,000 per hour, it would begin to earn its owners a substantial and unencumbered return.

After the Frankfurt airport and London's Heathrow, Amsterdam's Schiphol International Airport is Europe's largest airfreight depot site. KLM's operation at Schiphol is efficient and organized—dangerous goods here, live animals there, valuables (jewelry, currency, silver bars, uncut gemstones) over here, drugs in yet another place. In this world, "perishable" refers to more than flowers, food, and newspapers; it includes everything in tenuous fashion: watches, video games, shades of lipstick, a cut of trouser—objects for which a few days' head start on store shelves is crucial.

On an upper half-floor of the cavernous out-bound-freight building—the main floor includes an open space perhaps 600 by 200 feet and 40 feet high—there is no one, only automated loading equipment, enslaved by a computerized sorting program that is updated continuously in response to aircraft schedule changes and new delivery priorities. The loaders, moving on floor tracks, pull standard-size pallets and cargo containers from steel shelves at just the right moment to launch them on paths terminating promptly at the cargo doors of their intended airplane. It is stark, bloodless work. On the main floor the tedium is relieved in three ways: in the buildup of single pallets, where workers arrange many small packages trimly in eight-by-ten-foot-square loads, at heights to fit either the upper or lower deck of a particular aircraft, and with one top edge rounded slightly to conform to the curve of the plane's sidewall; by the loading of oddly shaped or remarkable objects—a matched set of four dark blue Porsche 911s, a prefabricated California ranch-style home; and by the sheer variety of goods—bins of chilled horse meat, Persian carpets, diplomatic mail bound in sisal twine and sealed with red wax, bear testicles, museum art exhibitions, cases of explosives.

The impression one gets amid the tiers of briefly stored cargo and whizzing forklifts is of mirthless haste. A polite but impatient rectitude about the importance of commerce prevails, and it forestalls simple questions: Have they run out of mechanical pencils in Houston? Is the need for eelpout in Osaka now excruciating? Are there no more shirtmakers in Dakar?

The following day I departed the freezing rain and spitting snow of Amsterdam for Cape Town, 6,000 miles and an opposing season to the south, where one of KLM's smallest facilities operates on a decidedly different scale. We bring, among other things, eight white ear-tufted marmosets and two Goeldi's marmosets, both endangered, inbound from South America for a local attraction called Monkey Den.

When my escort completed our tour—a semi-enclosed metal shed, no automation—he very kindly suggested that we go for a drive. He felt harried by shippers' phone calls, cajoling for more space than he could provide on the outbound flight. I, too, wanted to get away from the clamor.

For the past six days I had been flying a heavy schedule, mostly in and out of the Far East. I was bewildered by the speed with which everything moved, by how quickly we came and went through the countries. In a few hours my plane would turn around and fly back to Johannesburg, pick up fresh flowers, hunting trophies, and raw diamonds, then return to Amsterdam.

We drove west through windblown sand scrub on the Cape Flats, rather quickly through Cape Town itself, and around to Clifton Bay on the west side of Table Mountain. The weather had been hot, but it was cooler now, seventy-two, with a brisk southeast wind, the one they call the Doctor.

For a long while I stood there on the bluff in the summer sunshine, staring into the transparent blue water of the Atlantic. I was acutely aware of history here at Bartolomeu Dias's Cabo Tormentoso (the Portuguese navigator's Cape of Storms, a foreboding appellation his king would later change to Cabo da Boa Esperanca, Cape of Good Hope). Cook and Darwin anchored here as did, in 1522, the remnant of that part of Magellan's crew under Sebastian del Cano. In those days it had taken as many months as it now takes hours to come this far south from Europe, and an indifferent sea swamped and crushed the Dutch jachts and Iberian caravels like a child's paper sailers. Robben Island, where Nelson Mandela spent so many years, was just to the north. A few miles to the southeast was Skildergat Cave, a 35,000-year-old early human site. All of this was once the country of the Khoikhoi people, long since gone now to Namibia and Botswana, where they are called San and among whom are the much studied !Kung.

My companion was speaking English with a friend. When he lapsed into Afrikaans I recalled how, over the past few days, I had been scrambling to get even the simplest grasp of Malay, Thai, Hindi. I was moving carelessly around the planet. Beneath the familiar jet lag I began to sense something else. I looked up past my shoulder at the quiet oak and pine forests of Table Mountain, da Gama's defining pivot. It had a peculiar time to it, as indigenous as its rock. I could not take that time with me, nor bring my own time here and drape it possessively over the mountain. In that moment I glimpsed the impunity with which I was traveling and the inseparability of time and space in geography. The dispensation I enjoyed from the historical restraints of immense distance had created an illusion about time: the earth's spaces might vary terrifically—the moonlight reflecting last night on Shatt Al-Melghir, a saline lake in barren eastern Algeria, was not the same moonlight shining back from the icy reaches of Cook Inlet in Anchorage—but time, until this moment, had seemed a seamless thing, never qualitatively different. Everywhere I went, time continued the same, an imperial present. At most, in these depots and their environs, I was resetting my watch.

As I stood there gazing at Table Mountain, then back at the transparent

Atlantic, I knew that the mountain's time was not my time. I was on this other, no-Sunday, no-night on-time, international commercial time. I sought out my friend and asked, "Shouldn't we be getting back?" I was beginning to behave as if the present were only a preparation for the future. When I phoned my wife to say that I was bewildered, that it was as though all the rests in a symphony had become threats, she said, "It's because you're not going anywhere, you're just going."

Two changes in the late 1980s boosted the growth of international airfreight. Up until then, shipping by air meant being assured that your goods would arrive at such-and-such an airport within forty-eight hours of a promised time. Today, for an average of one to four dollars per pound, a customer expects guaranteed, on-time delivery; and increasingly that service is door-to-door, not airport-to-airport. The largest airfreight operation in the world (though the bulk of what they haul is small packets) is Federal Express. Next, in descending order of tonnage carried, are Lufthansa, UPS, and Air France, then Korean Air and Northwest. (At present, profitability in the industry remains marginal while airlines continue to maneuver for market share.)

Most air cargo, according to an industry forecaster, now consists of "high-value, time-perishable, consumer items." The business is driven by three things: the growing expectation, worldwide, of having whatever one wants tomorrow, not next week or next month; by frequent changes in fashion and in the design of basic products; and by a great disparity in labor costs from one country to the next. Much of what one sees aboard a freighter is placeless merchandise; except for the cost of employing a person, it might have been manufactured almost anywhere, including the country of destination. A museum director in Los Angeles found it less expensive, for example, to have the museum's entire red sandstone facade quarried in India, airfreighted to Japan to be dressed, and then flown to Los Angeles than to have it quarried, dressed, and trucked in from Minnesota.

Companies ship phone books from the United States to India to have the names inexpensively keyed in on mailing lists. Automobile insurance claims travel by the boxful from Miami to Manila to be processed by people who are not only cheaper to employ but who make fewer mistakes than the clerks for hire in Miami. And air shippers, exploiting the same small margins that currency traders do, find it less costly to have, say, nine tons of rayon blouses machine cut in Hong Kong and flown to Beijing to be finished by hand than to have all the work done in Hong Kong—before the blouses are flown on to Frankfurt or Chicago.

On long eight- and ten-hour trips on the freighters, I often left the flight deck, though it seemed always to be offering me some spectacular view of the earth—Mt. Pinatubo smoldering in the depopulated Zambales Mountains on Luzon, or L'Anse aux Meadows, a stark site on the northern tip of Newfoundland, where the Norse established a community circa 1000 A.D. Leaving these, I'd climb down the narrow, folding aluminum stairs and stroll the perimeter aisles around the cargo load. Containerized or wrapped in plastic, tagged with coded routing labels, the shipments were frequently difficult to identify without the help of manifests or air waybills. One night out of Taipei: 17 cartons of basketballs for Boston; 5,898 pounds of sunglasses headed for Atlanta; 85 cartons of women's polyester pajamas for Columbus, Ohio; cameras, men's ties, battery-operated action heroes variously directed; and 312 pounds of wristwatches for New York. What I saw very often seemed the fulfillment of mail-order-catalogue dreams. The celebrity in air freight, in fact, and the airplane's ability to gather and distribute goods over huge distances in a matter of hours have made the growth of 800-number stores like J. Crew, Land's End, and Victoria's Secret possible. By promoting "just in time" delivery—neither a sweater, a comic book, nor a jet engine arrives until the moment it's needed—airfreight companies have also 1) changed the way businesses define inventory, 2) made it possible for stores to turn storage space into display space, and 3) forced governments to reconsider the notion of an inventory tax.

What planes carry, generally, is what people imagine they want. Right now.

Back at D. F. Malan International Airport in Cape Town, I watched a six-man crew load Cape wines, salted snook bound for New York, 3,056 pounds of ostrich meat for Brussels, and one Wheaton terrier named Diggs for Toronto.

My guide told me that the fellow shipping ostrich meat, frustrated by a lack of cargo space out of Cape Town, had a restaurant in California interested, but without the space he couldn't close the deal. We were looking at the aircraft I had come in on, a 747–400 passenger plane with about 5,900 cubic feet of tower-hold cargo space (passenger baggage might take up only 20 percent of this). Depending on the demand for passenger seating, KLM might occasionally fly a 747–400 Combi into Cape Town, an aircraft in which the aft section of the main deck is given over to seven pallets of freight, while passengers are seated in the forward section—an efficient way for airlines to take advantage of fluctuations in both passenger and freight markets.

Tons of fish, he said, let alone more ostrich meat, could be shipped from Cape Town if only he could guarantee his customers the room. Today he'd be happy to squeeze a surfboard into the bulk-cargo hold, the space farthest aft on the lower deck, a last-on, first-off, loose-loaded compartment, where mail, air waybills, crew baggage, and, today, the Wheaton terrier went. We continued to exchange stories about peculiar things one sees on board—a yacht headed for an America's Cup race; a tropical-hardwood bowling alley from Bangkok; in San Francisco enough boxed Bing cherries, tied three to a bunch and packed neat as flashlight batteries, to fill one 747 freighter after another (27,000 cubic feet). They're not supposed to, but one of the pilots told me he liked to sit in the Ferraris and Lamborghinis he flew. "I've driven them many miles," the pilot said, "and very fast."

Business was good, but strange, I told my guide. Two days ago, on what pilots call the Tashkent Route between Europe and the cities of Karachi, Delhi, Bangkok, Singapore, and Jakarta (via Afghanistan, Uzbekistan, Kazakhstan, and Russia, because the Himalayas are too high and Iranian air space too dangerous), I had seen rocket fire and streams of tracer ammunition in Kabul, Taleban "extremists" and their entrenched opponents. People were being shot dead below, but to the east a full moon was rising rapidly, orange and huge as the sun. It sharply silhouetted the sawtooth peaks of southern ranges in the Hindu Kush. Farther to the southeast, beyond the Khyber Pass and high above the Indus River, a hundred miles of lightning bolts flared and jangled along a storm front. With one glance I took it all in: rockets flaming across the streets below, the silent moon, rain falling in the Indus Valley from a ceiling of cloud, above which the black vault of the sky glittered with stars.

On the Tashkent Route, air-traffic controllers in Dushanbe, Tadzhikistan, pass you on to Lahore, skipping chaotic Kabul altogether. Their voices crackle on the high-frequency radio like explosions of glass, trilling aviation English in the high-pitched intonation of a muezzin. At Lahore, you can see the Pakistani border stretching away south into the Punjab, a beaded snake of security lighting. From here west all the way to Libya (whose air-traffic controllers reprimand you that it is not Libya but "Libyan Arab Jamahiriya Territory"), religious and political tension is pointedly apparent from the sky. Coming up from Dubai, we would swing far out to the west over Saudi Arabia to be wide of Iraq, then dogleg north across Jordan, keeping east of Israel. Leaving Lebanon, we'd enter disputed air space over eastern Cyprus. Greek Cypriot and Turkish Cypriot air-traffic controllers do not play dangerous games with commercial aircraft, but, together with the Syrians, they contest the right among themselves to assign you flight levels and headings. Once across Turkey we'd bear north to stay east of Bosnia-Herzegovina.

Every pilot I spoke with had a story of the white-orange flash of lethal fighting seen from above, the named and the unnamed wars of the modem era, fought in Timor, in the Punjab, in what were once called the lawless hinterlands but which are now as accessible as Detroit or Alice Springs.

On the return flight to Johannesburg from Cape Town, I glanced through data comparing this 747–400 with others in KLM's fleet.[3] Each 747, despite being built to the same specifications and being fitted with the same engines, consistently burns slightly more or less fuel, or "performs differently against the book," depending. Northwest Airlines currently flies eight 747-200 freighters into the Far East; I flew on four of them, trying to gain a feeling for their personalities. (With so much history, distance, and weather, I thought—so many accidents, repairs, and strange cargos—there had to be personality.) Once I stayed with a single aircraft from Hong Kong through Taipei to Tokyo, then on to Anchorage, Chicago, and New York before turning back for Seattle—in all, about 12,000 nautical miles in 56 hours. Reading the plane's operating certificates (posted on a lavatory bulkhead in the cockpit) and its logbooks, and after marking all its accessible spaces, what I found was distinctiveness, not personality.

It was two-thirty in the morning and raining when we landed in Seattle. After the dehydrating hours aloft, mildly hypoxic, my tissues swollen from undissolved nitrogen, I was glad for the wet, oxygen-rich air at sea level. With a security escort shifting from foot to foot at my side, I drew in the night air deeply and brushed rain across my face. I'd been with the plane through five crew changes, and an uncomplicated affection had built up for all it had done while the crews came and went.

The freighter's belly was glazed with a thin film of oil. In it, and in exhaust grime on the engine's housing, mechanics had finger-traced graffiti. (Inside, on cargo compartment walls, ground crews often scrawl insults, some of a sexual nature, aimed at ground crews in other cities. On inaccessible surfaces within the wings, I was told by riveters at the Boeing plant, some leave declarations of love.)

The fifteen-year-old plane's thin (.063 inches) tempered-aluminum skin was scraped and dented, and it bore a half dozen aluminum patches. (In an effort to keep the plane on schedule, some of these minor tears were first repaired provi-

---

3. KLM has five 747-400 passenger planes and eleven 747-400 Combis but no dedicated freighters. Virtually all wide-body passenger aircraft, however, carry, in addition, a diverse and often substantial belly cargo, not only of manufactured goods, flowers, fresh food, and live animals but, more and more, containers of personal effects and the coffins of returning nationals. At the end of 1994, about 1,000 freighters were flying. By 2014, the industry predicts, 2,080 freighters will be in operation, 38 percent of them aircraft the size of 747s, capable of carrying 120 to 150 tons. Smaller loads of similar goods will continue to fly aboard thousands of "passenger" aircraft.

sionally with "speed tape.") Its windows were micropitted, its 32-ply tires slightly worn, its livery paint chipped. Looking aft from a point near the turn of its flat, streaked belly, I realized for the first time that the plane had the curved flanks of a baleen whale, in a scale exact to the extended flukes of its horizontal stabilizer.

I first flew with horses on a Northwest flight, out of O'Hare on a bitterly cold February night.[4] Sixteen were headed for lives on Hokkaido ranches among the well-to-do: a Percheron stallion, twelve Appaloosas, and three quarter horses, accompanied by two handlers.

We were delayed getting out. The driver of one of the loaders, a steerable platform used to raise cargo fifteen feet to the rear cargo door, accidentally rammed the plane, punching a hole in a canoe fairing (a cover protecting a jackscrew that extends the plane's flaps and "fairs," or tapers, this protrusion into the wing). We also had to replace an exhaust-gas temperature gauge on the number-three engine, the sort of maintenance that goes on regularly.

The pilot made a shallow climb out of Chicago to lessen the strain on the horses' back legs. He headed out over Wisconsin and Minnesota on a slight zigzag that would take us from one way point to another en route to Anchorage. Planes rarely fly a direct route between airports unless the skies are relatively empty, usually late at night, the time when most freight moves. Freighter pilots, some of whom wear bat wings instead of eagle wings and refer to themselves as "freight dogs," call it "flying the backside of the clock."

Soon after we're airborne I go down to look at the horses. The animals are lined up in six stalls on the right side of the aircraft, the 2,100-pound black Percheron in the first stall with a bred quarter horse; behind them a leopard Appaloosa stallion with a bred Appaloosa; and behind them, downwind in the flow of air, four stalls of bred and "open" mares, with four fillies and colts. They aren't sedated, most are dozing. They've been left unshod to give them a better hold on the stall floor, and won't be watered or fed for twenty-four hours in transit. Hemmed in by the usual farrago—aortic valves, poultry-processing equipment, mainframe computers, golf clubs, men's knit underwear—the horses are strangely peaceful. I can't hear their breathing or stomach noises over the sound of the engines. I turn the lights out and leave them be.

---

4. Thoroughbred horses fly back and forth between the continents constantly during the respective national racing seasons. Slaughter horses, mostly young draft horses, are carried to the Far East from the United States and Canada with some regularity, 114 at a time. With a reduction in import duties on fresh meat in the Far East, slaughter cattle like those killed in the Anchorage crash have become less economical to fly live.

On the flight deck, a narrow space like a railcar living room, the handlers are slumped with novels in a single row of tourist-class seats toward the rear, the only passenger seats available besides the jump seat. The flight engineer has just brewed a fresh pot of coffee. I settle in behind the captain to peruse the freight manifests. I gaze out the window. Every few minutes I look at the instrument panel in front of the copilot and at the hydraulic, fuel, and electrical panels in front of the flight engineer sitting a few inches to my right.

The 747 is not the biggest freighter in the sky, but in every other way—making long hauls economically on a scheduled basis—it is unrivaled. The biggest plane in regular service is the Russian Antonov 124, a fuel-guzzling, hulking beast of an aircraft that works at the fringes of the world of air-freight, hauling unusual loads on a charter basis. The only way to move emergency equipment (oil-skimming boats, fire-fighting trucks) or large quantities of emergency supplies (medicine, food, gas masks, cots) quickly around the world is on air-freighters, and the Antonov 124 ferries such material routinely and many more unusual things: French fighter planes to Venezuela; 132 tons of stage equipment for a Michael Jackson concert in Bucharest; a Pepsi-Cola bottling plant, complete, to Buenos Aires; a 38-ton bull gear to repair an oil tanker stranded in the Persian Gulf; 36,000 cubic feet of cigarettes per flight on repeated trips between Amsterdam and Moscow in December 1992.

Once we gain 18,000 feet, the flight engineer sets our altimeters to read against an atmospheric pressure of 29.92 inches of mercury. We will measure altitude against this pressure until we descend on approach into Anchorage, a standardization that ensures that planes all over the world will figure their altitudes on the same basis once they leave the air space around an airport. We've also left local time behind. Now all our communications are based on Coordinated Universal Time (UTC, formerly Greenwich Mean Time or Zulu time, as it is still sometimes called, the earth's time zones having once been divided among the letters of the alphabet). Another universal grid we are fixed in is that of degrees and minutes of latitude and longitude. And altitude, of course. (The altimeter shows altitude above mean sea level; if the altimeter reads 7,500 feet over Mexico City, you are 100 feet off the ground.)

These grids provide a common reference, and their uniformity makes flying safer, but there are dissenters around the globe, especially where time zones are concerned. Tonga, along with Russia's Chukotski Peninsula, insists on occupying a twenty-fifth time zone. When it's 12:15 on Sunday morning in Tonga, it's 11:15 on Friday night in Western Samoa, a few hundred miles to the northeast. And against UTC whole hours, central Australia stays on the half hour, Nepal keeps to a three-quarter hour, and Suriname adheres to ten minutes before the hour.[5]

Virtually everyone communicates over the radio in English, but it is often heavily accented English, and outside customary requests and responses, English is of limited use in areas like China or in what pilots call Sea Asia. Russian pilots, for their part, are unique in insisting on the use of meters per second instead of knots for airspeed, and on meters instead of feet for altitude. In addition, Russian commercial planes don't use the Traffic Collision Avoidance System, which warns of approaching aircraft, nor do they send out a signal so that planes with the system know they're there. Pilots learn of the presence of Russian aircraft only through air-traffic controllers. To politely register their disapproval of these tenuous arrangements, European pilots flash their landing lights at approaching Russian planes and wait for a response.

The wide acceptance of such standardized measurements and procedures can lead to the impression that a generally convivial agreement obtains throughout the world. And when, in one week, you transport the same sorts of freight to Cairo, Melbourne, and Rio de Janeiro, it is also easy to draw the conclusion that people everywhere want more or less the same things. However pervasive, the view is illusory. The airplane's speed and geographic reach benefit the spread of a European and North American consumer ethic, but not all of the world's cultures can be folded into this shape. One need only leave the airport in Lima or Calcutta or Harare to see how true this is. It is not merely poverty and starvation you see, the ring of another music you hear, or inversions of Western intuition you observe. It is starkly different renderings of the valuable.

Again and again, stalled in boulevard traffic in hot, choking air, feeling the taxi bumped by a languid crosscurrent of beggars, I thought of the speed of the plane, of how much it could leave behind. If we fled quickly enough, I thought, nothing could catch up.

One morning at KLM's corporate headquarters near Amsterdam, I spoke with a vice president in his corner office. Beyond us, planes were taking off every couple of minutes like salvos. "When I was a boy," he said, "I was given my

---

5. It is largely forgotten today that the notion of "standard time" in the United States, as opposed to local time, was promulgated by railroad commissions to coordinate the needs of railroads and other businesses engaged in long-distance commerce. A nationwide system, enforced by railroads and then by factories, was entrenched by 1883. Congress eventually gave its official approval, although several states—Utah, Minnesota, California—fought the inconvenience until 1917. The principal objection was that standard time distorted the natural rhythms of human life for the sake of greater efficiency in business and commerce. Today Cincinnati lives, more or less complacently, by Boston's sunrise.

father's watch. I thought that would be my watch for the rest of my life. But I have five watches now, choose one in the morning to match my suit, my tie. You just buy them." He spread his hands, a gesture of lament and consternation. In an adjacent office, another vice president told me, "Speed is the word. Air cargo is the answer to speed, it makes speed happen." I could not tell from his piercing look whether he meant it as a summary or an indictment.

An oceanic expanse of gray-white below obscures a four-square grid of Saskatchewan grain fields, a snow plain nicked by the dark, unruly lines of woody swales. One might imagine that little is to be seen from a plane at night, but above the clouds the Milky Way is a dense, blazing arch. A full moon often lights the plane freshly, and patterns of human culture, artificially lit, are striking in ways not visible in daylight. One evening I saw the distinctive glows of Bhiwani, Rohtak, Ghaziabad, and a dozen other cities around Delhi, diffused like spiral galaxies in a continuous deck of stratus clouds far below us. In Algeria and on the Asian steppes, wind-whipped pennants of gas flared. The jungle burned in incandescent spots on peninsular Malaysia and in southern Brazil. One clear evening, at 20,000 feet over Manhattan, I could see, it seemed, every streetlight halfway to the end of Long Island. A summer lightning bolt once unexpectedly revealed thousands of bright dots on the ink-black veld of the northern Transvaal: sheep. Another night, off the eastern coast of Korea, I arose from a nap to see a tight throw of the brightest light I'd ever observed. I thought we were low over a city until I glanced at the horizon and saw the pallid glow of coastal towns between Yongdok and Samch'ok. The light directly below, brilliant as magnesium flares, were those of a South Korean fishing fleet.

Over Anchorage we slam into severe turbulence at 34,000 feet. The plane seems suddenly to shrink, and we are pitched through the sky like a wood chip for ten minutes before we get clear of it and divert to Fairbanks. When I go below with a handler, the horses appear to have come through the violence unfazed. The handler knows and speaks soothingly to each animal. As we go down the line he recalls their breeding histories. Draft horses like the Percheron, he says, are the calmest breed, and working quarter horses are bred for calmness. He isn't surprised that they are all right and that they settle down quickly.

If you ask pilots which loads they most remember, they mention either costly objects—a $319,000 Bentley, flying 70,000 pounds of gold into Riyadh—or animals. Most say that Vietnamese potbelly pigs are the worst creatures to haul, their stench so permeating that pilots have to strip off their uniforms, seal them in plastic bags, and fly in clothes that they later throw away. (As bad, they say, is a planeload of durians—pulpy, melon-sized fruit whose scent reminds most Westerners of vomit.)

When large animals—draft horses and bulls—kick their stalls in mid-flight, you can feel the plane shudder. Goats and ostriches chew at whatever cargo they can reach. One pilot told me that he went down one night to look at a white tiger. Believing she'd been sedated, he drew close to the bars to peer in. She charged as ferociously as the cage permitted, sending the pilot reeling onto his back. The animal's roar, he said, drowned out the sound of the engines and nearly stopped his heart.

Pilots remember animals in some detail—wolf puppies turned loose in the cockpit, a killer whale in a tank—because they are alive and making these formidable journeys. Like the pilots.

We wait in Fairbanks until the Anchorage weather quiets, then fly back, landing in light turbulence. A 747 freighter taking off just after we land hits a wind shear, and in less than two seconds accelerates from 210 to 260 knots. An hour later, on takeoff, we abruptly lose 20 knots of airspeed when a headwind collapses. We're barely airborne when the departure threshold on the runway passes under our wheels. Two hours later our automatic pilot malfunctions. The nose plunges violently and we are in a rapid descent. In one of the swiftest and most assured moves I've ever seen a person make, the pilot recovers the plane and brings us back level before we fall 500 feet.

When I again accompany the handlers below, we find the horses awakened by the fall and spooked by our soundless approach. They glare awhile, then doze off.

In these same minutes the sun has just risen (at 30,000 feet it clears the horizon about twenty-two minutes earlier than it does when seen from a spot on the earth directly below), but the moon has not yet set, and for a while I hold both in the same gaze, in a sky that goes from azure to milk-blue between horizons. We are pushing against a 120-knot headwind, common this time of year over the North Pacific. When I ask whether the pilots have names for these winds aloft around the world, the captain says, "No, we haven't been flying long enough."

Far beneath us the winds are calmer. The burnished ocean surface seven miles below appears as still as a slab of stone, crinkled like an elephant's skin. I see one ship headed southwest against the Okhotsk Current, far off the coast of Kamchatka, its wake flared at the characteristic thirty-nine-degree angle.

When Japan looms I feel suddenly very tired. I haven't slept for thirty hours—traveling to Chicago, then caught up in events surrounding the horses, anticipating the appearance of the aurora borealis en route to Anchorage, listening to the pilots tell stories, looking out the window at the remoteness of Alaska, at the spectacle of clouds. Beneath us, every day, I'd seen buttermilk, mare's tail, and mackerel skies, then looked in vain through phrase books and small dictionaries for what they are called in Korean, Spanish, Dutch.

We touch down at Narita International Airport at 12:42 P.M. local standard time. At 12:45 we set the plane's parking brake at Gate 211.[6] At 12:54 Japanese officials open the door and a quarantine officer boards to inspect the horses. Once he is assured of their good health, he leads us down the air stairs where, one by one, we step gingerly through a plastic basin of disinfectant. The horse handlers, wearing fine-looking western boots, hesitate a moment.

The wood stalls are to be burned. The horses will be in quarantine here for three weeks before being flown to Hokkaido. I remember the snorts of steam and billowing breath on the ramp at O'Hare and wish I could see them now, standing, like us, in the sunshine and balmy breezes outside the plane.

From my accustomed seat, just behind and slightly to the left of the pilot, I have a clear view to the southeast over the South China Sea. Though it is slightly awkward to manage, I often lean into this window; just those few inches closer and my view widens appreciably. I look back at the port wing, the sleek gape of the engines, at a pinpoint of nuclear light opening and closing on a windshield ten miles away. At night, if I rotate my gaze 180 degrees, holding the upper edge of the slanted window against the stars, the world and the plane itself seem utterly still, immobile.

Now far to the south a ribbon of sunlit cumulus towers, fumaroles and hay-stacks, great pompadour waves of clouds. I never tire of seeing them, the most dominating evanescent form on the planet. We have seen a great range of them since leaving Tokyo. East of Honshu, over the Pacific, the ocean was occluded by a vast sheet of wool-nap cumulus. When that flat plain opened hundreds of miles later into a lattice, the formation appeared serried in three dimensions. These puffs eventually thinned, and I thought the sky cloudless until I looked up to see a rice-paper layer of cirrostratus. Then it, too, thinned to blue space, and for a while there was nothing but an occasional fair-weather cumulus, built up over a distant Pacific atoll, until we came to this rampart of heaped clouds: cumulus congestus. For all their beauty, the impossibly slow tai chi of their movement, clouds are of almost no help, claim the pilots, in anchoring a sense of depth or distance in the troposphere. They accentuate, however, the peculiar and insistent, ethereal nature of the sky.

---

6. Pilots use different methods to compute their actual (as distinct from scheduled) flying time. One is "block to block," or from the pulling of the nosewheel chocks at one end to the setting of them at the other end. Northwest pilots are limited to 82.5 hours of flying per month and to no more than 30 hours in any seven-day period.

I need to stretch. None of the three pilots wants anything from the galley,[7] so I raise the smoke door (which would give us some protection in the event of a maindeck fire) and descend the stairs to take a turn around the cargo. Unlike the pilots, I cannot resist a look each time the plane's contents change. I am drawn by the promise of revelation in the main hold. "Used clothing" might refer to a boutique-bound consignment of East German military uniforms. A fabled rumor of cargo might be confirmed. But the pilots, who speak animatedly about circus tigers, Lamborghini Diablos, and small wooden pallets of gold bars, each in its own burlap bag, seem uninterested or vaguely embarrassed by the bulk of what fills the space behind their heads.[8]

The specter of a fire down here is, of course, terrifying, as is the thought of a printing press or a stack of steel pipe breaking loose in turbulence. For this reason the contents of air shipments are carefully reviewed and documented; pilots receive written notification of even the smallest quantities of corrosives, explosives, and radioactive materials on board—anything that could start a fire. Cargo loads are tightly secured and neatly arranged so as to be accessible in flight. The flight engineer's last responsibility on his walk-around before departure is to check each piece of fire-fighting equipment and make sure that each pallet and container is secure; the ones I watched were thorough about it.

On flights to North America from the Far East's "new tigers"—Jakarta, Singapore, Bangkok, Hong Kong, Taipei—the planes ferry (in descending order, by weight) personal computers, sound-recording equipment, athletic shoes, photocopying equipment, and clothes. Traveling from North America to the Far East are comparable loads of motors and engines, personal computers, tele-

---

7. The heritage of oceangoing vessels is preserved in the language and some of the design of modern airplanes. Pilots frequently call the plane a ship; its fuselage, a hull. Its interior space is divided into decks that extend fore and aft. The captain might refer to starting an engine as turning a wheel. He steers the plane on the ground with a tiller and speaks of docking the ship, after which, on a freighter, cargo is always taken off the main deck on the port side (originally, the side of a ship desired for use in port). A rudder in the plane's vertical stabilizer changes its course. Waterline numbers stenciled on the interior hull indicate height above the ground. Sailboat fairings taper engine mounts into wings that bear green running lights to starboard, red lights to ports

8. About 4:00 A.M. one December night in Hong Kong, I stood at the top of our air stairs with my binoculars, scanning nearby office buildings. Christmas trees twinkled on a dozen floors. I had seen Christmas trees banked with brightly wrapped gift boxes in Muslim Dubai and in the Buddhist city of Bangkok, as well as in Amsterdam and Houston. The displays, of course, had nothing to do with the Christianity of, say, Joseph Arimathea. "This time of year," one pilot told me while we waited in Hong Kong, "we're flying freighters out of here wingtip to wingtip."

communications equipment, and tractor parts. Such commodities formed the bulk of most shipments I accompanied, but it was the condiments, so to speak, that made a load memorable: two hundred styrofoam cases of live tropical fish from Manila (labeled LTF) swimming in bags of oxygenated water, bound for Los Angeles; two Cadillac Eldorados for Osaka; canvas bags of home-bound paper bills (the accumulation of currency exchanges); munitions of war (MUW) for Khartoum; bundles of mesquite wood, for cooking, out of Houston; and noisome industrial chemicals (OBX).

In a fully loaded 747–200, cargo is palletized on thin aluminum "cookie sheets," wrapped tightly in clear plastic weatherproofing (or opaque plastic, to discourage thieves), and secured against shifting by webs or rope nets. Twenty-two rectangular sealed containers and pallets, dogged to a floor of steel casters and roller track with red latches, stand in pairs down the middle of the airplane, leaving narrow outboard aisles. Two additional units, canted to the taper of the plane, extend along the starboard wall into the nose. In the tail, aft of a ten-foot-wide cross aisle directly opposite a cargo door, stand another four units. A twenty-ninth unit stands behind them, near the open wall rack that holds the plane's Flight Data Recorder and Cockpit Voice Recorder.

I sideslip by containers and pallets on the port side and look back from the cross aisle at our freight for Singapore and Bangkok. It shimmies in the cobble-stone turbulence of what Wilbur Wright called "the infinite highway of the air," a rickety but firm, continuous vibration. From a viewport on the flight deck, with this area lit dimly by only a few safety lights, the plastic-wrapped cargo looks like a double row of huge jellyfish strung up in a freezer.

Moving forward up the starboard aisle, I finally stand in an eerie place at the forward edge of the main deck, looking at the back side of the fiberglass radar dome that fills the plane's nose. I look down into an open bay framed on either side by large jackscrews that push the nose out and up for loading through the front. The lip of this precipice, which I grip with my toes, is as close as one can get to standing on the bow of a ship. I spread my arms wide for balance, shut my eyes, and lean into the velocity of the plane. The sound of the engines is behind me, inaudible over the scream of air.

Chief pilots, or captains, men in their early fifties, "in the left-hand seat," tend to gaze to some purpose out the windows, while copilots, or first officers, men (and, rarely, women) in their mid-thirties, remain focused within the plane.

In the evolution of modem jet flight, there has been a dramatic shift away from the use of navigational references outside the plane, such as rivers, to using electronically displayed information within the plane. Some of the co-pilots I spoke with, in fact, had only hazy notions of the geography they flew over. They were inclined to fly "heads down," studying the route map, reviewing the flight plan (a sequence of way points, an expected fuel burn, the speed and direction of winds aloft), and watching their instruments and screens. On the most advanced commercial aircraft, it is the copilots who are frequently caught up in the protracted task of programming the plane's computers. ("I don't fly anymore," they joke, "but I can type sixty words a minute.")[9]

The chief pilots, many of them, possess a notable unique knowledge of how the earth has changed over the past thirty years: how far south, for example, the Sahara Desert has extended, how much the Aral Sea has shrunk, how far center-pivot irrigation has spread in Saudi Arabia. It's a knowledge that predates satellite imagery and often is more historically integrated. Many of these pilots learned the earth's surfaces when older planes held them to lower altitudes, when ground marks like pipelines and lakes were more important to navigation. Today, in advanced aircraft, they routinely fly high above the weather on automatic pilot and seldom descend for fuel. A dispatcher in a windowless international office half a world away will organize a sense of geography for them and radio in or even telephone with any changes due, say, to increased storm activity. There's little need to watch the weather, or anything else.

Pilots say they "fly by wire" now, no longer sensing the plane's response in their hands and feet. They refer to "cockpit management skills" more often than to their "stick and rudder" ability. In the 747–400, they monitor six separate cathode-ray screens, mesmerizing as small televisions. In this kind of self-absorbed travel, built on a dashboard knowledge of one's surroundings, a sense of both geographic scale and particularity is ruptured. Flights cover huge distances in a few hours; matriculation at a hotel, often reached on a crew bus driven down an advertising corridor similar to the airport's passenger corridors, is brief. English is spoken everywhere. Seven-Up, Anacin, Rambo, CNN, Ray-Ban, and Time are omnipresent. Reality outside the plane slowly merges with the comforting, authoritative, and self-referential world within it.

Jet lag is popularly construed as an affliction of the unseasoned traveler, a preventable distraction. No pilot I talked to regarded it as such but rather as a sort of temporal and spatial abuse that, by the time you reached your fifties, could overwhelm you on a single trip.

---

9. Pilots refer to newer planes like the Boeing 777 and the Airbus 320 synecdochically as "glass cockpits," planes in which the information most frequently reviewed is displayed in color overlays on video-like screens. The instrument cluster in older jet aircraft is referred to collectively as "steam gauges."

Over many days of flight, I fought my own idiosyncratic battle with jet lag, following the common advice of pilots to sleep when you're tired and eat when you're hungry. When I got home, after traveling 30,000 or 40,000 miles in ten days, I would fall into bed like an iron ingot dropped in the dust. On the road, like the pilots, I endured the symptoms of a jagged, asynchronous life. No matter how exhilarating a trip might have been, I sensed upon leaving the plane that a thrashing like the agitation of a washing machine had ended and that, slightly dazed, I was now drifting off my path, a yawing ship. My tissues felt leaden. Memory seemed a pea suspended in the empty hull of my body. I had the impression that my mind was searching for the matching ends of myriad broken connections and that it was vaguely panicked by the effort. The fabric of awareness felt discontinuous. Time shoaled, losing its familiar depth and resonance. I craved darkness and stillness. I believed that without stillness no dreams would come and that without dreams there would be no recovery. Once, in a hotel, I slept on solely to dream.

The physical hazards of long-term flying are relatively minor—an increased incidence of cataracts, high-frequency hearing loss—or unknown: the effect, for example, of regular exposure to high doses of cosmic radiation. Pilots more than copilots will tell you that whatever health hazards they may face, they love flying too much to give it up. Many think that jet lag is the principal cause of chronic moodiness, a prime source of tension in their domestic relationships. But they view separation and divorce as grim contemporary realities, and say resignedly that they are very well paid for what they do.

I liked the pilots I flew with. They had a remarkable ability to relax for hours in a state of alertness (pilots describe the job as "hours of boredom punctuated by minutes of terror"). They seemed able to monitor an instrument's unwavering reading and run technical checklists repeatedly without mentally wandering from or re-imagining the information. Their hand movements were smooth, slow, direct; they concentrated on precision and routine, on thoroughness. The virtues they admired—dedication to one's job, loyalty, allegiance to a code—were more military than corporate. Some, like generals, carried with them a peculiar, haggard isolation.

Standing between the pilots on the Singapore flight, my neck bowed beneath the overhead instrument panel, I could take the most commanding view possible of space outside the plane. Over the South China Sea, I could see outlying islands in the Spratly Archipelago to the southeast. To the northwest were the distant Mouths of the Mekong: Cua Tranh De, Cua Dinh An, Cua Ham Luong. A while later, Indonesia's Bunguran Selatan Archipelago loomed off the port side, the translucent sea turquoise over its reefs. Afternoon light from the bare orb of the sun filled the clear air at 37,000 feet with a tangible effulgence that made the island of Subi and the water seem closer. We looked down from the keep of our own wind, through layers of wind, to wind on the water; below that the surface current ran counter to currents deeper still. Toward Karimata Strait, between Borneo and Belitung Island to the south, a single layer of thin stratus cast its shadow over a hundred square miles of water. Beyond it the sea was brilliant. The effect was as if I were looking from today across the night and into tomorrow.

Ending a long silence in the cockpit, the captain said, "The earth is beautiful."

On our approach to Singapore, smoke began pouring out of the window vents—warm humid air from outside condensing in our dry interior. The pilots enjoyed my alarm.

On the ground, while the plane was unloaded, and then reloaded for Bangkok and Tokyo, I strolled through mown grass in an adjacent field. Two common mynah birds landed on the port wing.

The hotel in Seoul was just west of Mt. Namsan Park in Yongsan-Ku, in the city's southwest quarter. The crew bus would not leave for the airport for four hours, and I had risen before sunrise to take a long walk. I wanted to see things that couldn't be purchased.

I walked north through a cramped residential district. Seoul is a city of granite hills, of crags and pinnacles. On this winter morning it filled gradually with a diffuse gray light under heavy, overcast skies. As I wandered the narrow streets, I endeavored not to seem too curious about what was displayed on the shelves of small stores attached to small two-story houses. Instead I observed what sort of bicycles people rode, what kind of clothing they wore against the cold—indigenous solutions to common problems. I studied the spines of books displayed in a window, the Chinese, Japanese, and Korean titles mixed. I could not see past a street reflection in the window glass whether a companion volume was in Arabic.

Some Westerners traveling today in the Middle East may experience what they take for irritation over religious differences; in Seoul—or Bangkok or Wuhan—the look a Westerner may get while walking through residential streets seems more often one of resentment or bewilderment at the imposition of economic change. You are the one responsible, the looks imply, for swift, large-scale, painful alterations in my culture; you see them as improvements, but they are designed only to make business—your sort of business—flow more smoothly. It is you, they seem to say, who define, often and titanically, what is of value.

What I felt—the discomforting gospel of a world-encircling consumerism of which I was an inadvertent symbol—I could have felt as an indictment in any of a dozen other cities. What I had hoped for here was relief from the impact of culture I felt every time the plane landed.

Some in the West see in such rearrangements net gains; others, net losses. I do not lean strongly either way, though I'm saddened, as a traveler, by the erosion of languages, the diminishment of other systems of aesthetics, and the loss of what might be called a philosophy of hand tools. It is easy to rue the lack of restraint in promoting consumption as a way of life, but we daily accept myriad commercial solutions to our own discontent—the assuagement of new clothing, new investments, new therapies to ease our disaffection. Some who endure such accelerated living (our advertising presumes) find it a relief periodically to sweep everything into the past, making room for less obligating, more promising products or situations. But it is a rare consumer who has any sense of what such inclinations require of the world around him.

It is not difficult to disparage the capitulation in such manic living; what is hard to avoid is the impulse to blame or the instinct to exempt oneself. Getting dressed at the hotel, I had to smile at the labels in my clothing: J. Crew, GAP, The Territory Ahead, Patagonia. My shoes, dark brown suede wing tips, had been made in Korea.

Once, suspended over the North Pacific, I held the image of a loom in my mind. If these flights back and forth across the Pacific are the weft, I wondered, what is the warp, the world already strung, through which my shuttle cuts back and forth? And what pattern is the weave producing?

The plane I boarded out of Seoul was a passenger flight with a lower hold full of cargo for Narita. There I boarded a freighter bound for New York via Anchorage. In the Jeppesen Manual that most United States pilots carry—a two-inch-thick ring binder of tissue-thin pages containing detailed information about airports—Anchorage is described as a consistently dangerous place to get in and out of. The near-by area experiences a lot of wind shear and turbulence; icing is common in winter.[10]

Pilots recall with little prompting the details of commercial airplane crashes going back many years. Each one is a warning. Their interest is almost entirely technical and legal, not macabre. While I was flying in the Middle East, a freighter crashed in Kansas City, killing the three pilots aboard. Although the

---

10. The turbulence over Anchorage that we encountered on the flight with the horses was the worst that one of the pilots had ever experienced. On another flight out of Anchorage, the freighter built up the heaviest loads of ice the chief pilot had ever had to contend with.

crew I was with read the story in the International Herald Tribune, no one commented. The pilots presume such reports are always confused and therefore misleading. They wait instead for the National Transportation Safety Board findings to appear in Aviation Week and Space Technology.

We had no trouble getting into or out of Anchorage, and we enjoyed an undisturbed flight to New York, with spectacular views of the Canadian Rockies. On the next leg, from JFK to San Francisco, I fell into conversation with the pilot about the history of aerodynamic design that produced the 747. Like many pilots, he had an intuitive sense of the volume of abstract space and was a gazer-out-of-windows. It was about one in the morning. Air-traffic control in New York had given us a direct path to San Francisco. Our flight plan showed no areas of turbulence ahead, and no one in front of us was reporting any. The moonless sky was glimmering, deep. I asked the pilot if he had ever heard of James Turrell. He hadn't.

I'd hoped for weeks to speak with someone who had. Turrell is best known for an enormous project called Roden Crater near Flagstaff in northern Arizona. He reconformed the crater with bulldozers and road graders, believing celestial space actually had shape, that one could perceive the "celestial vault" above the earth, and that a view from within the crater would reveal that architecture by so disposing the viewer. Turrell, a pilot, once said, "For me, flying really dealt with these spaces delineated by air conditions, by visual penetration, by sky conditions; some were visual, some were only felt. These are the kinds of space I wanted to work with."

People who have come to Roden Crater—heavy-equipment operators as well as museum curators—say, yes, you do see that the sky has shape from the crater. I told the pilot I'd like to go.

After a while the pilot turned around in his seat and said, "He's right. I know what he's talking about. The space you fly the plane through has shape." I asked if he thought that time had boundary or dimension, and told him what I had felt at Cape Town, that time pooled in every part of the world as if in a basin. The dimension, the transparency, and the agitation were everywhere different. He nodded, as if together we were working out an equation.

A while later he said, "Being 'on time' is like being on fire."

One of my last flights takes me to Buenos Aires, seat of the old viceroyalty on the Rio de la Plata, the river of silver. Here, as in other places I visited, the people in the freight depot are friendly and open, and sometimes quite sophisticated about ironies in the airfreight business. I go to lunch with four men who treat me to a meal of Argentine beef and a good Argentine red wine. Affecting philosophical detachment, they explain the non-European way to conduct business in Buenos Aires, the paths money might take here.

We laugh. Then three of us go to a strong room to inspect a shipment of gold bullion.

Afterward, I walk out onto the tarmac with the KLM freight manager, who is directing the loading of flight 798 from Buenos Aires to Amsterdam, a thirteen-hour run. In the crackle blast of combusting kerosene, swept by hot winds, I watch the pallets go aboard. These, I have come to understand, are the goods. This lovely, shrieking behemoth, the apotheosis of modern imagination and invention, is being filled yet again with what we believe in. I watch, as agnostics must once have watched at Chartres, for a sign, a confirmation of faith. I see frozen trout; fresh strawberries; eighty cases of live worms; seventy-three pounds of gold for Geneva packed in light green metal boxes sealed with embossed aluminum bands, wrapped in clear plastic, banded again with steel strapping. An armed security officer stands by until the bulk-cargo door is closed, then stands at a distance, watching.

The last load in the aft compartment is four tons of horse meat. The temperature is set at fifty-three degrees, and the door is closed. The last load in the forward compartment will be 175 penguins. They have come in on the plane from Santiago and are headed for Tokyo. They've been waiting in the noise and heat around the airplane for freight in the forward compartment to be rearranged, the weight more evenly distributed.

The penguins stand in separate cells, packed five to a wooden crate. A wire-mesh panel on the front of each box, beginning at chest level, slants up and back, reaching the top of the box just above head height. So constructed, air can circulate to those on the inside of the load when all the crates are stacked in tiers on a single pallet. The gangs of five face in four directions; some see us, some see one another, some the back or another box. I recognize magellanic and rockhopper penguins. If they are making any noise I can't hear it over the jet engines. A few strike at the wire mesh with their bills. Some of the rockhoppers rise on their feet, cramping their heads, and flap their flippers repeatedly against the dividers.

After they are loaded, the temperature of their compartment is set at forty-three degrees and the door is closed.

KL 798, a passenger flight, takes us up the south coast of Brazil, above the Serra do Mar and Serra do Espinhaco and out over the Atlantic near Natal. There is a lightning storm near Recife, on the coast. I send my worn letter of introduction up to the cockpit to see if it would be possible to watch and talk for a while. The purser comes back with a smile. Yes.

From the cockpit, we watch cobra strikes of yellow and blue light on the starboard horizon. Against the display of lightning I hesitate to speak. I'm aware of my faith in the integrity of the aircraft. I recognize the familiar, impetuous hurtling toward a void, a space to be filled only briefly, then to yawn again, hopeful and acquisitive.

Out over the Atlantic I lean forward and ask the captain how long he's been flying, which routes he knows best. I think of the penguins two decks below, standing up on their toes and slamming flippers that once were wings against the walls of their pens.

Thomas Lynch

THE UNDERTAKING

THOMAS LYNCH 's collections of poems include *Skating with Heather Grace*, *Grimalkin & Other Poems*, and *Still Life in Milford*. *The Undertaking*, his first book of nonfiction, won the American Book Award, and the Heartland Prize for Nonfiction, and was a finalist for the National Book Award. *Bodies in Motion and at Rest* won the Great Lakes Book Award, and *Booking Passage* was named a 2006 Notable Book by the Library of Michigan. He is also the author of a book of short stories titled *Late Fictions*. His work has appeared in *Harper's, The New Yorker, Newsweek, Esquire, The New York Times, The Times of London*, and *The Irish Times* and has been broadcast by NPR, the BBC, and RTE in Ireland. He has read and lectured across the United States, throughout Europe, Canada, Australia, and New Zealand and is an adjunct professor with the Graduate Department of English at the University of Michigan, Ann Arbor. Lynch lives in Milford, Michigan, where he has been the funeral director since 1974, and in Moven, County Clare, Ireland, where he keeps an ancestral cottage.

Every year I bury a couple hundred of my townspeople. Another two or three dozen I take to the crematory to be burned. I sell caskets, burial vaults, and urns for the ashes. I have a sideline in headstones and monuments. I do flowers on commission.

Apart from the tangibles, I sell the use of my building: eleven thousand square feet, furnished and fixtured with an abundance of pastel and chair rail and crown moldings. The whole lash-up is mortgaged and remortgaged well into the next century. My rolling stock includes a hearse, two Fleetwoods, and a minivan with darkened windows our pricelist calls a service vehicle and everyone in town calls the Dead Wagon.

I used to use the *unit pricing method*—the old package deal. It meant that you had only one number to look at. It was a large number. Now everything is itemized. It's the law. So now there is a long list of items and numbers and italicized disclaimers, something like a menu or the Sears Roebuck Wish Book, and sometimes the federally-mandated options begin to look like cruise control or rear-window defrost. I wear black most of the time, to keep folks in mind of the fact we're not talking Buicks here. At the bottom of the list there is still a large number.

In a good year the gross is close to a million, five percent of which we hope to call profit. I am the only undertaker in this town. I have a corner on the market.

The market, such as it is, is figured on what is called *the crude death rate*—the number of deaths every year out of every thousand persons.

Here is how it works.

Imagine a large room into which you coax one thousand people. You slam the doors in January, leaving them plenty of food and drink, color TVs, magazines, and condoms. Your sample should have an age distribution heavy on baby boomers and their children—1.2 children per boomer. Every seventh adult is an old-timer, who, if he or she wasn't in this big room, would probably be in Florida or Arizona or a nursing home. You get the idea. The group will include fifteen lawyers, one faith healer, three dozen real-estate agents, a video technician, several licensed counselors, and a Tupperware distributor. The rest will be between jobs, middle managers, ne'er-do-wells, or retired.

Now for the magic part—come late December when you throw open the doors, only 991.6, give or take, will shuffle out upright. Two hundred and sixty will now be selling Tupperware. The other 8.4 have become the crude death rate.

Here's another stat.

Of the 8.4 corpses, two-thirds will have been old-timers, five percent will be children, and the rest (slightly less than 2.5 corpses) will be boomers—realtors and attorneys likely—one of whom was, no doubt, elected to public office during the year. What's more, three will have died of cerebral-vascular or coronary difficulties, two of cancer, one each of vehicular mayhem, diabetes, and domestic violence. The spare change will be by act of God or suicide—most likely the faith healer.

The figure most often and most conspicuously missing from the insurance charts and demographics is the one I call The Big One, which refers to the number of people out of every hundred born who will die. Over the long haul, The Big One hovers right around . . . well, dead nuts on one hundred percent. If this were on the charts, they'd call it *death expectancy* and no one would buy futures of any kind. But it is a useful number and has its lessons. Maybe you will want to figure out what to do with your life. Maybe it will make you feel a certain kinship with the rest of us. Maybe it will make you hysterical. Whatever the implications of a one hundred percent death expectancy, you can calculate how big a town this is and why it produces for me a steady if unpredictable labor.

They die around the clock here, without apparent preference for a day of the week, month of the year; there is no clear favorite in the way of season. Nor does the alignment of the stars, fullness of moon, or liturgical calendar have very much to do with it. The whereabouts are neither here nor there. They go off upright or horizontally in Chevrolets and nursing homes, in bathtubs, on the interstates, in ERs, ORs, BMWs. And while it may be that we assign more equipment or more importance to deaths that create themselves in places marked by initials—ICU being somehow better than Greenbriar Convalescent Home—it is also true that the dead don't care. In this way, the dead I bury and burn are like the dead before them, for whom time and space have become mortally unimportant. This loss of interest is, in fact, one of the first sure signs that something serious is about to happen. The next thing is they quit breathing. At this point, to be sure, a *gunshot wound to the chest* or *shock and trauma* will get more ink than a CVA or ASHD, but no cause of death is any less permanent than the other. Any one will do. The dead don't care.

Nor does *who* much matter, either. To say, "I'm OK, you're OK, and by the way, he's dead!" is, for the living, a kind of comfort.

It is why we drag rivers and comb plane wrecks and bomb sites.

It is why MIA is more painful than DOA.

It is why we have open caskets and all read the obits.

Knowing is better than not knowing, and knowing it is you is terrifically better than knowing it is me. Because once I'm the dead guy, whether you're OK or he's OK won't much interest me. You can all go bag your asses, because the dead don't care.

Of course, the living, bound by their adverbs and their actuarials, still do. Now, there is the difference and why I'm in business. The living are careful and oftentimes caring. The dead are careless, or maybe it's care-less. Either way, they don't care. These are unremarkable and verifiable truths.

My former mother-in-law, herself an unremarkable and verifiable truth, was always fond of holding forth with Cagneyesque bravado—to wit: "When I'm dead, just throw me in a box and throw me in a hole." But whenever I would remind her that we did substantially that with everyone, the woman would grow sullen and a little cranky.

Later, over meatloaf and green beans, she would invariably give out with: "When I'm dead just cremate me and scatter the ashes."

My former mother-in-law was trying to make carelessness sound like fearlessness. The kids would stop eating and look at each other. The kids' mother would plead, "Oh Mom, don't talk like that." I'd take out my lighter and begin to play with it.

In the same way, the priest that married me to this woman's daughter—a man who loved golf and gold ciboria and vestments made of Irish linen; a man who drove a great black sedan with a wine-red interior and who always had his eye on the cardinal's job—this same fellow, leaving the cemetery one day, felt called upon to instruct me thus: "No bronze coffin for me. No sir! No orchids or roses or limousines. The plain pine box is the one I want, a quiet Low Mass and the pauper's grave. No pomp and circumstance."

He wanted, he explained, to be an example of simplicity, of prudence, of piety and austerity—all priestly and, apparently, Christian virtues. When I told him that he needn't wait, that he could begin his ministry of good example even today, that he could quit the country club and do his hacking at the public links and trade his brougham for a used Chevette; that free of his Florsheims and cashmeres and prime ribs, free of his bingo nights and building funds, he could become, for Christ's sake, the very incarnation of Francis himself, or Anthony of Padua; when I said, in fact, that I would be willing to assist him in this, that I would gladly distribute his savings and credit cards among the worthy poor of the parish, and that I would, when the sad duty called, bury him for free in the manner he would have, by then, become accustomed to; when I told your man these things, he said nothing at all, but turned his wild eye on me in the way that the cleric must have looked on Sweeney years ago, before he cursed him, irreversibly, into a bird.

What I was trying to tell the fellow was, of course, that being a dead saint is no more worthwhile than being a dead philodendron or a dead angelfish. Living is the rub, and always has been. Living saints still feel the flames and stigmata of this vale of tears, the ache of chastity and the pangs of conscience. Once dead, they let their relics do the legwork, because, as I was trying to tell this priest, the dead don't care.

Only the living care.

And I am sorry to be repeating myself, but this is the central fact of my business—that there is nothing, once you are dead, that can be done *to you* or *for you* or *with you* or *about you* that will do you any good or any harm; that any damage or decency we do accrues to the living, to whom your death happens, if it really happens to anyone. The living have to live with it. You don't. Theirs is the grief or gladness your death brings. Theirs is the loss or gain of it. Theirs is the pain and the pleasure of memory. Theirs is the invoice for services rendered and theirs is the check in the mail for its payment.

And there is the truth, abundantly self-evident, that seems, now that I think of it, the one most elusive to the old in-laws, the parish priest, and to perfect strangers who are forever accosting me in barber-shops and cocktail parties and parent-teacher conferences, hell-bent or duty-bound to let me in on what it is they want done with them when they are dead.

Give it a rest is the thing I say.

Once you are dead, put your feet up, call it a day, and let the husband or the missus or the kids or a sibling decide whether you are to be buried or burned or blown out of a cannon or left to dry out in a ditch somewhere. It's not your day to watch it, because the dead don't care.

Another reason people are always rehearsing their obsequies with me has to do with the fear of death that anyone in their right mind has. It is healthy. It keeps us from playing in traffic. I say it's a thing we should pass on to the kids.

There is a belief—widespread among the women I've dated, local Rotarians, and friends of my children—that I, being the undertaker here, have some irregular fascination with, special interest in, inside information about, even attachment to, *the dead*. They assume, these people, some perhaps for defensible reasons, that I want their bodies.

It is an interesting concept.

But here is the truth.

Being dead is one—the worst, the last—but only one in a series of calamities that afflicts our own and several other species. The list may include, but is not limited to, gingivitis, bowel obstruction, contested divorce, tax audit, spiritual vexation, cash flow problems, political upheaval, and on and on and on some more. There is no shortage of misery. And I am no more attracted to the dead than the dentist is to your bad gums, the doctor to your rotten innards, or the accountant to your sloppy expense records. I have no more stomach for misery than the banker or the lawyer, the pastor or the politico—because misery is careless and is everywhere. Misery is the bad check, the ex-spouse, the mob in the street, and the IRS—who, like the dead, feel nothing and, like the dead, *don't care*.

Which is not to say that the dead do not matter.

They do. They do. Of course they do.

Last Monday morning Milo Hornsby died. Mrs. Hornsby called at 2 A.M. to say that Milo had *expired* and would I take care of it, as if his condition were like any other that could be renewed or somehow improved upon. At 2 A.M., yanked from my REM sleep. I am thinking, put a quarter into Milo and call me in the morning. But Milo is dead. In a moment, in a twinkling,

Milo has slipped irretrievably out of our reach, beyond Mrs. Hornsby and the children, beyond the women at the laundromat he owned, beyond his comrades at the Legion Hall, the Grand Master of the Masonic Lodge, his pastor at First Baptist, beyond the mailman, zoning board, town council, and Chamber of Commerce; beyond us all, and any treachery or any kindness we had in mind for him.

Milo is dead.

X's on his eyes, lights out, curtains.

Helpless, harmless.

Milo's dead.

Which is why I do not haul to my senses, coffee and quick shave, Homburg and great coat, warm up the Dead Wagon, and make for the freeway in the early o'clock for Milo's sake. Milo doesn't have any sake anymore. I go for her—for she who has become, in the same moment and the same twinkling, like water to ice, the Widow Hornsby. I go for her—because she still can cry and care and pray and pay my bill.

The hospital that Milo died in is state-of-the-art. There are signs on every door declaring a part or a process or bodily function. I like to think that, taken together, the words would add up to The Human Condition, but they never do. What's left of Milo, the remains, are in the basement, between SHIPPING & RECEIVING and LAUNDRY ROOM. Milo would like that if he were still liking things. Milo's room is called PATHOLOGY.

The medical-technical parlance of death emphasizes disorder.

We are forever dying of failures, of anomalies, of insufficiencies, of dysfunctions, arrests, accidents. These are either chronic or acute. The language of death certificates—Milo's says "Cardiopulmonary Failure"—is like the language of weakness. Likewise, Mrs. Hornsby, in her grief, will be said to be breaking down or falling apart or going to pieces, as if there were something structurally awry with her. It is as if death and grief were not part of The Order of Things, as if Milo's failure and his widow's weeping were, or ought to be, sources of embarrassment. "Doing well" for Mrs. Hornsby would mean that she is bearing up, weathering the storm, or being strong for the children. We have willing pharmacists to help her with this. Of course, for Milo, doing well would mean he was back upstairs, holding his own, keeping the meters and monitors bleeping.

But Milo is downstairs, between SHIPPING & RECEIVING and LAUNDRY ROOM, in a stainless-steel drawer, wrapped in white plastic top to toe, and—because of his small head, wide shoulders, ponderous belly, and skinny legs, and the trailing white binding cord from his ankles and toe tag—he looks, for all the world, like a larger than life-size sperm.

I sign for him and get him out of there. At some level, I am still thinking Milo gives a shit, which by now, of course, we all know he doesn't—because the dead don't care.

Back at the funeral home, upstairs in the embalming room, behind a door marked PRIVATE, Milo Hornsby is floating on a porcelain table under fluorescent lights. Unwrapped, outstretched, Milo is beginning to look a little more like himself—eyes wide open, mouth agape, returning to our gravity. I shave him, close his eyes, his mouth. We call this *setting the features*. These are the features—eyes and mouth—that will never look the way they would have looked in life when they were always opening, closing, focusing, signaling, telling us something. In death, what they tell us is that they will not be doing anything anymore. The last detail to be managed is Milo's hands—one folded over the other, over the umbilicus, in an attitude of ease, of repose, of retirement.

They will not be doing anything anymore, either.

I wash his hands before positioning them.

When my wife moved out some years ago, the children stayed here, as did the dirty laundry. It was big news in a small town. There was the gossip and the goodwill that places like this are famous for. And while there was plenty of talk, no one knew exactly what to say to me. They felt helpless, I suppose. So they brought casseroles and beef stews, took the kids out to the movies or canoeing, brought their younger sisters around to visit me. What Milo did was send his laundry van around twice a week for two months, until I found a housekeeper. Milo would pick up five loads in the morning and return them by lunchtime, fresh and folded. I never asked him to do this. I hardly knew him. I had never been in his home or his laundromat. His wife had never known my wife. His children were too old to play with my children.

After my housekeeper was installed, I went to thank Milo and pay the bill. The invoices detailed the number of loads, the washers and the dryers, detergent, bleaches, fabric softeners. I think the total came to sixty dollars. When I asked Milo what the charges were for pick-up and delivery, for stacking and folding and sorting by size, for saving my life and the lives of my children, for keeping us in clean clothes and towels and bed linen, "Never mind that" is what Milo said. "One hand washes the other."

I place Milo's right hand over his left hand, then try the other way. Then back again. Then I decide that it doesn't matter. One hand washes the other either way.

The embalming takes me about two hours.

It is daylight by the time I am done.

Every Monday morning, Ernest Fuller comes to my office. He was damaged in some profound way in Korea. The details of his damage are unknown to the locals. Ernest Fuller has no limp or anything missing so everyone thinks it was something he saw in Korea that left him a little simple, occasionally perplexed, the type to draw rein abruptly in his day-long walks, to consider the meaning of litter, pausing over bottle caps and gum wrappers. Ernest Fuller has a nervous smile and a dead-fish handshake. He wears a baseball cap and thick eyeglasses. Every Sunday night Ernest goes to the supermarket and buys up the tabloids at the checkout stands with headlines that usually involve Siamese twins or movie stars or UFOs. Ernest is a speed reader and a math whiz but because of his damage, he has never held a job and never applied for one. Every Monday morning, Ernest brings me clippings of stories under headlines like: 601 LB MAN FALLS THRU COFFIN—A GRAVE SITUATION or EMBALMER FOR THE STARS SAYS ELVIS IS FOREVER. The Monday morning Milo Hornsby died, Ernest's clipping had to do with an urn full of ashes, somewhere in East Anglia, that made grunting and groaning noises, that whistled sometimes, and that was expected to begin talking. Certain scientists in England could make no sense of it. They had run several tests. The ashes' widow, however, left with nine children and no estate, is convinced that her dearly beloved and greatly reduced husband is trying to give her winning numbers for the lottery. "Jacky would never leave us without good prospects," she says. "He loved his family more than anything." There is a picture of the two of them, the widow and the urn, the living and the dead, flesh and bronze, the Victrola and the Victrola's dog. She has her ear cocked, waiting.

We are always waiting. Waiting for some good word or the winning numbers. Waiting for a sign or wonder, some signal from our dear dead that the dead still care. We are gladdened when they do outstanding things, when they arise from their graves or fall through their caskets or speak to us in our waking dreams. It pleases us no end, as if the dead still cared, had agendas, were yet alive.

But the sad and well-known fact of the matter is that most of us will stay in our caskets and be dead a long time, and that our urns and graves will never make a sound. Our reason and requiems, our headstones or High Masses, will neither get us in nor keep us out of heaven. The meaning of our lives, and the memories of them, belong to the living, just as our funerals do. Whatever being the dead have now, they have by the living's faith alone.

We heat graves here for winter burials, as a kind of foreplay before digging in, to loosen the frost's hold on the ground before the sexton and his backhoe do the opening. We buried Milo in the ground on Wednesday. The mercy is that what we buried there, in an oak casket, just under the frost line, had ceased to be Milo. Milo had become the idea of himself, a permanent fixture of the third person and past tense, his widow's loss of appetite and trouble sleeping, the absence in places where we look for him, our habits of him breaking, our phantom limb, our one hand washing the other.

Lee Martin

SORRY

LEE MARTIN is the author of the novels *The Bright Forever*, a finalist for the 2006 Pulitzer Prize in Fiction, and *Quakertown*; two memoirs, *From Our House* and *Turning Bones*; and a short story collection, *The Least You Need to Know*. His fiction and nonfiction have appeared in *Harper's*, *Ms.*, *Creative Nonfiction*, *The Georgia Review*, *Story*, *DoubleTake*, *The Kenyon Review*, *Fourth Genre*, *River Teeth*, *The Southern Review*, and *Glimmer Train*. He is a winner of the Mary McCarthy Prize in Short Fiction and fellowships from the National Endowment for the Arts and the Ohio Arts Council, as well as the 2006 Ohio State University Alumni Award for Distinguished Teaching. He is professor of English and director of creative writing for the MFA Program at Ohio State University.

When I was a boy on our farm in southern Illinois, a family named Jent lived to our north. There were three brothers—David, Donnie, and Dan, in descending order—and a sister my age named Katrina. I was an only child of older parents, so all my cousins were young adults by the time I came along. Katrina was the first girl ever to come into my life, and she fascinated me. Sometimes she and Dan walked across our fields and we spent the afternoon at play. On occasion, I made the trip to their house, although I didn't like walking across the fields alone. There were barbed-wire fences to climb over or crawl through, and I was always afraid I would snag myself on one of the sharp barbs. I preferred to let Katrina come for me and then accompany me through the fields, holding the barbed wire apart so I could make my way safely to the other side.

I was like my mother, timid and not meant for the rough ways of farm life. There was so much that frightened me: the barbed wire, the water moccasins at the Jents' pond, the bulls in their pasture, the bees that hovered over the clover blossoms. Everything seemed dangerous. I was particularly afraid of the Jents' dog, a terrier that growled at me and nipped at my ankles. Whenever I came to visit, Katrina locked the dog in the shed, and no matter how much Dan protested, she insisted that the dog stay there so I wouldn't be afraid.

In my own home, my father whipped me at the least provocation. He used his belt, and sometimes a yardstick or a persimmon switch. When I was barely a year old, he lost both his hands when a corn picker mangled them beyond repair. He wore prosthetic hooks, their steel as cold and as hard as the regret that shadowed his life. There was so much to disappoint him. He had lost his hands because of his own carelessness; he had tried to clear the picker's shucking box without first shutting down the tractor's power takeoff, the device that sent the shucking box's rollers spinning, the rollers that pulled in his hands. Only a year before, I had come into his life abruptly, a surprise, when he was forty-two and my mother was forty-five. Obviously they hadn't planned on having children, and when they did, I turned out to be the sort of son I'm sure my father wouldn't have chosen. I was afraid of the dark, of the sparrows that sometimes got into our house, of the snakes that slithered through our yard. My father's response to my fainthearted nature was one of anger. Sometimes when he whipped me, I tried to run away, and he chased me about our farmyard, the air filling with our shouts.

"Goodness," my mother said once. "The Jents will think there's murder going on."

It shamed me to think that Katrina might be outside listening to the ugly shouts and screams and curses coming from our farm. What would she think of me? That I was, as my father often claimed, a heathen? I feared that the next time I saw her she would turn away from me in disgust. But she didn't. If she knew my trouble, she never mentioned it.

We were kids, only six years old, and we lived on farms separated by wide expanses of fields and pastures. I used to stand outside my house and gaze across those flat fields, hoping to catch some sign of Katrina in her farmyard that rested atop a hill—a flash of a red jacket, perhaps, the sparkle of the gold barrettes that she wore in her curled black hair—and then I would hope that she might walk across those fields to me. She was the sister I never had, the one I looked for as an adult in every new place I lived. She was a kind and merciful presence at the time of my father's rage, and for that, I loved her.

Because my father had no hands, he sometimes hired men to help him on our farm. My mother was as much help as she could be—driving grain trucks, greasing machinery, doctoring cattle and hogs—and my father could do many of the tasks that he had been able to perform before his accident. He could drive our International H tractor, plowing and disking and harrowing our fields. He could drive a combine and a corn picker at harvesttime. But still there was work that neither he nor my mother could manage—baling hay, making certain repairs to machinery—and, when that was the case, my father paid someone to do the chore. I remember a succession of such men, hay hands and mechanics—jacks-of-all-trades—men who weren't prosperous and had to scrabble from odd job to odd job. I never knew whom to feel more sorry for, the men who had to hire themselves out or my father, a handicap, who had to rely on their skills.

He always treated the hired men well, paid them whatever they asked, and insisted that they stay for a meal. Before they sat at our table, they washed their faces and hands at our basin and left my mother's towels streaked with oil and grease and grime. They rolled up their sleeves until the white flesh of their biceps showed. They took off their caps, and their foreheads were pale. These men were timid as my father encouraged them to eat more chicken, more potatoes, more bread. "You worked a ton," he said. "You need to get your belly full."

I was always surprised at how shy the hired men were at our table, how humble, how hesitant, despite my father's urging, to help themselves to seconds and thirds. These men, who had wrestled hay bales, yanked on wrenches, cursed stubborn nuts and bolts, were like children at our table, and my father, who was often so angry with me, was genuinely pleased to have them gathered there. I was happy, too, because as long as the men were there, I felt protected from my father. In their presence, his temper lay dormant the way thistles and horse-weed and wild garlic died back at frost. On the days when the hired men came into our house, I wished that my father could always be as relaxed, as jolly as he was then.

But eventually the men would leave, drive up our lane in rattletrap cars or trucks, and sooner or later, I would do something to irritate my father, and he would pull off his belt and use it to lash me. I would wish that I had some skill like those men, something that my father couldn't do without, something that would make him treat me more kindly.

I wonder now whether he enjoyed hosting the hired men only because he was grateful and wanted to show them how much he appreciated all they had done—our barn's loft stacked with bales of clover hay, hydraulic leaks repaired on our tractor—or whether it also satisfied him to make a display of his charity, to tap his hook against a meat platter and tell someone, "Dig in. Don't be bashful. If you go away hungry, you've got no one to blame but yourself."

How desperately he must have wanted to be one of them, a whole man, free from those hooks and the stumps of his arms that he slipped into the hooks' hard plastic holsters. Each day, he must have wished to be rid of the harness of canvas straps, the cable wires, the thick bands made of rubber, the ache in his shoulders where he contracted his muscles to tug at the wires, stretch the bands, and open the hooks. I wonder whether he ever dreamed himself whole again, his hands agile and strong, and whether, in those dreams, he touched me with tenderness. I can't imagine what it would have been like had he been able to do that. I knew only the cold steel of his hooks, the prickly cable wires, the snap of those pincers as they sprang shut.

During recess at school, we often played red rover. Two lines of children, human chains formed by spacing ourselves just far apart enough so we could grasp the hand of the classmates to our left and right, faced each other some twenty feet apart on the playground. One line called out to the other, "Red Rover, Red Rover. Send Bobby right over." The person called ran toward the opposite chain and tried to break through. I always hoped that Katrina and I would be on the same team. When we were, I tried to arrange it so we were next to each other. I loved the feel of her hand in mine. If an opponent dashed toward our link in the chain, I held her hand as tightly as I could, determined not to feel it slip from my grasp.

In those days, I was starved for tactile sensations, and Katrina, with whom I shared a double desk in our classroom, was the source of so much that pleased me: the warmth of her hand, the soft fuzz of her angora sweater, the airy billow of her empress sleeves. Sometimes, when we were at her house, we rode her horse, Lightning. I sat in the saddle behind Katrina, my arms wrapped around her waist. I was often secretly frightened by Lightning's gallop, but delighted, too, because I was holding onto Katrina. I was determined not to let her know that I was afraid.

Once, on a rainy afternoon, she and Dan and I were in their basement playing a game of Sorry. Dan and I were sitting cross-legged on the cool cement floor; Katrina was lying on her stomach, propped up on her elbows. I felt cozy there in the dry basement, looking up from time to time at the rain-blurred windows above us. It was raining, as my father would have said, "like pouring piss out of a boot." I could hear the rainwater gushing from the downspouts and puddling in the dirt. The thunderclaps were muffled and sounded far away because we were underground, insulated and dry, protected from the storm. We rolled our dice and moved our pieces over the game board, and the easy rhythm we fell into—the dice clicking, the tokens thumping—pleased me.

Then Dan started to pester Katrina. He was sitting next to her, and he kept pinching her leg. "Skeeters are out," he kept saying. "Bsst! There's another one."

Katrina squirmed about and slapped at his hand. "Quit it, Dan."

"I'm not doing anything," he said. "It's those skeeters."

Because I was an only child, I had no knowledge of the give-and-take between siblings. I knew nothing about their rivalries and affections. When I saw Dan pinching Katrina—when I took note of her mounting anger—I thought I understood perfectly: Dan was the villain; Katrina was his innocent victim, a damsel in distress.

Now, when I remember Dan, I call to mind a slight boy, so much smaller than other boys his age. "He's the runt of that litter," my father said.

And it was true. Dan, who was three years older than I, was perhaps an inch shorter. His brothers were both tall and beefy, but Dan was elfin, a sprout yet to take root and grow. I imagine now that he must have resented those of us who were younger. Here he is in our class photo, sitting cross-legged on the floor with the rest of the pipsqueaks, while his chums, the fourth graders, loom over us. Even though he was generally good-humored and friendly (in fact, I can recall several times when he defended me against the teasing of older boys), surely anytime we had to assume a line at school, he must have grown tired of always having to join the first graders, or at Christmastime having to be one of Santa's pint-sized helpers in the school pageant.

I wonder, too, if perhaps he resented Katrina because she was the only girl in the family, a sweet, good-hearted child who claimed everyone's attention. Maybe that's why he was pestering her in the basement on that rainy afternoon. Or maybe he was pinching Katrina's leg because he loved her deeply and couldn't say it, could show it only with a gesture that he considered playful and harmless. Or maybe he was just bored, frustrated with the rain that kept us confined to the basement.

I didn't understand, then, the complicated crosscurrents that run through a family's affections, though eventually I would figure out that even in my father's anger and my anguish as a result of it lay a wellspring of genuine love. Why else would we have been so disappointed with each other, so ashamed after an ugly scene? Why else would we have longed for a life more considerate and kind?

All I knew that day in the basement was that Katrina didn't like what Dan was doing to her any more than I liked their terrier nipping at my ankles.

"Leave her alone," I said. I shoved at Dan's shoulder, momentarily knocking him off balance.

"I'm not hurting her," he said, when he had regained his balance. Then he shoved me back. "Don't be a baby."

I don't remember exactly what happened next, only that we were wrestling. On Saturday nights, my father let me stay up late so we could watch *Championship Wrestling* together on channel seven. It was one of the few times I felt close to him, both of us rooting for Rip Hawk or Dick the Bruiser. It seems so ironic to me now, but perhaps natural, too, in a perverse way, that we would unite as spectators of violence, staged as it most surely was, when so many times my father had left stripes on my skin with his belt. Watching the wrestling matches, I learned holds and moves: the hammerlock, the headlock, the body scissors, the reverse toehold, the abdominal stretch, the flying mule kick.

I believe it was the headlock that I eventually used on Dan that day in the basement, and somehow in his attempt to escape it, he fell back and banged his head on the cement floor.

It's difficult ever to forget the sound of a skull hitting concrete, especially when you're in some way to blame for it. I stood over Dan, stunned. He lay motionless for a moment. Then he sat up, sheepishly rubbing his head, looking dazed, not injured nearly as badly as I had at first feared.

"You hurt him." Katrina was drumming her fists into my back. I spun around, surprised, and she hit me in the chest. "You're awful," she said, and then, as if she never wanted to have anything to do with me, she ran up the stairs, leaving Dan and me alone.

"Are you all right?" I asked him

"Yeah, I'm okay."

I felt such an emptiness inside, similar to the sinking sensation I got riding in a car that crested a hill too fast and dipped down the other side. "Hold onto your gizzard," my mother always said. I wondered whether this emptiness was what my father felt after he had whipped me, sorry that he had let his temper get the better of him, sorry that he had gone too far, sorry that the world he thought he had a hold on had slipped out from under him.

From time to time, in public, I had to help him with some chore. In stores, I took his billfold from his shirt pocket, and, at his instruction, fished out the appropriate bills and coins to settle our accounts. In the barbershop, if it was winter, I helped him off with his coat and cap. While we waited our turn for haircuts, I fetched him a Pepsi from the cooler and held it by the neck so he could grasp the bottle with the pincers of his hook. Sometimes, when he was finished drinking, he wouldn't be able to let go of the bottle. The pincers would be open so wide, he wouldn't be able to muster enough strength in his shoulder to open them a fraction more. "I'm fast," he would say to me then, humbled by his inadequacy, and I would have to work the bottle free from his hook.

I always felt that I was on display whenever he called on me to do something he couldn't. "Roy, who's your helper?" someone might say to him.

"That's my boy," he would say, and despite all the trouble between us, there would be an affectionate lilt to his voice, and I would believe that in his heart of hearts where he was whole and without temper or regret, he loved me.

"He looks like a good helper," someone would say, and my father would answer, "Well, sure he is. He's my right-hand man."

I would forget, then, the whippings he had given me, would convince myself that there wouldn't be any others, that we were moving into a better part of our lives. I was his helper, his right-hand man. That was my job.

Then, one summer, there came a time when I could do nothing to help him. A fisherman had drowned in the Jents' pond. He had leaned out too far to reel in a catch and had fallen from his boat. He had sunk to the bottom and never come up.

The first we knew of it was when his buddy, a skinny boy, gasping for air, came to our door begging for help. It was toward evening, the sun a reddish-orange ribbon in the west, just beginning to sink below the horizon. Water ran from the boy and puddled on our front porch. He had dove and dove, he told us, hoping to find his buddy, but had come up empty-handed.

"Mister," he said to my father. "Please. You've got to do something."

What could my father do but turn to other men for help? He told my mother to call the sheriff and then Mack Jent.

Earlier that summer, when a mountain lion had been killing livestock, a group of men at the Berryville Store had formed a hunting party and gone out with rifles. My father had gone with them, a bundle of rope looped over his shoulder, looking ineffectual among the men and their guns.

The evening the boy came to tell us his buddy had fallen into the pond, I got the same feeling that had come over me the night my father had marched off with the men: a tender pity for him and all he lacked. He would never be the one whom people could depend on in a time of crisis. He would never shoot a mountain lion, never rescue a drowning man. He would never be Lucas Mc-Cain from *The Rifleman*, or Paladin from *Have Gun, Will Travel*, television characters who always saved the day.

What made me especially sad was the knowledge that inside my father was exactly that kind of man—decisive, resourceful, courageous—and had he only had hands he would have been better able to demonstrate those qualities. He would have been freed from the clumsy movements of his hooks. How many times had he mourned a physical action he once performed with ease, now lost to him forever?

That evening, as dusk gathered, he could only stand on the bank of the Jents' pond while Mack and his oldest boy, David, and the skinny boy went out in the rowboat and dropped a tangle of barbed wire, tied to a rope, down into the water. They hoped that the barbed wire would snag the drowned man's clothing and then the three of them might be able to haul the body to the surface.

I stood beside my father as the dark came on. I could hear the boat moving on the pond, the oars creaking in their locks, the blades slapping the water.

Then Mack shouted, "I think we've got something."

My father said to me, "You go on home. You don't need to be here to see this."

I wonder now whether he was thinking of the moment when a farmer driving past my father's field heard his cries for help and freed him from the corn picker, brought him from the field, his hands mangled to pulp.

"I'll stay with you," I said. I wondered how long he had stood in the field, his hands caught in the rollers of the picker's shucking box, before the other farmer had happened by.

"You do like I say." My father's voice was angry now. "Or do you want me to blister your ass?"

I ran across the field toward the lights burning in our farmhouse. I was crying because I had to leave my father there, alone in the dark—helpless. All he could do was wait while Mack and David and the skinny boy pulled the drowned man from the pond.

One day not long afterward, my mother accepted a teaching position in the northern part of the state, and just like that, we were moving. My father sold our livestock. Trucks rumbled up our lane and took away our cattle and hogs. Suddenly, the pens and pastures were empty.

We were moving because my mother had lost her job teaching at Claremont Grade School, and my father was willing to move three hundred miles north to a suburb of Chicago in exchange for the extra income the new teaching position would bring. He leased our farm to Mack Jent and became an absentee landlord.

It gave me an odd feeling to think of Mack Jent farming our ground because I knew that my father didn't completely approve of his way of doing things. He planted too close to the fence lines, my father said. More than once he complained that Mack had planted over our property line. And he didn't keep his beans cultivated, or his machinery in tip-top shape. And he cut his wheat when it was still damp with dew, and on and on.

He had also brought a lawsuit against another farmer whose pickup truck had come up too fast behind Mack's tractor on the County Line Road and rear-ended him. It hadn't been a serious accident, but Mack had claimed whiplash and back injuries and had won a settlement.

It was practically unheard of in those days for one member of our rural community to sue another member. It was considered bad form—unneighborly and unchristian. Good neighbors would find a way to work out their differences without involving the courts.

So Mack Jent had a reputation of someone not to be trusted. Why my father handed over our farm to him, even allowing him the use of our machinery, I still don't know unless it was merely because the arrangement was convenient. Time was short and someone had to be found. Mack was close and eager for the chance.

To me, he was like their terrier dog—tightly wound and tenacious, full of growl and snap. He wasn't ill-tempered or abusive the way my father often was; he was dangerous for a different reason. He was a wiseacre. When he joked with me, his barbs often stung. He teased me about being afraid of their dog, or having to double with Katrina when we rode her horse. Maybe I ought to try riding sidesaddle, he suggested. I know his teasing was meant to be good-natured, but I was a sensitive boy, one who suspected, even then, that I would never be the sort of man he was—gung-ho and brazen, unwilling to calculate risk and consequences.

He worked for Marathon Oil and did his farming at night and on the weekends. Everything about him said that he was ready to go, man, go. He wore overalls with nothing beneath them but bare skin and boxer shorts. He kept his hair in a sharp-bristled flattop. A Winston cigarette jounced from his lower lip as he gabbed. Maybe he talked his way into leasing our farm, the way he would eventually try to convince my father to sell him the whole kit and caboodle. By this time, my father had come to regret the fact that he had ever allowed Mack to sink a plowshare into our eighty acres. From time to time, he would say, "I don't ever want this place sold to Mack Jent, or to any of his heirs." He had never accepted Mack's farming methods, and once, while Mack was our tenant, a spark from one of his Winstons had started a fire, and our International H tractor had burned to ruin.

"You see what you get," my father said, "when you're careless."

I never stopped, then, to consider the irony of his statement. What right did he have to accuse Mack when he himself had been careless with the corn picker and had ended up losing his hands? I thought only of the afternoon in the Jents' basement, when I had gone off half-cocked and wrestled Dan until he fell and hit his head. I had been reckless. I had thought I was defending Katrina and had ended up making her angry. Although we eventually put the incident behind us, the way children do, it seemed to mark the end of the way we had always known each other. Suddenly we were just two kids who went to the same school and happened to live near each other. There was nothing special between us. We may have even begun to pick up on the subtle tensions that smoldered between our fathers. We were moving in different directions. Then I was gone to Chicago, and though I saw Katrina in the summers when we came back to our farm, we were never the same. When we were around each other, there was, at least for me, the feeling that I was a stranger, had perhaps always been one, allowed a momentary place in Katrina's world only through her deliberate kindness. I had ruined that; I would know it forever.

The last time I saw her was in 1988 at my mother's funeral. It was January, and southern Illinois was in the midst of a bitter cold spell. The temperature had dropped into the teens. The wind howled. Dusty ribbons of snow snaked across the streets. I imagined the wind moaning in the stovepipes of our deserted farmhouse.

My father had died six years earlier. We had made our peace. Through the grace of my mother's faith in goodness, we had managed to get beyond the anger that had raged between us for years. My mother—who had always been loving and kind, who had believed in God and redemption—had been slipping away from us a little at a time over the past three years. Small strokes—sometimes no more than a tingle in her lip, a loss of balance—had been destroying brain cells until, finally, she lay, aphasic, in a nursing home. I lived far away from her and on my visits—usually two or three times a year—I was always shaken by how much her condition had worsened. She had stood by, silent, while my father had whipped me, while in my teen years our anger had spurred physical confrontations. She had always seemed so helpless in my father's house. All she could do was endure and trust to God. Eventually, the thousands of prayers that she must have said saved us. But I could do nothing to save her from the strokes that were taking her away.

I knew little of Katrina's own journey from childhood, only that she had married young, as soon as she had graduated from high school, that her mother had died from cancer soon after, that Katrina had worked for a time in a shelter care facility for mentally and physically challenged youths. I knew those facts, but they told me nothing of what she carried inside her—what private pains, demons, joys, fears. Once, I had felt as close to her as I would have a sister, but I couldn't see, then, the span of our adult lives, stretching out ahead of us like the long shadows our child bodies made when we were at play in the late afternoon sunlight. I didn't know the different directions a life could take, how far someone could spin away from home, from himself, from the people he swore he knew and loved.

"Lee."

I heard my name and turned, and there she was. Although more than twenty-five years had passed since the days when she had come for me and escorted me across the fields to her house, I recognized her immediately. Her dark hair was flecked with gray, but her face was still the face I had cherished all those years ago at a time in my life when I had needed her bright eyes, her kind smile.

"Hello, Katrina," I said, and I felt something open inside me, a door back to the boy I had been, timid and afraid.

"You remember me," she said, and I was stunned to think that she had imagined I wouldn't.

She introduced me to her husband, a friendly man who seemed as if he would be at ease in whatever situation he found himself. He wouldn't be afraid of barbed wire snagging him as he crawled through a fence, or bees stinging him, or terrier dogs nipping at his ankles. And, if trouble found him, he wouldn't turn into a madman, wrestle someone to the floor, bang his foe's head on the cement.

Katrina told a story about the day I fell off her horse. "Do you remember that?" she asked me. She was smiling, her eyes sparkling, and I could see that she was taking great pleasure in telling this story.

"No," I said, and it was true. I had absolutely no memory of the event she described.

"I boosted you up, and I told you to hold on to the reins. Before I could get on, Lightning took off at a gallop. He hadn't gone but a few feet when you fell off."

Her husband chuckled, the way he must have on the drive to the funeral home when Katrina had surely told him the same story. "You don't remember that?" he asked.

"I really don't." I wasn't sure which would be more shameful: to acknowledge the event or to display a faulty memory of it. "Was I hurt?" I asked Katrina.

"No, you weren't hurt. You were just scared. Poor little guy."

At one time, I would have given anything for her sympathy. Oddly enough, on the day of my mother's funeral, I wanted none of it. I wanted no reminder of the timid boy I had been, the one for whom Katrina had felt sorry. Both of my parents were now dead. I was the last to survive our turmoil, our shame. I was on the verge of the rest of my adult life, and the last thing I needed was to be reminded of what a "poor little guy" I had been.

"You know where we live," Katrina said to me. "Out on the highway. That big white house on King's Hill. Stop in and see us sometime."

"I will," I told her, but, of course, I never did.

Rebecca McClanahan

INTERSTELLAR

REBECCA MCCLANAHAN has published nine books, most recently *Deep Light: New and Selected Poems 1987–2007* and *The Riddle Song and Other Rememberings*, which won the 2005 Glasgow Prize in nonfiction. She has also authored four previous books of poetry and two books of writing instruction, including *Word Painting: A Guide to Writing More Descriptively*. McClanahan's work has appeared in *The Best American Poetry*, *The Best American Essays*, *Kenyon Review*, *Georgia Review*, *Gettysburg Review*, and numerous other publications. She has received the Wood Prize from *Poetry*, a Pushcart Prize in fiction, and (twice) the Carter Prize for the essay from *Shenandoah*. McClanahan lives in New York City and teaches in the low-residency MFA program at Queens University, Charlotte.

To be the sister of a sad and beautiful woman is to lie down in the memory of a grandparents' attic, your ear pressed to the floor vent. The grownups are talking, arranging the family constellation—your sister the luminous star, chased by a tail of stuttering light (that would be you).

Not that she is older, that is not why you chase her. It is her beauty, wanting to be close to something that shines. You are the age when dolls are real. You touch your sister's cheeks, her soft hands. You look into her brown eyes. You want to protect her, to claim her, to lift her up like some glittering bauble so that others will smile at you. She fills your lap.

You'll ruin your eyes, your mother says, but you decide the books are worth it. This one is about stars: Stars appear to be fixed, maintaining the same pattern in the skies year after year. You close your pale eyes and think about this a while. Your sister runs for the waves, bronzed goddess in yellow bikini. You dig your head deeper into the sand of the book, pull the umbrella closer, adjust the hat, button the long shirt, pull its collar high. You are aware of your neck, gooselike, awkward: quack quack honk. You look down at your white thighs, the rivers of blue veins. Your mother has them too, but the doctor says he's never seen them—childbearing veins, he calls them—in someone so young. You suspect you will never have children. You decide you will never wear shorts again.

Your sister begins to win contests. Once, for her perfect posture, she wins an expensive king-size mattress, which she presents to your parents. They sleep on it for years and years. In the meantime, you win fifteen dollars in an essay contest sponsored by the Women's Christian Temperance Union in which you make an admirable case against alcohol, which you have never tasted. From the bedroom you share, your sister has begun disappearing at night, climbing out the window and leaving pillows molded into her shape.

You watch her closely. Does she polish her skin? How can it shine just so? When you answer the door for your own first date, you feel her warmth passing behind you in the hall and you watch his eyes wander, watch them travel over your shoulder. All evening you are sure he is elsewhere, that when he looks into your face, he is trying to locate her.

Not that he will ever find her. *You* can't even find her. Sometimes you try, you ask Where have you been, I've been worried, but she doesn't answer. She talks in her sleep and you listen but it never makes sense. Your mother says you talk in your sleep too, that sometimes when she passes the door to your room you are both talking in your sleep to each other, making no sense.

To be the sister of a beautiful girl is to answer the phone and take messages. Boys are calling, modeling agents are calling, they are taking her picture, her portfolio is filling. Because she is too young to manage such beauty, your mother accompanies her to photo shoots to be sure no one takes advantage. The phone keeps ringing, and you keep leaving your book to answer it. When you return to *Our Town*, Emily is asking her mother if she's pretty. Pretty enough for all normal purposes, her mother answers. You wonder what normal purposes are.

One glory crowns you, though, and it keeps growing. You imagine the boys climbing it like Rapunzel's tower. You brush it every night and arrange it as though it belonged to a doll: chignons, braids, French twists. Sometimes you set it free, toss your head so that the sun will grab the hair, set it to shining like the *shook foil* in Hopkins' poem about the grandeur of God. Sometimes you allow it to fall down around your face as you study the books in the library.

What makes her even more lovely is that she doesn't realize she is. She is like the girl in the Richard Wilbur poem you are reading, the girl coming down the winding staircase, "perfectly beautiful, perfectly ignorant of it." There is a large heart at your sister's center, a pulsating bright heart, but no one bothers to see it. Beauty is its own excuse for being, why look farther, deeper? Sometimes you feel her heart beating wildly inside *you*—as she caresses a kitten's ears or gathers stray puppies into her arms, or knits, stitch by patient stitch, afghans to give away. If I looked like her, you think, I wouldn't worry with any of that. If I had what she had, I would just sit all day and shine.

When you are a beautiful girl turning into a beautiful woman, others want to hold you, to possess you. Some want to hurt you for your beauty. It is too bright: they will show you. Sometimes when she climbs back through the window and into the bed you share, you feel a great sadness radiating from her center. In the pillows it finds its voice in ragged breaths and tears that bruise the air. Twenty years from now she will tell you about the boys in the van, what they did to her. But in this moment all those years are ahead of you. The night, as the song on the radio is saying, has a thousand eyes. But you don't, and when the tears finally stop, she turns her back to you and floats away. The distance is immeasurable.

Certain stars which appear single to the naked eye are, in fact, double, and share a mutual revolution. You are in the library again, your hair falling over a book. Someone notices. He notices so hard that after a few months he names it love, and because love has set you free and it is April, you put on a pair of shorts and walk toward the door. You're not wearing shorts out in public, are you? he says, staring down at your veins. Of course not, you say. On the honeymoon he makes you promise you will never cut your hair. You promise, and you don't, but he leaves anyway. You sign the papers that arrive in the mail, thinking fine, I'll be fine, if that's the way it must be. Then one morning you cannot get out of bed, it hurts to breathe and why bother anyway, you want to die but it's too much trouble. Stay right there, your sister says over the phone. Then she is there in the room, smelling sweet like she's been rolling in flowers. She takes off her shoes, crawls in beside you, covers your hand with hers, and begins to rock you back and forth. You can't die, she says, you don't want to die. Don't talk like that, she says.

Not long after the divorce you discover to your surprise that the goose neck you've been hiding beneath turtlenecks and scarves might be precisely what the bookstore owner said it was. The day was hot and dusty, as were the books: *One type of double star is the eclipsing variable, composed of bright and dark components. Sometimes the dark star eclipses the bright one.* Finally, in heat and desperation, you removed the scarf. My my, the bookstore owner said in a foreign accent that made what followed sound almost like cool water flowing over rocks: You have the neck of a swan. How beautiful. Another day, passing beneath trees, a man tells you your eyes are the most incredible green. So you learn to wear that shade, to walk beneath trees, submerge your white body in lakes, your face bobbing just so, above the green water. In your mind you divide the spectrum of luminous radiation, the way you once divided the bedroom you shared with your sister. She can have the warm side, the sun bronzed oranges, yellows, reds, browns. You'll keep the cool greens and blues.

Man after man circles her, chases her light. Sometimes they look for her in the wrong places and find her there. Maybe he's not what he seems, you tell her. I am afraid for you. What if? It's my life, she says, as if your life and hers could never touch.

Man after man, it does not work out for you, though you wear long gowns and dim the lights. Then one night, one man, it does. Moonlight is streaming through the window, the stars are too bright to turn down, and he lifts the long gown over your ankles, your knees, over your white, perfectly imperfect thighs. He kisses your veins, one by one. It is a proposal, and you accept.

At the foot of the birthing bed you stand beside her husband and smooth the sheets. The nurse has placed a golden light above your sister and her swaddled, dark-eyed daughter: luminosity no astronomer could chart. It's what your sister was meant for, what will save her, you think. No more mornings when you find her exhausted, the bedroom drapes drawn shut. No more phone calls waking you from sleep, her husband's voice in the background, words flying.

Stars are not made of heavenly ether, but of the same corruptible elements that comprise earth.

One rainy March morning two years later, the phone rings. Do you want the Indian pictures? she says. Their eyes make me sad. Because of her voice, you rush over. When she answers the door, the framed pictures of the chief and the brave are stacked by the door, the babies are crying, kittens are mewing, and darkness circles your sister's eyes. You hope it is from sleeplessness but you're not sure. I've got to do something about all this, she says, spreading her arms to include the brown sofa, the vinyl chair, her husband's tray of stale ashes. She has five dollars in her purse. You have twenty. Today, she says. We have to do something today. You pack the children into the car seats and pull away from the curb in search of spring. Clots of leftover snow dot the street. The sky is pewter. Not one crocus, one daffodil, surprises you along the way. At the discount fabric store you choose shiny green with huge flowers and hummingbirds sipping nectar. All day you measure, cut, stretch, staple until the sofa is covered in spring. It won't last, you're sure of that, but it will get her through the day.

To be her sister is to lie beside your husband as he reads your mother's memoirs, one daughter *distant, beautiful, mysterious,* the other *dependable, reliable, sure.* "I knew it," he laughs. "I married the Maytag." One evening you go with your mother to a restaurant where your sister works part time to make ends meet. Your sister is still married, but barely. She wears the uniform of such places, a white blouse and a short skirt. Even after two children, her legs are smooth and finely muscled, not a vein in sight. The men cannot take their eyes off her. I don't know where she got those legs, your mother says. Later that night your sister is chilly. You loan her your best green sweater, and *you* cannot takes your eyes off her.

You can't blame them for chasing her light. Her laughter is liquid, she gathers her bright afghans around her, and the children and the stray cats and dogs. She tosses her beautiful head, and who wouldn't want to follow? Certainly not that man, or that one—the one who appears at her door days after her divorce is final. Every night he brings flowers and wine and more wine, she glows from within, and why spoil it for her, but still you must say it. I don't care, she says, how long it lasts. But his drinking, you say. I'm afraid for you. What if.

In the Al-Anon circle where you gather once a week, you say your name but not the rest. Everyone's here for the same reason, anyway. Still, they want you to say it aloud. You don't, and maybe you never will. No one can make you. It feels like a betrayal, it's no one's business anyway. Besides, what good would it do, it's her life not yours, she chose him. Still, when the others stand you stand with them, grabbing hands and circling, closing eyes and asking: the wisdom to know the difference.

To be the sister of a sad and beautiful woman is to be the aunt of beautiful nieces who belong to your sister or to your brothers who married women who look like your sister. You started to write, about your nieces, "each one lovelier than the next," but why pass on that burden? At the family reunion, the nieces flip through the pictures. They ooh and ah over your hair. They can't believe it was ever that long, that thick. What happened? they say. You tell them Just Wait. They discover your sister's portfolio. Wow, she was a knockout, they say. You tell them to stop using the past tense, that you are both still alive, thank you, in the present tense.

Though you've moved to a city light years from your sister, at home on your desk are the letters that have begun making their way to you: your sister is afraid for her future, she is raking up the dead leaves of the past. It's hard work, she writes. Some days it's all I can do to lift my head. Last week she sent you a picture of a goose-necked woman. You have never been fond of Klimt's women, but your sister is, and has written beside the picture: The beautiful white neck and shoulders reminded me of you. See what lasts?

When your nieces come to visit, you walk with them on city streets, recalling again how to step aside, to become the pal in the old movie, the one who lifts the bridal train, smoothes down the sheets so that the lovely one can get the beauty sleep she does not need. You now understand why a woman of a certain age chooses to walk alone, or with only a dog, and carefully selects the backdrop against which she will move. Green is good, but it's winter now, and in a cold city like yours, where sometimes only faces show, the bodies bundled beneath, you learn how to throw a look in someone's direction, making the kind of contact only eyes can make. And you learn how to carry in your eyes, in your glance, in a toss of your head, something the old ones call experience or character. Okay, all right, you'll settle for that. At home is a husband, who, after all these years, still kisses your veins. And beside him are your books and the words waiting to be written, your hidden heart still beating.

At a bookstore on the east side of the city, where aging beauties wear rouged cheeks beneath mink hats, you notice a table labeled *Hurt Art*: stacks of Renoir, Michelangelo, Monet, the covers torn or missing, spines broken, the pages water stained or burnt slightly at the edges as if they'd ventured too close to the flame. You want to buy all the books, to remove them from public shame. Someone has drawn a mustache on the Mona Lisa—a young girl perhaps, making her own mark? And why not hurt the art that holds a secret beneath its lips, a code you cannot begin to crack. You want to take your beautiful nieces aside and warn them. You want to spin back light years from today, hold your sister on your lap, rock her luminous beauty in your arms until it stops hurting.

Erin McGraw

BAD EYES

ERIN MCGRAW is the author of four books of fiction, including *The Good Life*. Her essays have appeared in *The Gettysburg Review*, *The Southern Review*, *The Missouri Review*, and *Ladies' Home Journal*. She teaches creative writing at Ohio State University.

> Seeing less than others can be a great strain.
> —Robert Lowell

The subject veers almost uncontrollably toward metaphor, but I mean to take it literally: I have unusually poor vision, minus 1300 diopters and still losing ground, ordinary progressive myopia that never stopped progressing. In me, the process by which light is supposed to focus images at the back of the eye has gone berserk, and the point of focus shifts ever closer to the front, like the projection of a movie falling short of its screen.

My eyeballs aren't round, like marbles or baseballs, but instead are oblongs, little footballs. This awkward shape puts so much strain on the retinas that a rip has developed in my left one, a patch where the tissue gave out like exhausted cloth. Now my ophthalmologist carefully includes a retina evaluation at annual checks, and I have a list of warning signs that indicate a significant rupture: sudden, flashing lights; floaters showering into my vision like rain.

Mostly, though, nothing about my vision is so fraught or dramatic. I'm shortsighted, is all, mope-eyed, gravel-blind, blind-buck and Davy. A squinter, the sort who taps her companions at plays and baseball games. "What just happened? I missed that." There's metaphor again, leaning in the doorway and clearing its throat meaningfully. But I'm still being literal, aiming to describe a world in which objects collapse into haze and through which I navigate, beyond the narrow realm that my contact lenses permit me to see clearly, by memory and assumption.

Here are some of the things I can't see, even with my contacts in: a baseball

in play, birds in trees, numbers and subtitles on TV, roads at night, constella-
tions, anything by candlelight, street signs, faces of people in cars, faces of people twenty feet away. One of my consistent embarrassments comes from
snubbing friends who stood more than a shadow's length from me, friends I
didn't even nod to because I couldn't tell who they were. So I've adopted a genial
half smile that I wear when I walk around my neighborhood or down the corridors of the department where I work. I have the reputation of being a very
friendly person.

Here are some of the things I can find when I narrow my eyes and look: tiny
new weeds in the front garden, fleas scurrying across my dog's belly, gray hairs.
My mother, watching me struggle before the bathroom mirror for ten minutes
while I spray and brush and bobby-pin to hide the worst of the gray, comments,
"I don't know why you bother. You don't have much. No one even sees it."

"I see it every time I look in the mirror."

"Well, you see what you're looking for."

She's told me this all my life. I roll my eyes and keep working the bobby
pins.

The glasses I remember best and loved most arrived when I was eight years
old. They were my second pair; the first were brown with wings at the corners,
the eyeglass equivalent to orthopedic shoes. I was delighted when the doctor
announced that they needed to be replaced.

My parents didn't share my delight—only a year had passed since we'd gotten that first pair. For six months, unconsciously, I'd been moving books closer
to my face and inching nearer the TV. Nothing was said about it. I think my
parents assumed that I must have been aware of a development so obvious to
them, but I was a dreamy, preoccupied child, and hadn't noticed that the edges
of illustrations in my books were no longer crisp. When I was moved to the
front row of my classroom, it never occurred to me to ponder why.

I was pleased to be there, though, and preened in my new glasses. Sleek cat
eyes, the white plastic frames featuring jaunty red stripes, they were 1965's cutting edge. I often took them off to admire them. When my correction needed
to be stepped up again, I insisted on using the same frames, even though by
then I had to keep the glasses on all the time, and could take pleasure in the
candy-cane stripes only if I happened to pass a window. In my school pictures
for three years running I wore these same glasses. By the third year they were
clearly too small for my face, and my eyes practically disappeared behind the
thick glass.

Every six months my mother took me to the eye doctor, and nearly every
visit meant a prescription for new, slightly heavier lenses. At first I resented
only the hours spent in the waiting room where I was often the only child,

but gradually I began to dread the examination itself, the stinging dilation drops and my frustrating attempts to read the eye chart. While I struggled to focus on letters that seemed to slip and buckle on the far wall, fear bloomed in my stomach.

"T," I would begin rashly, remembering that much from the visit before, but then I strained to make out the next wobbly shape. "U, maybe, or C. It could be O." Not bothering to comment, the doctor tilted back my chair, pulled around one of the clicking, finicky machines, and began the measurements for the next set of lenses. Both he and I ignored my quick, anxious breathing and dry mouth, but when he was finished I burst out of the office as if I were making a jail break.

Back in the world, panic dropped away, and my worsening vision seemed nothing more than an inconvenience. Perhaps if I'd been an outdoorsy kind of child, a girl who noticed leaves or clouds or insect life, I might have grieved the first time I was unable to detect a distant, sly animal. But I wasn't especially fond of the offerings of the natural world, which was too hot or too cold and full of things that made me itch. And the steady loss of detail—my inability first to make out the petals of a flower, and before long to discern the flower at all without glasses to help me—felt unimportant. I jammed on my glasses first thing in the morning, took them off after turning out my light at night, now and then remembered to clean them. Easy enough.

Only occasionally did I get the sense that I was hampered. The sisters at my Catholic school made me take my glasses off before games at recess, a sensible precaution; I was a terrible athlete, who reliably stopped dead in front of any moving object, so I was hit in the face by kickballs, tetherballs, basketballs, and once, memorably, by a softball bat that caught me square on the cheek. The sister blew her whistle and bustled toward me, already scolding. Why hadn't I gotten out of the way?

I didn't cry when the bat hit me, although it hurt, but her chiding made my lips start to quiver. I hadn't *seen* it, I protested. All of a sudden something had hit my face; the blow came out of nowhere.

It came out of the batter's box, the sister pointed out. I shouldn't have been standing so close. I knew that I couldn't see clearly and therefore had all the more reason to be cautious.

She handed me my glasses and let me go to the nurse's office, where I walked sulkily, coddling my sense of injustice. The nurse, used to seeing me, examined my cheek and pronounced that all I had suffered was a bruise. She had me back on the playground before the end-of-recess bell rang.

Still, I couldn't easily dismiss the incident. Up to that point, no one had told me, *You are at risk. And it is up to you to take precautions.* Back at home, I took my glasses off and looked at the house across the street. I recognized its shape and details, but that hardly required vision. I saw the house every day and could have drawn from memory its long, flat roof and the row of bunkerlike windows in the bathroom.

So I walked up the street, turned onto a cul-de-sac that I didn't know well, and took off my glasses again. Instantly, the turquoise stucco bungalow before me smeared into a vague blue box. I could make out windows but couldn't tell if the curtains were open or closed; could find the front door but not the mail slot, the wrought-iron handrail but not the steps it accompanied.

A shout erupted and I spun around, shoving my glasses back on to find that the shout had nothing to do with me: a couple of boys were playing catch at the top of the street. Nevertheless, my heart was whapping now, hurting me. I was foolish to stand so publicly, blinking and helpless, right in the middle of the sidewalk. Anyone could have sneaked up, knocked me to the ground, and taken my wallet, if I'd had a wallet.

I thought of comic-strip blind beggars on city streets, their canes kicked away, their tin cups stolen. For the first time, my bad eyes took on meaning: They were an invitation to bullies, and the fact that no one had yet taken my glasses and knocked me down was just dumb luck. Pressing my glasses in place, I ran home.

This new notion of myself seized my imagination, and I fell asleep for several nights imagining scenarios in which I was unfairly set upon, a lamb before wolves. I saw myself suffering nobly and remembered reverently. And then I forgot about my experiment in front of the blue house. I continued to play games without glasses at school, continued to get smacked with kickballs, continued not to be accosted by glasses-snatching bullies. Finally tired of my red and white striped glasses, I zipped through half a dozen new pairs, trying out granny glasses in three different shapes, including ones with octagonal lenses that made me look unnervingly like John Lennon.

By the time I was entering junior high, though, I was tired of wearing glasses. More precisely, I was tired of my bespectacled reflection, how glasses made my eyes look tiny and dim, my nose like a tremendous landmass. So I initiated a campaign to get contact lenses, which were just becoming widely available, although not usually for twelve-year-olds. To my astonishment, my cautious, conservative ophthalmologist immediately agreed.

"Contacts help sometimes, with myopia like this," he explained to my skeptical mother. "The theory is that the contact flattens the lens of the eye. It can slow down the disease's progress." I was so elated that I hardly flinched when he called what I had a "disease," a word we usually avoided. And so, a month later, we began a regime that I was in no way ready for.

These were the days when the only contact lenses were made of inflexible plastic, thick by today's standards, hard, immovable foreign bodies that had to be introduced to the protesting eyes at gradual intervals. The first day, the wearer put them in for two hours, then took them out for an hour of recovery, then in again, out, in, out. The second day, three hours.

The optometrist guided my shaking hand, showing me how to slip the lens directly in place. Before I could even look up, I had blinked the contact out; it bounced off the counter beneath us and hit the floor. My mother hissed. The optometrist ordered me not to move; he gently dropped to his knees and patted the linoleum until he found the lens and laboriously cleaned it again.

I blinked the lenses out twice more before he could get them centered on my corneas. Then, tentatively, he stepped back and asked, "How's that?" I was too stunned to answer. For all the talk about wearing schedules and tolerance, no one had told me that contact lenses would *hurt*. Each eye felt as though a hair had been coiled precisely on top of it, and hot, outraged tears poured out. Although the optometrist kept telling me to look up so that he could take measurements, I couldn't keep my eyes from snapping shut. Light was like a blade.

"It always takes a little while," he was telling my mother, "but she'll get used to them. Just take it easy. Don't let her overdo."

No fear of that. I was already frantic to take the lenses back out again, and the remaining hour and forty-five minutes of my first wearing period seemed unimaginable, an hour and forty-five minutes of torment. My mother had to lead me back out to the car by the hand; even with the sunglasses the optometrist had given me, I had to close my eyes. Light bouncing off of car windows and storefronts was searing.

For the next month, all I could think about was my eyes. As the optometrist had promised, they began to accommodate to the contacts, but accommodation wasn't what anyone could call comfort. My eyes stung, lightly, all the time. Every blink set the lenses shifting, and that slight movement felt as if it were grinding a ridge into the moist corneal tissue. The irritation made me blink again, shifting the contacts some more.

I spent the summer steeped in resentment. I refused invitations to parties and shopping trips because I had to put my contacts in and take them out, in and out, none of which would have happened if I'd had reasonable eyes to begin with. Even after I built up some expertise and didn't have to spend ten minutes tugging the corners of my eyes raw to dislodge the lenses, the contacts kept falling out on their own, vaulting away from my eyes, forcing me to freeze in midstep. With slow, scared care I would sink to my knees and begin patting first my clothes, then the ground around me, feeling for the tiny, mean-spirited disk.

For the first year I spent a lot of time apologizing about lost lenses, ones I rinsed down the drain or cracked, one that the dog snuffled up, and ones that simply shot out of my eyes and disappeared. My parents were understandably exasperated, and I became familiar with the dread that curled through me as soon as I felt one of the lenses begin to shimmy, the indicator that it would soon try for a getaway.

But that dread, at least, was practical. Cresting through me like high tide was the other dread, the one I'd forgotten about and put off for years. With the contacts ejecting themselves at malicious whim, I was constantly aware that my next breath might leave me marooned, half blind, vulnerable. The fact that no one ever treated me with anything but solicitude—often strangers got down on their hands and knees with me—did nothing to soften my fear. I started to walk more slowly, to avoid shag carpeting, to sit with my head tilted slightly back, hoping gravity would keep the contacts in place. Outside, I lingered by the sides of buildings.

By now the myopia was at a full gallop, and the world I saw without any lenses was no longer blurry; it was pure blur. If, for some reason, I had to walk across a room without glasses or contacts, I shuffled like a blind girl, groping for handholds, batting at the air in case something—a lamp, a shelf, some pot hanging from the ceiling—might be ready to strike. Smudged, bulging shapes crowded against me. I imagined fists or rocks or sudden, steep edges, threats from dreams that seemed probable in this shapeless landscape.

At visits to the ophthalmologist, I strained and fought to see the eye chart, memorizing E F O T Z and F X I O S C before the doctor caught on. I paid closer attention to the toneless way he informed my mother that I needed, again, a stronger correction, and felt my throat clench. My mother said, "I thought the contacts were supposed to slow this down."

"They might be doing that," he said. "There's no way of telling. She might be going downhill even faster without them." He bent over to write notes on my chart, which was half an inch thick by now. My eyes were good enough to see that.

I could see other things, of course, too. I could see the expression on my friend's face when I came to spend the night and unpacked all my cumbersome equipment: cleansing solution, wetting solution, saline solution, and the heat-sterilization unit that had to be plugged in for two hours. I could also see her expression after I emerged from the bathroom wearing my glasses. "Let me try them on," she said. I handed them over to let her giggle and bang into walls, and tried not to betray how anxious I was to get them back.

In biology class, I saw my teacher's impatient look when I told her that I couldn't draw the cells clustered on the microscope's slide. "Just close one eye and draw what you see," she said, and so, hopelessly, I did, even though I knew no cell ever had such peculiar zigzags. When I got my lab book back, the teacher had written, "You obviously have trouble seeing enough. Or correctly."

Maybe it was that prim, striving-for-accuracy last phrase that caught me. Or the clinical tone. Whichever, instead of feeling embarrassed or crushed, I was relieved. In a voice that didn't whine or tremble, her note offered me an interesting new self-definition. I grabbed it.

With relief, I gave up trying to make out faces across a football field and stopped straining to read the face of a bell tower clock, tasks I'd been using to gauge my vision's deterioration. By this time I was wearing a new, flexible kind of contact lens made out of silicone, far more comfortable and also less apt to fall out, so I was confident enough to stroll across parks and thickly carpeted rooms. I started asking the people around me what words were written on the blackboard, what images flicking by on the TV screen, and people told me. I was a person who had trouble seeing enough, or correctly, so they filled me in on the nuances I would miss on my own.

At a movie, nodding at the screen, my friend whispered, "She keeps noticing that clock. That clock has something to do with the murder." Or, gesturing at the teacher the next day in class: "She's smiling; she's in a good mood. I'll bet she's started smoking again."

I was being given not only facts but also interpretation. Those who could see sharply gave me shadow as well as object, context in addition to text. Did I resent all of these explanations and asides, pronounced extra slowly as if for the dim-witted? Not on your life. Friends and family were making things easy for me, and after years of constant unease, I was ready.

I drew other people's opinions over me like a blanket. Sight, it seemed, blended right into insight, and to perceive anything was to make a judgment call. Since the people around me had the first kind of sight, I was willing to grant that they had the second. And then the corollary: Since I lacked the one, I surely lacked the other.

Anybody with half an eye can see where this story is going: I got lazy. Knowing that many details were going to be lost to me anyway, I stopped even trying to see them. I could get the notion of a landscape but not the trees it contained, and recognized a skyline, if not the clear shape of a single building in it. I was all big picture, untroubled by the little stuff.

During my junior year in college, when I was an exchange student in England, I traveled to public gardens and scenic overlooks and took pictures. Only when the pictures were developed did I find out that candy wrappers had clogged the shrubbery, and that across the top slat of the pretty green park bench somebody had carved BOLLOX. These weren't microscopic flaws; they were clear to anybody, even myopic me. I'd been fully able to see the candy wrappers but hadn't bothered to. My photo album from that year is a catalog of England's trash, none of which I saw until the pictures came back. Then I felt outraged and—this is the kicker—betrayed.

Somewhere, at a juncture I can't pinpoint, I made a tactical shift in how I used my bad eyes. Not only had I given up trying to see the actual, physical world, but I had begun to let myself see a better world, one cut to my taste and measure, a world that, just for starters, didn't contain flyaway Snickers wrappers. And I believed in that world firmly enough to feel cheated when the wrappers got caught on the thorns of barberry bushes.

By this time, I know, the metaphorical implications are murmuring too loudly to be ignored. For I was fully as self-deceiving—delusional doesn't seem too strong a word—in my mental perceptions, my mind's eye. When I came home from that year abroad, I saw myself as English and annoyed the daylights out of my friends for months by calling the place we lived a flat (although it was in fact a house), stowing groceries in the car's boot, and pulling everybody's beer out of the refrigerator. Now, twenty years later, I imagine a photo that might have been taken of me at that time, highway trash wrapped around my ankles, BOLLOX scrawled on my forehead.

Permitting someone with so shaky a grasp of reality to enter relationships was just asking for trouble. The catalog of my romances from those years is unrelievedly dreary—boys taking short vacations from their long-term girl-friends, boys who didn't like girls, boys who needed a place to stay and someone to do the cooking. And then the hurt boys, the ones whose long-term girl-friends had left them, who called their therapists twice a day, who were too depressed to go to class. By this point I hardly need add that I saw nothing inappropriate about any of these choices.

When, at twenty-one, I announced my intention to marry a man I knew only slightly and understood less, dismayed family members and friends ringed around me, trying to make me see how inappropriate the choice was, how poorly we were matched, how little pleasure we took, even then, in each other's company. Their attempts hardened my resolve. I looked into the eyes of my intended and saw a soul misunderstood by the world, whose inability to hold a steady job indicated his need for a supportive wife, and whose vague visions of success I could share without quite having to get into focus.

The marriage lasted seven years—longer than it should have. Even when it finally collapsed, its flimsy walls giving way under disappointment, disillusion, and broken promises on both sides, I still couldn't make sense of the ruin, or understand why it had happened. I couldn't *see*, I wailed to a therapist, week after week.

"If you want to see, you have to look," she told me.

"I do look. But I can't see."

"Then you don't know how to look," she said.

Irritated by the smug shrinkishness of her answer, I said, "Okay. Fine. Tell me how to look."

"This isn't some kind of mystical thing. Just pay attention. Your only problem is that you don't pay attention."

As always when I am handed an accurate piece of information about myself, I was stung. Days had to pass before I calmed down and heard the invitation behind the therapist's words, weeks before I was willing to act on them. Not that I knew how to act. All I knew was that at my perceptions' farthest horizons, a new world was taking shape, still distant and faint, but just, barely, visible.

Five years ago my second husband and I bought a house, the first I've ever owned, and with it came property. The house sits on an ordinary suburban lot; we're not talking about Sissinghurst here. Still, space had to be filled up in gardens and around trees, and I learned, generally by error, about bloom time, soil acidity, shade tolerance, and zone hardiness.

Like most chores, gardening teaches me about myself, and I've learned that I'm never going to be a prize-winning gardener, one whose lilies glisten and whose roses scent the air a block away. At best, I'm a tidy gardener. I make time to stake perennials and deadhead the coreopsis; I struggle to preserve clean edges around the beds.

And I'm a heroic weeder, a merciless one, driven. I sometimes come into department stores with dirt under my fingernails from digging out knotweed from the parking lot planting strips. Many gardening tasks are too heavy for me, or require too delicate a touch, but weeding means the staving off of brute chaos, a task I approach with brio.

A year or so after I started gardening, I visited my mother, who has a garden of her own. Stooping to pluck weeds as we talked, I sought out the infant tufts of Bermuda grass that hadn't yet had a chance to sprawl and colonize. "How can you even *see* those tiny things?" my mother asked, and I was so startled that I paused for a moment, still crouched at plant level.

How *can* I even see those tiny things? I can spot an errant sprig of clover from halfway across the yard but can't make out the face of a good friend five rows down in an auditorium. I can see my gray hairs as if they were outlined in neon but can't read a football scoreboard on TV. The college co-ed who didn't notice trash and graffiti has become a woman who scours every scene, vigilant in her pursuit of jarring notes, infelicitous detail. She has learned to look and to pay attention. But she still can't see the picture itself, or the happy accidents it might contain.

Bad eyes pick out the bad—it makes sense. Put like that, the condition sounds dire, requiring corrective lenses for the brain or soul. But my myopia is physical before anything else; I'm truly unable make out the face of my friend in that auditorium, however much I might want to see her. A hinge exists between the literal and the metaphorical reality of my crummy vision. I can bear in mind that my vision is untrustworthy, but I can't change it.

All of which brings me back to my high-school biology teacher, God bless her, who diagnosed me more accurately than anyone else. I am a person who has trouble seeing enough, or correctly. Knowing this, I must go forth with useful caution, avoiding quick turns and snap decisions.

And, truly, I do all right. I haven't yet stepped off a cliff or driven into a pedestrian, and my judgments in recent years seem little worse than anyone else's. I just have to look, then look again. I have to remember that I'm seeing only part of the picture. I remind myself to allow for my margin of error and then bear in mind that the world is, always, more populous and bright and bountifully landscaped than it appears.

John McPhee

THE SEARCH FOR MARVIN GARDENS

JOHN MCPHEE, born in Princeton, New Jersey, was educated at Princeton and Cambridge. His writing career began at *Time* magazine and led to his long association with *The New Yorker*, where he has been a staff writer since 1965. His books include *A Sense of Where You Are, The Headmaster, Oranges, The Pine Barrens, A Roomful of Hovings and Other Profiles, The Crofter and the Laird, Levels of the Game, Encounters with the Archdruid, The Deltoid Pumpkin Seed, The Curve of Binding Energy, Pieces of the Frame, The Survival of the Bark Canoe, Coming into the Country, Giving Good Weight, Basin and Range, In Suspect Terrain, La Place de la Concorde Suisse, Table of Contents, Rising from the Plains, Heirs of General Practice, The Control of Nature, Looking for a Ship, Assembling California, The Ransom of Russian Art, Irons in the Fire*, and two *John McPhee Reader*s. Both *Encounters with the Archdruid* and *The Curve of Binding Energy* were nominated for National Book Awards in science. McPhee has received numerous awards, including the Award in Literature from the American Academy of Arts and Letters. He lives in Princeton, New Jersey, where he teaches writing at Princeton University.

Go. I roll the dice—a six and a two. Through the air I move my token, the flatiron, to Vermont Avenue, where dog packs range.

The dogs are moving (some are limping) through ruins, rubble, fire damage, open garbage. Doorways are gone. Lath is visible in the crumbling walls of the buildings. The street sparkles with shattered glass. I have never seen, anywhere, so many broken windows. A sign—"Slow, Children at Play"—has been bent backward by an automobile. At the lighthouse, the dogs turn up Pacific and disappear. George Meade, Army engineer, built the lighthouse—brick upon brick, six hundred thousand bricks, to reach up high enough to throw a beam twenty miles over the sea. Meade, seven years later, saved the Union at Gettysburg.

I buy Vermont Avenue for $100. My opponent is a tall, shadowy figure, across from me, but I know him well, and I know his game like a favorite tune. If he can, he will always go for the quick kill. And when it is foolish to go for the quick kill he will be foolish. On the whole, though, he is a master assessor of percentages. It is a mistake to underestimate him. His eleven carries his top hat to St. Charles Place, which he buys for $140.

The sidewalks of St. Charles Place have been cracked to shards by through-growing weeds. There are no buildings. Mansions, hotels once stood here. A few street lamps now drop cones of light on broken glass and vacant space behind a chain-link fence that some great machine has in places bent to the ground. Five plane trees—in full summer leaf, flecking the light—are all that live on St. Charles Place.

Block upon block, gradually, we are cancelling each other out—in the blues, the lavenders, the oranges, the greens. My opponent follows a plan of his own devising. I use the Hornblower & Weeks opening and the Zuricher defense. The first game draws tight, will soon finish. In 1971, a group of people in Racine, Wisconsin, played for seven hundred and sixty-eight hours. A game begun a month later in Danville, California, lasted eight hundred and twenty hours. These are official records, and they stun us. We have been playing for eight minutes. It amazes us that Monopoly is thought of as a long game. It is possible to play to a complete, absolute, and final conclusion in less than fifteen minutes, all within the rules as written. My opponent and I have done so thousands of times. No wonder we are sitting across from each other now in this best-of-seven series for the international singles championship of the world.

On Illinois Avenue, three men lean out from second-story windows. A girl is coming down the street. She wears dungarees and a bright-red shirt, has ample breasts and a Hadendoan Afro, a black halo, two feet in diameter. Ice rattles in the glasses in the hands of the men.

"Hey, sister!"

"Come on up!"

She looks up, looks from one to another to the other, looks them flat in the eye.

"What for?" she says, and she walks on.

I buy Illinois for $240. It solidifies my chances, for I already own Kentucky and Indiana. My opponent pales. If he had landed first on Illinois, the game would have been over then and there, for he has houses built on Boardwalk and Park Place, we share the railroads equally, and we have cancelled each other everywhere else. We never trade.

In 1852, R. B. Osborne, an immigrant Englishman, civil engineer, surveyed the route of a railroad line that would run from Camden to Absecon Island, in New Jersey, traversing the state from the Delaware River to the barrier beaches of the sea. He then sketched in the plan of a "bathing village" that would surround the eastern terminus of the line. His pen flew glibly, framing and naming spacious avenues parallel to the shore—Mediterranean, Baltic, Oriental, Ventnor—and narrower transsecting avenues: North Carolina, Pennsylvania, Vermont, Connecticut, States, Virginia, Tennessee, New York, Kentucky, Indiana, Illinois. The place as a whole had no name, so when he had completed the plan Osborne wrote in large letters over the ocean, "Atlantic City." No one ever challenged the name, or the names of Osborne's streets. Monopoly was invented in the early nineteen-thirties by Charles B. Darrow, but Darrow was only transliterating what Osborne had created. The railroads, crucial to any player, were the making of Atlantic City. After the rails were down, houses and hotels burgeoned from Mediterranean and Baltic to New York and Kentucky. Properties—building lots—sold for as little as six dollars apiece and as much as a thousand dollars. The original investors in the railroads and the real estate called themselves the Camden & Atlantic Land Company. Reverently, I repeat their names: Dwight Bell, William Coffin, John DaCosta, Daniel Deal, William Fleming, Andrew Hay, Joseph Porter, Jonathan Pitney, Samuel Richards—founders, fathers, forerunners, archetypical masters of the quick kill.

My opponent and I are now in a deep situation of classical Monopoly. The torsion is almost perfect—Boardwalk and Park Place versus the brilliant reds. His cash position is weak, though, and if I escape him now he may fade. I land on Luxury Tax, contiguous to but in sanctuary from his power. I have four houses on Indiana. He lands there. He concedes.

Indiana Avenue was the address of the Brighton Hotel, gone now. The Brighton was exclusive—a word that no longer has retail value in the city. If you arrived by automobile and tried to register at the Brighton, you were sent away. Brighton-class people came in private railroad cars. Brighton-class people had other private railroad cars for their horses—dawn rides on the firm sand at water's edge, skirts flying. Colonel Anthony J. Drexel Biddle—the sort of name that would constrict throats in Philadelphia—lived, much of the year, in the Brighton.

Colonel Sanders' fried chicken is on Kentucky Avenue. So is Clifton's Club Harlem, with the Sepia Revue and the Sepia Follies, featuring the Honey Bees, the Fashions, and the Lords.

My opponent and I, many years ago, played 2,428 games of Monopoly in a single season. He was then a recent graduate of the Harvard Law School, and he was working for a downtown firm, looking up law. Two people we knew— one from Chase Manhattan, the other from Morgan, Stanley—tried to get into the game, but after a few rounds we found that they were not in the conversation and we sent them home. Monopoly should always be *mano a mano* anyway. My opponent won 1,199 games, and so did I. Thirty were ties. He was called into the Army, and we stopped just there. Now, in Game 2 of the series, I go immediately to jail, and again to jail while my opponent seines property. He is dumbfoundingly lucky. He wins in twelve minutes.

Visiting hours are daily, eleven to two; Sunday, eleven to one; evenings, six to nine. "NO MINORS, NO FOOD, Immediate Family Only Allowed in Jail." All this above a blue steel door in a blue cement wall in the windowless interior of the basement of the city hall. The desk sergeant sits opposite the door to the jail. In a cigar box in front of him are pills in every color, a banquet of fruit salad an inch and a half deep—leapers, co-pilots, footballs, truck drivers, peanuts, blue angels, yellow jackets, redbirds, rainbows. Near the desk are two soldiers, waiting to go through the blue door. They are about eighteen years old. One of them is trying hard to light a cigarette. His wrists are in steel cuffs. A military policeman waits, too. He is a year or so older than the soldiers, taller, studious in appearance, gentle, fat. On a bench against a wall sits a good-looking girl in slacks. The blue door rattles, swings heavily open. A turnkey stands in the doorway. "Don't you guys kill yourselves back there now," says the sergeant to the soldiers.

"One kid, he overdosed himself about ten and a half hours ago," says the M.P.

The M.P., the soldiers, the turnkey, and the girl on the bench are white. The sergeant is black. "If you take off the handcuffs, take off the belts," says the sergeant to the M.P. "I don't want them hanging themselves back there." The door shuts and its tumblers move. When it opens again, five minutes later, a young white man in sandals and dungarees and a blue polo shirt emerges. His hair is in a ponytail. He has no beard. He grins at the good-looking girl. She rises, joins him. The sergeant hands him a manila envelope. From it he removes his belt and a small notebook. He borrows a pencil, makes an entry in the notebook. He is out of jail, free. What did he do? He offended Atlantic City in some way. He spent a night in the jail. In the nineteen-thirties, men visiting Atlantic City went to jail, directly to jail, did not pass Go, for appearing in topless bathing suits on the beach. A city statute requiring all men to wear full-length bathing suits was not seriously challenged until 1937, and the first year in which a man could legally go bare-chested on the beach was 1940.

Game 3. After seventeen minutes, I am ready to begin construction on over-priced and sluggish Pacific, North Carolina, and Pennsylvania. Nothing else being open, opponent concedes.

The physical profile of streets perpendicular to the shore is something like a playground slide. It begins in the high skyline of Boardwalk hotels, plummets into warrens of "side-avenue" motels, crosses Pacific, slopes through church missions, convalescent homes, burlesque houses, rooming houses, and liquor stores, crosses Atlantic, and runs level through the bombed-out ghetto as far—Baltic, Mediterranean—as the eye can see. North Carolina Avenue, for example, is flanked at its beach end by the Chalfonte and the Haddon Hall (908 rooms, air-conditioned), where, according to one biographer, John Philip Sousa (1854–1932) first played when he was twenty-two, insisting, even then, that everyone call him by his entire name. Behind these big hotels, motels—Barbizon, Catalina—crouch. Between Pacific and Atlantic is an occasional house from 1910—wooden porch, wooden mullions, old yellow paint—and two churches, a package store, a strip show, a dealer in fruits and vegetables. Then, beyond Atlantic Avenue, North Carolina moves on into the vast ghetto, the bulk of the city, and it looks like Metz in 1919, Cologne in 1944. Nothing has actually exploded. It is not bomb damage. It is deep and complex decay. Roofs are off. Bricks are scattered in the street. People sit on porches, six deep, at nine on a Monday morning. When they go off to wait in unemployment lines, they wait sometimes two hours. Between Mediterranean and Baltic runs a chain-link fence, enclosing rubble. A patrol car sits idling by the curb. In the back seat is a German shepherd. A sign on the fence says, "Beware of Bad Dogs."

Mediterranean and Baltic are the principal avenues of the ghetto. Dogs are everywhere. A pack of seven passes me. Block after block, there are three-story brick row houses. Whole segments of them are abandoned, a thousand broken windows. Some parts are intact, occupied. A mattress lies in the street, soaking in a pool of water. Wet stuffing is coming out of the mattress. A postman is having a rye and a beer in the Plantation Bar at nine-fifteen in the morning. I ask him idly if he knows where Marvin Gardens is. He does not. "HOOKED AND NEED HELP? CONTACT N.A.R.C.O." "REVIVAL NOW GOING ON, CONDUCTED BY REVEREND H. HENDERSON OF TEXAS." These are signboards on Mediterranean and Baltic. The second one is upside down and leans against a boarded-up window of the Faith Temple Church of God in Christ. There is an old peeling poster on a warehouse wall showing a figure in an electric chair. "The Black Panther Manifesto" is the title of the poster, and its message is, or was, that "the fascists have already decided in advance to murder Chairman Bobby Seale in the electric chair." I pass an old woman who carries a bucket. She wears blue sneakers, worn through. Her feet spill out. She wears red socks, rolled at the knees. A white handkerchief, spread over her head, is knotted at the corners. Does she know where Marvin Gardens is? "I sure don't know," she says, setting down the bucket. "I sure don't know. I've heard of it somewhere, but I just can't say where." I walk on, through a block of shattered glass. The glass crunches underfoot like coarse sand. I remember when I first came here—a long train ride from Trenton, long ago, games of poker in the train—to play basketball against Atlantic City. We were half black, they were all black. We scored forty points, they scored eighty, or something like it. What I remember most is that they had glass backboards—glittering, pendent, expensive glass backboards, a rarity then in high schools, even in colleges, the only ones we played on all year.

I turn on Pennsylvania, and start back toward the sea. The windows of the Hotel Astoria, on Pennsylvania near Baltic, are boarded up. A sheet of unpainted plywood is the door, and in it is a triangular peephole that now frames an eye. The plywood door opens. A man answers my question. Rooms there are six, seven, and ten dollars a week. I thank him for the information and move on, emerging from the ghetto at the Catholic Daughters of America Women's Guest House, between Atlantic and Pacific. Between Pacific and the Boardwalk are the blinking vacancy signs of the Aristocrat and Colton Manor motels. Pennsylvania terminates at the Sheraton-Seaside—thirty-two dollars a day, ocean corner. I take a walk on the Boardwalk and into the Holiday Inn (twenty-three stories). A guest is registering. "You reserved for Wednesday, and this is Monday," the clerk tells him. "But that's all right. We have *plenty* of rooms." The clerk is very young, female, and has soft brown hair that hangs below her waist. Her superior kicks her.

He is a middle-aged man with red spiderwebs in his face. He is jacketed and tied. He takes her aside. "Don't say 'plenty,'" he says. "Say 'You are fortunate, sir. We have rooms available.'"

The face of the young woman turns sour. "We have all the rooms you need," she says to the customer, and, to her superior, "How's that?"

Game 4. My opponent's luck has become abrasive. He has Boardwalk and Park Place, and has sealed the board.

Darrow was a plumber. He was, specifically, a radiator repairman who lived in Germantown, Pennsylvania. His first Monopoly board was a sheet of linoleum. On it he placed houses and hotels that he had carved from blocks of wood. The game he thus invented was brilliantly conceived, for it was an uncannily exact reflection of the business milieu at large. In its depth, range, and subtlety, in its luck-skill ratio, in its sense of infrastructure and socioeconomic parameters, in its philosophical characteristics, it reached to the profundity of the financial community. It was as scientific as the stock market. It suggested the manner and means through which an underdeveloped world had been developed. It was chess at Wall Street level. "Advance token to the nearest Railroad and pay owner twice the rental to which he is otherwise entitled. If Railroad is unowned, you may buy it from the Bank. Get out of Jail, free. Advance token to nearest utility. If unowned, you may buy it from Bank. If owned, throw dice and pay owner a total ten times the amount thrown. You are assessed for street repairs: $40 per house, $115 per hotel. Pay poor tax of $15. Go to Jail. Go directly to Jail. Do not pass Go. Do not collect $200."

The turnkey opens the blue door. The turnkey is known to the inmates as Sidney K. Above his desk are ten closed-circuit-TV screens—assorted viewpoints of the jail. There are three cellblocks—men, women, juvenile boys. Six days is the average stay. Showers twice a week. The steel doors and the equipment that operates them were made in San Antonio. The prisoners sleep on bunks of butcher block. There are no mattresses. There are three prisoners to a cell. In winter, it is cold in here. Prisoners burn newspapers to keep warm. Cell corners are black with smudge. The jail is three years old. The men's block echoes with chatter. The man in the cell nearest Sidney K. is pacing. His shirt is covered with broad stains of blood. The block for juvenile boys is, by contrast, utterly silent—empty corridor, empty cells. There is only one prisoner. He is small and black and appears to be thirteen. He says he is sixteen and that he has been alone in here for three days.

"Why are you here? What did you do?"

"I hit a jitney driver."

. . .

The series stands at three all. We have split the fifth and sixth games. We are scrambling for property. Around the board we fairly fly. We move so fast because we do our own banking and search our own deeds. My opponent grows tense.

Ventnor Avenue, a street of delicatessens and doctors' offices, is leafy with plane trees and hydrangeas, the city flower. Water Works is on the mainland. The water comes over in submarine pipes. Electric Company gets power from across the state, on the Delaware River, in Deepwater. States Avenue, now a wasteland like St. Charles, once had gardens running down the middle of the street, a horse-drawn trolley, private homes. States Avenue was as exclusive as the Brighton. Only an apartment house, a small motel, and the All Wars Memorial Building—monadnocks spaced widely apart—stand along States Avenue now. Pawnshops, convalescent homes, and the Paradise Soul Saving Station are on Virginia Avenue. The soulsaving station is pink, orange, and yellow. In the windows flanking the door of the Virginia Money Loan Office are Nikons, Polaroids, Yashicas, Sony TVs, Underwood typewriters, Singer sewing machines, and pictures of Christ. On the far side of town, beside a single track and locked up most of the time, is the new railroad station, a small hut made of glazed firebrick, all that is left of the lines that built the city. An authentic phrenologist works on New York Avenue close to Frank's Extra Dry Bar and a church where the sermon today is "Death in the Pot." The church is of pink brick, has blue and amber windows and two red doors. St. James Place, narrow and twisting, is lined with boarding houses that have wooden porches on each of three stories, suggesting a New Orleans made of salt-bleached pine. In a vacant lot on Tennessee is a white Ford station wagon stripped to the chassis. The windows are smashed. A plastic Clorox bottle sits on the driver's seat. The wind has pressed newspaper against the chain-link fence around the lot. Atlantic Avenue, the city's principal thoroughfare, could be seventeen American Main Streets placed end to end—discount vitamins and Vienna Corset shops, movie theatres, shoe stores, and funeral homes. The Boardwalk is made of yellow pine and Douglas fir, soaked in pentachlorophenol. Downbeach, it reaches far beyond the city. Signs everywhere—on windows, lampposts, trash baskets—proclaim "Bienvenue Canadiens!" The salt air is full of Canandian French. In the Claridge Hotel, on Park Place, I ask a clerk if she knows where Marvin Gardens is. She says, "Is it a floral shop?" I ask a cabdriver, parked outside. He says, "Never heard of it." Park Place is one block long, Pacific to Boardwalk. On the roof of the Claridge is the Solarium, the highest point in town—panoramic view of the ocean, the bay, the saltwater ghetto. I look down at the rooftops of the side-avenue motels and into swimming pools. There are hundreds of people around the rooftop pools, sunbathing, reading—many more people than are on the beach. Walls, windows, and a block of sky are all that is visible from these pools—no sand, no sea. The pools are craters, and with the people around them they are counter-sunk into the motels.

The seventh, and final, game is ten minutes old and I have hotels on Oriental, Vermont, and Connecticut. I have Tennessee and St. James. I have North Carolina and Pacific. I have Boardwalk, Atlantic, Ventnor, Illinois, Indiana. My fingers are forming a "V." I have mortgaged most of these properties in order to pay for others, and I have mortgaged the others to pay for the hotels. I have seven dollars. I will pay off the mortgages and build my reserves with income from the three hotels. My cash position may be low, but I feel like a rocket in an underground silo. Meanwhile, if I could just go to jail for a time I could pause there, wait there, until my opponent, in his inescapable rounds, pays the rates of my hotels. Jail, at times, is the strategic place to be. I roll boxcars from the Reading and move the flatiron to Community Chest. "Go to Jail. Go directly to Jail."

The prisoners, of course, have no pens and no pencils. They take paper napkins, roll them tight as crayons, char the ends with matches, and write on the walls. The things they write are not entirely idiomatic; for example, "In God We Trust." All is in carbon. Time is required in the writing. "Only humanity could know of such pain." "God So Loved the World." "There is no greater pain than life itself." In the women's block now, there are six blacks, giggling, and a white asleep in red shoes. She is drunk. The others are pushers, prostitutes, an auto thief, a burglar caught with pistol in purse. A sixteen-year-old accused of murder was in here last week. These words are written on the wall of a now empty cell: "Laying here I see two bunks about six inches thick, not counting the one I'm laying on, which is hard as brick. No cushion for my back. No pillow for my head. Just a couple scratchy blankets which is best to use it's said. I wake up in the morning so shivery and cold, waiting and waiting till I am told the food is coming. It's on its way. It's not worth waiting for, but I eat it anyway. I know one thing when they set me free I'm gonna be good if it kills me."

How many years must a game be played to produce an Anthony J. Drexel Biddle and chestnut geldings on the beach? About half a century was the original answer, from the first railroad to Biddle at his peak. Biddle, at his peak, hit an Atlantic City streetcar conductor with his fist, laid him out with one punch. This increased Biddle's legend. He did not go to jail. While John Philip Sousa led his band along the boardwalk playing "The Stars and Stripes Forever" and Jack Dempsey ran up and down in training for his fight with Gene Tunney, the city crossed the high curve of its parabola. Al Capone held conventions here—upstairs with his sleeves rolled, apportioning among his lieutenant governors the states of the Eastern seaboard. The natural history of an American resort proceeds from Indians to French Canadians via Biddles and Capones. French Canadians, whatever they may be at home, are Visigoths here. Bienvenue Visigoths!

My opponent plods along incredibly well. He has got his fourth railroad, and patiently, unbelievably, he has picked up my potential winners until he has blocked me everywhere but Marvin Gardens. He has avoided, in the fifty-dollar zoning, my increasingly petty hotels. His cash flow swells. His railroads are costing me two hundred dollars a minute. He is building hotels on States, Virginia, and St. Charles. He has temporarily reversed the current. With the yellow monopolies and my blue monopolies, I could probably defeat his lavenders and his railroads. I have Atlantic and Ventnor. I need Marvin Gardens. My only hope is Marvin Gardens.

There is a plaque at Boardwalk and Park Place, and on it in relief is the leonine profile of a man who looks like an officer in a metropolitan bank—"Charles B. Darrow, 1889–1967, inventor of the game of Monopoly." "Darrow," I address him, aloud. "Where is Marvin Gardens?" There is, of course, no answer. Bronze, impassive, Darrow looks south down the Boardwalk. "Mr. Darrow, please, where is Marvin Gardens?" Nothing. Not a sign. He just looks south down the Boardwalk.

My opponent accepts the trophy with his natural ease, and I make, from notes, remarks that are even less graceful than his.

Marvin Gardens is the one color-block Monopoly property that is not in Atlantic City. It is a suburb within a suburb, secluded. It is a planned compound of seventy-two handsome houses set on curvilinear private streets under yews and cedars, poplars and willows. The compound was built around 1920, in Margate, New Jersey, and consists of solid buildings of stucco, brick, and wood, with slate roofs, tile roofs, multi-mullioned porches, Giraldic towers, and Spanish grilles. Marvin Gardens, the ultimate outwash of Monopoly, is a citadel and sanctuary of the middle class. "We're heavily patrolled by police here. We don't take no chances. Me? I'm living here nine years. I paid seventeen thousand dollars and I've been offered thirty. Number one, I don't want to move. Number two, I don't need the money. I have four bedrooms, two and a half baths, front den, back den. No basement. The Atlantic is down there. Six feet down and you float. A lot of people have a hard time finding this place. People that lived in Atlantic City all their life don't know how to find it. They don't know where the hell they're going. They just know it's south, down the Boardwalk."

Brenda Miller

THE DATE

BRENDA MILLER is the author of *Season of the Body*, a finalist for the PEN American Center Book Award in Creative Nonfiction. She has received four Pushcart Prizes, and her essays have appeared in *The Sun, Shenandoah, Fourth Genre, Creative Nonfiction, Brevity, Utne Reader*, and *The Georgia Review*. She coauthored, with Suzanne Paola, the textbook *Tell It Slant: Writing and Shaping Creative Nonfiction*. Her work has also appeared in numerous anthologies and retrospectives devoted to the personal essay, including *The Pushcart Book of Essays*, a selection of the best essays published in the Pushcart Prize anthologies in the last twenty-five years. She is associate professor of English at Western Washington University and serves as editor in chief of *The Bellingham Review*.

> When I return naked to the stone porch,
> there is no one to see me glistening.
> —Linda Gregg

A man I like is coming for dinner tonight. This means I sleep very little, and I wake up in the half-light of dawn, disoriented, wondering where I am. I look at my naked body stretched diagonally across the bed; I look at the untouched breasts, the white belly, and I wonder. I don't know if this man will ever touch me, but I wonder.

I get up, and I make coffee. While I wait for the water to boil I vaguely study the pictures and poems and quotes held in place by magnets on my refrigerator. I haven't really looked at these things in a long time, my gaze usually blinking out as I reach for the refrigerator door. This morning I try to look at these objects clearly, objectively, as if I were a stranger, trying to figure what this man will think of them and so, by extension, what he will make of me.

He'll see pictures of my three nieces, my nephew, my godson. He'll see my six women friends hiking in a slot canyon of the San Rafael swell, straddling the narrow gap with their strong thighs, their muscular arms. He'll see the astrological forecast for Pisces ("There's never been a better moment to turn your paranoia into *pronoia*," it insists), and the Richard Campbell quote which tells me if I'm to live like a hero I must be ready at any moment, "there is no other way." He'll see Rumi: "Let the Beauty we love be what we do. There are hundreds of ways to kneel and kiss the ground." He'll see me kayaking with my friend Kathy in the San Juan Islands, and then, if his gaze moves in a clockwise direction, he'll see me sitting with my parents inside the Oasis Cafe in Salt Lake City. He'll glance at me standing on the estate of Edna St. Vincent Millay, my arms around my fellow artist colonists, grinning as if I were genuinely happy.

Who is this person on my refrigerator door? Every morning, these bits and pixels try to coalesce into a coherent image, a picture for me to navigate by as I move solitary through my morning routine of coffee, juice, cereal, a few moments of blank rumination out the stained-glass kitchen window. I suppose we put these things on our refrigerators as subliminal reminders of self, to fortify those parts of the self most necessary to get us through a day. But I've seen these fragments so often they've come to mean nothing to me; I barely see them, and I know this collage exists only for others, a constructed persona for the few people who make it this far into my house, my kitchen, my life. *Look*, it says, *look how athletic/spiritual/creative/loved I am*. And my impulse, though I stifle it, is to rearrange all these items: delete some, add others, in order to create a picture I think this man will like.

But how could I know? How would I keep from making a mistake? Besides, I tell myself, a mature woman would never perform such a silly and demeaning act. So I turn away from the fridge, leave things the way they are. I drink my coffee and gaze out the window. It's February, and the elm trees are bare, the grass brown under patches of snow. Tomorrow is Valentine's Day, a fact I've been avoiding. I think about the blue tulips I planted in the fall, still hunkered underground, and the thought of them in the darkness, their pale shoots nudging the hard-packed soil, makes me a little afraid.

I'm thirty-eight years old, and I've been alone for almost three years now, have dated no one since leaving my last boyfriend, who is now marrying someone else in California. Sometimes I like to be alone; I come into my bedroom, pleased by the polish of light through the half-closed venetian blinds. I lie on my bed at odd hours of the day with a small lavender pillow over my eyes, like the old woman I think I'm becoming. At times like these, the light in my bedroom seems a human thing, kind and forgiving, and my solitude a position to be envied, guarded even if it means I will remain unpartnered for life.

But this feeling of "unpartneredness" can set me adrift in a way that frightens me. I gaze into my bedroom and see no light, smell no lavender. Instead, the empty room throbs like a reproach—dark, unyielding. I can't move beyond the threshold; I stand there, paralyzed, panic gnawing beneath my skin. I try to breathe deeply, try to remember the smiling self on my refrigerator door, but that person seems all surface, a lie rehearsed so many times it bears faint semblance to truth. I cry as if every love I've known has been false somehow, a trick.

At these times I want only to be part of the coupled universe, attached to some cornice that might solidify my presence in a world which too often renders me invisible. In my parents' house an entire wall is devoted to formal family photographs, and the family groupings fall into neat, symmetrical lines: my older brother, his wife and two children flanking one side of my parents; my younger brother, his wife and two children balance out the other. When I lived with my boyfriend Keith for five years, my parents insisted we take a portrait as well, and we did: me in a green T-shirt and multicolored beads, Keith in jeans and a denim shirt, standing with our arms entwined. So for a while, my photo, and my life, fit neatly into the familial constellation.

Keith and I split up, but the photo remained on the wall a year longer, staring down at me when I came to visit for Hanukkah. "You have to take that down," I finally told them, and they nodded sadly, said "we know." Now a portrait of myself, alone, hangs in its place—a nice photograph, flattering, but it still looks out of line amid the growing and changing families that surround it. Whenever I visit, my young nephew asks me, "Why aren't you married?" and gazes at me with a mixture of wonder and alarm.

A man I like is coming to dinner, and so I get out all my cookbooks and choose and discard recipes as if trying on dresses. I want something savory yet subtle, not too messy, not too garlicky, just in case we kiss. I don't know if we'll kiss, but just in case. I don't know much about this man at all. I know he has two young daughters, an ex-wife; he writes poetry, and teaches a hundred high school students every day. I don't know how old he is, but I suspect he's younger than I am, and so I need to be careful not to reveal too much too fast.

It will be our third date, this dinner. From what I've heard, the third date's either the charm or the poison. I have a friend who in the last five years has never "gotten past the third date." She calls me at 10:30 on a Friday night. "Third date syndrome," she sighs. She describes the sheepish look on her date's face as she returns to the table after a trip to the Ladies' room. She tells me about the "Let's just be friends speech" that by now she has memorized: "You're great. I enjoy your company, but a) I don't have a lot of time right now, b) I'm not looking for a relationship, c) I'm going to be out of town a lot in the next couple of months." My friend sighs and tells me: "I just wish one of them would come right out and say, 'Look, I don't really like you. Let's just forget it.' It would be a relief."

I listen to her stories with a morbid fascination, the way I might listen to a friend's travel adventures: the wrong turn into the Men's bathroom in a bus station in Turkey, the fish heads staring out at you from a plate of stew in Italy. I listen to her stories with both wonder and relief, as if she is traveling in some dangerous land to which I've, thankfully, been denied a visa.

But then we hang up and I turn back to my empty house, the bed whose wide expanse looks accusatory in my bedside light, the pile of books that has grown lopsided and dangerous. I stare at my fish, a fighting fish named Betty, who flares his gills at me and swims in vicious circles around his plastic hexagon, whips his iridescent body back and forth. My friend Connie tells me this behavior indicates love, that my fish is expressing his masculinity so I might want to mate with him. I take this explanation as a compliment.

A man I like is coming to dinner, which means I need to do the laundry and wash the sheets, just in case. I don't know how long it's been since I washed the sheets. There's been no need to keep track. It's just me here after all, and I'm always clean when I go to bed, fresh from the bath; nothing happens in that bed to soil it. When I lived with Seth, or Keith, I washed the sheets every week, but then I had someone in the laundromat to help me fold them when they were dry.

As I dangle the dry sheets over the Laundromat's metal table, I realize that I've never really dated before. I've always been transparent: approach me and you see inside. Touch me and I will open, like a door made of rice paper, light and careless. It's difficult to remember the beginnings of things; was there always this dithering back and forth, this wondering, this not-knowing? On my first date with my first boyfriend, Kevin, we took LSD and sat in a tree for five hours. We were eighteen years old. We communicated telepathically, kept our legs intertwined, sinewy as the branches of a madrone.

Now I have to weigh everything: to call or not to call. To wait three days, five days, six. To ask everyone who might know him for information, to take this information and form a strategic plan. I shave my legs and my underarms, I make an appointment for a haircut, a manicure, all of which will make no difference if nothing is bound to happen. I don't know if anything will happen, but I plan for it anyway. I think about condoms, and blush, and wonder if he will buy any, wonder where they are in the store, how much they cost these days. I wonder about the weight of a man's hands on my shoulders, on my hair. Marilynne Robinson, in *Housekeeping*, writes that "need can blossom into all the compensations it requires. . . . To wish for a hand on one's hair is all but to feel it. So whatever we may lose, very craving gives it back to us again."

I want to believe her, so I crave the hand. I close my eyes and try to picture this man's wrists, to feel the soft underside of his wrist against my mouth. A man's wrists have always been the key to my lust; something rouses me in the power of a hand concentrated in that hinge. And yes, I feel it. Yes, my breath catches in my throat, as if he stroked his thumb against the edge of my jaw. My body's been so long without desire I've almost forgotten what it means to be a sexual being, to feel this quickening in my groin. And it's all I need for now: this moment of desire unencumbered by the complications of fulfillment. Because craving only gives rise to more craving; desire feeds on itself, and cannot be appeased. It is *my* desire after all, *my* longing, more delicious than realization, because over this longing I retain complete control.

I lied. I changed everything on my refrigerator, on my bulletin board, on my mantelpiece. I casually put up a picture, half-hidden, of myself on a good day, my tan legs long, my skin flawless as I pose in front of a blazing maple bush on Mill Creek. I try to suppress an unbidden fantasy: a photograph of me and this man and his two daughters filling in the empty place on my parents' wall. I know this is a dangerous and futile image, but it lodges anyway in my head.

I call my friend every half hour or so with updates on my frame of mind, asking for reassurance that I am not a terrible person. I ask questions as if she were a representative of the tourist board: "On what date does one start holding hands? Kissing? If I ask him out and he says yes, how do I know if he's just being polite?" If there were a phrasebook, I would buy it; a class, I would take it.

Yesterday I discussed this imminent dinner with my hairstylist, Tony, as he bobbed my hair. Tony has a new boyfriend, they're essentially married, but he's had his share of dating and he gives me both sides: "Well on the one hand, you've *got* to play the game," he says, waving the blow dryer away from my hair, "but on the other hand you need to show some honesty, some of the real you. You don't want to scare him off. This is a good lesson for you. Balance."

Tony is my guru. When I came to him the first time, a month after moving to Salt Lake City, I told him my hair was in a transition: not long, not short, just annoying. "You can't think of it," said Tony, cupping my unwanted flip, "as a transition. This is what your hair wants to be right now. There are no transitions. This is *it*, right now."

Yesterday, he cupped my newly coiffed hair in his slender fingers, gazed at me somberly in the mirror. I smiled uncertainly, cocked my head. "Good?" he asked. "Good," I replied. He whisked bits of hair off my shoulders with a stiff brush. "Don't worry," he said. "Play it cool." I nodded, gazing at myself in the mirror which always makes my cheeks look a little too pudgy, my lips too pale. Whenever I look at myself too long, I become unrecognizable, my mouth slightly askew, a mouth I can't imagine kissing or being kissed. I paid Tony, then walked carefully out of the salon, my head level, a cold breeze against my bare neck. In the car, I did not resist the urge to pull down the rear-view mirror and look at myself again. I touched my new hair. I touched those lips, softly, with the very tips of my fingers.

A date. The word still brings up visions of Palm Springs, California and the date orchards on the outskirts of town, the sticky sweetness of the dark fruit. We drove through the orchards on car trips during the summers, my family hot and irritable in the blue station wagon. The stores had giant dates painted on their awnings, and when we stopped, our misery was forgotten. My mother doled the fruit out to us from the front seat, her eyes already half-closed in pleasure. The dates—heavy, cloying, dark as dried blood—always made the roof of my mouth itch, but I ate them anyway because they came in a white box like candy. I ate them because I was told they were precious, the food of the gods.

A man I like is coming to dinner. In two hours. The chicken is marinating, and the house is clean, and if I take a shower now and get dressed I'll have an hour and a half to sit fidgeting on my living room chair, talking to myself and to the fish, whose water, of course, I've changed. "Make a good impression," I plead with him. "Mellow out." He swims back and forth, avoiding my eyes, butting his pinhead against his bowl. I call my friend: Do I light candles? A fire in the fireplace? Do I use the cloth napkins? She says yes to the napkins, nix to everything else. I must walk the line between casual and serious, between cool and aflame. Perfume? Yes. Eyeliner? No. I remake the bed, only now realizing how misshapen my comforter is, all the feathers bunched into one end, so the coverlet lies forlornly against my pillows. It's yellowed at the edges, and my pillowcases are mismatched. Skirts or pants? I ask my friend. Wine or beer? My friend listens, a saint, then finally says: "Why are you asking me? I never get past the third date!" Suddenly I want to get off the phone as quickly as possible.

Handwritten marginal annotations: "Thought process?" (top); "Avoiding the topic?"; "Fighting w/ herself?"; "Did she want to distract herself?"; "Comic relief?"; "Memory why?"

the fruit or the occasion?

. . .

A man I like is coming to dinner. He's late. I sit on the edge of my bed, unwilling to stand near the front windows where he might see me waiting. My stomach hurts, and is not soothed by the smell of tandoori chicken overcooking in the oven. My hands, like a cliché, are sweating. I lie back on the bed, at this point not caring if I mess my hair, or wrinkle my green rayon dress, chosen for its apparent lack of effort. My name is painted in Japanese above my black bureau. Pieces of myself are scattered all around me: a blue kilim from Turkey, a seashell from Whidbey Island, a candlestick from Portugal. Pale light sifts through the venetian blinds at an angle just right for napping or making love. If I had to choose right now, I'd choose a nap, the kind that keeps me hovering on the edge of a consciousness so sweet it would seem foolish to ever resurface. My lavender eye pillow is within reach. My house is so small; how could it possibly accommodate a man, filling my kitchen chairs, peering at my refrigerator door?

On my bedside table is *The Pillow Book* of Sei Shonagan, a Japanese courtesan of the eleventh century, a woman whose career consisted in waiting. In this expectant state, she observed everything around her in great detail, found some of it to her liking and some not. I idly pick the book up and allow it to fall open. I read, "When a woman lives alone, her house should be extremely dilapidated, the mud wall should be falling to pieces, and if there is a pond, it should be overgrown with water plants. It is not essential that the garden be covered with sage-brush; but weeds should be growing through the sand in patches, for this gives the place a poignantly desolate look."

I close the book. I look around this apartment, this house where I live alone. My room feels clean, new, expectant. Now I want nothing more than to stay alone, to hold myself here in a state of controlled desire. But if this man doesn't show, I know my house will quickly settle into the dilapidation Shonagan saw fit for a single woman; the line between repose and chaos is thinner than I once thought. Despite all I've tried to learn in these years alone—about the worthiness of myself as an independent woman, about the intrinsic value of the present moment, about defining myself by my own terms, not by someone else's—despite all this, I know that my well-being this moment depends on a man's hand knocking on my door. *He surprises him*

The doorbell rings, startling me into a sitting position. I clear my throat, which suddenly seems ready to close altogether, to keep me mute and safe. I briefly consider leaving the door unanswered; I imagine my date waiting, looking through the kitchen window, then backing away and into his car, shaking his head, wondering. Perhaps he would think me crazy, or dead. Perhaps he

Tells part like Hemingway
Makes us guess.

would call the police, tell them there's a woman he's worried about, a woman who lives alone. Or, more likely, he would drive to a bar, have a beer, forget about me. The thought of his absence momentarily pleases me, bathes me with relief. But of course I stand up and glance in the mirror, rake my hands through my hair to see it feather into place, and casually walk out to greet this man I like, this man who's coming to dinner.

o The plot is sporadic
↳ Resembles the train of thought
↳ Take away   ↗ See thru her eyes
   - Details are interesting and in depth
o Structure is successful

o Mentions quick little things about her past, but
delves deep into her present.

                    Focus?

o Felt like, kitchen wasn't her, but a reflection of
her life? Her future?

→ Repetition
      ↳ She rambles
              ↳ frazzled.

o Calling her friend that didn't help

o Explored average
      ↳ Creating new lense

Writing Prompt.
comes w/ discussion.
Creative → Narrative
Apparent subject : going on a date.
Deeper subject Body image?, Curating self-image?
What to communicate w/ not yourself, but your space. Who are you?
→ Coming to accept herself.

Apparent subject: Fathers in general
Deeper subject: Relationship w/ his father

Dinty W. Moore

SON OF MR. GREEN JEANS
A Meditation on Fathers

Expectations vs. Reality
of culture

DINTY W. MOORE is the author of the forthcoming memoir *Between Panic & Desire*. His other books include *The Accidental Buddhist, Toothpick Men, The Emperor's Virtual Clothes*, and the writing guide *The Truth of the Matter: Art and Craft in Creative Nonfiction*. He edits *Brevity*, the online journal of concise creative nonfiction, and was once trampled by a retired circus elephant.

ALLEN, TIM

saying alot. Very few words.

Best known as the father on ABC's *Home Improvement* (1991–99), the popular comedian was born Timothy Allen Dick on June 13, 1953. When Allen was eleven-years-old, his father, Gerald Dick, was killed by a drunk driver while driving home from a University of Colorado football game.

BEES

"A man, after impregnating the woman, could drop dead," critic Camille Paglia suggested to Tim Allen in a 1995 interview. "That is how peripheral he is to the whole thing."

"I'm a drone," Allen responded. "Like those bees?"

"You are a drone," Paglia agreed. "That's exactly right."

CARP

After the female Japanese carp gives birth to hundreds of tiny babies, the father carp remains nearby. When he senses approaching danger, he will suck the helpless babies into his mouth and hold them safely there until the coast is clear.

Idealized.
sitcoms & nature

DIVORCE

University of Arizona psychologist Sanford Braver tells the story of a woman who felt threatened by her husband's close bond with their young son. The husband had a flexible work schedule, but the wife did not, so the boy spent the bulk of his time with the father.

The mother became so jealous of the tight father-son relationship that she eventually filed for divorce and successfully fought for sole custody. The result was that instead of being in the care of his father while the mother worked, the boy was now left in day care.

EMPEROR PENGUINS

Once an emperor penguin male has completed the act of mating, he remains by the female's side for the next month to determine if he is indeed about to become a father. When he sees a single greenish white egg emerge from his mate's egg pouch, he begins to sing.

Scientists have characterized his song as "ecstatic."

FATHER KNOWS BEST

In 1949, Robert Young began *Father Knows Best* as a radio show. Young played Jim Anderson, an average father in an average family. The show later moved to television, where it was a substantial hit, but Young's successful life ended in a tragedy of alcohol and depression.

In January 1991, at age eighty-three, Young attempted suicide by running a hose from his car's exhaust pipe to the interior of the vehicle. The attempt failed because the battery was dead and the car wouldn't start.

GREEN GENES

In Dublin, Ireland, a team of geneticists has been conducting a study to determine the origins of the Irish people. By analyzing segments of DNA from residents across different parts of the Irish countryside, then comparing this DNA with corresponding DNA segments from people elsewhere in Europe, the investigators hope to determine the derivation of Ireland's true forefathers.

HUGH BEAUMONT

The actor who portrayed the benevolent father on the popular TV show *Leave It to Beaver* was a Methodist minister. Tony Dow, who played older brother Wally, reports that Beaumont didn't care much for television and actually hated kids. "Hugh wanted out of the show after the second season," Dow told the *Toronto Sun*. "He thought he should be doing films and things."

Relationships w/ his father

INHERITANCE

My own Irish forefather was a newspaperman, owned a popular nightclub, ran for mayor, and smuggled rum in a speedboat during Prohibition. He smoked, drank, ate nothing but red meat, and died of a heart attack in 1938.

His one son—my father—was only a teenager when his father died. I never learned more than the barest details about my grandfather from my father, despite my persistent questions. Other relatives tell me that the relationship had been strained.

My father was a skinny, eager to please little boy, battered by allergies, and not the tough guy his father had apparently wanted. My dad lost his mother at age three and later developed a severe stuttering problem, perhaps as a result of his father's sharp disapproval. My father's adult vocabulary was outstanding, due to his need for alternate words when faltering over hard consonants like *B* or *D*.

The stuttering grew worse over the years, with one noteworthy exception: after downing a few shots of Canadian whiskey, my father could muster a stunning, honey-rich Irish baritone. His impromptu vocal performances became legend in local taverns, and by the time I entered the scene my father was spending every evening visiting the working-class bars. Most nights he would stumble back drunk around midnight; some nights he was so drunk he would stumble through a neighbor's back door, thinking he was home.

Our phone would ring. "You'd better come get him."

As a boy, I coped with the embarrassment of all this by staying glued to the television—shows like *Father Knows Best* and *Leave It to Beaver* were my favorites. I desperately wanted someone like Hugh Beaumont to be my father, or maybe Robert Young.

Hugh Brannum, though, would have been my absolute first choice. Brannum played Mr. Green Jeans on *Captain Kangaroo*, and I remember him as kind, funny, and extremely reliable.

JAWS

My other hobby, besides watching other families on television, was an aquarium. I loved watching as my tropical fish drifted aimlessly through life, and I loved watching guppy mothers give birth. Unfortunately, guppy fathers, if not moved to a separate tank, will often come along and eat their young.

KITTEN

Kitten, the youngest daughter on *Father Knows Best*, was played by Lauren Chapin.

LAUREN CHAPIN

Chapin's father, we later learned, molested her, and her mother was a severe alcoholic. After *Father Knows Best* ended in 1960, Chapin's life came apart. At age sixteen, she married an auto mechanic. At age eighteen, she became addicted to heroin and began working as a prostitute.

MASCULINITY

Wolf fathers spend the daylight hours away from the home—hunting—but return every evening. The wolf cubs, five or six to a litter, rush out of the den when they hear their father approaching and fling themselves at their dad, leaping up to his face. The father will back up a few feet and disgorge food for the cubs, in small, separate piles.

NATURAL SELECTION

When my wife, Renita, confessed to me her desire to have children, the very first words out of my mouth were "You must be crazy." Convinced that she had just proposed the worst imaginable idea, I stood from my chair, looked straight ahead, and literally marched out of the room.
This was not my best moment.

OZZIE

Oswald Nelson, at thirteen, was the youngest person ever to become an Eagle Scout. Oswald went on to become Ozzie Nelson, the father in *Ozzie and Harriet*. Though the show aired years before the advent of reality television, Harriet was Ozzie's real wife, Ricky and David were his real sons, and eventually Ricky's and David's wives were played by their actual spouses. The current requirements for Eagle Scout make it impossible for anyone to ever beat Ozzie's record.

PENGUINS, AGAIN

The female emperor penguin "catches the egg with her wings before it touches the ice," Jeffrey Moussaieff Masson writes in his book *The Emperor's Embrace*. She then places the newly laid egg on her feet, to keep it from contact with the frozen ground.

At this point, both penguins will sing in unison, staring at the egg. Eventually, the male penguin will use his beak to lift the egg onto the surface of his own feet, where it will remain until hatching.

Not only does the penguin father endure the inconvenience of walking around with an egg balanced on his feet for months on end, but he also will not eat for the duration. *Sacrifices*

QUIZ

1. What is Camille Paglia's view on the need for fathers?
2. Why did Hugh Beaumont hate kids, and what was it he would have rather been doing than counseling The Beav?
3. Who played Mr. Green Jeans on *Captain Kangaroo*?
4. Who would you rather have as your father: Hugh Beaumont, Hugh Brannum, a wolf, or an emperor penguin?

RELIGION

In 1979, Lauren Chapin, the troubled actress who played Kitty, had a religious conversion. She credits her belief in Jesus with saving her life. After *his* television career ended, Methodist Minister Hugh Beaumont became a Christmas tree farmer.

SPUTNIK

On October 4, 1957, *Leave It to Beaver* first aired. On that same day, the Soviet Union launched Sputnik I, the world's first artificial satellite. Sputnik I was about the size of a basketball, took roughly ninety-eight minutes to orbit the Earth, and is often credited with escalating the Cold War and launching the U.S.-Soviet space race.

Later, long after *Leave It to Beaver* ended its network run, a rumor persisted for years that Jerry Mathers, the actor who played Beaver, had died at the hands of the Soviet-backed communists in Vietnam. Actress Shelley Winters went so far as to announce it on the *Tonight Show*. But the rumor was false.

TOILETS

Leave It to Beaver was the first television program to show a toilet.

USING DRUGS

The presence of a supportive father is essential to helping children avoid drug problems, according to the National Center of Addiction and Substance Abuse at Columbia University. Lauren Chapin may be a prime example here. Tim Allen would be one, too. Fourteen years after his father died at the hands of a drunk driver, Allen was arrested for dealing drugs and spent two years in prison.

I also fit the gloomy pattern. Though I have so far managed to avoid my father's relentless problems with alcohol, I wasted about a decade of my life hiding behind marijuana, speed, and various hallucinogens.

VASECTOMIES

I had a vasectomy in 1994. *Wanted to end the cycle of fathers?*

WARD'S FATHER

In an episode titled "Beaver's Freckles," we learn that Ward Cleaver had "a hittin' father," but little else is ever revealed about Ward's fictional family. Despite Wally's constant warning—"Boy, Beav, when Dad finds out, he's gonna clobber ya!"—Ward does not follow his own father's example and never hits his sons on the show. This is an example of xenogenesis.

XENOGENESIS

(zen'*u*-jen'*u*-sis), n. *Biol.* 1. heterogenesis 2. the supposed generation of offspring completely and permanently different from the parent.

Believing in xenogenesis—though at the time I couldn't define it, spell it, *or* pronounce it—I changed my mind about having children about four years after my wife's first suggestion of the idea.

Luckily, this was five years before my vasectomy.

Y-CHROMOSOMES

The Y-chromosome of the father determines a child's gender, and is unique, because its genetic code remains relatively unchanged as it passes from father to son. The DNA in other chromosomes is more likely to get mixed between generations, in a process called recombination. What this means, apparently, is that boys have a higher likelihood of directly inheriting their ancestral traits.

Once my wife convinced me to risk being a father—this took many years and considerable prodding—my Y-chromosomes took the easy way out. Our only child is a daughter.

Maria, so far, has inherited many of what people say are the Moore family's better traits—humor, a facility with words, a stubborn determination.

It is yet to be seen what she will do with the negative ones. =) His?

ZAPPA

Similar to the "Beaver died in Vietnam" rumor of the late 1960s, during the late 1990s, Internet discussion lists were filled with assertions that the actor who played Mr. Green Jeans, Hugh "Lumpy" Brannum, was in fact the father of musician Frank Zappa. Brannum, though, had only one son, and that son was neither Frank Zappa nor this author.

Too bad.

Uses alphabet.
sectioned it into digestable pieces
cant find something working use form.

Kathleen Norris

CELIBATE PASSION

KATHLEEN NORRIS's books of poetry include *Little Girls in Church, How I Came to Drink, My Grandmother's Piano*, and *The Year of Common Things*. Her nonfiction books include *Dakota: A Spiritual Geography, The Cloister Walk, Amazing Grace: A Vocabulary of Faith*, and *The Virgin of Bennington*. A Benedictine oblate since the late sixties, Norris's essays on monasticism have appeared in the *Gettysburg Review, The Hungry Mind Review, The Massachusetts Review*, and the *North Dakota Quarterly*.

> The Cherub was stationed at the gate of the earthly paradise
> with his flaming sword to teach us that no one will enter the
> heavenly paradise who is not pierced with the sword of love.
> —St. Francis de Sales,
> *Treatise on the Love of God*

Celibacy is a field day for ideologues. Conservative Catholics, particularly those who were raised in the pre-Vatican II church, tend to speak of celibacy as if it were an idealized, angelic state, while feminist theologians such as Uta Ranke-Heinemann say, angrily, that "celibate hatred of sex is hatred of women." That celibacy constitutes the hatred of sex seems to be a given in the popular mythology of contemporary America, and we need only look at newspaper accounts of sex abuse by priests to see evidence of celibacy that isn't working. One could well assume that this is celibacy, impure and simple. And this is unfortunate, because celibacy practiced rightly is not at all a hatred of sex; in fact it has the potential to address the sexual idolatry of our culture in a most helpful way.

One benefit of the nearly ten years that I've been a Benedictine oblate has been the development of deep friendships with celibate men and women. This has led me to ponder celibacy that works, practiced by people who are fully aware of themselves as sexual beings but who express their sexuality in a celibate way. That is, they manage to sublimate their sexual energies toward another

396

purpose than sexual intercourse and procreation. Are they perverse, their lives necessarily stunted? Cultural prejudice would say yes, but I have my doubts. I've seen too many wise old monks and nuns whose lengthy formation in celibate practice has allowed them to incarnate hospitality in the deepest sense. In them, the constraints of celibacy have somehow been transformed into an openness that attracts people of all ages, all social classes. They exude a sense of freedom. They also genderbend, at least in my dreams. Sister Jeremy will appear as a warrior on horseback, Father Robert as a wise old woman tending a fire.

The younger celibates of my acquaintance are more edgy. Still contending mightily with what one friend calls "the raging orchestra of my hormones," they are more obviously struggling to contain their desires for intimacy, for physical touch, within the bounds of celibacy. Often they find their loneliness intensified by the incomprehension of others. In a culture that denies the value of their striving, they are made to feel like fools, or worse.

Americans are remarkably tone-deaf when it comes to the expression of sexuality. The sexual formation that many of us receive is like the refrain of an old Fugs' song: "Why do ya like boobs a lot—ya gotta like boobs a lot." The jiggle of tits and ass, penis and pectorals, assault us everywhere—billboards, magazines, television, movies. Orgasm becomes just another goal; we undress for success. It's no wonder that in all this powerful noise, the quiet tones of celibacy are lost; that we have such trouble comprehending what it could mean to dedicate one's sexual drives in such a way that genital activity and procreation are precluded. But celibate people have taught me that celibacy, practiced rightly, does indeed have something valuable to say to the rest of us. Specifically, they have helped me better appreciate both the nature of friendship, and what it means to be married.

They have also helped me recognize that celibacy, like monogamy, is not a matter of the will disdaining and conquering the desires of the flesh but a discipline requiring what many people think of as undesirable, if not impossible— a conscious form of sublimation. Like many people who came into adulthood during the sexually permissive 1960s, I've tended to equate sublimation with repression. But my celibate friends have made me see the light; accepting sublimation as a normal part of adulthood makes me more realistic about human sexual capacities and expression. It helps me to respect the bonds and boundaries of marriage.

Any marriage has times of separation, ill-health, or just plain crankiness, in which sexual intercourse is ill-advised. And it is precisely the skills of celibate friendship—fostering intimacy through letters, conversation, performing mundane tasks together (thus rendering them pleasurable), savoring the holy simplicity of a shared meal, or a walk together at dusk—that can help a marriage survive the rough spots. When you can't make love physically, you figure out other ways to do it.

Monastic people are celibate for a very practical reason: the kind of community life to which they aspire can't be sustained if people are pairing off. Even in churches in which the clergy are often married—Episcopal and Russian Orthodox, for example—their monks and nuns are celibate. And while monastic novices may be carried along for a time on the swells of communal spirit, when that blissful period inevitably comes to an end, the loneliness is profound. One gregarious monk in his early thirties told me that just as he thought he'd settled into the monastery, he woke up in a panic one morning, wondering if he'd wake up lonely every morning for the rest of his life.

Another monk I know regards celibacy as an expression of the essential human loneliness, a perspective that helps him as a hospital chaplain, when he is called upon to minister to the dying. I knew him when he was still resisting his celibate call—it usually came out as anger directed toward his abbot and community, more rarely as misogyny—and I was fascinated to observe the process by which he came to accept the sacrifices that a celibate, monastic life requires. He's easier to be with now; he's a better friend.

This is not irony so much as grace, that in learning to be faithful to his vow of celibacy, the monk developed his talent for relationship. It's a common occurence. I've seen the demands of Benedictine hospitality—that they receive all visitors as Christ—convert shy young men who fear women into monks who can enjoy their company. I've witnessed this process of transformation at work in older monks as well. One friend, who had entered the monastery very young, was, when I first met him, still suffering acutely from an inadequate and harmful sexual formation. Taught that as a monk he should avoid women, he faced a crisis when he encountered women as students and colleagues on a college faculty. Fear of his own sexual desires translated all too easily into misogyny. As a good Benedictine, however, he recognized, prayed over, and explored the possibilities for conversion in this situation. Simply put, he's over it now. I'm one of many women who count him as a dear friend, including several who became serious scholars because he urged them on.

One reason I enjoy celibates is that they tend to value friendship very highly. And my friendships with celibate men, both gay and straight, give me some hope that men and women don't live in alternate universes. In 1990s America, this sometimes feels like a countercultural perspective. Male celibacy, in particular, can become radically countercultural if it is perceived as a rejection of the consumerist model of sexuality, a model that reduces women to the sum of her parts. I have never had a monk friend make an insinuating remark along the lines of, "You have beautiful eyes" (or legs, breasts, knees, elbows, nostrils), the usual catalogue of remarks that women grow accustomed to deflecting. A monk is supposed to give up the idea of possessing anything and, in this culture, that includes women.

Ideally, in giving up the sexual pursuit of women (whether as demons or as idealized vessels of purity), the male celibate learns to relate to them as human beings. That many fail to do so, that the power structures of the Catholic church all but dictate failure in this regard, comes as no surprise. What is a surprise is what happens when it works. Once, after I'd spent a week in a monastery, I boarded a crowded Greyhound bus and took the first available seat. My seat-mate, a man, soon engaged me in conversation, and it took me a while to realize that he wasn't simply being friendly, he was coming on to me. I remember feeling foolish for being so slow to catch on. I remember thinking, "No wonder this guy is acting so strange; he didn't take a vow of celibacy."

When it works, when men have truly given up the idea of possessing women, healing can occur. I once met a woman in a monastery guest house who had come there because she was pulling herself together after being raped, and said she needed to feel safe around men again. I've seen young monks astonish an obese and homely college student by listening to her with as much interest and respect as to her conventionally pretty roommate. On my fortieth birthday, as I happily blew out four candles on a cupcake ("one for each decade," a monk in his twenties cheerfully proclaimed), I realized that I could enjoy growing old with these guys. They were helping me to blow away my fears of middle age.

As celibacy takes hold in a person, over the years, as monastic values supersede the values of the culture outside the monastery, celibates become people who can radically affect those of us out "in the world," if only because they've learned how to listen without possessiveness, without imposing themselves. With someone who is practicing celibacy well, we may sense that we're being listened to in a refreshingly deep way. And this is the purpose of celibacy, not to attain some impossibly cerebral goal mistakenly conceived as "holiness" but to make oneself available to others, body *and* soul. Celibacy, simply put, is a form of ministry—not an achievement one can put on a résumé but a subtle form of service to others. In theological terms, one dedicates one's sexuality to God through Jesus Christ, a concept and a terminology I find extremely hard to grasp. All I can do is to catch a glimpse of people who are doing it, incarnating celibacy in a mysterious, pleasing, and gracious way.

The attractiveness of the celibate is that he or she can make us feel appreciated, enlarged, no matter who we are. I have two nun friends who invariably have that effect on me, whatever the circumstances of our lives on the infrequent occasions when we meet. The thoughtful way in which they converse, listening and responding with complete attention, seems always a marvel. And when I first met a man I'll call Tom, he had much the same effect on me. I wrote in my notebook, "such tenderness in a man . . . and a surprising, gentle, kindly grasp of who I am." (Poets aren't used to being listened to, let alone understood by, theologians.) As our friendship deepened, I found that even brief, casual conversations with him would often inspire me to dive into old, half-finished poems in an attempt to bring them to fruition.

I realized, of course, that I had found a remarkable friend, a Muse. I was also aware that Tom and I were fast approaching the rocky shoals of infatuation, a man and a woman, both decidedly heterosexual, responding to each other in unmistakably sexual ways. We laughed; we had playful conversations as well as serious ones; we took delight in each other. At times we were alarmingly responsive to one another, and it was all too easy to fantasize about expressing that responsiveness in physical ways.

The danger was real, but not insurmountable; I sensed that if our infatuation were to develop into love, that is, to ground itself in grace rather than utility, our respect for each other's commitments—his to celibacy, mine to monogamy— would make the boundaries of behavior very clear. We had few regrets, and yet for both of us there was an underlying sadness, the pain of something incomplete. Suddenly, the difference between celibate friendship and celibate passion had become all too clear to me; at times the pain was excruciating.

Tom and I each faced a crisis the year we met—his mother died, I suffered a disastrous betrayal—and it was the intensity of these unexpected, unwelcome experiences that helped me to understand that in the realm of the sacred, what seems incomplete or unattainable may be abundance, after all. Human relationships are by their nature incomplete—after twenty-one years, my husband remains a mystery to me, and I to him, and that is as it should be. Only hope allows us to know and enjoy the depth of our intimacy.

Appreciating Tom's presence in my life as a miraculous, unmerited gift helped me to place our relationship in its proper, religious context, and also to understand why it was that when I'd seek him out to pray with me, I'd always leave feeling so much better than when I came. This was celibacy at its best, a man's sexual energies so devoted to the care of others that a few words could lift me out of despair, give me the strength to reclaim my life. Abundance indeed. Celibate love was at the heart of it, although I can't fully comprehend the mystery of why this should be so. Celibate passion—elusive, tensile, holy.

Naomi Shihab Nye

THIS IS NOT WHO WE ARE

NAOMI SHIHAB NYE is the author of *Never in a Hurry* (essays); *Habibi* and *Going Going* (novels for teens); *Baby Radar* and *Sitti's Secrets* (picture books); and *You & Yours*, *Fuel*, *Red Suitcase*, *Words Under the Words*, and *Amaze Me* (books of poetry). She has edited seven anthologies of poetry for young readers, including *This Same Sky* and *The Space Between Our Footsteps: Poems and Paintings from the Middle East*.

I'm idling in the drive-through line at a fast-food franchise in Texas, the kind of place I usually avoid, because my hungry teenager needs a hamburger, when a curling strand of delicate violin rises from National Public Radio. I know immediately it's Simon Shaheen, the Arab-American virtuoso violinist, an elegant man who wears starched white shirts and black suits and plays like an angel.

A calm washes over me that I haven't felt in days. The commentator says his name. I raise the volume; our car fills up with grace. I place my head on the steering wheel, tears clouding my eyes.

"Mom! Are you all right? You are *so weird*!"

No. I am simply an Arab American in deep need of cultural uplift to balance the ugliness that has cast a deep shadow over our days.

Play Ali Jihad Racy, Um Kalthoum, Marcel Khalife, Hamza El Din, Matoub Lounes . . . any melodious Middle Eastern music to counteract the terrible sorrow of this time! With so many precious people and lands grieving and no way that we, simple citizens, can solve it or get our full minds around it, what shall we do with our souls?

I grew up in St. Louis in a tiny house full of large music—Mahalia Jackson and Marian Anderson singing majestically on the stereo, my German-American mother fingering "The Lost Chord" on the piano as golden light sank through trees, my Palestinian father trilling in Arabic in the shower each dawn. He held single notes so long we thought he might faint.

The world rang rich counterpoint, mixed melodies, fragrances, textures:

401

Not perfect linear narrative. *Don't time jump.*

crushed mint and garlic in the kitchen, cardamom brewing in the coffee, fabulously embroidered Palestinian pillows plumped on the couch. And always, a thrumming underchord, a hovering, hopeful note: Things had been bad, but they would get better. Our dad had lost his home, but he would make another one. People suffered everywhere, but life would improve.

I refuse to let go that hope.

Because men with hard faces do violent things, because fanaticism seizes and shrinks minds, is no reason for the rest of us to abandon our songs.

Maybe we need to sing them louder.

I hold in my heart so many sorrowing individuals. All families and friends of innocent victims everywhere. All dedicated advocates of peace—keep speaking out wherever you can! All people related to the Middle East who despise bad behavior. All gentle immigrants—how much harder their lives may be now. All citizens who trust the great potential of humanity. All children who want to be happy. All mothers and sisters of violent men.

I wish for world symbols more than SUVs wearing American flags like hula skirts—aren't images that embrace all humanity, all nations and variations, the only thing that will save us now? My friend Milli makes me an exquisite peace bracelet with a miniature globe on it, alongside an ivory dove and beads from many countries. I wear it every day.

A friend I don't know sends an email: "It is our duty to be hopeful."

The words of children console us, not the other way around. During a local poetry workshop with fourth graders, a girl hands me a folded note: "Poetry is eating all my problems." My great-niece stomps her foot. "Adults are forgetting how to have fun!"

I keep thinking, we teach children to use language to solve their disputes. We teach them not to hit and fight and bite. Then look what adults do!

I read about the Seeds of Peace teenagers, Arabs and Israelis who come together in Maine and Jerusalem for deepened dialogue and greater understanding. Their gatherings are not easy. They cry and fear and worry. But they emerge from their sessions changed. Every weapon on earth betrays their efforts, but we need them desperately, to balance the cruel tides.

Condolence cards fan out on my table—kind women I haven't seen in years, writing, "We care." Everyone advises me to stay balanced, practice yoga again, eat well, laugh out loud. They understand that an Arab American might be feeling sicker than most people these difficult days. I grip these lovely messages as if they were prescriptions from the best doctor. My wonderful Japanese-

American friend Margaret in Hawaii is particularly vigilant, writing, "How are you? You are strongly in our thoughts," every single week.

I treasure the welcoming world of women . . . laughing, tending, nourishing, mending, wrapping language around one another like a warm cloak. I try to think of supportive women in my community whom I could surprise—friends who might be able to use a bunch of red ranunculus, a plate of hot gingerbread when it is not even their birthday.

And I keep thinking of the Palestinian grandmother who lived to be 106 years old and didn't read or write, though she always said she could "read the sky" and the tea leaves in the bottoms of everyone's cups. She claimed she didn't want to die "until everyone she didn't like died first." We think she succeeded. The truth was, she was very popular. She liked everybody and they all loved her. The Israeli anthropologist who did an oral history project in her village found me years later to say, "Her warmth changed my life—I consider her my grandmother, too." Even though she had lost her home to Israel in 1948, she said, "I never lost my peace inside."

The only place she ever traveled beyond Palestine was Mecca, by bus. She was proud to be called a hajji, to wear layered white clothes afterward. In her West Bank village, she worked hard to get stains out of everyone's dresses—scrubbing them with a stone over a big tin tub in the courtyard, under her beloved lemon tree. If we told her, "You are very patient," she would joke, "What choice do I have?"

I think she would consider the recent tragedies a terrible stain on her religion. She would weep. She never fussed at my father for not praying five times a day in the traditional way. As she excused herself from our circle for her own prayers, he might say something like, "I'm praying all the time, every minute," and she would grin.

She wanted people to worship in whatever ways they felt comfortable. To respect one another, enjoy one another's company, tell good stories, sit around the fire drinking tea and cracking almonds, and never forget to laugh no matter what terrible things they had been through. Laughter was the power.

What wisdom did she possess that other people can't figure out?

I thought I was done writing about her—for years she starred in my essays and poems. But after September 11, she started poking herself into my dreams again, kindly, sorrowfully: "Say this is not who we are."

Apparently, the entire United States has taken to reading more poetry, which can only be a good sign. Journalists ask, "Why do you suppose people are finding strength in poetry now?" Those of us who have been reading poetry all our lives aren't a bit surprised. As a direct line to human feeling, empathetic experience, genuine language and detail, poetry is everything that headline news is not. It takes us inside situations, helps us imagine life from more than one perspective, honors imagery and metaphor—those great tools of thought—and deepens our confidence in a meaningful world.

I feast on *The Poetry of Arab Women*, a contemporary collection. Deema K. Shehabi wrote, "And where is that mountain / that will fold us inward slowly."

Then I read Coleman Barks's vibrant translations of Rumi, the thirteenth-century Sufi poet who has for the past few years been one of the best-selling poets in the United States. It's rumored he's also the poet most often read aloud on the radio in Afghanistan. Open *The Soul of Rumi* anywhere and find something helpful.

Yes. I breathe deeply, closing my eyes. *And how are we educated human beings so old and so stupid?*

Now that I have tears in my eyes even while making baba ghanouj, our famous eggplant dip, so what? This is my cultural sorrow—not the first ever in the world. Admit it and move on. There is still so much good work to do.

When a gentle man I don't know approaches me in a crowd at a literary conference to say, "I am afraid for my daughter to admit she is half Arab now. What should I do?" I am momentarily tongue-tied.

Later I wish I had told him, "Tell her never deny it. Maybe Arab Americans must say we are twice as sad as other people. But we are still proud, of everything peaceful and beautiful that endures. Then speak of beauty if we can—the beauty of culture, poetry, tradition, memory, family, daily life. Each day, live in honor of the ones who didn't have this luxury or time. We are not alone."

Lia Purpura

AUTOPSY REPORT

LIA PURPURA is the author of the essay collection *On Looking*, nominated for a National Book Critics Circle Award. Essays from that collection were awarded a Pushcart Prize and named Notable Essays in *The Best American Essays 2004* and *2005*. She was awarded an NEA Fellowship in Prose in 2004. *Increase*, her first collection of essays, won the Associated Writing Programs Award in Creative Nonfiction, and her collection of poems, *Stone Sky Lifting*, won the Ohio State University Press/*The Journal* Award. She is the author of *The Brighter the Veil* (winner of the Towson University Prize in Literature/Poetry) and *Poems of Grzegorz Musial: Berliner Tagebuch* and *Taste of Ash*, translated on a Fulbright year in Poland. Her poems and essays have appeared in many magazines, including *Agni, Double Take, Field, Georgia Review, Iowa Review, Orion, Parnassus: Poetry in Review*, and *Ploughshares*. Writer-in-residence at Loyola College in Baltimore, Purpura also teaches at the Rainier Writing Workshop's MFA Program. In 2007, she was Bedell Visiting Writer at the University of Iowa's MFA Program in Nonfiction.

I shall begin with the chests of drowned men, bound with ropes and diesel-slicked. Their ears sludge-filled. Their legs mud-smeared. Asleep belowdecks when a freighter hit and the river rose inside their tug. Their lashes white with river silt.

I shall stand beside sharp pelvic bones, his mod hip-huggers stretched tightly between them. His ribs like steppes, ice shelves, sandstone. His wide-open mouth, where a last breath came out. And there at his feet, the stuff of his death: a near-empty bottle of red cough syrup, yellow-labeled and bagged by police.

I shall touch, while no one is looking, the perfect cornrows, the jacket's wet collar. Soaked black with blood, his stiffening sleeve. And where the bullets passed neatly through, the pattern when his shirt's uncrumpled: four or five holes like ragged stars, or a child's cutout snowflake.

. . .

I shall note the blue earring, a swirled lapis ball in the old, yellowed man's ear, his underwear yellowed, his sunken face taut. The amber and topaz half-empty fifths his landlord found and gave to police.

The twenty-year alcoholic before us, a businessman. All the prescriptions for his hypertension bagged and unused near his black-socked, gold-toed foot. The first button open on his neat white shirt and, I shall confirm, the requisite pen in the pocket neatly clamped in.

"Oh, no," an assistant says. The gospel station's softly on, floaty in its mild joy; it's 7:45 on a rainy Sunday morning and so far I'm the only visitor. Turning briefly to me, he asks "What did you come here for?"
   Then, "Oh, no," he says again, "no more eighteen-year-olds," as he stops at the first body, surveying. Soon, the doctors gather in the hall, finish their dough-nuts, scrub, suit up, begin to read from the police reports, the facts meditative as any rote practice, marking and measuring, preparing ritual ground: *The last person to see him alive was his girlfriend. History: bipolar. Suspected: OD, heroin.* "Something too pure is killing these kids in the county," the doctor says. Of the boy's house, the report states "nice," "middle class," and "the deceased's bedroom is cluttered and dirty." Multiple generations at home. Bottle caps with resin in the trash. And here is a silver soup spoon, blue-black from the flame, encrusted where he cooked the stuff, its graceful stem embellished for nothing. As his body is—beautiful now, for nothing. Is olive-skinned, muscled, nicely propor-tioned. No, I shall say it, *is stunning*, as it turns to marble before us.

We walk back to the first body, unmingling stories. They divide up the bodies. They take the clothes off.

What I thought before seeing it all: *never again will I know the body as I do now.*
   And how, exactly, is that?

Have I thought of the body as sanctuary? A safe, closed place like the ark from which the Torah is taken and laid out on a table to be unscrolled. The two sides parted, opened like, soon I'd know, a rib cage, that a hand with a sharp-tipped pointer might lead the way over, reading toward depth.
   Here's the truth: when I first saw the bodies, I laughed out loud. The laugh burst forth, I could not stop it. *Forgive me*, I thought even then, but the scene, the weird gestures looked entirely staged. Such a response is sure measure of expectations, sure proof I held other images dear: shrouds, perhaps? Veils? A

pall hanging (and though I've never seen a pall, I know it is "cast over," that it shadows all that it touches). Had I assumed crisp sheets drawn up, as in surgery, to section off an operating theater around the site of death? Had somewhere an ideal been lodged: arms at sides in the position of sleep (not so birdlike, jutting, rigid); faces placid (mouths not slack, not black, empty sockets, dry shafts down, archaeological, beckoning, unquiet).

Was I awaiting some sign of passage, the strains of ceremony slapping in its wake? (There was the dime the police searched for, evidence caught in the body bag, bright and mud-smeared, I didn't point out. How meager against the royal cats, well-fed and gold-haltered, the canopic jars holding royal organs, the granaries built for the beautiful pharaohs ... *leave the dime in*, I thought, *that the boatman might row him across*.)

Did I expect, finally, the solemnity of procession? Death gowned and dancing, scythe raised and cape blowing, leading the others, at dusk, over a mountain. In silhouette. Fully cinematic.

And now that I've admitted laughing, I shall admit this, more unexpected still:

When the assistants opened the first body up, what stepped forth, unbidden, was calm.

It was in the assistants' manner of touching their material, their work, that delicacy. The precise, rote gestures feeling space and resistance; adjusting the arc of a blade to the bodies' proportions; cupping and weighing, knowing the slippage, anticipating it; the pressure, the estimate, the sure, careful exchange of hand and knife, the gesture performed so efficiently it looked like habit: easy, inevitable.

The calm came to me while the skin behind the ears and across the base of the skull was cut from its bluish integument. While the scalp was folded up and over the face like a towel, like a compress draped over sore eyes. While the skull was sawed open and a quarter of it lifted away, dust flying, the assistants working without masks. It was calm that came forth while the brain was removed, while the brain, heavy and gray and wet, was filleted with an enormous knife, one hand on top to keep it from jiggling. While the doctor found the ragged lesion in the thalamus and ruled the cause of death hypertension—not alcoholism. Calm, while the brain was slipped into a jar, and the skull refitted, the skin pulled back over to hold it all in again.

I suppose they expected queasiness, fear, short, labored breath—all death's effect. That I'd back away. That after the first, I'd have seen enough. Or the tears that followed fast, after the laughter—for the waste, the fine bones, because these were sons or fathers or would never be fathers—perhaps they expected the tears to return?

But when the bodies were opened up—how can I say this? The opening was familiar. As if I'd known before, this . . . what? Language? Like a dialect spoken only in childhood, for a short time with old-world relatives, and heard again many years later, the gist of it all was sensible. And though I couldn't reply, meanings hung on. A shapeliness of thought was apparent, all infection and lilt and tonal suggestion.

Nothing was too intimate: not the leaves stuck to the crewman's thigh, and higher up, caught in the leg of his underwear; the captain's red long johns and soaked, muddy sock. Their big stomachs and how reliably strong they still looked. Not the diesel fuel slicking their faces, stinking the building, dizzying us, or the pale, wrinkled soles of one's foot, waterlogged. Not the hair braided by some woman's hands, her knuckles hard against his head. The quarter-sized hole in his twisted gray sweat sock, sock he pulled on that morning, or afternoon, or whenever he rose while he lived and dressed without a thought to dressing.

Not the dime the police found and bagged. The buckshot pockmarking his face, his young face, the buccal fat still high, rounded and thick. Nothing was unfamiliar in the too-bright room. Not the men's nakedness, although I have never seen twelve men, naked, before me. Not the method by which the paths of bullets were measured: rods of different lengths pushed through each hole— I had to stop counting there were so many—until one came out the other side.

Not the phrase "exit wound."

And though I'd never seen a bullet hole, of course it would be shallow as the tissue underneath swelled uselessly back together. Of course blood pooled each blue-burnt circumference. *Of course*, I remember thinking.

The purpose the work comprised, the *opening*, was familiar.

It was familiar to see the body opened.

Because in giving birth, I knew the body opened beyond itself?

Because I have been opened, enough times now in surgery, once the whole length of me, and there are hundreds of stitches?

Then, when everything was lifted out—the mass of organs held in the arms, a cornucopia of dripping fruits hoisted to the hanging scale—there was the spine. I could look straight through the empty body, and there, as if buried in wet, red earth, there was the white length of spine. Shields of ribs were sawed out and saved to fix back into place. There were the yellow layers of fat, yellow as a cartoon sun, as sweet cream butter, laid thinly on some, in slabs on others. There were the ice-blue casings of large intestines, the small sloshing stomach, transparent, to be drained. The bladder, hidden, but pulled into view for my sake and cupped in hand like a water balloon. Cracks and snappings. The whisking and shushing of knives over skin, a sound like tearing silk. The snipping. The measuring jars filled with cubed liver. The intercostal blood vessel pulled out like a basted hem. The perforating branches of the internal thoracic artery leaving little holes behind in the muscle like a child's lace-up board. The mitral valves sealing like the lids of ice cream cups. And heavy in the doctor's hand, the spleen, shining, as if pulled from a river.

How easily the body opens.

How with difficulty does the mouth in awe, in praise. For there are words I cannot say.

If looking, though, is a practice, a form of attention paid, which is, for many, the essence of prayer, it is the sole practice I had available to me as a child. By seeing, I called to things, and in turn, things called me, applied me to their sight and we became each as treasure, startling to one another, and rare. Among my parents' art, their work, I moved in fields of color and gesture, cut parts built to make up wholes: mannequins' heads adorned with beads; plaster food, so real, so hard the mashed potatos hurt, and painted sandwiches of sponge grew stiff and scratched. Waxed fibers with feathers twisted into vessels. Lips and mouths and necks of clay were spun and pulled into being in air. With the play of distance, with hues close up, paintings roughened with weaves, softened with water, oil, turpentine, greens, fleshes, families of shapes grew until—better than the bodies of clouds, these forms stayed put—forms spoke, bent toward, nodded so that they came to happen again and again, and I played among them in their sight. And what went on between us was ineffable, untold and this was *the silent part of my life as a child.*

I never thought to say, or call this "God," which even then sounded like shorthand, a refusal to be speechless in the face of occurrences, shapes, gestures happening daily, and daily reconstituting sight. "God," the very attitude of the word—for the lives of words were also palpable to me—was pushy. Impatient. Quantifiable. A call to jettison the issue, the only issue as I understood it: the unknowable certainty of being alive, of being a body untethered from origin, untethered from end, but also so terribly *here.*

And *here*—for we went out to see often—was once constituted by enormous, black, elegiac shapes closed between black gashes or bars. And in the same day, *here* was also curved, colored shapes, airborne and hung from wire, like, ah! muted, lobed organs, so that *here* could be at once a gesture of mourning and a gesture of ease.

I went home and showered, showered and scrubbed in hottest water and threw away the old shoes I'd worn. Later that day, at the grocery store among the other shoppers, I saw all the scalps turned over faces, everyone's face made raw and meatlike, the sleek curves of skulls and bony plates exposed. I saw where to draw the knife down the chest to make the Y that would reveal.

I'd seen how easily we open, our skin not at all the boundary we're convinced of as we bump into each other, excuse ourselves. I'd seen how small a thing gone wrong need be: one sip, just one too many, mere ounces of water in the lungs too much. And the woman in front of me on the checkout line, the pale tendons in her neck, the fibers of muscle wrapping bone below her wool collar, her kidneys backed against my cart—how her spleen, so unexpectedly high in the body, was marked precisely by the orange flower on her sweater! And after seeing the assistants gather the organs up in their arms and arrange them on the aluminum table, after seeing such an abundance in there—here, too, was abundance: pyramids of lemons, red-netted sacks of oranges and papery onions, bananas fitting curve to curve, the dusty skins of grapes, translucent greens, dark roses, heavy purples.

Then, stepping out into the street with my bags, everything fresh and washed in the cold March rain, there was that scent hanging in the air—a fine film of it lingered, and I knew it to be the milky blueness I saw, just hours ago, cut free and swaying, barest breath and tether. That scrim, an opacity, clung to everyone, though they kept walking to cars, lifting and buckling children in. Packing their trunks, returning their carts. Yes, everything looked as it always had—bright and pearly, lush and arterial after the rain.

Richard Rhodes

WATCHING THE ANIMALS

RICHARD RHODES is the author or editor of twenty-two books, including *The Making of the Atomic Bomb*, which won a Pulitzer Prize in nonfiction, a National Book Award, and a National Book Critics Circle Award; *Dark Sun: The Making of the Hydrogen Bomb*, which was one of three finalists for a Pulitzer Prize in history; an investigation of the roots of private violence, *Why They Kill*; a personal memoir, *A Hole in the World*; a biography, *John James Audubon*; and four novels. He has received numerous fellowships for research and writing, including grants from the Ford Foundation, the Guggenheim Foundation, the MacArthur Foundation, and the Alfred P. Sloan Foundation. He has been a host and correspondent for documentaries on public television's *Frontline* and *American Experience* series. An affiliate of the Center for International Security and Cooperation at Stanford University, Rhodes lectures frequently to audiences in the United States and abroad. *The Inland Ground*, in which this essay appeared, was his first book.

> The loves of flint and iron are naturally a little rougher than those of the nightingale and the rose.
> Ralph Waldo Emerson

I remembered today about this country lake in Kansas where I live: that it is artificial, built at the turn of the century, when Upton Sinclair was writing *The Jungle*, as an ice lake. The trains with their loads of fresh meat from the Kansas City stockyards would stop by the Kaw River, across the road, and ice the cars. "You have just dined," Emerson once told what must have been a shocked Victorian audience, "and however scrupulously the slaughterhouse is concealed in the graceful distance of miles, there is complicity, expensive races—race living at the expense of race. . . ."

The I-D Packing Company of Des Moines, Iowa: a small outfit which subcontracts from Armour the production of fresh pork. Can handle about 450

411

pigs an hour. No beef or mutton. No smoked hams or hotdogs. Plain fresh pork. A well-run outfit, with federal inspectors alert on all the lines.

The kind of slaughterhouse Upton Sinclair was talking about doesn't exist around here any more. The vast buildings still stand in Des Moines and Omaha and Kansas City, but most of the operations are gone. The big outfits used to operate on a profit margin of 1.5 percent, which didn't give them much leeway, did it? Now they are defunct, and their buildings, which look like monolithic enlargements of concentration-camp barracks, sit empty, the hundreds of windows broken, dusty, jagged pieces of glass sticking out of the frames as if the animals heard the good news one day and leaped out the nearest exit. Even the stockyards, miles and miles of rotting weathered board pens, floors paved fifty years ago by hand with brick, look empty, though I am told cattle receipts are up compared to what they were a few years back. The new thing is small, specialized, efficient houses out where the cattle are, in Denver, in Phoenix, in Des Moines, especially in Texas, where the weather is more favorable to fattening cattle. In Iowa the cattle waste half their feed just keeping warm in the wintertime. But in Iowa or in Texas, the point of meatpacking today is refrigeration. It's cheaper to ship cold meat than live animals. So the packing plants have gone out to the farms and ranches. Are even beginning to buy up the ranches themselves so that they won't have to depend on the irregularities of farmers and cattlemen who bring their animals in only when the price is up or the ground too wet for plowing. Farmhouses stand empty all over America. Did you know that? The city has already won, never mind how many of our television shows still depict the hardy bucolic rural. I may regret the victory, but that's my lookout. We are an urban race now; and meat is something you buy shrink-wrapped at the supermarket.

There are no stockyards outside the I-D Packing Company. The pigs arrive by trailer truck from Sioux City and other places. Sometimes a farmer brings in two or three in the back of his pickup. Unloads them into the holding pens where they are weighed and inspected, goes into the office, and picks up his check. The men, except on the killing floor, are working on the cooled carcasses of yesterday's kill anyway, so there is time to even out the line. Almost everything in a packing house operates on a chainline, and for maximum profit that line must be full, 450 carcasses an hour at the I-D Packing Company, perhaps 300 heavies if today is heavies day—sows, overgrown hogs. Boars presumably escape the general fate. Their flesh is flavored with rut and tastes the way an unventilated gymnasium locker room smells.

Down goes the tailgate and out come the pigs, enthusiastic after their drive. Pigs are the most intelligent of all farm animals, by actual laboratory test. Learn the fastest, for example, to push a plunger with their foot to earn a reward of pelletized feed. And not as reliable in their instincts. You don't have to call cattle to dinner. They are waiting outside the fence at 4:30 sharp, having arrived as silently as the Vietcong. But perhaps that is pig intelligence too: let you do the work, laze around until the last minute and then charge over and knock you down before you can slop the garbage into the trough. Cattle will stroll one by one into a row of stalls and usually fill them in serial order. Not pigs. They squeal and nip and shove. Each one wants the entire meal for itself. Won't stick together in a herd, either. Shoot out all over the place, and you'd damned better have every gate closed or they'll be in your garden and on your lawn and even in your living room, nodding by the fire.

They talk a lot, to each other, to you if you care to listen. I am not romanticizing pigs. They always scared me a little on the farm, which is probably why I watched them more closely than the other animals. They do talk: low grunts, quick squeals, a kind of burn sometimes, angry shrieks, high screams of fear.

I have great respect for the I-D Packing Company. They do a dirty job and do it as cleanly and humanely as possible, and do it well. They were nice enough to let me in the door, which is more than I can say for the Wilson people in Omaha, where I first tried to arrange a tour. What are you hiding, Wilson people?

Once into the holding pen, the pigs mill around, getting to know each other. The I-D holding pens are among the most modern in the nation, my spokesman told me. Tubular steel painted tinner's red to keep it from rusting. Smooth concrete floors with drains so that the floors can be washed down hygienically after each lot of pigs is run through.

The pigs come out of the first holding pen through a gate that allows only one to pass at a time. Just beside the gate is a wooden door, and behind the door is the first worker the pigs encounter. He has a wooden box beside him filled with metal numbers, the shape of each number picked out with sharp needles. For each lot of pigs he selects a new set of numbers—2473, say—and slots them into a device like a hammer and dips it in non-toxic purple dye. As a pig shoots out of the gate he hits the pig in the side with the numbers, making a tattoo. The pig gives a grunt—it doesn't especially hurt, pigskin is thick, as you know— and moves on to one of several smaller pens where each lot is held until curtain time. The tattoo, my spokesman told me, will stay on the animal through all the killing and cleaning and cutting operations, to the very end. Its purpose is to identify any animal or lot of animals which might be diseased, so that the seller can be informed and the carcasses destroyed. Rather too proud of his tattooing process, I thought, but then, you know the tattoos I am thinking of, the Nazi ones.

It would be more dramatic, make a better story, if the killing came last, but it comes first. We crossed a driveway with more red steel fencing. Lined up behind it, pressing into it because they sensed by now that all was not well with them, were perhaps a hundred pigs. But still curious, watching us go by in our long white canvas coats. Everyone wore those, and hard plastic helmets, white helmets for the workers, yellow helmets for the foremen. I got to be a foreman.

Before they reach their end, the pigs get a shower, a real one. Water sprays from all angles to wash the farm off of them. Then they begin to feel crowded. The pen narrows like a funnel; the drivers behind urge the pigs forward, until one at a time they climb onto a moving ramp. The ramp's sides move as well as its floor. The floor is cleated to give the pigs footing. The sides are made of blocks of wood so that they will not bruise, and they slant inward to wedge the pigs along. Now they scream, never having been on such a ramp, smelling the smells they smell ahead. I do not want to overdramatize, because you have read all this before. But it was a frightening experience, seeing their fear, seeing so many of them go by. It had to remind me of things no one wants to be reminded of any more, all mobs, all death marches, all mass murders and extinctions, the slaughter of the buffalo, the slaughter of the Indian, the Inferno, Judgment Day, complicity, expensive races, race living at the expense of race. That so gentle a religion as Christianity could end up in Judgment Day. That we are the most expensive of races, able in our affluence to hire others of our kind to do this terrible necessary work of killing another race of creatures so that we may feed our oxygen-rich brains. Feed our children, for that matter.

At the top of the ramp, one man. With rubber gloves on, holding two electrodes that looked like enlarged curling irons except that they sported more of those needles. As a pig reached the top, this man jabbed the electrodes into the pig's butt and shoulder, and that was it. No more pain, no more fear, no more mudholes, no more sun in the lazy afternoon. Knocked instantly unconscious, the pig shuddered in a long spasm and fell onto a stainless-steel table a foot below the end of the ramp. Up came another pig, and the same result. And another, and another, 450 an hour, 3,600 a day, the belts returning below to coax another ride.

The pigs are not dead, merely unconscious. The electrodes are humane, my spokesman said, and, relatively speaking, that is true. They used to gas the pigs—put them on a conveyor belt that ran through a room filled with anesthetic gas. That was humane too. The electrodes are more efficient. Anesthesia relaxes the body and loosens the bowels. The gassed pigs must have been a mess. More efficient, then, to put their bodies in spasm.

They drop to the table, and here the endless chain begins. A worker takes the nearest dangling chain by its handle as it passes. The chain is attached at its top to a belt of links, like a large bicycle chain. At the bottom the dangling chain has a metal handle like the handle on a bicycle. The chain runs through the handle and then attaches to the end of the handle, so that by sliding the handle up the chain the worker forms a loop. Into the loop he hooks one of the pig's hind feet. Another worker does the same with the other foot. Each has his own special foot to grab, or the pig would go down the line backwards, which would not be convenient. Once hooked into the line, the pig will stay in place by the force of its own weight.

Now the line ascends, lifting the unconscious animal into the air. The pig proceeds a distance of ten feet to where a worker standing on a platform deftly inserts a butcher knife into its throat. They call it "sticking," which it is. Then all hell breaks loose, if blood merely is hell. It gushes out, at about a forty-five-degree angle downward, thick as a ship's hawser, pouring directly onto the floor. Nothing is so red as blood, an incandescent red and most beautiful. It is the brightest color we drab creatures possess. Down on the floor below, with a wide squeegee on a long handle, a worker spends his eight hours a day squeegeeing that blood, some of it clotted, jellied, now, into an open drain. It is cycled through a series of pipes directly into a dryer, later to be made into blood meal for animal feed.

The line swings around a corner, high above the man with the squeegee, around the drain floor, turns again left at the next corner, and begins to ascend to the floor above. This interval—thirteen seconds, I think my spokesman said, or was it thirty?—so that the carcass may drain completely before further processing. Below the carcass on the ascent is a trough like those lowered from the rear of cement trucks, there to catch the last drainings of blood.

Pigs are not skinned, as cattle are, unless you are after the leather, and we are after the meat. But the hair must be taken off, and it must first be scalded loose. Courteously, the line lowers the carcass into a long trough filled with water heated to 180 degrees. The carcass will float if given a chance, fat being lighter than water, so wooden pushers on crankshafts spaced equally along the scalding tank immerse and roll the carcasses. Near the end of the trough, my spokesman easily pulls out a tuft of hair. The line ascends again, up and away, and the carcass goes into a chamber where revolving brushes as tall as a man whisk away the hair. We pass to the other side of the chamber and find two workers with wide knives scraping off the few patches of hair that remain. The carcasses pass then through great hellish jets of yellowish-blue gas flame to singe the skin and harden it. The last step is polishing: more brushes. Our pig has turned pink and clean as a baby.

One of the small mercies of a slaughterhouse: what begins as a live animal loses all similarity as the processing goes on, until you can actually face the packaged meat at the exit door and admire its obvious flavor.

The polished carcasses swing through a door closed with rubber flaps, and there, dear friends, the action begins. Saws. Long knives. Butcher knives. Draw-knives. Boning knives. Wails from the saws, large and small, that are driven by air like a dentist's drill. Shouts back and forth from the men, jokes, announcements, challenges. The temperature down to fifty degrees, everyone keen. Men start slicing off little pieces of the head right inside the door, each man his special slice, throwing them onto one of several lines that will depart for special bins. A carcass passes me and I see a bare eyeball staring, stripped of its lids. Deft knives drop the head from the neck, leaving it dangling by a two-inch strip of skin. Around a corner, up to a platform, and three men gut the carcasses, great tubs of guts, each man taking the third carcass as it goes by. One of them sees me with my tape recorder and begins shouting at us something like "I am the greatest!" A crazy man, grinning and roaring at us, turning around and slipping in the knife and out comes everything in one great load flopped onto a stainless-steel trough. And here things divide, and so must our attention.

My spokesman is proud of his chitterling machine. "I call them chitlins, but they're really chitterlings." It is the newest addition to his line. A worker separates the intestines from the other internal organs and shoves them down a slide, gray and shiny. Another worker finds one end and feeds it onto a steel tube flushed with water. Others trim off connective tissue, webbings, fat. The intestines skim along the tube into a washing vat, shimmy up to the top of the machine where they are cooled, shimmy back down where they are cooled further, and come out the other side ready for the supermarket. A worker drops them into wax buckets, pops on a lid, and packs them into shipping boxes. That is today's chitlin machine. They used to have to cool the chitlins overnight before they could be packaged. Now five men do the work of sixteen, in less time.

The remaining organs proceed down a waist-high conveyor next to a walkway; on the other side of the same walkway, the emptied carcasses pass; on a line next to the organ line the heads pass. By now all the meat has been trimmed off each head. A worker sockets them one at a time onto a support like a foot-rest in a shoeshine parlor and a wedge neatly splits them in half. Out come the tongues, out come the brains, and at the end of the line, out come the pituitaries, each tiny gland being passed to a government inspector in white pants, white shirt, and a yellow hardhat, who looks it over and drops it into a wax bucket. All these pieces, the brain, the tongue, the oddments of sidemeat off the head and carcass, will be shipped to Armour to become "by-products": hotdogs, baloney, sausage. You are what you eat.

The loudest noise in the room comes from the big air-saw used to split the carcass in half down the backbone, leaving, again, connections at the butt end and between the shoulders. Other workers trim away interior fat, and then the carcasses proceed down their chain to the blast freezer, fifty miles an hour and twenty-five below zero, no place for mere mortals, to be chilled overnight.

Coming out of the freezer in another part of the room is yesterday's kill, cold and solid and smooth. A worker splits apart the two sides; the hams come off and go onto their own line; the shoulders come off and go onto theirs, to be made into picnics, shoulder roasts, trotters. Away goes the valuable loin, trimmed out deftly by a worker with a drawknife. Away goes the bacon. Chunks and strips of fat go off from everywhere in buckets carried on overhead hooks to a grinder that spins out worms of fat and blows them through a tube directly to the lard-rendering vats. Who uses lard anymore, I ask my spokesman. I don't know, he says, I think we export most of it.

At the end of all these lines men package the component parts of pig into waxpaper-lined cartons, load the cartons onto pallets, forklift the pallets into spotless aluminum trailers socketed right into the walls of the building, so that I did not even realize I was inside a truck until my spokesman told me, and off they go to Armour. Processing an animal is exactly the opposite of processing a machine: the machine starts out with components and ends up put together; the animal starts out put together and ends up components. No clearer illustration of the law of entropy has ever been devised.

And that is a tour of a slaughterhouse, as cheerful as I could make it.

But the men there. Half of them blacks, some Mexicans, the rest whites. It gets harder and harder to hire men for this work, even though the pay is good. The production line keeps them hopping; they take their breaks when there is a break in the line, so that the killing floor breaks first, and their break leaves an empty space ten minutes long in the endless chain, which, arriving at the gutting operation, allows the men there to break, and so on. Monday-morning absenteeism is a problem, I was told. Keeping the men under control can be a problem, too, I sensed: when the line broke down briefly during my tour, the men cheered as convicts might at a state license-plate factory when the stamping machine breaks down. It cannot be heartening to kill animals all day.

There is a difference, too, between the men who work with the live animals and hot carcasses and those who cut up the cold meat, a difference I remember from my days of butchering on the farm: the killing unsettles, while the cold cutting is a craft like carpentry or plumbing and offers the satisfactions of craftsmanship. The worker with the electrodes jammed them into the animal with anger and perverse satisfaction, as if he were knocking off the enemy. The worker at the guts acted as if he were wrestling bears. The hot workers talked to themselves, yelled at each other, or else lapsed into that strained silence you meet in deeply angry men; the cold workers said little, but worked with deftness and something like pride. They knew they were good, and they showed off a little, zip zip, as we toured by. They used their hands as if they knew how to handle tools, and they did.

The technology at the I-D Packing Company is humane by present standards, at least so far as the animals are concerned. Where the workers are concerned, I'm not so sure. They looked to be in need of lulling.

Beyond technology is the larger question of attitude. Butchering on the farm when I was a boy had the quality of a ceremony. We would select, say, a steer, and pen it separately overnight. The next morning several of us boys would walk the steer to a large compound and leave it standing near the concrete-floored area where we did the skinning and gutting. Then the farm manager, a man of great kindness and reserve, would take aim with a .22 rifle at the crosspoint of two imaginary lines drawn from the horns to the opposite eyes. And hold his head until the steer was entirely calm, looking at him, a certain shot, because this man did not want to miss, did not want to hurt the animal he was about to kill. And we would stand in a spread-out circle, at a respectful distance, tense with the drama of it, because we didn't want him to miss either.

The shot cracked out, the bullet entered the brain, and the animal instantly collapsed. Then the farm manager handed back the rifle, took a knife, ran forward, and cut into the throat. Then we dragged the steer onto the concrete, hooked its back legs through the Achilles tendons to a cross tree, and laboriously winched it into the air with a differential pulley. Four boys usually did the work, two older, two younger. The younger boys were supposed to be learning this skill, and you held your stomach together as best you could at first while the older boys played little tricks like, when they got there in the skinning, cutting off the pizzle and whipping it around your neck, but even these crudities had their place: they accustomed you to contact with flesh and blood.

And while the older boys did their work of splitting the halves with a backsaw, you got to take the guts, which on the farm we did not save except for the liver, the heart, and the sweetbreads, in a wheelbarrow down to the back lane, where you built, with wood you had probably cut yourself, a most funereal pyre. Doused the guts with gasoline, tossed in a match, and Whoosh! off they went. And back on the concrete, the sawing done, the older boys left the sides hanging overnight in the winter cold to firm the meat for cutting.

By now it was noon, time for lunch, and you went in with a sort of pride that you had done this important work, and there on the table was meat some other boys had killed on some other ceremonial day. It was bloody work, of course, and sometimes I have wondered how adults could ask children to do such work, but it was part of a coherent way of life, as important as plowing or seeding or mowing or baling hay. It had a context, and I was literary enough even then to understand that burning the guts had a sacrificial significance. We could always have limed them and dumped them into a ditch. Lord knows they didn't burn easily.

I never saw our farm manager more upset than the day we were getting ready to butcher five pigs. He shot one through the nose rather than through the brain. It ran screaming around the pen, and he almost cried. It took two more bullets to finish the animal off, and this good man was shaking when he had finished. "I hate that," he said to me. "I hate to have them in pain. Pigs are so damned hard to kill clean."

But we don't farm any more. The coherence is gone. Our loves are no longer the loves of flint and iron, but of the nightingale and the rose, and so we delegate our killing. Our farm manager used to sleep in the sheep barn for nights on end to be sure he was there to help the ewes deliver their lambs, ewes being so absent-minded they sometimes stop labor with the lamb only halfway out. You saw the beginning and the end on the farm, not merely the pre-packaged middle. Flint and iron, friends, flint and iron. And humility, and sorrow that this act of killing must be done, which is why in those days good men bowed their heads before they picked up their forks.

Bill Roorbach

SHITDIGGERS, MUDFLATS, AND THE WORM MEN OF MAINE

BILL ROORBACH is the author of, most recently, *Temple Stream: A Rural Odyssey*, which won the 2006 Maine Literary Prize for nonfiction, the recipient of a Kaplan Foundation Furthermore grant. An NEA fellow and the winner of a 2002 O. Henry Award, Roorbach is the author of a novel, *The Smallest Color*, and a collection of short stories, *Big Bend*, winner of the Flannery O'Connor Award in 2001. His other books include *Into Woods, Summers with Juliet, A Place on Water*, and the bestselling book of instruction, *Writing Life Stories*. His short work has appeared in *Harper's, The Atlantic, The New York Times Magazine, Granta, New York*, and dozens of other magazines and journals, and also has been featured on the NPR program *Selected Shorts*. He has taught at Ohio State, Colby College, and the University of Maine at Farmington, and currently holds the Jenks Chair in Contemporary American Letters at the College of Holy Cross in Worcester, Massachusetts. He lives in Farmington, Maine.

"Hard work," says Dicky Butts, and we haven't even started yet.

"Get wet today," says Truman Lock. He pulls his graying beard, squints out over the bay. The blast of an offshore wind (strong enough to blow the boat and its no-lights trailer halfway into the oncoming lane as we made the drive over) is piling whitecaps, spraying their tops, bowing the trees around us, knocking my hat off my head, giving even the wormers pause.

Dicky says, "No fun today."

Walter—Truman's father—lets a long minute go by, says, "We do get some weather, Down East." He seems to know he's offering a cliché, works the rich inflections of his Maine twang extra hard: there's an observer here, myself, and no one (including me) knows exactly what the observer wants.

The night's rain has stopped and the cold front that caused it is finishing its push.

The dirt parking area at the shore access on Ripley Neck is nearly empty—

420

most of the wormers have decided to let this tide go—too much like March (here toward the last days of June), too wild, too easy to stay in bed. "Not a climber in the lot," Truey says, one of a constant stream of plain observations. It'll take me fifty conversations with twenty worm diggers before I figure out the obvious: a climber is a clammer. He means most of the usual guys aren't here today—clammers, crabbers, inside lobstermen, wormers—not even anybody picking weed. Just two cars in the lot—mature Subarus, both of them, no boat trailers.

We watch the tide. It will be a big one, Truey guesses, with the offshore wind blowing the bay empty. He's sitting at the wheel of his Chevy truck, Dicky at his side. Walter and I stand in the parking lot at their two windows. We all watch the bay. Low water is charted at 7:30 this morning. It's six now. We watch, and watch more. That's what we do, watch. No talking. Down on the mudflats a quarter mile away a couple of men are bent low, visibly chopping at the mud with their worm hoes. "Bloods," Truey says.

"Those boys are bloodwormers," Dicky says, deciding to pull me in a little, help me out here, whatever I'm up to. He's a stocky, good-looking man with a naked lady tattooed on one arm, a faded bird in a flower on the other. At thirty-three, he's the youngest of the team. He has a wide face and ought to look jolly, but he doesn't. Jolly you need to smile. He's taciturn and tough, burned and blown, his skin newly cooked over a deep spring tan, the creases of his neck white. He's got mud smears on the bill of his no-team baseball cap. You think maybe he's a little mean until he speaks and, yes, finally smiles, but it's a warm smile, not jolly at all in the wide face, a good father's smile, and you see how kindly he is, how helpful. This he wants to avoid showing. He pronounces the word *wormers*—names his profession—with softened *r*'s and extra vowels, points out the bent men, says, "Ten cents a worm." Back to taciturn.

Ten chops, ten deep turns of the mud, a pause to pull a worm, ten more chops, drop a worm in the bucket. Ten chops bent over the heavy muck and those guys out there get a dime, a dime a worm, a hundred weary chops to a dollar, a thousand chops for ten bucks, ten thousand chops to make the tide pay.

"Those fellows are Garneys," Walter says. He knows every wormer in Washington County by sight, and probably most in the state. He's been at this forever. He wants me to know that a Garney is any digger from Beals Island, which is just over the bridge from Jonesport, a few miles east. He wants me to know that the Beals Island boys are known for working in bad weather, and for working low tide all the way up to the beach, staying in the mud longer than maybe is good for the worm population. But then, every wormer wants you to know that every other wormer is a fuckhead. I'm thinking of a certain group of

Midcoast boys who told me how dumb and lazy the Down East boys are, including these very boys right here.

"Shitdiggers," Dicky spits. It sounds like genuine animosity, but if I said it I'd probably get a blood rake through the brain.

Truey pulls the muddy brim of his cap, patiently fills me in: "Sandworms, see, are but six cents, but it's faster getting. Those guys out there was here an hour before us. They'll be here an hour longer for their money, and rip the mud right to the weed line."

"It does takes a toll on your back," Walter says dreamily, apropos of nothing in particular.

Oh, fuck. I'm here on a magazine assignment: get to know these guys, these peculiar wormers, these strugglers at the extreme end of our great economy, write a poignant piece about their miserable lives. But they don't seem miserable. Not as miserable as I am, for example, doing a job I'm really anxious about, inside a nascent career I'm really anxious about, a shaky career that has me saying yes to assignments like this, so many cents a word, really not the kind of thing I'm good at. For one thing, I'm feeling horribly guilty, stealing these guys' lives from them, worried sick what they'll think of their portraits when the magazine hits the racks in town. No one likes his own picture.

But here we are, all of us doing our work in this beautiful, dramatic place. Which is their place, one they know intimately, a place they know themselves to belong. They are their own economy, efficient, dependable, always bears, always bulls. Get to know them? They aren't going to let that happen unless I'm willing to work a couple of years alongside them, and probably not then. I've found Truey after an unbelievably long series of phone conversations with mistrustful Yankees, Truey the one wormer in all of Down East Maine who said, sure, sure, come along and worm.

"Bloodworms," Truey sighs, not with malice, exactly, but with the supercilious pride of a specialist: these fellows dig sandworms, and even if maybe they are less hardy, less appealing to fish, less marketable and so less valuable, they're easier to come by. He keeps looking me up and down. I smile too much, smile now.

This is not my first day worming. I had a day up Midcoast with a bunch of mean-spirited mo-fos. Shitdiggers, for sure. The Midcoast boys abused me, rightfully so: what comes to them for talking to me? But more about them soon. Right now I'm Down East, anxious but hopeful. Months have passed since my Midcoast frolic without much progress on my story. My big break is slipping away. Truey and Dicky and Walter are my last chance. And a new strategy is in place: I haven't told them specifically about *Harper's*, only that I'm a professor at the University of Maine at Farmington, doing a kind of study of guys working, and that I'll write about them. All true. They maybe expected a pipe, a tweed jacket, elbow patches, a vaguely British accent. Instead they got me: UMF sweatshirt, long hair, guy basically their age, a classic summer dink and a flat-lander to boot.

Truey looks me over thoroughly, maybe trying to think what will interest me. He nods in the direction of one of the Subarus in the empty parking lot. "That's Porky Bob. He's a climber, most generally, but they just ain't any steamers, not anymore. He'll be digging bloods today."

I'm rumpled and desperately bleary, slept poorly maybe three hours in the Blueberry Motel, the only motel open this time of year anywhere near, lone customer, windy night.

"They would used to get ten bushels," Walter says, "a whole pickup load on a tide. Now you're lucky with a plateful for supper." He looks pained and weary. "It's the pollution. It's the runoff from the blueberry highlands."

This does interest me. I'm nodding my head earnestly.

"Some say sewerage," Truey says.

"No," Walter says. "That's the lie. The clam, he likes the sewage. What he don't like is the sewage treatment."

"Many a wormer was once a climber," Truey says.

The three men leave me out now, rapid shop talk. I hear it the way I hear Spanish: pick out words here and there, get the drift. They're speculating about the worm population at Pigeon Hill, which I know to be a beach up toward Hancock. They're bad-mouthing some climber. They're thinking the weather will clear. They're speculating about the take today. They're talking about ur-chins, near as I can tell, something spirited about sea urchins and the frukking Japanese. Walter would rather eat pussy than that stuff. But Jack Morrison made $2,800 in a day diving for 'em. And Truey's a certified diver. The rest sounds like daydreaming: all they need is scuba, an urchin boat (forty feet would do 'er), hot tanks for divers (the deep water in the Gulf of Maine is brutally cold in every season), some of that stuff is all, and you make $2,800 a day.

Without a word of transition, without a word at all, Truey is pulling his truck around in the ominously empty parking lot, listening all the while to some story Dicky is telling, then backing the Cox trailer smoothly and straight as a new ashen oar down the steep ramp to the bay. Walter plods down behind, thinking of something else, chewing a thumbnail. I march down after him, flopping in my new worming boots (the Down East salesman pronounced this women boots), anxious to be of use. But these aren't vacationers nervous at the winch of their thousand-buck trailer, this is Truey and Dicky knocking a scarred plank of junkyard lumber out from under the motor (a muddy Mercury 200, no messing around, a good old machine much reworked by Truey, who's a local stock car racer, and Dicky, who's his mechanic): knock the plank, unhook the cable, let the boat hit the water, no splash. Now three of us are at the gunwales (I imitate every gesture they make, trying to be useful), waiting for Truey to park his mostly orange truck and return.

Dicky grins at me. "Gonna get wet," he says. He sees my thin sweatshirt and that I don't have a raincoat and yells up to Truey to bring what they got. He's so solicitous I stop worrying about the high wind. I stop thinking about the low-down, bloodworming, shit-digging Midcoast boys who laughed and left me stuck in the mud, laughed derisively and chopped across the mud away from me, giggling like middle-aged and tattooed twelve-year-olds, dunking worms in their buckets, dunking worms. I stop thinking about my deadline, two weeks past, stop worrying that my worming story is going to get killed. (In the end, okay, it did get killed, but me, I've got the experience of worming under my belt, my fat kill fee, and my own bloodworm rake, which will hang forevermore in the shed at my inland house.)

"This weather'll clear by noon," Walter says, watching the sky. He's built small and strong, is always preoccupied, always has a subject in mind and an informed, unexpected opinion ("If them senators up in Washington was all women, we'd have our troubles solved"). He's not only a worm digger but his wife's partner as a minor worm dealer. His own dad (recently dead of diabetes, from which Walter also suffers) was a wormer, too, one of the originals up in Wiscasset with worming legends Bill and Artie Wanser and Frank Hammond—the first guys in the business back when the war was over and life was sweet and anybody could be Ernest Hemingway—go sportfishing in the ocean—anybody anywhere in the world: customers.

Truey returns with an armless orange sweatshirt and a torn yellow slicker for me. "All we have extra," he says, with real concern. He's got muscles and the same gruff demeanor as Dicky, and like Dicky he's warm and helpful and kind, all that just hiding behind a stern self-possession that you might read as distrust. But he's got a certain coldness to him, the bluff chill of the bad father. His cap says MRS. GIANT JIM'S STREET STOCK on it. Mrs. Giant Jim's Pizza, up on Route 1, is one of his racing sponsors. In Mrs. Giant Jim's they've got pictures of Truey in his lemon-yellow number five, holding the checkered flag after big wins at Bangor Speedway, never a smile for the camera. I gratefully put on the partial sweatshirt and ripped slicker and the three wormers look at me a long time the way they've been looking at the tide: not much they can do about either, not much at all. We get in the boat, a twenty-one-foot aluminum camo-painted Ouachita flat-bottom work boat full of worming stuff: four blood hoes, four sandworm hoes, three worm boxes, four buckets, several twisted blue gloves, one faded green one, three life preservers, first aid kit.

We're off. Truey's the helmsman, Dicky beside him, both of them standing. Walter and I are on the middle seat facing forward, taking the spray.

I examine my women boots. Last time out, with the japing Midcoast boys, I wore my flyfishing hip boots, which have thick felt soles for traction on mossy river rocks. The deep tidal mud down by Bar Harbor sucked them off my feet over and over again till they were gone. So now I've got better boots, the real thing, according to Walter (who has explained that they're "Number one in Maine"): tight-ankle LaCrosse hip waders. I've gotten them two sizes small to be sure of their snugness. I wonder if I should have tied strips of inner tube around the arches, as Walter also suggested, but I don't want to look like a total fucking dork. I start to tie and button the interior calf straps (a collar of eyes inside the boot below the knee that you tighten like shoelaces before you pull the thighs up), aware that Walter is too preoccupied to notice what I'm up to.

Dicky is staring. He says, "I myself personally prefer not to use the calf straps."

I say I don't want to get stuck in the mud, tell him the Midcoast story.

He and Truey grin at the picture of me floundering as the Midcoast boys leave me behind, especially the part where my ass is in the mud and I have to let go of my notebook and pen, losing them, then lose the boot. Har har har, then my new friends fall back into their default faces—pretty grim—let me finish tying the calves of my boots.

Dicky says, "If we go in you need to get them boots off pretty fast . . ."

"Ah," Truey says, "we ain't going in."

Walter isn't listening, is looking to where we are going. He points, says, "Some mud showing over there."

Truey says, "Benson Williams."

Dicky says, "Little Fred."

Truey says, "That fellow from Jackman."

These are people who have indeed "gone in." The tone isn't quite elegiac, but before I can ask for elaboration, Walter's telling Truey to slow down. There's a flotilla of lobster buoys, for one thing (which, to be sure, Truey has been missing expertly); for another, these waves will be big trouble if he gets the boat up planing. Truey nods with an irritated patience and you can see Walter has been giving him advice like this for a lifetime. Truey's forty now. His dad is fifty-seven. Truey's name is actually Walter, too—Walter Lock III—but he was born on Harry Truman's birthday.

We are in the estuarine bay of the Harrington River, heading for Foster Island below Ray Point. I've gotten these names off of maps, for in the manner of most people deeply familiar with their surroundings, Walter and Truey and Dicky can't quite remember the names of the islands and spits and necks around us, only that good worming can be found on the flats that will appear here shortly. They venture several guesses but can't agree on the names. Finally Walter says if you were to boat around the island you'd end up at Milbridge, the next town up the coast (up being toward Portland, which is a hundred miles south and west).

We're crashing over waves now. Truey and Dicky crouch a little but stay on their feet in the stern. The old gas tank, less than a quarter full, bounces around back there. Walter kneels on the middle seat beside me. We all look resolutely forward. The spray is ice-cold. I think of hackneyed Maine Coast paintings, proceed to compose one: five stripes of color—the gray plane of clouds, the green of the pines in the shore forest, the naked gray rocks, the brown rockweed exposed by the tide, water the gray of the sky but alive with whitecaps. We're the sole boat today; the scene is dramatic, timeless, lacks color, a Wyeth, which Wyeth I'm not sure.

Our beeline has brought us across Harrington Bay to several hundred yards off Foster Island. Truey lifts the motor and we skim onto the mud. Again we sit and watch. You can see disturbed places in the exposed muck. "That is yesterday," Dicky says. "That is us." The wind is so strong I have to pull my San Francisco Giants cap down to my eyebrows, cock my head. I don't know why San Francisco—it's just a hat, but Dicky looks at the logo all day rather than in my eyes, asks me on the way home if it's a Chinese character on there.

"See them two?" Truey says. He's pointing out men I hadn't noticed, crouched men chopping at the mud much closer to shore. I don't at first see their boat and ask how they got there.

"Canoe," Dicky says.

"Wouldn't be in a canoe today," Walter says. He hops out of the boat, overboard into the mud. From the bow he collects his sandworm hoe (what climbers might call a rake)—five claw-curved steel tines nineteen inches long, these welded onto a bar that is welded in turn onto a post that impales a wooden handle about nine inches long. The angle between handle and hoe is sharp; at work, one's knuckles are just behind the tines. Walter has shaped his handle to fit his stiffened fingers; the carving is artful: skin-smooth, oiled, comfortable. Next he hefts his worm box, a homemade fiberglass case like a carpenter's box mixed with a budget cooler, fitted at top with the wooden handle from a broom. Attached to one end is a big old coffee can—a vessel for bloodworms, which sandwormers view as incidental but which bring ten cents each, it's not like you're going to throw them away. He slides the box along the mud, leans forward, moves fast enough to keep from sinking beyond the point of suction. I study his style. He's a strong old guy, moves with grace through the mud.

"Watch him," Truey says. "He'll dig all around the mussel beds," this with a mix of affectionate pride and irritation at his dad's predictability. And sure enough, Walter is into the edges of the mussel bed, which is slowly coming exposed with the tide. He operates knee-deep in the muck, digging and stepping, moving his worm box along beside him. Each big flip of mud seems to produce a worm. He holds them up one by one for me to see.

"Rattlesnake," Truey says, making fun, since Walter claims the mussel-bed worms are bigger.

"Tinker," Dicky says.

"Shitdigger," Truey taunts, and we all briefly laugh. I miss the switch back to grim, find myself laughing alone.

Walter slogs speedily off across the mud to the next mussel bed. Dicky and Truey and I wait. We wait a little more. Truey points out the bloodwormers again. "Man in the red is the fastest wormer Down East," he says. "You watch him go." It's true, the man is chopping three strokes a second, stepping along the mud, a hundred yards ahead of his partner, hundreds of yards from his canoe.

"That fellow lost his son this spring," Dicky says. "Day pretty well like this."

We watch the man work. He does not straighten periodically as his partner does; he does not rest.

"Six hundred pounds of wrinkles," Truey says. "Boy and his partner. Was he twenty-one yet? Six hundred pounds of wrinkles in the bottom of their canoe. Six hundred pounds."

"Got turned by the wind," Dicky says. His own son is twelve, and for now Dicky gives him half the summer off. "The boy was not a swimmer. Though his partner made it all right."

"They should have went to college," Truey says. He's eyeing me closely, this professor, right here in his worm boat. Dicky, too, more subtly.

This is a test. I don't give a twitch, not a smile. I say, "That's a sad story."

We watch the bloodwormer, watch him digging like hell, plopping worms in his bucket, chopping the mud.

Dicky says, "College is not for everybody."

"True," I say. I'm off the hook.

The wind has picked up. It's singing in my ears, watering my eyes. I'm thinking of the boy sinking in his boots. I ask what wrinkles are, exactly. Truey sighs, twirls his finger to draw the creature in the air, makes me to understand that wrinkles are those little spiral-shelled snails, what I have always called periwinkles. He says, "The Japanese eat 'em. I wouldn't go near 'em." You can't quite tell if he means the snails or the Japanese. His sons are babies, still, two and four, products of his third marriage.

"Nor is worming," Dicky says. Nor is it for everybody, he means.

We watch the sky, watch the tide, sit in the boat in the wind. No warning and the guys are overboard, grabbing their worm boxes and hoes. Truey asks if I'm blooding or sanding. I say sanding—of course—and they give me a hoe and a bucket. I pull my women boots up to my thighs, tie the ties into my belt loops, and step overboard. I sink. I step. I've got the bucket and the hoe. I sink, step, sink, step, suckingly follow the men. Step, sink, looking for the little round holes that signal sandworm mud. When Dicky crouches to the task, I watch him. Strike the tines full depth into the mud (nineteen inches!), two hands to turn the heavy gray stuff, a quick grab to pick out the worms, one or two or three to every dig in this spot. Good mud. Three or four digs, then step.

"The trick is to keep moving," Truey says. The two of them are off, leaving four-foot-wide swaths of turned mud behind them, digging, digging, plucking worms, sliding the worm boxes—lean forward steeply and step—dig right, dig left, dig middle, pluck worms, step.

I use two hands, grunt and turn the mud. My back already hurts. Two worms. I tug on one where it's escaping back into its hole in the mud and it breaks, pull on the other more carefully and it comes free—a foot long, orangey brown, cilia down its length, appearance of a flattened and softened centipede, perhaps a half inch in diameter, diameter turning to width as the worm flattens trying to locomote out of my hand. Dicky has given me his gloves, so I'm not worried about the stingers hidden in the retracted head. I put the worm in my bucket. One. Next chop and I note the tunnels the worms leave—slightly discolored tubes in the mud. The worms can move very quickly into the un-dug, disappear. You chop and grab. You don't wait around. Two. You step. Three. I'm doing fine, not stuck, proud of my new boots. Chop, two hands. The stuff is heavy. I'm glad I'm strong, wish I were stronger, remember how I've bragged to Juliet that I'm in great shape. Four, five, six.

"Those little digs'll hurt your back," Truey advises kindly. He's ten feet ahead of me already.

Dicky has walked to a new spot, far to my right. "Try to make it all one scoop." He shows me: swoop, scoop, plops worms into his bucket.

I make a big dig, do it right, turn a great chunk of mud, watch the hole grow wet, look in there for movement. I pull out an odd, long, flat worm that just keeps coming—three feet long, at a guess.

"Tapeworm," Truey says. He very nearly smiles, because tapeworms are ridiculous, useless.

I dig again, showing Truey every worm I turn, trying to get the sense of an acceptable size. The worms expand in length then quickly retract, so you can't really put it in inches. You just have to know. Truey okays a couple, shrugs at a third. The shrug is as negative as he'll get with me. Next worm is a blood. Truey turns back to his work: the tide is low enough only for two and a half or three hours of digging this far out on the flat—you can't socialize. I examine the bloodworm, which is wholly different from a sandworm. No cilia, for one thing, and it's all pink translucence, smaller than a sand, more substantial than an earthworm, something deeply red beneath the surface of its skin. This one is smallish, not quite six inches, with a thickening at the head end, a bit of flattening at the tail. I roll it in my fingers. Abruptly, the head shoots out, a moist pink cylinder an inch long, ugly and sudden, unbenign, bulging and unfolding till the stingers show, four grasping needles in the circle of the nasty mouth. Walter has told me that if they get you in the webs between your fingers, your whole hand'll blow right up. I haven't been worred till now—how bad could a worm bite be? Bad, is the answer. I let the worm grasp at the air a moment, then throw it in with the sandworms in my bucket—a mistake, as I will discover: the bloods bite the sandworms in half, making them worthless.

Step and dig, dig and step; my legs are growing exhausted, forty feet from the boat. The digging style Truey showed me seems to be saving my back, though. Dig and step. I've lost count of my take, but it looks like a lot in there—a crawling, wriggling, spiraling mass, sunken in the quart of seawater I've added to the mix. There's quite a bit of mud in there too. Incredibly, I don't turn up a single clam. Incredibly, I forget about my assignment. My notebook never comes out of my pocket. I'm worming.

The wind is getting stronger yet, and colder, takes my San Francisco Giants cap. I lunge for it, fall in the mud, get the hat, put it dripping on my head, manage to stand by leaning hard on bucket with one hand, rake with the other. I wish for the sandy flats Walter has told me he used to work with his dad, up past Portland by George Bush's place, all along and up to Kennebunkport. You can't get near there now.

Step and dig. Dig and step. It's getting harder and harder to lift my feet. I keep needing to stand straight, but it's standing that gets you stuck. Suddenly, a mudhole boils in front of me. Before I can react, an eel pops out, leaps from his hole and into my face, struggles away, gets a few feet and pauses, gills gaping. I give a little scream of surprise.

"Oh, yes," Truey calls. He's farther away from me yet.

"Mud eel," Dicky shouts in the wind.

The seagulls descend, laughing. The eel slithers back in my direction.

"He's a meal," Truey shouts. He means the eel, for the seagulls.

I stop and watch the spectacle: seagulls, eel, the wind, the waves away off where the mud stops, the plane of dramatic clouds, the salty and sulfuric smell of the mud, the men working methodically away from me. I'm this close to having some sort of college professor epiphany when I realize I've gazed too long. I'm stuck.

I look back at the boat—it's far. I look at Dicky and Truman and know I've got to get out on my own. I hear in my head the Midcoast boys' derisive laughter. I struggle. My mud muscles—some rare strands in the sides and tops of my thighs—are exhausted, can't do it. I pull with my hands on the lip of my right boot, get it to move a little. I pull on my left, but my foot leaves the boot and won't go back in. I remember Truey's story about Crawford Peacham's moronic son—how the dumb kid got stuck and they had to cut his boots off 'im. How the kid was covered with mud, mud in his nostrils, mud in his mouth, mud halfway up the frukkin' wazoo. I wriggle and pull and both socks are off inside the boots and both boots are stuck and I'm not connected to them except at the calves, where I'm firmly laced. I fall over, go up to my elbows in the mud, then very slowly up to my biceps. Both arms, both legs. Soon it'll be my face. Deadline two weeks gone. I'm sinking.

"He's stuck," Truey calls.

Dicky looks back, and just when you think the laughter should erupt, the two of them are dropping their hoes and coming at me, almost racing. Truey gets there first and without a word pulls my arms out, stands me up, then puts his strong hands under my knees and yanks me free a leg at a time, oblivious of the gazes the bloodwormers downflat turn our way.

Dicky makes a forward-leaning race to the boat, pushes it over the mud in a mighty effort, brings it right up behind me so I can sit on the port gunwale. The two of them inspect me a moment, then go back to work without a tease of any kind. I sit in the boat a long time, getting my socks back on, getting my boots readjusted, resting my thighs and my back, getting the mud off my face. The whole time I keep my eye on a certain small hummock of mussels, watch it closely the way as a stock boy I used to watch the clock at the A&P, watch relieved as the hummock sinks in the returning tide.

"Did he quit?" Truey shouts over the wind.

"I think he quit," Dicky calls back. There's no doubt I better go back to work. I climb out of the boat, dig my way close around it in a big rectangle, afraid to move far from the safety of its gunwales. I chop and step and pluck and pull. It's like digging nickels out of the fetid mud, pennies. It's like freelance writing. Forget it.

Near Ellsworth, back in April, back when the deadline for my article was still months off, back before I'd found Truey and Walter and Dicky by telephone, back when I didn't know how many television stations and local papers and even *Yankee* magazine had done stories on worming using the same Midcoast boys repeatedly, back when my ridiculous plan was to go out on the flats alone, hoping to meet fellow wormers, back then I drove down to a town near Ellsworth that I shall call Wormville with no great prejudice, drove all morning to pop into the Town Hall in this little coastal town—Town Hall being a well-kept colonial-era house—popped in, all fake confidence, all grins and swagger, to ask about a worming license.

"Who're you digging for?" the Wormville town clerk said, all smiles herself. I faltered a little at the unexpected question, said, "Just digging?"

Now the town clerk was all frowns. She listened skeptically to my convoluted explanation of mission (UMF professor, writing about workingmen in Maine, meet the real guys out on the flats), but in the end she had to hand me a license application—all Maine residents are eligible—one form for all of the many Maine coast commercial fisheries.

Later, over a lobster lunch at Ruth and Wimpy's incredible Lobster Shack, I would check off the box for marine worm digging, add my birthdate, height and weight. Later still I'd cheerfully write a check for $43, cheerful because *Harper's* would pay (and pay for my worm rake, and various horrid motels, and maybe a dozen lobsters at Ruth and Wimpy's, at least that, even if the story got killed), cheerfully mail the whole thing off to the Department of Marine Resources in Augusta, which (as I would note with my newly acquired worm digger's churlishness) isn't even on the coast. But right now, having provided me with all I needed to get started, the good town clerk of Wormville walked me to the Town Hall door and pointed across the street to one of the few other commercial buildings in town, a modern one-story affair with a pair of handsomely carved and painted wood signs: the first, GULF OF MAINE BAIT COMPANY; the second, GULF OF MAINE WREATH COMPANY. She said, "Before you go drowning yourself on the flats, you'll want to talk to Nelson Forrest," and was rid of me.

I walked over and was intercepted in the parking lot by Nelson Forrest himself, energetically on his way somewhere else. I rather nervously explained what I was after, using the whole professor bit, interested in the work, etc., still saying nothing about *Harper's*, or any national article. But here, finally, after two weeks of fruitless phone calls looking for sources, looking for reporterly access to the world of worming, I had someone live to talk to. Mr. Forrest seemed preoccupied, even a little annoyed, but once he got me in his office—thin paneling, tidy old desk, real oil paintings (appealingly amateur), smell of the sea, a phone, a fax—he leaned back in his chair, lit a cigarette, became voluble, answering questions I hadn't asked: "State law says the worms must be dug by hand." He's well tanned and much creased, his eyes blue as the sky over Cadillac Mountain on

Mt. Desert Island (pronounced dessert), which is due south, just across French-man Bay. To folks in Wiscasset, Wormville is Down East. To folks Down East, Wormville is Midcoast. Wiscasset might as well be Massachusetts.

Mr. Forrest stares intently at me, talks rapidly, explains the business, answering his own questions: "We pay ten cents a worm for bloods. Six cents for sands. Up in Wiscasset they're paying twelve cents, but they have less shipping cost." The diggers, whom Forrest carefully calls independent contractors, bring the worms to one of ten or fifteen dealers—places like Gulf of Maine Bait—for counting, starting about an hour after low water. "They'll stagger in for hours after that," he says, then corrects himself: "Well, not stagger, exactly." On vinyl-covered tables the men (and a few women) count bloods rapidly into wooden trays of 250, then fill out a card:

250 BLOOD WORMS
dug and counted by:

_____

Forrest also deals sandworms, but far fewer: "I hate sandworms; they're so frigging fragile. They'll die if you look at 'em." He transfers the worms to news-paper-and-seaweed-lined cardboard flats, where they rest in the walk-in cooler to wait for the worm van, a service provided by several independent shippers (Great Northern Seafood, for one example: "Worm Transit, Maine to Mary-land"). Nelson's worms—three thousand to fifteen thousand a day—are driven to Logan airport, and from there flown to points south (Maryland, Virginia, North Carolina), west (California, especially Sacramento), and east (Mediter-ranean France, Spain, and Italy). "It's a unique business. You tell people you sell worms . . . they look at you." The wholesale buyers are either distributors who service bait shops or the captains of fishing charters. The final price out there in the world—some guy fishing for sea bass or spot or weakfish or flounder—is in the range of three to four dollars a dozen. Mr. Forrest nods proudly. "They do catch fish. See, they're two-thirds blood. Maybe it's the scent, we don't know." His competition, in his estimation, isn't other worm dealers, really, but twenty-four other ocean baits including eels, sea clams, herring, and squid. Of these, squid is probably the most effective, and, unlike worms, can be frozen for ship-ment, then frozen again by the fisherman after partial use. "Worms aren't the distributors' favorite," Mr. Forrest says. "They die, they're expensive . . . but they need 'em."

Terrible years, good years, the business seems to go on, though not like the old days. Nelson Forrest, who has never dug worms himself, wriggled into worming back in 1972—boom times. He shakes his head about the terrible years of the late eighties—tiny worms, and not many—won't venture a theory as to where the big ones went, though (like every cycle in business and nature), the sea-worm cycle does have its theorists. Pollution plays a role in many of these visions, overharvesting in others. Global warming gets a nod, and one strident wormer I talked to up near Wiscasset invoked Chernobyl (but oddly not the defunct Yankee nuclear facility, which is right in Wiscasset's backyard). Some don't see doom, particularly, just the well-known fact that sea worms are unpredictable. Some years there are plenty of big ones, the kind the fishermen like, some years there just ain't. Nelson Forrest would like to see some conservation—maybe close the mud in winter, maybe think more about size limits. "It's a constant battle to keep the guys out of the little ones . . . and we don't buy on Sundays." He pauses, considers. "Though that's no conservation measure; the guys just refrigerate Sunday worms, bring 'em in Monday." Then he shakes his head, lights the fifth cigarette of our conversation. "When I started, I worried I'd be out of worms in ten years." He looks at me carefully, to see that I'm not missing the point, shakes his head again. "But we're running out of fish first. The fish are gone. Pollution, commercial overfishing, this frigging economy—they do destroy sportfishing." And where sportfishing goes, the wormers will go.

That afternoon there's a 2:30 tide, and Mr. Forrest sets me up with one of his crews, the group I have been calling the Midcoast boys, these fellows who, I'll later learn, are practically worming poster boys they've been on TV so much. They love nothing more but jazzing a guy with a tie and a microphone. The wormers know something most reporters won't admit: they're getting used. But torturing a reporter for a tide can make up for it, make time fly.

One of the crew, my guide, gets me to follow him in my own vehicle—sixty miles an hour on back roads to one Thompson Island. I watch his head turn at every sight of the water; he's checking the size of the tide, driving off the road. We park on the main drag into Bar Harbor in front of an enormous fence that hides a gargantuan house.

After I've donned my flyfishing boots in the face of my guide's skeptical impatience (but no warnings), he trots me past two No Trespassing signs and through the summer-dink lawn, around a summer-dink gate and past two more summer-dink property signs, then along an old lane through a quiet wood, shore pines and pin oaks, lots of poison ivy. Past the fifth and sixth No Trespassing signs we break into a little meadow that is on a point thrust into the Mount Desert Narrows. Trap Rock is in sight, and Thomas Island. Seals play out there. There's a strong onshore breeze, the sound of waves crashing, white sprays of foam thrown up on rocks out there. It's gorgeous.

In the cover of some scruffy pines and under yet another No Trespassing sign, three grim guys await. My guide offers no introductions. I pull out my little notebook filled with little questions to ask, but every one of them looks and sounds like it was written at four in the morning in the worst motel in Ellsworth.

We all of us stand among boulders and birch trees and watch the tide, which for me means picking out a particular rock and keeping track of how wet it is.

I smile my rube's smile. "So what are your all's names?"

Nothing.

"You. Hi. Where do you live?"

Nada.

"How much can a good wormer expect to make on the average tide?"

Silence.

"Ever get into fights over territory?"

Here we go. They all look at me. My guide says, "Old days you'd have a hell of brawl. Now we see guys from Wiscasset or someplace, we might holler some."

"Tell 'em to go the fuck home," the next guy says, real fury.

My guide says, "Used to be you'd shoot holes in a guy's boat."

Another gently says, "Tires do get slashed. But some years the worms are one place and not another and fellows travel."

"Where're you from?" the go-the-fuck-home guy says. Everyone looks at me closely.

Me, I don't say a thing, just look out at the tide.

"He's from the college," my guide says. "Farmington, up there."

"I thought only queers lived up that way!"

I'm supposed to defend Farmington, I guess. But I don't. What am I going to say? Well, yes, we have some gay citizens, of course, about 10 percent, I believe, something along those lines, same as Wormville, same as anywhere. Nice folks, our queers!

We stand on the rocks. We watch the tide. The breeze itself feels tense, carries drops of rain. Where's the story? I don't say a word. The men around me stiffen.

Shop talk saves the day. My guide says, "She gonna go out?"

The gentle man says, "Somewhat, I think." That onshore wind will keep the tide small.

The angry fellow says, "Probably under eight feet."

My guide: "Shit tide."

The angry fellow: "I'll give you ten bucks you bail out the bay."

They all snigger and have a look at me to see if I believe that's possible. I notice for the first time that the silent man is a young teen. He looks as if he feels sorry for me. I love him for that, gangly kid. He stands half behind the protection of his dad's back (his dad is the gentle one), holding a bloodworm hoe (six tines nine inches long, short wooden handle), dangles it at the end of one limp arm, an empty joint-compound bucket dangles at the end of the other, the tools of the trade looking like mittens someone has pinned to his jacket.

"You like worming?" I ask him inanely.

"I'm just doing it so my dad don't get pissed off when I ask for money."

His dad doesn't laugh, stares the boy down.

Around a corner on the rocky mud toward the mainland a lone figure comes aslogging, a stately, slow march through the muck, his bucket in one hand, hoe in the other. On shore he'd look weary; on firm land he'd look gimpy and stiff; on dry land he'd be another old salt spitting stories; but on the flats there's a grandeur about him. He pauses and looks at the mud, continues on, pauses and looks at the mud, stoops, begins to dig. His style is large, operatic: big strokes, very slowly made. He doesn't seem to be turning up many worms. "He's way inside," the angry man says.

"It's Binky Farmer," my guide says. "He's seventy-seven years old, that one."

"Way inside," the angry one repeats, but no one else seems to want to indict old Binky, whose only pension is a tide a day.

"Shoot him," the angry one says. "I mean it. Shoot him. It's the ethics of the thing."

My guide says, "It's not Binky who should be shot. It's these schoolteachers who come along in summah, trying to strike it rich during their taxpayer vacation."

All the boys turn subtly. Binky's off the spot. I'm back on. They eye me closely.

I pull out my pen, my little notebook, write down chunks of conversation, to remind everyone what I'm here for.

My guide looks on curiously, but no way he'll penetrate my handwriting.

He offers a quote, is visibly pleased when I write it down: "We'll all need boats before long with all these No Trespassing signs."

"Fucking summer dinks," says the angry one. "Just try to keep me off this fucking point!" He swipes his rake at the air. "I been coming out here since I was seven." He swipes the rake in my direction again, for emphasis, ready to pop my summer-dink skull, find the worm within.

We watch the tide. It's going nowhere at all.

Five more wormers come into the meadow. No greetings, just nods, men who've known each other a long time. The new fellows take note of a stranger's presence, remain utterly silent, drift off to watch the tide from their own vantage points around the point. The rest of us watch the bay, watch the sky, watch old Binky as he straightens up, rests; we watch the seagulls, watch the island out there, watch as Binky goes back to work. Suddenly, no word said, they're all rolling up their sleeves. Suddenly, the tide is right. I can't find my indicator rock—suddenly there are a million rocks. The new guys are off and moving through the mud. The father-and-son team hike off across the meadow to the other side of the neck, disappear. I had hoped to work near them, in the warmth of their kindness. My guide and the angry fellow step over the seaweed-covered rocks and into the mud right in front of us. Resolutely I follow, uninvited. It may not be much of a tide, it may not be deep mud, but after a short twenty minutes, I'm stuck good.

The angry guy looks back, laughs, shouts something.

"What?" I shout.

"I said, 'You are a queer!'"

"Leave him for the tide," my guide shouts. The two of them are laughing hard, moving away from me.

"What?" I shout.

"Mud eel bite your cock off!" says the angry guy.

"What?" I shout.

"He won't get but four cents for that worm!"

I'm alone. I struggle, still sinking. I drop my notebook, reach for it, lose my pen. I thrash after the notebook, quickly exhausted, then lose my hat, lose my sunglasses. I don't want to lose my Orvis wading boots, but after a struggle, I do lose them, abandon them there in the mud, socks too. The notebook is the one thing I manage to recover, and with it stuffed in my shirt I crawl and slither and drag myself to a rock near shore, pull myself puffing up onto it, sit heavily, watch the wormers move out and away chopping at the mud, warmed to their work, no thought of me in their heads.

"Fucking queers!" I shout. I'm reaching for an insult they might mind.

But they can't hear me. They're already hundreds of yards away in the wind, which comes at my face.

"Fucking winter dinks!"

They don't even turn their heads.

I drag myself rock to rock through the mud and to shore and slog my way back up the point through the yard of the summer mansion. All the No Trespassing signs have been torn down, torn to bits by those fellows who came after, strewn in bits everywhere along the way as if by some furious wind.

Dicky Butts's wife drives the town school bus, part time. Health insurance? No way. Pension plan? Ha. They live in town, a quiet and genuine Maine place, a working town—no stores, no tourist facilities—just a village made of houses and trailers and shacks and sheds. Dicky's good little house is neatly kept, painted blue, on a small piece of an old family lot. His grandmother lives nearby, and his sister too, and his mom and dad, and his aunts and uncles and cousins and many a good friend. Their propinquity is his security, his insurance, his retirement plan.

Truey's house is on a corner of the property down by the road, next turn up from the worm shed. It's a small place, a ranch house, bedrooms in the basement. In the yard he's got an old army truck rebuilt to serve as a log skidder, huge tires draped with tractor chains—winter work. There are logs everywhere. Some cut, some tree length, all of them a season old, valuably waiting. Beside the skidder is his speedway trailer—high rack of worn racing slicks—leaning into the weather. The car itself, the estimable number five, is in a home-built garage, and in the garage is where you'll find Truey and Dicky most high tides, mired in oil, changing engines, packing bearings, knocking out dents (of which in number five there are always plenty). Behind the garage in tall grass are a couple of car bodies—what's left of wrecks Truman and Dicky have used as parts for the racer. And there's kid stuff for the little boys—plenty of toys, a swing set, a play pool. Truey's wife is a nurse at the hospital in Calais, fifteen miles down Route 1. Her job provides the family with health insurance and a retirement plan. Her job also gives insurance of another kind: proof against bad worming.

Delores and Walter's house is at the top of a long, narrow lwan, a couple of football fields up the hill from the road and the worm shed. It's newish, set back on the hill, modern lines, tall windows, peaked ceiling, furniture-showroom furniture. It's all very tidy, with an entire wall devoted to a wallpaper mountain scene, anything but the ocean.

It's well-known, according to Walter, well-known around the flats Down East, that Delores runs the Walter Lock Jr. Bait Company. He means he's damn proud of her business acumen and not afraid to say so. Delores is tanned and short and built delicately around the ankles and knees, bigger and sturdier on top. She wears large, round eyeglasses, gives an occasional smile, looks closely at you as you speak, her bullshit detector set on stun. Walter says she's tough, she's the one to sell something—sell a car, sell a house, sell the worms ("If these senators up in Washington was just women," he says again, has said it five or six times since I've known him). There's a sign in her handsome handwriting in the worm shed: "No more short counts. There will be no warning." I know it's her handwriting, because she's written me at the university, inviting me to come on back down, see the business end of things. It's her sense that I didn't quite get what I needed from the men, she wrote, in so many words, quite a few words.

And today she's gone out of her way to answer all my questions, even suggesting questions to ask. She knows I want some color for my write-up (she calls it), so she has told me that she and Walter tried a couple of winters in Florida, picking oranges (piecework, like worms), but lately it's been back to year-round Maine. As for Truey, Truey may seem like a tough guy, but Truey is her little love bunny.

While Walter and Truey are out on the flats, she's on the phone and watching the fax—getting orders from distributors and retailers all over, filling them. She shows me how everything works. Charts and graphs and order sheets. The volume of her sales gets translated into limits: if she's got orders for ten thousand bloodworms and five thousand sandworms on a given day, that's as many as she'll buy from her diggers. A five-hundred-worm limit means a digger can make no more than $50 that day, no matter how prolific the mud. Some families, the ones Delores likes, can get around the limits by bringing spouses and sons and daughters into the picture.

In the worming shed—the windowless cinder-block basement of a truck garage (the garage now converted to an apartment—the days when they could afford to run their own trucks are over)—she washes the counting trays, packs the worms. She hasn't stopped moving since I arrived. The worms go in the usual cardboard flats for the distributors, 125 sands or 250 bloods in a bed of seaweed. Also, increasingly, Delores makes a special fisherman's ten-pack for bait shops to sell, her own invention. A little maidenhair seaweed, ten carefully counted worms to a small, clear, plastic bag, a twist tie, then into a partitioned shipping box, cardboard lined with styrofoam: LIVE SEA WORMS. RUSH!

A lot of work, something she didn't have to do in the past.

It's impossible to talk to her when she's counting; she doesn't hear or see, waits till the little bag she's working on is completely and neatly packed. She doesn't move quickly, even though it's familiar work; rather, she's elegant with it, as if she were cooking a fancy French dish. Between ten-packs she gives a small shrug, a smile, talks a snippet of politics, a bit of worm theory, tells a quick story, offers a confession: "Back when we were paying two and three cents a worm I'd kill 'em when they stung me. Now we're paying ten, I just pack the biters in like the rest." She likes her diggers loyal, she says, doesn't appreciate someone who's over limit trying to sell to other dealers, though she'll buy spare worms from almost anybody if she's got the orders.

Delores has two years of college, University of Southern Maine, thirty-some years back, cannot remember what major, did not get the degree. At this, I just shrug. For that, she likes me more. And I like her. She knows exactly who I am. She keeps me at her side, introduces me to everyone as a scientist. I don't correct her, and in some weird way my actual physical stance changes.

The look on my face feels scientific. Even my questions change. I'm a new man. Give me a lab coat. I peer at the worms a whole new way, as if through some delicate instrument. For the first time among wormers I don't feel like an idiot. That's Delores.

In the hours after the tide the wormers come in, quietly, tiredly, make their counts. There's no banter, no conversation, no braggadocio. The diggers just come in. There's Jordon LeMieux, whom Walter has called an ace blood digger. There's Spooky Nick, another ace, and Clarissa Larssen—the best woman wormer in Maine, in Walter's estimation. Squeak Snodgras comes in and counts his worms wordlessly, hands in his count slip, wordlessly leaves. There's a cool-looking teen boy, a hottie—Nike Air sneakers, T-shirt that says SLAM DUNK, inner-city haircut—standing by his long-haired and tattooed dad, and in the counting room at prom time the boy is attentive, engaged, watches carefully as Pop counts his allowance worm by worm into the tray. Another father stands beside his daughter, an athletic and serious young woman of sixteen—very, very pretty—with mud to her eyelashes. They count. No one talks, not even all the young guys—a dozen of them in their twenties (their muddy pants low on their hips, showing the cracks of their fannies: wormer's cleavage). No chatter. No high fives. Nothing but the counting, the exchanging of slips, this scientist watching. There are two guys with ponytails like mine (that is, scraggly), a bunch with tattoos, several apparent body builders, a thin fellow with JESUS LOVES YOU on his sweatshirt. The wormers straggle in for a couple of hours, dumping their worms, counting them fast under fluorescent light, filling out their slips, collecting their cash or watching Delores put their counts in her book for a paycheck at the end of the week. In a couple of months some of the boys will have to start blueberry picking up on the highlands; a few weeks past that some will go off logging. Some have skills like welding for whoever comes needing it; some will clean houses or leave town with construction crews or take temporary work at a mill. In December there's firewood chopping, even knickknack carving, and many an individual scheme. Then the new year: time to start thinking about the mud. Some guys will have to get out there in January—break the ice, dig the worms. Some will luxuriate till February. Some—the diggers with luck, or skills that match this year's needs, or spouses who work good jobs—won't have to go out till March.

My first trip with the Down East boys proved a good one for them, Walter and Dicky both counting 1,500 sands—$90 each, plus enough bloods to carry the take over a hundred dollars for the tide. Truey, always a little more aggressive, got 1,650 sands that day. Dicky was kind enough to count my worms for me, and after culling about 50 (too small, or diseased, or broken by the bloods I'd thrown in with them), my count for the tide was an unspectacular 155 worms: $9.30. The five killer bloods in there brought my payday up to $9.80. I refused the cash, but Delores refused my refusal, and so—after a spot of negotiating, and a suggestion by Dicky—I became a minor sponsor of Truey's big number five, glory of the Bangor Speedway.

Still trying, I make yet another worming trip, drive down from Farmington the night before a tide Truey thinks'll be a good one, eat a diner dinner, stay at the Blueberry Motel. It's a nice late low tide, and I sleep in, eat a big breakfast. Truey broke a camshaft in the race Saturday night and wrecked his engine, so there's extra incentive for a big day for all of us. My boots are tight; I've been out on my own in the mud below Milbridge, practicing. I've bought myself a sandworm hoe. I have my own gloves, a proper shirt. I know the Harrington River mud, now, and the Harrington River mud knows me. I'm ready to leave the ranks of professors, even scientists, ready to move up to shitdigger. The day is auspicious, the parking lot at Ripley Neck entirely full. Walter points out a Garney across the way, hovering in a workboat. "Spyglass," he says. "He'll sit there and wait to see where the real wormers go."

We cross the bay in good weather. The talk is briefly of cranberries. Walter has had a brainstorm: he'll dig a homemade bog in the woods up behind his house, grow cranberries. Dicky and Truey don't have much to say about that, then Truey invokes sea urchins, and they're off on that good subject again. Twenty-eight hundred dollars a day, and you can go all winter. Twenty-eight hundred a day, and you don't have to worry about the worm market drying up, and you don't have to cut wood, or make wreaths, or shovel snow, or work blueberries. You just get in your diving gear, bring up the urchins, get your body heat back in the hot tank on the deck of your boat, dive and dive and dive again, get rich on the Japanese.

"It's a hard winter in this county," as Walter says. Here in June, the Down East boys are already thinking about ice.

That fucking spyglass Garney is going ashore in the neighborhood of some Milbridge boys. The sun is hot. Thunderheads are building up. You think of lightning, then you think of yourself plugged into the mud, the highest thing for hundreds of yards around, a lightning rod. Workboats are tooling every which way, and Truey and Dicky and Walter know everyone. "That fellow there is Minton Frawley. He went out to Arizona one winter and got himself in the movies. Did you see *Stir Crazy*? He's the guy looking up the girl's crotch in that bar scene."

"He's back worming," Dicky says.

"Scared of lightning," Truey says, meaning Freddy. "He'll run at the first boom-boom. Watch him."

"Winter does take a toll," Walter says, drifting on his own raft of thought. When we hit the mud, Walter gets in it, immediately marches to a big mussel flat, and begins to dig its borders. Dicky and Truey and I wait. Like most worm-ers, they like to watch the tide, size it up, have a chat. "Ask your daddy how many orders he's got," Dicky says. "I need some ambition."

He does look tired.

Truey just watches his father at work.

Dicky sizes up the tide, pretends a discouragement that looks real. "I don't think this is going to be a profitable day, Truey."

My deadline is long gone, my story's a kill, but here I am. The guys don't pay much attention to me anymore, negative or positive. I'm up to about forty bucks in Truey's race car. Maybe one Saturday soon I'll go to the races, hang in the pit, a scientist, see, interested in speed. Maybe *Harper's* will like that story!

There's a rumble of thunder not far distant. Truey smiles briefly at Dicky's joking, goes over the gunwales, gets himself ready to worm. Dicky reluctantly follows. I'm so reluctant I just sit in the boat and watch them start. More thun-der.

"There he goes," Truey says. Sure enough, movie star Frawley has turned his boat around and is heading back in.

Truey takes off his shirt, and you have to wonder if his naked-lady tattoo is by the same artist as Dicky's. It's the same woman, same colors, same thick lines. I climb into the mud. Today I plan to up my sponsorship of the glorious num-ber five to serious partnership proportions. Today I want to dig like a Down East boy.

Truey is already at it, working hard.

Dicky can't seem to get started. "Help," he says. A plaintive joke. He doesn't feel like it today. In the end, though, he'll get 1,900 sandworms, 120 bloods: $126, a super tide. Truey will get 2,100 sands, 50 bloods. A money tide, a mon-ster. Walter will do as well as Dicky. I will get 210 sandworms, zero bloods, working as hard as I've ever worked, chopping and stomping and picking legs sore as hell from previous outings, shoulders aching, mind blank, struggling in the mud, turning it, panting, mucking along, pulling worms: $12.60.

Truey hikes off far away across the mud. Later, when the tide comes up, we'll have to go pick him up. Walter is chopping away at some distant mussel mound. Dicky doesn't range too far, gradually gets his rhythm, digs faster and faster, coming into the worms. I never get a rhythm at all, stay close to the boat, trying to get a whole tide in, no breaks, no getting stuck. I know how to walk now, don't pause long enough to sink, but march forward, ever forward, chop left, chop middle, chop right, pulling worms from the mud. To me, they seem scarce today. To me, they seem terribly fragile. I break every third worm, miss a million that zip into their holes before I can get hold. The thunder booms a little closer.

Late in the tide, Dicky starts saying, "Help," again, just kind of saying it out loud every twenty steps or so, groaning comically. He's found some good mud, is plunking worms into his box three and four at a dig. "Help," he moans, kidding around. Then he shouts, "Truey, let's quit." It's an old joke, and from across the flat Truman Lock gives Dicky the finger. Dicky excavates his way through the mud, pulling worms, pulling worms, dunking them in his box, saying, "Help, Truey. Truey, help," a mantra for the dig. Then he bellows, loud as hell across the mud, "Truey, get me outta here," and then he shouts it again.

David Sedaris

REPEAT AFTER ME

DAVID SEDARIS is the author of *Barrel Fever* and *Holidays on Ice*, as well as collections of personal essays, *Naked, Me Talk Pretty One Day*, and *Dress Your Family in Corduroy and Denim*. His essays appear regularly in *Esquire* and *The New Yorker*. Sedaris and his sister, Amy Sedaris, have collaborated under the name "The Talent Family" and have written several plays that have been produced at La Mama, Lincoln Center, and the Drama Department in New York City. These plays include *Stump the Host, Stitches, One Woman Shoe*, which received an Obie Award, *Incident at Cobbler's Knob*, and *The Book of Liz*. Sedaris's original radio pieces can often be heard on *This American Life*. In 2001, Sedaris became the third recipient of the Thurber Prize for American Humor. He was named by *Time* magazine as Humorist of the Year in 2001. He has also edited *Children Playing Before a Statue of Hercules: An Anthology of Outstanding Stories*. In 2005, Sedaris was nominated for two Grammy Awards for Best Spoken Word Album, *Dress Your Family in Corduroy & Denim*, and Best Comedy Album, *David Sedaris: Live at Carnegie Hall*.

> Give me your life, your pain, your bottomless sorrow—
> it's not like you're going to do anything with it.

Although we'd discussed my upcoming visit to Winston-Salem, my sister and I didn't make exact arrangements until the eve of my arrival, when I phoned from a hotel in Salt Lake City.

"I'll be at work when you arrive," she said, "so I'm thinking I'll just leave the key under the hour ott near the ack toor."

"The what?"

"Hour ott."

I thought she had something in her mouth until I realized she was speaking in code.

"What are you, on a speakerphone at a methadone clinic? Why can't you just tell me where you'll put the goddamned house key?"

Her voice dropped to a whisper. "I just don't know that I trust these things."

"Are you on a cell phone?"

"Of course not," she said. "This is just a regular cordless, but still, you have to be careful."

When I suggested that, actually, she didn't have to be careful, Lisa resumed her normal tone of voice, saying, "Really? But I heard . . ."

My sister's the type that religiously watches the fear segments of her local Eyewitness News broadcasts, retaining nothing but the headlines. She remembers that applesauce can kill you but forgets that in order to die, you have to inject it directly into your bloodstream. Announcements that cell-phone conversations may be picked up by strangers mix with the reported rise of both home burglaries and brain tumors, meaning that as far as she's concerned, all telecommunication is potentially life threatening. If she didn't watch it on the news, she read it in *Consumer Reports* or heard it thirdhand from a friend of a friend of a friend whose ear caught fire while dialing her answering machine. Everything is dangerous all of the time, and if it's not yet been pulled off the shelves, then it's certainly under investigation—so there.

"Okay," I said. "But can you tell me which hour ott? The last time I was there, you had quite a few of them."

"It's ed," she told me. "Well . . . eddish."

I arrived at Lisa's house late the following afternoon, found the key under the flowerpot, and let myself in through the back door. A lengthy note on the coffee table explained how I might go about operating everything from the television to the waffle iron, each carefully detailed procedure ending with the line, "Remember to turn off and unplug after use." At the bottom of page 3, a postscript informed me that if the appliance in question had no plug—the dishwasher, for instance—I should make sure it had completed its cycle and was cool to the touch before leaving the room. The note reflected a growing hysteria, its subtext shrieking, Oh, my God, he's going to be alone in my house for close to an hour! She left her work number, her husband's work number, and the number of the next-door neighbor, adding that she didn't know the woman very well so I probably shouldn't bother her unless it was an emergency. "P.P.S. She's a Baptist, so don't tell her you're gay."

The last time I was alone at my sister's place, she was living in a white-brick apartment complex occupied by widows and single, middle-aged working women. This was in the late seventies, when we were supposed to be living in dorms. College hadn't quite worked out the way she'd expected, and after two years in Virginia she'd returned to Raleigh and taken a job at a wineshop. It was a normal enough life for a twenty-one-year-old, but being a dropout was not

Parents told them this?

what she had planned for herself. Worse than that, it had not been planned for her. As children, we'd been assigned certain roles—leader, bum, troublemaker, slut—titles that effectively told us who we were. Since Lisa was the oldest, smartest, and bossiest, it was assumed that she would shoot to the top of her field, earning a master's degree in manipulation and eventually taking over a medium-sized country. We'd always known her as an authority figure, and while we took a certain joy in watching her fall, it was disorienting to see her with so little confidence. Suddenly she was relying on other people's opinions, following their advice and withering at the slightest criticism.

"Do you really think? Really?" She was putty.

My sister needed patience and understanding, but more often than not I found myself wanting to shake her. If the oldest wasn't who she was supposed to be, then what did it mean for the rest of us?

Lisa had been marked Most Likely to Succeed, so it confused her to be ringing up gallon jugs of hearty burgundy. I had been branded Lazy and Irresponsible, so it felt right when I, too, dropped out of college and wound up back in Raleigh. After being thrown out of my parents' house, I went to live with Lisa in her white-brick complex. It was a small studio apartment—the adult version of her childhood bedroom—and when I eventually left her with a broken stereo and an unpaid eighty-dollar phone bill, the general consensus was, "Well, what did you expect?"

I might reinvent myself to strangers, but to this day, as far as my family is concerned, I'm still the one most likely to set your house on fire. While I accepted my lowered expectations, Lisa fought hard to regain her former title. The wineshop was just a temporary setback, and she left shortly after becoming manager. Photography interested her, so she taught herself to use a camera, ultimately landing a job in the photo department of a large international drug company, where she took pictures of germs, viruses, and people reacting to germs and viruses. On weekends, for extra money, she photographed weddings, which really wasn't that much of a stretch. Then she got married herself and quit the drug company in order to earn an English degree. When told there was very little call for thirty-page essays on Jane Austen, she got a real estate license. When told the housing market was down, she returned to school to study plants. Her husband, Bob, got a job in Winston-Salem, so they moved, buying a new three-story house in a quiet suburban neighborhood.

My sister's home didn't really lend itself to snooping, so I spent my hour in the kitchen, making small talk with Henry. It was the same conversation we'd had the last time I saw him, yet still I found it fascinating. He asked how I was doing. I said I was all right, and then, as if something might have drastically changed within the last few seconds, he asked again.

Of all the elements of my sister's adult life—the house, the husband, the sudden interest in plants—the most unsettling is Henry. Technically he's a blue-fronted Amazon, but to the layman, he's just a big parrot, the type you might see on the shoulder of a pirate.

"How you doing?"

The third time he asked, it sounded as if he really cared. I approached his cage with a detailed answer, and when he lunged for the bars, I screamed like a girl and ran out of the room.

"Henry likes you," my sister said a short while later. She'd just returned from her job at the plant nursery and was sitting at the table, unlacing her sneakers. "See the way he's fanning his tail? He'd never do that for Bob. Would you, Henry?"

Bob had returned from work a few minutes earlier and immediately headed upstairs to spend time with his own bird, a balding green-cheeked conure named Jose. I'd thought the two of them might enjoy an occasional conversation, but it turns out they can't stand each other. "Don't even mention Jose in front of Henry," Lisa whispered. Bob's bird squawked from the upstairs study, and the parrot responded with a series of high, piercing barks. It was a trick he'd picked up from Lisa's border collie, Chessie, and what was disturbing was that he sounded exactly like a dog. Just as, when speaking English, he sounded exactly like Lisa. It was creepy to hear my sister's voice coming from a beak, but I couldn't say it didn't please me.

"Who's hungry?" she asked.

"Who's hungry?" the voice repeated.

I raised my hand, and she offered Henry a peanut. As he took it in his claw, his belly sagging to the perch, I understood what someone might see in a parrot. Here was this strange little fatso living in my sister's kitchen, a sympathetic listener turning again and again to ask, "So, really, how are you?'"

I'd asked her the same question, and she'd said, "Oh, fine, you know." She's afraid to tell me anything important, knowing I'll only turn around and write about it. In my mind, I'm like a friendly junkman, building things from the little pieces of scrap I find here and there, but my family's started to see things differently. Their personal lives are the so-called pieces of scrap I so casually pick up, and they're sick of it. Our conversations now start with the words, "You have to swear you will never repeat this." I always promise, but it's generally understood that my word is no better than Henry's.

I'd come to Winston-Salem to address the students at a local college, and also to break some news. Sometimes when you're stoned, it's fun to sit around and think of who might play you in the movie version of your life. What makes it fun is that no one is actually going to make a movie of your life. Lisa and I no longer get stoned, so it was all the harder to announce that my book had been optioned, meaning that, in fact, someone was going to make a movie of our lives—not a student, but a real director people had heard of.

"A what?"

I explained that he was Chinese, and she asked if the movie would be in Chinese.

"No," I said. "He lives in America. In California. He's been here since he was a baby."

"Then what does it matter if he's Chinese?"

"Well," I said, "he's got . . . you know, a sensibility."

"Oh, brother," she said.

I looked to Henry for support and he growled at me.

"So now we have to be in a movie?" She picked her sneakers off the floor and tossed them into the laundry room. "Well," she said, "I can tell you right now that you're not dragging my bird into this."

The movie was to be based on our preparrot years, but the moment she put her foot down, I started wondering who we might get to play the role of Henry. "I know what you're thinking," she said, "and the answer is no."

Once, at a dinner party, I met a woman whose parrot had learned to imitate the automatic ice maker on her new refrigerator. "That's what happens when they're left alone," she said. This was the most disturbing bit of information I'd heard in quite a while. Here was this creature, born to mock its jungle neighbors, and it wound up doing impressions of man-made kitchen appliances. I repeated the story to Lisa, who told me that neglect had nothing to do with it. She then prepared a cappuccino, setting the stage for Henry's pitch-perfect imitation of the milk steamer. "He can do the blender, too," she said.

She opened the cage door, and as we sat down to our coffees, Henry glided down onto the table. "Who wants a kiss?" She stuck out her tongue, and he accepted the tip gingerly between his upper and lower beak. I'd never dream of doing such a thing, not because it's across-the-board disgusting, but because he would have bitten the shit out of me. While Henry might occasionally have fanned his tail in my direction, it was understood that he was loyal to only one person, which, I think, is another reason my sister is so fond of him.

"Was that a good kiss?" she asked. "Did you like that?"

I expected a yes or no answer and was disappointed when he responded with the exact same question: "Did you like that?" Yes, parrots can talk, but unfortunately they have no idea what they're actually saying. When she first got him, Henry spoke the Spanish he'd learned from his captors. Asked if he'd had a good night's sleep, he'd simply say hola, much like the Salvadoran women I used to clean with in New York. He goes through phases, favoring an often repeated noise or sentence, and then he moves on to something else. When our mother died, Henry learned how to cry. He and Lisa would set each other off, and the two of them would go on for hours. A few years later, in the midst of a brief academic setback, she trained him to act as her emotional cheerleader. I'd call and hear him in the background screaming, "We love you Lisa!" and "You can do it!" This was replaced, in time, with the far more practical "Where are my keys?"

[handwritten annotation: ↳ she has grown a bit. Can do it alone.]
[handwritten annotation: Used to be confident → she became insecure → Gaining it back]

[handwritten annotation in left margin: Implied character arc.]

After we finished our coffees, Lisa drove me to Greensboro, where I delivered my scheduled lecture. This is to say that I read stories about my family. After the reading, I answered questions about them, thinking all the while how odd it was that these strangers seemed to know so much about my brother and sisters. In order to sleep at night, I have to remove myself from the equation, pretending that the people I love voluntarily choose to expose themselves. It's a delusion much harder to maintain when a family member is actually in the audience.

The day after the reading, Lisa called in sick, and we spent the afternoon running errands. Winston-Salem is a city of plazas, midsize shopping centers each built around an enormous grocery store. I was looking for cheap cartons of cigarettes, so we drove from plaza to plaza, comparing prices and talking about our sister Gretchen. A year earlier, she'd bought a pair of flesh-eating Chinese box turtles with pointed noses and spooky translucent skin. The two of them lived in an outdoor pen and were relatively happy until raccoons dug beneath the wire and chewed the front legs off the female and the rear legs off her husband. "I may have the order wrong," Lisa said, "but you get the picture."

The couple survived the attack and continued to track the live mice that constituted their diet, propelling themselves forward like a pair of half-stripped Volkswagens.

"The sad part is that it took her two weeks to notice it," Lisa said. "Two weeks!" She shook her head and drove past our exit. "I'm sorry, but I don't know how a responsible pet owner could go that long without noticing a thing like that. It's just not right."

According to Gretchen, the turtles had no memories of their former limbs, but Lisa wasn't buying it. "Oh, come on," she said. "They must at least have phantom pains. I mean, how can a living creature not mind losing its legs?" Her eyes misted, and she wiped them with the back of her hand. "My little collie gets a tick and I go crazy." Lisa's a person who once witnessed a car accident saying, "I just hope there isn't a dog in the backseat." Human suffering doesn't faze her much, but she'll cry for days over a sick-pet story.

"Did you see that movie about the Cuban guy?" she asked. "It played here for a while, but I wouldn't go. Someone told me a dog gets killed in the first fifteen minutes, so I said forget it."

I reminded her that the main character died as well, horribly, of AIDS, and she pulled into the parking lot, saying, "Well, I just hope it wasn't a real dog."

I wound up buying cigarettes at Tobacco USA, a discount store with the name of a theme park. Lisa had officially quit smoking ten years earlier and might have taken it up again were it not for Chessie, who, according to the vet, was predisposed to lung ailments. "I don't want to give her secondhand emphysema, but I sure wouldn't mind taking some of this weight off. Tell me the truth: Do I look fat to you?"

"Not at all."

She turned sideways and examined herself in the window of Tobacco USA. "You're lying."

"Well, isn't that what you want me to say?"

"Yes. But I want you to really mean it."

But I had meant it. It wasn't the weight I noticed so much as the clothing she wore to cover it up. The loose, baggy pants and oversized shirts falling halfway to her knees: This was the look she'd adopted a few months earlier, after she and her husband had gone to the mountains to visit Bob's parents. Lisa had been sitting beside the fire, and when she scooted her chair toward the center of the room, her father-in-law said, "What's the matter, Lisa? Getting too fat—I mean hot. Getting too hot?"

He had tried to cover his mistake, but it was too late. The word had already been seared into my sister's brain.

"Will I have to be fat in the movie?" she asked me.

"Of course not. You'll be just . . . like you are."

"Like I am according to who?" she asked. "The Chinese?"

"Well, not all of them," I said. "Just one."

Normally, if at home during a weekday, Lisa likes to read eighteenth-century novels, breaking at 1:00 to eat lunch and watch a television program called *Matlock*. By the time we finished with my errands, the day's broadcast had already ended, so we decided to go to the movies—whatever she wanted. She chose the story of a young Englishwoman struggling to remain happy while trying to lose a few extra pounds, but in the end she got her plazas confused and we arrived at the wrong theater just in time to watch *You Can Count on Me*, the Kenneth Lonergan movie in which an errant brother visits his older sister. Normally Lisa's the type who talks from one end of the show to the other. A character will spread mayonnaise onto a chicken sandwich and she'll lean over, whispering, "One time, I was doing that? And the knife fell into the toilet."

Then she'll settle back in her seat and I'll spend the next ten minutes wondering why on earth someone would make a chicken sandwich in the bathroom. This movie reflected our lives so eerily that for the first time in recent memory, she was stunned into silence. There was no resemblance between us and the main characters—the brother and sister were younger and orphaned—but like us they'd stumbled to adulthood playing the worn, confining roles assigned to them as children. Every now and then one of them would break free, but for the most part they behaved not as they wanted to but as they were expected to. In brief, a guy shows up at his sister's house and stays for a few weeks until she kicks him out. She's not evil about it, but having him around forces her to think about things she'd rather not, which is essentially what family members do, at least the family members my sister and I know.

On leaving the theater we shared a long, uncomfortable silence. Between the movie we'd just seen and the movie about to be made, we both felt awkward and self-conscious, as if we were auditioning for the roles of ourselves. I started in with some benign bit of gossip I'd heard concerning the man who'd played the part of the brother but stopped after the first few sentences, saying that, on second thought, it wasn't very interesting. She couldn't think of anything, either, so we said nothing, each of us imagining a bored audience shifting in its seats.

We stopped for gas on the way home and were parking in front of her house when she turned to relate what I've come to think of as the quintessential Lisa story. "One time," she said, "one time I was out driving . . ." The incident began with a quick trip to the grocery store and ended, unexpectedly, with a wounded animal stuffed into a pillowcase and held to the tailpipe of her car. Like most of my sister's stories, it provoked a startling mental picture, capturing a moment in time when one's actions seem both unimaginably cruel and completely natural. Details were carefully chosen and the pace built gradually, punctuated by a series of well-timed pauses. "And then . . . and then . . ." She reached the inevitable tailpipe, and just as I started to laugh, she put her head against the steering wheel and fell apart. It wasn't the gentle flow of tears you might release when recalling an isolated action or event, but the violent explosion that comes when you realize that all such events are connected, forming an endless chain of guilt and suffering.

I instinctively reached for the notebook I keep in my pocket, and she grabbed my hand to stop me. "If you ever," she said, "ever repeat that story, I'll never talk to you again."

In the movie version of our lives, I would have turned to offer her comfort, reminding her, convincing her, that the action she'd described had been kind and just. Because it was. She's incapable of acting otherwise.

In the real version of our lives, my immediate goal was simply to change her mind. "Oh, come on," I said. "The story's really funny, and, I mean, it's not like you're going to do anything with it."

Your life, your privacy, your bottomless sorrow—it's not like you're going to do anything with it. Is this the brother I always was or the brother I have become?

I'd worried that, in making the movie, the director might get me and my family wrong, but now a worse thought occurred to me: What if he gets us right?

Dusk. The camera pans an unremarkable suburban street, moving in on a parked four-door automobile where a small, evil man turns to his sobbing sister, saying, "What if I use the story but say that it happened to a friend?"

But maybe that's not the end. Maybe before the credits roll, we see this same man getting out of bed in the middle of the night, walking past his sister's bedroom and downstairs into the kitchen. A switch is thrown, and we notice, in the far corner of the room, a large standing birdcage covered with a tablecloth. He approaches it carefully and removes the cover, waking a blue-fronted Amazon parrot, its eyes glowing red in the sudden light. Through everything that's come before this moment, we understand that the man has something important to say. From his own mouth the words are meaningless, so he pulls up a chair. The clock reads 3:00 A.M., then 4:00, then 5:00, as he sits before the brilliant bird repeating slowly and clearly the words, "Forgive me. Forgive me: Forgive me."

Reflects on meaning of parrot scaring him.
Language & Dialogue is successful.
↳ Code Language → childish.
Exploring people's lives & family dynamic.

Richard Selzer

IMELDA

RICHARD SELZER, the son of a family doctor, was born in Troy, New York. He attended Union College in Schenectady, New York, and earned an MD at Albany Medical College in 1953. He is the author of *Rituals of Surgery*, a collection of short stories; two volumes of essays, *Mortal Lessons* and *Confessions of a Knife*; and a volume of essays and fiction, *Letters to a Young Doctor*. In 1991, he contracted Legionnaires' disease and went on to document his recovery in *Raising the Dead: A Doctor's Encounter with His Own Mortality*. He retired from practicing surgery and teaching at Yale Medical School in 1986.

I heard the other day that Hugh Franciscus had died. I knew him once. He was the Chief of Plastic Surgery when I was a medical student at Albany Medical College. Dr. Franciscus was the archetype of the professor of surgery—tall, vigorous, muscular, as precise in his technique as he was impeccable in his dress. Each day a clean lab coat monkishly starched, that sort of thing. I doubt that he ever read books. One book only, that of the human body, took the place of all others. He never raised his eyes from it. He read it like a printed page as though he knew that in the calligraphy there just beneath the skin were all the secrets of the world. Long before it became visible to anyone else, he could detect the first sign of granulation at the base of a wound, the first blue line of new epithelium at the periphery that would tell him that a wound would heal, or the barest hint of necrosis that presaged failure. This gave him the appearance of a prophet. "This skin graft will take," he would say, and you must believe beyond all cyanosis, exudation and inflammation that it would.

He had enemies, of course, who said he was arrogant, that he exalted activity for its own sake. Perhaps. But perhaps it was no more than the honesty of one who knows his own worth. Just look at a scalpel, after all. What a feeling of sovereignty, megalomania even, when you know that it is you and you alone who will make certain use of it. It was said, too, that he was a ladies' man. I don't know about that. It was all rumor. Besides, I think he had other things in mind than mere living. Hugh Franciscus was a zealous hunter. Every fall during the season he drove upstate to hunt deer. There was a glass-front case in his office where he showed his guns. How could he shoot a deer? we asked. But he knew better. To us medical students he was someone heroic, someone made up of several gods, beheld at a distance, and always from a lesser height. If he had grown accustomed to his miracles, we had not. He had no close friends on the staff. There was something a little sad in that. As though once long ago he had been flayed by friendship and now the slightest breeze would hurt. Confidences resulted in dishonor. Perhaps the person in whom one confided would scorn him, betray. Even though he spent his days among those less fortunate, weaker than he—the sick, after all—Franciscus seemed aware of an air of personal harshness in his environment to which he reacted by keeping his own counsel, by a certain remoteness. It was what gave him the appearance of being haughty. With the patients he was forthright. All the facts laid out, every question anticipated and answered with specific information. He delivered good news and bad with the same dispassion.

I was a third-year student, just turned onto the wards for the first time, and clerking on Surgery. Everything—the operating room, the morgue, the emergency room, the patients, professors, even the nurses—was terrifying. One picked one's way among the mines and booby traps of the hospital, hoping only to avoid the hemorrhage and perforation of disgrace. The opportunity for humiliation was everywhere.

It all began on Ward Rounds. Dr. Franciscus was demonstrating a cross-leg flap graft he had constructed to cover a large fleshy defect in the leg of a merchant seaman who had injured himself in a fall. The man was from Spain and spoke no English. There had been a comminuted fracture of the femur, much soft tissue damage, necrosis. After weeks of débridement and dressings, the wound had been made ready for grafting. Now the patient was in his fifth postoperative day. What we saw was a thick web of pale blue flesh arising from the man's left thigh, and which had been sutured to the open wound on the right thigh. When the surgeon pressed the pedicle with his finger, it blanched; when he let up, there was a slow return of the violaceous color.

"The circulation is good," Franciscus announced. "It will get better." In several weeks, we were told, he would divide the tube of flesh at its site of origin, and tailor it to fit the defect to which, by then, it would have grown more solidly. All at once, the webbed man in the bed reached out, and gripping Franciscus by the arm, began to speak rapidly, pointing to his groin and hip. Franciscus stepped back at once to disengage his arm from the patient's grasp.

"Anyone here know Spanish? I didn't get a word of that."

"The cast is digging into him up above," I said. "The edges of the plaster are rough. When he moves, they hurt."

Without acknowledging my assistance, Dr. Franciscus took a plaster shears from the dressing cart and with several large snips cut away the rough edges of the cast.

"Gracias, gracias." The man in the bed smiled. But Franciscus had already moved on to the next bed. He seemed to me a man of immense strength and ability, yet without affection for the patients. He did not want to be touched by them. It was less kindness that he showed them than a reassurance that he would never give up, that he would bend every effort. If anyone could, he would solve the problems of their flesh.

Ward Rounds had disbanded and I was halfway down the corridor when I heard Dr. Franciscus' voice behind me.

"You speak Spanish." It seemed a command.

"I lived in Spain for two years," I told him.

"I'm taking a surgical team to Honduras next week to operate on the natives down there. I do it every year for three weeks, somewhere. This year, Honduras. I can arrange the time away from your duties here if you'd like to come along. You will act as interpreter. I'll show you how to use the clinical camera. What you'd see would make it worthwhile."

So it was that, a week later, the envy of my classmates, I joined the mobile surgical unit—surgeons, anesthetists, nurses and equipment—aboard a Military Air Transport plane to spend three weeks performing plastic surgery on people who had been previously selected by an advance team. Honduras. I don't suppose I shall ever see it again. Nor do I especially want to. From the plane it seemed a country made of clay—burnt umber, raw sienna, dry. It had a dead-weight quality, as though the ground had no buoyancy, no air sacs through which a breeze might wander. Our destination was Comayagua, a town in the Central Highlands. The town itself was situated on the edge of one of the flat-lands that were linked in a network between the granite mountains. Above, all was brown, with only an occasional Spanish cedar tree; below, patches of luxuriant tropical growth. It was a day's bus ride from the airport. For hours, the town kept appearing and disappearing with the convolutions of the road. At last, there it lay before us, panting and exhausted at the bottom of the mountain.

That was all I was to see of the countryside. From then on, there was only the derelict hospital of Comayagua, with the smell of spoiling bananas and the accumulated odors of everyone who had been sick there for the last hundred years. Of the two, I much preferred the frank smell of the sick. The heat of the place was incendiary. So hot that, as we stepped from the bus, our own words did not carry through the air, but hung limply at our lips and chins. Just in front of the hospital was a thirsty courtyard where mobs of waiting people squatted or lay in the meager shade, and where, on dry days, a fine dust rose through which untethered goats shouldered. Against the walls of this courtyard, gaunt, dejected men stood, their faces, like their country, preternaturally solemn, leaden. Here no one looked up at the sky. Every head was bent beneath a wide-brimmed straw hat. In the days that followed, from the doorway of the dispensary, I would watch the brown mountains sliding about, drinking the hospital into their shadow as the afternoon grew later and later, flattening us by their very altitude.

The people were mestizos, of mixed Spanish and Indian blood. They had flat, broad, dumb museum feet. At first they seemed to me indistinguishable the one from the other, without animation. All the vitality, the hidden sexuality, was in their black hair. Soon I was to know them by the fissures with which each face was graven. But, even so, compared to us, they were masked, shut away. My job was to follow Dr. Franciscus around, photograph the patients before and after surgery, interpret and generally act as aide-de-camp. It was exhilarating. Within days I had decided that I was not just useful, but essential. Despite that we spent all day in each other's company, there were no overtures of friendship from Dr. Franciscus. He knew my place, and I knew it, too. In the afternoon he examined the patients scheduled for the next day's surgery. I would call out a name from the doorway to the examining room. In the courtyard someone would rise. I would usher the patient in, and nudge him to the examining table where Franciscus stood, always, I thought, on the verge of irritability. I would read aloud the case history, then wait while he carried out his examination. While I took the "before" photographs, Dr. Franciscus would dictate into a tape recorder:

"Ulcerating basal cell carcinoma of the right orbit—six by eight centimeters—involving the right eye and extending into the floor of the orbit. Operative plan: wide excision with enucleation of the eye. Later, bone and skin grafting." The next morning we would be in the operating room where the procedure would be carried out.

We were more than two weeks into our tour of duty—a few days to go—when it happened. Earlier in the day I had caught sight of her through the window of the dispensary. A thin, dark Indian girl about fourteen years old. A figurine, orange-brown, terra-cotta, and still attached to the unshaped clay from which she had been carved. An older, sun-weathered woman stood behind and somewhat to the left of the girl. The mother was short and dumpy. She wore a broad-brimmed hat with a high crown, and a shapeless dress like a cassock. The girl had long, loose black hair. There were tiny gold hoops in her ears. The dress she wore could have been her mother's. Far too big, it hung from her thin shoulders at some risk of slipping down her arms. Even with her in it, the dress was empty, something hanging on the back of a door. Her breasts made only the smallest imprint in the cloth, her hips none at all. All the while, she pressed to her mouth a filthy, pink, balled-up rag as though to stanch a flow or buttress against pain. I knew that what she had come to show us, what we were there to see, was hidden beneath that pink cloth. As I watched, the woman handed down to her a gourd from which the girl drank, lapping like a dog. She was the last patient of the day. They had been waiting in the courtyard for hours.

"Imelda Valdez," I called out. Slowly she rose to her feet, the cloth never leaving her mouth, and followed her mother to the examining-room door. I shooed them in.

"You sit up there on the table," I told her. "Mother, you stand over there, please." I read from the chart:

"This is a fourteen-year-old girl with a complete, unilateral, left-sided cleft lip and cleft palate. No other diseases or congenital defects. Laboratory tests, chest X ray—negative."

"Tell her to take the rag away," said Dr. Franciscus. I did, and the girl shrank back, pressing the cloth all the more firmly.

"Listen, this is silly," said Franciscus. "Tell her I've got to see it. Either she behaves, or send her away."

"Please give me the cloth," I said to the girl as gently as possible. She did not. She could not. Just then, Franciscus reached up and, taking the hand that held the rag, pulled it away with a hard jerk. For an instant the girl's head followed the cloth as it left her face, one arm still upflung against showing. Against all hope, she would hide herself. A moment later, she relaxed and sat still. She seemed to me then like an animal that looks outward at the infinite, at death, without fear, with recognition only.

Set as it was in the center of the girl's face, the defect was utterly hideous—a nude rubbery insect that had fastened there. The upper lip was widely split all the way to the nose. One white tooth perched upon the protruding upper jaw projected through the hole. Some of the bone seemed to have been gnawed away as well. Above the thing, clear almond eyes and long black hair reflected the light. Below, a slender neck where the pulse trilled visibly. Under our gaze the girl's eyes fell to her lap where her hands lay palms upward, half open. She was a beautiful bird with a crushed beak. And tense with the expectation of more shame.

"Open your mouth," said the surgeon. I translated. She did so, and the surgeon tipped back her head to see inside.

"The palate, too. Complete," he said. There was a long silence. At last he spoke.

"What is your name?" The margins of the wound melted until she herself was being sucked into it.

"Imelda." The syllables leaked through the hole with a slosh and a whistle.

"Tomorrow," said the surgeon, "I will fix your lip. *Mañana*."

It seemed to me that Hugh Franciscus, in spite of his years of experience, in spite of all the dreadful things he had seen, must have been awed by the sight of this girl. I could see it flit across his face for an instant. Perhaps it was her small act of concealment, that he had had to demand that she show him the lip, that he had had to force her to show it to him. Perhaps it was her resistance that intensified the disfigurement. Had she brought her mouth to him willingly, without shame, she would have been for him neither more nor less than any other patient.

He measured the defect with calipers, studied it from different angles, turning her head with a finger at her chin.

"How can it ever be put back together?" I asked.

"Take her picture," he said. And to her, "Look straight ahead." Through the eye of the camera she seemed more pitiful than ever, her humiliation more complete.

"Wait!" The surgeon stopped me. I lowered the camera. A strand of her hair had fallen across her face and found its way to her mouth, becoming stuck there by saliva. He removed the hair and secured it behind her ear.

"Go ahead," he ordered. There was the click of the camera. The girl winced.

"Take three more, just in case."

When the girl and her mother had left, he took paper and pen and with a few lines drew a remarkable likeness of the girl's face.

"Look," he said. "If this dot is A, and this one B, this, C and this, D, the incisions are made A to B, then C to D. CD must equal AB. It is all equilateral triangles." All well and good, but then came X and Y and rotation flaps and the rest.

"Do you see?" he asked.

"It is confusing," I told him.

"It is simply a matter of dropping the upper lip into a normal position, then crossing the gap with two triangular flaps. It is geometry," he said.

"Yes," I said. "Geometry." And relinquished all hope of becoming a plastic surgeon.

In the operating room the next morning the anesthesia had already been administered when we arrived from Ward Rounds. The tube emerging from the girl's mouth was pressed against her lower lip to be kept out of the field of surgery. Already, a nurse was scrubbing the face which swam in a reddish-brown lather. The tiny gold earrings were included in the scrub. Now and then, one of them gave a brave flash. The face was washed for the last time, and dried. Green towels were placed over the face to hide everything but the mouth and nose. The drapes were applied.

"Calipers!" The surgeon measured, locating the peak of the distorted Cupid's bow.

"Marking pen!" He placed the first blue dot at the apex of the bow. The nasal sills were dotted; next, the inferior philtral dimple, the vermilion line. The *A* flap and the *B* flap were outlined. On he worked, peppering the lip and nose, making sense out of chaos, realizing the lip that lay waiting in that deep essential pink, that only he could see. The last dot and line were placed. He was ready.

"Scalpel!" He held the knife above the girl's mouth.

"O.K. to go ahead?" he asked the anesthetist.

"Yes."

He lowered the knife.

"No! Wait!" The anesthetist's voice was tense, staccato. "Hold it!"

The surgeon's hand was motionless.

"What's the matter?"

"Something's wrong. I'm not sure. God, she's hot as a pistol. Blood pressure is way up. Pulse one eighty. Get a rectal temperature." A nurse fumbled beneath the drapes. We waited. The nurse retrieved the thermometer.

"One hundred seven . . . no . . . eight." There was disbelief in her voice.

"Malignant hyperthermia," said the anesthetist. "Ice! Ice! Get lots of ice!" I raced out the door, accosted the first nurse I saw.

"Ice!" I shouted. "*Hielo!* Quickly! *Hielo!*" The woman's expression was blank. I ran to another. "*Hielo! Hielo!* For the love of God, ice."

"*Hielo?*" She shrugged. "*Nada.*" I ran back to the operating room.

"There isn't any ice," I reported. Dr. Franciscus had ripped off his rubber gloves and was feeling the skin of the girl's abdomen. Above the mask his eyes were the eyes of a horse in battle.

"The EKG is wild . . ."

"I can't get a pulse . . ."

"What the hell . . ."

The surgeon reached for the girl's groin. No femoral pulse.

"EKG flat. My God! She's dead!"

"She can't be."

"She is."

The surgeon's fingers pressed the groin where there was no pulse to be felt, only his own pulse hammering at the girl's flesh to be let in.

. . .

It was noon, four hours later, when we left the operating room. It was a day so hot and humid I felt steamed open like an envelope. The woman was sitting on a bench in the courtyard in her dress like a cassock. In one hand she held the piece of cloth the girl had used to conceal her mouth. As we watched, she folded it once neatly, and then again, smoothing it, cleaning the cloth which might have been the head of the girl in her lap that she stroked and consoled.

"I'll do the talking here," he said. He would tell her himself, in whatever Spanish he could find. Only if she did not understand was I to speak for him. I watched him brace himself, set his shoulders. How could he tell her? I wondered. What? But I knew he would tell her everything, exactly as it had happened. As much for himself as for her, he needed to explain. But suppose she screamed, fell to the ground, attacked him, even? All that hope of love . . . gone. Even in his discomfort I knew that he was teaching me. The way to do it was professionally. Now he was standing above her. When the woman saw that he did not speak, she lifted her eyes and saw what he held crammed in his mouth to tell her. She knew, and rose to her feet.

"*Señora*," he began, "I am sorry." All at once he seemed to me shorter than he was, scarcely taller than she. There was a place at the crown of his head where the hair had grown thin. His lips were stones. He could hardly move them. The voice dry, dusty.

"No one could have known. Some bad reaction to the medicine for sleeping. It poisoned her. High fever. She did not wake up." The last, a whisper. The woman studied his lips as though she were deaf. He tried, but could not control a twitching at the corner of his mouth. He raised a thumb and forefinger to press something back into his eyes.

"*Muerte*," the woman announced to herself. Her eyes were human, deadly.

"*Sí, muerte*." At that moment he was like someone cast, still alive, as an effigy for his own tomb. He closed his eyes. Nor did he open them until he felt the touch of the woman's hand on his arm, a touch from which he did not withdraw. Then he looked and saw the grief corroding her face, breaking it down, melting the features so that eyes, nose, mouth ran together in a distortion, like the girl's. For a long time they stood in silence. It seemed to me that minutes passed. At last her face cleared, the features rearranged themselves. She spoke, the words coming slowly to make certain that he understood her. She would go home now. The next day her sons would come for the girl, to take her home for burial. The doctor must not be sad. God has decided. And she was happy now that the harelip had been fixed so that her daughter might go to Heaven without it. Her bare feet retreating were the felted pads of a great bereft animal.

. . .

The next morning I did not go to the wards, but stood at the gate leading from the courtyard to the road outside. Two young men in striped ponchos lifted the girl's body wrapped in a straw mat onto the back of a wooden cart. A donkey waited. I had been drawn to this place as one is drawn, inexplicably, to certain scenes of desolation—executions, battlefields. All at once, the woman looked up and saw me. She had taken off her hat. The heavy-hanging coil of her hair made her head seem larger, darker, noble. I pressed some money into her hand.

"For flowers," I said. "A priest." Her cheeks shook as though minutes ago a stone had been dropped into her navel and the ripples were just now reaching her head. I regretted having come to that place.

"*Sí, sí,*" the woman said. Her own face was stitched with flies. "The doctor is one of the angels. He has finished the work of God. My daughter is beautiful."

What could she mean! The lip had not been fixed. The girl had died before he would have done it.

"Only a fine line that God will erase in time," she said.

I reached into the cart and lifted a corner of the mat in which the girl had been rolled. Where the cleft had been there was now a fresh line of tiny sutures. The Cupid's bow was delicately shaped, the vermilion border aligned. The flattened nostril had now the same rounded shape as the other one. I let the mat fall over the face of the dead girl, but not before I had seen the touching place where the finest black hairs sprang from the temple.

"*Adiós, adiós . . .*" And the cart creaked away to the sound of hooves, a tinkling bell.

There are events in a doctor's life that seem to mark the boundary between youth and age, seeing and perceiving. Like certain dreams, they illuminate a whole lifetime of past behavior. After such an event, a doctor is not the same as he was before. It had seemed to me then to have been the act of someone demented, or at least insanely arrogant. An attempt to reorder events. Her death had come to him out of order. It should have come after the lip had been repaired, not before. He could have told the mother that, no, the lip had not been fixed. But he did not. He said nothing. It had been an act of omission, one of those strange lapses to which all of us are subject and which we live to regret. It must have been then, at that moment, that the knowledge of what he would do appeared to him. The words of the mother had not consoled him; they had hunted him down. He had not done it for her. The dire necessity was his. He would not accept that Imelda had died before he could repair her lip. People who do such things break free from society. They follow their own lonely path. They have a secret which they can never reveal. I must never let on that I knew.

How often I have imagined it. Ten o'clock at night. The hospital of Comayagua is all but dark. Here and there lanterns tilt and skitter up and down the corridors. One of these lamps breaks free from the others and descends the stone steps to the underground room that is the morgue of the hospital. This room wears the expression as if it had waited all night for someone to come. No silence so deep as this place with its cargo of newly dead. Only the slow drip of water over stone. The door closes gassily and clicks shut. The lock is turned. There are four tables, each with a body encased in a paper shroud. There is no mistaking her. She is the smallest. The surgeon takes a knife from his pocket and slits open the paper shroud, that part in which the girl's head is enclosed. The wound seems to be living on long after she has died. Waves of heat emanate from it, blurring his vision. All at once, he turns to peer over his shoulder. He sees nothing, only a wooden crucifix on the wall.

He removes a package of instruments from a satchel and arranges them on a tray. Scalpel, scissors, forceps, needle holder. Sutures and gauze sponges are produced. Stealthy, hunched, engaged, he begins. The dots of blue dye are still there upon her mouth. He raises the scalpel, pauses. A second glance into the darkness. From the wall a small lizard watches and accepts. The first cut is made. A sluggish flow of dark blood appears. He wipes it away with a sponge. No new blood comes to take its place. Again and again he cuts, connecting each of the blue dots until the whole of the zigzag slice is made, first on one side of the cleft, then on the other. Now the edges of the cleft are lined with fresh tissue. He sets down the scalpel and takes up scissors and forceps, undermining the little flaps until each triangle is attached only at one side. He rotates each flap into its new position. He must be certain that they can be swung without tension. They can. He is ready to suture. He fits the tiny curved needle into the jaws of the needle holder. Each suture is placed precisely the same number of millimeters from the cut edge, and the same distance apart. He ties each knot down until the edges are apposed. Not too tightly. These are the most meticulous sutures of his life. He cuts each thread close to the knot. It goes well. The vermilion border with its white skin roll is exactly aligned. One more stitch and the Cupid's bow appears as if by magic. The man's face shines with moisture. Now the nostril is incised around the margin, released, and sutured into a round shape to match its mate. He wipes the blood from the face of the girl with gauze that he has dipped in water. Crumbs of light are scattered on the girl's face. The shroud is folded once more about her. The instruments are handed into the satchel. In a moment the morgue is dark and a lone lantern ascends the stairs and is extinguished.

Six weeks later I was in the darkened amphitheater of the Medical School. Tiers of seats rose in a semicircle above the small stage where Hugh Franciscus stood presenting the case material he had encountered in Honduras. It was the highlight of the year. The hall was filled. The night before he had arranged the slides in the order in which they were to be shown. I was at the controls of the slide projector.

"Next slide!" he would order from time to time in that military voice which had called forth blind obedience from generations of medical students, interns, residents and patients.

"This is a fifty-seven-year-old man with a severe burn contracture of the neck. You will notice the rigid webbing that has fused the chin to the presternal tissues. No motion of the head on the torso is possible. . . . Next slide!"

"Click," went the projector.

"Here he is after the excision of the scar tissue and with the head in full extension for the first time. The defect was then covered. . . . Next slide!"

"Click."

". . . with full-thickness drums of skin taken from the abdomen with the Padgett dermatome. Next slide!"

"Click."

And suddenly there she was, extracted from the shadows, suspended above and beyond all of us like a resurrection. There was the oval face, the long black hair unbraided, the tiny gold hoops in her ears. And that luminous gnawed mouth. The whole of her life seemed to have been summed up in this photograph. A long silence followed that was the surgeon's alone to break. Almost at once, like the anesthetist in the operating room in Comayagua, I knew that something was wrong. It was not that the man would not speak as that he could not. The audience of doctors, nurses and students seemed to have been infected by the black, limitless silence. My own pulse doubled. It was hard to breathe. Why did he not call out for the next slide? Why did he not save himself? Why had he not removed this slide from the ones to be shown? All at once I knew that he had used his camera on her again. I could see the long black shadows of her hair flowing into the darker shadows of the morgue. The sudden blinding flash . . . The next slide would be the one taken in the morgue. He would be exposed.

In the dim light reflected from the slide, I saw him gazing up at her, seeing not the colored photograph, I thought, but the negative of it where the ghost of the girl was. For me, the amphitheater had become Honduras. I saw again that courtyard littered with patients. I could see the dust in the beam of light from the projector. It was then that I knew that she was his measure of perfection and pain—the one lost, the other gained. He, too, had heard the click of the camera, had seen her wince and felt his mercy enlarge. At last he spoke.

"Imelda." It was the one word he had heard her say. At the sound of his voice I removed the next slide from the projector. "Click" . . . and she was gone. "Click" again, and in her place the man with the orbital cancer. For a long moment Franciscus looked up in my direction, on his face an expression that I have given up trying to interpret. Gratitude? Sorrow? It made me think of the gaze of the girl when at last she understood that she must hand over to him the evidence of her body.

"This is a sixty-two-year-old man with a basal cell carcinoma of the temple eroding into the bony orbit . . ." he began as though nothing had happened.

At the end of the hour, even before the lights went on, there was loud applause. I hurried to find him among the departing crowd. I could not. Some weeks went by before I caught sight of him. He seemed vaguely convalescent, as though a fever had taken its toll before burning out.

Hugh Franciscus continued to teach for fifteen years, although he operated a good deal less, then gave it up entirely. It was as though he had grown tired of blood, of always having to be involved with blood, of having to draw it, spill it, wipe it away, stanch it. He was a quieter, softer man, I heard, the ferocity diminished. There were no more expeditions to Honduras or anywhere else.

I, too, have not been entirely free of her. Now and then, in the years that have passed, I see that donkey-cart cortège, or his face bent over hers in the morgue. I would like to have told him what I now know, that his unrealistic act was one of goodness, one of those small, persevering acts done, perhaps, to ward off madness. Like lighting a lamp, boiling water for tea, washing a shirt. But, of course, it's too late now.

Sue William Silverman

THE PAT BOONE FAN CLUB

SUE WILLIAM SILVERMAN's first memoir, *Because I Remember Terror, Father, I Remember You*, won the Association of Writers and Writing Programs award series in creative nonfiction. *Love Sick: One Woman's Journey Through Sexual Addiction* is her second memoir. Her poetry collection is *Hieroglyphics in Neon*. Her essays have won literary competitions sponsored by *Hotel Amerika*, *Mid-American Review*, and *Water~Stone Journal*. Other work has appeared in such places as *Prairie Schooner*, *Chicago Tribune*, *Detroit Free Press*, *Redbook*, *Chronicle of Higher Education*, and *The Writer's Chronicle*. She's associate editor of *Fourth Genre: Explorations in Nonfiction*, and she teaches in the low-residency MFA in Writing Program at Vermont College.

Skimming the *Holland Sentinel*, a local newspaper in west Michigan, I see a man who has haunted me for years. Pat Boone. Once again I gaze at him in alluring black and white, just like the photograph I treasured in ninth grade. According to the article, he will be performing the first Saturday night in May at the Calvary Reformed Church as part of Tulip Time Festival. I order a ticket immediately.

On the night of the concert, Pat Boone dazzles onto the stage in white bucks, tight white pants, a white jacket emblazoned with red and blue sequined stars across the shoulders. Though he began as a '50s and '60s pop singer, he has aged into a Christian music icon favored by—I'm sure—Republicans. That I am a Jewish atheist liberal Democrat gives me no pause, not even as he performs in this concrete megachurch weighted with massive crosses. In fact, growing up, these very symbols gave me comfort.

I sit in the balcony, seats empty in the side sections. It's hardly a sold-out crowd. While we enthusiastically clap after the opening number, there are no whistles or shrieks from this mostly elderly, sedate audience. There is no dancing in the aisles, no rushing the stage. If a fan swoons from her upholstered pew, it will more likely be from stroke than idolatry. The cool, unscented air in the auditorium feels polite as a Sunday worship service—rather than a Saturday-night-rock-and-roll-swaggering-Mick-Jagger kind of concert.

Yet I am certainly worshipful. Of him. I am transfixed. It's as if his photograph—that paper image—is conjured to life. Through binoculars, breathless, I watch only him, me in my own white jacket, as if I knew we'd match.

I'm not surprised he still affects me. In fact, during the days leading up to tonight, I plotted how I might meet him after the concert, for I must finally tell him what I failed to say last time we met. But in case security guards stop me, I've written a letter that explains the role he played in my life. At the very least I'll ask a guard to hand-deliver my letter. To further prove my loyalty, I've retrieved, from an old scrapbook, my "i am a member of the pat boone fan club" card, printed on blue stock, which I've put in my pocket. But regardless of the letter or fan-club card, I'm determined to get close enough to touch him, the way I once touched that other photograph, years ago. Time collapses as if, even now, it's not too late for him to save me from my Jewish family, save me from a childhood long ended.

I curled up on the baby-blue bedspread in my home in Glen Rock, New Jersey, a magnifying glass in my teenage hand. Slowly I scanned the glass across black-and-white photographs of Pat Boone in the latest issue of *Life* magazine. In one, he, his wife, Shirley, and four daughters perch on a tandem bicycle in front of their New Jersey home, not many miles from my own. I was particularly drawn to the whiteness of the photos. Pat Boone's white-white teeth beamed at me, his white bucks spotless. I savored each cell of his being, each molecule, as I traced my finger across his magnified image. I believed I felt skin, the pale hairs on his forearms. Only a membrane of paper separated me from a slick fingernail, a perfectly shaped ear, the iris of his eye. Surely the wind gusted his hair, his family's hair, but in the photograph all movement was frozen, the bicycle wheels stationary, never to speed away from me. The family itself was in tandem, legs pumping in perfect, still arcs. It was this crisp, clean, unchanging certainty that I craved.

The hands on his wristwatch were stopped at 3:40. I glanced at my own watch, almost 3:40. I didn't move, waiting for the minute hand to reach the eight, as if I could will time itself to stop, entranced by the notion that we would both endlessly exist in this same segment of time. For even as I tumbled inside the photograph, we remained static on this one particular day, suspended at 3:40 . . . trapped together, me on the tandem bike directly behind him, leaning toward him. Now inside the black-and-white photo, I see lilacs, maple trees, shutters on the windows. But I'm never distracted by scents or colors. I never inhale the Ivory soap of his shirt, never sense warm friction of rubber beneath the wheels of the bike, never have to feel loss or know that seasons change. My ponytail, streaming behind my back, is frozen, captured with him and his family—now my consistent and constantly loving family.

For hours I fantasized living inside this black-and-white print, unreachable. This immaculate universe was safe, far away from my father's messy flesh-and-blood hands, hands that hurt me at night.

Through my bedroom window, sun glinted off the glass I held inches from his face. Round magnifier. Beam of light. Halo. I placed my hand, fingers spread, beneath the glass, hovering just above the paper, as if glass, hand, photograph, him—all existed in disembodied heavenly light.

As the bus rumbled across the George Washington Bridge, over the Hudson River, I clutched a ticket to his television show in one hand, a copy of his book, *'Twixt Twelve and Twenty*, in the other. Silently, I sang the words, his words, with which he closed his weekly program, "See the USA in your Chevrolet," a show I watched religiously on our black-and-white Zenith. With the darkness of New Jersey behind me, the gleaming lights of Manhattan before me, I felt as if I myself were a photograph slowly being developed into a new life. In just an hour I would see him. I wanted to be with him—be his wife, lover, daughter, houseguest, girlfriend, best friend, pet. Interchangeable. Any one of these relationships would do.

Sitting in the studio during the show, I waited for it to end. Mainly, I waited for the time when we would meet. Yes, I suppose I loved his voice, his music. At least, if asked, I would claim to love his songs. What else could I say since there was no language at that moment to specify what I most needed from Pat Boone? How could I explain to him—to anybody—that if I held that magnifying glass over my skin, I would see my father's fingerprints? I would see skin stained with shame. I would see a girl who seemed marked by her very Jewishness. Since my Jewish father misloved me, what I needed in order to be saved was an audience with Pat Boone.

Here in this audience, I was surrounded by girls crying and screaming his name. But I was different from these fans. Surely he knew this, too, sensed my silent presence, the secret life we shared. Soon, I no longer heard the girls, no longer noticed television cameras, cue cards, musicians. No longer even heard his voice or which song he sang. All I saw was his face suffused in a spotlight, one beam that seemed to emanate from a darkened sky.

After the show, I queued up with other fans outside the stage door. I waited with my Aqua Net–flipped hair, Peter Pan collar, circle pin, penny loafers. Slowly the line inched forward, girls seeking autographs.

But when I reached him, I was too startled to speak. Now I faced him in living color. Pink shirt. Brown hair. Suede jacket. His tan hands moved; his brown eyes actually blinked. I could see him breathe. I forgot my carefully rehearsed words: "Will you adopt me?"

Besides, if I spoke, I feared he wouldn't even hear me. My voice would be too low, too dim, too insignificant, too tainted. He would know I was too distant to be saved. I felt as if I'd fallen so far from that photograph that my own image was out of focus. I was a blur, a smudged Jewish blur of a girl, mesmerized by a golden cross, an amulet on a chain around his neck. Speechless, I continued to stand, unmoving, holding up the line. Finally he smiled and asked, "Is that for me?" He gestured toward the book. I held it out to him. Quickly he scrawled his name.

Later, alone in my bedroom, lying on my blue bedspread, I trailed a fingertip over his autograph. I spent days learning to copy his signature. I traced it, duplicated it. Using black India ink, I forged the name "Pat Boone" on my school notebooks. I wrote his name on my white Keds with a ballpoint pen. At the Jersey Shore I scrawled my own love letters in the sand. But I had missed my chance to speak to him. For years those words I wanted to say remained unspoken.

Now, watching him through binoculars in the Calvary Reformed Church in Holland, Michigan, I again scan every cell of his face, his neck. I'm sure I can observe individual molecules in his fingers, palms, hands, wrists. He wears a gold pinkie ring, a gold-link bracelet. And a watch! That watch? I wonder if it's the same 3:40 watch. In his presence I am once again tranced—almost as if we've been in a state of suspension together all this time.

He doesn't even appear to have aged—much. Boyish good looks, brown hair. Yet this grandfather sings his golden oldies, tributes to innocence and teenage love: "Bernadine," "Love Letters in the Sand," "Moody River," "Friendly Persuasion," "Tutti Frutti." His newer songs are about God and country. Well, he sings, after all, to a white Christian audience, mainly elderly church ladies with tight gray curls, pastel pantsuits, sensible shoes. I know I am the only one here who voted for President Clinton, who wears open-toed sandals, who doesn't believe in God. But nothing deters me. I feel almost like that teenage girl yearning to be close to him, closer.

From the piano, he retrieves a bouquet of tulips wrapped in cellophane, telling the audience that at each concert he gives flowers to one young girl. Peering into the darkened auditorium, he asks, half joking, whether any girls have actually come to the concert. "Have any of you mothers or grandmothers brought your granddaughter with you?"

I lean forward, looking around. In one section—members of a tour bus, no doubt—is a group of older women all wearing jaunty red hats. At least twenty of these hats turn in unison as if searching the audience. No one else moves. The row in front of me seems to be mother-and-daughter pairs, but most of the daughters wear bifocals, while some of the mothers, I noticed earlier, used canes to climb the stairs. After a moment of silence, Pat Boone, cajoling, lets us know he found one young girl at his earlier, four o'clock show. He lowers the microphone to his side, waiting.

Me. I want it to be me.

A girl, her neck bent, silky brown hair shading her face, finally walks forward from the rear of the auditorium. Pat Boone hurries down the few steps, greeting her before she reaches the stage. He holds out the flowers, but she doesn't seem to realize she's supposed to take them.

"What's your name?" he asks.

"Amber." She wears ripped jeans and a faded sweatshirt.

"Here." Again he urges the tulips toward her hands. "These are for a lovely girl named Amber."

As strains of "April Love" flow from the four-piece band, she finally takes the flowers. His arm encircles her waist. Facing her, he sings as if just to her, "April love is for the very young . . ." The spotlight darkens, an afterglow of sunset. The petals of the tulips, probably placed on stage hours earlier, droop.

After the song, Pat Boone beams at her and asks for a kiss. "On the cheek, of course." He laughs, reassuring the audience, as he points to the spot. The girl doesn't move. "Oh, please, just one little peck." His laugh dwindles to a smile.

I lean back, sliding down in my seat. I lower the binoculars to my lap.

Kiss him, I want to whisper to the girl, not wanting to witness Pat Boone embarrassed or disappointed.

No, walk away from him. Because he's old enough to be your father, your grandfather.

Instead, he leans forward and quickly brushes his lips on her cheek. With the bouquet held awkwardly in her arms, she escapes down the aisle to her seat.

Now his voice needs to rest, perhaps. The lights on stage are extinguished. Images of Pat Boone in the Holy Land flash on two large video screens built into the wall behind the pulpit. The introduction to the theme song from *Exodus* soars across the hushed audience. Atop the desert fortress Masada—the last outpost of Jewish zealots who chose mass suicide rather than Roman capture— a much younger Pat Boone, in tan chinos, arms outstretched, sings, "So take my hand and walk this land with me," lyrics he, himself, wrote. The real Pat Boone sits on a stool watching the video pan to Israeli children wearing kibbutz hats, orchards of fig trees, camels, the Sea of Galilee, Bethlehem, the old city in Jerusalem. The Via Dolorosa. The Wailing Wall. The Dead Sea.

"Until I die, this land is mine."

A final aerial shot circles a sweatless and crisp Pat Boone on Masada. Desert sand swelters in the distance.

This land is mine . . .

For the first time I wonder what he means by these words he wrote. Does he mean, literally, he thinks the Holy Land is his, that it belongs to Christianity? Or, perhaps, is he momentarily impersonating an Israeli, a Zionist, a Jew? Or maybe this appropriation is just a state of mind.

Pat Boone, Pat Boone. Who are you? I always thought I knew.

The lights flash on. Arising from his stool, Pat Boone is smiling. The band hits the chords as he proclaims we'll all have "A Wonderful Time up There."

Periodically, growing up, I frequented churches, immersing myself in hymns and votive candles. Once I even owned a cross necklace and a garnet rosary, superficially believing Catholic and Christian amulets offered luck and protection. So I'm more familiar with Christian songs than those of my own religion even though at one time in my life, in elementary school, I attended Jewish services.

Saturday mornings, when we lived on the island of St. Thomas, my parents and I drove up Synagogue Hill, parking by the wrought-iron gate leading to the temple. We entered the arched stucco doorway where my father paused to don a yarmulke. Here the air was cool, shaded from tropical sun. In my best madras dress, I trailed behind my parents down the aisle, the floor thick with sand. My feet in my buffalo-hide sandals etched small imprints beside the tracks left by my father's heavy black shoes. I sat between my parents on one of the benches. The rabbi, standing before the mahogany ark containing the six Torahs, began to pray. I slid from the bench to sit on the sandy floor.

The sand was symbolic in this nineteenth-century synagogue, founded by Sephardic Jews from Spain. During the Spanish Inquisition, Jews, forced to worship in secret, met in cellars where they poured sand on floors to muffle footsteps, mute the sound of prayers. Otherwise, if caught, they would be killed. This was almost all I knew of Judaism except stories my mother told me about the Holocaust when bad things happened to Jews—little Jewish girls, too.

Throughout the service, I sprinkled sand over me as if at the beach. I trailed it down my bare legs. I slid off my sandals, submerging my toes beneath grains of coral. Lines of sand streaked the sweaty crooks of my elbows. Small mounds cupped my knees. I even trickled it on my head until it caught in the weave of my braids. I leaned against one of the cool, lime-washed pillars, smudging my dress as well. No one in the congregation, not even my parents, ever seemed to notice. Perhaps they were too engrossed by readings from the Torah to see me . . . while, to me, none of their prayerful chants were as lovely as sand. Instead, I watched wands of light beam through arched windows glinting off mica in the sand, off me. I felt as if I, myself, could become one with whitewash, with sand, with light. Then, later that night, home in bed, maybe my father wouldn't find me, wouldn't be able to see or distinguish me. Maybe if I poured enough sand over my body I could discover how to hide all little Jewish girls, make us invisible. Instead, it seemed to be my own father's footsteps that were muffled, for no one in the congregation ever heard or saw him. Not as he really was.

After the concert, I slowly walk through the church lobby, exhausted. At the sales booth, buying a CD, I ask whether Pat Boone will be signing autographs. No one seems to know. A gray-haired man limps past, the word SECURITY stenciled on his black T-shirt. The church ladies stream out the door, not seeming to expect anything more of the evening.

I could follow them.

But at the far corner of the lobby is a hallway that seems to lead to the back of the auditorium, behind the stage. It is empty. No one guards the entrance. I turn down its plush, blue-carpeted stillness. My footsteps are silent. It is a hush that might precede a worship service. Solemn, scentless air. Dim sconces line the walls. I had thought there would be a throng of grandmothers lining up for autographs and snapshots. But I am alone gripping his CD in one hand, my letter to him in the other.

At the end of the corridor are two wide doors, shut. I assume they're locked, but as I grasp the knob it turns. Another hallway. I pass another T-shirted guard, this one holding a silent walkie-talkie, his ear plugged with a hearing aid. I assume he'll stop me. But my straight solid footsteps, the determined look on my face seem to grant me entrance. I must look as if I belong here. I act as if I know what I'm doing.

I do belong here. I do know what I'm doing.

Beyond another set of doors I reach a small group dressed in Dutch costumes, wooden clogs, including the mayor and his wife, who were on stage earlier to thank Pat Boone for celebrating the Tulip Time Festival. Beside them is another security guard, this one a teenage boy, murmuring into his walkie-talkie. I approach, wanting to ask him where I might find Pat Boone. I decide to throw myself on his mercy. I'm prepared to beg, plead, cry. I will say I've been waiting my whole life. I will say the Voice of God Himself told me to speak to Pat Boone.

The guard continues to mumble into his walkie-talkie. For a few more minutes I patiently wait for him to finish, until anxiety floods me. Suppose I miss him? He might be preparing to leave the building right this minute. He'll disappear before I find him. Then, as if pulled by unseen forces, I turn away from the guard. I retrace my footsteps back through the set of doors.

I glimpse a white shirt. The back of a man's head. Brown hair. Him.

He and another man are just opening a door farther down the corridor.

I yell, "Mr. Boone. Pat Boone."

I rush after him, grabbing the door about to shut behind him. We're in a small foyer just behind the stage. Not understanding the force of my need, the other man tries to shoo me away. I ignore him, pleading, "Mr. Boone. I have to speak to you. Just for a minute. I've been waiting. Pat Boone."

I push past the assistant and stand right in front of Pat Boone. His red and blue sequined jacket is off. He's in his white shirt, white pants, white shoes. His face is still in makeup. He has few wrinkles. His eyes are almost expressionless. It's as if his whole life all he's practiced is his public smile, and the rest of his face is frozen—but familiar to me—the way he looked in the photograph. And there they are as he smiles at me, albeit tentatively: his white-white teeth.

My words are garbled, rushed, confused. I don't know how much time I have, when I will be removed. So much to explain. I hardly know where to start. I tell him how much I loved the photograph in *Life* magazine.

"Oh, yes, that tandem bicycle," he says. "I remember that."

"But you saved my life," I say.

I am telling him about my father, what happened with my father, that it was he, Pat Boone . . . just knowing he existed kept me going . . . just seeing his photograph helped me stay alive . . . that he represented—what word do I use? "Safety?" "Holiness"? "Purity"? He has taken a step back, away from me. His smile may have dimmed by one decibel. Am I acting like a crazy woman? Am I the first woman who has ever pursued him to confess that her father once hurt her, and that he, Pat Boone, represented hope? Just thinking that one day he might . . .

"Well, I'm glad to know that I did something good," he says. "That I helped someone."

"Oh, yes," I say. "You were everything. Your family. Your daughters."

"I guess these things happen a lot," he says. "To children. It's terrible."

"Here." I give him the letter. "This will explain how I felt."

He takes the letter, folded in an envelope. That hand—those clean fingers I studied by the hour.

"I'll write back to you," he says. "After I read it."

My audience with him is over. "Thank you," I whisper, turning to leave.

I pause in the parking lot in the damp spring night. The massive walls of the church loom over me. Busloads of grandmothers rumble from the lot.

I was too overwhelmed to tell him about the magnifying glass or his wristwatch. Nor did I say, "I want you to adopt me"—the one thing I've most wanted. Of course, even I know how crazy that would sound. Besides, is it even still true?

I get in my car and shut the door. But I continue to watch the church. Maybe I'll catch one last glimpse of him. Him. Did he help sustain me all those years? Did he offer hope?

Yes. His image. His milky-white image.

That sterile pose. I conjured him into the man I needed him to be: a safe father. By my believing in that constant image, he did save me, without my being adopted, without my even asking.

At the end of the concert, the mayor of Holland and his wife came on stage to present Pat Boone with a special pair of wooden clogs painted to resemble his trademark bucks. Again, I had to lower the binoculars, embarrassed for him, unable to watch, just as when he gave the tulips to that young girl.

I wonder if anyone else in the audience felt uncomfortable when this father, this grandfather, tried to coerce a kiss from that adolescent girl? Or did anyone notice her embarrassment, her shame? No, that's not a thought that would trouble any of Pat Boone's fans in Calvary. But Calvary doesn't exist for me, cannot be made to exist for me—even by Pat Boone.

Pat Boone! Those two short syllables have stretched the length of my life. So regardless of religion or illusion, his love letters offered me improbable safety—grooved in vinyl, etched in sand.

Floyd Skloot

A MEASURE OF ACCEPTANCE

FLOYD SKLOOT was born in Brooklyn, New York, in 1947. He is the author of four books of nonfiction, including a trilogy of memoirs: *In the Shadow of Memory*, winner of the PEN Center USA Literary Award and a finalist for both the Barnes & Noble Discover Award and PEN Award for the Art of the Essay; *A World of Light*; and *The Wink of the Zenith*. His essays have been included in *The Best American Essays*, *The Best American Science Writing*, *The Pushcart Prize Anthology*, *The Best Food Writing*, *The Art of the Essay*, and *The Fourth Genre*, and in such publications as *The New York Times Magazine*, *American Scholar*, *Antioch Review*, *Boulevard*, *Creative Nonfiction*, *Sewanee Review*, *Southwest Review*, *Virginia Quarterly Review*, and *Witness*. He has also published six collections of poetry and four novels. Skloot lives in Portland, Oregon.

The psychiatrist's office was in a run-down industrial section at the northern edge of Oregon's capital, Salem. It shared space with a chiropractic health center, separated from it by a temporary divider that wobbled in the current created by opening the door. When I arrived, a man sitting with his gaze trained on the spot I suddenly filled began kneading his left knee, his suit pants hopelessly wrinkled in that one spot. Another man, standing beside the door and dressed in overalls, studied the empty wall and muttered as he slowly rose on his toes and sank back on his heels. Like me, neither seemed happy to be visiting Dr. Peter Avilov.

Dr. Avilov specialized in the psychodiagnostic examination of disability claimants for the Social Security Administration. He made a career of weeding out hypochondriacs, malingerers, fakers, people who were ill without organic causes. There may be many such scam artists working the disability angle, but there are also many legitimate claimants. Avilov worked as a kind of hired gun, paid by an agency whose financial interests were best served when he determined that claimants were not disabled. It was like having your house appraised by the father-in-law of your prospective buyer, like being stopped by a traffic cop several tickets shy of his monthly quota, like facing a part-time judge who

473

works for the construction company you're suing. Avilov's incentives were not encouraging to me.

I understood why I was there. After a virus I contracted in December of 1988 targeted my brain, I became totally disabled. When the Social Security Administration had decided to reevaluate my medical condition eight years later, they exercised their right to send me to a doctor of their own choosing. This seemed fair enough. But after receiving records, test results and reports of brain scans, and statements from my own internal medicine and infectious diseases physicians, all attesting to my ongoing disability, and after requiring twenty-five pages of handwritten questionnaires from me and my wife, they scheduled an appointment for me with Avilov. Not with an independent internal medicine or infectious diseases specialist, not with a neurologist, but with a shrink.

Now, twelve years after first getting sick, I've become adept at being brain damaged. It's not that my symptoms have gone away: I still try to dice a stalk of celery with a carrot instead of a knife, still reverse *p* and *b* when I write, or draw a primitive hourglass when I mean to draw a star. I call our *bird feeder* a *bread-winner* and place newly purchased packages of frozen corn in the dishwasher instead of the freezer. I put crumpled newspaper and dry pine into our wood-stove, strike a match and attempt to light the metal door. Preparing to cross the "main street" in Carlton, Oregon, I looked both ways, saw a pickup truck a quarter mile south, took one step off the curb, and landed flat on my face, cane pointing due east.

So I'm still much as I was in December of 1988, when I first got sick. I spent most of a year confined to bed. I couldn't write and had trouble reading anything more complicated than *People* magazine or the newspaper's sports page. The functioning of memory was shattered, bits of the past clumped like a partly assembled jigsaw puzzle, the present a flicker of discontinuous images. Without memory, it was impossible for me to learn how to operate the new music system that was meant to help me pass the time, or figure out why I felt so confused, or take my medications without support.

But in time I learned to manage my encounters with the world in new ways. I shed what no longer fit the life: training shoes and road-racing flats, three-piece suits and ties, a car. I bought a cane. I seeded my home with pads and pens so that I could write reminders before forgetting what I'd thought. I festooned my room with color-coded Post-it notes telling me what to do, whom to call, where to locate important items. I remarried, finding love when I imagined it no longer possible. Eventually, I moved to the country, slowing my external life to match its internal pace, simplifying, stripping away layers of distraction and demands.

Expecting the unexpected now, I can, like an improvisational actor, incorporate it into my performance. For instance, my tendency to use words that are close to—but not exactly—the words I'm trying to say has led to some surprising discoveries in the composition of sentences.

A freshness emerges when the mind is unshackled from its habitual ways. In the past, I never would have described the effect of a viral attack on my brain as being "geezered" overnight if I hadn't first confused the words *seizure* and *geezer.* It is as though my word-finding capacity has developed an associative function to compensate for its failures of precision, so I end up with *shellac* instead of *plaque* when trying to describe the gunk on my teeth. Who knows, maybe James Joyce was brain damaged when he wrote *Finnegans Wake* and built a whole novel on puns and neologisms that were actually symptoms of disease.

It's possible to see such domination of the unexpected in a positive light. So getting lost in the familiar woods around our house and finding my way home again adds a twist of excitement to days that might seem circumscribed or routine because of my disability. When the natural food grocery where we shop rearranged its entire stock, I was one of the few customers who didn't mind, since I could never remember where things were anyway. I am less hurried and more deliberate than I was; being attentive, purposeful in movement, lends my life an intensity of awareness that was not always present before. My senses are heightened, their fine-tuning mechanism busted: spicy food, stargazer lilies in bloom, birdsong, heat, my wife's vivid palette when she paints have all become more intense and stimulating. Because it threatens my balance, a sudden breeze is something to stop for, to let its strength and motion register. That may not guarantee success—as my pratfall in Carlton indicates—but it does allow me to appreciate detail and nuance.

One way of spinning this is to say that my daily experience is often spontaneous and exciting. Not fragmented and intimidating, but unpredictable, continuously new. I may lose track of things, or of myself in space, my line of thought, but instead of getting frustrated I try to see this as the perfect time to stop and figure out what I want or where I am. I accept my role in the harlequinade. It's not so much a matter of making lemonade out of life's lemons but rather of learning to savor the shock, taste, texture, and aftereffects of a mouthful of unadulterated citrus.

Acceptance is a deceptive word. It suggests compliance, a consenting to my condition and to who I have become. This form of acceptance is often seen as weakness, submission. We say *I accept my punishment.* Or *I accept your decision.* But such assent, while passive in essence, does provide the stable, rocklike foundation for coping with a condition that will not go away. It is a powerful passivity, the Zen of Illness, that allows for endurance.

There is, however, more than endurance at stake. A year in bed, another year spent primarily in my recliner—these were times when endurance was the main issue. But over time, I began to recognize the possibilities for transformation. I saw another kind of acceptance as being viable, the kind espoused by Robert Frost when he said "Take what is given, and make it over your own way." That is, after all, the root meaning of the verb to *accept*, which comes from the Latin *accipere*, or "take to oneself." It implies an embrace. Not a giving up but a welcoming.

People encourage the sick to resist, to fight back; we say that our resistance is down when we contract a virus. But it wasn't possible to resist the effects of brain damage. Fighting to speak rapidly and clearly, as I always had in the past, leads only to more garbling of meaning; willing myself to walk without a cane or climb a ladder leads only to more falls; demanding that I not forget something only makes me angrier when all I can remember is the effort not to forget. I began to realize that the most aggressive act I could perform on my own behalf was to stop struggling and discover what I could really do.

This, I believe, is what the Austrian psychotherapist Viktor E. Frankl refers to in his classic book, *The Doctor and the Soul*, as "spiritual elasticity." He says, speaking of his severely damaged patients, that "man must cultivate the flexibility to swing over to another value-group if that group and that alone offers the possibility of actualizing values." Man must, Frankl believes, "temper his efforts to the chances that are offered." Such shifts of value, made possible by active acceptance of life as it is, can only be achieved alone. Doctors, therapists, rehabilitation professionals, family members, friends, lovers cannot reconcile a person to the changes wrought by illness or injury, though they can ease the way. Acceptance is a private act, achieved gradually and with little outward evidence. It also seems never to be complete; I still get furious with myself for forgetting what I'm trying to tell my daughter during a phone call, humiliated when I blithely walk away with another shopper's cart of groceries or fall in someone's path while examining the lower shelves at Powell's Bookstore.

But for all its private essence, acceptance cannot be expressed purely in private terms. My experience did not happen to me alone; family, colleagues and friends, acquaintances were all involved. I had a new relationship with my employer and its insurance company, with federal and state government, with people who read my work. There is a social dimension to the experience of illness and to its acceptance, a kind of reciprocity between self and world that goes beyond the enactment of laws governing handicapped access to buildings, or rules prohibiting discrimination in the workplace. It is in this social dimension that, for all my private adjustment, I remain a grave cripple and, apparently, a figure of contempt. At least the parties involved agreed that what was wrong with me was all in my head. However, mine was a disability arising from organic damage to the brain caused by a viral attack, not from psychiatric illness. The distinction matters; my disability status would not continue if my condition were psychiatric. It was in the best interests of the Social Security Administration for Dr. Avilov to say my symptoms were caused by the mind, were psychosomatic rather than organic in nature. And what was in their interests was also in Avilov's.

On hi-tech scans, tiny holes in my brain make visually apparent what is clear enough to anyone who observes me in action over time: I no longer have "brains." A brain, yes, with many functions intact, but I'm not as smart or as quick or as steady as I was. Though I may not look sick and I don't shake or froth or talk to myself, after a few minutes it becomes clear that something fundamental is wrong. My losses of cognitive capability have been fully measured and recorded. They were used by the Social Security Administration and the insurance company to establish my total disability, by various physicians to establish treatment and therapy programs, by a pharmaceutical company to establish my eligibility for participation in the clinical field trial of a drug that didn't work. I have a handicapped parking placard on the dashboard of my car; I can get a free return-trip token from the New York City subway system by flashing my Medicaid card. In this sense, I have a public profile as someone who is disabled. I have met the requirements.

Further, as someone with quantifiable diminishment in IQ levels, impaired abstract reasoning and learning facility, scattered recall capacities and aptitudes that decrease as fatigue or distraction increases, I am of scientific use. When it serves their purposes, various institutions welcome me. Indeed, they pursue me. I have been actively recruited for three experimental protocols run by Oregon Health Sciences University. One of these, a series of treatments using DMSO, made me smell so rancid that I turned heads just by walking into a room. But when it does not serve their purpose, these same institutions dismiss me. Or challenge me. No matter how well I may have adjusted to living with brain damage, the world I often deal with has not.

When money or status is involved, I am positioned as a pariah. So would Avilov find that my disability was continuing, or would he judge me as suffering from mental illness? Those who say that the distinction is bogus, or that the patient's fear of being labeled mentally ill is merely a cultural bias and ought not matter, are missing the point. Money is at stake; in our culture, this means it matters very much. To all sides.

Avilov began by asking me to recount the history of my illness. He seemed as easily distracted as I was; while I stared at his checked flannel shirt, sweetly ragged mustache, and the pen he occasionally put in his mouth like a pipe,

Avilov looked from my face to his closed door to his empty notepad and back to my face, nodding. When I had finished, he asked a series of diagnostic questions: did I know what day it was (hey, I'm here on the right day, aren't I?), could I name the presidents of the United States since Kennedy, could I count backward from 100 by sevens? During this series, he interrupted me to provide a list of four unconnected words (such as *train argue barn vivid*), which I was instructed to remember for later recall. Then he asked me to explain what was meant by the expression, "People who live in glass houses should not throw stones." I nodded, thought for a moment, knew that this sort of proverb relied on metaphor, which as a poet should be my great strength, and began to explain. Except that I couldn't. I must have talked for five minutes, in tortuous circles, spewing gobbledygook about stones breaking glass and people having things to hide, shaking my head, backtracking as I tried to elaborate. But it was beyond me, as all abstract thinking is beyond me, and I soon drifted into stunned silence.

Crashing into your limitations this way hurts; I remembered as a long-distance runner hitting the fabled "wall" at about mile twenty-two of the Chicago Marathon, my body depleted of all energy resources, feeding on its own muscle and fat for every additional step, and I recognized this as being a similar sensation.

For the first time, I saw something clear in Avilov's eyes. He saw me. He recognized this as real, the blathering of a brain-damaged man who still thinks he can think. It was at this moment that he asked, "Why are you here?" I nearly burst into tears, knowing that he meant I seemed to be suffering from organic rather than mental illness. Music to my ears. "I have the same question."

The rest of our interview left little impression. But when the time came for me to leave, I stood to shake his hand and realized that Avilov had forgotten to ask me if I remembered the four words I had by then forgotten. I did remember having to remember them, though. Would it be best to walk out of the room, or should I remind him that he forgot to have me repeat the words I could no longer remember? Or had I forgotten that he did ask me, lost as I was in the fog of other failures? Should I say *I can't remember if you asked me to repeat those words, but there's no need because I can't remember them*?

None of that mattered because Avilov, bless his heart, had found that my disability status remained as it was. Such recommendations arrive as mixed blessings; I would much rather not be as I am, but since I am, I must depend upon on receiving the legitimate support I paid for when healthy and am entitled to now. There was little time to feel relieved because I soon faced an altogether different challenge, this time from the company that handled my disability insurance payments. I was ordered to undergo a "Two Day Functional

Capacity Evaluation" administered by a rehabilitation firm they hired in Portland. A later phone call informed me to prepare for six and a half hours of physical challenges the first day, and three hours more the following day. I would be made to lift weights, carry heavy boxes, push and pull loaded crates, climb stairs, perform various feats of balance and dexterity, complete puzzles, answer a barrage of questions. But I would have an hour for lunch. Wear loose clothes. Arrive early.

With the letter had come a warning: "You must provide your best effort so that the reported measurements of your functional ability are valid." Again, the message seemed clear: no shenanigans, you! We're wise to your kind. I think the contempt that underlies these confrontations is apparent. The patient— or, in the lingo of insurance operations, the claimant—is approached not only as an adversary but as a deceiver. *You can climb more stairs than that! You can really stand on one leg, like a heron; stop falling over, freeloader! We know that game.* Paranoia rules; here an institution seems caught in its grip. With money at stake, the disabled are automatically supposed to be up to some kind of chicanery, and our displays of symptoms are viewed as untrustworthy. Never mind that I contributed to Social Security for my entire working life, with the mutual understanding that if I were disabled, the fund would be there for me. Never mind that both my employer and I paid for disability insurance with the mutual understanding that if I were disabled, payments would be there for me. Our doctors are suspect, our caregivers are implicated, and *we've got our eyes on you!*

The rehab center looked like a combination gym and children's playground. The staff was friendly, casual; several were administering physical therapy so that the huge room into which I was led smelled of sweat. An elderly man at a desk worked with a small stack of blocks. Above the blather of Muzak, I heard grunts and moans of pained effort: a woman lying on mats, being helped to bend damaged knees; a stiff-backed man laboring through his stretches; two women side by side on benches, deep in conversation as they curled small weights.

The man assigned to conduct my Functional Capacity Evaluation looked enough like me to be a cousin. Short, bearded, thick hair curling away from a lacy bald spot, Reggie shook my hand and tried to set me at ease. He was good at what he did, lowering the level of confrontation, expressing compassion, concerned about the effect on my health of such strenuous testing. I should let him know if I needed to stop. Right then, before the action began, I had a moment of grave doubt. I could remain suspicious, paranoia begetting paranoia, or I could trust Reggie to be honest, to assess my capacities without prejudice. The presence of patients being helped all around me seemed a good sign. This firm didn't appear dependent upon referrals for evaluation from insurance companies.

They had a lucrative operation, independent of all that. And if I could not trust a man who reminded me of a healthier version of myself, it seemed like bad karma. I loved games and physical challenges. But I knew who and what I was now; it would be fine if I simply let him know as well. Though much of my disability results from cognitive deficits, there are physical manifestations too, so letting Reggie know me in the context of a gymlike setting felt comfortable. Besides, he was sharp enough to recognize suspicion in my eyes anyway, and that would give him reason to doubt my efforts. We were both after the same thing: a valid representation of my abilities. Now was the time to put all I had learned about acceptance on the line. It would require a measure of acceptance on both sides.

What I was not prepared for was how badly I would perform in every test. I knew my limitations but had never measured them. Over a dozen years, the consequences of exceeding my physical capabilities had been made clear enough that I learned to live within the limits. Here, I was brought repeatedly to those limits and beyond; after an hour with Reggie, I was ready to sleep for the entire next month. The experience was crushing. How could I comfortably manage only 25 pounds in the floor-to-waist lift repetitions? I used to press 150 pounds as part of my regular weekly training for competitive racing. How could I not stand on my left foot for more than two seconds? You should've seen me on a ball field! I could hold my arms up for no more than 75 seconds, could push a cart loaded with no more than 40 pounds of weights, could climb only 66 stairs. I could not fit shapes to their proper holes in a form board in the time allotted, though I distinctly remember playing a game with my son that worked on the same principles and always beating the timer. Just before lunch, Reggie asked me to squat and lift a box filled with paper. He stood behind me and was there as I fell back into his arms.

I may not have been clinically depressed, as Dr. Avilov attested earlier, but this evaluation was almost enough to knock me into the deepest despair. Reggie said little to reveal his opinions. At the time, I thought that meant that he was simply being professional, masking judgment, and though I sensed empathy I realized that could be a matter of projection on my part.

Later, I believed that his silence came from knowing what he had still to make me do. After lunch, and an interview about the Activities of Daily Living form I had filled out, Reggie led me to a field of blue mats spread across the room's center. For a moment, I wondered if he planned to challenge me to a wrestling match. That thought had lovely symbolic overtones: wrestling with someone who suggested my former self; wrestling with an agent of THEM, a man certain to defeat me; or having my Genesis experience, like Jacob at Peniel, wrestling with Him.

Which, at least for Jacob, resulted in a blessing and a nice payout.

But no. Reggie told me to crawl.

In order to obtain "a valid representation" of my abilities, it was necessary for the insurance company to see how far, and for how long, and with what result, I could crawl. It was a test I had not imagined. It was a test that could, in all honesty, have only one purpose. My ability to crawl could not logically be used as a valid measure of my employability. And in light of all the other tasks I had been unable to perform, crawling was not necessary as a measure of my functional limits. It would test nothing, at least nothing specific to my case, not even the lower limits of my capacity. Carrying the malign odor of indifference, tyranny's tainted breath, the demand that I crawl was almost comical in its obviousness: the paternal powers turning someone like me, a disabled man living in dependence upon their finances, into an infant.

I considered refusing to comply. Though the implied threat (*you must provide your best effort . . .*) contained in their letter crossed my mind, and I wondered how Beverly and I would manage without my disability payments, it wasn't practicality that made me proceed. At least I don't think so. It was, instead, acceptance. I had spent the morning in a public confrontation with the fullness of my loss, as though on stage with Reggie, representing the insurance company, as my audience. Now I would confront the sheer heartlessness of the System, the powers that demanded that I crawl before they agreed temporarily to accept my disability. I would, perhaps the first time, join the company of those far more damaged than I am, who have endured far more indignity in their quest for acceptance. Whatever it is that Reggie and the insurance company believed they were measuring as I got down on my hands and knees and began a slow circuit of the mats in the center of that huge room, I believed I was measuring how far we still had to go for acceptance.

Reggie stood in the center of the mats, rotating in place as I crawled along one side, turned at the corner, crossed to the opposite side, and began to return toward the point where I had started. Before I reached it, Reggie told me to stop. He had seen enough. I was slow and unsteady at the turns, but I could crawl fine. I never received a follow-up letter from the insurance company. I was never formally informed of their findings, though my disability payments have continued.

At the end of the second day of testing, Reggie told me how I'd done. In many of the tests, my results were in the lower 5–10 percent for men my age. My performance diminished alarmingly on the second day, and he hadn't ever tested anyone who did as poorly on the dexterity components. He believed that I had given my best efforts and would report accordingly. But he would not give me any formal results. I was to contact my physician, who would receive Reggie's report in due time.

When the battery of tests had first been scheduled, I'd made an appointment to see my doctor a few days after their completion. I knew the physical challenges would worsen my symptoms and wanted him to see what had resulted. I knew I would need his help. By the time I got there, he too had spoken to Reggie and knew about my performance. But my doctor never got an official report either.

This was familiar ground. Did I wish to request a report? I was continuing to receive my legitimate payments; did I really want to contact my insurance company and demand to see the findings of my Functional Capacity Evaluation? Risk waking the sleeping dragon? What would be the point? I anticipated no satisfaction in reading that I was in fact disabled, or in seeing how my experience translated into numbers or bureaucratic prose. It seems that I was of interest only when there was an occasion to rule me ineligible for benefits. Found again to be disabled, I wasn't even due the courtesy of a reply. The checks came; what more did I need to show that my claims are accepted? There was no need for a report. Through the experience, I had discovered something more vital than the measures of my physical capacity. The measure of public acceptance that I hoped to find, that I imagined would balance my private acceptance, was not going to come from a public agency or public corporation. It didn't work that way, after all. The public was largely indifferent, as most people, healthy or not, understand. The only measure of acceptance would come from how I conducted myself in public, moment by moment. With laws in place to permit handicapped access to public spaces, prevent discrimination, and encourage involvement in public life, there is general acceptance that the handicapped live among us and must be accommodated.

But that doesn't mean they're not resented, feared, or mistrusted by the healthy. The disability racket! I had encountered the true, hard heart of the matter. My life in the social dimension of illness is governed by forces that are severe and implacable. Though activism has helped protect the handicapped over the last four decades, there is little room for reciprocity between the handicapped person and his or her world. It is naïve to expect otherwise.

I would like to think that the insurance company didn't send an official letter of findings because they were abashed at what they'd put me through. I would like to think that Dr. Avilov, who no longer practices in Salem, hasn't moved away because he found too many claimants disabled and lost his contract with the Social Security Administration. That my experience educated

Reggie and his firm, and that his report educated the insurance company, so everyone now understands the experience of disability, or of living with brain damage.

But I know better. My desire for reciprocity between self and world must find its form in writing about my experience. Slowly. This essay has taken me eleven months to complete, in sittings of fifteen minutes or so. Built of fragments shaped after the pieces were examined, its errors of spelling and of word choice and logic ferreted out with the help of my wife or daughter or computer's spell-checker. It may look to a reader like the product of someone a lot less damaged than I claim to be. But it's not. It's the product of someone who has learned how to live with his limitations, and work with them. And when it's published, if someone employed by my insurance company reads it, I will probably get a letter in the mail demanding that I report for another battery of tests. After all, this is not how a brain-damaged man is supposed to behave.

Lauren Slater

BLACK SWANS

LAUREN SLATER is a three-time American Society of Magazine Editors Award nominee—twice in the essay category, once in the profile category—who has published several highly acclaimed books of nonfiction. Her essays and articles have appeared in *Harper's*, *The New York Times Magazine*, and *Elle*, among others; her work has also been picked numerous times for *The Best American Essays* series. She is a 2004 winner of a National Endowment for the Arts grant in creative nonfiction. A psychologist, she works in Boston, Massachusetts.

snow

There is something satisfying and scary about making an angel, lowering your bulky body into the drowning fluff, stray flakes landing on your face. I am seven or eight and the sky looms above me, gray and dead. I move my arms and legs—expanding, contracting—sculpting snow before it can swallow me up. I feel the cold filter into my head, seep through the wool of my mittens. I swish wider, faster, then roll out of my mold to inspect its form. There is the imprint of my head, my arms which have swelled into white wings. I step back, step forward, pause and peer. Am I dead or alive down there? Is this a picture of heaven or hell? I am worried about where I will go when I die, that each time I swallow, an invisible stone will get caught in my throat. I worry that when I eat a plum, a tree will grow in my belly, its branches twining around my bones, choking. When I walk through a door I must tap the frame three times. Between each nighttime prayer to Yahweh I close my eyes and count to ten and a half.

She's like 7 or P

And now I look down at myself sketched in the snow. A familiar anxiety chews at the edges of my heart, even while I notice the beauty of the white fur on all the trees, the reverent silence of this season. I register a mistake on my angel, what looks like a thumbprint on its left wing. I reach down to erase it, but unable to smooth the snow perfectly, I start again on another angel, lowering myself, swishing and sweeping, rolling over—no. Yet another mistake, this time the symmetry in the wingspan wrong. A compulsion comes over me. I do it again, and again. In my memory hours go by. My fingers inside my mittens get wrinkled and raw. My breath comes heavily and the snow begins to blue. A moon rises, a perfect crescent pearl whose precise shape I will never be able to re-create. I ache for something I cannot name. Someone calls me, a mother or a father. *Come in now, come in now.* Very early the next morning I awaken, look out my bedroom window, and see the yard covered with my frantic forms— hundreds of angels, none of them quite right. The forms twist and strain, the wings seeming to struggle up in the winter sun, as if each angel were longing for escape, for a free flight that might crack the crystal and ice of her still, stiff world.

Looking back on it now, I think maybe those moments in the snow were when my OCD began, although it didn't come to me full-fledged until my mid-twenties. OCD stands for obsessive-compulsive disorder, and some studies say more than three million Americans suffer from it. The "it" is not the commonplace rituals that weave throughout so many of our lives—the woman who checks the stove a few times before she leaves for work, or the man who combs his bangs back, and then again, seeking symmetry. Obsessive-compulsive disorder is pervasive and extreme, inundating the person's life to the point where normal functioning becomes difficult, maybe even impossible.

For a long time my life was difficult but not impossible. Both in my childhood and my adulthood I'd suffered from various psychiatric ailments— depressions especially—but none of these were as surreal and absurd as the obsessive-compulsive disorder that one day presented itself. Until I was twenty-five or so, I don't think I could have been really diagnosed with OCD, although my memory of the angels indicates I had tendencies in that direction. I was a child at once nervous and bold, a child who loved trees that trickled sap, the Vermont fields where grass grew the color of deep-throated rust. I was a child who gathered earthworms, the surprising pulse of pink on my fingers, and yet these same fingers, later in the evening, came to prayer points, searching for safety in the folds of my sheets, in the quick counting rituals.

Some mental health professionals claim that the onset of obsession is a response to an underlying fear, a recent trauma, say, or a loss. I don't believe that is always true because, no matter how hard I think about it, I remember nothing unusual or disorienting before my first attack, three years out of college. I don't know exactly why at two o'clock one Saturday afternoon what felt like a seizure shook me. I recall lying in my apartment in Cambridge. The floors were painted blue, the curtains a sleepy white. They bellied in and out with the breezes. I was immersed in a book, *The Seven Storey Mountain*, walking my way through the tale's church, dabbing holy water on my forehead. A priest was crooning. A monk moaned. And suddenly this: a thought careening across my cortex. I

Positive feedback mechanism.

CAN'T CONCENTRATE. Of course the thought disturbed my concentration, and the monk's moan turned into a whisper, disappeared.

I blinked, looked up. I was back in Cambridge on a blue floor. The blue floor suddenly frightened me; between the planks I could see lines of dark dirt and the sway of a spider crawling. Let me get back, I thought, into the world of the book. I lowered my eyes to the page, but instead of being able to see the print, there was the thought blocking out all else: I CAN'T CONCENTRATE.

Now I started to panic. Each time I tried to get back to the book the words crumbled, lost their sensible shapes. I said to myself, *I must not allow that thought about concentration to come into my mind anymore*, but, of course, the more I tried to suppress it, the louder it jangled. I looked at my hand. I ached for its familiar skin, the paleness of its palm and the three threaded lines that had been with me since birth, but as I held it out before my eyes, the phrase I CAN'T CONCEN-TRATE ON MY HAND blocked out my hand, so all I saw was a blur of flesh giving way to the bones beneath, and inside the bones the grimy marrow, and in the grimy marrow the individual cells, all disconnected. Shattered skin.

Began

very quick

My throat closed up with terror. For surely if I'd lost the book, lost language, lost flesh, I was well on my way to losing the rest of the world. And all because of a tiny phrase that forced me into a searing self-consciousness, that plucked me from the moment into the meta-moment, so I was doomed to think about thinking instead of thinking other thoughts. (My mind devouring my mind.)

I tried to force my brain onto other topics, but with each mental dodge I became aware that I was dodging, and each time I itched I became aware that I was itching, and with each inhalation I became aware that I was inhaling, and I thought, *If I think too much about breathing, will I forget how to breathe?*

I ran into the bathroom. There was a strange pounding in my head, and then a sensation I can only describe as a hiccup of the brain. My brain seemed to be seizing as the phrase about concentration jerked across it. I delved into the medicine cabinet, found a bottle of aspirin, took three, stood by the sink for five minutes. No go. Delved again, pulled out another bottle—Ativan, a Valium-like medication belonging to my housemate, Adam. Another five minutes, my brain still squirting. One more Ativan, a tiny white triangle that would put me to sleep. I would sleep this strange spell off, wake up me again, sane again. I went back to my bed. The day darkened. The Ativan spread through my system. Lights in a neighboring window seemed lonely and sweet. I saw the shadow of a bird in a tree, and it had angel wings, and it soared me someplace else, its call a pure cry.

"What's wrong with you?" he said, shaking my shoulder. Adam stood over me, his face a blur. Through cracked eyelids I saw a wavering world, none of its outlines resolved: the latticed shadow of a tree on a white wall, my friend's face

Dialogue

a streak of pink. I am O.K., I thought, for this was what waking up was always like, the gentle resurfacing. I sat up, looked around.

"You've been sleeping for hours and hours," he said. "You slept from yesterday afternoon until now."

I reached up, gently touched a temple. I felt the faraway nip of my pulse. My pulse was there. I was here.

"Weird day yesterday," I said. I spoke slowly, listening to my words, testing them on my tongue. So far so good.

I stood up. "You look weird," he said, "unsteady." → *differentiates*

"I'm O.K.," I said, and then, in that instant, a surge of anxiety. I had lied. I had not been O.K. Say *"God I'm sorry" fourteen times*, I ordered myself. *This is crazy*, I said to myself. *Fifteen times*, a voice from somewhere else seemed to command. "You really all right?" Adam asked. I closed my eyes, counted, blinked back open.

"O.K.," I said. "I'm going to shower."

But it wasn't O.K. As soon as I was awake, obsessive thoughts returned. What before had been inconsequential behaviors, such as counting to three before I went through a doorway or checking the stove several times before bed, now became imperatives. There were a thousand and one of them to follow: rules about how to step, what it meant to touch my mouth, a hot consuming urge to fix the crooked angles of the universe. It was constant, a cruel nattering. *There, that tilted picture on the wall. Scratch your head with your left hand only.* It was noise, the beak of a woodpecker in the soft bark of my brain. But the worst by far were the dread thoughts about concentrating. I picked up a book but couldn't read, so aware was I of myself reading, and the fear of that awareness, for it meant a cold disconnection from this world.

I began to avoid written language because of the anxiety associated with words. I stopped reading. Every sentence I wrote came out only half coherent. I became afraid of pens and paper, the red felt tip bleeding into white, a wound. What was it? What was I? I could not recognize myself spending hours counting, checking, avoiding. Gods seemed to hover in their air, inhabit me, blowing me full of their strange stellar breaths. I wanted my body back. Instead, I pulsed and stuttered and sparked with a glow not my own.

I spent the next several weeks mostly in my bedroom, door closed, shades drawn. I didn't want to go out because any movement might set off a cycle of obsessions. I sat hunched and lost weight. My friend Adam, who had some anxiety problems of his own and was a real pooh-pooher of "talk therapy," found me a behaviorist at McLean.

"These sorts of conditions," the behavioral psychologist, Dr. Lipman, told me

Rhythmic beat.

as I sat one day in his office, "are associated with people who have depressive temperaments, but unlike depression, they do not yield particularly well to more traditional modes of psychotherapy. We have, however, had some real success with cognitive/behavioral treatments."

Outside it was a shining summer day. His office was dim, though, his blinds adjusted so only tiny gold chinks of light sprinkled through, illuminating him in patches. He was older, maybe fifty, and pudgy, and had tufts of hair in all the wrong places, in the whorls of his ears and his nostrils. I had a bad feeling about him.

Nevertheless, he was all I had right now. "What is this sort of condition exactly?" I asked. My voice, whenever I spoke these days, seemed slowed, stuck, words caught in my throat. I had to keep touching my throat, four times, five times, six times, or I would be punished by losing the power of speech altogether.

"Obsessive-compulsive disorder," he announced. "Only you," he said, and lifted his chin a little proudly, "have an especially difficult case of it."

This, of course, was not what I wanted to hear. "What's so especially difficult about my case?" I asked.

He tapped his chin with the eraser end of his pencil. He sat back in his leather seat. When the wind outside blew, the gold chinks scattered across his face and desk. Suddenly the world cleared a bit. The papers on his desk seemed animated, rustling, sheaves full of wings, books full of birds. I felt creepy, despondent, and excited all at once. Maybe he could help me. Maybe he had some special knowledge.

He then went on to explain to me how most people with obsessive thoughts— *my hands are filthy*, for instance—always follow those thoughts with a compulsive behavior, like hand washing. And while I did have some compulsive behaviors, Dr. Lipman explained, I had also reported that my most distressing obsession had to do with concentration, and that the concentration obsession had no clear-cut compulsion following in its wake.

"Therefore," he said. His eyes sparkled as he spoke. He seemed excited by my case. He seemed so sure of himself that for a moment I was back with language again, only this time it was his language, his words forming me. "Therefore, you are what we call a primary ruminator!"

A cow, I thought, chewing and chewing on the floppy scum of its cud. I lowered my head.

He went on to tell me about treatment obstacles. Supposedly, primary ruminators are especially challenging because, while you can train people to cease compulsive behaviors, you can't train them nearly as easily to tether their thoughts. His method, he told me, would be to use a certain instrument to desensitize me to the obsessive thought, to teach me not to be afraid of it, so when it entered my mind, I wouldn't panic and thereby set off a whole cycle of anxiety and its partner, avoidance.

"How will we do it?" I asked.

And that is when he pulled "the instrument" from his desk drawer, a Walkman with a tiny tape in it. He told me he'd used it with people who were similar to me. He told me I was to record my voice saying "I can't concentrate I can't concentrate" and then wear the Walkman playing my own voice back to me for at least two hours a day. Soon, he said, I'd become so used to the thought it would no longer bother me.

He looked over at the clock. About half the session had gone by. "We still have twenty more minutes," he said, pressing the red Record button, holding the miniature microphone up to my mouth. "Why don't you start speaking now."

I paid Dr. Lipman for the session, borrowed the Walkman and the tape, and left, stepping into the summer light. McLean is a huge, stately hospital, buildings with pillars, yawning lawns. The world outside looked lazy in the sweet heat of June. Tulips in the garden lapped at the pollen-rich air with black tongues. A squirrel chirped high in the tuft of a tree. For a moment the world seemed lovely. Then, from far across the lawn, I saw a shadow in a window. Drawn to it for a reason I could not articulate, I stepped closer, and closer still. The shadow resolved itself into lines—two dark brows, a nose. A girl, pressed against glass on a top-floor ward. Her hands were fisted on either side of her face, her curls in a ratty tangle. Her mouth was open, and though I could not hear her, I saw the red splash of her scream.

Behavior therapy is in some ways the antithesis of psychoanalysis. Psychoanalysis focuses on cause, behavior therapy on consequence. Although I've always been a critic of old-style psychoanalysis with its fetish for the past, I don't completely discount the importance of origins. And I have always believed in the mind as an entity that at once subsumes the body and radiates beyond it, and therefore in need of interventions surpassing the mere technical—interventions that whisper to mystery, stroke the soul.

The Walkman, however, was a purely technical intervention. It had little red studs for buttons. The tape whirred efficiently in its center like a slick dark heart. My own voice echoed back to me, all blips and snaky static. I wondered what the obsession with concentration meant. Surely it had some significance beyond the quirks in my neuronal wiring. Surely the neuron itself—that tiny pulse of life embedded in the brain's lush banks—was a God-given charge. When I was a girl, I had seen stalks of wheat filled with a strange red light.

When I was a girl, I once peeled back the corn's green clasps to find yellow pearls. With the Walkman on, I closed my eyes, saw again the prongs of corn, the wide world, and myself floating out of that world, in a place above all planets, severed even from my own mind. And I knew the obsession had something to do with deep disconnection and too much awe.

"There may be no real reasons," Dr. Lipman repeated to me during my next visit. "OCD could well be the result of a nervous system that's too sensitive. If the right medication is ever developed, we would use that."

Because the right medication had not yet been found, I wore the Walkman. The earplugs felt spongy. Sometimes I wore it to bed, listening to my own voice repeat the obsessive fear. When I took the earphones off, the silence was complete. My sheets were damp from sweat. I waited. Shadows whirled around. Planets sent down their lights, laying them across the blue floor. Blue. Silver. Space. *I can't concentrate.*

I did very little for the next year. Dr. Lipman kept insisting I wear the Walkman, turning up the volume, keeping it on for three, now four hours at a time. Fear and grief prevented me from eating much. When I was too terrified to get out of bed, Dr. Lipman checked me into the local hospital, where I lay amidst IV drips, bags of blood, murmuring heart machines that let me know someone somewhere near was still alive.

It was in the hospital that I was first introduced to psychiatric medications, which the doctors tried out on me, to no avail. The medications had poetic names and frequently rhymed with one another—nortriptyline, desipramine, amitriptyline. Nurses brought me capsules in miniature paper cups or oblong shapes of white that left a salty tingle on my tongue. None of them worked, except to make me drowsy and dull.

And then one day Dr. Lipman said to me, "There's a new medication called Prozac, still in its trial period, but it's seventy percent effective with OCD. I want to send you to a Dr. Stanley, here at McLean. He's one of the physicians doing trial runs."

I shrugged, willing to try. I'd tried so much, surely this couldn't hurt. I didn't expect much though. I certainly didn't expect what I finally got.

In my memory, Stanley is the Prozac Doctor. He has an office high in the eaves of McLean. His desk gleams. His children smile out from frames lined up behind him. In the corner is a computer with a screen saver of hypnotic swirling stars. I watch the stars die and swell. I watch the simple gold band on Stanley's hand. For a moment I think that maybe in here I'll finally be able to escape the infected repetitions of my own mind. And then I hear a clock tick-tick-ticking. The sound begins to bother me; I cannot tune it out. *The clock is ruining my con-*

centration, I think, and turn toward it. The numbers on its face are not numbers but tiny painted pills, green and white. A chime hangs down, with another capsule, probably a plastic replica, swinging from the end of it. Back. Forth. Back. Back.

The pads of paper on Stanley's desk are all edged in green and white, with the word "Prozac" scripted across the bottom. The pen has "Prozac" embossed in tiny letters. He asks me about my symptoms for a few minutes, and then uses the Prozac pen to write out a prescription.

"What about side effects?" I ask.

"Very few," the Prozac Doctor answers. He smiles. "Maybe some queasiness. A headache in the beginning. Some short-term insomnia. All in all it's a very good medication. The safest we have."

"Behavior therapy hasn't helped," I say. I feel I'm speaking slowly, for the sound of that clock is consuming me. I put my hands over my ears.

"What is it?" he asks.

"Your—clock."

He looks toward it.

"Would you mind putting it away?"

"Then I would be colluding with your disease," he says. "If I put the clock away, you'll just fixate on something else."

"Disease," I repeat. "I have a disease."

"Without doubt," he says. "OCD can be a crippling disease, but now, for the first time, we have the drugs to combat it."

I take the prescription and leave. I will see him in one month for a follow-up. Disease. Combat. Collusions. My mind, it seems, is my enemy, my illness an absurdity that has to be exterminated. I believe this. The treatment I'm receiving, with its insistence upon cure—which means the abolition of hurt instead of its transformation—helps me to believe this. I have, indeed, been invaded by a virus, a germ I need to rid myself of.

Looking back on it now, I see this belief only added to my panic, shrunk my world still smaller.

On the first day of Prozac I felt nothing, on the second and third I felt nauseated, and for the rest of that week I had headaches so intense I wanted to groan and lower my face into a bowl of crushed ice. I had never had migraines before. In their own way they are beautiful, all pulsing suns and squeezing colors. When I closed my eyes, pink shapes flapped and angels' halos spun. I was a girl again, lying in the snow. Slowly, one by one, the frozen forms lifted toward the light.

And then there really was an angel over me, pressing a cool cloth to my forehead. He held two snowy tablets out to me, and in a haze of pain I took them.

"You'll be all right," Adam said to me. When I cried it was a creek coming from my eyes.

I rubbed my eyes. The headache ebbed.

"How are you?" he asked.

"O.K.," I said. And waited for a command. *Touch your nose, blink twelve times, try not to think about think about concentrating.*

The imperatives came—I could hear them—but from far far away, like birds beyond a mountain, a sound nearly silent and easy to ignore.

"I'm . . . O.K.," I repeated. I went out into the kitchen. The clock on the stove ticked. I pressed my ear against it and heard, this time, a steady, almost soothing pulse.

Most things, I think, diminish over time, rock and mountain, glacier and bone. But this wasn't the nature of Prozac, or me on Prozac. One day I was ill, cramped up with fears, and the next day the ghosts were gone. Imagine having for years a raging fever, and then one day someone hands you a new kind of pill, and within a matter of hours sweat dries, the scarlet swellings go down, your eyes no longer burn. The grass appears green again, the sky a gentle blue. *Hello hello. Remember me?* the planet whispers.

But to say I returned to the world is even a bit misleading, for all my life the world has seemed off-kilter. On Prozac, not only did the acute obsessions dissolve; so too did the blander depression that had been with me since my earliest memories. A sense of immense calm flooded me. Colors came out, yellow leaping from the light where it had long lain trapped, greens unwinding from the grass, dusk letting loose its lavender.

By the fourth day I still felt so shockingly fine that I called the Prozac Doctor. I pictured him in his office, high in the eaves of McLean. I believed he had saved me. He loomed large.

"I'm well," I told him.

"Not yet. It takes at least a month to build up a therapeutic blood level."

"No," I said. "It doesn't." I felt a rushing joy. "The medicine you gave me has made me well. I've—I've actually never felt better."

A pause on the line. "I suppose it could be possible."

"Yes," I said. "It's happened."

I became a "happening" kind of person. Peter Kramer, the author of *Listening to Prozac*, has written extensively on the drug's ability to galvanize personality change as well as to soothe fears or elevate mood. Kramer calls Prozac a cosmetic medication, for it seems to reshape the psyche, lift the face of the soul.

One night, soon after the medication had kicked in, I sat at the kitchen table with Adam. He was stuck in the muck of his master's thesis, fearful of failure.

"It's easy," I said. "Break the project down into bits. A page a day. Six days, one chapter. Twelve days, two. One month, presto." I snapped my fingers. "You're finished."

Adam looked at me, said nothing. The kitchen grew quiet, a deliberate sort of silence he seemed to be purposefully manufacturing so I could hear the echo of my own voice. Bugs thumped on the screen. I heard the high happy pitch of a cheerleader, the sensible voice of a vocational counselor. In a matter of moments I had gone from a fumbling, unsure person to this—all pragmatism, all sure solutions. For the first time on Prozac I felt afraid.

I lay in bed that night. From the next room I heard the patter of Adam's typewriter keys. He was stuck in the mire, inching forward and falling back. Where was I? Who was I? I lifted my hand to my face, the same motion as before, when the full force of obsession had struck me. The hand was still unfamiliar, but wonderfully so now, the three threaded lines seams of silver, the lights from passing cars rotating on my walls like the swish of a spaceship softly landing.

In space I was then, wondering. How could a drug change my mind so abruptly? How could it bring forth buried or new parts of my personality? The oldest questions, I know. My brain wasn't wet clay and paste, as all good brains should be, but a glinting thing crossed with wires. I wasn't human but machine. No, I wasn't machine but animal, linked to my electrified biology more completely than I could have imagined. We have lately come to think of machines and animals, of machines and nature, as occupying opposite sides of the spectrum—there is IBM and then there's the lake—but really they are so similar. A computer goes on when you push its button. A gazelle goes on when it sees a lynx. Only humans are supposedly different, above the pure cause and effect of the hard-wired primitive world. Free will and all.

But no, maybe not. For I had swallowed a pill designed through technology, and in doing so, I was discovering myself embedded in an animal world. I was a purely chemical being, mood and personality seeping through serotonin. We are all taught to believe it's true, but how strange to feel that supposed truth bubbling right in your own tweaked brainpan. Who was I, all skin and worm, all herd? For the next few weeks, amidst feelings of joy and deep relief, these thoughts accompanied me, these slow, simmering misgivings. In dreams, beasts roamed the rafters of my bones, and my bones were twined with wire, teeth tiny silicon chips.

I went to Drumlin Farm one afternoon to see the animals. A goose ate grass in an imperturbable rhythm. Sheep braved robotically, their noses pointing toward the sky. I reached out to touch their fur. Simmering misgivings, yes, but my fingers alive, feeling clumps of cream, of wool.

Every noon I took my pill. Instead of just placing it on my tongue and swallowing with water, I unscrewed the capsule. White powder poured into my hands. I tossed the plastic husk away, cradled the healing talc. I tasted it, a burst of bitterness, a gagging. I took it that way every day, the silky slide of Prozac powder, the harshness in my mouth.

Mornings now, I got up early to jog, showered efficiently, then strode off to the library. I was able to go back to work, cutting deli part-time at Formaggio while I prepared myself for divinity school the next year by reading. I read with an appetite, hungry from all the time I'd lost to illness. The pages of the books seemed very white; the words were easy, black beads shining, ebony in my quieted mind.

I found a book in the library's medical section about obsessive-compulsive disorder. I sat in a corner, on a corduroy cushion, to read it. And there, surrounded by pages and pages on the nature of God and mystery, on Job who cried out at his unfathomable pain, I read about my disorder from a medical perspective, followed the charts and graphs and correlation coefficients. The author proposed that OCD was solely physical in origin, and had the same neurological etiology as Tourette's. Obsessive symptoms, the author suggested, are atavistic responses left over from primitive grooming behaviors. We still have the ape in us; a bird flies in our blood. The obsessive person, linked to her reptilian roots, her mammalian ancestors, cannot stop picking parasites off her brother's back, combing her hair with her tongue, or doing the human equivalent of nest building, picking up stick after stick, leaf after leaf, until her bloated home sits ridiculously unstable in the crotch of an old oak tree.

Keel keel, the crow in me cries. The pig grunts. The screen of myself blinks on. Blinks off. Darkens.

Still, I was mostly peaceful, wonderfully organized. My mind felt lubed, thoughts slipping through so easily, words bursting into bloom. I was reminded of being a girl on the island of Barbados, where we once vacationed. My father took me to a banquet beneath a tropical sky. Greased black men slithered under low poles, their liquid bodies bending to meet the world. Torches flared, and on a long table before me steamed food of every variety. *A feast*, my father said, *all the good things in life*. Yes, that was what Prozac was first like for me, all the good things in life: roasted ham, delicate grilled fish, lemon halves wrapped in yellow waxed paper, fat plums floating in jars.

I could, I thought, do anything in this state of mind. I put my misgivings aside—how fast they would soon come back! how hard they would hit!—and ate into my days, a long banquet. I did things I'd never done before: swimming at dawn in Walden Pond, writing poetry I knew was bad and loving it anyway.

I applied for and was awarded a three-month grant to go to Appalachia, where I wanted to collect oral histories of mountain women. I could swagger anywhere on the Zack, on Vitamin P. Never mind that even before I'd ever come down with OCD I'd been the anxious, tentative sort. Never mind that unnamed trepidations, for all of my life, had prevented me from taking a trip to New Hampshire for more than a few days. Now that I'd taken the cure, I really could go anywhere, even off to the rippling blue mountains of poverty, far from a phone or a friend.

A gun hung over the door. In the oven I saw a roasted bird covered with flies. In the bathroom, a fat girl stooped over herself, without bothering to shut the door, and pulled a red rag from between her legs.

Her name was Kim, her sister's name was Bridget, and their mother and father were Kat and Lonny. All the females were huge and doughy, while Lonny was a single strand of muscle tanned to the color of tobacco. He said very little, and the mother and daughters chattered on, offering me Cokes and Cheerios, showing me to my room, where I sat on a lumpy mattress and stared at the white walls.

And then a moon rose. A storm of hurricane force plowed through fields and sky. I didn't feel myself here. The sound of the storm, battering just above my head, seemed far far away. There was a whispering in my mind, a noise like silk being split. Next to me, on the night table, my sturdy bottle of Prozac. I was fine. So long as I had that, I would be fine.

I pretended I was fine for the next couple of days, racing around with manic intensity. I sat heavy Kat in one of her oversized chairs and insisted she tell me everything about her life in the Blue Ridge Mountains, scribbling madly as she talked. *I am happy happy happy*, I sang to myself. I tried to ignore the strange sounds building in my brain, kindling that crackles, a flame getting hot.

And then I was taking a break out in the sandy yard. It was near one hundred degrees. The sun was tiny in a bleary sky. Chickens screamed and pecked.

In one swift and seamless move, Lonny reached down to grab a bird. His fist closed in on its throat while all the crows cawed and the beasts in my bones brayed away. He laid the chicken down on a stump, raised an ax, and cut. The body did its dance. I watched the severing, how swiftly connections melt, how deep and black is space. Blood spilled.

I ran inside. I was far from a phone or a friend. Maybe I was reminded of some pre-verbal terror: the surgeon's knife, the violet umbilical cord. Or maybe the mountain altitudes had thrown my chemistry off. I don't really know why, or how. But as though I'd never swallowed a Prozac pill, my mind seized and clamped and the obsessions were back.

I took a step forward and then said to myself. *Don't take another step until you count to twenty-five.* After I'd satisfied that imperative, I had to count to twenty-five again, and then halve twenty-five, and then quarter it, before I felt safe enough to walk out the door. By the end of the day, each step took over ten minutes to complete. I stopped taking steps. I sat on my bed.

"What's wrong with you?" Kat said. "Come out here and talk with us."

I tried, but I got stuck in the doorway. There was a point above the doorway I just had to see, and then see again, and inside of me something screamed *back again back again*, and the grief was very large.

For I had experienced the world free and taken in colors and tasted grilled fish and moon. I had left one illness like a too tight snakeskin, and here I was, thrust back. What's worse than illness is to think you're cured—partake of cure in almost complete belief—and then with no warning to be dashed on a dock, moored.

Here's what they don't tell you about Prozac. The drug, for many obsessives who take it, is known to have wonderfully powerful effects in the first few months when it's new to the body. When I called the Prozac Doctor from Kentucky that evening, he explained to me how the drug, when used to treat OCD as opposed to depression, peaks at about six months and then loses some of its oomph. "Someday we'll develop a more robust pill," Dr. Stanley said. "In the meantime, up your dose."

I upped my dose. No relief. Why not? Please. Over the months I had come to need Prozac in a complicated way, had come to see it as my savior, half hating it, half loving it. I unscrewed the capsules and poured their contents over my fingers. Healing talc, gone. Dead sand. I fingered the empty husks.

"You'll feel better if you come to church with us," Kat said to me that Sunday morning. She peered into my face, which must have been white and drawn. "Are you suffering from some city sickness?"

I shrugged. My eyes hurt from crying. I couldn't read or write; I could only add, subtract, divide, divide again.

"Come to church," Kat said. "We can ask the preacher to pray for you."

But I didn't believe in prayers where my illness was concerned. I had come to think, through my reading and the words of doctors, and especially through my brain's rapid response to a drug, that whatever was wrong with me had a simplistic chemical cause. Such a belief can be devastating to sick people, for on top of their illness they must struggle with the sense that illness lacks any creative possibilities.

I think these beliefs, so common in today's high-tech biomedical era in which the focus is relentlessly reductionistic, rob illness of its potential dignity. Illness can be dignified: we can conceive of pain as a kind of complex answer from an elegant system, an arrow pointing inward, a message from soil or sky.

Not so for me. I wouldn't go to church or temple. I wouldn't talk or ask or wonder, for these are distinctly human activities, and I'd come to view myself as less than human.

An anger rose up in me then, a rage. I woke late one night, hands fisted. It took me an hour to get out of bed, so many numbers I had to do, but I was determined.

And then I was walking outside, pushing past the need to count before every step. The night air was muggy, and insects raised a chorus.

I passed midnight fields, a single shack with lighted windows. Cows slept in a pasture.

I rounded the pasture, walked up a hill. And then, before me, spreading out in moonglow, a lake. I stood by its lip. My mind was buzzing and jerking. I don't know at what point the swans appeared—white swans, they must have been, but in silhouette they looked black. They seemed to materialize straight out of the slumbering water. They rose to the surface of the water as memories rise to the surface of consciousness. Hundreds of black swans suddenly, floating absolutely silent, and as I stood there the counting ceased, my mind became silent, and I watched. The swans drifted until it seemed, for a few moments, that they were inside of me, seven dark, silent birds, fourteen princesses, a single self swimming in a tepid sea.

I don't know how long I stood there, or when, exactly, I left. The swans disappeared eventually. The counting ticking talking of my mind resumed.

Still, even in chattering illness I had been quieted for a bit; doors in me had opened; elegance had entered.

This thought calmed me. I was not completely claimed by illness, nor a prisoner of Prozac, entirely dependent on the medication to function. Part of me was still free, a private space not absolutely permeated by pain. A space I could learn to cultivate.

Over the next few days, I noticed that even in the thicket of obsessions my mind sometimes swam into the world, if only for brief forays. There, while I struggled to take a step, was the sun on a green plate. *Remember that,* I said to myself. And here, while I stood fixated in a doorway, was a beetle with a purplish shell, like eggplants growing in wet soil. *Appreciate this,* I told myself, and I can say I did, those slivers of seconds when I returned to the world. I loved the beetle, ached for the eggplant, paddled in a lake with black swans.

And so a part of me began to learn about living outside the disease, cultivating appreciation for a few free moments. It was nothing I would have wished for myself, nothing to noisily celebrate. But it was something, and I could choose it, even while mourning the paralyzed parts of me, the pill that had failed me.

A long time ago, Freud coined the term "superego." A direct translation from German is "over I." Maybe what Freud meant, or should have meant, was not a punitive voice but the angel in the self who rises above an ego under siege, or a medicated mind, to experience the world from a narrow but occasionally gratifying ledge.)

I am thirty-one now, and I know that ledge well. It is a smaller space than I would have wished for myself—I who would like to possess a mind free and flexible. I don't. Even after I raised my dose, the Prozac never worked as well as it once had, and years later I am sometimes sad about that, other times strangely relieved, even though my brain is hounded. I must check my keys, the stove; I must pause many times as I write this and do a ritual count to thirty. It's distracting, to say the least, but still I write this. I can walk and talk and play. I've come to live my life in those brief stretches of silence that arrive throughout the day, working at what I know is an admirable speed, accomplishing all I can in clear pauses, knowing those pauses may be short-lived. I am learning something about the single moment, how rife with potential it is, how truly loud its tick. I have heard clocks and clocks. Time shines, sad and good.

And what of the unclear, mind-cluttered stretches? These, as well, I have bent to. I read books now, even when my brain has real difficulty taking in words. Half a word, or a word blurred by static, is better than nothing at all. There is also a kind of stance I've developed, detaching my mind from my mind, letting the static sizzle on while I walk, talk, read, while the obsessive cycles continue and I, stepping aside, try to link my life to something else. It is a meditative exercise of a high order, and one I'm getting better at. Compensations can be gritty gifts.

Is this adaptation a spiritual thing? When I'm living in moments of clarity, have I transcended disease, or has disease transformed me, taught me how to live in secret niches? I don't know.

A few nights ago, a man at a party, a psychologist, talked about the brain. "The amazing thing," he said, "is that if you cut the corpus callosum of small children, they learn without the aid of medication or reparative surgery how to transfer information from the left to the right hemisphere. And because we know cerebral neurons never rejuvenate, that's evidence," he said, "for a mind that lives beyond the brain, a mind outside of our biologies."

Perhaps. Or perhaps our biologies are broader than we ever thought. Perhaps the brain, because of its wound, has been forced into some kink of creativity we can neither see nor explain. This is what the doctors didn't tell me about illness: that an answer to illness is not necessarily cure, but an ambivalent compensation. Disease, for sure, is disorganization, but cure is not necessarily the synthetic, pill-swallowing righting of the mess. To believe this is to define brain function in rigid terms of "normal" and "abnormal," a devastating definition for many. And to believe this, especially where the psyche is concerned, may also mean dependence on psychotropic drugs, and the risk of grave disappointment if the drugs stop working.

I think of those children, their heads on white sheets, their corpus callosa exposed and cut. I wonder who did that to them, and why. I'm sure there is some compelling medical explanation—wracking seizures that need to be stopped—but still, the image disturbs me. I think more, though, of the children's brains once sewn back inside the bony pockets of skull. There, in the secret dark, between wrenched hemispheres, I imagine tiny tendrils growing, so small and so deep not even the strongest machines can see them. They are real but not real, biological but spiritual. They wind in and out, joining left to right, building webbed wings and rickety bridges, sending out messengers with critical information, like the earliest angels who descended from the sky with news and challenge, wrestling with us in nighttime deserts, straining our thighs, stretching our bodies in pain, no doubt, until our skin took on new shapes.

Strength. sensory adjectives. Imagery: effective.

weakness: Her transitions were weak.

Uses reflection well.

Apparent subject: a woman living with OCD.

Deeper subject:

Cheryl Strayed

THE LOVE OF MY LIFE

CHERYL STRAYED has published award-winning stories and essays in more than a dozen magazines and anthologies. She is the author of a novel, *Torch*. Born in Pennsylvania, raised in rural Minnesota, Strayed now lives in Portland, Oregon. She holds an MFA in fiction writing from Syracuse University.

The first time I cheated on my husband, my mother had been dead for exactly one week. I was in a café in Minneapolis watching a man. He watched me back. He was slightly pudgy, with jet-black hair and skin so white it looked as if he'd powdered it. He stood and walked to my table and sat down without asking. He wanted to know if I had a cat. I folded my hands on the table, steadying myself; I was shaking, nervous at what I would do. I was raw, fragile, vicious with grief. I would do anything.

"Yes," I said.

"I thought so," he said slowly. He didn't take his eyes off me. I rolled the rings around on my fingers. I was wearing two wedding bands, my own and my mother's. I'd taken hers off her hand after she died. It was nothing fancy: sterling silver, thick and braided.

"You look like the kind of girl who has a cat."

"How's that?" I asked.

He didn't answer. He just kept looking at me steadily, as if he knew everything about me, as if he owned me. I felt distinctly that he might be a murderer.

"Are you mature?" he asked intently.

I didn't know what he meant. I still don't. I told him that I was.

"Well, then, prove it and walk down the street with me."

We left the café, his hand on my arm. I had monstrous bruises on my knees from how I'd fallen on them after I walked into my mother's hospital room and first saw her dead. He liked these. He said he'd been admiring them from across the room. They were what had drawn him to me. Also, he liked my boots. He thought I looked intriguing. He thought I looked mature. I was twenty-two. He

500

was older, possibly thirty. I didn't ask his name; he didn't ask mine. I walked with him to a parking lot behind a building. He stopped and pressed me against a brick wall and kissed me, but then he wasn't kissing me. He was biting me. He bit my lips so hard I screamed. *→ code word?*

"You lying cunt," he whispered into my ear. "You're not mature." He flung me away from him and left.

I stood, unmoving, stunned. The inside of my mouth began to bleed softly. Tears filled my eyes. I want my mother, I thought. My mother is dead. I thought this every hour of every day for a very long time: I want my mother. My mother is dead.

It was only a kiss, and barely that, but it was, anyway, a crossing. When I was a child I witnessed a leaf unfurl in a single motion. One second it was a fist, the next an open hand. I never forgot it, seeing so much happen so fast. And this was like that—the end of one thing, the beginning of another: my life as a slut. *{Metaphor}*

When my mother was diagnosed with cancer, my husband, Mark, and I took an unspoken sexual hiatus. When she died seven weeks later, I couldn't bear for Mark to touch me. His hands on my body made me weep. He went down on me in the gentlest of ways. He didn't expect anything in return. He didn't make me feel that I had to come. I would soak in a hot bath, and he would lean into it to touch me. He wanted to make me feel good, better. He loved me, and he had loved my mother. Mark and I were an insanely young, insanely happy, insanely in love married couple. He wanted to help. No, no, no, I said, but then sometimes I relented. I closed my eyes and tried to relax. I breathed deep and attempted to fake it. I rolled over on my stomach so I wouldn't have to look at him. He fucked me and I sobbed uncontrollably. *Intimacy affected ⇒ relationship.*

"Keep going," I said to him. "Just finish." But he wouldn't. He couldn't. He loved me. Which was mysteriously, unfortunately, precisely the problem.

? I wanted my mother. *Oedipus/Electra complex*

We aren't supposed to want our mothers that way, with the pining intensity of sexual love, but I did, and if I couldn't have her, I couldn't have anything. Most of all I couldn't have pleasure, not even for a moment. I was bereft, in agony, destroyed over her death. To experience sexual joy, it seemed, would have been to negate that reality. And more, it would have been to betray my mother, to be disloyal to the person she had been to me. A survivor of her marriage to my troubled father, and then a single mother afterward, working hard to raise my brother and sister and me. My stepfather had loved her and been a good husband to her for ten years, but shortly after she died, he'd fallen in love with someone else. His new girlfriend and her two daughters moved into my mother's house, took her photos off the walls, erased her. I needed my stepfather to be the *→ lacking deprived*

[handwritten: Taking on other roles?]

kind of man who would suffer for my mother, unable to go on, who would carry a torch. And if he wouldn't do it, I would. *[handwritten: who is "we"?]*

We are not allowed this. We are allowed to be deeply into basketball, or Buddhism, or *Star Trek*, or jazz, but we are not allowed to be deeply sad. Grief is a thing that we are encouraged to "let go of," to "move on from," and we are told specifically how this should be done. Countless well-intentioned friends, distant family members, hospital workers, and strangers I met at parties recited the famous five stages of grief to me: denial, anger, bargaining, depression, and acceptance. I was alarmed by how many people knew them, how deeply this single definition of the grieving process had permeated our cultural consciousness. Not only was I supposed to feel these five things, I was meant to feel them in that order and for a fairly prescribed amount of time. I did not deny. I did not get angry. I didn't bargain, become depressed, or accept. I fucked. I sucked. Not my husband, but people I hardly knew, and in that I found a glimmer of relief. *[handwritten: Afraid or desperate to connect?]* The people I messed around with did not have names; they had titles: the Prematurely Graying Wilderness Guide, the Technically Still a Virgin Mexican Teenager, the Formerly Gay Organic Farmer, the Quietly Perverse Poet, the Failing but Still Trying Massage Therapist, the Terribly Large Texas Bull Rider, the Recently Unemployed Graduate of Juilliard, the Actually Pretty Famous Drummer Guy. Most of these people were men; some were women. With them, I was not in mourning; I wasn't even me. I was happy and sexy and impetuous and fun. I was wild and enigmatic and terrifically good in bed. I didn't care about them or have orgasms. We didn't have heart-to-heart talks. I asked them questions about their lives, and they told me everything and asked few questions in return; they knew nothing about me. Because of this, most of them believed they were falling instantly, madly in love with me. *[handwritten: Ambiguity]*

I did what I did with these people, and then I returned home to Mark, weak-kneed and wet, bleary-eyed and elated. I'm alive, I thought in that giddy, postsex daze. My mother's death has taught me to live each day as if it were my last, I said to myself, latching on to the nearest cliché, and the one least true. I didn't *[handwritten: Cliché]* *[handwritten: she knows its a lie]* stop to think: What if it had been my last day? Did I wish to be sucking the cock of an Actually Pretty Famous Drummer Guy? I didn't think to ask that because I didn't want to think. When I did think, I thought, I cannot continue to live without my mother.

I lied—sometimes to the people I messed around with (some of them, if they'd known I was married, would not have wanted to mess around with me), but mostly to Mark. I was not proud of myself. I was in love with him and wanted to be faithful to him and wanted to want to have sex with him, but something in me wouldn't let me do it. We got into the habit of fucking in the middle of the night, both of us waking from a sound sleep to the reality of our bodies wet and hard and in the act. The sex lasted about thirty seconds, and we would almost always both come. It was intensely hot and strange and surreal and darkly funny and ultimately depressing. We never knew who started it. Neither of us recalled waking, reaching for each other. It was a shard of passion, and we held on to it. For a while it got us through.

We like to say how things are, perhaps because we hope that's how they might actually be. We attempt to name, identify, and define the most mysterious of matters: sex, love, marriage, monogamy, infidelity, death, loss, grief. We want these things to have an order, an internal logic, and we also want them to be connected to one another. We want it to be true that if we cheat on our spouse, it means we no longer want to be married to him or her. We want it to be true that if someone we love dies, we simply have to pass through a series of phases, like an emotional obstacle course from which we will emerge happy and content, unharmed and unchanged.

After my mother died, everyone I knew wanted to tell me either about the worst breakup they'd had or all the people they'd known who'd died. I listened to a long, traumatic story about a girlfriend who suddenly moved to Ohio and to stories of grandfathers and old friends and people who lived down the block who were no longer among us. Rarely was this helpful.

Occasionally I came across people who'd had the experience of losing someone whose death made them think, I cannot continue to live. I recognized these people: their postures, where they rested their eyes as they spoke, the expressions they let onto their faces and the ones they kept off. These people consoled me beyond measure. I felt profoundly connected to them, as if we were a tribe. *[Misery loves company]*

It's surprising how relatively few of them there were. People don't die anymore, not the way they used to. Children survive childhood; women, the labors of birth; men, their work. We survive influenza and infection, cancer and heart attacks. We keep living on and on: 80, 90, 103. We live younger, too; frightfully premature babies are cloistered and coddled and shepherded through. My mother lived to the age of forty-five and never lost anyone who was truly beloved to her. Of course, she knew many people who had died, but none who made her wake to the thought: I cannot continue to live.

And there is a difference. Dying is not your girlfriend moving to Ohio. Grief is not the day after your neighbor's funeral, when you felt extremely blue. It is impolite to say this. We act as if all losses are equal. It is un-American to behave otherwise: we live in a democracy of sorrow. Every emotion felt is validated and judged to be as true as any other.

But what does this do to us, this refusal to quantify love, loss, grief? Jewish tradition states that one is considered a mourner when one of eight people dies: father, mother, sister, brother, husband, wife, son, or daughter. This definition

[Bigger point delving into emotional validity.]

doesn't fulfill the needs of today's diverse and far-flung affections; indeed, it probably never did. It leaves out the steprelations, the long-term lovers, the chosen family of a tight circle of friends, and it includes the blood relations we perhaps never honestly loved. But its intentions are true. And, undeniably, for most of us that list of eight does come awfully close. We love and care for oodles of people, but only a few of them, if they died, would make us believe we could not continue to live. Imagine if there were a boat upon which you could put only four people, and everyone else known and beloved to you would then cease to exist. Who would you put on that boat? It would be painful, but how quickly you would decide: You and you and you and you, get in. The rest of you, good-bye. *?*

For years, I was haunted by the idea of this imaginary boat of life, by the desire to exchange my mother's fate for one of the many living people I knew. I would be sitting across the table from a dear friend. I loved her, him, each one of these people. Some I said I loved like family. But I would look at them and think, Why couldn't it have been you who had died instead? You, good-bye.

I didn't often sleep with Mark, but I slept beside him, or tried to. I dreamed incessantly about my mother. There was a theme. Two or three times a week she made me kill her. She commanded me to do it, and I sobbed and got down on my knees, begging her not to make me, but she would not relent. In each dream, like a good daughter, I ultimately complied. I tied her to a tree in our front yard, poured gasoline over her head, and lit her on fire. I made her run down the dirt road that passed by the house where I'd grown up, and I ran her over with my truck; I dragged her body, caught on a jagged piece of metal underneath, until it came loose, and then I put my truck in reverse and ran her over again. I took a miniature baseball bat and beat her to death with it. I forced her into a hole I'd dug and kicked dirt and stones on top of her and buried her alive. These dreams were not surreal. They took place in the plain light of day. They were the documentary films of my subconscious and felt as real to me as life. My truck was really my truck; our front yard was our actual front yard; the miniature baseball bat sat in our closet among the umbrellas. I didn't wake from these dreams crying; I woke shrieking. Mark grabbed me and held me. He wetted a washcloth with cool water and put it over my face. These dreams went on for months, years, and I couldn't shake them. I also couldn't shake my infidelities. I couldn't shake my grief.

What was there to do with me? What did those around me do? They did what I would have done, what we all do when faced with the prospect of some-one else's sorrow: they tried to talk me out of it, neutralize it, tamp it down, make it relative and therefore not so bad. We narrate our own lesser stories of loss in an attempt to demonstrate that the sufferer is not really so alone. We make grossly inexact comparisons and hope that they will do. In short, we insist on ignoring the precise nature of deep loss because there is nothing we can do to change it, and by doing so we strip it of its meaning, its weight, its own fiercely original power.

The first person I knew who died was a casual friend of my mother's, named Barb. Barb was in her early thirties, and I was ten. Her hair was brown and shoulder length, her skin clear and smooth as a bar of soap. She had the kind of tall body that made you acutely aware of the presence of its bones: a long, knobby nose; wide, thin hips; a jaw too pointed to be considered beautiful. Barb got into her car and started the engine. Her car was parked in a garage and all the doors were closed and she had stuffed a Minnesota Vikings cap into a small hole in the garage wall to make it even more airtight. My mother explained this to me in detail: the Vikings hat, the sitting in the car with the garage door closed on purpose. I was more curious than sad. But in the months that followed, I thought of Barb often. I came to care for her. I nurtured an inflated sense of my connection to her. Recently, another acquaintance of mine died. He was beautiful and young and free-spirited and one hell of a painter. He went hiking one day on the Oregon coast and was never seen again. Over the course of my life, I have known other people who've died. Some of them have died the way we hoped they would—old, content, at their time; others, the way we hoped they wouldn't—by murder or suicide, in accidents, or too young of illnesses. The deaths of those people made me sad, afraid, and angry; they made me question the fairness of the world, the existence of God, and the nature of my own existence. But they did not make me suffer. They did not make me think, I cannot continue to live. In fact, in their deaths I felt more deeply connected to them, not because I grieved them but because I wanted to attach myself to what is interesting. It is interesting to be in a Chinese restaurant and see a poster of the smiling face of an acquaintance, who is one hell of a painter, plastered on the front door. It is interesting to be able to say, I know him, to feel that a part of something important and awful and big. The more connections like this we have, the more interesting we are.

There was nothing interesting to me about my mother's death. I did not want to attach myself to it. It was her life that I clung to, her very, very interesting life. When she died, she was about to graduate from college, and so was I. We had started together. Her college was in Duluth, mine in Minneapolis. After a lifetime of struggle and sacrifice, my mother was coming into her own. She wanted to major in six subjects, but the school wouldn't let her, so she settled on two.

My mother had become pregnant when she was nineteen and immediately married my father, a steelworker in western Pennsylvania when the steel plants were shutting down, a coal miner's son born about the time that the coal was

[handwritten marginal note: care about a woman who is already dead?]

⌐ abused

running out. After three children and <u>nine years of violence</u>, my mother left him. My father had recently moved us to a small town near Minneapolis in pursuit of a job prospect. When they divorced, he went back to Pennsylvania, but my mother stayed. She worked as a waitress and in a factory that made small plastic containers that would eventually hold toxic liquids. We lived in apartment complexes full of single mothers whose children sat on the edges of grocery store parking lots. We received free government cheese and powdered milk, food stamps and welfare checks. *⇒ Background*

After a few years, my mother met my stepfather, and when he fell off a roof on the job and hurt his back, they took the $12,000 settlement and spent every penny on forty acres of land in northern Minnesota. There was no house; no one had ever had a house on this land. My stepfather built a one-room tarpaper shack, and we lived in it while he and my mother built us a house from scrap wood and trees they cut down with the help of my brother, my sister, and me. We moved into the new house on Halloween night. We didn't have electricity or running water or a phone or an indoor toilet. Years passed, and my mother was happy—happier than she'd ever been—but still, she hungered for more.

Just before she died, she was thinking about becoming a costume designer or a professor of history. She was profoundly interested in the American pioneers, the consciousness of animals, and the murders of women believed to be witches. She was looking into graduate school, though she feared that she was too old. She couldn't believe, really, that she was even getting a degree. I'd had to convince her to go to college. She'd always read books but thought that she was basically stupid. To prepare, she shadowed me during my senior year of high school, doing all the homework that I was assigned. She photocopied my assignment sheets, wrote the papers I had to write, read the books. I graded her work, using my teacher's marks as a guide. My mother was a shaky student at best.

She went to college and earned straight A's.

Why not help?

She died on a Monday during spring break of our senior year. After her funeral, I immediately went back to school because she had begged me to do so. It was the beginning of a new quarter. In most of my classes, we were asked to introduce ourselves and say what we had done over the break. "My name is Cheryl," I said. "I went to Mexico." <u>I lied not to protect myself but because it would have been rude not to. To express loss on that level is to cross a boundary, violate personal space</u>, to impose emotion in a nonemotional place.

We did not always treat grief this way. Nearly every culture has a history, and some still have a practice, of mourning rituals, many of which involve changes in the dress or appearance of those in grief. The wearing of black clothing or mourning jewelry, hair cutting, and body scarification or ritual tattooing all made the grief-stricken immediately visible to the people around them. Although it is true that these practices were sometimes ridiculously restrictive and not always in the best interest of the mourner, it is also true that they gave us something of value. They imposed evidence of loss on a community and forced that community to acknowledge it. If, as a culture, we don't bear witness to grief, the burden of loss is placed entirely upon the bereaved, while the rest of us avert our eyes and wait for those in mourning to stop being sad, to let go, to move on, to cheer up. And if they don't—if they have loved too deeply, if they do wake each morning thinking, I cannot continue to live—well, then we pathologize their pain: we call their suffering a disease. We do not help them; we tell them that they need to get help.

Nobody knew about my sexual escapades. I kept waiting for them to cure me, or for something to cure me of them. Two years had passed since my mother's death, and I still couldn't live without her, but I also couldn't live with myself. I decided to tell Mark the truth. The list was long. I practiced what I would say, trying to say it in the least painful way. It was impossible. It was time.

Mark sat in the living room playing his guitar. He was working as an organizer for a nonprofit environmental agency, but his real ambition was to be a musician. He had just formed his first band and was writing a new song, finding it as he went along. I told him that I had something to tell him and that it was not going to be easy. He stopped playing and looked at me, but he kept his hands on the guitar, holding it gently. This man whom I'd loved for years, had loved enough to marry, who had been with me through my mother's death and the aftermath, who'd offered to go down on me in the gentlest of ways, who would do anything, anything for me, listened as I told him about the Technically Still a Virgin Mexican Teenager, the Prematurely Graying Wilderness Guide, the Recently Unemployed Graduate of Juilliard.

He fell straight forward out of his chair onto his knees and then facedown onto the floor. His guitar went with him and it made clanging, strumming, hollow sounds as it went. I attempted to rub his back. He screamed for me to get my hands off him. Later, spent, he calmly told me that he wanted to kill me. He promised he would if I'd given him AIDS.

Women are used to the bad behavior of men. We eroticize and congratulate it and in return we brace ourselves to be dissatisfied, duped, deceived, dumped, and dicked around. I had broken the rules. Even among our group of alternative, left-wing, hippie, punk-rock, artsy politicos, I was viewed by many as the worst kind of woman: the whore, the slut, the adulteress, the liar, the cheat. And to top it all off, I had wronged the best of men. Mark had been faithful to me all along.

[handwritten: → good, perfect even.]

[handwritten: can't use behavior (awful) to only use social satire of a way of defending it.]

He moved out and rented a room in the attic of a house. Slowly we told our friends. The Insanely Young, Insanely Happy, Insanely in Love Married Couple was coming apart. First, they were in disbelief. Next, they were mad, or several of them—not at us, but at me. One of my dearest friends took the photograph of me she kept in a frame in her bedroom, ripped it in half, and mailed it to me. Another made out with Mark. When I was hurt and jealous about this I was told that perhaps it was exactly what I needed: a taste of my own medicine. I couldn't rightfully disagree, but still my heart was broken. I lay alone in our bed feeling myself almost levitate from the pain.

We couldn't decide whether to get divorced or not. We went to a marriage counselor and tried to work it out. Months later, we stopped the counseling and put the decision on hold. Mark began to date. He dated one of those women who, instead of a purse, carried a teeny-weeny backpack. He dated a biologist who also happened to be a model. He dated a woman I'd met once who'd made an enormous pot of very good chili of which I'd eaten two bowls.

His sex life temporarily cured me of mine. I didn't fuck anyone, and I got crabs from a pair of used jeans I'd bought at a thrift store. I spent several days eradicating the translucent bugs from my person and my apartment. Then the Teeny-Weeny Backpack Woman started to play tambourine in Mark's budding band. I couldn't take it anymore. I went to visit a friend in Portland and decided to stay. I met a man: a Punk Rocker Soon to Be Hopelessly Held Under the Thumb of Heroin. I found him remotely enchanting. I found heroin more enchanting. Quickly, without intending to, I slipped into a habit. Here, I thought. At last.

By now Mark pretty much hated me, but he showed up in Portland anyway and dragged me back home. He set a futon down for me in the corner of his room and let me stay until I could find a job and an apartment. At night we lay in our separate beds fighting about why we loved and hated each other so much. We made love once. He was cheating on someone for the first time. He was back with the Biologist Who Also Happened to Be a Model, and he was cheating on her with his own wife. Hmmm, we thought. What's this?

But it was not to be. I was sorry. He was sorry. I wasn't getting my period. I was really, really, really sorry. He was really, really, really mad. I was pregnant by the Punk Rocker Soon to Be Hopelessly Held Under the Thumb of Heroin. We were at the end of the line. We loved each other, but love was not enough. We had become the Insanely Young, Insanely Sad, Insanely Messed-up Married Couple. He wanted me gone. He pulled the blankets from my futon in his room and flung them down the stairs.

I sat for five hours in the office of an extremely overbooked abortion doctor waiting for my abortion. The temperature in the room was somewhere around fifty-six degrees. It was packed with microscopically pregnant women who were starving because we had been ordered not to eat since the night before. The assistants of the Extremely Overbooked Abortion Doctor did not want to clean up any puke.

At last, I was brought into a room. I was told to undress and hold a paper sheet around myself. I was given a plastic breast and instructed to palpate it, searching for a lump of cancer hidden within its depths, while I waited for my abortion. I waited, naked, palpating, finding the cancer over and over again. The Extremely Overbooked Abortion Doctor needed to take an emergency long-distance phone call. An hour went by. Finally, she came in.

I lay back on the table and stared at a poster on the ceiling of a Victorian mansion that was actually composed of miniature photographs of the faces of a hundred famous and important women in history. I was told to lie still and peacefully for a while and then to stand up very quickly and pull on my underwear while an assistant of the Extremely Overbooked Abortion Doctor held me up. I was told not to have sex for a very long time. The procedure cost me $400, half of which I was ridiculously hoping to receive from the Punk Rocker Soon to Be Hopelessly Held Under the Thumb of Heroin. I went home to my new apartment. The light on my answering machine said I had three messages. I lay on my couch, ill and weak and bleeding, and listened to them.

There was a message from the Punk Rocker Soon to Be Hopelessly Held Under the Thumb of Heroin, only he didn't say anything. Instead he played a recording of a few lines from the Radiohead song, "Creep."

There was a message that consisted of a thirty-second dial tone because the person had hung up.

There was a message from Mark wondering how I was.

My mother had been dead for three years. I was twenty-five. I had intended, by this point in my life, to have a title of my own: the Incredibly Talented and Extraordinarily Brilliant and Successful Writer. I had planned to be the kind of woman whose miniature photographed face was placed artfully into a poster of a Victorian mansion that future generations of women would concentrate on while their cervixes were forcefully dilated by the tip of a plastic tube about the size of a drinking straw and the beginnings of babies were sucked out of them. I wasn't anywhere close. I was a pile of shit.

Despite my mother's hopes, I had not graduated from college. I pushed my way numbly through that last quarter, but I did not, in the end, receive my bachelor's degree because I had neglected to do one assignment: write a five-page paper about a short story called "The Nose," by Nikolay Gogol. It's a rollicking tale about a man who wakes up one morning and realizes that his nose is gone. Indeed, his nose has not only left him but has also dressed in the man's clothes, taken his carriage, and gone gadding about town. The man does what anyone would do if he woke up and found that his nose was gone: he goes out to find it. I thought the story was preposterous and incomprehensible. Your nose does not just up and leave you. I was told not to focus on the unreality of it. I was told that the story was actually about vanity, pretentiousness, and opportunism in nineteenth-century Russia. Alternately, I could interpret it as a commentary upon either male sexual impotency or divine Immaculate Conception. I tried dutifully to pick one of these concepts and write about it, but I couldn't do it, and I could not discuss with my professor why this was so. In my myopic, grief-addled state, the story seemed to me to be about something else entirely: a man who woke up one morning and no longer had a nose and then went looking for it. There was no subtext to me. It was simply a story about what it was about, which is to say, the absurd and arbitrary nature of disappearance, our hungry ache to resurrect what we've lost, and the bald truth that the impossible can become possible faster than anyone dreams.

All the time that I'd been thinking, I cannot continue to live, I also had the opposite thought, which was by far the more unbearable: that I would continue to live, and that every day for the rest of my life I would have to live without my mother. Sometimes I forgot this, like a trick of the brain, a primitive survival mechanism. Somewhere, floating on the surface of my subconscious, I believed—I still believe—that if I endured without her for one year, or five years, or ten years, or twenty, that she would be given back to me, that her absence was a ruse, a darkly comic literary device, a terrible and surreal dream.

What does it mean to heal? To move on? To let go? Whatever it means, it is usually said and not done, and the people who talk about it the most have almost never had to do it. I cannot say anything about healing, but I can say that something happened as I lay on the couch bleeding and listening to my answering machine play the Radiohead song and then the dial tone and then Mark's voice wondering how I was: I thought about writing the five-page paper about the story of the man who lost his nose. I thought about calling Mark and asking him to marry me again. I thought about becoming the Incredibly Talented and Extraordinarily Brilliant and Successful Writer. I thought about taking a very long walk. I decided to do all of these things immediately, but I did not move from the couch. I didn't set out the next day either to write the paper about the guy who lost his nose. I didn't call Mark and ask him to marry me again. I didn't start to work on becoming the Incredibly Talented and Extraordinarily Brilliant and Successful Writer. Instead I ordered pizza and listened to that one Lucinda Williams CD that I could not ever get enough of, and, after a few days, I went back to my job waiting tables. I let my uterus heal and then slept at least once with each of the five guys who worked in the kitchen. I did, however, hold on to one intention, and I set about fulfilling it: I was going to take a long walk. One thousand six hundred and thirty-eight miles, to be exact. Alone. Mark and I had filed the papers for our divorce. My stepfather was going to marry the woman he'd started dating immediately after my mother died. I wanted to get out of Minnesota. I needed a new life and, unoriginally, I was going west to find it. I decided to hike the Pacific Crest Trail—a wilderness trail that runs along the backbone of the Sierra Nevada and the Cascade mountains, from Mexico to Canada. I decided to hike a large portion of it—from the Mojave Desert in California to the Columbia River at the Oregon-Washington border. It would take me four months. I'd grown up in the country, done a good amount of camping, and taken a few weekend backpacking trips, but I had a lot to learn: how, for example, to read a topographical map, ford a river, handle an ice axe, navigate using a compass, and avoid being struck by lightning. Everyone who knew me thought that I was nuts. I proceeded anyway, researching, reading maps, dehydrating food and packing it into plastic bags and then into boxes that would be mailed at roughly two-week intervals to the ranger stations and post offices I'd occasionally pass near.

I packed my possessions and stored them in my stepfather's barn. I took off my wedding ring and put it into a small velvet box and moved my mother's wedding ring from my right hand to my left. I was going to drive to Portland first and then leave my truck with a friend and fly to LA and take a bus to the start of the trail. I drove through the flatlands and Badlands and Black Hills of South Dakota, positive that I'd made a vast mistake.

Deep in the night, I pulled into a small camping area in the Big Horn Mountains of Wyoming and slept in the back of my truck. In the morning I climbed out to the sight of a field of blue flowers that went right up to the Tongue River. I had the place to myself. It was spring and still cold, but I felt compelled anyway to go into the river. I decided I would perform something like a baptism to initiate this new part of my life. I took off my clothes and plunged in. The water was like ice, so cold it hurt. I dove under one time, two times, three times, then dashed out and dried off and dressed. As I walked back to my truck, I noticed my hand: my mother's wedding ring was gone.

At first I couldn't believe it. I had believed that if I lost one thing, that I would then be protected from losing another, that my mother's death would inoculate me against further loss.

It is an indefensible belief, but it was there, the same way I believed that if I endured long enough, my mother would be returned to me.

A ring is such a small thing, such a very small thing.

I went down on my hands and knees and searched for it. I patted every inch of ground where I had walked. I searched the back of my truck and my pockets, but I knew. I knew that the ring had come off in the river. Of course it had; what did I expect? I went to the edge of the water and thought about going back in, diving under again and again until I found it, but it was a useless idea, and I was defeated by it before I even began. I sat down on the edge of the water and cried. Tears, tears, so many kinds of tears, so many ways of crying. I had collected them, mastered them; I was a priestess, a virtuoso of crying.

I sat in the mud on the bank of the river for a long time and waited for the river to give the ring back to me. I waited and thought about everything. I thought about Mark and my boat of life. I thought what I would say to him then, now, forever: You, get in. I thought about the Formerly Gay Organic Farmer and the Quietly Perverse Poet and the Terribly Large Texas Bull Rider and the Five Line Cooks I Had on Separate Occasions Over the Course of One Month. I thought about how I was never again going to sleep with anyone who had a title instead of a name. I was sick of it. Sick of fucking, of wanting to fuck the wrong people and not wanting to fuck the right ones. I thought about how if you lose a ring in a river, you are never going to get it back, no matter how badly you want it or how long you wait.

I leaned forward and put my hands into the water and held them flat and open beneath the surface. The soft current made rivulets over my bare fingers. I was no longer married to Mark.

I was no longer married to my mother. I was no longer married to my mother. I couldn't believe that this thought had never occurred to me before: that it was her I'd been wed to all along and I knew that I couldn't be faithful anymore.

Incest?

If this were fiction, what would happen next is that the woman would stand up and get into her truck and drive away. It wouldn't matter that the woman lost her mother's wedding ring, even though it was gone to her forever, because the loss would mean something else entirely: that what was gone now was actually her sorrow and the shackles of grief that had held her down. And in this loss she would see, and the reader would know, that the woman had been in error all along. That, indeed, the love she had for her mother was too much love, really, too much love and also too much sorrow. She would realize this and get on with her life. There would be what happened in the story and also everything it stood for: the river, representing life's constant changing; the tiny blue flowers, beauty; the spring air, rebirth. All of these symbols would collide and mean that the woman was actually lucky to have lost the ring, and not just to have lost it, but to have loved it, to have ached for it, and to have had it taken from her forever. The story would end, and you would know that she was the better for it. That she was wiser, stronger, more interesting, and most of all, finally starting down her path to glory. I would show you the leaf when it unfurls in a single motion: the end of one thing, the beginning of another. And you would know the answers to all the questions without being told. Did she ever write that five-page paper about the guy who lost his nose? Did she ask Mark to marry her again? Did she stop sleeping with people who had titles instead of names? Did she manage to walk 1,638 miles? Did she get to work and become the Incredibly Talented and Extraordinarily Brilliant and Successful Writer? You'd believe the answers to all these questions to be yes. I would have given you what you wanted then: to be a witness to a healing.

But this isn't fiction. Sometimes a story is not about anything except what it is about. Sometimes you wake up and find that you actually have lost your nose. Losing my mother's wedding ring in the Tongue River was not okay. I did not feel better for it. It was not a passage or a release. What happened is that I lost my mother's wedding ring and I understood that I was not going to get it back, that it would be yet another piece of my mother that I would not have for all the days of my life, and I understood that I could not bear this truth, but that I would have to.

Healing is a small and ordinary and very burnt thing. And it's one thing and one thing only: it's doing what you have to do. It's what I did then and there. I stood up and got into my truck and drove away from a part of my mother. The part of her that had been my lover, my wife, my first love, my true love, the love of my life.

[handwritten annotations:]

She loved her mom WAY too much . . . . .

Apparent subject: Woman cheating on her husband

Deeper subject: Meditation on grief.
↳ Lack of understanding.

Amy Tan

MOTHER TONGUE

AMY TAN was born in the United States to immigrant parents from China. Her novels are *The Joy Luck Club*, *The Kitchen God's Wife*, *The Hundred Secret Senses*, *The Bonesetter's Daughter*, and *Saving Fish from Drowning*, all *New York Times* bestsellers and the recipient of various awards. She is also the author of a memoir, *The Opposite of Fate*; two children's books, *The Moon Lady* and *Sagwa*; and numerous articles for magazines, including *the New Yorker*, *Harper's*, and *National Geographic*. Her current work includes writing a new novel, collaborating on a television pilot with director Wayne Wang and cowriter Ron Bass, and creating the libretto for *The Bonesetter's Daughter*, which premieres in September 2008 with the San Francisco Opera. Tan's other musical work for the stage is limited to serving as lead rhythm dominatrix, backup singer, and second tambourine with the literary garage band the Rock Bottom Remainders, whose members include Stephen King, Dave Barry, and Scott Turow. In spite of their dubious talent, their yearly gigs have managed to raise more than $1 million for literacy programs. Tan lives in San Francisco and New York.

I am not a scholar of English or literature. I cannot give you much more than personal opinions on the English language and its variations in this country or others.

I am a writer. And by that definition, I am someone who has always loved language. I am fascinated by language in daily life. I spend a great deal of my time thinking about the power of language—the way it can evoke an emotion, a visual image, a complex idea, or a simple truth. Language is the tool of my trade. And I use them all—all the Englishes I grew up with.

Recently, I was made keenly aware of the different Englishes I do use. I was giving a talk to a large group of people, the same talk I had already given to half a dozen other groups. The nature of the talk was about my writing, my life, and my book, *The Joy Luck Club*. The talk was going along well enough, until I remembered one major difference that made the whole talk sound wrong. My mother was in the room. And it was perhaps the first time she had heard me give a lengthy speech, using the kind of English I have never used with her. I was saying things like, "The intersection of memory upon imagination" and "There is an aspect of my fiction that relates to thus-and-thus"—a speech filled with carefully wrought grammatical phrases, burdened, it suddenly seemed to me, with nominalized forms, past perfect tenses, conditional phrases, all the forms of standard English that I had learned in school and through books, the forms of English I did not use at home with my mother.

Just last week, I was walking down the street with my mother, and I again found myself conscious of the English I was using, the English I do use with her. We were talking about the price of new and used furniture and I heard myself saying this: "Not waste money that way." My husband was with us as well, and he didn't notice any switch in my English. And then I realized why. It's because over the twenty years we've been together I've often used that same kind of English with him, and sometimes he even uses it with me. It has become our language of intimacy, a different sort of English that relates to family talk, the language I grew up with.

So you'll have some idea of what this family talk I heard sounds like, I'll quote what my mother said during a recent conversation which I videotaped and then transcribed. During this conversation, my mother was talking about a political gangster in Shanghai who had the same last name as her family's, Du, and how the gangster in his early years wanted to be adopted by her family, which was rich by comparison. Later, the gangster became more powerful, far richer than my mother's family, and one day showed up at my mother's wedding to pay his respects. Here's what she said in part:

"Du Yusong having business like fruit stand. Like off the street kind. He is Du like Du Zong—but not Tsung-ming Island people. The local people call putong, the river east side, he belong to that side local people. That man want to ask Du Zong father take him in like become own family. Du Zong father wasn't look down on him, but didn't take seriously, until that man big like become a mafia. Now important person, very hard to inviting him. Chinese way, came only to show respect, don't stay for dinner. Respect for making big celebration, he shows up. Mean gives lots of respect. Chinese custom. Chinese social life that way. If too important won't have to stay too long. He come to my wedding. I didn't see, I heard it. I gone to boy's side, they have YMCA dinner. Chinese age I was nineteen."

You should know that my mother's expressive command of English belies how much she actually understands. She reads the *Forbes* report, listens to *Wall Street Week*, converses daily with her stockbroker, reads all of Shirley MacLaine's books with ease—all kinds of things I can't begin to understand. Yet some of my friends tell me they understand 50 percent of what my mother says. Some say they understand 80 to 90 percent. Some say they understand none of it, as if she were speaking pure Chinese. But to me, my mother's English is perfectly clear, perfectly natural. It's my mother tongue. Her language, as I hear it, is vivid, direct, full of observation and imagery. That was the language that helped shape the way I saw things, expressed things, made sense of the world.

Lately, I've been giving more thought to the kind of English my mother speaks. Like others, I have described it to people as "broken" or "fractured" English. But I wince when I say that. It has always bothered me that I can think of no way to describe it other than "broken," as if it were damaged and needed to be fixed, as if it lacked a certain wholeness and soundness. I've heard other terms used, "limited English," for example. But they seem just as bad, as if everything is limited, including people's perceptions of the limited English speaker.

I know this for a fact, because when I was growing up, my mother's "limited" English limited *my* perception of her. I was ashamed of her English. I believed that her English reflected the quality of what she had to say. That is, because she expressed them imperfectly her thoughts were imperfect. And I had plenty of empirical evidence to support me: the fact that people in department stores, at banks, and at restaurants did not take her seriously, did not give her good service, pretended not to understand her, or even acted as if they did not hear her.

My mother has long realized the limitations of her English as well. When I was fifteen, she used to have me call people on the phone to pretend I was she. In this guise, I was forced to ask for information or even to complain and yell at people who had been rude to her. One time it was a call to her stockbroker in New York. She had cashed out her small portfolio and it just so happened we were going to go to New York the next week, our very first trip outside California. I had to get on the phone and say in an adolescent voice that was not very convincing, "This is Mrs. Tan."

And my mother was standing in the back whispering loudly, "Why he don't send me check, already two weeks late. So mad he lie to me, losing me money."

And then I said in perfect English, "Yes, I'm getting rather concerned. You had agreed to send the check two weeks ago, but it hasn't arrived."

Then she began to talk more loudly. "What he want, I come to New York tell him front of his boss, you cheating me?" And I was trying to calm her down, make her be quiet, while telling the stockbroker, "I can't tolerate any more excuses. If I don't receive the check immediately, I am going to have to speak to your manager when I'm in New York next week." And sure enough, the following week there we were in front of this astonished stockbroker, and I was sitting there red-faced and quiet, and my mother, the real Mrs. Tan, was shouting at his boss in her impeccable broken English.

We used a similar routine just five days ago, for a situation that was far less humorous. My mother had gone to the hospital for an appointment, to find out about a benign brain tumor a CAT scan had revealed a month ago. She said she had spoken very good English, her best English, no mistakes. Still, she said, the hospital did not apologize when they said they had lost the CAT scan and she had come for nothing. She said they did not seem to have any sympathy when she told them she was anxious to know the exact diagnosis, since her husband and son had both died of brain tumors. She said they would not give her any more information until the next time and she would have to make another appointment for that. So she said she would not leave until the doctor called her daughter. She wouldn't budge. And when the doctor finally called her daughter, me, who spoke in perfect English—lo and behold—we had assurances the CAT scan would be found, promises that a conference call on Monday would be held, and apologies for any suffering my mother had gone through for a most regrettable mistake.

I think my mother's English almost had an effect on limiting my possibilities in life as well. Sociologists and linguists probably will tell you that a person's developing language skills are more influenced by peers. But I do think that the language spoken in the family, especially in immigrant families which are more insular, plays a large role in shaping the language of the child. And I believe that it affected my results on achievement tests, IQ tests, and the SAT. While my English skills were never judged as poor, compared to math, English could not be considered my strong suit. In grade school I did moderately well, getting perhaps B's, sometimes B-pluses, in English and scoring perhaps in the sixtieth or seventieth percentile on achievement tests. But those scores were not good enough to override the opinion that my true abilities lay in math and science, because in those areas I achieved A's and scored in the ninetieth percentile or higher.

This was understandable. Math is precise; there is only one correct answer. Whereas, for me at least, the answers on English tests were always a judgment call, a matter of opinion and personal experience. Those tests were constructed around items like fill-in-the-blank sentence completion, such as, "Even though Tom was _____, Mary thought he was _____," And the correct answer always seemed to be the most bland combinations of thoughts, for example, "Even though Tom was shy, Mary thought he was charming," with the grammatical structure "even though" limiting the correct answer to some sort of semantic opposites, so you wouldn't get answers like, "Even though Tom was foolish, Mary thought he was ridiculous." Well, according to my mother, there were very few limitations as to what Tom could have been and what Mary might have thought of him. So I never did well on tests like that.

The same was true with word analogies, pairs of words in which you were supposed to find some sort of logical, semantic relationship—for example, "*Sunset* is to *nightfall* as _____ is to _____." And here you would be presented with a list of four possible pairs, one of which showed the same kind of relationship: *red* is to *stoplight*, *bus* is to *arrival*, *chills* is to *fever*, *yawn* is to *boring*. Well, I could never think that way. I knew what the tests were asking, but I could not block out of my mind the images already created by the first pair, "*sunset* is to *nightfall*"—and I would see a burst of colors against a darkening sky, the moon rising, the lowering of a curtain of stars. And all other pairs of words—red, bus, stoplight, boring—just threw up a mass of confusing images, making it impossible for me to sort out something as logical as saying: "A sunset precedes nightfall" is the same as "a chill precedes a fever." The only way I would have gotten that answer right would have been to imagine an associative situation, for example, my being disobedient and staying out past sunset, catching a chill at night, which turns into feverish pneumonia as punishment, which indeed did happen to me.

I have been thinking about all this lately, about my mother's English, about achievement tests. Because lately I've been asked, as a writer, why there are not more Asian Americans represented in American literature. Why are there few Asian Americans enrolled in creative writing programs? Why do so many Chinese students go into engineering? Well, these are broad sociological questions I can't begin to answer. But I have noticed in surveys—in fact, just last week—that Asian students, as a whole, always do significantly better on math achievement tests than in English. And this makes me think that there are other Asian-American students whose English spoken in the home might also be described as "broken" or "limited." And perhaps they also have teachers who are steering them away from writing and into math and science, which is what happened to me.

Fortunately, I happen to be rebellious in nature and enjoy the challenge of disproving assumptions made about me. I became an English major my first year in college, after being enrolled as pre-med. I started writing nonfiction as a freelancer the week after I was told by my former boss that writing was my worst skill and I should hone my talents toward account management.

But it wasn't until 1985 that I finally began to write fiction. And at first I wrote using what I thought to be wittily crafted sentences, sentences that would finally prove I had mastery over the English language. Here's an example from the first draft of a story that later made its way into *The Joy Luck Club*, but without this line: "That was my mental quandary in its nascent state." A terrible line, which I can barely pronounce.

Fortunately, for reasons I won't get into today, I later decided I should envision a reader for the stories I would write. And the reader I decided upon was my mother, because these were stories about mothers. So with this reader in mind—and in fact she did read my early drafts—I began to write stories using all the Englishes I grew up with: the English I spoke to my mother, which for lack of a better term might be described as "simple"; the English she used with me, which for lack of a better term might be described as "broken"; my translation of her Chinese, which could certainly be described as "watered down"; and what I imagined to be her translation of her Chinese if she could speak in perfect English, her internal language, and for that I sought to preserve the essence, but neither an English nor a Chinese structure. I wanted to capture what language ability tests can never reveal: her intent, her passion, her imagery, the rhythms of her speech and the nature of her thoughts.

Apart from what any critic had to say about my writing, I knew I had succeeded where it counted when my mother finished reading my book and gave me her verdict: "So easy to read."

The purpose for writing.

↳ She makes a clear decision.
↳ She knows what she wants to happen.

She uses known images.
Used broken language => successful.

Ryan Van Meter

IF YOU KNEW THEN
WHAT I KNOW NOW

RYAN VAN METER is currently an MFA candidate in the Nonfiction Writing Program at the University of Iowa. His work has been previously published in *River Teeth* and *Quarterly West*, and is forthcoming from *Indiana Review* and the *Iowa Review*.

In your sixth grade social studies class, fourth hour, when Mrs. Perry assigns the group project on European world capitals, don't look at Mark. Don't look at Jared. See if there's another group you can get into. The quiet girl who sits in front of you needs someone to work with, too. If you could avoid working on this project with those two boys, you could avoid all of this.

If you do end up in a group with Mark and Jared you should insist that you meet at the library. If you could meet at the library then they couldn't do what they are planning to do. If you do agree to meet with them at Mark's house then I don't know what to tell you. If you meet there it's probably all going to happen the way it's going to happen.

You will show up at Mark's. His sister will answer the door. Your backpack will weigh down on your back, and his Dad will be watching football in the living room, but you don't see him, you only hear the dull roar of the TV crowd. His sister will point you down the hallway, "first room on the right" she will say, "across from the bathroom." You'll knock on the closed door. You'll think it's odd that the door is closed. They know you're coming over. They know it's the day before the project is due. They know all of this. You will hear whispering on the other side of door, and then it's swung open, and Mark stands there, smiling. Jared is flung across the bed reading a magazine. The television glows in the corner. A video game is on, but the action is paused, a figure with winged shoes and a bow and arrow frozen in the middle of the arc of his jump. You've played this game before. You're good at it.

You'll let your backpack slump to the floor, unzip it, and pull out your books.

You'll balance them in your lap, split open folders and pull out the assignment worksheet. "OK," you will say. You read over the assignment, the social studies project you're supposed to be working on, and you won't notice that they aren't listening to you. You won't notice they are mouthing words to each other. You won't know their plan is about to take shape.

And you won't know when they ask you to grab the box of Hostess cupcakes on the kitchen counter that they really don't care about the cupcakes. They just need you out of the room for a second. Of course you'll do it. You'll hop up and head to the kitchen. You're so excited to be over at Mark's house, hanging out with other boys. It's what your mother has been telling you to do for years: "You need to spend more time with boys. You should do more things that boys like to do. Why are you always just hanging around girls?" That's why what you see when you walk back in the room will be so confusing. You'll think, "this isn't what boys do, this isn't what I thought we were supposed to do."

The door will be shut when you return from the kitchen, though you'll know you certainly didn't shut it as you left. The rest of the house will be quiet, but you can still hear the football game from the living room. You will twist the knob and push open the door, and you will see them, on the bed. Jared will be under Mark, and they are turned so you can't see their faces, not the front of their faces anyway, and they are pretending to kiss. Mark's thick forearms will be stiffly curled around Jared, Jared's glasses will be folded, shoved in the corner of the windowsill. Both of them will peek under not-quite-closed eyelids. You will know right off they aren't really kissing because one of them—it's hard to tell if it's Mark or if it's Jared—will slide a flat palm in between their wet mouths so their lips can't touch. But they hope you will think they are kissing, and that's the idea behind this. You will know they aren't kissing, but you will also know they want to pretend they are kissing. You will guess correctly when you think the project isn't going to be worked on today.

They will pull away after you've stood there for a second. You will start to step away, though you don't really know where to go, and they will say, "come back, come back in, we're sorry." You are back in the room, and they are sitting on Mark's navy blue comforter holding hands. You'll feel immediately nervous, your face will feel suddenly hot and pink. There's no way now for you to cover your skin for them not to see the blushing color and for them not to see how you try to swallow, though your throat is too dry.

They will start talking about it, which you were afraid they would do. "What's wrong?" Jared will ask you. Mark will ask, "Yeah, what's wrong, Ryan?" They will look at each other and down at their hands, one flopped over the other. "We hope you don't mind us doing this stuff. This is just something we do," Jared says, and he will shrug as if it's normal, as normal as note passing. "Don't you ever do stuff like this, Ryan?" Mark will ask you, and here you are, at the point of all this. "You like to kiss guys, right, Ryan?" They are trying to get you to say things about yourself that you won't be ready to say for several more years, and that's what will hurt the most about this afternoon. Hurt more than never hanging out with Mark or Jared again. Hurt more than anything anybody will say at school about what actually happened in Mark's bedroom. It will hurt most when you realize they saw something in you that you thought you'd hidden so well you couldn't even see it yourself anymore. They found something in you before you did. They saw it, and there it will be, holding a box of cupcakes.

Years after, you will wonder how you managed to get through the rest of junior high and high school without ever speaking to Mark or Jared again, but somehow you will do it. In high school Jared will trade his brown glasses for contacts, and you will overhear girls in hallways whispering to each other about how pretty his eyes are. Mark will begin hanging out with the boys who wear dark jackets throughout the whole school year, no matter the weather, the boys who smoke in the sunken garden behind the school building, sitting on rotted railroad ties, sharing cigarettes every morning before the bell rings and after lunch. You will eventually find your own friends, and from that afternoon in sixth grade to the evening of your high school graduation you will never tell another person about Mark and Jared's kiss.

One day someone will ask you about the first time you kissed a boy, and you will think of this kiss, the one between Mark and Jared, the kiss that isn't really a kiss and isn't really yours. You could almost laugh. It will be funny to you, in a way, how important this kiss will be—it was the first kiss between two men, however young they were, you will have seen. Funny how of all the kisses in your life this is the one you will think most about. It will be the biggest kiss you ever saw.

Before you will ever be able to actually tell another person about this kiss you will try to write it as fiction. You will try to recast it as a short story. You will have moved to Chicago by then, after college and college creative writing classes, and you will spend evenings sitting in cafés, working, bent over a legal pad, and one night this kiss will come to you, and you will think, "now that's a good story." You will begin by vividly describing it, the class project and the bedroom door and the glasses on the windowsill. There will be something about watching it happen on the page, about having control over the afternoon and these three boys. You will try to rename them, but you will never find the perfect substitutes for the names *Mark* or *Jared*. Without *Mark* or *Jared* the story somehow won't work. You will read over it, you will witness the afternoon again, and it won't seem real. You will try to change the layout of Mark's house, change the ages of the boys, move them through time, make them years older or younger. The boy in the story holding the cupcakes—even in the fictional version, you include the cupcakes—just standing there, blushing, his stunned silence, is something you yourself can't believe. You will think this doesn't seem real, it doesn't sound like something that would really happen.

Finally you decide to just tell it. It will be almost eleven years from that sixth-grade afternoon. You will sit with three close friends and together drink several bottles of wine. None of them will have gone to your high school, and none of them will have heard of Mark or Jared. You will sit in an old armchair, a plastic cup of wine hanging from your hand. Votive candles will be scattered on a coffee table, their dull lights reflecting across the bare hardwood floor in the dim apartment. When you begin to tell the story you will feel the rise of a familiar panic. There will be the dry throat and the same flushed and sweating neck. Your friends will watch your face turn. And it will feel silly, your body still affected, still intimidated. A man in his twenties afraid of two twelve-year-old boys on a bed, miles away and years gone.

If you can't stop any of this, if you can wait sixteen years, it will end well, or at least, better than you'd guess. At your ten-year high school reunion, near the night's end, on the crowded patio, Jared will approach you.

At the reunion, throughout the evening, you will have noticed that most of the boys from your high school—the football players and basketball players, the class officers and the prom king—are quickly balding or already bald and somehow all shorter. Everyone's life is sort of rearranged: the quarterback walks on prosthetic feet now, and the class president is a Dallas Cowboys cheerleader. You are taller than you were then, and your classmates look at you and look again and tell you that you look grown-up. And instead of hiding a part of yourself from them like you did in school you will have decided to bring your boyfriend.

You stand next to him. The open bar is closed. Classmates make plans to meet at nearby bars, promise to e-mail each other, send letters, and exchange photos of children to keep in touch. Your best friend and your boyfriend are smoking cigarettes. You are standing outside with them on a patio overlooking a courtyard, waiting to walk back to your hotel room and look through the senior yearbook you brought, to point at pictures and talk about the faces. Out of the clump of classmates and spouses Jared suddenly walks up to you. You already knew he was at the reunion, and you almost thought you'd made it through the night without talking to him. He looks like he did in high school—big and thick, a round chest, thick stump legs, a spread-out face with large, wet eyes—only he's losing his hair, and his skin is lined with age. He has a wife;

she's extremely thin. Jared extends his hand, and you shake it. He says "Hey, Ryan," like he's surprised to see you. The patio is very dark. Classmates crowd around you both, squeezing the space away, their faces covered in shadows. Jared's nametag—like your nametag, with a scan of your senior picture printed on it—is stuck to his shirt, a crease down its center and dotted by drops of beer.

Your boyfriend and your best friend drop away, leaning to each other in their own conversation; they won't notice Jared. He asks you the customary questions, the ones answered this evening already a hundred times. Where do you live now, how are you doing, what are you doing, do you like Chicago? You tell him, wondering why he's talking to you. You are still afraid of Jared. Or at least you are still afraid of that Jared, the one with the glasses on an afternoon in sixth grade. The conversation comes to an end, once you've exhausted the usual, casual exchange. Then Jared lifts his big arm to your shoulder. He says, "Hey, listen, you probably won't even remember what I am talking about, but there was this time, at fuckin' Mark's house, when—" and you stop him.

"I know what you're going to say."

"You do?"

"I know exactly what you're going to say." You are surprised, too.

"I don't have to say it?"

"No," you say, and actually you don't want him to say it, you don't want to hear him tell it. It would seem too easy, too obvious for this tormentor to apologize at your reunion. You wouldn't even test this moment on the page—if it was a story you could write—since no reader would believe it. "It couldn't really happen this way," you think, standing in front of Jared, watching it happen.

"Well, look, I just want to say that what we did, it was stupid. I'm really sorry. We were just asshole kids."

You think it's strange that you assumed you were the only boy hurt by that kiss in Mark's bedroom. But you see that Jared carries that day with him like you do; he carries a shame not very different from yours. Somehow you've shared a scar for this many years. You say to Jared that just knowing he remembers that afternoon is enough. He thanks you and grabs you again. On your shoulder his hand feels a little like the warmth of comfort, and a little like the squeeze of danger.

[handwritten: New journalism]

[handwritten: How is this different compared to other pieces?]

David Foster Wallace

CONSIDER THE LOBSTER

[handwritten: Read the footnotes → what do they do? Work? Undercut?]

DAVID FOSTER WALLACE is author of the novel *The Broom of the System* and the meganovel *Infinite Jest*, as well as the short story collections *Girl with Curious Hair*, *Brief Interviews with Hideous Men*, and *Oblivion: Stories*, and the essay collections *A Supposedly Funny Thing I'll Never Do Again* and *Consider the Lobster: And Other Essays*. He has received a Guggenheim Fellowship, a Whiting Writers' Award, the John Traine Humor Prize from the *Paris Review*, an Illinois Arts Council Award for Non-Fiction, a Quality Paperback Book Club's New Voices Award in Fiction, and a Lannan Foundation Award for Literature. He is the Roy E. Disney Endowed Professor of Creative Writing and professor of English at Pomona College.

The enormous, pungent, and extremely well-marketed Maine Lobster Festival *[handwritten: advertised]* is held every late July in the state's midcoast region, meaning the western side of Penobscot Bay, the nerve stem of Maine's lobster industry. What's called the midcoast runs from Owl's Head and Thomaston in the south to Belfast in the north. (Actually, it might extend all the way up to Bucksport, but we were never able to get farther north than Belfast on Route 1, whose summer traffic is, as you can imagine, unimaginable.) The region's two main communities are Camden, with its very old money and yachty harbor and five-star restaurants and phenomenal B&Bs, and Rockland, a serious old fishing town that hosts the Festival every summer in historic Harbor Park, right along the water.*

Tourism and lobster are the midcoast region's two main industries, and they're both warm-weather enterprises, and the Maine Lobster Festival represents less an intersection of the industries than a deliberate collision, joyful and lucrative and loud. The assigned subject of this *Gourmet* article is the Fifty-sixth Annual MLF, 30 July–3 August 2003, whose official theme this year was "Lighthouses, Laughter, and Lobster." Total paid attendance was over one hun-

---

* There's a comprehensive native apothegm: "Camden by the sea, Rockland by the smell."

dred thousand, due partly to a national CNN spot in June during which a senior editor of *Food & Wine* magazine hailed the MLF as one of the best food-themed festivals in the world. The 2003 Festival highlights: concerts by Lee Ann Womack and Orleans, annual Maine Sea Goddess beauty pageant, Saturday's big parade, Sunday's William G. Atwood Memorial Crate Race, annual Amateur Cooking Competition, carnival rides and midway attractions and food booths, and the MLF's Main Eating Tent, where something over twenty-five thousand pounds of fresh-caught Maine lobster is consumed after preparation in the World's Largest Lobster Cooker near the grounds' north entrance. Also available are lobster rolls, lobster turnovers, lobster sauté, Down East lobster salad, lobster bisque, lobster ravioli, and deep-fried lobster dumplings. Lobster Thermidor is obtainable at a sit-down restaurant called the Black Pearl, on Harbor Park's northwest wharf. A large all-pine booth sponsored by the Maine Lobster Promotion Council has free pamphlets with recipes, eating tips, and Lobster Fun Facts. The winner of Friday's Amateur Cooking Competition prepares Saffron Lobster Ramekins, the recipe for which is now available for public downloading at www.mainelobsterfestival.com. There are lobster T-shirts and lobster bobblehead dolls and inflatable lobster pool toys and clamp-on lobster hats with big scarlet claws that wobble on springs. Your assigned correspondent saw it all, accompanied by one girlfriend and both his own parents—one of which parents was actually born and raised in Maine, albeit in the extreme northern inland part, which is potato country and a world away from the touristic midcoast.*

For practical purposes, everyone knows what a lobster is. As usual, though, there's much more to know than most of us care about—it's all a matter of what your interests are. Taxonomically speaking, a lobster is a marine crustacean of the family Homaridae, characterized by five pairs of jointed legs, the first pair terminating in large pincerish claws used for subduing prey. Like many other species of benthic carnivore, lobsters are both hunters and scavengers. They have stalked eyes, gills on their legs, and antennae. There are a dozen or so different kinds worldwide, of which the relevant species here is the Maine lobster, *Homarus americanus*. The name "lobster" comes from the Old English *loppestre*, which is thought to be a corrupt form of the Latin word for locust combined with the Old English *loppe*, which meant spider.

Moreover, a crustacean is an aquatic arthropod of the class Crustacea, which comprises crabs, shrimp, barnacles, lobsters, and freshwater crayfish. All this is

---

*N.B. All personally connected parties have made it clear from the start that they do not want to be talked about in this article.

right there in the encyclopedia. And an arthropod is an invertebrate member of the phylum Arthropoda, which phylum covers insects, spiders, crustaceans, and centipedes/millipedes, all of whose main commonality, besides the absence of a centralized brain-spine assembly, is a chitinous exoskeleton composed of segments, to which appendages are articulated in pairs.

The point is that lobsters are basically giant sea-insects.* Like most arthropods, they date from the Jurassic period, biologically so much older than mammalia that they might as well be from another planet. And they are—particularly in their natural brown-green state, brandishing their claws like weapons and with thick antennae awhip—not nice to look at. And it's true that they are garbagemen of the sea, eaters of dead stuff,† although they'll also eat some live shellfish, certain kinds of injured fish, and sometimes each other.

But they are themselves good eating. Or so we think now. Up until sometime in the 1800s, though, lobster was literally low-class food, eaten only by the poor and institutionalized. Even in the harsh penal environment of early America, some colonies had laws against feeding lobsters to inmates more than once a week because it was thought to be cruel and unusual, like making people eat rats. One reason for their low status was how plentiful lobsters were in old New England. "Unbelievable abundance" is how one source describes the situation, including accounts of Plymouth pilgrims wading out and capturing all they wanted by hand, and of early Boston's seashore being littered with lobsters after hard storms—these latter were treated as a smelly nuisance and ground up for fertilizer. There is also the fact that premodern lobster was cooked dead and then preserved, usually packed in salt or crude hermetic containers. Maine's earliest lobster industry was based around a dozen such seaside canneries in the 1840s, from which lobster was shipped as far away as California, in demand only because it was cheap and high in protein, basically chewable fuel.

Now, of course, lobster is posh, a delicacy, only a step or two down from caviar. The meat is richer and more substantial than most fish, its taste subtle compared to the marine gaminess of mussels and clams. In the U.S. pop-food imagination, lobster is now the seafood analogue to steak, with which it's so often twinned as Surf 'n' Turf on the really expensive part of the chain steakhouse menu.

In fact, one obvious project of the MLF, and of its omnipresently sponsorial Maine Lobster Promotion Council, is to counter the idea that lobster is unusually luxe or unhealthy or expensive, suitable only for effete palates or the occa-

---

* Midcoasters' native term for a lobster is, in fact, "bug," as in "Come around on Sunday and we'll cook up some bugs."
† Factoid: Lobster traps are usually baited with dead herring.

sional blow-the-diet treat. It is emphasized over and over in presentations and pamphlets at the Festival that lobster meat has fewer calories, less cholesterol, and less saturated fat than chicken.* And in the Main Eating Tent, you can get a "quarter" (industry shorthand for a 1¼-pound lobster), a 4-ounce cup of melted butter, a bag of chips, and a soft roll w/butter-pat for around twelve dollars, which is only slightly more expensive than supper at McDonald's.

Be apprised, though, that the Maine Lobster Festival's democratization of lobster comes with all the massed inconvenience and aesthetic compromise of true democracy. See, for example, the prenominate Main Eating Tent, for which there is a constant Disneyland-grade queue, and which turns out to be a square quarter-mile of awning-shaded cafeteria lines and rows of long institutional tables at which friend and stranger alike sit cheek to jowl, cracking and chewing and dribbling. It's hot, and the sagged roof traps the steam and the smells, which latter are strong and only partly food-related. It is also loud, and a good percentage of the total noise is masticatory. The suppers come in Styrofoam trays, and the soft drinks are iceless and flat, and the coffee is convenience-store coffee in more Styrofoam, and the utensils are plastic (there are none of the special long skinny forks for pushing out the tail meat, though a few savvy diners bring their own). Nor do they give you near enough napkins considering how messy lobster is to eat, especially when you're squeezed onto benches alongside children of various ages and vastly different levels of fine-motor development—not to mention the people who've somehow smuggled in their own beer in enormous aisle-blocking coolers, or who all of a sudden produce their own plastic tablecloths and try to spread them over large portions of tables to try to reserve them (the tables) for their own little groups. And so on. Any one example is no more than a petty inconvenience, of course, but the MLF turns out to be full of irksome little downers like this—see, for instance, the Main Stage's headliner shows, where it turns out that you have to pay twenty dollars extra for a folding chair if you want to sit down; or the North Tent's mad scramble for the Nyquil-cup-sized samples of finalists' entries handed out after the cooking competition; or the much-touted Maine Sea Goddess pageant finals, which turn out to be excruciatingly long and to consist mainly of endless thanks and tributes to local sponsors. Let's not even talk about the grossly inadequate Port-A-San facilities or the fact that there's no place to wash your hands before or after eating. What the Maine Lobster Festival really is is a midlevel county fair with a culinary hook, and in this respect it's not unlike

---

* Of course, the common practice of dipping the lobster meat in melted butter torpedoes all these happy fat-specs, which none of the council's promotional stuff ever mentions, any more than potato industry PR talks about sour cream and bacon bits.

[handwritten margin note: Make tourists seem like lazy fat people]

Tidewater crab festivals, Midwest corn festivals, Texas chili festivals, etc., and shares with these venues the core paradox of all teeming commercial demotic events: it's not for everyone.* Nothing against the euphoric senior editor of *Food & Wine*, but I'd be surprised if she'd ever actually been here, in Harbor Park, watching people slap canal-zone mosquitoes as they eat deep-fried Twinkies and watch Professor Paddywhack, on six-foot stilts in a raincoat with plastic lobsters protruding from all directions on springs, terrify their children.

Lobster is essentially a summer food. This is because we now prefer our lobsters fresh, which means they have to be recently caught, which for both tactical and economic reasons takes place at depths less than 25 fathoms. Lobsters tend to be hungriest and most active (i.e., most trappable) at summer water temperatures of 45 to 50 degrees. In the autumn, most Maine lobsters migrate out into deeper water, either for warmth or to avoid the heavy waves that pound New England's coast all winter. Some burrow into the bottom. They might hibernate;

[handwritten note: making digs @ tourism using lobsters.]

---

*In truth, there's a great deal to be said about the differences between working-class Rockland and the heavily populist flavor of its Festival versus comfortable and elitist Camden with its expensive view and shops given entirely over to two-hundred-dollar sweaters and great rows of Victorian homes converted to upscale B&Bs. And about these differences as two sides of the great coin that is U.S. tourism. Very little of which will be said here, except to amplify the above-mentioned paradox and to reveal your assigned correspondent's own preferences. I confess that I have never understood why so many people's idea of a fun vacation is to don flip-flops and sunglasses and crawl through maddening traffic to loud, hot, crowded tourist venues in order to sample a "local flavor" that is by definition ruined by the presence of tourists. This may (as my Festival companions keep pointing out) all be a matter of personality and hard-wired taste: the fact that I do not like tourist venues means that I'll never understand their appeal and so am probably not the one to talk about it (the supposed appeal). But, since this FN will almost surely not survive magazine-editing anyway, here goes:

As I see it, it probably really is good for the soul to be a tourist, even if it's only once in a while. Not good for the soul in a refreshing or enlivening way, though, but rather in a grim, steely-eyed, let's-look-honestly-at-the-facts-and-find-some-way-to-deal-with-them way. My personal experience has not been that traveling around the country is broadening or relaxing, or that radical changes in place and context have a salutary effect, but rather that intranational tourism is radically constricting, and humbling in the hardest way—hostile to my fantasy of being a true individual, of living somehow outside and above it all. (Coming up is the part that my companions find especially unhappy and repellent, a sure way to spoil the fun of vacation travel:) To be a mass tourist, for me, is to become a pure late-date American: alien, ignorant, greedy for something you cannot ever have, disappointed in a way you can never admit. It is to spoil, by way of sheer ontology, the very unspoiledness you are there to experience. It is to impose yourself on places that in all noneconomic ways would be better, realer, without you. It is, in lines and gridlock and transaction after transaction, to confront a dimension of yourself that is as inescapable as it is painful: as a tourist, you become economically significant but existentially loathsome, an insect on a dead thing.

nobody's sure. Summer is also lobsters' molting season—specifically, early to mid-July. Chitinous arthropods grow by molting, rather the way people have to buy bigger clothes as they age and gain weight. Since lobsters can live to be over a hundred, they can also get to be quite large, as in 25 pounds or more—though truly senior lobsters are rare now, because New England's waters are so heavily trapped.* Anyway, hence the culinary distinction between hard- and soft-shell lobsters, the latter sometimes a.k.a. shedders. A soft-shell lobster is one that has recently molted. In midcoast restaurants, the summer menu often offers both kinds, with shedders being slightly cheaper even though they're easier to dismantle and the meat is allegedly sweeter. The reason for the discount is that a molting lobster uses a layer of seawater for insulation while its new shell is hardening, so there's slightly less actual meat when you crack open a shedder, plus a redolent gout of water that gets all over everything and can sometimes jet out lemonlike and catch a tablemate right in the eye. If it's winter or you're buying lobster someplace far from New England, on the other hand, you can almost bet that the lobster is a hard-shell, which for obvious reasons travel better.

As an à la carte entrée, lobster can be baked, broiled, steamed, grilled, sautéed, stir-fried, or microwaved. The most common method, though, is boiling. If you're someone who enjoys having lobster at home, this is probably the way you do it, since boiling is so easy. You need a large kettle w/ cover, which you fill about half full with water (the standard advice is that you want 2.5 quarts of water per lobster). Seawater is optimal, or you can add two tbsp. salt per quart from the tap. It also helps to know how much your lobsters weigh. You get the water boiling, put in the lobsters one at a time, cover the kettle, and bring it back to a boil. Then you bank the heat and let the kettle simmer—ten minutes for the first pound of lobster, then three minutes for each pound after that. (This is assuming you've got hard-shell lobsters, which, again, if you don't live between Boston and Halifax is probably what you've got. For shedders, you're supposed to subtract three minutes from the total.) The reason the kettle's lobsters turn scarlet is that boiling somehow suppresses every pigment in their chitin but one. If you want an easy test of whether the lobsters are done, you try pulling on one of their antennae—if it comes out of the head with minimal effort, you're ready to eat.

A detail so obvious that most recipes don't even bother to mention it is that each lobster is supposed to be alive when you put it in the kettle. This is part of

---

*Datum: In a good year, the U.S. industry produces around eighty million pounds of lobster, and Maine accounts for more than half that total.

lobster's modern appeal: it's the freshest food there is. There's no decomposition between harvesting and eating. And not only do lobsters require no cleaning or dressing or plucking, but they're relatively easy for vendors to keep alive. They come up alive in the traps, are placed in containers of seawater, and can—so long as the water's aerated and the animals' claws are pegged or banded to keep them from tearing one another up under the stresses of captivity*—survive right up until they're boiled. Most of us have been in supermarkets or restaurants that feature tanks of live lobster, from which you can pick out your supper while it watches you point. And part of the overall spectacle of the Maine Lobster Festival is that you can see actual lobstermen's vessels docking at the wharves along the northeast grounds and unloading fresh-caught product, which is transferred by hand or cart 150 yards to the great clear tanks stacked up around the Festival's cooker—which is, as mentioned, billed as the World's Largest Lobster Cooker and can process over one hundred lobsters at a time for the Main Eating Tent.

So then here is a question that's all but unavoidable at the World's Largest Lobster Cooker, and may arise in kitchens across the United States: Is it all right to boil a sentient creature alive just for our gustatory pleasure? A related set of concerns: Is the previous question irksomely PC or sentimental? What does "all right" even mean in this context? Is it all just a matter of personal choice?

As you may or may not know, a certain well-known group called People for the Ethical Treatment of Animals thinks that the morality of lobster-boiling is not just a matter of individual conscience. In fact, one of the very first things we hear about the MLF . . . well, to set the scene: We're coming in by cab from the almost indescribably odd and rustic Knox County Airport† very late on the night before the Festival opens, sharing the cab with a wealthy political consul-

---

*N.B. Similar reasoning underlies the practice of what's termed "debeaking" broiler chickens and brood hens in modern factory farms. Maximum commercial efficiency requires that enormous poultry populations be confined in unnaturally close quarters, under which conditions many birds go crazy and peck one another to death. As a purely observational side note, be apprised that debeaking is usually an automated process and that the chickens receive no anesthetic. It's not clear to me whether most *Gourmet* readers know about debeaking, or about related practices like dehorning cattle in commercial feed lots, cropping swine's tails in factory hog farms to keep psychotically bored neighbors from chewing them off, and so forth. It so happens that your assigned correspondent knew almost nothing about standard meat-industry operations before starting work on this article.

†The terminal used to be somebody's house, for example, and the lost-luggage-reporting room was clearly once a pantry.

tant who lives on Vinalhaven Island in the bay half the year (he's headed for the island ferry in Rockland). The consultant and cabdriver are responding to informal journalistic probes about how people who live in the midcoast region actually view the MLF, as in, Is the Festival just a big-dollar tourist thing, or is it something local residents look forward to attending, take genuine civic pride in, etc.? The cabdriver (who's in his seventies, one of apparently a whole platoon of retirees the cab company puts on to help with the summer rush, and wears a U.S.-flag lapel pin, and drives in what can only be called a very deliberate way) assures us that locals do endorse and enjoy the MLF, although he himself hasn't gone in years, and now come to think of it no one he and his wife know has, either. However, the demi-local consultant's been to recent Festivals a couple times (one gets the impression it was at his wife's behest), of which his most vivid impression was that "you have to line up for an ungodly long time to get your lobsters, and meanwhile there are all these ex-flower children coming up and down along the line handing out pamphlets that say the lobsters die in terrible pain and you shouldn't eat them."

And it turns out that the post-hippies of the consultant's recollection were activists from PETA. There were no PETA people in obvious view at the 2003 MLF,* but they've been conspicuous at many of the recent Festivals. Since at least the mid-1990s, articles in everything from the *Camden Herald* to the *New York Times* have described PETA urging boycotts of the Maine Lobster Festival, often deploying celebrity spokesmen like Mary Tyler Moore for open letters and ads saying stuff like "Lobsters are extraordinarily sensitive" and "To me, eating a lobster is out of the question." More concrete is the oral testimony of

---

*It turned out that one Mr. William R. Rivas-Rivas, a high-ranking PETA official out of the group's Virginia headquarters, was indeed there this year, albeit solo, working the Festival's main and side entrances on Saturday, 2 August, handing out pamphlets and adhesive stickers emblazoned with "Being Boiled Hurts," which is the tagline in most of PETA's published material about lobster. I learned that he'd been there only later, when speaking with Mr. Rivas-Rivas on the phone. I'm not sure how we missed seeing him in situ at the Festival, and I can't see much to do except apologize for the oversight—although it's also true that Saturday was the day of the big MLF parade through Rockland, which basic journalistic responsibility seemed to require going to (and which, with all due respect, meant that Saturday was maybe not the best day for PETA to work the Harbor Park grounds, especially if it was going to be just one person for one day, since a lot of diehard MLF partisans were off-site watching the parade [which, again with no offense intended, was in truth kind of cheesy and boring, consisting mostly of slow homemade floats and various midcoast people waving at one another, and with an extremely annoying man dressed as Blackbeard ranging up and down the length of the crowd saying "Arrr" over and over and brandishing a plastic sword at people, etc.; plus it rained]).

Dick, our florid and extremely gregarious rental-car liaison,* to the effect that PETA's been around so much during recent years that a kind of brittlely tolerant homeostasis now obtains between the activists and the Festival's locals, e.g.: "We had some incidents a couple years ago. One lady took most of her clothes off and painted herself like a lobster, almost got herself arrested. But for the most part they're let alone. [Rapid series of small ambiguous laughs, which with Dick happens a lot.] They do their thing and we do our thing."

This whole interchange takes place on Route 1, 30 July, during a four-mile, fifty-minute ride from the airport† to the dealership to sign car-rental papers. Several irreproducible segues down the road from the PETA anecdotes, Dick— whose son-in-law happens to be a professional lobsterman and one of the Main Eating Tent's regular suppliers—articulates what he and his family feel is the crucial mitigating factor in the whole morality-of-boiling-lobsters-alive issue: "There's a part of the brain in people and animals that lets us feel pain, and lobsters' brains don't have this part."

Besides the fact that it's incorrect in about eleven different ways, the main reason Dick's statement is interesting is that its thesis is more or less echoed by the Festival's own pronouncement on lobsters and pain, which is part of a Test Your Lobster IQ quiz that appears in the 2003 MLF program, courtesy of the Maine Lobster Promotion Council:

> *The nervous system of a lobster is very simple, and is in fact most similar to the nervous system of the grasshopper. It is decentralized with no brain. There is no cerebral cortex, which in humans is the area of the brain that gives the experience of pain.*

Though it sounds more sophisticated, a lot of the neurology in this latter claim is still either false or fuzzy. The human cerebral cortex is the brain part that deals with higher faculties like reason, metaphysical self-awareness, language, etc. Pain reception is known to be part of a much older and more primitive system of nociceptors and prostaglandins that are managed by the brain

---

*By profession, Dick is actually a car salesman; the midcoast region's National Car Rental franchise operates out of a Chevy dealership in Thomaston.

†The short version regarding why we were back at the airport after already arriving the previous night involves lost luggage and a miscommunication about where and what the midcoast's National franchise was—Dick came out personally to the airport and got us, out of no evident motive but kindness. (He also talked nonstop the entire way, with a very distinctive speaking style that can be described only as manically laconic; the truth is that I now know more about this man than I do about some members of my own family.)

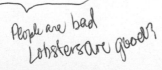

People are bad
Lobsters are good?

stem and thalamus.* On the other hand, it is true that the cerebral cortex is involved in what's variously called suffering, distress, or the emotional experience of pain—i.e., experiencing painful stimuli as unpleasant, very unpleasant, unbearable, and so on.

Before we go any further, let's acknowledge that the question of whether and how different kinds of animals feel pain, and of whether and why it might be justifiable to inflict pain on them in order to eat them, turn out to be extremely complex and difficult. And comparative neuroanatomy is only part of the problem. Since pain is a totally subjective mental experience, we do not have direct access to anyone or anything's pain but our own; and even just the principles by which we can infer that other people experience pain and have a legitimate interest in not feeling pain involve hardcore philosophy—metaphysics, epistemology, value theory, ethics. The fact that even the most highly evolved nonhuman mammals can't use language to communicate with us about their subjective mental experience is only the first layer of additional complication in trying to extend our reasoning about pain and morality to animals. And everything gets progressively more abstract and convoluted as we move farther and farther out from the higher-type mammals into cattle and swine and dogs and cats and rodents, and then birds and fish, and finally invertebrates like lobster.

apes

Why use girl here Image?

The more important point here, though, is that the whole animal-cruelty-and-eating issue is not just complex, it's also uncomfortable. It is, at any rate, uncomfortable for me, and for just about everyone I know who enjoys a variety of foods and yet does not want to see herself as cruel or unfeeling. As far as I can tell, my own main way of dealing with this conflict has been to avoid thinking about the whole unpleasant thing. I should add that it appears to me unlikely that many readers of *Gourmet* wish to think hard about it, either, or to be queried about the morality of their eating habits in the pages of a culinary monthly. Since, however, the assigned subject of this article is what it was like to attend the 2003 MLF, and thus to spend several days in the midst of a great mass of Americans all eating lobsters, and thus to be more or less impelled to think hard about lobster and the experience of buying and eating lobster, it turns out that there is no honest way to avoid certain moral questions.

---

* To elaborate by way of example: The common experience of accidentally touching a hot stove and yanking your hand back before you're even aware that anything's going on is explained by the fact that many of the processes by which we detect and avoid painful stimuli do not involve the cortex. In the case of the hand and stove, the brain is bypassed altogether; all the important neurochemical action takes place in the spine.

There are several reasons for this. For one thing, it's not just that lobsters get boiled alive, it's that you do it yourself—or at least it's done specifically for you, on-site.* As mentioned, the World's Largest Lobster Cooker, which is highlighted as an attraction in the Festival's program, is right out there on the MLF's north grounds for everyone to see. Try to imagine a Nebraska Beef Festival† at which part of the festivities is watching trucks pull up and the live cattle get driven down the ramp and slaughtered right there on the World's Largest Killing Floor or something—there's no way.

The intimacy of the whole thing is maximized at home, which of course is where most lobster gets prepared and eaten (although note already the semiconscious euphemism "prepared," which in the case of lobsters really means killing them right there in our kitchens). The basic scenario is that we come in from the store and make our little preparations like getting the kettle filled and boiling, and then we lift the lobsters out of the bag or whatever retail container they came home in ... whereupon some uncomfortable things start to happen. However stuporous the lobster is from the trip home, for instance, it tends to come alarmingly to life when placed in boiling water. If you're tilting it from a container into the steaming kettle, the lobster will sometimes try to cling to the container's sides or even to hook its claws over the kettle's rim like a person trying to keep from going over the edge of a roof. And worse is when the lobster's fully immersed. Even if you cover the kettle and turn away, you can usually hear the cover rattling and clanking as the lobster tries to push it off. Or the creature's claws scraping the sides of the kettle as it thrashes around.

---

* Morality-wise, let's concede that this cuts both ways. Lobster-eating is at least not abetted by the system of corporate factory farms that produces most beef, pork, and chicken. Because, if nothing else, of the way they're marketed and packaged for sale, we eat these latter meats without having to consider that they were once conscious, sentient creatures to whom horrible things were done. (N.B. "Horrible" here meaning really, really horrible. Write off to PETA or peta.org for their free "Meet Your Meat" video, narrated by Mr. Alec Baldwin, if you want to see just about everything meat-related you don't want to see or think about. [N.B.₂ Not that PETA's any sort of font of unspun truth. Like many partisans in complex moral disputes, the PETA people are fanatics, and a lot of their rhetoric seems simplistic and self-righteous. But this particular video, replete with actual factory-farm and corporate-slaughterhouse footage, is both credible and excruciating.])

† Is it significant that "lobster," "fish," and "chicken" are our culture's words for both the animal and the meat, whereas most mammals seem to require euphemisms like "beef" and "pork" that help us separate the meat we eat from the living creature the meat once was? Is this evidence that some kind of deep unease about eating higher animals is endemic enough to show up in English usage, but that the unease diminishes as we move out of the mammalian order? (And is "lamb"/"lamb" the counterexample that sinks the whole theory, or are there special, biblico-historical reasons for that equivalence?)

The lobster, in other words, behaves very much as you or I would behave if we were plunged into boiling water (with the obvious exception of screaming).* A blunter way to say this is that the lobster acts as if it's in terrible pain, causing some cooks to leave the kitchen altogether and to take one of those little light-weight plastic oven timers with them into another room and wait until the whole process is over.

There happen to be two main criteria that most ethicists agree on for determining whether a living creature has the capacity to suffer and so has genuine interests that it may or may not be our moral duty to consider.† One is how much of the neurological hardware required for pain experience the animal comes equipped with—nociceptors, prostaglandins, neuronal opioid receptors, etc. The other criterion is whether the animal demonstrates behavior associated with pain. And it takes a lot of intellectual gymnastics and behaviorist hairsplitting not to see struggling, thrashing, and lid-clattering as just such pain behavior. According to marine zoologists, it usually takes lobsters between thirty-five and forty-five seconds to die in boiling water. (No source I could find talked about how long it takes them to die in superheated steam; one rather hopes it's faster.)

There are, of course, other ways to kill your lobster on-site and so achieve maximum freshness. Some cooks' practice is to drive a sharp heavy knife point-first into a spot just above the midpoint between the lobster's eyestalks (more or less where the Third Eye is in human foreheads). This is alleged either to kill the lobster instantly or to render it insensate, and is said at least to eliminate some of the cowardice involved in throwing a creature into boiling water and then fleeing the room. As far as I can tell from talking to proponents of the knife-in-

---

*There's a relevant populist myth about the high-pitched whistling sound that sometimes issues from a pot of boiling lobster. The sound is really vented steam from the layer of seawater between the lobster's flesh and its carapace (this is why shedders whistle more than hard-shells), but the pop version has it that the sound is the lobster's rabbitlike death scream. Lobsters communicate via pheromones in their urine and don't have anything close to the vocal equipment for screaming, but the myth's very persistent—which might, once again, point to a low-level cultural unease about the boiling thing.

† "Interests" basically means strong and legitimate preferences, which obviously require some degree of consciousness, responsiveness to stimuli, etc. See, for instance, the utilitarian philosopher Peter Singer, whose 1974 *Animal Liberation* is more or less the bible of the modern animal-rights movement:

> It would be nonsense to say that it was not in the interests of a stone to be kicked along the road by a schoolboy. A stone does not have interests because it cannot suffer. Nothing that we can do to it could possibly make any difference to its welfare. A mouse, on the other hand, does have an interest in not being kicked along the road, because it will suffer if it is.

language is gruesome voice is patronizing

the-head method, the idea is that it's more violent but ultimately more merciful, plus that a willingness to exert personal agency and accept responsibility for stabbing the lobster's head honors the lobster somehow and entitles one to eat it. (There's often a vague sort of Native American spirituality-of-the-hunt flavor to pro-knife arguments.) But the problem with the knife method is basic biology: lobsters' nervous systems operate off not one but several ganglia, a.k.a. nerve bundles, which are sort of wired in series and distributed all along the lobster's underside, from stem to stern. And disabling only the frontal ganglion does not normally result in quick death or unconsciousness.

Another alternative is to put the lobster in cold saltwater and then very slowly bring it up to a full boil. Cooks who advocate this method are going on the analogy to a frog, which can supposedly be kept from jumping out of a boiling pot by heating the water incrementally. In order to save a lot of research-summarizing, I'll simply assure you that the analogy between frogs and lobsters turns out not to hold—plus, if the kettle's water isn't aerated seawater, the immersed lobster suffers from slow suffocation, although usually not decisive enough suffocation to keep it from still thrashing and clattering when the water gets hot enough to kill it. In fact, lobsters boiled incrementally often display a whole bonus set of gruesome, convulsionlike reactions that you don't see in regular boiling.

Ultimately, the only certain virtues of the home-lobotomy and slow-heating methods are comparative, because there are even worse/crueler ways people prepare lobster. Time-thrifty cooks sometimes microwave them alive (usually after poking several extra vent holes in the carapace, which is a precaution most shellfish-microwavers learn about the hard way). Live dismemberment, on the other hand, is big in Europe: some chefs cut the lobster in half before cooking; others like to tear off the claws and tail and toss only these parts into the pot.

And there's more unhappy news respecting suffering-criterion number one. Lobsters don't have much in the way of eyesight or hearing, but they do have an exquisite tactile sense, one facilitated by hundreds of thousands of tiny hairs that protrude through its carapace. "Thus," in the words of T. M. Prudden's industry classic *About Lobster*, "it is that although encased in what seems a solid, impenetrable armor, the lobster can receive stimuli and impressions from without as readily as if it possessed a soft and delicate skin." And lobsters do have nociceptors,* as well as invertebrate versions of the prostaglandins and major neurotransmitters via which our own brains register pain.

---

*This is the neurological term for special pain receptors that are "sensitive to potentially damaging extremes of temperature, to mechanical forces, and to chemical substances which are released when body tissues are damaged." (The quoted phrase is from a textbook.)

Lobsters do not, on the other hand, appear to have the equipment for making or absorbing natural opioids like endorphins and enkephalins, which are what more advanced nervous systems use to try to handle intense pain. From this fact, though, one could conclude either that lobsters are maybe even _more_ vulnerable to pain, since they lack mammalian nervous systems' built-in analgesia, or, instead, that the absence of natural opioids implies an absence of the really intense pain sensations that natural opioids are designed to mitigate. I for one can detect a marked upswing in mood as I contemplate this latter possibility. It could be that their lack of endorphin/enkephalin hardware means that lobsters' raw subjective experience of pain is so radically different from mammals' that it may not even deserve the term "pain." Perhaps lobsters are more like those frontal-lobotomy patients one reads about who report experiencing pain in a totally different way from you and I. These patients evidently do feel physical pain, neurologically speaking, but don't dislike it—though neither do they like it; it's more that they feel it but don't feel anything _about_ it—the point being that the pain is not distressing to them or something they want to get away from. Maybe lobsters, who are also without frontal lobes, are detached from the neurological-registration-of-injury-or-hazard we call pain in just the same way. There is, after all, a difference between (1) pain as a purely neurological event, and (2) actual suffering, which seems crucially to involve an emotional component, an awareness of pain as unpleasant, as something to fear/dislike/want to avoid.

Still, after all the abstract intellection, there remain the facts of the frantically clanking lid, the pathetic clinging to the edge of the pot. Standing at the stove, it is hard to deny in any meaningful way that this is a living creature experiencing pain and wishing to avoid/escape the painful experience. To my lay mind, the lobster's behavior in the kettle appears to be the expression of a _preference_; and it may well be that an ability to form preferences is the decisive criterion for real suffering.* The logic of this (preference → suffering) relation may be easiest to see in the negative case. If you cut certain kinds of worms in half, the halves will often keep crawling around and going about their vermiform business as if nothing had happened. When we assert, based on their post-op behavior, that these worms appear not to be suffering, what we're really saying is that there's no sign that the worms know anything bad has happened or would _prefer_ not to have gotten cut in half.

---

*"Preference" is maybe roughly synonymous with "interests," but it is a better term for our purposes because it's less abstractly philosophical—"preference" seems more personal, and it's the whole idea of a living creature's personal experience that's at issue.

Dont boil lobsters.

Lobsters, though, are known to exhibit preferences. Experiments have shown that they can detect changes of only a degree or two in water temperature; one reason for their complex migratory cycles (which can often cover one-hundred-plus miles a year) is to pursue the temperatures they like best.* And, as mentioned, they're bottom dwellers, and do not like bright light: if a tank of food-lobsters is out in the sunlight or a store's fluorescence, the lobsters will always congregate in whatever part is darkest. Fairly solitary in the ocean, they also clearly dislike the crowding that's part of their captivity in tanks, since (as also mentioned) one reason why lobsters' claws are banded on capture is to keep them from attacking one another under the stress of close-quarter storage.

In any event, at the Festival, standing by the bubbling tanks outside the World's Largest Lobster Cooker, watching the fresh-caught lobsters pile over one another, wave their hobbled claws impotently, huddle in the rear corners, or scrabble frantically back from the glass as you approach, it is difficult not to sense that they're unhappy, or frightened, even if it's some rudimentary version of these feelings . . . and, again, why does rudimentariness even enter into it? Why is a primitive, inarticulate form of suffering less urgent or uncomfortable for the person who's helping to inflict it by paying for the food it results in? I'm not trying to give you a PETA-like screed here—at least I don't think so. I'm trying, rather, to work out and articulate some of the troubling questions that arise amid all the laughter and saltation and community pride of the Maine Lobster

---

*Of course, the most common sort of counterargument here would begin by objecting that "like best" is really just a metaphor, and a misleadingly anthropomorphic one at that. The counterarguer would posit that the lobster seeks to maintain a certain optimal ambient temperature out of nothing but unconscious instinct (with a similar explanation for the low-light affinities upcoming in the main text). The thrust of such a counterargument will be that the lobster's thrashings and clankings in the kettle express not unpreferred pain but involuntary reflexes, like your leg shooting out when the doctor hits your knee. Be advised that there are professional scientists, including many researchers who use animals in experiments, who hold to the view that nonhuman creatures have no real feelings at all, merely "behaviors." Be further advised that this view has a long history that goes all the way back to Descartes, although its modern support comes mostly from behaviorist psychology.

To these what-look-like-pain-are-really-just-reflexes counterarguments, however, there happen to be all sorts of scientific and pro-animal rights counter-counterarguments. And then further attempted rebuttals and redirects, and so on. Suffice to say that both the scientific and the philosophical arguments on either side of the animal-suffering issue are involved, abstruse, technical, often informed by self-interest or ideology, and in the end so totally inconclusive that as a practical matter, in the kitchen or restaurant, it all still seems to come down to individual conscience, going with (no pun) your gut.

Festival. The truth is that if you, the Festival attendee, permit yourself to think that lobsters can suffer and would rather not, the MLF begins to take on the aspect of something like a Roman circus or medieval torture-fest.

Does that comparison seem a bit much? If so, exactly why? Or what about this one: Is it possible that future generations will regard our own present agribusiness and eating practices in much the same way we now view Nero's entertainments or Aztec sacrifices? My own initial reaction is that such a comparison is hysterical, extreme—and yet the reason it seems extreme to me appears to be that I believe animals are less morally important than human beings*; and when it comes to defending such a belief, even to myself, I have to acknowledge that (a) I have an obvious selfish interest in this belief, since I like to eat certain kinds of animals and want to be able to keep doing it, and (b) I haven't succeeded in working out any sort of personal ethical system in which the belief is truly defensible instead of just selfishly convenient.

Given this article's venue and my own lack of culinary sophistication, I'm curious about whether the reader can identify with any of these reactions and acknowledgments and discomforts. I am also concerned not to come off as shrill or preachy when what I really am is more like confused, uneasy. For those *Gourmet* readers who enjoy well-prepared and -presented meals involving beef, veal, lamb, pork, chicken, lobster, etc.: How much do you think about the (possible) moral status and (probable) physical suffering of the animals involved? If so, what ethical convictions have you worked out that permit you not just to eat but to savor and enjoy flesh-based viands (since of course refined *enjoyment*, rather than just ingestion, is the whole point of gastronomy)? If, on the other hand, you'll have no truck with confusions or convictions and regard stuff like the previous paragraph as just so much fatuous navel-gazing, what makes it feel OK, inside, to just dismiss the whole thing out of hand? That is, is your refusal to think about any of this the product of actual thought, or is it just that you don't want to think about it? And if the latter, then why not? Do you ever think, even idly, about the possible reasons for your reluctance to think about it? I am not trying to bait anyone here—I'm genuinely curious. After all, isn't being extra aware and attentive and thoughtful about one's food and its overall context part of what distinguishes a real gourmet? Or is all the gourmet's extra attention and sensibility just supposed to be sensuous? Is it really all just a matter of taste and presentation?

---

*Meaning *a lot* less important, apparently, since the moral comparison here is not the value of one human's life versus the value of one animal's life, but rather the value of one animal's life versus the value of one human's taste for a particular kind of protein. Even the most diehard carniphile will acknowledge that it's possible to live and eat well without consuming animals.

These last few queries, though, while sincere, obviously involve much larger and more abstract questions about the connections (if any) between aesthetics and morality—about what the adjective in a phrase like "The Magazine of Good Living" is really supposed to mean—and these questions lead straightaway into such deep and treacherous waters that it's probably best to stop the public discussion right here. There are limits to what even interested persons can ask of each other.

Talks about lobsters

Uses them to explore the morality & ethics surrounding the food industry.

There is a POV.
First person
More journalism

Descriptive grammar
Philosophy - reflect how usage is how people actually speak

Prescriptivist: Ain't is not a word.

Joy Williams

HAWK

JOY WILLIAMS is the author of four novels—the most recent, *The Quick and the Dead*, was a finalist for the Pulitzer Prize in 2001—and two collections of stories, as well as a book of essays, *Ill Nature*, a finalist for the National Book Critics Circle Award for criticism. Among her many honors are the Rea Award for the short story and the Strauss Living Award from the American Academy of Arts and Letters. She lives in Key West, Florida, and Tucson, Arizona.

"Hawk was in a hundred photographs. He was my sweetie pie, my honey, my handsome boy, my love. On the following day he would attack me as though he wanted to kill me."

Glenn Gould bathed his hands in wax and then they felt new. He didn't like to eat in public. He was personally gracious. He was knowledgeable about drugs. He loved animals. In his will, he directed that half his money be given to the Toronto Humane Society. He hated daylight and bright colours. His piano chair was fourteen inches high. His music was used to score *Slaughterhouse-Five*, a book he did not like. After he suffered his fatal stroke, his father waited a day to turn off the respirator because he didn't want him to die on his stepmother's birthday. When Glenn Gould wrote cheques he signed them Glen Gould because he was afraid that by writing the second n he would make too many squiggles. He took prodigious amounts of Valium and used make-up. He was once arrested in Sarasota, Florida, for sitting on a park bench in an overcoat, gloves and muffler. He was a prodigy, a genius. He had dirty hair. He had boring dreams. He probably believed in God.

My mind said *You read about Glenn Gould and listen to Glenn Gould constantly but you don't know anything about music. If he were alive you wouldn't have anything you could say to him ...*

A composer acquaintance of mine dismissed Glenn as a *performer*.

Glenn Gould loved the idea of the Arctic but he had a great fear of the cold. He was a virtuoso. To be a virtuoso you must have an absolutely fearless attitude toward everything but Glenn was, in fact, worried, frightened and phobic. The

542

dogs of his youth were named Nick and Banquo. As a baby, he never cried but hummed. He thought that the key of F minor expressed his personality.

You have no idea what that means my mind said. *You don't really know what it is he's doing. You don't know why he's brilliant.*

He could instantly play any piece of music from memory. On the whole he did not like works that progressed to a climax, and then to a reconciliation. The Goldberg Variations, which Glenn is most widely known for, were written by Bach for harpsichord. Bach was visiting one of his students, Johann Goldberg, who was employed by a Count von Keyserling, the Russian ambassador to the court of Saxony. The Count had insomnia and wanted some music that would help him through the dark hours. The first notes of the Goldberg Variations are inscribed on Glenn's tombstone.

My dog rose from his bed and walked beneath the table, which he barely cleared. He put his chin on my knee. He stood there for a few moments, not moving. I could see nothing but his nose. I loved kissing his nose. It was my hobby. He was a big black German Shepherd with accents of silver and brown. He had a beautiful face. He looked soulful and dear and alert. He was born on October 17, 1988 and had been with us since Christmas Day of that year. He was now almost nine years old. He weighed one hundred pounds. His name was Hawk. He seemed to fear nothing. He was always looking at me, waiting for me. He just wanted to go where I was going. He could be amusing, he had a sense of humour, but mostly he seemed stoic and watchful and patient. If I was in a room, he was in that room, no other. Of course we took long walks together and many cross-country trips. He was adept at ferry crossings and checking into motels. When he could not accompany me, I would put him in a kennel, once for as long as two weeks. I felt that it was good for him to endure the kennel occasionally. Life was not all good, I told him. Though mostly life was good. He had had a series of collars over the years. His most recent one was lavender in colour. He had tags with his various addresses and phone numbers on them and a St. Francis medal with the words protect us. He had a collection of toys. A softball, and squeaky toys in the shapes of a burglar, a cat, a shark, a snowman, and a hedgehog that once made a snuffling noise like a hedgehog but not for long. They were collected in a picnic basket on the floor and when he was happy he would root through the basket and select one. He preferred the snowman. His least favourite was a large green and red toy—its shape was similar to a large bone but it was an abstraction, it lacked charm. Hawk was in a hundred photographs. He was my sweetie pie, my honey, my handsome boy, my love. On the following day he would attack me as though he wanted to kill me.

. . .

As regards to life it is much the best to think that the experiences we have are necessary for us. It is by means of experience that we develop and not through our imagination. Imagination is nothing. Explanation is nothing. One can only experience and somehow describe—with, in Camus's phrase, lucid indifference. At the same time, experience is fundamentally illusory. When one is experiencing emotional pain or grief, one feels that everything that happens in life is unreal. And this is a right understanding of life.

I loved Hawk and Hawk loved me. It was the usual arrangement. Just a few days before, I had said to him, This is the life, isn't it honey. We were picnicking on Nantucket. We were on the beach with a little fire. There was a beautiful sunset. Friends had given us their house on the island, an old farmhouse off the Polpis Road. Somehow, on the first night at the house, Hawk had been left outside. When he was on the wrong side of a door he would never whine or claw at it, he would stare at it fixedly. I had fallen into a heavy sleep.

I was exhausted. I was always exhausted but I didn't go to a doctor. I had no doctor, no insurance. If I was going to be very sick, I would just die, I thought. Hawk would mourn me. Dogs are the best mourners in the world, as everyone knows. In my sleep, in the strange bed in the old farmhouse, I saw a figure at the door. It was waiting there clothed in a black garbage bag and bandages. Without hesitation I got up and went to the door and opened it and Hawk came in. Oh I'm sorry, I said to him. He settled down at the foot of the bed with a great comfortable sigh. His coat was cool from the night. I felt that he had tried to project himself through to me, that he had been separated from me through some error, some misunderstanding, and this, clearly, was something neither of us wanted. It had been a bad transmission, but it had done the job and done it without frightening me. What a resourceful boy! I said to him. Oh there are ghosts in that house, our friends said later. Someone else said, You know, ghosts frequently appear in bandages.

Before Hawk, I had had a number of dogs that died before their time, from grim accident or misfortune, taken from me unprepared in the twinkling of an eye. Shadrach, Nichodemus, Angel . . . Nichodemus wasn't even old enough to have learned to lift his leg. They were all good dogs, faithful. They were innocents. Hawk was the only one I didn't name from the Bible. I named him from Nature, wild Nature. My parents always had dogs too, German shepherds, and my mother would always say, You have to talk to a dog, Joy, you've got to talk to them. It ended badly for my mother and father's dogs over the years and then for my mother and father. My father was a Congregational minister. I am a Christian. Kierkegaard said that for the Christian, the closer you keep to God and the more involved you get with him, the worse for you. It's as though God was saying . . . you might as well go to the fair and have a good time with the rest. Don't get involved with me—it will only bring you misery. After all, I abandoned my own child, I allowed him to be killed. Christianity, Kierkegaard said, is related only to the consciousness of sin.

We were in Nantucket during the dies caniculares, the dog days of summer, but it was a splendid time. Still, there was something wrong with me. My body had turned against me and was full of browsing, shifting pain. The pain went anywhere it wanted to. My head ached, my arms and legs and eyes, my ribs hurt when I took a deep breath. Still, I walked with Hawk, we kept to our habits. I didn't want to think about it but my mind said you have to, you have to do something, you can't just do nothing you know . . . Some days were worse than others. On those days, I felt crippled. I was so tired. I couldn't think, couldn't concentrate. Even so, I spent long hours reading and listening to music. Bach, Mahler, Strauss. Glenn thought that the "Metamorphosen" of Strauss was the ultimate. I listened to Thomas de Hartmann play the music of Gurdjieff. I listened to Kathleen Ferrier sing Mahler and Bach and Handel and Gluck. She sang the famous aria from Gluck's opera, *Orfeo ed Euridice*—"What Is Life." We listened to the music over and over again.

Hawk had engaging habits. He had presence. He was devoted to me. To everyone, this was apparent. But I really knew nothing of his psychology. He was no Tulip or Keeper or Bashan who had been analysed by their writers. He knew sit, stay, down, go to your place. He was intelligent, he had a good memory. And surely, I believed, he had a soul.

The friends who had given us the house on Nantucket insisted that I see a doctor about my malady. They made an appointment for me with their doctor in New York. We would leave the Island, return to our own home for a few days, then put Hawk into the kennel and drive into the city, a little over two hours away.

I can't remember our last evening together.

On the morning my husband and I were to drive into the city, I got up early and took Hawk for a long walk along accustomed trails. I was wearing a white sleeveless linen blouse and poplin pants. My head pounded, I could barely put one foot ahead of the other. How about Lupus? my mind said. How about Rheumatoid Arthritis? Well, we'll know more soon . . . We drove then to the kennel. It was called Red Rock and Hawk had been there before, they liked him there, he'd always been a gentleman there. When we drove in, Hawk looked disconsolate yet resigned. I left him in the car while I went into the office. I was looking for Fred, big, loud, gruffly pleasant Fred, but he didn't appear. One of his assistants did, a girl named Lynn. Lynn knew Hawk. He's only going to be here for one night, right? Lynn said. I went out to get him. I put the leash on him, his blue, rather grimy leash, and he jumped out of the car and we walked into the office. Lynn had opened another door that led to a row of cement runs. We stood in that doorway, Hawk and I. All right then, I said. I was bent forward slightly. He turned and looked at me and rose and fell upon me, seizing my breast. Immediately, as they say, there was blood everywhere. He tore at my breast, snarling, I think, I can't remember if he was snarling. I turned, calling his name, and he turned with me, my breast still in his jaws. He then shifted and seized my left hand, and after an instant or two, my right, which he ground down upon, shifting, getting a better grip, always getting a better grip with his jaws. I was trying to twist his collar with my bleeding left hand but I was trying not to move either. Hawk! I kept calling my darling's name, Hawk! Then he stopped chewing on my hand and he looked at me coldly. Fred had been summoned by then and had a pole and a noose, the rig that's used for dangerous dogs, and I heard him say, He's stopped now. I fled to the car. My blouse was soaked with blood, it was dripping blood. I drove home sobbing. I've lost my dog, I've lost my Hawk. My mind didn't say anything. It was all it could do to stay with me as I sobbed and drove, my hands bleeding on the wheel.

I thought he had bitten off my nipple. I thought that when I took off my blouse and bra, the nipple would fall out like a diseased hibiscus bud, like the eraser on a pencil. But he hadn't bitten it off. My breast was bruised black and there were two deep punctures in it and a long raking scratch across it and that was all. My left hand was bleeding hard from three wounds. My right hand was mauled.

At home I stood in the shower, howling, making deep ugly sounds. I had lost my dog. The Band-Aids we put over my cuts had cartoon characters all over them. We didn't take our medicine cabinet very seriously. For some reason I had papered it with newspaper pictures of Bob Dole's hand clutching its pen. I put clean clothes on but the blood seeped around the Band-Aids and stained them too. I put more Goofy and Minnie Band-Aids on and changed my clothes again. I wrapped my hand in a dish towel. Hawk's water dish was still in the kitchen, his toys were scattered around. I wanted to drive into the city and keep my appointment with the doctor, he could look at my hand. It seemed only logical. I just wanted to get in the car and drive away from home. I wouldn't let my husband drive. We talked about what happened as being unbelievable. We hadn't yet started talking about it as being a tragedy. I'll never see him again, I've lost my dog, I said. Let's not talk about that now, my husband said. As we approached the city I tried to compose myself for the doctor. Then I was standing on the street outside his office which was on East Eighty-fifth Street trying to compose myself. I looked dishevelled, my clothes were stained, I was wearing high-top sneakers. Some people turned as they were walking by and made a point of staring at me.

He was a cheerful doctor. He put my hand in a pan of inky red sterilizing solution. He wanted to talk about my malady, the symptoms of my malady, but he was in fact thinking about the hand. He went out of the office for a while and when he came back he said, I've made an appointment for you to see an orthopaedic surgeon. This doctor was on East Seventy-third Street. You really have to do something about this hand, the first doctor said.

The surgeon was of the type Thomas Mann was always writing about, a doctor out of *The Magic Mountain,* someone whom science had cooled and hardened. Still, he seemed to take a bit of pleasure in imagining the referring doctor's discomfort at my messy wounds. People are usually pretty well cleaned up by the time Gary sees them, he said. He took X-rays and looked at them and said, I will be back in a moment to talk with you about your hand. I sat on the examining table and swung my feet back and forth. One of my sneakers was blue and the other one green. It was a little carefree gesture I had adopted for myself some time ago. I felt foolish and dirty. I felt that I must not appear to be very bright. The doctor returned and asked when the dog had bitten me and frowned when I told him it had been six hours ago. He said, This is very serious, you must have surgery on this hand today. I can't do it here, it must be done under absolutely sterile conditions at the hospital. The bone could become infected and bone infections are very difficult to clear up. I've reserved a bed in the hospital for you and arranged for another surgeon to perform the operation. I said, Oh, but . . . He said, The surgery must be done today. He repeated this, with beats between the words. He was stern and forbidding and, I thought, pessimistic. Good luck, he said.

The surgeon at Lenox Hill Hospital was a young good-looking Chinese man. He spoke elegantly and had a wonderful smile. He said, The bone is fractured badly in several places and the tendon is torn. Because it was caused by a dog's bite, the situation is actually life-threatening. Oh, surely . . . I began. No, he said, it's very serious, indeed, life-threatening, I assure you. He smiled.

I lay in a bed in the hospital for a few hours and at one in the morning the hand was operated on and apparently it went well enough. Long pins held everything together. You will have some loss of function in your hand but it won't be too bad, the doctor said, presenting his wonderful smile. I used to kiss Hawk's nose and put my hands in his jaws in play. People in the hospital wanted to talk about my dog biting me. That's unusual, isn't it, they said, or, That's strange isn't it, or, I thought that breed was exceptionally loyal. One nurse asked me if I had been cruel to him.

My hand would not be the same. It would never be strong and it would never again stroke Hawk's black coat.

CREDITS

"The Fourth State of Matter" by Jo Ann Beard. First appeared *The New Yorker*, June 1996. Later published in *The Boys of My Youth* (Back Bay Books, 1999).

"Getting Along with Nature" from *Home Economics* by Wendell Berry. Copyright © 1987 by Wendell Berry. Reprinted by permission of North Point Press, a division of Farrar, Straus and Giroux, LLC.

"The Pain Scale" by Eula Biss first appeared in the *Seneca Review*, vol. 35, no. 1 (spring 2005). A shorter version later appeared in *Harper's Magazine*, vol. 310, no. 1861 (June 2005).

"The Unwanted Child" in *All But the Waltz: A Memoir of Five Generations in the Life of a Montana Family*, by Mary Clearman Blew, pages 159–177.

"Torch Song," copyright © 1999 by Charles Bowden. Originally published in *Harper's Magazine*, August 1998, vol. 297, no. 1779, p. 43. Reproduced by permission of Anderson Literary Management.

"Embalming Mom" by Janet Burroway, originally published *Apolachee Quarterly*, 1985, no. 22, pp. 2–13.

"Physical Evidence" by Kelly Grey Carlisle. From *River Teeth*, vol. 7, no. 1 (fall 2005) by permission of the University of Nebraska Press. Copyright © 2005 by the University of Nebraska Press.

"The Glass Essay" by Anne Carson, from *Glass, Irony, and God*, copyright © 1995 by Anne Carson. Reprinted by permission of New Directions Publishing Corp.

"Burl's" by Bernard Cooper. Originally appeared in *Los Angeles Times Magazine*, Nov. 1994.

"Visitor" by Michael W. Cox. Originally published *New Letters*, 64.2, 1998, pp. 7–16.

"The Art of French Cooking" by E. J. Levy. *Salmagundi*, vol. 144–145 (fall 2004/ winter 2005), pp. 188–198.

"Portrait of My Body" by Phillip Lopate. From *Portrait of my Body*, Anchor Books, 1996, pp. 18–31.

"Flight" by Barry Lopez. Reprinted by permission of SLL/Sterling Lord Literistic, Inc. Copyright by Barry Lopez.

"The Undertaking" by Thomas Lynch. From *The Undertaking: Life Studies from the Dismal Trade*, W. W. Norton, 1997.

"Sorry" by Lee Martin. From *Turning Bones* by Lee Martin by permission of the University of Nebraska Press. Copyright © 2003 by Lee Martin.

"Interstellar" copyright © 2007 by Rebecca McClanahan.

"Bad Eyes" by Erin McGraw. Originally published in *The Gettysburg Review*, vol. 11, no. 1 (1998), pp. 89–98.

"The Search for Marvin Gardens" from *Pieces of the Frame* by John McPhee. Copyright © 1975, renewed 2003 by John McPhee. Reprinted by permission of Farrar, Straus and Giroux, LLC.

Brenda Miller, "The Date" from *Season of the Body: Essays*. Copyright © 2002 by Brenda Miller. Reprinted with the permission of Sarabande Books, www.sarabandebooks.org.

"Son of Mr. Green Jeans" by Dinty W. Moore. *Crazyhorse*, n. 63 (Spring 2003), pp. 49–53.

"Celibate Passion," from *The Cloister Walk* by Kathleen Norris, copyright © 1996 by Kathleen Norris. Used by permission of Riverhead Books, an imprint of Penguin Group (USA) Inc.

"This Is Not Who We Are" by Naomi Shihab Nye. First appeared in *O Magazine* (April 2002), p. 83–86.

"Autopsy Report" by Lia Purpura. First published in *The Iowa Review*, vol. 33, no. 3, (2003–2004). Later published in *On Looking*, 2006, Sarabande Books, pp. 1–8.

"Watching the Animals" by Richard Rhodes. Reprinted from *The Inland Ground: An Evocation of the American Middle West*, © 1969, 1991 by Richard Rhodes.

"Shitdiggers, Mudflats, and the Worm Men of Maine" by Bill Roorbach. *Into Woods*, 2002. University of Notre Dame Press, pp. 49–76; *Creative Nonfiction* 9 (1998), pp. 40–55.